The Stone Age Archaeology of Southern Africa

STUDIES IN ARCHEOLOGY

Consulting Editor: Stuart Struever

Department of Anthropology
Northwestern University
Evanston, Illinois

The Stone Age Archaeology of Southern Africa

C. GARTH SAMPSON

Department of Anthropology
Southern Methodist University
Dallas, Texas

ACADEMIC PRESS   New York and London

A Subsidiary of Harcourt Brace Jovanovich, Publishers

ACADEMIC PRESS, INC.
111 Fifth Avenue, New York, New York 10003

United Kingdom Edition published by
ACADEMIC PRESS, INC. (LONDON) LTD.
24/28 Oval Road, London NW1

Sampson, Clavil Garth, Date
    The stone age archaeology of southern Africa.

    (Studies in archeology series)
    Bibliography: p.
    1.   Stone age—Africa, southern.   2.   Africa, southern
—Antiquities.   I.   Title.
GN865.S52S25   916.8'03'2   73-205441
ISBN 0-12-785759-1

. . . that to turn the Book only was so hard and intricate a matter, that many times there was more business to find out what should be read, than to read it when it was found out.

These inconveniences therefore considered, here is set forth such an Order whereby the same shall be redressed.

THOMAS CRANMER
The Book of Common Prayer   1549

I will not offer to solve such problems, said Pantagruel; for it is somewhat ticklish, and you can hardly handle it without coming off scurvily; but I will tell you what I have heard.

FRANÇOIS RABELAIS
Gargantua and Pantagruel   1535
(the Urquhart translation)

Contents

11 Doubts and Speculations

Preface

This book has two aims, one less virtuous than the other. The first (and virtuous) one is to provide a service to professional archaeologists and other scholars with interests in Paleolithic studies. Almost all of us who have hoped to learn something of southern African prehistory have at some time in our search been frustrated by the inaccessibility of the sources. All too often an important contribution in this field has been buried in some small provincial journal, which, to an outsider, must seem so outrageously obscure that it becomes almost quotable for this perverse reason alone. Many other papers when eventually tracked down to be too trivial to justify the unfortunate searcher's efforts. In order to overcome these difficulties, I have attempted to take the best of the literature, extract from it what seems to me to be the most useful facts and to present them in the most complete format which space will allow. So, the book is in part a compendium of information about stratigraphy, artifacts, fauna, skeletons, and sediments which should be of use to professionals, students, and amateur archaeologists alike. I should add here that I have a very low opinion of annotated bibliographies and source books and this work is neither of those things. The references in it have been selected for their factual basis and the text deals mainly with the critical evaluation, organization and interpretation of the facts, such as they are.

This leads me to the book's second function, which is certainly less worthy. It attempts to revise the Stone Age record completely and contains an extensive revision of the orthodox framework used in such studies, As a synthesis, it is a very personal one. It contains several interpretations that have not been aired before, and I have tampered with much of the terminology in what should be cheerfully confessed to be a rather high-handed manner. Hopefully the reader may concede that at least some of this tampering has been necessary in order to tidy up the chaotic array of different terms currently in use to describe the same things. I do not feel especially defensive about any of the ideas or new terms offered here. However, it would be good to see some alternative (and better) ideas produced to replace them, as well as the tediously destructive arguments which inevitably greet new (and therefore unfashionable) interpretations.

Next, it will be apparent that I have repeatedly strayed into fields which are not strictly archaeology in the narrow meaning of stone tools, pots, dates, and stratigraphy. Whereas all these things appear in the work, it also touches (lightly —my grasp of these subjects being hardly vicelike) upon physical anthropology, vertebrate paleontology, palynology, and sedimentology. Frankly, the material remains of Stone Age cultures are pretty dull when treated in isolation, and the techniques of artifact typology applied to them by paleolithic specialists hardly bring them to life. However, when set against a background of past variations in environment, food sources, and human anatomy, the artifact studies become a little more palatable. Had these adjacent studies been omitted from the book, it could not have been written: sheer boredom would have intervened before its completion.

Then there is the problem, shared with all syntheses, of keeping up with current research results. Impressive fieldwork programs have been just completed in eastern Zambia, Swaziland, and the southern Cape coast, but their results are not yet available. Several older and equally impressive projects are still in press. It is likely that abundant new information will be pouring out of this region in the next five years and this work may require substantial revisions. It is essentially a statement of results acquired up to 1971.

Each chapter deals with a particular industry and its associations, problems, distribution, and environmental setting. The chapters proceed in chronological order starting with the earliest traces of Stone Age remains and ending with the protohistoric population of South Africa in contact with incoming Iron Age groups. The sequence is presented by some introductory remarks on terminology, methods and the like, and is closed with a short chapter of pure speculations which should provide excellent ammunition for weary and justified detractors.

Acknowledgments

Actually, the book has been far too long in the making. It was started in 1968 and has developed in fits and starts, written mostly at night and occasionally abandoned thanks to the pressures of two unrelated research projects and full-time teaching responsibilities. Bits of the manuscript were written in Oxford, Berkeley, Eugene, and Dallas. It has traveled too long and too far, and I take full responsibility or its flaws. Among those who have helped me to patch it up, I am enormously grateful to several friends for their secretarial help. These include Evelyn Brew, Beatrix Cameron, Hazel Gilboe, Flora Kalious, Mary Sampson, Paula Spurlock, and Barbara Winters. I am especially indebted to Beatrix Cameron whose stylistic comments were of great help, and also to William Singleton who assisted in the laborious business of cross-checking the bibliography and who made several useful comments on the manuscript. The illustrations I regard as an essential and equally important part of the whole work and I owe a debt of gratitude to Lucy Addington who drew all the stone artifacts, Linda Verrett who drew the ceramics and organic tools, and to Sally McBrearty and Tom Ryan who helped me with some of the skeletal illustrations and diagrams.

Ultimately any synthesis depends on the work and advice of one's colleagues in several countries. They are so numerous that I must ask to be excused from enumerating all of them for fear of omitting a few. I would, however, like to thank Basil Cooke, whose critical comments on the australopithecine sections have been a great help, as have been the comments and suggestions of Clark Howell and Richard Klein, who reviewed the manuscript for the publisher. I would also like to acknowledge a real intellectual debt to Ray Inskeep and Charles McBurney who were my past mentors and whose standards and ideas have indirectly influenced the writing of this work in all its stages. Any errors of fact or awkwardness in handling the material are of course of my own making.

Introduction

1

Of all the regions of the world that have been explored by archaeologists, southern Africa must surely be among those with the longest Stone Age record. Current estimates place the first traces of prehistoric Man in South Africa at about 3 million years Before Present, at which time the techniques of simple stone tool manufacture are barely discernable in an archaeological context. From this period until the late nineteenth century A.D. there is evidence for apparently continuous habitation by groups who relied entirely on stone and various organic materials for the manufacture of their tools and weapons. At least one isolated band of such people may have persisted until quite recently. Through out this period hunting and gathering formed the basis for survival. Exposure to the techniques of cultivation or stock rearing did not come about until the advent of Iron Age immigrants after about A.D. 100. Even after this time it is doubtful whether the alternative way of life was widely embraced by the Stone Age population, who nevertheless acquired some of the trappings of Iron Age material culture such as ceramics, glass beads, and a few iron weapons. Written records of their activities began in the seventeenth century A.D., but most of the early accounts tend to document only their decimation by European pioneers and farmers. Among the few valuable exceptions are the nineteenth century records of dwindling and hard-pressed "Bushmen" bands who held out in the mountains of the Cape Province. Only from accounts such as these can we glean details of their daily life, social organization, systems of belief, and material culture. Even here we find that important questions go unanswered and the necessary information must be recovered from the archaeological record. Investigations into the preceding centuries must depend more on archaeological data than documents, and all enquiry before the seventeenth century must perforce be conducted through the excavation of prehistoric remains.

The material traces of Stone Age activities in the remote past are ephemeral and frequently elude the untrained observer. At best they occur in dense accumulations (sites) composed of flaked stone, charcoal, and food debris representing temporary encampments of hunter–gatherer groups. Such accumulations are excessively vulnerable to destruction by the elements and fail to survive intact unless rapidly covered by protective deposits. This may occur through natural processes in a very restricted range of environments such as stream banks, lake shores, active thermal spring margins, and areas with unstable sand dunes.

Caves and rock shelters provide another shielding situation, whereas man-made accumulations of shellfish food debris (shell middens) provide a third type of insulation against the elements. But such preservation is the exception rather than the rule in southern Africa, where vast tracts of countryside are subjected to intensive surface erosion. This is caused by seasonal or irregular rainfall patterns, weakly developed soils, vulnerable and unstable vegetation cover, and a long history of overgrazing by European and Iron Age stock farmers. In such erosive environments all the organic remains in the Stone Age site will be lost, leaving only the more resistant stone artifacts scattered over the eroded surface. Even the original deployment of flaked stone about the encampment is thus destroyed. The disadvantages of surface sites for prehistoric research are therefore obvious.

By contrast, the suitably protected site, if excavated by professionally controlled methods, may yield information on lithic technology, diet, contemporary climatic conditions, and the deployment of different activities about the original encampment. Sites in this condition are said to be in primary or archaeological context, whereas sealed sites that have been partially destroyed or disorganized prior to burial are in secondary or geological context. Secondary-context sites are sometimes difficult to recognize and may be misleading. It is likely that the horizontal arrangement of materials in any sealed site has been partly disorganized during burial, and not even the finest primary-context "floors" are entirely exempt from such disruptions. The distinction between a primary- and secondary-context occurrence therefore is blurred. It is hardly surprising that professional archaeologists in this field are increasingly concerned with recognizing the amount and type of disturbance in sealed sites. Serious disruption before burial may lead to false associations between objects and result in misinterpretation of the site as a whole.

Surprisingly few sealed sites contain the debris of only one brief occupation. Usually the sheltered nature of the locality has attracted human habitation repeatedly over very long periods so that the deposits contain numerous super-imposed occupation levels. Such multilevel sites are essential for the chronological ordering of the Stone Age record. Analysis of the stratigraphy of a layered deposit should yield a relative time scale in which the lowest levels are shown to be earlier than those overlying them. Such procedures for relative dating nowadays frequently are supplemented by absolute dating of individual layers. Charcoal or other organic materials taken from the layer are processed by the carbon-14 method to yield an absolute date within stipulated limits of probability. The technique has been shown to be effective for materials up to about 60,000 years old and perhaps beyond this date. Thus, the carbon-14 method has provided a basic chronological framework within which the later and most complex portion of the Stone Age record may be explained.

Multilevel sites can be subjected to the same kinds of disturbance and disorganization of objects already discussed. Not only must natural agents be considered but also the scuffling effects of human feet which may have displaced objects horizontally or trodden them down into earlier occupation levels. Wheareas vertical displacement of objects in a single-occupation site will only break up the pattern of the floor scatter, serious mixing of layers can take place in multilevel deposits. Thus, objects of disparate ages may be found in a close but false association, which cannot always be detected by even the most skillful and experienced excavator. Unfortunately, charcoals are subject to the same vertical mixing so that younger carbon samples may migrate downwards into older levels and vice versa. The carbon-14 readings from a multilevel site may flatly contradict the stratigraphic evidence when younger dates underlie older ones. Such "inverted dates" may provide some measure of the degree of disturbance within the deposits. Dating inversions are unhappily a far too common feature of stratified sites in southern Africa, where clear visible layering of the deposits is often entirely absent.

The excavating procedures adopted to cope with this situation have varied considerably in the past. Without visible strata to control the thickness of individual excavated levels, arbitrary spits have been removed and their archaeological contents treated as single cultural units. Thus, the thickness of a single excavated spit is frequently determined by the whim of the excavator, who may take into account the richness of the deposit, local stratified features in the spit, or apparent changes in the content of the spit. All too frequently other nonarchaeological factors have been allowed to enter the excavator's decision about a particular spit depth. Another common practice is to combine the contents of several superimposed spits in the final presentation of excavated data. Thus, cultural debris covering perhaps several millenia are presented as a single cultural unit without any indication of stylistic changes through that period. The reason behind such presentation is usually the excavator's opinion that the contents of all the combined spits are identical. No attempt is made to justify the opinion by presenting a spit-by-spit analysis of what was actually excavated. Such details would also help to demonstrate what portions of the cultural and food debris were kept for analysis after the excavations were completed.

Before the advent of numerical analytical procedures in Stone Age archaeology, it was fairly common practice among excavators to jettison all but the most obvious artifacts plus a representative sample of food waste. In southern Africa such selective habits have unfortunately persisted into quite recent times, and many analyses remain incomplete for want of adequate information on less spectacular items in the Stone Age record. Typical of this category are the flaking by-products of stone tool manufacture and the smaller animals that formed part of the prehistoric diet. Inevitably the uneven standards applied in excavations, analysis, and presentation of archaeological data have greatly influenced the rate at which prehistoric research has advanced.

Archaeological site reports also vary widely in quality and detail. A few extremely haphazard or selective excavations have been reported in more detail than is really necessary since the provenance of so many described objects is either unknown or in doubt for want of adequate field records. A far greater number of well-controlled excavations have received cursory descriptions in "preliminary reports" that have never been followed up by full-scale analysis. Much information remains to be gleaned from archaeological collections excavated over the last twenty years and now stored in various institutions. Final reports that meet with acceptable international methods of presentation are regrettably few, but have increased in number during recent years and promise a general improvement in standards. However, long delays between final excavations and full reporting may continue to plague the progress of this field. Archaeology has come to rely increasingly on a wide range of specialists whose major interests do not necessarily include prehistory. Biologists, geologists, soil chemists, and others are frequently asked to contribute to these studies with what time they can spare from their own research, thus contributing to delayed publication.

Many pitfalls therefore await the prehistorian intent upon synthesizing and interpreting the archaeological record of this region. So varied is the quality of all the primary sources upon which he must draw that almost any attempt at interpretation can be criticized as overambitious or even rash. This book, while directing the reader's attention to the relative value of different sources, will nonetheless put forward a number of interpretations not previously considered. These are presented, together with a revised terminology, in the hope of provoking more vigorous critical discussion of overall interpretation—a field which has been sadly neglected over the past fifteen years.

In an area the size of southern Africa—taken here to include the territory of Zambia, Angola, and all the land to the south of these two countries—excavated sites are still sparsely distributed. This may be expected in an area of some 2.5

million square miles in which archaeological research has been pursued for barely fifty years and at no time by more than a dozen full-time professional archaeologists. Thus, our ideas about prehistoric events are almost all vulnerable in the sense that they are supported by too little information. With very few exceptions, the interpretation made possible by the available evidence could all be modified to some extent by the next decade's research. Such changes have taken place repeatedly during this century.

Attempts to interpret the whole Stone Age record in this area have been undertaken on several occasions before, and each work reflects the methods and preoccupations of the times. The pioneer efforts of Johnson in *The Stone Age Implements of South Africa* (1907b) and *The Pre-Historic Period in South Africa* (1907a) are concerned primarily with the classification of surface finds in the terms developed in southwestern France in the nineteenth century. Peringuey's "The Stone Ages of South Africa" (1911) shows a similar concern. Not until Burkitt's *South Africa's Past in Stone and Paint* (1928) with Goodwin's and van Riet Lowe's "The Stone Age Cultures of South Africa" (1929) do we find a break with the French terminology and an attempt to isolate groups of associated artifacts referred to as "cultures." The need for sites showing a stratified series of "cultures" that would demonstrate their relative ages was realized by these authors, but most of their earliest field evidence came from surface sites or collections taken from ancient river terrace sequences. Later works such as Leakey's *Stone Age Africa* (1936) and Alimen's *Prehistoric Africa* (1957) reflect greater concern with the correct sequence of "cultures" in relation to a hypothetical framework of "pluvials" or periods of increased rainfall, now realized to be inadequately supported by field evidence.

It is now over ten years since the first appearance of Clark's excellent paperback edition of *The Prehistory of Southern Africa* (1959a), and it remains a valuable introduction to the subject, although still based on the suspect "pluvial" chronology then in use. The pioneer terminology of Goodwin, van Riet Lowe, and Burkitt was skillfully adapted to a geographical approach based on regional comparisons—a model which has continued in use to the present time. The work appeared in time to use the first results of the carbon-14 dating technique, but it nevertheless remains committed to an environmental approach, with less emphasis on stratigraphy, chronology, and stone artifact analysis. Since its publication many new sites have been excavated, the "pluvial" framework has been abandoned in favor of carbon-14 dates, and numerical analysis has been widely adopted for describing Stone Age material.

ARTIFACT CLASSIFICATION

The raw materials of Stone Age research include stone artifacts, rare wooden or bone tools and ornaments, animal bones, very rare human bones, plant remains, and other ephemera such as traces of dwellings, hearths, paintings, or

engravings. Associated with these remains we may find charcoal and possible
environmental indicators in the form of soil features or traces of fossil pollen.
From each of these it may be possible to obtain information about the human
past: skills, ability to work with stone and other raw materials, changing fash-
ions in artifact design, the diet, hunting ability, butchery techniques, physical
appearance, burial practices, settlement patterns, hunting-group size, aesthetic
concepts, possibly some insight into supernatural beliefs, absolute age, the contemporary environment (flora, fauna, rainfall, etc.), and systems for exploiting
food sources in that environment. This list reflects the *maximum* information
that might be obtained from the archaeological record of an ancient illiterate
hunter–gatherer society. Any one Stone Age site almost never provides the full
range of materials giving such information, and this is especially true of southern Africa where conditions of preservation vary widely from place to place.
Stone artifacts, being the most durable, therefore constitute the largest part of
the material record.

This work will follow the procedures for artifact classification proposed at the
Burg Wartenstein Symposium on Terminology in 1967 (Clark 1968). The basic
terminology is summarized briefly as follows.

A buried mass of similiar artifacts in primary context are thought to reflect the
skills, aims, and needs of a single prehistoric human group. The single mass represents a small part of the much larger body of refuse left by that group over a
wider hunting territory. Groups in different parts of the country may show similar habits of artifact design. Thus, the artifacts buried at one site represent a
minute proportion of a much larger artifact population spread over a wide area.
By excavating the single mass the archaeologist is taking a sample of the whole
population. This collection of artifacts is therefore called a *sample*. The place
where it is found is called a *site,* which may yield several samples from different
depths in the deposit. One sample in a multilayer deposit may be referred to as
a *horizon*. A group of similar samples found at numerous sites perhaps hundreds
of miles apart is called an *industry*. Unhappily the Burg Wartenstein agreement has not provided a term to indicate chronological subdivisions of an industry. It will become apparent in later chapters that the styles, shapes, and size of
artifacts in most industries change with time, and these changes may be reflected
in a buried sequence of superimposed samples. Such vertical or chronological
subdivisions will be referred to as *phases*. Finally, the largest entity is a group
of similar industries covering a very large area. This is termed an *industrial
complex*. For the sake of brevity the term *complex* will be used in the present
work. It may include samples found thousands of miles apart that shared many
features. This similarity cannot possibly be the result of direct contact between
the two groups that made the samples; yet it shows that they belong to the same
technical tradition.

It will be useful at this stage to outline the basic procedures of artifact analysis. Analysis is based on the assumption that an unselected stone artifact sample can be divided into three categories: tools, cores, and waste. The tools are those specimens with traces of damage, usually on sharp margins or edges, that suggest use, resharpening, or deliberate shaping before use. These are considered to reflect a variety of activities by the makers, but the exact use of most tools remains problematical. They also form a wide variety of shapes and sizes that lend themselves to further subdivision. There is general agreement that the tools provide more useful information than the other two categories. The cores, which are pieces from which sharp flakes have been struck, were seldom used, but they are thought to provide information about the basic techniques of flaking. Elaborate preparation of cores took place in order to obtain flakes of specific shapes and sizes, and different techniques of preparation have been widely recognized. The cores, therefore, can also be subdivided, and again there is debate on how this should be done, although less interest is taken in this field than in the classification of tools. The waste category comprises an unusually large portion of the sample and contains flakes without any trace of marginal damage, deliberate trimming, or other signs of use. Most archaeologists agree that waste should be included in the analysis, but this has seldom been done.

After the artifact sample has been subdivided into clusters of tool types and core types, the numbers of each cluster are recorded. Each type may be quoted as a percentage of the tool total, and the same may be done for the cores. These percentages reflect the relative proportions of different tools in the sample and the relative importance of different flaking techniques among the cores. They represent the range of stylistic preferences of the group(s) that made the sample, and the percentages can be directly compared with those of other samples. Thus, a certain degree of objective comparison is made possible, given that an identical system of classification or *typology* is applied to all samples.

Certain features of individual tool types may repay closer examination such as size, shape, or the angle of some working edge, and to this end some specimens may be measured in order to determine the range of variability displayed by one type. The purpose of the classification is to determine the similarities and differences among samples from various areas and to detect changes in artifact proportions with time. The chronological changes provide information about the phases of the industry, and in a wider sense about the sequence of different industries. For this information we rely on the stratigraphy of multilayered sites. The paucity of standardized typologies in southern Africa makes it difficult to present a complete numerical breakdown of all known samples in any one industry. However, it is possible to list the range of types from most samples in terms of "present" or "absent" rather than as percentage ratios. Where figures are available, these are quoted in tables or graphs as a basis for discussion of what is thought to be significant.

NOMENCLATURE

In 1957 the Third Pan-African Congress of Prehistory proposed an arrangement of entities that may be summarized as follows (Clark 1957b):

	Chronological stage	Industries and variants
5.	Later Stone Age	Wilton, Smithfield, *Strandloper*
4.	Second Intermediate	*Magosian*, Howiesonspoort, *Modderpoort*
3.	Middle Stone Age	Stillbay, Pietersburg, Mossel Bay, *Mazelspoort, Alexandersfontein*
2.	First Intermediate	Sangoan and *Fauresmith*
1.	Earlier Stone Age	*Pre-Chelles–Acheuls, Chelles–Acheuls*

The framework rests on a five-stage chronology, although it was pointed out that certain industries could be subdivided—usually on the "early, middle, and later" basis at stratified sites where deposits were unusually deep. The Burg Wartenstein Symposium has agreed to abolish the five-stage nomenclature in favor of a sequence of complexes based on sealed and stratified field data (Clark *et al.* 1968b).

To conduct such a revision it is necessary that several names used to describe industries in the preceding tabulation be abandoned. All those listed in *italics* are represented by numerically distorted or mixed collections, most of which come from surface scatters or other suspect contexts. Terms like "Chelles–Acheul" and "Strandloper" do not represent actual sites or samples to which other materials may be referred or compared.

In erecting a revised framework of industrial complexes composed of various industries, much new excavated evidence must be taken into consideration. So many sealed samples have become available during the past fifteen years that several new terms are needed to describe entities which were not previously recognized or were completely unknown. The revised nomenclature proposed in the present work is given in Table 1.

This is obviously a more elaborate framework than that proposed in 1957 and contains more than a dozen (*italicized*) terms not previously used in the literature of the southern African Stone Age. The justification for adopting these terms is presented in the appropriate chapters on each complex. When considering the number of terms already dropped from the literature, the introduction of so many new ones inevitably will be criticized. It should be stressed here that the nomenclature in this field must perforce remain flexible as fieldwork increases and more results become known. The new terminology proposed here is designed to reflect the present state of research and will be subject to alteration itself as more information is made available. Whether the above terms are thought suitable or not, it is evident that a functional vocabulary will be essential to describe the numerous artifact samples that recent excavations have produced.

TABLE 1

Revised Nomenclature Proposed by Stone Age Industrial Complexes of Southern Africa

Complex	Industry	Phase
11. *Coastal*	Sandy Bay	*Preceramic* and *Ceramic*
10. Smithfield	?	*Preceramic* and *Ceramic*
9. Wilton	Coastal and *Interior* Wilton, Matopan, Pfupian, Zambian Wilton, Nachikufan	*Early–Classic–Developed–Ceramic*
8. *Oakhurst*	*Oakhurst, Lockshoek*, Pomongwan	Early and Late
7. ?	Howiesonspoort, Umguzan	—
6. ?	"post-Howiesonspoort"	—
5. Bambata	Bambata, Mwulu, Florisbad, Stillbay?	—
4. Pietersburg	Pietersburg, *Orangian*, Mossel Bay	Early and Late
3. Sangoan	Sangoan	Early and Late (Charaman)
2. Acheulian	—	Typical, Late, and *Final*
1. Oldowan	—	Typical and Developed

As a general procedure, a new term was adopted only after a group of related sealed samples had been recognized to share numerous distinctive features that may include typology and geographical distribution. The actual name then is chosen to represent a site from which a sealed, numerically undistorted sample has been excavated by controlled methods. If several such sites exist, that from which the first sample was taken is adopted as it has historical precedence over the others. A few older terms like "Acheulian," "Sangoan," and "Smithfield" have been retained since they are deeply entrenched in the literature and are so widely used that their removal would serve no useful purpose.

STRATIFIED SITES AND THEIR CORRELATION

The sequence of complexes and industries outlined above is derived entirely from the excavation of stratified sites in which samples of two or more industries can be chronologically separated. Thus, typology, stratigraphy, and carbon-14 dating have been adopted as the only reliable framework within which to trace the sequence of prehistoric events in different regions of the subcontinent. The distribution of such excavations is shown to be largely restricted to the eastern portion of the subcontinent (see the endpapers). Whereas single-level sites have been excavated in the western Cape, South-West Africa, Botswana, and Angola, virtually nothing is known of archaeological stratigraphy in the west.

Correlations between multilevel sites proceed on the assumption that the same sequence of industries is represented in deposits which may be hundreds of miles apart. The main objective is to establish a sequence of prehistoric culture changes for individual regions and to compare cultural differences between regions during single periods in the past. Only when this space–time framework

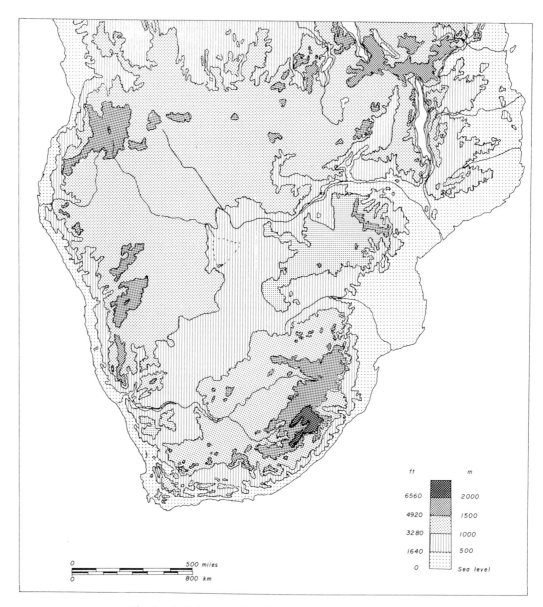

ft		m
6560		2000
4920		1500
3280		1000
1640		500
0		Sea level

Fig. 1. Relief map and major rivers of southern Africa.

has been firmly erected, can we reach any understanding of the processes underlying prehistoric culture changes in southern Africa.

The correlation chart on the endpapers includes several *regions* that corre-
spond partly to geographical or political subdivisions, but also take into
account the relative abundance of stratified sites. The complex pattern of cul-

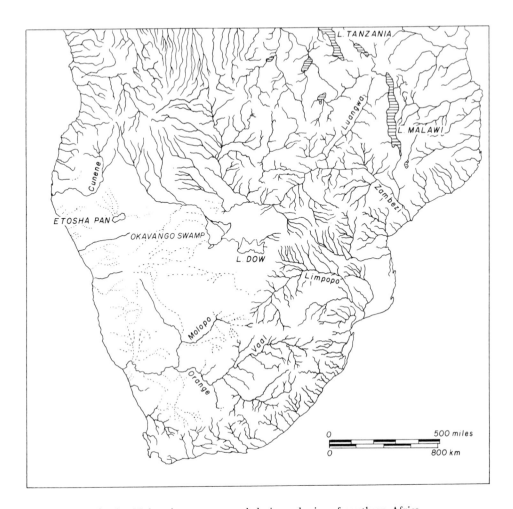

Fig. 2. Major river systems and drainage basins of southern Africa.

ture changes suggested by this chart reveals that some industries and even complexes overlap in time but are restricted to different regions. In a few examples,
industries appear to overlap in the same region, and these situations are discussed in the appropriate chapters where supporting evidence from the
carbon-14 dating technique is also introduced.

Finally, the reader unfamiliar with the physical geography of the subcontinent
may find the group of maps dealing with relief, river systems, vegetation, mean
annual rainfall, and temperature of some assistance (Figs. 1–5). Political boundaries and major drainage basins will be mentioned frequently, as well as provincial territories and special physiographic regions. All the most commonly quoted
areas are mapped for the reader's convenience in Fig. 6.

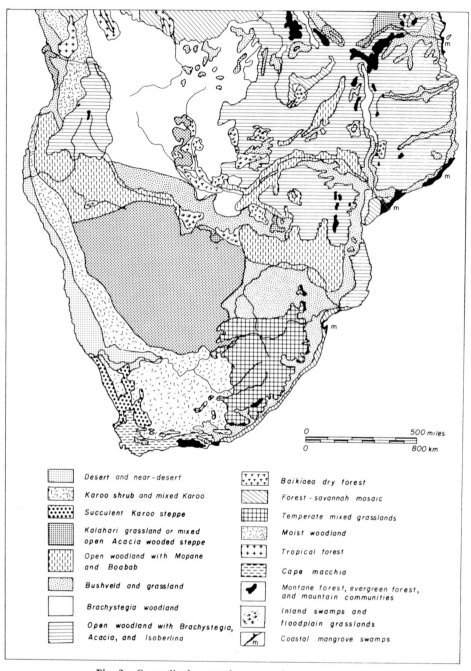

Fig. 3. Generalized vegetation map of southern Africa.

Legend:

- Desert and near-desert
- Karoo shrub and mixed Karoo
- Succulent Karoo steppe
- Kalahari grassland or mixed open Acacia wooded steppe
- Open woodland with Mopane and Boabab
- Bushveld and grassland
- Brachystegia woodland
- Open woodland with Brachystegia, Acacia, and Isoberlina
- Baikiaea dry forest
- Forest-savannah mosaic
- Temperate mixed grasslands
- Moist woodland
- Tropical forest
- Cape macchia
- Montane forest, evergreen forest, and mountain communities
- Inland swamps and floodplain grasslands
- Coastal mangrove swamps

0   500 miles
0   800 km

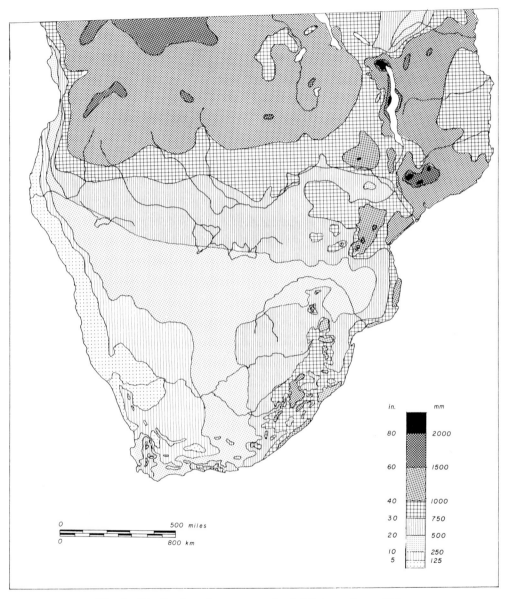

in.	mm
80	2000
60	1500
40	1000
30	750
20	500
10	250
5	125

0   500 miles

0   800 km

Fig. 4. Distribution of mean annual rainfall in southern Africa.

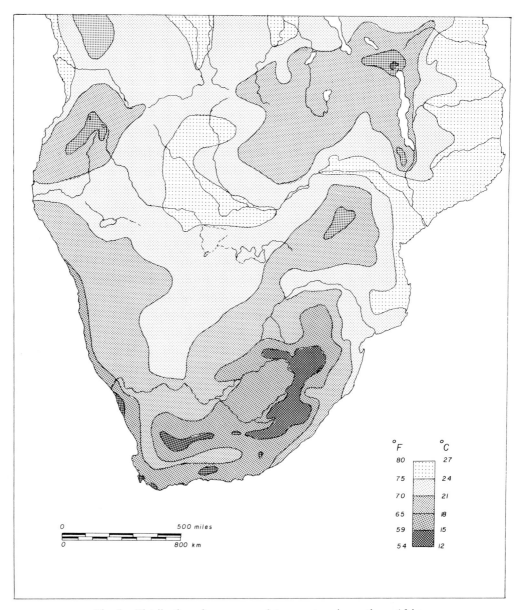

Fig. 5. Distribution of mean annual temperature in southern Africa.

Fig. 6. Political boundaries, provinces, capitals, and major cities in southern Africa.

15

2

The Earliest
Hominid Sites

INTRODUCTION

Fossil remains of the earliest known hominids have been found in five ancient caverns in South Africa (see Fig. 7). Abundant fragments representing over 100 individuals have been recovered from the hard cemented deposits that accumulated in each cave over a period estimated to fall between about 3 million and 500,000 years ago. In the same deposits occur fragmentary fossils of a wide variety of extinct and modern animals, and three sites have yielded small but important samples of stone artifacts. Together, these five sites constitute the largest single body of evidence available for the study of human origins, and, as such, their importance cannot be exaggerated.

Field research has been carried on sporadically over nearly fifty years during which one site was destroyed completely by commercial limeworkings and the others were extensively damaged. Since four of the caverns are formed in the coarse limestones or dolomites of the Transvaal system, they also contain layers of pure reconstituted limestone together with the fossil-rich deposits. Commercial exploitation of these lime beds led to the original exposure of the fossil deposits, parts of which were blasted out and dumped on the surface. Thousands of fossils have been recovered from the dumps, and the exact position in the deposits of most of these is not known. The recovery of fossils is extremely slow; they must be chiseled out or developed in acetic acid baths, which release the bone from its rocky matrix.

Fieldwork continues at three of the five sites, and new discoveries may alter some of the conclusions and tentative interpretations that appear at the end of this chapter. Doubtless, many more papers will be added to the already vast literature on these sites. Although few original interpretations are offered, the synthesis attempts to isolate problems for future research.

DOLOMITE CAVE FORMATION

A detailed study of the evolution of caverns in dolomite has been carried out by Brain (1958, 1967e), who has also proposed a system for classifying the breccias and other deposits found in some of them.

A chamber can be formed in dolomite below the water table in an area of structural weakness. If the level of the water table is lowered, the cavern may be scoured by flowing water and further dissolved by percolating surface water rich in carbonic acids. Any vertical joints in the rock forming the roof of the cavern may be widened by percolating groundwaters. These widened joints are called *avens*. During this period some indirect link with the surface may develop through adjacent tunnels and caverns already opened to the air. Mild ventilation allows moisture to evaporate so that carbonates are deposited from the percolating groundwater to form flowstone (travertine) on the cavern floor, or even stalactites and stalagmites if the carbonate precipitation is relatively rapid. A by-product of dolomite solution is a residue of insoluble, very angular chert grains released from the rock. These may be precipitated as lenses of residual cave earth in the travertine.

Eventually an aven will widen sufficiently to form a vertical shaft linking the cavern with the surface. Surface debris will pass down the shaft and accumulate very slowly over the basal travertine. With this, there may occur high concentrations of bone material resulting from activities around the mouth of the funnel at the surface. Agents of bone accumulation may include leopards, porcupines, hyenas, owls, possibly saber-tooth cats, and primitive hominids. This accumulation also receives percolating water rich in carbonates which cement the deposit into a *Phase I breccia.*

The increased widening of the shaft allows the rapid accumulation of surface soil and rubble over the Phase I breccia. Because this infilling is relatively quick there is less time for bones to accumulate, and these are usually scarce in the upper deposit, which is known as *Phase II breccia.*

1925). The geologist R. B. Young visited the limeworks in 1924 and was given the breccia blocks containing the fossil hominid. These were salvaged during blasting operations by a quarryman named M. de Bruyn, who was able to show Young the exact locality from the quarry face (Dart 1925a, 1926); the skull was shown to have come from a reddish travertine overlaid by a sterile red sand body in the cavity (Young 1925). De Bruyn's eyewitness account of the exact locality is the only one available. In published photographs it is marked as the lower left portion of the cavity fill, some 50 ft below modern ground level and about 200 ft in from the original travertine cliff face.

Soon after Dart had developed the specimen and published his now famous account of its manlike features (Dart 1925a), the eminent anthropologist A. Hrdlička visited the site, but found that the original cavity had been completely quarried away (Hrdlička 1925). The entire working face had advanced some 50 yd beyond the original cavity, and a narrow breccia-filled fissure in the quarry floor was all that remained of it. In the new quarry face he observed another distinctive cave filling at almost exactly the same level as the original one. He excavated part of this, recovering numerous fossil animal bones but no further hominid remains. The quarrymen left "Hrdlička's Cave" intact, removed some travertine from around it, then moved their working face to a lower level further back. This enabled R. Broom to collect further fossils from the site in 1937, when he identified a third fossiliferous cavity called "Spier's Cave," now also destroyed (Broom and Schepers 1946).

In 1948 F. E. Peabody led a research team from the University of California, which reopened the excavations at "Hrdlička's Cave," and plotted the stratigraphy in some detail (Peabody 1954). At the base of the cavity filling was a "massive red sandy limestone" containing fossil remains of tortoise, baboon, small antelope, shrews, rodents, small carnivores, bats, hyrax, and blocks containing "the track-marks of small animals." Over this was a "pure lime" with lenses of red sandy limestone containing only baboon and small antelope, and the remaining cavity was filled to the roof with semicemented sterile red sand (see Fig. 8). Peabody placed a climatic interpretation on all three layers (dry–wet–dry), which is now unacceptable in the light of Brain's study of the development of limestone cavity deposits already mentioned. There is a definite consensus between Dart, Broom, and Peabody that the original cave and "Hrdlička's Cave" were two exposures of a single tunnel-shaped cavity, or at least two arms of the same cave system. They occurred at the same level, and both yielded a fauna dominated by small animals. Microscopic examination of breccia enclosing the hominid skull showed that its mineral constituents were identical to those from the basal sandy limestone at "Hrdlička's Cave." Peabody stressed that the state of preservation of the skull was more in keeping with that of the fossils from the overlying "pure lime." These fossils were covered with a drusy calcite similar to that covering one side of the hominid brain cast, but such crystalline formations were not found on the fossils from the basal sandy limestone.

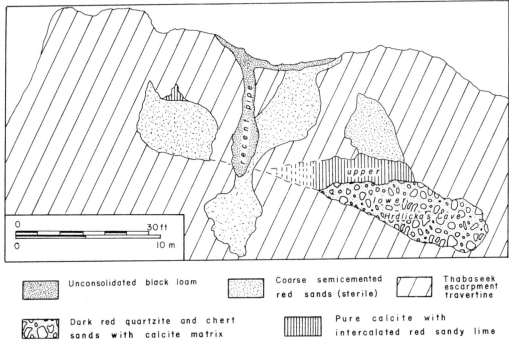

Unconsolidated black loam

Coarse semicemented red sands (sterile)

Thabaseek escarpment travertine

Dark red quartzite and chert sands with calcite matrix

Pure calcite with intercalated red sandy lime

Fig. 8. Section through the north quarry face at Taung. The upper and lower Hrdlička's Cave run parallel to the Thabaseek escarpment. The quarry floor is 45 ft below the surface. The position of the Taung skull is at the same level, but 110 ft west of Hrdlička's Cave. Probably the skull cave and Hrdlička's Cave belong to the same gallery system. (After Peabody 1954.)

Although some doubt will always surround the exact locality and associations of the Taung hominid, the field research that took place after the initial discovery in no way contradicts the verbal report of de Bruyn, who identified the find spot.

MAKAPAN

The Makapan Limeworks, also known as Makapansgat, have yielded remains extensively discussed by Dart in numerous papers over the past twenty years. Abundant faunal remains, several australopithecine fragments, and numerous fractured stones have been recovered from the site. Out of this material Dart has generated three controversial hypotheses almost as important as his initial claims for the Taung child. These are: (1) australopithecines made controlled use of fire; (2) they made systematic use of animal bones as tools; (3) they flaked and used stones brought into the site from elsewhere, as well as local stalagmite and cobbles in the cave. Although the hominid skeletal remains found here are not as impressive as those from other sites, the evidence relating to the behavior and cultural status of the australopithecines is of great importance. Before these can be adequately discussed, it is necessary to examine the stratigraphy and circumstances of the various finds.

The limeworks are about 10 miles east northeast of Potgietersrus in the central Transvaal and the site is on the south slope of the valley that contains Makapan Stream, a tributary of the Magalakwin River. Within the dolomite limestones of the lower valley slopes, several solution cavities and their fills have been exposed by erosion, and one, in particular, was found to contain a deep and pure cave travertine, varying in depth between 5 and 40 ft. This deposit was commercially exploited by White Limes Ltd. in the 1920s, and the overlying fossiliferous breccia was exposed for the first time.

W. I. Eitzman sent a collection of blackened bone fragments and a few ungulate teeth to Dart, who suspected that they had been burned. Analysis revealed that free carbon was present, and he concluded that the bones had been accumulated by man (Dart 1925b). In 1947 J. Kitching discovered an australopithecine occiput—now easily recognized by the numerous discoveries from other sites—and a systematic search of the breccia blocks in the limeworkers' reject dumps was started (Dart 1948a). Abundant fauna and several more australopithecine fragments were recovered. (Dart 1948b; Boné and Dart 1955). During geological work on the quarry faces Brain extracted fractured pebbles and stones thought by van Riet Lowe to be of human manufacture (Brain, van Riet Lowe, and Dart 1955), a conclusion regarded with skepticism by almost all other prehistorians. It was pointed out that the stratum from which the stones had been collected in fact overlay the bone breccia and was therefore later than the australopithecines, but A. Hughes, who had been systematically searching the breccias, soon discovered a hominid maxilla in breccia above, and therefore later than the stony horizon (Dart 1955b). By 1958 all the limeworkers' dump material had been searched, and further hominid remains were recovered (Dart 1958c, 1962a, b, c), including an almost complete australopithecine cranium found *in situ* (Dart 1959a, b).

In an attempt to resolve the numerous problems and uncertainties presented by this site, systematic excavation of the breccia is now in progress. Indisputable flaked stone artifacts have been recovered from the residual soil in deep solution cavities weathered into the surface of the breccia, and specimens have recently been recovered from the breccia itself (Dart 1965a; Partridge 1965). Numerous weathered cobbles and scree blocks from these potholes have been examined by B. Maguire, who is directing the excavations. He has concluded that several have been utilized (Maguire 1965).

The geology and stratigraphy of the site have been discussed in several papers. An early interpretation (Bosazza, Adie, and Brenner 1946) suggested successive invasions of wind-blown sands into an open cave where they became calcified. In 1947 Dart read a paper giving details of the cave fills, but accepting their eolian origin (Dart 1952). A geomorphological interpretation was applied by later authors (Barbour 1949; King 1951). In 1955 Brain began a detailed investigation of the deposits which culminated in a definitive monograph on all the Transvaal australopithecine-bearing deposits (Cooke and Wells 1957; Brain 1958). Brain's summary of the Makapan stratigraphy was essentially similar to that of Dart's some ten years earlier, but Brain's meticulous analysis of the sediments showed that they were not entirely of wind-blown origin. His description of the geology and formation of the deposits has been widely acknowledged as a definitive account, and some recent investigations have only slightly altered his original conclusions (Brain 1965).

It appears that a solution cavity first was formed in the dolomite, probably below the water table and without access to the surface. As the cavity became enlarged, a massive roofblock subsided, filling the lower part of the cavity and leaving a typical cleavage surface on the roof where the block became detached. Percolating water deposited pure travertine over the fallen block, and a small opening at the north end of the cavity permitted the slow accumulation of a typical Phase I breccia. This "lower Phase I" is composed of travertine with layers of residual cave earth and calcified surface sands. In places there are red calcified muds and patches of bone-rich gray or buff breccia and localized "rodent breccia." The "upper Phase I" is a hard pink breccia with fewer bones but abundant dolomite blocks. It is likely that the entrance had enlarged by this stage to allow a more rapid accumulation of deposits from the surface. The next stage is thought to coincide with a massive roof collapse, which caused a sudden enlargement of the cave mouth so that surface soil could be washed in rapidly. This "Phase II" breccia is a red-brown color very similar to surface soil in the area. It contains several stone horizons from which the questionable "artifacts" were obtained. Subsequent surface erosion of the valley flank has cut away most of the original dolomite roof so that upper Phase I and Phase II breccias are now exposed on the surface. For a summary of this development, see Fig. 9.

The limeworkers dug four irregular pits through the breccia to reach the basal travertine, which was then quarried away by lateral working until the original dolomite walls of the cavern were reached. It is now possible to walk on the original dolomite cavern floor below the overhanging upper Phase I breccia. During the course of quarrying most of the fossil-rich lower Phase I deposit was blasted away, leaving the harder pink upper Phase I breccia to form the roof of the cutting.

It has been pointed out (Haughton 1964) that the vast majority of specimens from the lower Phase I deposits were found in blocks on the quarry dumps and were not recovered *in situ*. Fortunately this gray breccia is easily distinguishable from the overlying pink (upper Phase I) and red-brown stony (Phase II) deposits so that the stratigraphic provenance of the contained material is reasonably certain. A much larger proportion of specimens has been recovered *in situ* from pink and red breccias, either by controlled excavation or extraction from

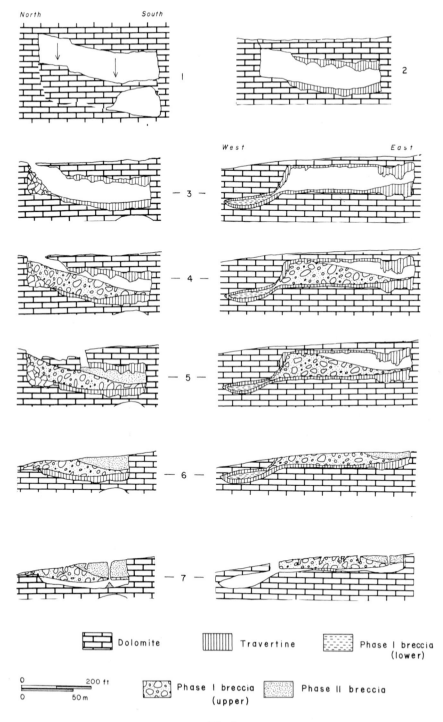

North   South

West   East

— 1 —
— 2 —
— 3 —
— 4 —
— 5 —
— 6 —
— 7 —

Dolomite   Travertine   Phase I breccia
(lower)

0   200 ft
0   50 m

Phase I breccia
(upper)   Phase II breccia

Fig. 9

24

TABLE 2

Makapan Breccia Deposits and Associated Finds

Phase [a]	Deposit	Finds	Context
Phase II	Sandy red-brown breccia, poorly consolidated, with dolomite pebble bands, collapsed into cavity left by travertine quarry. Full section exposed.	Australopithecine maxilla, Stone "artifacts" from pebble bands.	*In situ.*
Unconformity			
Upper Phase I	Hard pink consolidated breccia with abundant dolomite blocks. Extensive vertical sections. Deep solution cavities in exposed surface, filled with residual earth and dolomite, quartz, and chert blocks.	Complete australopithecine cranium, fragments. Stone artifacts from solution cavities. Abundant baboon remains.	*In situ,* some from dumps.
Lower Phase I	Banded travertines, calcified sands, residual cave earth, localized patches of gray or buff fossil-rich breccias.	Australopithecine fragments. Abundant bovid fauna. No stone artifacts.	Almost all from dumps, rarely *in situ.*
Basal	Travertine	Sterile	

[a] After Brain (1958).

exposed quarry faces. The reliability and association of the stone specimens and rare bones presently being excavated from pothole infillings of the upper Phase II breccias are still open to some doubt. It is likely that the carbonate of the original breccia has dissolved locally around tree roots that have long since disappeared.

The specimens found in the soft cavity fill would therefore be *in situ* and not washed in from the surface. As the breccia has dissolved away during the course of surface erosion, the more resistant quartz and chert blocks in the breccia have been concentrated in what is now the surface soil over the breccia. It is also

Fig. 9. Reconstructed geological sections through the Makapan cavern system, showing suggested stages in development: (1) roof collapse forming main cavern; (2) formation of avens and travertines on cavern roof and floor; (3) further roof collapse and wider opening to the surface; (4) lower Phase I (gray) breccia accumulates in the west end of the system, followed by upper Phase I (pink) breccias; (5) roof collapses continue, partly filling cavern with Phase II (red-brown) breccia; (6) erosion of surface hillslope removes remnants of collapsed dolomite roof, exposing breccias; (7) present situation after removal of basal travertines and Phase I breccia, with collapse cone of Phase II and dissolution cavities formed by tree roots in breccia surfaces. (After Brain 1958.)

possible that scree rubble containing artifacts could have washed down from up-slope, and the specimens are not therefore truly associated with the breccia. Recent verbal reports confirm that artifacts have been found embedded in the concentrated breccia walls of the potholes, suggesting that the association is in fact valid. The various deposits and their contexts are summarized in Table 2.

STERKFONTEIN

Extensive controlled excavations have been carried out over long periods at this site by archaeologists and palaeontologists, resulting in more reliable information than is available at present from Makapan. Sterkfontein has yielded probably the most complete australopithecine remains.

The site is one of three situated in the shallow valley of the Blaauwbank River, an upper tributary of the Crocodile River in the Transvaal. All three breccia exposures are located about 6 miles north of Krugersdorp in a limited area defined by an outcrop of the dolomite series belonging to the Transvaal system. The dolomite rests conformably on the Black Reef series, which are composed of quartzite and shale—a geological setting very similar to that of Makapan.

The entrance to the Sterkfontein caverns is situated in the northern flank of a small hill on the south bank of the Blaauwbank Stream. Further up this same slope limeworkings have opened up a massive breccia outcrop, part of which forms a roof to one of the subterranean caverns. These were first reported by explorers and prospectors in the 1890s, and the breccia was opened up by lime-workers in the 1930s. Its fossiliferous content was not noticed until 1935, when T. Jones recovered fossilized baboon remains from the workings (T. R. Jones 1936). His discovery drew the attention of the paleontologist, R. Broom, who was at that time virtually the only firm supporter of Dart's claim for the Taung skull (Broom 1925). He located further fauna in the breccia (Broom 1937a, b), and very soon located fragments of an adult primate that he suspected might be australopithecine. Further searching yielded the front two-thirds of a brain cast and several parts of the skull. Broom named this specimen *Plesianthropus transvaalensis* (Broom 1936a). Several other specimens were obtained in 1937, some of which came from deep in the breccia some 30 ft below the surface.

Further work was interrupted until 1946, when Broom recovered a virtually complete adult skull of an australopithecine, close to the spot where he had found the original specimen. By 1949 when he moved to another site, Broom had obtained the remains of not less than 15 individuals from this site as well as a substantial sample of fauna. Much of this material had been recovered by controlled blasting and excavation during 1947–1949, when Broom was assisted by J. Robinson (Broom and Robinson 1950b; Broom, Robinson, and Schepers 1950).

In 1954 Brain began his excavation of the breccia deposits and two years later he found stone artifacts in loose breccia on the surface, some 60 ft west of the main fossiliferous area, or "Type Site," which had never yielded any traces of foreign stones. Mason and Brain stripped off the overburden from this "Extension Site" area, finding several more artifacts (Robinson and Mason 1957). The exposed breccia itself was excavated by Robinson, who found artifacts, fauna, and australopithecine remains associated in the consolidated body of the breccia, as well as evidence for stratigraphy within the breccia (Robinson 1962b) which had, until then, been thought to comprise a single homogenous deposit.

The geology of the site was first published by H. B. S. Cooke (1938), who pointed out that the fossil-rich part of the breccia was in the upper portion only. This upper part lay at a steep angle, suggesting a talus slope. The bones therefore had been washed into the deposit from an upper cavity, now completely eroded away. The first accurate plan of the site (Broom *et al.* 1950) showed a fissure in the dolomite about 175 ft long on a southeast–northwest axis and about 45 ft wide with a roughly rectangular shape (Fig. 10). Part of the original dolomite cave roof runs along the northeast face of the fissure, whereas that in the opposite face has been blasted away.

Brain (1958) suggested that this cavern had developed when a subterranean cavity collapsed, leaving another cavity closer to the surface. This then filled with near-sterile breccia. In the last stages of infilling, a bone accumulation was washed in via the sloping dolomite roof, thus filling it completely. However, J. T. Robinson's (1962b) recent study has revealed a more complex stratigraphic situation (Fig. 11).

An upper- and a lower-solution cavity were formed in the dolomite without any connecting passage between them. The upper cavity was eventually opened to the surface by erosion and filled with surface rubble, which became calcified into a sterile pink breccia, the upper part of which contains abundant fossils and about 90% of all the australopithecine remains from the site. After the upper cavern had been completely filled, the wall of the *lower* cavern, which meanwhile had been expanding through dissolution processes, collapsed so that some of the upper cavern pink breccia tumbled into the newly opened deep cavity. The slumping formed an air space in the breccia close to the roof of the upper cavern, which again was filled, this time with a red-brown breccia containing stone artifacts, fauna, and some australopithecine remains. During this second phase of infilling, lumps of pink breccia still clinging to the roof fell into the red-brown sediment and were cemented in place by calcification. When the cavern had again filled up, minor subsidence caused further air spaces under the roof so that a third phase of infilling took place to form a chocolate-brown breccia with rare fauna and possible traces of stone artifacts. Subsequent surface erosion has cemented some of the original dolomite roof to expose all three of these distinct phases of infilling.

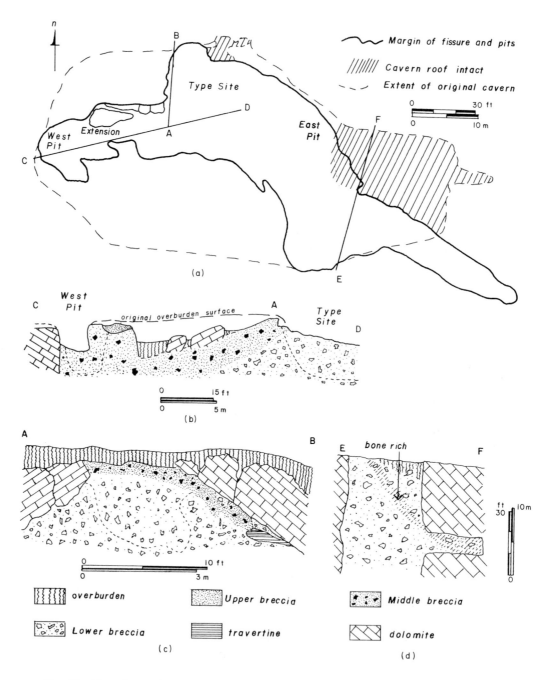

Fig. 10. Plan (a) and three sections (b, c, d) through the Sterkfontein locality. (After Brain 1958; J. T. Robinson 1962b; Tobias and Hughes 1969.)

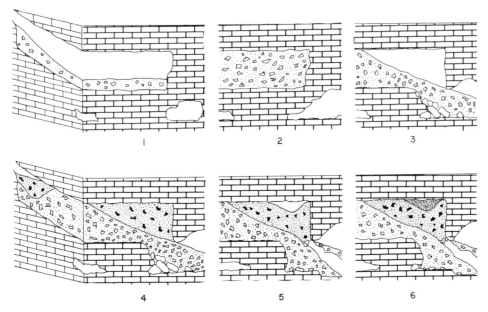

Fig. 11. Reconstructed sections through Sterkfontein, following Robinson (1962b). Suggested sequence of collapses and infilling of the cave system: (1) Formation of Phase I breccia through fissure entrance. (2) Total infilling of cavern by Lower (pink) breccia. (3) Cavern floor collapses into lower cavity, leaving space above Phase I breccia. (4) Space filled with Middle (red-brown) breccia. (5) Further settling of breccias, leaving smaller space below cavern roof; formation of travertine lenses in Lower (Type Site) breccia. (6) Formation of Upper (dark brown) breccia in spaces below dolomite roof. Butzer (1971) suggests that this is a weathered portion of the Middle breccia surface formed after erosion of the roof.

The deposits of the first phase have been called the *Lower breccia* by Robinson. Most of this material is near sterile except the upper, sloping band, which was excavated by Broom and Robinson in an area of the breccia exposure known as the "Type Site." The abundant fauna and most of the australopithecines come from this band. The Lower breccia is also sometimes called the Type Site breccia, pink breccia, or reddish breccia. It has yielded no stone tools.

The second phase of infilling is called the *Middle breccia* and is exposed at the western end of the fissure only. This area is known as the "West Pit" and the "Extension Site," and the Middle breccia is sometimes called the red-brown breccia or the artifact breccia. *Equus* is present in the small faunal sample.

The final phase is known as the *Upper breccia*, also the chocolate-brown or dark brown breccia. Remains of this are restricted to a small patch in the Extension Site near the north wall of the fissure, and it is only about 3 ft deep. A single stone artifact has been discovered in this deposit, and *Equus* remains are more abundant here than in the Middle breccia.

It should be noted that there is general agreement among most writers concerned with this site that the upper cavern was not actually occupied by either animals or man. It is assumed that the faunal, hominid, and cultural remains were washed in via a funnel at the back of some upper shelter or cave long since completely removed by surface erosion of the dolomite hillside. None of the occurrences is therefore in primary context.

Although artifacts have been excavated from the Middle breccia in direct association with australopithecine teeth, it should be noted that large blocks of fossiliferous Lower breccia fell into the deposit prior to solidification. As the upper part of the Lower breccia contains abundant australopithecine remains, there is a remote possibility that the Middle breccia teeth were in fact dissolved out of one of these intrusive lumps. If this were the case, the teeth would not be associated with the tools, but would be earlier. This problem may be resolved during the course of present excavations by Hughes, who has reexamined all the breccia dumps around the fissure margin, finding numerous further artifact and fossil remains including australopithecine teeth (Tobias and Hughes 1969).

SWARTKRANS

This site is generally recognized as the richest of all the known australopithecine breccias, having yielded some 15,000 diagnostic animal bones and the largest sample of the robust australopithecine *Paranthropus robustus*, together with relatively scarce but important remains of a new hominid form called *Homo sp.* Not only is this the only site where the two hominids are in association, but it has also yielded a fine sample of stone artifacts similar to those from the Sterkfontein Extension Site.

Swartkrans is a breccia exposure on the south flank of a low isolated hill on the north bank of the Blaauwbank River, and less than 1 mile west of Sterkfontein. Like the other two sites in this valley, the breccia was formed in a solution cavity in the dolomite series of the Transvaal system. However, the shape of this cavern system has not been determined by the bedding phases of the limestone, as is the case at all the other sites. The Swartkrans hill has two large faults crossing it roughly at right angles, and part of the fault breccia has dissolved to form an irregular cavern network that does not conform with the structure of the surrounding rock. Before quarrying began here, the surface of the breccia was exposed in a large narrow fissure.

It was first blasted in the 1930s by a prospector named Knowlan, who back-filled the quarry cavity with breccia. The fill became overgrown with vegetation so that later workers were unaware that the site had been disturbed (Brain 1967c, 1968). It was not until 1948 that Broom shifted his excavations from Sterkfontein and began work at Swartkrans for the first time, with the assistance of the University of California Africa Expedition. Almost immediately, the molar of a new hominid named *Paranthropus* was recovered, and numerous other fragments were soon obtained. In 1949 they also found a very large *Paranthropus* mandible and the jaws of a new genus called *Telanthropus,* but now considered to belong to the genus *Homo.* During these excavations a very thick band of pure white travertine was exposed, thus attracting the attention of limeworkers to the site once more. Nothing could be done to prevent them from blasting this and the adjacent breccia for commercial purposes, and they virtually wrecked the site by 1950. In the following two years the scanty remains of the fossiliferous breccia were systematically removed by Broom and Robinson, and the site was then abandoned. Only in 1965, when Brain resumed work on the breccia dumps here, was Knowlan's back-filled quarry found. This is packed with lumps of fossiliferous breccia and its removal has exposed further standing faces of *in situ* breccia. The extent of the site is therefore greater than previously realized, and work is still in progress to develop the newly discovered dump material.

The stratigraphy of the breccias was at first considered to be similar to that of Makapan (King 1951). This viewpoint was extensively reviewed by J. T. Robinson (1952b), who pointed out that the entire mass of breccia lay on top of a basal travertine and that the main breccia was not of eolian origin, but was similar to modern surface soil (Brain and Robinson 1953). The formation of the cavern system and its breccias has been studied in detail by Brain (1958).

The site divides into three features; a lower cave and two upper cavities known as the inner and outer caves. The lower cave contains no breccia and is linked to the surface cavities by two near-vertical shafts located at the east end of the outer cave floor (Fig. 12). The outer cave is an irregular fissure almost 130 ft long, and the inner cave is protected by a dolomite roof. A thick travertine occurred on the floors of the two upper caves, with a very thick travertine base near the junction of the two caves. A pink, richly fossiliferous, ungraded breccia was found in the outer cave, and this was overlaid unconformably by a stratified rocky brown breccia that dipped in the direction of the inner cave and almost entirely filled it. This later brown breccia is almost sterile.

Brain has postulated that the upper and lower caves were developed at almost the same time, and a small funnel connected the outer cave with the surface This allowed the formation of a thick travertine base, which cut off the inner cave from the outer and caused residual cave earth at the east end of the outer cave. A slight widening of the funnel caused a Phase I breccia deposit to develop in the southeast corner of the outer cave, and owl pellets worked their way down the funnel to form a rich rodent breccia. Slight widening of the funnel increased the ventilation and permitted the formation of the main pink breccia in the outer cave with its rich fossil content, including *"Telanthropus"* and *Paranthropus.* It is stressed that the cavern was never used by the hominids, who presumably occupied a surface shelter or cave connected to the top of the funnel, but which has now been completely destroyed by surface erosion of the hillside.

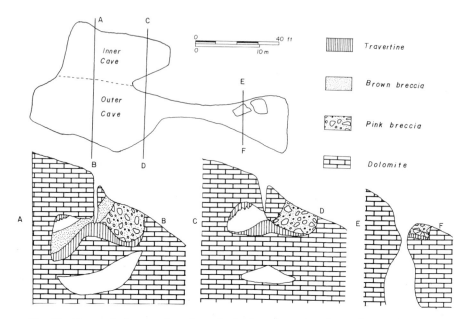

Fig. 12. Plan and three sections through the Swartkrans locality. (After Brain 1958.)

After the outer cave had been completely filled with pink breccia, the dolomite floor separating the upper and lower caverns partially collapsed, so that the travertine barrier between the inner and outer caves was broken through. By this stage the surface opening had been widened considerably, and the newly opened inner cave filled fairly rapidly with semisterile surface material, which became calcified into the brown breccia. Further minor subsidence of the dolomite floor caused narrow fissures in both breccias, and these cracks have filled up with relatively recent soil.

All the important hominid, faunal, and artifact remains have been recovered from the pink breccia in the outer cave. Brain (1968) has argued cogently that only a small part of the material is debris from human occupation at the mouth of the funnel leading down to the outer cave. It is probable that most of the fauna and the hominid remains result from leopard kills, which had been dragged up into trees that usually grow at fissure openings in this otherwise open grassland country. The content of the pink breccia is therefore in a geological context and only partially reflects the activities of the early hominids.

KROMDRAAI

Although a rich fossil fauna, a few reliable stone artifacts, and several fragments of *Paranthropus* have been recovered from the Kromdraai deposits, their association remains in some doubt since relatively little systematic work has taken place here. Much of the breccia still remains to be excavated and the bottom of the deposit has not yet been reached.

The site comprises two elongated fissures each about 80 ft long and 70 ft wide near the crest of a low hill on the south bank of the Blaauwbank River and only 1 mile from Sterkfontein. The form of the fissures conforms with the local structure of the dolomite in which they occur and there is general agreement among Broom, Robinson, and Brain that they both developed by a similar process and may possibly belong to the same cavern system. For convenience they have been labeled *Kromdraai A* and *B*.

In 1938 a schoolboy, G. Terblanche, picked up a fossilized hominid palate which he passed on to G. W. Barlow, the limeworks manager at Sterkfontein. The specimen was sold to Broom, who realized it did not come from Sterkfontein. He was taken to the find spot (now called Site B) and was given several other fragments, which he was able to piece together to form the type specimen of *Paranthropus robustus* (Broom 1939a, 1951). This specimen came from a loose decomposed block of breccia lying on the surface. In 1941, Broom placed a trial blast in a small circular patch of breccia exposed earlier by lime prospectors only a few feet away from where the block had been found. A juvenile *Paranthropus* mandible was found in the newly exposed breccia, thus supporting the claim that the type specimen truly belongs in Site B (Broom 1941a). However, very few faunal remains were recovered; he soon reached a stony sterile breccia and decided to abandon the site. Instead he turned to Site A in 1947, recovering a large sample of well-preserved fauna but no trace of any australopithecine remains. Brain returned to Site B in 1955–1956 in the hope of recovering a fauna with the *Paranthropus*. His work revealed that the deposits were more extensive than realized, but he nevertheless recovered only fragmentary bones together with several *Paranthropus* teeth, all in the upper 10 ft of the deposit. Both sites have yet to be fully excavated but at present show little promise of abundant material. Brain has recovered at least one whole chert artifact from Site B, and further work may prove useful (Brain 1958).

Since neither site has been excavated to its full depth, nothing definite is known about their stratigraphy or development. Both fissures contain a sandy reddish-brown breccia with a stony breccia at the east end of each. The near-vertical contact between the sandy and stony breccia strongly suggests that both fissures were connected to the surface by a vertical funnel that has been removed by surface erosion. The mode of accumulation, therefore, is similar to that of the other two sites in the valley, and none of the material is in primary context.

It is also apparent that the faunal sample from this site is *not* in direct association with the hominid remains, but a single reliable stone artifact has been recovered in direct association with Site B. Brain and Robinson have tentatively accepted that the two fissures may be coeval, but any consideration of the dating of the Kromdraai *Paranthropus* based on fauna should be treated with considerable reserve at present.

DATING AND CORRELATING THE DEPOSITS

Several different assessments of the relative ages of the deposits have been published. In the absence of any materials in the breccias that may be used for calculations of an absolute age, most authors have used the partly studied faunal
assemblages to obtain relative dates. The mammalian fauna from each site contains both extinct and living specimens of African game animals, carnivores, and
microfauna. When faunal assemblages from two different sites are being compared, the assemblage with the larger proportion of extinct specimens is generally accepted to be the older of the two. Conversely, the assemblage with the
larger number of living species is taken to be the younger. Using this basic prin-
ciple, it should be possible to arrange the various breccias in order of decreasing
age. Unfortunately, several difficulties have hampered the success of this apparently straightforward approach.

No complete or exhaustive classification of any of the five faunal assemblages
has appeared yet. The fauna samples from Makapan, Swartkrans, and Sterkfontein are being steadily enlarged by new finds, and final studies on these are not
possible. Published information on the fauna shows that certain groups of animals have been studied more closely than others and the data are therefore of
uneven quality.

Theoretical difficulties also arise from attempts to compare the fauna. The
modern environment surrounding Taung supports a semiarid thornbush vegetation in contrast to the Blaauwbank River valley, which is in grassveld country, and
Makapan, which is now situated in partly wooded so-called "highveld." Under
modern conditions it is clear that these three different habitats would not all
support the same range of animal species, and it is probable that they differed in
this respect in the past even during periods of fluctuating mean annual rainfall.
It is possible on theoretical grounds that certain extinct species are absent from
Taung because the local environment could not support them, and not because
Taung is a relatively "recent" site. It is clear, therefore, that species adapted to
restricted or specialized habitats (for example, *Hippopotamus*) are of limited
use in relative dating.

Another recurrent difficulty in assessing the relative ages of the breccias has
been the concern to align them within different chronological frameworks. Many
authors have attempted to arrange the sites within the time scale set up for the
Pleistocene sequence of eastern Africa, which was based on a series of "pluvials"
or prolonged periods of increased rainfall. Since this sequence is not supported
by adequate evidence in eastern Africa, it cannot be usefully applied in the
South. Detailed analysis of the different papers on this problem would serve little useful purpose since the pluvial framework has been abandoned. The various
(and conflicting) interpretations of the correct sequence of breccias can be summarized in historical order (see Table 3).

TABLE 3

History of the Sequential Dating of the Australopithecine Sites

"Pluvial" terminology	Haughton (1947)	H. B. S. Cooke (1952)[a]	Oakley (1954)	Howell (1955)	Ewer (1956a, 1957b)	Oakley (1957a)	Wells and Cooke (1957)	Brain (1958)	J. T. Robinson (1961)
Kamasian (second) pluvial	All sites	All	Kromdraai Swartkrans	Kromdraai Swartkrans Makapan (gray)	Kromdraai Swartkrans	Kromdraai Swartkrans	Kromdraai Swartkrans Makapan	Kromdraai	Kromdraai Swartkrans
Interpluvial	same age	sites same			Makapan Taung	Makapan Sterkfontein	Makapan Sterkfontein	Swartkrans Makapan Sterkfontein	Sterkfontein (Extension) Makapan Sterkfontein (Type)
Kageran (first) pluvial	(Makapan not mentioned)	age	Sterkfontein and Taung Makapan	Taung Sterkfontein (pink)	Sterkfontein	Taung	Taung		

[a] H. B. S. Cooke (personal communication, 1973) has pointed out that H. B. S. Cooke (1952) is misleading. The actual paper given at the Nairobi meeting (1947) was rather long, and the editors cut it without reference to the author. The original table survived in the published version and showed overlapping sequences for Makapan and the Sterkfontein area. This was the first attempt to separate the deposits, and it undoubtedly influenced Oakley, Howell, and Ewer, each of whom had the full text at their disposal as well as the table.

Recent assessments of the correct breccia sequence still rely mainly on Ewer's site-to-site comparison of selected groups of fauna; primates (17 species), insectivores (3), hyraxes (2), carnivores (29), and suids (4). Ewer points out that Makapan and Sterkfontein share nine species, and five of these are not found at any other sites. Swartkrans has more species in common with Makapan than it has with Sterkfontein and should therefore be placed later in the sequence. Kromdraai has least in common with Sterkfontein and Makapan and should be placed last in sequence after Swartkrans with which it has more in common. Exact placing of Taung has proved difficult because of ecological differences, but it is closer to Sterkfontein–Makapan than it is to the other two. The basic order: Sterkfontein–Makapan–Swartkrans–Kromdraai has been adopted by subsequent authors with minor adaptations. The results of Brain's granulometric study of Phase II breccias (see page 40) showed that Sterkfontein and Makapan were accumulating during periods apparently drier than the present. This evidence together with the findings of Cooke and Wells, who analyzed the vast bovid sample from Makapan (not considered in Ewer's analysis), caused the repositioning of the sequence seen in the chart. The basic order was slightly adjusted to accommodate the Sterkfontein Middle breccia in the sequence, after Robinson's analysis.

It is apparent that this site sequence, still widely quoted as proven, is based on an analysis carried out fifteen years ago on the evidence then available. Since Ewer's first published analysis other animal groups have been studied, and the original sequence needs to be considered in the light of this more recent work.

TABLE 4

Faunal Species Associated with the Early Hominid Sites [a]

	Taung		Sterkfontein		Makapan		Swartkrans		Kromdraai A	
Insectivores	3	(1)	11	(1)	4	(1)	5		5	(2)
Bats		(1)	—			(1)	—		2	(1)
Primates	7		5		6		7		5	
Hares		(1)	—			(1)		(1)	—	
Rodents	15	(4)	12	(8)	18	(8)	3		10	(6)
Carnivores		(1)	6		6		16	(2)	15	
Hyraxes	2		2		2		2		2	
Horses	—		—		2		1		4	(1)
Rhino	—		—		3	(2)	—		—	
Bovids	4	(1)	6	(1)	24	(11)	2		1	
Total no. of species present	34		42		67		37		44	
Living modern species		(9)		(10)		(24)		(3)		(10)
Modern species (%)	26.5		23.8		35.8		8.1		22.7	
Extinct species (%)	73.5		76.2		64.2		91.9		77.3	

[a] Numbers in brackets, living species.

The most up-to-date faunal lists are those presented by Cooke (1964) in which all the known species are included. Much more remains to be published. Table 4 summarizes these results. These faunas cannot all be compared with each other. The lists from Sterkfontein and Taung are similar in character with abundant microfauna, several primate species, and only scarce bovids. Also Kromdraai and Swartkrans share many characters, particularly the abundant carnivores. The Makapan list cannot be compared readily with the other two pairs since it includes abundant bovids and rodents.

Taung and Sterkfontein have only 12 species in common although the broad composition of their fauna appears to be similar. Ecological differences between the sites are frequently invoked by various authors to explain the small proportion of shared species (12 out of 59, about 20% shared). Taung appears to be the more arid habitat, as reflected in the microfauna, which contains several arid and semiarid species not present at Sterkfontein. Also, the factors causing the bone accumulations at both sites are very imperfectly understood. Another serious difficulty in comparing these assemblages is that the Sterkfontein species lists have never distinguished between the Lower and Middle breccia bone samples. These are two chronologically distinct assemblages at a single site that may display important differences. Until this distinction is made, it will remain impossible to determine whether Taung has more in common with the Lower or Middle breccia of Sterkfontein. The fact that Taung has a higher proportion of extinct rodents may suggest that it has more in common with the Lower breccia at Sterkfontein. This possibility is supported by the fact that only *Australopithecus africanus* has been found at both deposits and that stone artifacts are absent. Horse remains are absent from Taung and present in Sterkfontein Lower breccia, *Equus* also has been reported from the Middle breccia.

Comparisons between Swartkrans and Kromdraai A create different problems. Both sites share the same habitat, and the broad composition of their fauna is similar, but the Bovidae have not been studied. Both assemblages come from single stratigraphic units. They have only 18 species in common out of a total of 61 (29.5% species shared). As ecological separation cannot be invoked, the differences in species content must have arisen because they were deposited (1) at different times (2) by different processes. Swartkrans contains more extinct species, whereas Kromdraai A contains more living species, particularly rodents. Horse remains are present at both sites, but a greater number of species is present at Kromdraai A, which is almost certainly later than Swartkrans. However, the Kromdraai A fauna cannot be used to date the Kromdraai B hominid site. The microfauna from Kromdraai B contains as many extinct species as the Makapan sample and may be of comparable age (see page 91).

There is general agreement that the Taung–Sterkfontein faunas are older than the Swartkrans–Kromdraai A samples. However, these two pairs cannot be compared with much confidence because of differences in content. Kromdraai has the same population of extinct species as Taung–Sterkfontein, whereas

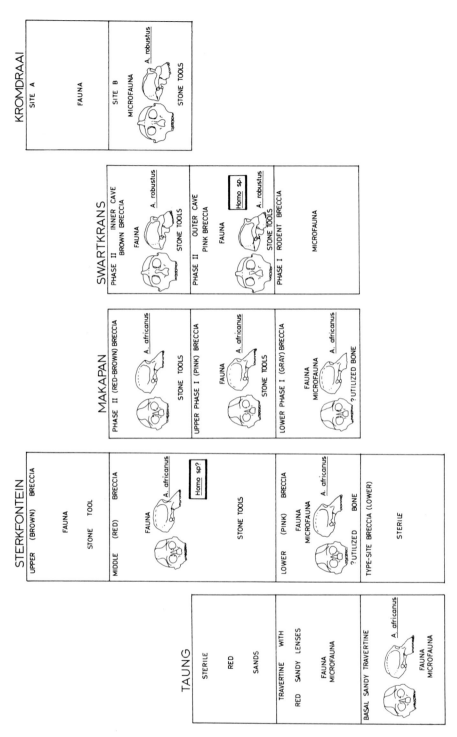

Fig. 13. Tentative correlation of the various geological units of the five australopithecine sites. The units at the bottom of the diagram are earliest and those at the top are latest in the sequence. The artifactual, faunal, and hominid content of each unit is displayed.

38

Swartkrans has a considerably higher percentage of extinct forms than any of the other sites. Considered in isolation, this may be taken to indicate that Swartkrans is the oldest, and that Kromdraai may be of similar age to Taung and Sterkfontein. However, this argument ignores the fact that *Equus,* which appears relatively late in the African faunal record, is abundant in Kromdraai and Swartkrans, suggesting that these are indeed the younger pair. Unfortunately, the bovids from these two are imperfectly reported, and it is expected that these, when eventually published, will reduce the population of extinct species at both sites (H. B. S. Cooke 1968). It is possible that Swartkrans and Sterkfontein Middle breccia may prove to be broadly contemporary when their faunas are compared.

The list for Makapan is certainly the most complete, but no attempt has been made yet to distinguish between the faunas of the lower Phase I breccia and the upper Phase I or overlying Phase II deposits. With so many modern species present (including *Equus*) it is possible that this fauna has more in common with Kromdraai and Swartkrans. Actually, Makapan has only 11 out of 94 species (12%) in common with Swartkrans and more in common with Sterkfontein: 17 out of 59 (29%). This discrepancy is overcome by Ewer, who placed Makapan between Sterkfontein and Swartkrans in the site sequence.

Clearly, there are still several discrepancies in the arguments put forward to support the established site sequence: Sterkfontein–Makapan–Swartkrans–Kromdraai A. Basically, this arrangement fails to admit the strong possibility that certain deposits may *overlap* in time. The faunas have been treated as single chronological units, whereas each faunal assemblage probably took an enormous length of time to accumulate. Phase I and Phase II faunas can be isolated and listed separately. When these are published together with complete analysis of the bovids from Swartkrans and Kromdraai, an accurate correlation between the sites may be sought.

A tentative overlapping correlation model for the five sites is shown in Fig. 13. The possibility that Swartkrans is the same age as the Phase II breccias from Sterkfontein and Makapan can be supported by granulometric data, which have been claimed to indicate similar fluctuations in past rainfall (see page 42).

This revised arrangement of the deposits permits a relatively straightforward sequence of the hominid finds: Taung and Sterkfontein Lower breccia, and Makapan Phase I breccia contain remains of a relatively gracile australopithecine without any evidence of stone toolmaking. The later group of deposits contains a more robust australopithecine, stone artifacts, and traces of a more "developed" hominid. Kromdraai B cannot be placed in the sequence with any certainty unless it is accepted on faith that the Kromdraai A fauna provides a true date for the hominid.

The problem of absolute dates for these sites is still being investigated (Tobias 1969; Tobias and Hughes 1969). An intensive search of the breccias has been made for materials that might prove amenable to dating by the potassium–argon, fission-track, and paleomagnetic techniques, but none has been found so far. The possibility of protactinium–thorium dating remains to be investigated.

Most authors agree that the faunal analysis places all the sites within the Lower Pleistocene or Villafranchian period, except Kromdraai A, which may be Middle Pleistocene. Broom (1945b), who made the first attempt to date the sites, suggested a Middle Pliocene age for Taung and Upper Pliocene for Sterkfontein. More recent work on fossil African mammals has shown this proposal to be unacceptable. Kurtén (1960, 1962) attempted to compare the incompletely reported breccia faunas with the European Pleistocene faunal sequence and suggested that they were post-Villafranchian and shared more in common with the so-called "Cromerian" faunas. It is unlikely that such long-range comparisons will prove useful, although detailed comparisons with potassium–argon dated faunas from eastern Africa should give valuable guides to their absolute age.

Climatic Deductions from Phase II Breccia Analysis

Phase II breccias, being composed of cemented surface materials from the outside hill slope should be expected to reflect surface conditions during the period of their accumulation. Realizing this, Brain (1957, 1958) undertook an intense study of dolomitic hillside soils in areas of widely differing rainfall. After grading these samples, he extracted the sand fraction from each and examined the washed grains under a microscope. These consisted of silicon (chert) grains only, and other mixed constituents in the sand were removed. He discovered that soils from dry climates contained a large proportion of well-rounded grains, and those from wetter regions contained a higher proportion of angular grains. Brain developed a technique for measuring the mean angularity of a sand-grain sample by determining the volume of airspace between the grains. A compacted sample of angular grains produces more air spaces than a similar sample of rounded or subrounded ones. Thus, the quantity of air space or *porosity* of the sand fraction in the soil is thought to be a direct reflection of rainfall conditions.

Phase II breccia samples were taken at various depths from all the sites, and the silica sand fraction was extracted by dissolving the carbonates with hydrochloric acid. The porosity of several samples from each level in a breccia was measured so that an average figure could be obtained, together with a minimum and maximum reading. These porosity readings could then be compared with those for the modern dolomite soil at the site entrance. The results are summarized in Fig. 14.

Brain also discovered that the breccia sands contained varying quantities of quartz grains derived from the Black Reef quartzites. At Sterkfontein, Swartkrans, and Kromdraai the nearest outcrop is about a mile away so the grains must have been carried by wind action. Thus, a high percentage of quartz in the

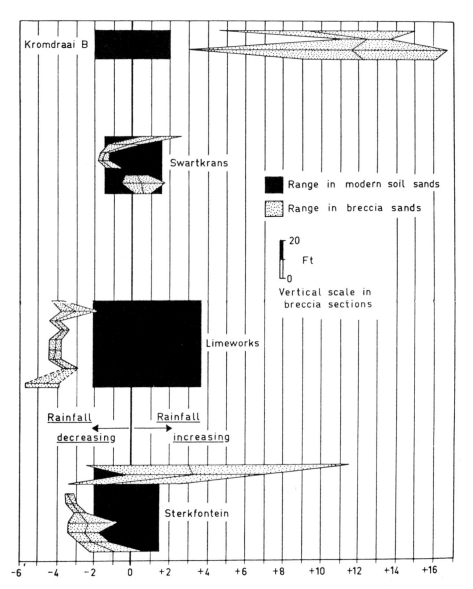

Fig. 14. Phase II breccias: 35–60 mesh sand—deviation in percentage porosity from zero, which represents average present-day conditions (28 inches of rainfall per year). The sand-grain porosity curves from Brain (1958) suggested this correlation. The fluctuation in sand-grain porosity (and implied rainfall) were thought to fit a hypothetical series of "pluvial" periods (see Table 3, page 35) now known to be unsupported by adequate field data.

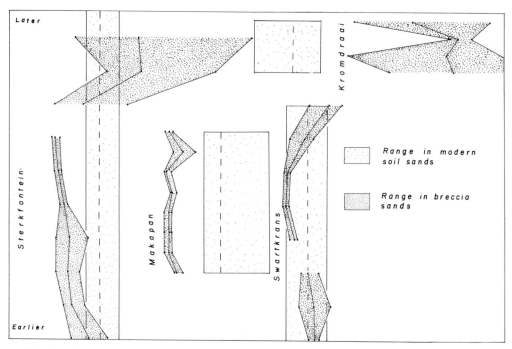

Fig. 15. Tentative correlations of porosity and chert–quartz ratio curves, showing the chronological overlap between Phase II breccias in different sites. The same data shown in Fig. 14 are arranged to fit the tentative correlation suggested in Fig. 13 (page 38). It is apparent that the chronological curves for sand-grain porosity can be made to correlate in this system also.

sample might reflect poor vegetation cover and a relatively dry climate. By counting the ratio of quartz to chert grains in each breccia sample and comparing these figures in the same way with the modern local soil, Brain was able to propose a climatic chart based on an entirely independent method. Both the porosity test and the quartz–chert ratio test show a high degree of correlation.

The Sterkfontein and Swartkrans deposits suggest dry-phase oscillations, beginning with conditions similar to the present day, then becoming increasingly arid and returning to present-day conditions at the top of the deposit. The Makapan Phase II breccia suggests conditions permanently drier than the present climate, whereas Kromdraai B suggests a rainfall considerably greater than the present, possibly tending toward present-day conditions near the top of the deposit.

If the Swartkrans and Sterkfontein Phase II breccias were deposited during the same period, it should be expected that both display similar granulometric curves (see Fig. 15). The graphs for quartz–chert ratios are remarkably similar, but the porosity curves are only generally similar. The Makapan Phase II breccia can only be compared by the porosity test since quartz occurs in the vicinity of the cavern and need not reflect wind transport if found in the breccia. The Makapan curve has more in common with the middle portions of Sterkfontein and Swartkrans. Kromdraai B cannot be equated with any of the other sites. It may partially overlap with the top of the Sterkfontein deposit which suggests a trend toward wetter conditions. The correlation cannot be verified by faunal analysis at present.

Butzer (1971) has pointed out that factors such as dolomitic soil development and changes in hillslope gradient may have contributed more towards the discovered fluctuations than climatic changes, but this claim requires further investigation. A straightforward climatic interpretation of the curves may need to be revised in the future.

THE HOMINID REMAINS

Before discussing the affinities and cultural status of the various hominids, it is necessary to summarize the range and state of preservation of the skeletal evidence from each site.

Taung

The Taung material comprises an almost complete juvenile skull with mandible attached (See Fig. 16). Parts of the specimen were found in three breccia blocks that fitted together. These yielded the brain cast, the frontal portion, and the lower left fragment of the mandible. When rejoined and developed, they produce an almost perfect endocranial cast with the left side incomplete, but covered in calcite crystals. Surrounding the frontal portion of the cast is a complete face and dentition. Another block contained fragments of a distal radius and ulna and phalanges fragments, never described (Dart 1925a; Broom 1925). These postcranial fragments are now recognized to be those of a baboon.

The skull is well rounded without any trace of supraorbital ridges or frontal flattening, and the glabella is prominent. The foramen magnum is set forward under the skull. The face has a concave profile with flattened nasal bones and prognathous maxillae (Sollas 1926). The orbits are relatively large and semicircular. The rami of the mandible are missing, but the milk dentition is complete. The front part of the mandible shows neither a chin nor a simian shelf, but the body is relatively thick. The teeth include upper and lower first permanent molars in the process of eruption, and the rest are deciduous. These are hardly worn or damaged. The canines are notably small, and there is no diastema between canines and the first premolars. The stage of eruption of the teeth suggest an age at death of about 6 years (Dart 1929, 1934; Broom 1936b; Abel 1931).

The brain capacity was originally calculated at 520 cc, but later estimates place it at around 500 cc (Keith 1931). Dart named the specimen *Australopithecus africanus*.

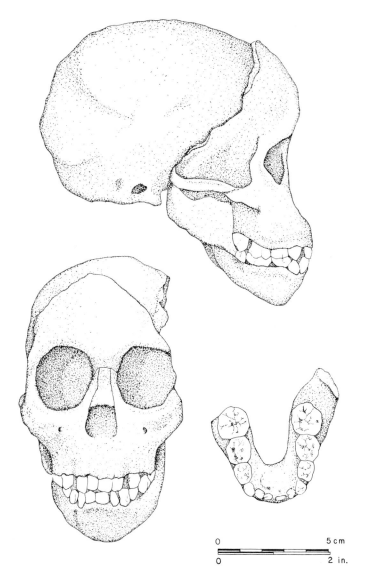

Fig. 16. Right lateral and frontal views of the Taung infant skull and mandible of *Australopithecus africanus*. Bottom right: upper view of the manibular arch. Much of the calvarium is missing, but a natural cranial of the right side of the brain has been preserved.

Makapan

The skeletal remains from Makapan may be conveniently described in three stratigraphic units: the lower Phase I or gray breccia, the upper Phase I or pink breccia, and the Phase II or red-brown breccia.

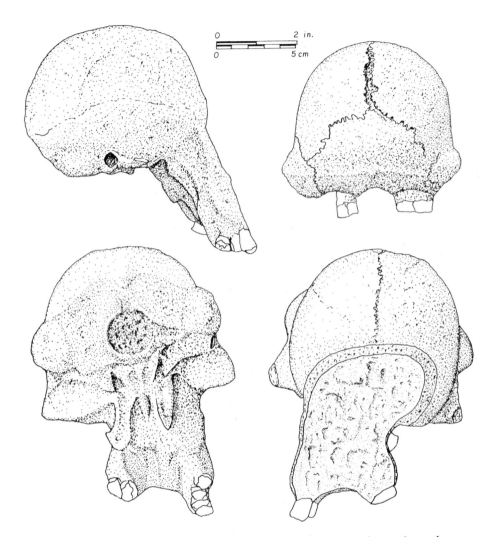

Fig. 17. The most complete adult cranium of *Australopithecus africanus* from the upper Phase I pink breccia at Makapan. The specimen was developed from an eroded breccia block near the surface. The facial region had been entirely eroded away before the block was discovered.

The largest sample of skeletal remains comes from the lower Phase I breccia. Among these, the skull is represented by an adult occiput (Dart 1948a, b, e) with a poorly developed torus, a second occipital fragment (Boné 1955b), and a juvenile right parietal (Boné 1956); an adult right maxilla with part of the face (Dart 1949a) with molars and premolars still in place, but the canine and third molar are both damaged; another adult right maxilla lacking the third molar and canine (Dart 1949d); a few isolated permanent and deciduous molars. A total of ten mandibular fragments have been recorded from this deposit: an adolescent mandible without rami but with complete deciduous dentition less the incisors, which were missing from their sockets before fossilization. Like the Taung specimen it is chinless and lacks a simian shelf, but the jawbone and teeth are more massive (Dart 1948c, d). An adult right mandible (Dart 1962b) contains all the right dentition including the canine; the ramus is complete. Nine other adult mandible fragments represent at least four individuals. One of these specimens contains a complete right dentition together with the whole set of incisors (Dart 1954a, b, 1962b). The postcranial bones include a clavicle (Boné 1955a) and pelvic fragments. There is an almost complete left ilium and a large fragment of a right ischium. Both came from one breccia block and are considered to belong to the same adolescent individual, presumed to be male (Dart 1949b, c). Another adolescent left ilium is considered to be female (Dart 1958c).

From the upper Phase I pink breccia comes an almost complete cranium together with the base of the skull, the rear part of the palate, and the rear molars (see Fig. 17). The frontal and the entire face have been weathered away by surface exposure (Dart 1962a, c). The specimen is well rounded and lacks an occipital torus. The palate and other facial fragments suggest a moderately prognathous jaw.

Only one specimen has been recovered from the Phase II breccia. This is a damaged and weathered maxilla (Dart 1955b).

All the specimens have been attributed to one type, named by Dart as *Australopithecus prometheus,* a term no longer used since the firemaking capacity of this hominid is not yet proved. Robinson (1954a) has renamed this material *Australopithecus africanus transvaalensis* since it falls within the range of variation of the Sterkfontein material called by that name.

Sterkfontein

The Sterkfontein hominid material may also be divided into two stratigraphic units: (1) the larger sample from the top of Lower or pink breccia found just beneath the sloping dolomite cavern roof at the Type Site; (2) the small sample recovered *in situ* with stone artifacts from the Middle or red-brown breccia, which is of a later date than the Type Site material.

The Type Site sample contains the almost complete skull of an adult female (Broom and Robinson 1950b). (See Fig. 18.) The specimen displays a rounded vault, a moderately developed supraorbital ridge, and a prominent glabella. There is no trace of a saggittal crest, and the occipital crest is poorly developed. The foramen magnum is set well forward, and the face is markedly prognathous. All the teeth are missing, but the palate and sockets are intact. Several other damaged and incomplete crania have been recovered as well as several maxillae and facial fragments (Broom 1936a, 1937c; Broom, *et al.* 1950). There are several mandible fragments and one almost complete specimen that is

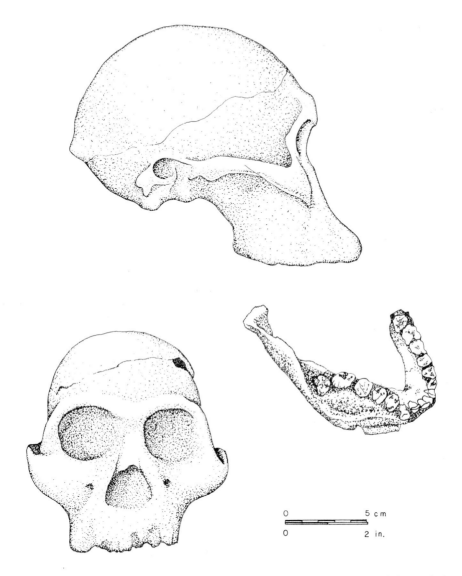

Fig. 18. The almost complete and undistorted adult cranium (all teeth missing) of *Australopithecus africanus* from the top of the Lower (pink) breccia at Sterkfontein Type Site. Lower left: an oblique view of the most complete adult mandible (not of the same individual) from the same deposits. Some doubt remains about the exact position of the skull which is either from the top of the Lower breccia or the bottom of the Middle breccia.

slightly crushed on the right side. The body of the jaw is thick, the rami are tall, and there is no chin or simian shelf (Broom 1947; Broom and Robinson 1949d). The sample also includes more than 100 socketed or isolated teeth, which have been described and discussed by several authors (Gregory and Hellman 1939; Shaw 1939b, 1940; von Koeningswald 1948; Robinson 1956; Boné 1959). The permanent upper incisors and canines are relatively small, and the premolars are bicuspid with four roots. The upper molars are all rhomboidal in shape with little difference in crown size. The lower canines and premolars have asymmetrical crowns, and the third molars are triangular in shape.

Among the postcranial remains there is a damaged scapula, a proximal humerus, numerous vertebrae and fragments, and several rib fragments. A complete pelvis has been reconstructed from a virtually whole right innominate and parts of the left, and the right proximal femur was also recovered. Three other distal femora have been recovered as well as a capitate bone and phalanges (Broom and Robinson 1949a; Kern and Straus 1949). Several other postcranial bones have·not been described yet.

The positions of the foramen magnum, the morphology of the vertebral column, and the positions of the muscular attachments of the pelvis and femora are widely accepted as evidence of bipedal gait and hominid status for the australopithecines, although the calculated brain capacities are only 482 cc (Broom and Robinson 1948), 435 cc (Broom and Schepers 1946), and 480–520 cc (Broom *et al.* 1950) for four measurable specimens. The small brain size has caused some authors to doubt its hominid status (Ashton and Zuckerman 1951), but this appears to be a minority view at present (Le Gros Clark 1952).

The later and much smaller sample from the overlying Middle breccia includes a juvenile maxilla fragment, with the newly erupted first permanent molar in pristine condition and two worn deciduous molars. Isolated teeth include a lower canine, an upper molar, and two molar fragments (Robinson 1962b). As this material is said to fall within the range of variation for the Type Site sample, it has been accepted as belonging to the same hominid, now named *Australopitheus africanus transvaalensis*.

Swartkrans

The hominid material from Swartkrans is virtually restricted to the Phase I breccia from the elongated outer cave, but it has been divided into two groups based on taxonomic differences.

By far the largest of the two groups is that ascribed to *Paranthropus crassidens* by Broom (1949a, b). Broom and Robinson (1952) describe most of the material, and Brain (1970) lists all the known specimens. Among these are a nearly complete adult cranium, the left side of a second adult cranium with both maxillae, one nearly complete juvenile skull, and one damaged adolescent cranium. The incisors are missing from all these specimens. The two adult specimens show concave foreheads, greatly enlarged supraorbital ridges, well-developed sagittal crests, and massive upper molars. The occipital crest is well

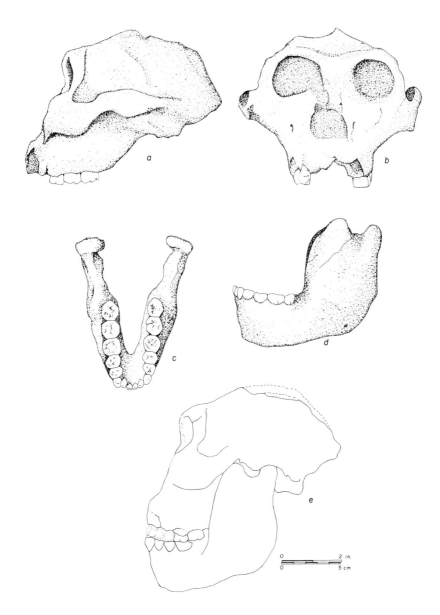

Fig. 19. The most complete adult cranium (a, b) and jaw (c, d) of separate individuals of *Australopithecus (Paranthropus) robustus* from the pink breccia of the outer cave of Swartkrans. (e) Left lateral reconstuction of occluded jaw and skull.

Kromdraai

The *Kromdraai* material comprises the left half of an adult cranium together with the left maxilla, zygomatic arch, and sphenoid (see Fig. 21). A broken right maxilla was also recovered. The skull is relatively small with thick bones and the foramen magnum is set well forward under the base of the skull. The maxilla is only moderately prognathous, and the brow ridges have not been preserved. The mandible is massive and displays neither a chin nor a simian shelf (Broom 1938, 1939a). Only the upper molars and premolars are known. Robinson (1956) considers the dentition to be closely related to that of the paranthropines from Swartkrans, and his opinion is supported by the lower teeth and the deciduous dentition of a juvenile mandible with an almost complete tooth row (Broom 1941a).

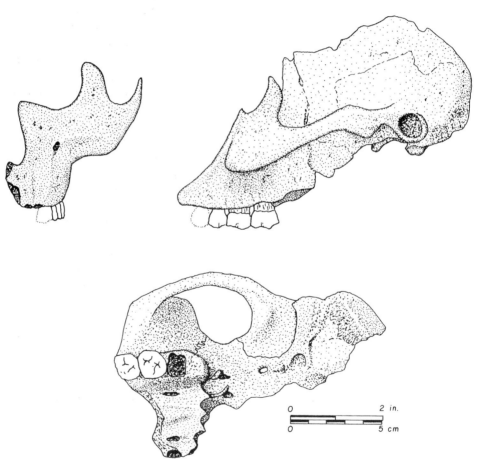

Fig. 21. The most complete fragment of *Australopithecus (Paranthropus) robustus* from Kromdraai B.

Among the postcranial hominid specimens there is a right distal humerus (Le Gros Clark 1947; Straus 1948) and an ulna fragment found close to it. There are also two hand bones (Broom 1942) including a left second distal metacarpal and a finger proximal phalanx, and a group of foot bones including a talus, a left fifth proximal phalanx, and a second (or third) distal phalanx.

Broom named all this material *Paranthropus robustus* and the name has been retained. It is now used to describe the larger group of Swartkrans specimens as well, but the two are distinguished at subspecific level, thus : *Paranthropus robustus robustus* from Kromdraai and *Paranthropus robustus crassidens* from Swartkrans (J. T. Robinson 1954a; Campbell 1964).

This completes the summary of all the presently known skeletal remains from the five sites. Most of the controversial points that have arisen out of this study of the material are caused by the fragmentary nature of the remains. Large samples of teeth are available for some types, but cranial and postcranial bones are still poorly represented. The three major fields of controversy are: the hominid status of the australopithecines, the meaning of the skeletal differences between *Australopithecus* and *Paranthropus,* and the true status of the *"Telanthropus"* material.

Evidence for Erect Posture*

The most impressive body of evidence used to justify the hominid status of the australopithecines is the list of features demonstrating that these creatures walked permanently upright on their hind limbs. This characteristic is perhaps the most vital distinction between Man and the anthropoid apes, which are able to stand and run unsupported by the forelimbs for only brief periods. Permanent bipedalism frees the forelimbs of the burden of supporting the body, thus allowing more extensive experimentation with the raw materials of the environment. This experimentation is thought to have led to systematic manipulation of materials and, ultimately, toolmaking—another supposed distinction between Apes and Man.

That the australopithecines were fully erect is adequatly proved by the position of the foramen magnum in all the skull fragments retaining the occiput, and also by the morphology of an almost complete pelvis, numerous pelvic fragments, and the proximal end of the femur. There are enough vertebrae to reconstruct almost the complete vertebral column, although the sample of foot and hand bones is not yet sufficient to allow accurate reconstructions.

The occiput and foramen magnum is set far forward under the base of the skull, unlike that of the apes, which is set in the lower back of the cranium. The australopithecine head was therefore poised on a nearly vertical backbone—an

---

* A substantial revision of the evidence for australopithecine posture and gait is currently under way (J. T. Robinson, in press).

arrangement demonstrated by the available vertebrae (J. T. Robinson 1954b). The shape of the pelvis agrees closely with that of other hominids: the innominate is short and broad with a deep sciatic notch, and the sacrum is broad (Chopra 1962). The femur shaft displays a marked lateral lean from the vertical when the distal end is placed on a horizontal surface, thus providing additional evidence for a broad sacrum. It has been argued (J. T. Robinson 1962c) that the muscle *gluteus maximus* acted as an extensor of the thigh, whereas the *gluteus medius* was an abductor. The well-developed lower iliac spine suggests a strong *rectus femoris,* part of the muscle complex supporting a bipedal posture. Another attachment below that for *rectus femoris* reflects a very strong ligament joining the femur to the ilium, and it has been argued that the knee joint could be locked in such a position that the leg would be straight. The functioning of the *gluteus maximus* in Man as an extensor is vital for efficient locomotion particularly in the second half of the stride. When it functions as an abductor only, bipedalism is only possible in the form of a brief shuffling run, frequently observed among anthropoid apes.

Differences between Australopithecus and Paranthropus

The material from Taung, Makapan, and Sterkfontein has been placed in the genus *Australopithecus,* whereas that from Swartkrans and Kromdraai has been labeled *Paranthropus.* It has been argued at length by several authors that there are sufficient differences between the two groups of material to justify retaining them in different genera. The most important differences are given in Table 5

TABLE 5

Differences between *Autstralopithecus* and *Paranthropus*

Feature	*Australopithecus*	*Paranthropus*
Forehead	Weakly developed	Absent
Supraorbital ridge	Pronounced	Present
Face	Bony, moderately flat	Flat or concave
Zygomatic arch	Moderately developed	Strongly developed
Palate	Even depth	Deeper at back
Temporal fossa	Medium	Large
Pterygoid plate	Small	Large
Sagittal crest	Absent or very weak	Present in males and some females
Ascending ramus	Moderate height, slope backwards	High, vertical
Tooth-row size proportions	Front and back harmonious	Front smaller than back
Canines	Relatively large	Small
Maxillary front tooth row	Parabolic curve	Almost straight across front of palate
Lower deciduous first molar	Incompletely molarized	Completely molarized

A considerable body of metrical data exists to support these differences (Broom 1939b; Senyürek 1941; J. T. Robinson 1956; Tobias 1967a), but less information is available for differences between the postcranial bones.

Robinson, who has consistently supported the "two-genera" hypothesis (J. T. Robinson 1949, 1952a, 1954a, 1962a, c, 1967), has cogently argued that many of the special enlargements in the *Paranthropus* facial and mouth region are functionally related to the very massive molars. The weight and thickness of the mandible and the high ascending ramus require strongly developed mastication muscles, which in turn require strong attachments provided by the sagittal crest (J. T. Robinson 1954c, 1958a). As the molars of mature specimens are heavily worn, it is argued that the grinding which brought about the wear was caused by an essentially vegetarian diet. The mastication of plant foods and particularly roots would introduce sand between the molar surfaces, thus causing intensive abrasion. The markedly reduced canines and small incisors are quoted as additional evidence pointing to a noncarnivorous diet.

By contrast, the harmoniously proportioned tooth row of *Australopithecus* with its relatively large canines and smaller molars is thought to be truly omnivorous with a possibly predatory behavior pattern. It has also been claimed that the teeth display more chipping (as opposed to grinding) than the *Paranthropus* dentition, possibly indicating the chewing of bones. Since these differences have not been accurately measured, and nuts and other vegetable foods might also cause chipping, this argument cannot be seriously considered at present. The possibility of postmortem chipping must also be considered since all the material is in a derived context.

The "One-Genus" Hypothesis

Washburn and Patterson (1951) were the first to propose that the two groups of specimens might belong to a single genus, and this view has been supported by Oakley (1954b), Dart (1955a), and Le Gros Clark (1955). In recent years this opinion has been adopted by many students of human origins, after the detailed reexamination of the material by Tobias (1967a).

Tobias has stressed that differences between the two groups, as cited by Robinson, are almost all related to differences in tooth dimensions: because the cheek teeth of *Paranthropus* (*sensu stricto*) are so massive, the shape of the face is flattened; the zygomatic arch is strongly developed to accommodate the enlarged masseter muscles; the large temporal fossa is related to the enlarged temporalis muscle; enlarged pterygoid plates relate to larger pterygoid muscles; the sagittal crest is necessary to anchor the large temporalis muscle; the palate is deeper at the rear to accommodate the larger molar roots; the height and angle of the ramus is related to the size of the dentition, as is the thickness and height of the mandible and density of bone around the molar roots. It is argued that all these differences are of secondary importance in defining the two groups. They are merely functional differences arising out of the size of the teeth in each group. Tooth size is therefore the critical factor that separates them (see Fig. 22).

After reexamining all the available teeth, Tobias conceded that the *Paranthropus* upper canines are indeed very small in relation to the cheek teeth, which are mostly larger than those found in *Australopithecus*. He also agreed that the *Paranthropus* lower canines are smaller than those in *Australopithecus*. However, the paranthropine incisors are only slightly smaller. Tobias does not believe that any of these differences are great enough to justify the claim that *Paranthropus* was adapted to a vegetarian diet, and he points out that chipping occurs on the molars from both *Australopithecus* and *Paranthropus* samples. He also suggests that the incisors from both groups wear at a similar rate, and demonstrates that the range of tooth-size variation is similar in each. There is therefore, no reliable evidence to suggest that we are dealing with two distinct patterns of diet, as reflected in the teeth. Since there is no evidence available to suggest that the two groups differ in brain capacity or complexity, Tobias concludes that all the material belongs to a single genus, *Australopithecus*, but that the two groups represent species: A. *africanus* Dart and *A. robustus* Broom. At present the postcranial remains are too poorly represented to help in defining the two taxa, but Tobias argues that slight differences may be detected in the pelvis.

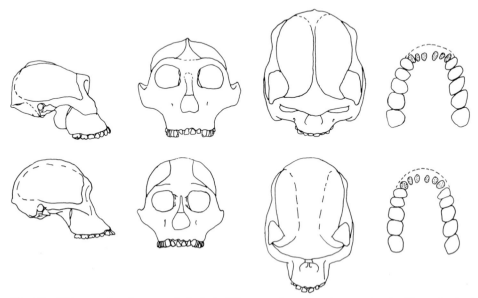

Fig. 22. Diagram showing morphological differences between (top row) *A. (Paranthropus) robustus* and (bottom row) *A. africanus*. Left to right: left lateral view, frontal view, top view, dental arch of palate.

More recent discoveries of *Paranthropus*-like specimens with postcranial material from eastern Africa should help to clarify this problem. New estimates of cranial capacity (Holloway 1970) suggest that *A. robustus* brain size is comparable with that of the modern gorilla. Limb bones, particularly the head of femur and phalanges are presently being studied in order to determine whether or not *A. robustus* was truly bipedal or a part-time "knuckle-walker" (Tuttle 1967). Should this prove to be the case, separate generic status (that is, *Paranthropus*) may again be justified.

The Status of "Telanthropus" at Swartkrans

A set of six specimens (mandible, mandible fragment, premolar, premaxilla fragment, radius, and metacarpal fragment) differ in size and morphology from the large *A. robustus* (*Paranthropus*) sample. Broom and Robinson (1949c) referred them to a new genus and species: *Telanthropus capensis* (Robinson 1953a, b).

The new hominid, although found in the same deposits as *A. robustus,* differs from it as follows: the upper canine root is shorter; the lower part of the nasal cavity has a distinct "floor" separated from the palate and its structure suggests a greater projection of the nose from the face; the mandible is shorter and less robust, and the ascending ramus (reconstructed) is shorter and smaller; the lower molars and premolars are smaller and M_3 is greatly reduced and slightly smaller than M_2; the postcanine teeth have a characteristic rectangular plan form, not found in the other Swartkrans hominid material.

Dart (1955a) argued that this hominid differed so slightly from the gracile australopithecines at Makapan that separate generic status was not justified. He pointed out that the specimens may represent females of the gracile form of australopithecines. A similar interpretation had been tentatively suggested by Straus (1950) in a discussion of the position of the mylohyoid groove in relation to the mandibular foramen in the jaw. More recently Wolpoff (1968, 1971) has insisted that *"Telanthropus"* should be brought within the australopithecine taxon which should be extended to accommodate this specimen. His claim has yet to meet with general acceptance. Their shared opinion has been overlooked in favor of Simonetta's classification (1957), placing the material in the *Homo erectus* group, which also includes *Sinanthropus* from Choukoutien in China, *Pithecanthropus* from Java, *Atlanthropus* from Rabat and Ternifine in Northern Africa, and probably Hominid 9 from Olduvai Gorge, Tanzania. This view has been supported by Robinson (1961) and also by Tobias and von Koenigswald (1964).

These conflicting interpretations merely reflect the fact that too few specimens were available for study, but this situation is now altered. The new material reported by Clarke, Howell, and Brain (1970) includes a left temporal fragment, which joins to a left facial fragment composed of palate, orbital region,

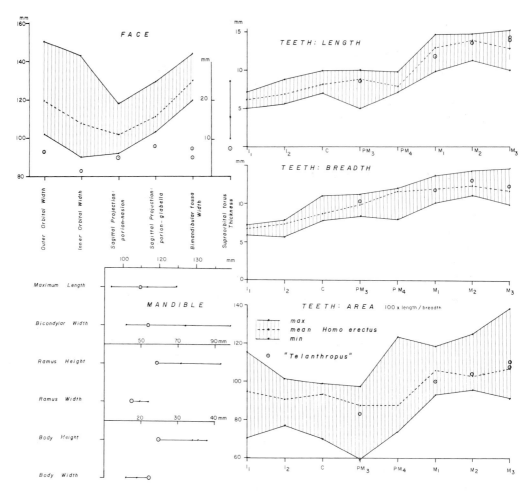

Fig. 23. Diagram comparing facial, mandibular and dental measurements of *Homo* sp. *(Telanthropus)* with the range of measurements for *Homo erectus* specimens from northern Africa and Southeast Asia. The Swartkrans specimen is evidently within the range of dental size for *H. erectus,* but the face and mandible clearly differ.

and much of the zygomatic arch. The edge of the palate makes a perfect fit with the original *"Telanthropus"* maxilla so that it has proved possible to reconstruct the face of an adult individual. The near-complete *"Telanthropus"* mandible articulates with the reconstructed skull but does not belong to the same individual. This more complete specimen clearly differs in several features from both the robust and gracile australopithecine forms. These features may be summarized as follows: the supraorbital ridge is thicker and the frontal sinus is larger, the postorbital constriction is only moderately developed, the angle between the supraorbital ridge and frontal squama is more pronounced; the frontal bone

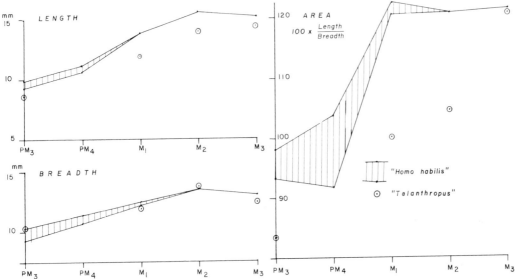

Fig. 24. Tooth measurements of *Homo* sp. *(Telanthropus)* compared with those of *Homo habilis* from Olduvai Gorge. The Swartkrans specimen falls outside the range of *H. habilis*, which is probably too narrow since the available sample of teeth is still too small.

rises more steeply from behind the ridge; the posterior margin of the zygomatic process of the frontal is *not* well defined; the nasal profile confirms Robinson's original diagnosis that the bony nose was prominent.

In profile, the individual clearly differs from the australopithecines, and the authors are confident in referring it to the genus *Homo*. However, they have sensibly delayed ascribing it to a species until more material becomes available.

If it belongs with the *Homo erectus* group, as previously suggested for the jaw material, it remains to be demonstrated that the available fragments fall within the range of metrical variation for *H. erectus*. Very few mandibular measurements can be compared throughout the *H. erectus* corpus of material since different authors have stressed particular dimensions for each specimen. *"Telanthropus"* measurements are compared in Fig. 23, with the range of variation for the few *H. erectus* measurements taken for all reported specimens.

It has also been tentatively suggested that the jaw material might eventually be ascribed to *Homo habilis* when more materials and metrical data become available (Leakey, Tobias, and Napier 1964). Robinson (1965) has challenged the validity of the proposed species *H. habilis*, pointing out that the fragmentary remains from Olduvai Gorge, Tanzania (which are quoted as "type" specimens) partly overlap with the range of variation of *A. africanus* and should be referred to that group. He suggests instead that *"Telanthropus"* occupies a position comparable with the early stages of *H. erectus* development (Tobias and Robinson 1966). The initial suggestion that *"Telanthropus"* remains may be similar to *H.*

habilis has not been repeated although Tobias has continued to defend vigorously the validity of *H. habilis* at Olduvai (for example, Tobias, 1964, 1965, 1968). Comparable measurements for *"Telanthropus"* and *H. habilis* jaw materials show no striking similarities (Fig. 24).

Minority Views: Two Extremes

Although there is no concensus about the most appropriate way to subdivide the australopithecine material, there is widespread agreement that (1) they belong to the Hominidae and (2) they are distinct from modern Man. However, there are two conflicting opinions which deny even these basic assumptions about the taxonomic status of the australopithecines: the first claims that they are *not* hominids, but have more in common with the apes; the second argues that they cannot be separated from modern Man and should be incorporated in a single genus, namely *Homo*.

The hominid status of the australopithecines was challenged by Zuckerman (1928) who presented metrical evidence to demonstrate that the estimated brain capacity for the Taung child (500 cc) fell within the range of variation for cranial capacity of the adult male chimpanzee. Studies in the growth rate of the chimpanzee suggested that an adult representative of the Taung skull would have a brain capacity of about 556.5 cc if male, and 515 cc if female. Both these estimates are outside the upper limit of adult chimpanzee brain size, but within the range of the gorilla. He also demonstrated that the length and breadth of the Taung skull fell "almost within range" of the chimpanzee, but the height of the skull above the Frankfurt plane was greater than the maximum for the chimpanzee.

When more fossil material was recovered, he again challenged the hominid status of the australopithecine remains (Zuckerman 1950a, b, c, 1951a, b). Taking 75 dental characters of *"Plesianthropus"* (the near-complete *A. africanus* skull from Sterkfontein) he demonstrated that only four characters differed from the gorilla and none differed from the orangutan. Twenty-six dental characters of *"A. prometheus"* (*A. africanus* from Makapan) differed in no way from gorillas or orangutans. A tooth-by-tooth comparison suggested that almost every specimen in the collections could fit the range of variation for the equivalent pongid teeth. He also pointed out that the australopithecine teeth bore less resemblance to the teeth of modern Man than they did to the great apes. The new data on australopithecine cranial capacity was analyzed by Ashton (1950), who pointed out that almost all the new skulls and endocranial casts were larger than the maximum capacity for chimpanzee, but were within the range of gorillas. Because they were all smaller than the *"Pithecanthropus"* brain capacity, he suggested that they were closer to the Apes than to Man.

Ashton and Zuckerman (1951) next compared selected cranial indices of the fossil material. They found that: the height of the nuchal musculature above the

Frankfurt plane was close to modern Man; the height of the cranial vault above the orbital margin was similar to Man and gorillas, but greater than other apes; the position of the occipital condyles was similar to that of the gorilla, but intermediate between Man and the other Apes (Ashton and Zuckerman 1952). They suggested that all three indices are functionally related to posture of the skull in relation to the body. If the australopithecines walked upright, the head was not balanced in the same way as modern Man.

In a series of subsequent papers they point out that: the australopithecine brain does not differ significantly in size or conformation from the gorilla; there is no real evidence of reduction in the jaws or teeth; the skull is balanced on the vertebral column as in apes and not as in humans; the innominate bones do not suggest upright gait identical to that in Man; the pelvic bones suggest more apelike features than human ones. From this evidence, they are forced to conclude that they were apelike rather than manlike creatures and need not occupy a position intermediate between Apes and Man (Zuckerman 1954; Ashton and Zuckerman 1956a, b). They have continued to support this claim in subsequent studies of the cranial casts (Ashton and Zuckerman 1956c) and in an unpublished multivariate analysis of the innominate bones (Zuckerman, Ashton, Oxnard, and Spence 1967).

Nine features of the pelvis were selected for comparison, each being functionally related to the main blocks of muscle acting upon the hip joint. Their analysis reveals that the length of the australopithecine ischium "is such as to give the extensors of the hip the greater mechanical advantage that is typical of the quadrupeds." They also claim that the iliac blade, although broad, was orientated so that *gluteus medius* and *gluteus minimus* were extensors of the hip as in quadrupeds rather than abductors as in humans. This, they suggest, may indicate that the australopithecines were never bipedal in the human sense, but at best could manage the shuffling gait observed among the great apes.*

Similar multivariate studies of the fragmentary Sterkfontein scapula have led Oxnard (1968, 1969) to suggest that this specimen shows many characteristics with the scapula of the gibbon and chimpanzee. This analysis also suggests that the human shoulder evolved from an oranglike form rather than from shapes comparable with other primates.

This recital of the apelike features by Zuckerman and the members of his team reflects a methodologically unsound approach to the problem. If the earliest hominids have in fact evolved from some apelike ancestor, it is to be expected that they will retain numerous simian features. The possibility that they display more simian than human characters does not necessarily make them apes. By isolating individual features and refusing to view the total range of morphological elements, they have failed to notice that the *combination* of features found in the australopithecines cannot be found in any living or early

---

*Presently under revision (J. T. Robinson, in press).

Pleistocene apes. Given their chronological position within the hominid fossil record, it is the relatively scarce human features that are most remarkable, rather than the numerous pongid ones. Nevertheless, the team has provided a wealth of comparative metrical data and have applied a variety of sophisticated statistical analyses, some of which may prove extremely valuable when fully published. As Campbell (1968) has pointed out: "The most sophisticated techniques will only give dusty answers to badly designed questions."

An extreme contrast to the position of Zuckerman and his co-workers is that taken up by Mayr (1949, 1951), who suggests that the hominids have only speciated once and that all fossil hominids, including the australopithecines, should be grouped with the single genus: *Homo*.

In 1950 the South African "fossil ape-man" material was published under no less than three genera and five species names. Mayr pointed out that this naming procedure was peculiar to paleoanthropologists, who gave generic and specific names to each new find without much concern for its relationships to other types already known. This was not the practice among taxonomists in other fields of biology, and the naming procedures for fossil man were clearly at fault when measured by the standards customary in most branches of zoology. The "type concept" of species was still in use among paleoanthropologists, who erected species on the basis of morphological differences among fossil specimens. The three published "genera" were based on one infant skull, one adult female, and one adult male, and diagnostic features were therefore obscured by age and sex differences.

Mayr proposed that the "biological species concept" be applied to the material instead. Using this model, a species is defined as "a group of interbreeding natural populations that are reproductively isolated from other such groups." Species must also differ in ecological requirements so that they can live alongside each other. Within a species, every population is adapted to the conditions of its respective local environment. New species arise from isolated and much modified portions of the parental species (Mayr 1942). This concept recognizes that most species are polytypic and great diversity of morphology within the species is therefore to be expected.

The evidence derived from palaeontology and zoogeography demonstrates that speciation is an exceedingly slow process taking at least several hundred thousands of years and averaging perhaps over 1 million years, roughly 30,000 human generations. The same evidence shows that the process is a very gradual one, and there is no evidence for mutational jumps or "macromutations." Mayr argued that there was indeed insufficient time for more than one significant speciation which separated *Homo* from the parental primate stock. The vital diagnostic features that distinguishes *Homo* is permanent bipedalism, which led to a chain of subsequent developments such as toolmaking and increase in brain capacity. Geographical speciation could not take place since Man was able to adapt to most ecological niches with the aid of cultural developments. However, phyletic speciation did occur, but only one species of Man was present on earth at any given moment in time. In a later publication (Mayr 1964) he raised the number of contemporary species to two. On this basis, all the known human fossils should be classified as *Homo,* of which the australopithecine population was an early species.

Although Mayr's arguments have not been accepted entirely, they nevertheless sparked off a process of "lumping" the fossil material, which has proved to be of lasting value. At present, two genera (*Australopithecus* and *Homo*) are recognized by most scholars. The advent of potassium–argon dating in the last decade has shown that *Australopithecus* was present in eastern Africa at least 3 and probably 5 million years ago, and adequate time was therefore available for further speciation.

TOOLMAKING: THE "OSTEODONTOKERATIC" PROBLEM

It has been claimed that the earliest evidence of true cultural activity in the form of toolmaking is present in the gray breccia at Makapan. Dart (1949a, c, f, 1954c, 1956b) observed that the animal bones from this deposit were broken in consistent patterns and that certain parts of the skeleton were more abundant than others. This he interpreted as deliberate selection and breakage of bone by the australopithecines. It was postulated that certain bones had been broken to facilitate their use as tools or weapons, and he pointed out that some of the long bones displayed "spiral fractures," which he claimed were produced by twisting the bone in order to split it longitudinally. These, he suggested, were used as ripping and gouging tools, whereas bones with heavy epiphyses (some of which displayed damaged condyles) were used as bludgeons. Mandibles and maxillae fragments, he suggested were used as saws and scrapers; horn cores acted as daggers, and scapulae as axes. Therefore, bone, teeth, and horns (but not stone) formed the earliest raw materials for toolmaking activities, and the term "osteodontokeratic" culture was coined by translating "bone–teeth–horn." To support his case, Dart cited several baboon skulls found in the Taung and Sterkfontein breccias that had twin indentations in the frontal bones. These fractures apparently occurred before fossilization, and it was shown that the battered condyles of certain antelope humerus distals fitted closely with the indentation.

The strongest objections raised against Dart's claim were that the samples of bone were too small to justify such interpretation. He therefore undertook a near-total recovery of all bone fragments from the grey breccia dumps and presented his case once again (Dart 1957a), this time bringing forward abundant numerical data (Dart 1957b, 1958a). Criticism of his interpretations persisted even after the discovery of a similar assemblage in direct association with stone tools of a much later period at Kalkbank in the Transvaal (Dart and Kitching 1958; Dart 1960c). Numerous subsequent papers have repeated his earlier claims

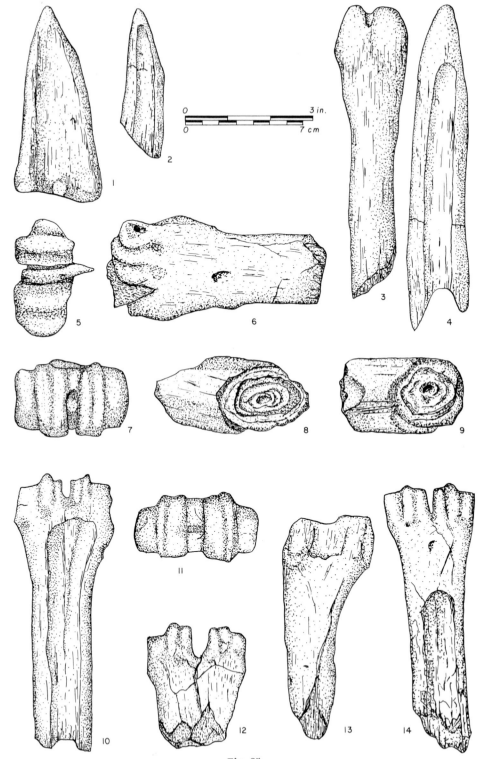

0   3 in.

0   7 cm

Fig. 25

64

while stressing various aspects such as the ratio of humeri to femora, and proximal to distal fragments (Dart 1959c). Ethnographic parallels have been cited to support the interpretation of certain bone fragments as "scoops" (Dart 1959d, 1960a, b, 1961a), and it has been further suggested that an australopithecine proximal humerus was used for the same purpose (Dart 1961b). He has also claimed that stalagmite fragments, apparently showing signs of battering, were used as pounders to break up the bones (Dart 1962d, e, 1965c).

It is still widely believed that Dart's interpretations go far beyond the legitimate evidence presented by the Makapan Phase I bone collection, and recent papers on the supposed use of a "ritual kudu-skull chalice" (Dart 1967) and "Australopithecine cordage and thongs" (Dart 1965b) have done little to dispel the antipathy towards his earlier claims.

However, numerous scholars partially support the hypothesis (Wolberg 1970). Among these, Tobias has stressed that there are several features in the gray breccia that are not easily explained as the by-products of predatory or bone-accumulating animals (Tobias 1965, 1967b, 1969): There are five times as many humeri as there are femora, and among the humeri there are ten times more distal ends than proximals. Hyena and porcupine tooth marks are extremely rare and easily recognized. About 80% of a sample of nearly 60 baboon skulls from Makapan, Sterkfontein, and Taung show prefossilization fractures of the skull or jaw, and battered distal humeri fit some of the skull fractures. Certain bone splinters (mislabeled "flakes") have *localized* damage or wear on one edge. A few larger long-bone shafts have smaller bone or horn cores, or dolomite chips wedged between the condyles (Fig. 25). The stalagmites are unlikely to have been broken off by natural agents. Quartz pebbles and fragments were derived from some distance outside the cave. Tobias (1967b) has also presented impressive photographic evidence for localized wear on the edges of certain bone fragments. He points out that over 40 hominid fragments have been found in the gray breccia and all of these belong to *Australopithecus*. It is therefore reasonable to postulate that these creatures were responsible for the peculiar features of the bone assemblage. They therefore practiced an extremely simple form of toolmaking as seen in the regular patterns of bone breakage. He also cites indirect evidence for toolmaking behavior among australopithecines, such as upright posture, formation of the hand bones, brain capacity, and dental crowding. This feature may

---

Fig. 25. Bovid limb bone fragments from the lower Phase I (gray) breccia at Makapan that Tobias (1967b) selected for their undoubted traces of manipulation and surface damage: (1, 2, 4) bone shaft fragments split and worn to pointed shapes; (3) heavily worn epiphysis; (5) cannon bone with pointed bone splinter wedged between the condyles; (7) distal view of undamaged cannon bone condyles; (8, 9) two shaft fragments wedged one inside the other; (11, 12) distal and lateral view of cannon bone with artificially widened condyles; (10) split and (14) crushed shafts of distal ends of cannon bones forming the "apple scoop" design proposed by Dart (1959d); (13) distal end of antelope humerus with prefossilization damage of the condyles.

Fig. 26. Diagram summarizing all the bone-accumulating agents other than *Australopithecus* that may have contributed material to the bone breccias. They include leopard forms (in tree), which probably contributed most damaged bone material, and at least three species of hyena (right of fissure mouth). Whereas porcupines contributed a small percentage of the bones and owls contributed most (perhaps all) of the microfauna, it remains uncertain whether cheetahs (left of fissure mouth) and lions made any contribution.

only be present when the teeth have ceased to function as weapons (reduced canines), and the jaw is reduced also, when its functions are at least partly replaced by tools (Oppenheimer 1964).

Contrary to the position of Dart, Tobias, and others there remains the possibility that the massive bone accumulations are *not* the result of australopithecine activities. It has been suggested that bone-collecting animals, particularly the hyena and porcupine, either entered the cavern itself or the mouth of a fissure leading to the cavern. Bones would have accumulated in lairs at the fissure opening, possibly at the back of a shelter, and migrated down into the cavern below (Fig. 26). Since the fissure was narrow, very little soil was carried down, and the Phase I accumulation therefore consisted of massive bone heaps accumulated over many thousands of years. At times the predators themselves may have accidentally fallen down the fissure while attempting to reach a pool of water in the back of the shelter. Other animals may have been trapped in a similar manner

(Brain 1958). The australopithecine remains may represent part of the predator's diet and are not entirely responsible for the bone heaps.

The case for hyenas as agents of bone accumulation has been poorly documented until recently. The only detailed report of a brown hyena lair was a bone heap including 14 impala skulls, several baboon skulls, guinea fowl bones, a tree-snake skeleton, and skulls of "two chitas" (sic) (Maberly 1951). It seemed unlikely that the latter would have been killed or scavenged by hyenas, and it was later learned that hyenas were never observed entering or leaving the lair (Hughes 1954a). One observation of a hyena carrying a skull away from a kill could not be followed up (Washburn 1957), and only a few undoubted hyena lairs have been systematically reported. These were found to be without bone accumulations (Hughes 1954b, 1958). However, the small amount of negative evidence available at present need not be taken as absolute proof that hyenas *never* collect bones, as claimed by Dart (1956a). More recently, Brain (1968) closely observed the scavenging activities of both brown and spotted hyenas in open country. Both species extensively scatter and destroy nearly all bones by crushing so that very little of the skeleton remains.

The bone-gathering activities of porcupines are well attested (Alexander 1956), and the characteristic gnaw marks left on bones by the incisors of this animal are easily recognized. The presence of porcupine bones in the Phase I bone heap, the extreme scarcity of gnawed bones, and the presence of large bones (particularly giraffe femora) outside the carrying capacity of the porcupine all suggest that this animal played only a minor role in the accumulation process (Dart 1958b). Recent studies of porcupine lairs (Hughes 1958; Hendey and Singer 1965) suggest that these may contain a very large number of bones. One lair on the Nossob River has been closely observed by Hughes, who estimates a growth rate of about 30 bones per year (Brain 1968). Over a period of several thousand years it is theoretically possible for porcupines to accumulate a mass of bones as large as the Makapan Phase I bone heaps. However, the modern lair material shows distinctive gnawing marks formed by the porcupine incisors on about 70% of all the bones. Such gnaw marks occur on less than 1% of the Makapan material and under 5% of the Swartkrans bones.

The possibility that cheetah or saber-tooth cats may have contributed some of the bone material has also been investigated by Brain (1970). Controlled feeding experiments with cheetahs reveal that no bone damage is caused by the sharp meat-slicing dentition of these carnivores. As saber-tooth dentition is similarly adapted to slicing rather than bone crushing, it is argued that these creatures could not be responsible for the damaged bones found in the breccias.

The case for leopards as agents of bone accumulation and systematic bone damage is much stronger. Brain (1968, 1969b, 1970) reports that leopards in the Kruger National Park, Transvaal very frequently drag their kills into the branches of a tree to avoid harrassment from hyenas. These may otherwise drive the leopard off its kill and devour or scatter most of the bones. If the carcass is

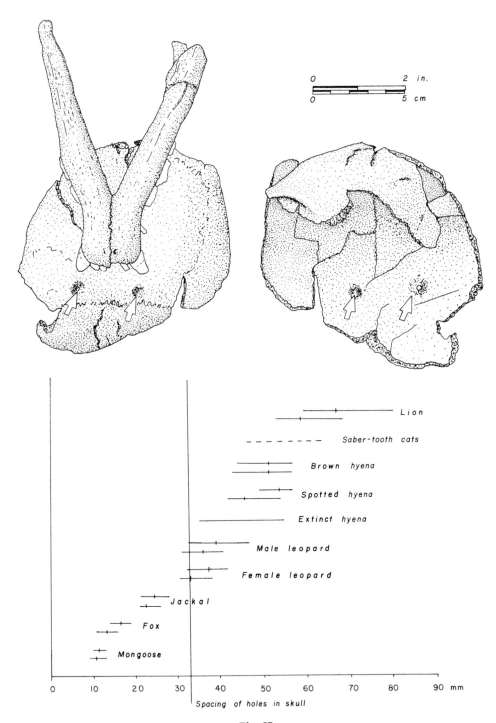

Fig. 27

safely lodged in a tree, the hyenas are unable to reach it even if the leopard temporarily leaves the area. Usually the carcass is draped over a branch with the head and limbs dangling. It is "eaten out" in a 3–4 day period during which the vertebrae and ribs are virtually destroyed and the pelvis and scapulae are extensively damaged. When eventually abandoned, the skull, horns, and extremities of the limbs are left hanging in the skin. If the prey is a baboon, the leopard frequently drags it with the back of the skull firmly clenched in its jaws. In this case, the entire skeleton is devoured and only the skull remains, with clear puncture marks or even indentations formed by the leopard canines during the process of dragging it into the tree. The cranium may also be smashed for extraction of the brain. Hyenas are dealt with in a similar manner, but no canine holes occur in the crushed skull.

Observations of leopard kills in South-West Africa (in areas where hyenas are absent) reveal that leopards do not take the kill into a tree. Only the fleshy parts of the carcass are eaten, and the kill is abandoned without any substantial damage to the bones. It is apparent that the peculiar habits of leopards mentioned above are restricted to areas where the hyena population is relatively dense and there is some competition between carnivores.

Brain points out that both leopard and hyena remains are present at Swartkrans, and it is reasonable to assume such competition at the time that the breccia was forming. However, large trees are absent from the grassveld region of the Blaauwbank River except in occasional deep fissures in the dolomite slopes. The fissures provide protection to young saplings from wind and grass fires and also provide additional ground moisture for the root system which is able to penetrate deeper. The two forms found most frequently in fissure openings are the wild fig, *Ficus,* and the white stinkwood, *Celtis kraussiana.* Such a restricted distribution of large trees would greatly increase the probability that the bones of leopard kills would be brought into the vicinity of a fissure mouth. After the carcass has been selectively eaten out and abandoned, the remaining bones hanging in the skin would eventually drop as the hide rotted. A large proportion of these would drop right down the fissure into the deposits of the underground cavern below. At Swartkrans, the bones are dispersed thinly through the whole deposit, suggesting that they were introduced to the cavern over a very long period, possibly reflecting sporadic use of large trees by leopards. This hypothesis would also explain the high frequency of limb bones and skulls among the Swartkrans animal bones. It may also explain the almost total absence of postcranial bones of baboon and australopithecines. These are represented almost

Fig. 27. Cranial fragment Sk-54 of an adolescent *Australopithecus robustus* from Swartkrans betraying two punctate marks (arrows) in the occipital region. Both the spacing and diameters of these holes fit the rejoined mandibular canines of an extinct leopard jaw from the same deposit. Bottom: means and ranges of maxillary (upper) and mandibular (lower) canines of various carnivores. The spacing of the holes in Sk-54 falls within the range of leopards only. (After Brain 1970.)

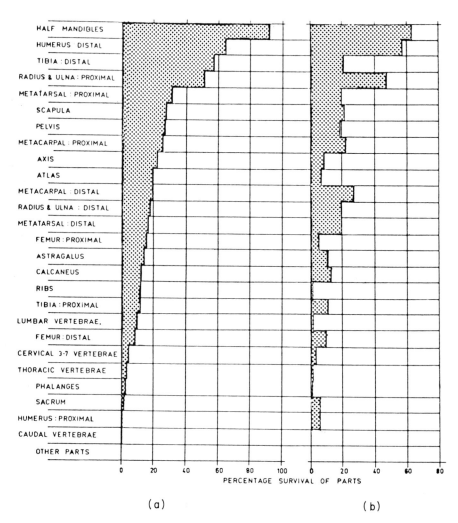

Fig. 28. Histogram of percentage survivals of (a) parts of goat skeletons from the Kuiseb River, based on 64 individuals, and (b) parts of bovid skeletons from Phase I breccia at Makapansgat.

entirely by skull fragments. Of great interest is the young *A. robustus* skull labeled Sk-54, which has two round holes punctured in the cranium. The spacing of these two holes matches the spacing of the lower canines of an adult fossil leopard jaw, but not of any other carnivore (Fig. 27).

Unfortunately, the "leopard hypothesis" cannot adequately explain the Makapan Phase I bone accumulations, which are highly concentrated in the deposits. The relative abundance of trees in the Makapan valley may preclude the possibility of repeated use of some hypothetical fissure mouth at this site, even though the valley may have been drier at the time of accumulation.

In order to understand the patterns of bone breakage in the Makapan collection, it is necessary to compare it with a bone sample known to have been damaged by a limited number of agents. Brain (1967a, b, 1969a) was able to obtain a sample of goat bones from eight Hottentot villages on the Kuiseb River in the Namib Desert. Goats are periodically slaughtered by the villagers for celebrations, and the pattern of butchery was recorded in detail. The only damage caused by human activity was: (1) the horns were chopped from the skull, (2) the neck vertebrae were chopped through, (3) the larger limb bones were smashed so that the marrow could be extracted. No further damage was done to the bones, and no part of the skull or skeleton was used as an implement. After the flesh had been boiled and eaten, the bones were discarded on the open sand surface.

At this stage a second agent contributes to bone damage. Small jackal-sized dogs scavenge the discarded material and selectively chew on certain bones. The rate of survival of different limb-bone epiphyses is directly related to the age at which they fuse to the shaft. If the animal is not quite mature, certain epiphyses will be destroyed completely by dogs and by climatic elements. It is apparent that the age at which the animal is killed is an important factor in determining which epiphyses survive, since not all limb-bone ends fuse at the same age.

One of the important features of the Makapan collection is the obvious disproportion of body parts among the bovid bones. Dart explained these disproportions in terms of human selection of certain bones for use. Different bones were either brought back to the "cave" or left outside because they had some specific use. Figure 28 shows the relative proportions of different body parts that survived in the Makapan sample in descending order. A similar graph for the Kuiseb goat bone collection is placed next to it. The overall trend for the modern sample is similar to that from Makapan. From this it is possible to conclude, with some reservations, that the distortion of body parts in the Makapan sample could be explained in terms of scavenging activity, *possibly* mixed with some damage resulting from hominids. A few striking anomalies in the graph are: (1) the larger number of distal tibiae at Makapan, (2) the larger number of atlas–axis vertebrae at Makapan. Anomaly (1) may reflect the fact that *old* goats were rarely killed by the Hottentots. The distal tibias of an immature animal may be more readily destroyed by a scavenger. Since younger goats dominate the sample, this may distort the ratio of epiphyses which are present. Anomaly (2), the low percentage of axis–atlas vertebrae among the goats, may be the result of damage when the head is severed from the spine by the Hottentots before the head is boiled. It should be noted, however, that there are many young animals in the Makapan sample also.

Therefore, it is possible that most of the anomalies in the Makapan sample may be explained in terms of scavenger activities, particularly hyenas and jackals, with a minor contribution from porcupines. One feature that cannot be explained in these terms is the localized wear or smoothing on certain bone fragments from Makapan. Similar specimens have been reported from Sterkfontein

(Robinson 1959) and from Olduvai Gorge, Tanzania (L. S. B. Leakey 1960). Identical specimens are not found among the Kiuseb goat bones, although bone "pseudotools" can be produced in the sand surrounding the waterholes near the villages. These evenly polished and tapered "tools" are produced when bone fragments are repeatedly trampled and moved in the sand by the large goat herds that visit the water holes each day. None of these specimens displays *localized* wear and polish. The process produces an even polish along all edges of the bone fragment. At present it is impossible to explain away the Makapan and Sterkfontein examples as the product of some natural process. It has been suggested that the localized wear was caused by rubbing the edge on a soft material such as skin (Brain 1967d).

Three other factors of the Makapan collection cannot be explained away as the product of natural processes: the "battered" stalagmite fragments, the cannon-bone distals with bone or limestone fragments wedged between the condyles, and the bone shafts with horn cores or smaller shafts rammed into the marrow cavities. Admittedly these specimens form a very small proportion of the whole bone assemblage, but they cannot be regarded as "accidental" phenomena. At present it appears probable that they may be the result of deliberate manual manipulation by hominids. Since the only hominid remains found in the grey breccia are australopithecine, it may be tentatively assumed that these creatures deliberately (and systematically?) used bone fragments as tools at a period for which there is no clear evidence of stone toolmaking. Unfortunately, at Makapan, and probably at other sites, the evidence for this activity is "diluted" by bone damage caused by scavengers and (at Swartkrans) by leopards.

THE STONE ARTIFACTS

True stone tools have been reported from the Phase II breccias of Makapan and Sterkfontein. At Swartkrans they occur at variable depths in the deposit, and one specimen is claimed from Kromdraai B (Brain, 1958).

At *Makapan* they were first reported to come from the Phase II or red-brown breccia, which overlies the gray breccia (Brain, van Riet Lowe, and Dart 1955). This was a small sample of fractured dolomite fragments extracted from the lower rubble layers of the deposit, but their validity has been challenged (von Koenigswald 1961).

Further intensive study of the Phase II breccias has yielded a sample of 5755 pebbles and slabs from the upper rubble exposed in the collapsed cone of breccia found within the cave (Mason 1962a, 1965). Another sample of 14,118 pebbles was recovered by excavation from the lower rubble of the same breccia. Almost all the pebbles and slabs were dolomite, with very few chert specimens. Both rock types occur in the immediate vicinity of the cavern and were probably not transported any distance to the deposit. However, very rare waterworn quartzite pebbles also occur with the chert and dolomite. The nearest surface outcrop of quartz is a few hundred yards upslope from the cavern exposure on the hillside, and quartzite pebbles also occur in the stream bed at the bottom of the slope.

In both the upper and lower rubble–gravel samples of the Phase II breccia there are 2.1 and 2.2%, respectively, fragments and pebbles with distinct conchoidal fracture scars suggesting possible human workmanship. However, several features argue against this interpretation: the conchoidal or "flake" scars occur haphazardly on the rock surface; scars are not restricted to any particular size of rock but may be found on both enormous and minute specimens (16–0.5-inch diameter); only three "flakes" have been found with the apparently flaked specimens. The ratio of fractured slab–cobbles to true flakes is 99.4:0.6%. This ratio is very similar to that found in ancient rubble deposits of extreme geological age —that is, before the advent of hominids. This would indicate that although flaked stones are present in the rubble, their character would suggest a natural origin. All other true man-made flaked stone assemblages contain much higher ratios of flakes (Partridge 1965).

Controlled excavations into the surface of the Phase II rubbles revealed deep solution cavities in the breccia, probably caused by ancient tree roots. Each cavity is filled with a mixture of surface rubble and dissolved breccia together with fractured stones, rare flakes, and battered cobbles. Rock types other than the local dolomite and chert occur in large numbers. The proportions of different exotic rocks are: quartzite 96%, quartz 2.5%, and the residue composed of diorite, sandstone, and shale. Maguire (1965, 1968) claims that several hundred specimens show signs of localized battering. This takes the form of crushed edges, flake scars, and localized changes in surface texture. He has also isolated groups of rocks with similar shapes. Certainly a few published specimens are unquestionable artifacts, but most of the available drawings and photographs remain unconvincing. Some specimens came from *in situ* positions in the consolidated breccia but the greater part of the sample comes from the surface soil and the fillings of the solution cavity. The association between many artifacts and the breccia is therefore still open to question. The argument that the specimens in the loose soil have dissolved out of the breccia remains an opinion rather than a fact. When a large enough sample is obtained from within the breccia itself, the surface soil material can be discarded.

The claim that many of these rocks have been used as pounders depends mainly on ethnographic evidence (Dart 1965c; Boshier 1965). The possibility that similar battering might occur on rocks in natural hill-wash deposits on the valley slopes has not been investigated. The available evidence suggests that a few doubtful artifacts (Leakey 1970) have been found definitely *in situ* in the red-brown breccia, but this case has been partly obscured by a large number of ambiguous data.

Sterkfontein first yielded foreign stones with definite and clear flake scars in some loose surface breccia to the west of the main quarry (Brain 1956). Controlled excavations in this area exposed solid breccia with numerous solution cavities in its surface. During the course of this work, several more flaked stones were found in the overburden (Robinson and Mason 1957). The hard breccia exposed by this work was then excavated to form what is now called the West Pit. A large sample of flaked stones together with a few flakes was recovered from within the breccia itself (Robinson 1958b; Mason 1962b).

About 130 lb of foreign rock was recovered, and a further 2736 specimens have been removed from the limeworkers' dumps surrounding the West Pit (Tobias and Hughes 1969). The proportions of rock types found in the excavated sample are: quartzite 57%, quartz 38.4%, chert 2.5%, diabase 2.1%. All these materials are available in the adjacent Blaauwbank River, and Mason argues that all the material was carried from the source up to the original cave. Certain points argue against this interpretation:

1. Brain (1970) reported that gravel patches occur on the adjacent slopes of the valley. It is possible that some foreign rock material would have washed into the cavern from one of these high-level gravel patches.

2. Of 98 definite stone tools, only 3 are convincing flakes. Mason has suggested that the flakes were carried away from the site to be used elsewhere, but it could be argued with equal force that flaking would occur at the stream bed to save the effort of carrying heavy cobbles up to the cave.

The validity of the published specimens is reasonably secure. Their size range is restricted between 170 and 60 mm, and all show clear signs of deliberate and systematic flaking. The scars are relatively large, radial scars. The few flakes also display clear cones, platforms, and dorsal ridges. The sample has been subdivided into the following types: 3 whole flakes, 4 broken flakes, 2 choppers, 3 (?) proto-hand-axes, 1 spheroid, 39 cores, and numerous blocks with a few flake scars but no apparent design. (The material recovered from the limeworkers' dumps has not been published yet.) Six specimens are abraded, suggesting that at least some of the material may have been washed in from an adjacent gravel patch on the valley slopes. It is possible therefore that the sample is derived and numerically distorted. Bearing this in mind, together with the relatively small number of tools in the published sample, Mason's claim that it belongs to the "Lower Acheulian" may be based on too little evidence (Mason, 1961a, b, 1962a). The only control sample of "Lower Acheulian" with which the Sterkfontein tools have been compared is itself a rolled and derived sample from the gravel beds of the Blaauwbank River (Mason 1962a, b). The presence of the proto-hand axe at Sterkfontein may suggest that the sample more closely resembles the "Developed Oldowan" of Bed II at Olduvai Gorge (M. Leakey 1970).

Swartkrans first yielded stone artifacts from the limeworkers' debris (Brain 1958), and large numbers of tools and foreign stones have been recovered during later work. Data on these are conveniently summarized in Table 6.

TABLE 6

Swartkrans Stone Artifacts [a]

Rock type	Count (%)	Weight (gm)	Waterworn	Flaked pieces
Quartzite	3148 (75.9)	507	87	33
Quartz	36 (18.5)	226	3	8
Diabase	6 (3.1)	450	1	5
Other	5 (2.5)	166	0	5
Totals:	195 (100.0)	1349	91	51

[a] From Brain (1970).

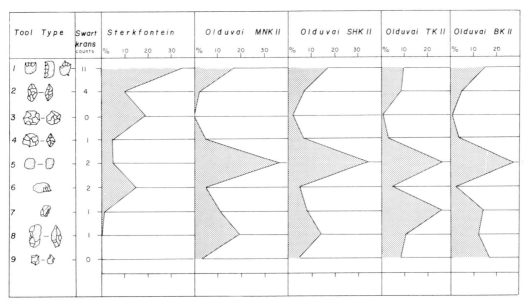

Fig. 29. Percentage distributions of nine tool types in the Developed Oldowan from Sterkfontein and Olduvai Gorge localities (the Swartkrans sample is too small to be converted to percentages): (1) choppers; (2) bifaces; (3) polyhedrals; (4) discoids; (5) spheroids; (6) heavy-duty scrapers; (7) light-duty scrapers; (8) other heavy-duty tools; (9) other light-duty tools. (After M. D. Leakey 1970.)

The distribution of raw materials is broadly similar to that of Sterkfontein, but the percentage values for quartz and quartzite differ. The numerous water-worn specimens suggest that the material was derived from gravel patches located on the valley slopes and was washed into the fissure opening leading to the Swartkrans caverns. The flaked pieces include 30 specimens that have multiple

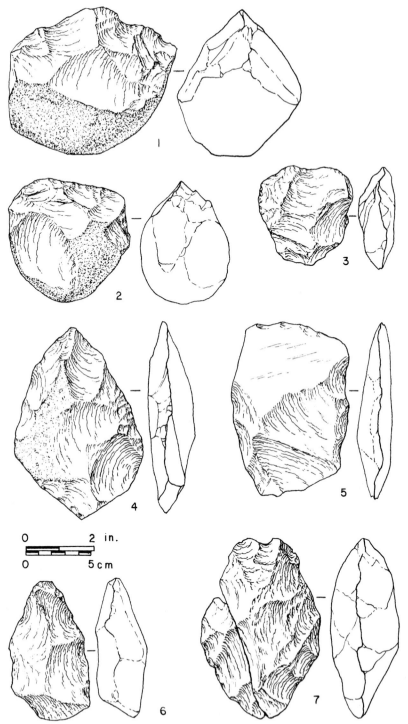

Fig. 30. Artifacts from Swartkrans: (1, 2) choppers; (3) discoids; (4, 6, 7) bifaces; (5) cleaver. (After M. D. Leakey 1970.)

76

flaking and are unquestionable artifacts. All of these come from the pink breccia, and their context is not in doubt. M. Leakey (1970) has classified them according to the criteria used for analysis of the Developed Oldowan so that direct comparisons are possible between Sterkfontein, Swartkrans, and the Developed Oldowan of Olduvai Gorge (Fig. 29).

Both samples are broadly similar even though they contain relatively few specimens. Swartkrans has a cleaver, pick, pointed chopper, and anvils not found at Sterkfontein. It is uncertain whether these differences are at all significant, considering the small size of each sample. Compared with the Developed Oldowan, the Sterkfontein sample obviously falls outside the range of variation for this industry, but it still resembles it more closely than any other known stone artifact assemblages (Fig. 30).

EVIDENCE FOR FIRE: *Australopithecus "prometheus"?*

Among the specimens sent to Dart in 1925 from Makapan was "a charred and comminuted ungulate bone breccia" (Dart 1948b). Suspecting that this material represented fragments of a very ancient hearth, Dart sent specimens to be analyzed at the South African Government Chemical Laboratory and also to the Institute for Medical Research in Johannesburg. He reports that the two independent assays revealed the presence of "numerous black particles" resembling carbon in the dried acid-insoluble residue. Most of this black material was transformed (presumably by combustion?) into carbon dioxide. These results, derived from two independent sources, prompted Dart to propose that the presence of true carbon had been demonstrated and that fireplaces had been present in the breccia, presumably made by very early men, as he had predicted in an earlier paper (Dart 1925b). Dart also reported that a third set of "detailed chemical analyses of glassy and ashy materials and microscopic examination of these fluxes" was carried out by Dr. V. L. Bosazza. These analyses corroborated the findings of the other two laboratories. Unfortunately no detailed account of any of these three assays was ever published and we have no numerical data on the relative proportions of the elements found in the breccia.

Twenty years after these tests were run, Kitching found the first australopithecine occiput in the dump material derived from the Phase I breccia. Dart concluded that this was the hominid responsible for the "hearths" and named the new find *Australopithecus prometheus* after the Greek mythical hero who captured fire for the use of man.

A few years later, Oakley (1956) tested several new samples of breccia and ascertained that no free carbon could be found in any of them. The blackening of the bone fragments had been caused mainly by deposition of manganese dioxide. He suggested that the samples tested earlier had been contaminated either by modern charcoal hearths or by an accident of blasting. Since no account of the original tests is available, it remains uncertain whether all the carbonate cement was completely dissolved from the "numerous black patches." If some carbonate cement had remained, this might explain the subsequent production of carbon dioxide. However, there is no indication that Oakley's samples come from the same position in the breccia as the original material, and there must remain a small residual doubt that free carbon may have been present in isolated patches of the breccia. Even if this were ultimately proved, it need not automatically prove that the australopithecines were firemakers since natural bush fires may have caused similar occurrences.

ASSOCIATED FAUNA

Abundant fossil remains of animals have been recovered from the breccias of all five sites but complete lists of the animals present in each deposit are not yet available. Accurate identifications have been hampered often by the fragmentary nature of the bone material and many individual specimens have been reclassified as more complete material came to light. This process has led to confused terminology and frequent regrouping or renaming of specimens. Over seventy papers have been published on various aspects of the fauna by more than thirty specialists. The faunal samples from Makapan, Sterkfontein, and Swartkrans continue to accumulate more material from fieldwork in progress. Bone breccia blocks must be developed by hand or dissolved in dilute acetic acid in order to free specimens from the hard matrix. Both methods are slow and literally tons of breccia remain to be processed so that a "complete" study will not be possible in the near future.

Much of the bone material comes from the limeworkers' dumps and was not recovered *in situ* in the original deposits. Only a few authors mention the color and texture of the matrix adhering to the fossils which they describe, thus giving some clue of the original stratigraphic position. Thus far, it has not proved possible to divide the fauna sample from a site between into two or more stratigraphic units. It is impossible, therefore, to study faunal changes within a single site through time. The most complete lists of animal species present (H. B. S. Cooke 1964) treat each site as one unit, as do most earlier descriptions. All analyses deal exclusively with mammals, and the fairly abundant bird and reptile fossils remain to be studied.

The larger mammals will be discussed first. These include primates, carnivores, perissodactyls, and the numerous artiodactyls. They are followed by the smaller mammals or microfauna, including insectivores, bats, hares, and numerous rodents. These, together with the undescribed nonmammalian fauna, are the best indicators of the varied environments in which the earliest hominids were able to survive.

Nonhuman Primates

Primates occur in relatively large numbers at all the sites and probably form the highest percentage of animals represented at Taung. At all sites they are represented almost exclusively by damaged skulls, muzzles and mandible fragments. Dart (1957b) lists for Makapan a minimum of 45 individuals, represented by skull and jawbone fragments. Only two postcranial fragments were recovered from the sample. Comparable figures have not been published for other sites, but postcranial bones are reported to be extremely rare. Dart (1949e, f) suggested that this disproportion reflected australopithecine hunting activities, while Brain (1968) points out that the patterns of skull damage and the absence of postcranial bones are reproduced exactly by modern leopards after eating out a baboon carcass.

No living primates are represented in the breccias and the nomenclature of the extinct forms has passed through several revisions since the earliest notes on the Taung material (Haughton 1925). The most complete and thorough study of all the primate material recognizes 13 species (Freedman 1957) to which an additional species from Taung can now be added (Freedman 1961b, 1965). The number of diagnostic specimens of each species is listed for individual sites in Table 7.

Except *Cercopithecoides,* all these are extinct baboonlike forms. The genus *Parapapio* has a dental morphology that closely resembles *Papio,* but it also differs from *Papio* in the profile shape of the muzzle, which may be shorter. *Parapapio* also lacks the clear sexual dimorphism seen in the supraorbital and maxillary ridges of *Papio.* The other extinct baboons all differ from these in dental characteristics, muzzle profile, and skull morphology.

The Taung primates are considered to be the most primitive group. *Parapapio antiquus* includes specimens originally described under three names: *Papio antiquus* (Haughton 1925); *Papio africanus* (Gear 1926; Broom 1934; T. R. Jones 1936); and *Parapapio africanus* (Broom 1940; Dart 1949e; Hopwood and Hollyfield 1954). The second form from Taung, *Parapapio jonesi,* (Broom 1940) is a relatively small baboon that appears at all the sites and evidently survived over a considerable period. *Parapapio whitei* (Broom 1940) is the largest form, evidently larger than any living baboon. *Papio izodi* resembles *Parapapio antiquus* in many features and Freedman (1957) has suggested that the Taung breccia may have accumulated at a time shortly after divergence of the *Papio* and *Parapapio* lines. *Papio wellsi* (Freedman 1961a) is the same size as *Papio izodi,* but differs from the others in facial profile and the transverse section of the muzzle. *Cercopithecoides williamsi* (Mollett 1947) is an extinct colobine monkey with an unusually foreshortened face.

The Sterkfontein primates include numerous specimens of *Parapapio jonesi, P. whitei,* and *C. williamsi* and another monkey *C. moletti* (Freedman 1957), which is still imperfectly known since no complete skulls are available for study.

TABLE 7

Nonhuman Primate Remains from Early Hominid Sites [2]

Genus and species	Taung	Sterkfontein	Makapan	Swartkrans	Kromdraai
Parapapio antiquus	22	—	—	—	—
Parapapio jonesi	1	24	15	3	2
Parapapio broomi	—	42	34	—	—
Parapapio whitei	3	13	4	—	—
Papio izodi	4	—	—	—	—
Papio wellsi	8	—	—	—	—
Papio robinsoni	—	—	—	93	1
Simopithecus darti	—	—	20	—	—
Papio angusticeps	—	—	—	—	14
Simopithecus danieli	—	—	—	18	—
Dinopithecus ingens	—	—	—	37	—
Gorgopithecus major	—	—	—	—	12
Ceropithecoides williamsi	1	17	6	?	—
Ceropithecoides molletti	—	1	—	3	—

[2] From Freedman (1957, 1961b).

The most abundant specimens are of *Parapapio broomi* (T. R. Jones 1936). This group now includes specimens previously named *P. makapani* (Broom and Hughes 1949) and *Brachygnathopithecus peppercorni* (Kitching 1952). Like *P. whitei,* they show a distinct size increase, but no major changes in skull morphology.

At Makapan the large *Parapapio whitei* is absent, but another giant baboon with a distinctive detention is present: *Simopithecus darti* (Broom and Jensen 1946). No complete skulls have been described, and the sample includes fragmentary specimens previously called *Papio darti* (Broom and Jensen 1946; Mollett 1947; Kitching, Wells, and Westphal 1948; Broom and Robinson 1949b; Dart 1949e), *Dinopithecus* sp. (Broom and Hughes 1949), *Brachygnathopithecus peppercorni* (Kitching 1952), *Gorgopithecus wellsi,* and *G. darti* (Kitching 1953).

Swartkrans has a few specimens of the diminutive *P. jonesi* and some *C. moletti,* but the sample is otherwise dominated by giant forms not present in the previous three sites. *Papio robinsoni* (Freedman 1957) includes specimens first published as *Dinopithecus ingens* (Broom 1940), *Parapapio* sp. (Robinson 1952b), and *Papio* sp. (Oakley 1954a). The next most abundant giant form is *Dinopithecus ingens* (Broom 1937a) of which female specimens are more abundant. Next is *Simopithecus danieli* of which all the available specimens are female. The remarkable scarcity of males in the Swartkrans sample has not been reported from other sites. Possibly the giant males were less likely to be attacked by carnivores. If it is accepted that Swartkrans is younger than Makapan, there

appears to be a definite trend toward increased size among the primate population in which *S. darti* is replaced by the larger *S. danieli* and *C. williamsi* is replaced by a bigger form of *C. molletti*.

At Kromdraai there is an apparent reversal in this trend. *Papio angusticeps*
(Broom 1940) is dentally similar to *P. robinsoni* but the shape of the muzzle is
closest to the living baboon *P. ursinus*. However, *P. angusticeps* is smaller than
even the living form. The other new form, *Gorgopithecus major* (Broom 1940),
is a large baboon, but smaller than *D. ingens*. It has a very distinctive skull
shape with massive brow ridges and large canines well demonstrated in a virtually intact male skull. Referred to the group are specimens previously published as *Parapapio major* (Broom 1940), *Simopithecus* sp. (Oakley 1954b),
Simopithecus major (Hopwood and Hollyfield 1954). *Parapapio corunatus*
comes from a soil pocket in the breccia and is not reliably associated with the
other material (Broom and Robinson 1950a).

Remarkably few species are shared by any two sites and this disparity is taken
by most authors to indicate that they are of different ages. However, several
other variables may be invoked to partly explain the differences: the three distinct habitats of Taung, the Blaauwbank River valley and Makapan, climatic
fluctuations through time, and shifts in primate population in response to other
animal population changes, particularly carnivores. Other important factors are
the vagaries of sampling and survival: Dart (1949e) mentions that the limeworks foreman at Makapan, a certain Mr. Darling, deliberately incinerated any
breccia block that appeared to contain a primate skull since this offended his
fundamentalist beliefs. Hundreds of primate specimens (certainly including numerous australopithecine remains) have been lost from this site. Also it is unknown whether the carnivores, thought to be responsible for the primate bone
accumulation, were in any way responsible for selecting individuals from the actual primate populations. It remains uncertain whether modern leopards take
"random samples" of the baboon populations upon which they prey. In spite of
all these unknowns, the fossil evidence nonetheless suggests quite different primate populations in the vicinity of each site. In three adjacent sites of the
Blaauwbank River valley the differences can be explained as the result of population shifts with time, but this is less certain for explaining discrepancies between
sites in different environments. Evidently, the past baboon population of the
Transvaal has been extremely varied and no fossil evidence has been presented
which might suggest a continuous evolving population through time. The
changes are still interpreted as "population shifts" in response to environmental
factors (Freedman 1957).

Carnivores

H. B. S. Cooke (1963) lists 31 species of which only three are represented by living populations. They include wild dogs, jackals, foxes, herpestines, hyenas, fe-
lids, and saber-tooth cats. The numbers of diagnostic specimens, minimum totals

TABLE 8

Carnivore Counts and Body Parts from Makapan [a]

	Minimum no. of individuals	Limb-bone fragments	Cranial and teeth
Wild dogs	1	1	0
Jackals	1	1	0
Hyaenids	17	5	78
Leopards	1	2	0
Saber-tooth cats	1	0	4
"Medium carnivores"	2	3	0
"Small carnivores" (herpestines?)	7	7	17

[a] From Dart (1957b).

TABLE 9

Numbers of Carnivore Species Present at Early Hominid Sites

Genus	Description	Taung	Sterk-fontein	Makapan	Swart-krans	Krom-draai
Canis	Extinct jackal, wolf, wild dog	1	2	1	1	3
Vulpes	Extinct fox	—	—	?	1	1
Herpestes	Extinct mongoose-like form	—	—	—	—	1
Crossarchus	Extinct mongoose-like form	—	—	—	—	1
Cynictus	Yellow mongoose-like form	—	—	1	1	—
Lycaena	Primitive predatory hyaenid	—	2	—	2	—
Leecyaena	Small short-faced hyaenid	—	—	—	1	—
Crocuta	Ancestral predatory hyaenids	—	—	1	2	2
Hyaena	Ancestral scavenging hyaenids	—	—	1	2	1
Felis	Extinct serval-like form	—	—	—	—	1
Therailurus (*Dinofelis*)	Large saber-tooth–leopard form	—	1	1	?	1
Panthera	Ancestral lion–leopard	—	—	—	3	2
Meganteron	Saber-tooth cat	—	1	1	1	1

for individuals, age at death, and sex of this material have not been surveyed, and no systematic study of surviving body parts has been carried out. Most descriptions concentrate on skulls and dentition, whereas postcranial specimens are mentioned only when in close association with diagnostic skull parts. Dart (1957b) provides data on body parts and individual counts for Makapan (Table 8). Unfortunately, comparable figures are not available from other sites and it is not clear whether hyenids dominate the carnivores from Swartkrans or Kromdraai. As Table 9 shows, this group has not been recorded from Taung and Sterkfontein.

Canid specimens are relatively rare, with jackals best represented in the group The Taung collection contains only one fragment doubtfully referred to *C. mesomelas,* the black-backed jackal. The specimen is probably an ancestral form related to the living species but not identical with it and the classification is not accepted by Ewer (1956c), who described the canid material. Sterkfontein has another form, *Canis mesomelas pappos* (Ewer 1956c), which differs from the living form in a few dental characters. It is present at all sites except Taung. Another species found only at Sterkfontein is *C. brevirostris,* a small jackal with short, stout canines and a shortened premolar series probably adapted to an omnivorous diet. Kromdraai has two new species: *C. atrox* (Broom 1948b), poorly represented but dentally distinctive; *C. terblanchi* (Broom 1948b) was the same size as the striped jackal but differs from it in skull and dental morphology. *Vulpes pulcher* (Broom 1937a) is represented only by mandible fragments, and the Makapan specimen comprises the back of the skull and cannot be referred to a species.

The herpestine or mongooselike forms come from Swartkrans and Kromdraai only. *Herpestes mesotes* (Ewer 1956e) at Kromdraai is an ancestral form of the living marsh mongoose. Also from Kromdraai, *Crossarchus transvaalensis* (Broom 1937b) is dentally distinct and slightly larger than the living mongoose. Swartkrans has material identical to the living yellow mongoose, *Cynictes penicillata,* and a closely related extinct form named *C. penicillata brachydon* (Ewer 1956e, 1957c), which is the same size but has shorter, wider carnassials.

The lycaenids from Swartkrans and Sterkfontein are *L. silberbergi* (Broom 1945a) with a primitive tooth row lacking any trace of a lower second molar, and *L. nitidula* (Ewer 1955a), which is the same size but has distinctive cheek teeth adapted to shearing rather than crushing. This is taken to indicate more predatory activity and less scavenging. *Leecyaena forfex* (Ewer 1955a) is related to the lycaenids but has a shorter skull with a strongly developed crest. It was slightly smaller than the brown hyena.

Five species of *Crocuta* have been recognized. Ewer (1954a) points out that the dentition of this genus differs from that of *Hyaena* in that it is adapted to meat cutting or shearing rather than bone smashing. *Crocuta* cf. *brevirostris* (Toerien 1952) comes from Makapan only and is poorly represented by a small jaw fragment. Swartkrans has *C. crocuta angella* (Ewer 1955b) similar to the living spotted hyena except for the teeth, which include large upper first molars. *Crocuta venustula* (Ewer 1955b) from Swartkrans is a smaller animal with a lighter mandible than living hyenas. *Crocuta spelea* (Broom 1939c) from Kromdraai has a high sagittal crest, and *C. ultra* (Ewer 1954b) is smaller than the living spotted hyena, with a short snout, low broad forehead, and a compressed incisor row.

Hyena species include *H. makapani* (Toerien 1952) from Makapan. This is well represented by fossil remains. The teeth differ from those of living hyenas in size and morphology, but the creature was about the same size as the striped hyena. Swartkrans has remains of the living brown hyena and an antecedent of the living species. *Hyaena bellax* (Ewer 1954b) from Kromdraai is larger than any of the living or fossil forms and it has massive mandibles to accommodate unusually large bone-smashing molars. The organization of the South African hyaenid fossil material is shown in Fig. 31.

Only two fragmentary specimens of *Felis crassidens* (Broom 1948b) are known from Kromdraai, and the other catlike forms are all larger. *Therailurus barlowi* (*Dinofelis*) occurs at Makapan, Sterkfontein, and possibly at Swartkrans. It was first published as *Meganteron barlowi* (Broom 1937a) and later reclassified by Ewer (1955c). It is larger than the living adult male leopard, with a short broad mouth, long curved incisors and extremely large canines. *Therailurus piveteaui* (Ewer 1955c) from Kromdraai is about the same size and shape, but the canines are slightly shorter and the carnassials have a very different shape. It has been suggested that this form should be reclassified as *Dinofelis zdansky* as it closely resembles a European saber-tooth cat (von Hemmer 1965).

True lion- or leopardlike fossils are reported from Swartkrans and Kromdraai. *Panthera shawi* (Broom 1937b) is represented by loose teeth only and remains a doubtful classification, but the fragmentary remains of *P.* aff. *leo* (Ewer 1956d)

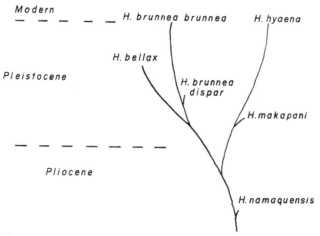

Fig. 31. Organization of the fossil hyenids. (After Ewer 1955b.)

do suggest some resemblance to the living lion. *Panthera pardus incurva* (Ewer 1956d) is relatively abundant at Swartkrans (minimum, 13 individuals) and may be represented by isolated fragments from Sterkfontein and Kromdraai. This form is closely related to the living leopard, but has smaller cheek teeth and other minor differences in dental morphology.

Saber-tooth cats are present in all the sites (except Taung). *Meganteron gracile* (Broom 1948b) from Sterkfontein is the smallest form and is represented by only a few fragments. *Meganteron* sp. nov. (H. B. S. Cooke 1969) from Makapan was reported as *Machaerodus darti* (Toerien 1955) and is represented by a mouth and mandible fragments only. *Meganteron eurynodon* (Ewer 1955c) is found at Swartkrans and Kromdraai. It is a medium-sized saber-tooth with a relatively short, flat canine without the crenulations on the anterior edge—a common feature in other species. A specimen was recovered from Kromdraai that included a crushed skull, mandible and associated vertebrae, scapula, and humerus fragments.

This brief survey of the carnivore material also suggests that widely different populations existed in the vicinity of each site. Taung and Sterkfontein have very few specimens, whereas Makapan has more material, dominated by hyena. Swartkrans and Kromdraai have the most varied carnivore material but share only 5 species from a list of 24 of both sites. Ewer (1955a) suggests that the Swartkrans carnivores are only slightly more recent in age than the Sterkfontein (Type Site), sample, whereas Kromdraai follows Swartkrans considerably later in time. This chronological arrangement does not account for the fact that Swartkrans has at least three (possibly four) modern species, whereas Kromdraai has only one possibly extant form.

The presence of large carnivores in the breccias poses important problems about the mode of bone accumulations at each site. If Brain's hypothesis applies to other sites besides Swartkrans—that leopard kills are the main source of bone material—the presence of leopard and other large carnivore remains must be explained. Brain has observed a hyena fall accidentally to its death into a limestone fissure during panic flight, and it may be agreed that hyenas might be killed relatively frequently during the harrassment of leopards near the fissure mouth. (This has not been reported by modern observers.) If accidents account for most of the large carnivore remains, it might be expected that more of the animal skeleton would have survived beside the cranial fragments. At present, little is known about cannibalism among large carnivores, and the possibility that *some* of the remains reflect early hominid predation cannot be ruled out entirely.

Perissodactyls

This group includes rhinoceros and horse remains. Rhinoceros is present at Makapan only (Hooijer 1959), possibly reflecting a dense-bush environment not present near the other four sites today. Almost all the fossil remains are teeth.

Out of a total of 99 known teeth, 94 are deciduous (milk) molars of young animals. These are closely related to the milk dentition of the modern white rhino, *Ceratotherium simum* (minimum total, 28 individuals present) and the black rhino *Diceros bicornis* (6 individuals). Only one adult jaw fragment has been found. The prevalence of juveniles in this sample is remarkable and reflects some form of selection. This effectively rules out accidental deaths which would produce a random age distribution. Either carnivore or hominid activity may be invoked to explain this activity, but the published evidence for systematic damage to the teeth (Anderson 1968) remains unconvincing without a parallel study of modern specimens collected under controlled conditions.

Horse remains have been recently surveyed by Churcher (1970), who lists the four species given in Table 10. The small three-toed horse *Hipparion steytleri* is represented by cheek teeth only and has been reported previously as *Stylohipparion steytleri* (van Hoepen 1930; H. B. S. Cooke 1950) or *S. lybicum* (Singer and Boné 1966). Dart (1957a) lists 44 specimens from Makapan.

The very large horse *Equus capensis* (Broom 1909) is the most abundant form at Swartkrans and Kromdraai A. H. B. S. Cooke (1964) hints at its presence at Makapan, but presents no supporting evidence, and Ewer (1958b) omits it altogether. Within this taxon Churcher now groups all material previously published as *E. helmei, E. cawoodi, E. kuhni,* and *E. zeitsmani.* Also included are some teeth of *E. harrisi* and *E. plicatus.* The breccia specimens tabulated above are represented by abundant cheek teeth, some incisors, and canines. Postcranial survivals include phalanges only.

The zebra *E. burchelli* was diagnosed from relatively few damaged teeth (Mendrez 1966). In historical times this species occurred in most parts of South Africa except the Lesotho and Cape mountains. It now has a greatly restricted distribution, unlike *E. quagga,* which is now extinct. The habitat of the diminutive zebrine formerly included most of the Orange Free State and Cape Province

TABLE 10

Perissodactyl Remains with Early Hominid Sites [a]

Genus and species	Sterkfontein Type	Sterkfontein extension	Makapan	Swartkrans	Kromdraai A
Hipparion steytleri, Pleistocene hipparion	—	—	5	1	1
Equus capensis, extinct, giant Cape horse	7	—	?	13	23
E. burchelli, Burchell's zebra	—	2	—	—	7
E. quagga, quagga	—	—	—	12	1?
Total individuals:	7	2	5	26	32

[a] From Churcher (1970).

TABLE 11

Age at Death of *Equus* Specimens [a]

	Sterkfontein Type	Sterkfontein Extension	Makapan	Swartkrans	Kromdraai A
Old mature	2	—		6	10
Mature	2	1		7	8
Young mature	—	1	No	2	6
Colt	3	—	data	10	3
Colt (milk dentition)	—	—		—	2
Total individuals:	7	2	5	25	29

[a] From Churcher (1970).

during the advent of European settlement. The Swartkrans sample includes many teeth, and an articulated left forefoot including metacarpals and phalanges. The Kromdraai specimen is damaged and shares some characters with *E. burchelli*.

The distribution of species among the five deposits indicates that Sterkfontein Extension, Swartkrans, and Kromdraai A sites contain extant species and are therefore younger than Sterkfontein Type and Makapan. More precise ranking of the deposits is not possible. Churcher's (1970) valuable assessment of the age at death of each specimen is summarized in Table 11.

Unlike many of the other larger mammalian species from the breccias, the horses display a surprising bias in favor of mature or even old specimens. If this bias reflects selective preference by predatory leopards, no such selection of modern zebras by leopard has been observed to support such an assumption. The fact that most of the mature and old specimens are of the giant *E. capensis* make the bias all the more surprising. Unfortunately, the Sterkfontein and Makapan samples are too small to permit any comment on chronological changes in age-at-death distributions for the horses. Similar details for other mammalian species would be of great value.

Makapan has also yielded a remarkable chalicothere named *Metaschizotherium transvaalensis* (George 1950) represented by relatively abundant limb-bone fragments and isolated teeth. At least 17 individuals have been isolated. The creature is larger than most herbivores and is distinct from them in having grazing dentition and short feet with claws instead of hooves (Webb 1965).

Artiodactyls

Within this order are the various pigs, hippo, giraffes, buffalo, alcelaphines, numerous antelope, and gazelle. Only the pigs have been intensively surveyed so far, and the Bovidae from Sterkfontein, Kromdraai, and Swartkrans remain unpublished, so that the group cannot be compared in detail between individual sites.

Only four species are listed for Taung (H. B. S. Cooke 1964): an extinct massive warthog, *Potamocheroides shawi* (Dale 1948); fragments related to the modern nyala, *Tragelaphus angasi;* also *Cephalophus parvus* (Broom 1934), a minute form even smaller than the living bluebuck; and *Oreotragus longiceps* (Broom 1934), an extinct neotragine antelope. Recently a juvenile kudu *Strepsiceros strepsiceros* also has been recovered (Freedman 1961a). No other material has been reported, and the marked absence of bovids from the site is taken to reflect a semidesert environment, capable of supporting primates and microfauna, but not big game.

Among the very few specimens thus far described from Sterkfontein are the two extinct bovids discussed below, *Hippotragus broomi* (H. B. S. Cooke 1947) an extinct roan, and *Makapania broomi* (Wells and Cooke 1957), a remarkable extinct alcelaphine with horns protruding sideways from immediately behind the orbits. The piglike forms have been studied by several specialists and their distribution is summarized in Table 12.

Nearly all these have been classified on dental morphology only, and most of the type material is in the form of loose teeth, or jaw and maxilla fragments (Dale and Tobiansky 1947). Dart (1957b) shows that postcranial bones are extremely scarce at Makapan, and no postcranial material has been published from other sites.

Rapid changes in molar shape and crown pattern take place in modern warthogs as they mature, and classification of fossil teeth may be hampered by lack of information on growth changes in extinct forms (Shaw 1938, 1939a). This discovery has led to the "lumping" of several earlier false identifications into the five forms listed above, and the initial phylogeny of the suids (H. B. S. Cooke 1949b) has been extensively revised (Ewer 1956b), and may need revision again in the near future.

Potamochoeroides hypsodon (Dale 1948) is poorly represented by teeth only. It is apparently larger than the living warthogs, but differs from *P. shawi* in dental structure, as the specific name implies. The *P. shawi* jaw fragments from Makapan have been sorted into "age groups" based on five stages of tooth eruption and crown wear. The sample contains a high frequency of young-mature animals

TABLE 12

Suid Species from Early Hominid Sites

Genus and species	Taung	Sterkfontein	Makapan	Swartkrans	Kromdraai
Potamochoeroides hypsodon	—	—	×	—	—
Potamochoeroides shawi	cf.	—	×	—	—
Tapinochoerus meadowsi	—	×	—	×	—
Potamocheorops antiquus	—	?	—	×	×
Notochoerus euilus	—	—	×	—	—

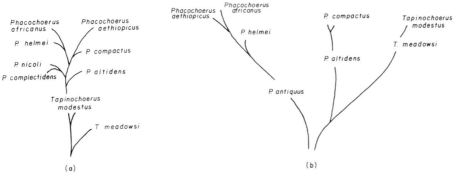

Fig. 32. Phylogeny of the South African fossil pigs (b) after Ewer (1956b) compared with (a) that of H. B. S. Cooke (1949b).

with fewer juveniles and very old specimens. This may reflect a random sample of the normal population and does not suggest deliberate selection of certain age groups. *Tapinochoerus meadowsi* (Broom 1937a) is another dentally distinct form represented only by jaw and skull fragments. *Notochoerus (Gerontochoerus) euilus* (Hopwood and Hollyfield 1954; Ewer 1958a) is also represented by numerous teeth and mandible fragments but is not represented by other parts. *Potamochoerops antiquus* (Broom 1948b) may be absent from Sterkfontein since the matrix adhering to this specimen is unlike the breccia from that site. This form closely resembles the recently extinct *Phacochoerus aethiopicus,* or southern warthog, and may be ancestral to it. The phylogeny suggested by Ewer (1956b) and H. B. S. Cooke (1949b) are compared in Fig. 32.

The only extensive survey of artiodactyls is for Makapan (Wells and Cooke 1956). They include:

Hippopotamus makapanensis (Kitching 1951): possibly closer to the modern hippo *H. amphibus*

Giraffa camelopardalis: teeth closely related to modern giraffe

Libytherium olduvaiensis cf. an extinct short-necked, giraffid (Cooke and Wells 1947)

Strepsiceros strepsiceros cf. the living kudu, some mature, 1 juvenile

Tragelaphus angasi cf. the living nyala

Taurotragus oryx cf. the living eland, mainly juvenile specimens

Syncerus caffer cf. the modern Cape or black buffalo, mainly juvenile specimens.

Cephalophus pricei: an extinct buck, about 1.5 times larger than the living duiker

Cephalophus caerulus cf. the living blue duiker

Redunca darti: the most abundant form present, an extinct reedbuck with relatively massive horn cores

Redunca arundinum cf. the living reedbuck

Redunca fulvorufula cf. the living mountain reedbuck, 1–2 individuals only

Oryx gazella cf. the modern gemsbok

Alcelaphus robustus cf. an extinct large hartebeest, represented by 3 teeth only

Alcelaphus helmei: an extinct hartebeest

Connochaetes taurinus cf. modern blue wildebeest

Makapania broomi: a large extinct alcelaphine, horns protrude laterally from behind the orbits

Oreotragus major (Wells 1951): a large extinct klipspringer

Aepyceros melampus cf. the modern impala

Phenacotragus vanhoepeni: an extinct neotragine antelope, the second most frequent species present

Gazella gracilior: a small extinct gazelle

The four most abundant forms are (in decreasing order) :

1. *Redunca darti:* extinct reedbuck
2. *Phenacotragus vanhoepeni:* extinct neotragine antelope
3. *Makapania broomi:* extinct hartebeestlike form
4. *Connochaetes* cf. *taurinus:* wildebeest

Less frequent than these, but moderately well represented are buffalo, eland, kudu, nyala, mountain reedbuck, and three relatively small extinct buck: *C. pricei, Oreotragus major,* and *Gazella gracilior.*

A third group of very rare species includes: blue duiker, oryx, impala, and two extinct hartebeest; rare traces of *Damalisus* cf. *albifrons* or tsessebe may be present, but this form is not listed by H. B. S. Cooke (1964).

This fauna is taken to reflect a well-watered hill-and-valley environment with some dense bush thinning out into adjacent dry plains capable of supporting open-country animals, particularly the gazelle. The body-parts analysis of the bovids is discussed on page 71.

The Makapan bovid sample was first thought to contain a relatively high proportion of extant species, thus giving the fauna a "modern" aspect not evident in the carnivores, primates, or pigs. When the bovid material (almost all *Antidorcas*) from Swartkrans, Kromdraai, and Sterkfontein is published, the chronological relationship between the sites can be usefully reexamined.

Hares, and Hyraxes, and Antbears

H. B. S. Cooke (1964) lists material related to two living hares: *Pronolagus randensis* from Makapan; and the Cape hare *Lepus capensis* from Taung and Swartkrans. Only two specimens are listed from Makapan (Dart 1957b), and they are probably rare occurrences at the other sites.

Hyraxes occur at all sites, but in relatively small numbers. These are *Procavia antiqua* (Broom 1934), which is considered to be ancestral to the modern Cape dassie, and *Procavia transvaalensis* (Shaw 1937), an extinct form about 1.5 times the size of the modern dassie. Material previously published as *P. robertsi* (Broom 1948b) has been reclassified as *P. antiqua* so that only two legitimate species are recognized (Churcher 1956).

Recently, a giant hyrax has been recovered from Makapan (Kitching 1965); *Gigantohyrax maguirei* is represented by a nearly complete skull considerably larger than any living or Pleistocene fossil hyrax.

	Skull length (mm)
Procavia capensis, modern Cape dassie	81.5
Procavia transvaalensis, extinct dassie	125.2
Gigantohyrax maguirei	200.0

Brain (1968) mentions that the fossil hyraxes are represented by skulls only. In all these specimens the skull cap and back of the skull is missing. A modern leopard when given a dassie carcass will devour the whole skeleton and crush the skull to extract the brain.

The antbear, *Orycteropus* cf. *afer*, is represented by two molars from the Makapan gray breccia (Kitching 1963).

Microfauna

These orders of small mammals are considered: insectivores, bats, and rodents. Over 40 species have been recognized (see Table 13). They dominate the Taung fauna and occur in relatively large quantities at other sites in dense patches of bone sometimes called "rodent breccia." The microfauna pockets in the breccia contain relatively few large animal bones and they have been interpreted by sevral authors as the product of owl pellets. The owl's digestive system is so designed to allow it to swallow small animals whole. Bones and fur are regurgitated from the crop in a ball known as the pellet (Chitty 1934; Davis 1959, 1962). Being nocturnal hunters, owls seek darkened perches during daylight hours, and caves provide an obvious refuge. There has been general agreement in the past that this process adequately explains the presence of the rodent breccias. However, the discovery of early hominid occupation floors near the shores of the Pleistocene lake at Olduvai in Tanzania has revealed small dense patches of microfauna on open exposed sites in close association with small animal bones, artifacts and hominid remains. L. S. B. Leakey (1968: 30) described the floor FLN from Bed I, Olduvai Gorge: "These patches are almost solid with the bones of small creatures. I am almost certain now as the result of experiment that they represent patches of human dung passed through the intestines."

The possibility that the FLN concentrations are the result of owl pellets is fairly remote since they occur in the open and actually within the area of a hominid occupation floor. This new evidence calls into question all previous assumptions about the origin of the "rodent breccias." It is still unknown whether

TABLE 13

Microfauna List for the Early Hominid Sites [a]

	Taung	Sterk-fontein	Maka-pan	Swart-krans	Krom-draai B
Insectivora					
Proamblysomus antiquus (Broom 1941b), golden mole	—	—	—	—	×
Chrysotricha hamiltoni (de Graaf 1958), golden mole	—	—	×	—	—
Chlorotalpa spelea (Broom 1941b), golden mole	—	×	—	×	—
Elephantulus langi (Broom 1937a), fossil elephant shrew	—	2.8	3.1	×	×
Elephantulus cf. *brachyrhyncus*,* short-snouted elephant shrew	×	—	—	×	—
Mylomygale spiersi (Broom 1948b), specialized elephant shrew	×	2.8	—	—	—
Crocidura taungsensis (Broom 1948b), small fossil shrew	9.0	—	—	—	—
Crocidura cf. *bicolor*,* tiny musk shrew	—	×	—	—	×
Suncus cf. *etruscus*,* dwarf shrew	—	8.5	3.1	×	×
Suncus cf. *orangiae** (Pocock 1969), Orange River dwarf shrew	—	×	—	—	—
Suncus cf. *gracilis** (Pocock 1969), smallest dwarf shrew	—	×	—	—	—
?*Myosorex robinsoni* (Meester 1955), extinct forest shrew	—	2.8	6.2	×	?
Chiroptera					
Rhinolophus cf. *capensis*,* Lichtenstein's horseshoe bat	×	—	×	—	—
Rhinolophus cf. *darlingi** (Pocock 1969), Darling's horse-shoe bat	—	×	—	—	—
Rhinolophus cf. *augur* (Pocock 1969), Geoffrey's horseshoe bat	—	×	—	—	—
Rodentia					
Pedetes gracile (Broom 1934), small spring hare	×	—	—	—	—
Mystromys antiquus (Broom 1948b), extinct rat	9.0	—	—	—	⎫ 71.5
Mystromys hausleitneri (Broom 1948b), extinct rat	—	26.7	9.3	—	⎭
Mystromys darti (Lavocat 1957b), extinct rat	—	—	×	—	—
Tatera cf. *brantsi** (Lavocat 1957a), Brant's gerbil	9.0	5.6	?	—	⎫ 2.5
Desmodillus auricularis, namaqua gerbil	×	—	—	—	⎭
Grammomys cf. *dolichurus*,* forest mouse	—	—	9.3	—	×
Dasymys bolti (Lavocat 1957a, b), swamp rat	—	?2.8	—	×	—
Pelomys cf. *falla*,* creek rat	—	2.8	3.1	—	—
Rhabdomys cf. *pumilio*, Cape striped fieldmouse	×	2.8	3.1	—	×
"*Rhabdomys minor*" (Pocock 1969), small extinct field-mouse	—	×	—	—	—
Aethomys cf. *namaquensis*,* bush rat	—	2.8	6.2	—	—
Aethomys cf. *chrysophilus* (Pocock 1969), bush rat	—	×	—	—	—
Thallomys debruyni (Broom 1937a), desert rat	×	—	—	—	—
Mastomys cf. *natalensis*,* multimammate mouse	4.5	5.6	3.1	—	×
Leggada cf. *minutoides** (Lavocat, 1957a, b), Cape dwarf mouse	—	2.8	3.1	—	—
Leggada cf. *major*,* wild mouse	—	×	—	—	—
Mus cf. *musculus** (Pocock 1969), house mouse	—	×	—	—	—

(continued)

TABLE 13 *(continued)*

	Taung	Sterk-fontein	Maka-pan	Swart-krans	Krom-draai B
Rodentia *(continued)*					
Dendromus antiquus (Broom 1948b), extinct climbing mouse	×	—	—	—	—
Dendromus cf. *mesomelas,* * climbing mouse	—	5.6	3.1	—	?1.0
Dendromus cf. *melanotis* * (Pocock 1969), grass-climbing mouse	—	×	—	—	—
Malacothrix cf. *typica* (Lavocat 1957a, b), long-eared mouse	×	—		—	×
?Malacothrix makapani (de Graaf 1961), extinct long-eared mouse	—	—	3.1	—	—
Steatomys cf. *pratensis,* * fat mouse	—	—	×	—	×
Palaeotomys gracilis (Lavocat 1957a, b), fossil vlei rat	59.5	22.8	41.1	×	18.4
Prototomys campbelli (Broom and Schepers 1946), fossil vlei rat	×	—	—	—	—
Graphiurus sp. (Pocock 1969), doormouse	—	×	—	—	—
Xenohystrix crassidens (Greenwood 1955), extinct porcupine form	—	—	×	—	—
Hystrix major (Greenwood 1955), one-third larger than living porcupine	—	—	×	—	—
Hystrix cf. *cristata* * (Greenwood 1955), ?modern porcupine	—	×	—	—	—
Hystrix africae-australis * (Greenwood 1955), modern porcupine	—	—	cf.	—	—
Petromus minor (Broom 1939d), extinct dassie rat	×	—	—	—	—
Gypsorhychus darti (Broom 1934), large sand mole	×	—	—	—	—
Gypsorhychus minor (Broom 1934), smaller extinct mole	×	—	—	—	—
Gypsorhychus makapani (Broom 1948a), larger mole	—	—	×	—	—
Cryptomys robertsi (Broom and Schepers 1946), extinct mole rat	4.5	2.8	3.1	×	×
Minimum total individuals[b]:	22	35	32	—	402

[a] Numerical values, percentages of minimum total individuals; ×, species present, but no numerical data available (H. B. S. Cooke 1963; Pocock 1969); *, similar to living species.

[b] From de Graaf (1961).

there are any consistent patterns in the microfauna found in owl pellets as opposed to human dung. The body-part analysis of microfauna from the breccia (de Graaf 1961) provides an excellent model for controlled experiments such as those Leakey mentions. Unfortunately, no analysis of Leakey's results have appeared yet. At present, the possibility that at least some of the "rodent breccia" derives from hominid dung deserves further investigation.

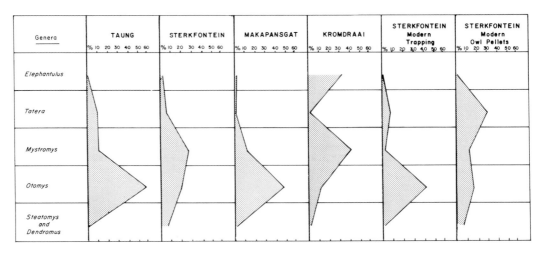

Fig. 33. Percentage frequencies of six genera (in terms of minimum numbers) of microfauna from the breccias. The two modern samples suggest selective sampling of the microfaunal population by modern owls. (Data from Cartmill 1967.)

Changes in the microfauna population through time have been suggested by Freedman (1961b), who points out that Cricetinae dominate over Murinae at Taung and Sterkfontein, but the ratio is reversed at Makapan, which is considered to be later. The microfauna from a much later deposit near Makapan has very few Cricetinae at all, suggesting a time trend toward increased Murinae in later deposits. Lavocat (1967) points out that the Kromdraai B sample is dominated by Cricetinae and does not fit the "trend" model.

The microfauna also indicates that the Taung environment was the driest of the sites. The occurrence of *Petromus minor,* and other "desert rat" forms such as *Thallomys debruyni* and *Crocidura taungensis,* as well as the spring hare *Pedetes gracile* and the gerbils *Tatera* and *Malacothrix,* all indicate a semiarid environment. The microfauna is from the same deposit reported to have yielded the hominid skull (de Graaf 1961). Ecological differences between the other sites are less obvious. Makapan contains numerous moist-loving insectivores and murids and a wider variety of porcupines. The littoral mole *Chrysotricha* also reflects a moist habitat, but arid elements are also present: *Thallomys* and *Malacothrix* presumably reflecting arid country beyond the Makapan valley.

Changes in microfauna populations through time at a *single site* cannot be investigated until adequate samples are recovered at intervals throughout the depth of the deposits. Time differences between the sites may be demonstrated by the microfauna on a tentative basis only. The suggested sequence Taung–Sterkfontein–Makapan (de Graaf 1961) is based on a preliminary study of samples with relatively small numbers of individuals. The more recent lists suggest Taung has the highest proportion of extinct species (74%), followed by

Sterkfontein (64%), then Makapan (56%), and Kromdraai B (53%). Swart-krans has not been fully studied. Clearly there is no legitimate difference between Makapan and Kromdraai B in this comparison. Cartmill (1967) has suggested that the percentage proportions of six genera listed in Fig. 33 demonstrate that the Kromdraai B environment was wetter than the earlier Sterkfontein environment, but the numerical basis for this case remains ambiguous.

Nonmammalian Fauna

No systematic survey has appeared. Taung has yielded remains of lizard, crab, and tortoise (Broom 1934). Sterkfontein is reported to contain numerous bird bones, including at least one large bird of prey (Broom 1937b) as well as snake, gecko, and two species of frogs (Pocock 1969). Makapan has yielded several birds reported as guinea fowl, shrike, vulture, and marabou stork as well as tortoise and water turtle (Dart 1957b). No lists for Swartkrans or Kromdraai have been published, nor are there quantitative data for the other three sites. It is assumed that all the forms are relatively rare. The presence of turtle at Makapan provides additional evidence of a relatively moist habitat.

SOME TENTATIVE CONCLUSIONS

The oldest group of deposits are Taung (Hrdlička's Cave), the lower Phase I breccia at Makapan and the lower or Type Site breccia at Sterkfontein. The correct time sequence for the three still cannot be determined with certainty since no absolute dating method can be applied to them. Analysis of the fauna for dating purposes has proved unreliable because the three sites occur in different environments and have very few species in common. All three sites have been claimed as the earliest by using this method, but all studies suggest that the three deposits are separated by short time intervals. Attempts to isolate them chronologically by this method serve no useful purpose and they may at best be considered broadly contemporary and partly overlapping in time.

All three contain remains of *Australopithecus africanus* only. No other hominid has been found in this period. *Australopithecus africanus* is therefore the oldest known hominid from South Africa and is represented by: the Taung child; fragmentary skulls and jaws of at least a dozen adults and adolescents at Makapan; numerous cranial fragments, maxillae, jaw fragments, and more than a hundred loose teeth from Sterkfontein. The complete adult female cranium from Sterkfontein may belong to this group also. Postcranial remains of *A. africanus* include: fragmentary pelves at Makapan, a complete pelvis at Sterkfontein, pelvic fragments, ribs, vertebrae, limb-bone fragments, and hand and ankle bones also from Sterkfontein.

All this material demonstrates that *A. africanus* was a small, delicate-boned hominid standing about 4.5 ft tall when fully grown. The brain capacity varies from about 435 cc for a juvenile specimen to about 530 cc for an adult. The pelvis, spine, and femora show clearly that they walked upright permanently, but lacked the walking efficiency of modern man. In efficient walking, the foot must be lifted from the ground as it is brought forward. This is brought about by a hip-rolling mechanism induced by the greater trochanter, a bony process adjacent to the head of the femur. The trochanter on the australopithecine femur is less developed than that of modern Man, indicating that the hip did not roll sufficiently to raise the foot entirely from the ground. To accomplish this, the knee had to be slightly bent at each step, thus producing a clumsy shuffling gait. It is probable that *A. africanus* was not an efficient runner. Also, the curvature of the australopithecine spine suggests that the center of gravity for the body (in the region of the thoracic vertebrae) was forward of the line joining the two iliac crests of the pelvic girdle. In modern Man the center of gravity is poised directly above this line, so that the upper body is perfectly balanced on the pelvis when the individual is standing at ease. In this position there is almost no energy loss. In contrast to this arrangement, the australopithecines were unable to stand "at rest" since balance could be maintained only by muscular flexing and subsequent energy loss.

Their facial appearance was superficially apelike, with a prognathous mouth region, no chin, a small, broad flattened nose, and pronounced eyebrow ridges attached to a low sloping forehead. Some slight sexual dimorphism is apparent in the skull formation, and it has been suggested that males display moderate sagittal and occipital ridges. In contrast to the outer facial formation, the arrangement of the teeth is distinctly human in character: the tooth row of the palate is organized in a parabolic curve, the molars and premolars decrease in size from back to front, the canines are relatively small, and the incisors are arranged in a distinct curve. The reduced canines and incisors suggest some adaptive trend moving away from the use of the front teeth as weapons of defence or predation. Tooth crowding also suggests a similar trend. Apparently, the defensive and predatory function of the teeth has shifted to the upper limbs and hands, which are permanently freed from the burden of supporting the upper body.

Bipedalism, freedom of the hands, reduction of the canines, and the presence of tooth crowding may all suggest that these creatures habitually used hard objects as tools to serve as more efficient extensions of the hands and nails. The complexity and size of the *A. africanus* brain in relation to its body size may also be invoked to argue that they systematically shaped hard materials to make them more efficient. Toolmaking has been observed among modern chimpanzees, and it may be reasonable to infer that similar behavior patterns existed among the australopithecines. Unfortunately, the archaeological evidence for toolmaking by *A. africanus* is surrounded by difficulties. No flaked stone tools have been recovered, but Makapan has yielded a few bone fragments with localized grinding and polishing which may suggest systematic working of some softer material such as skin. Other specimens that may indicate deliberate manual manipulation include limb-bone shafts with smaller shafts or horn cores rammed into the marrow cavities, distal cannon bones with bone or stone chips wedged between the condyle, battered stalagmite fragments, and foreign rocks derived from some distance away from the site.

The pattern of the *A. africanus* diet remains obscure in many details. Molar and premolar crown patterns are so designed that they reflect an unspecialized diet. The entire dentition suggests an adaptation to dealing with both plant and animal foods, but there is no indication of the proportions of these foods which comprised the diet. If *A. africanus* was predominantly vegetarian with only occasional meat eating (like modern chimpanzees), the molars might reflect special adaptation to a grinding process. This might take the form of large flattened crown surfaces, with chipping of the enamel by grit in the vegetable foods. However, such features are absent in *A. africanus,* which has relatively small cusped molars with rare chipping of the enamel. The canines, although small, are still larger than the other teeth. It is probably reasonable to infer from the dentition alone that meat formed part of the diet, but it is impossible to judge whether it formed the dominant food. Observations of occasional meat eating among chimpanzees and baboons (Dart 1963) may allow similar inferences.

It is also uncertain whether the australopithecines actually hunted any of the wide variety of fossil animals found in the breccias. Both the small size of *A. africanus* and the absence of stone tools from the breccias may be used to argue against the hypothesis that they could systematically hunt large game. Although there are consistent patterns of breakage among the animal bones and apparent "selection" of certain body parts, such features probably reflect the variable resistance of different bones and parts of bones to damage by carnivore gnawing. Any evidence of systematic butchery by australopithecines may be thus obscured. Agents responsible for the bone accumulations may include "accidents," hyenas, leopards, porcupines, owls, and *A. africanus.* Any food waste from the australopithecine diet would be diluted by materials introduced by the other agents.

At present it is difficult to judge the proportions of bones derived from these different sources. Porcupine gnaw marks enable us to isolate a small percentage of the total bone samples that may have been collected by that animal, and most of the microfauna probably derives from owl pellets. The remainder could have been introduced by leopards, hyenas, or australopithecines. Unfortunately it remains uncertain whether any of the three caves were actually used as shelters or lairs by any of these creatures. The "leopard-kill" model, which fits the Swartkrans evidence, does not explain the very dense bone accumulations at Makapan. This probably limits the number of agents at Makapan to hyenas and australopithecines. Either (or both) may have actually occupied the outer part of the cave near an entrance which has not been determined with certainty yet. Bone materials dropped at the entrance then were washed down and concentrated in the deeper recesses of the cavern. If australopithecines caused most of these accumulations, we must assume: (1) that they hunted in organized bands, using wooden weapons not preserved in the breccia, or (2) that they systematically scavenged parts of carcasses by driving off large carnivores from their kills. Neither assumption can be verified by the available evidence. It has been suggested that the high proportion of juvenile specimens among the large animals found at Makapan reflects the limited killing ability of the australopithecines. This may also reflect selection of younger prey by large carnivores.

There are different and conflicting interpretations of the available fossil evidence for the *A. africanus* hunting–scavenging activities. The more conservative view is that they were omnivorous hominids capable of killing only small animals such as rodents, hares, other primates, and very young antelope. They in turn were preyed upon by large carnivores that introduced their bones into the cave breccias. In this case, Taung might be viewed as an actual australopithecine habitation site since it contained bones of microfauna, primates, and small antelope only.

Opposed to this view is the hypothesis based on a more liberal use of the evidence—that they were organized game hunters who used the caverns for shelter and for the butchering of carcasses. Recent research on the patterns of carnivore damage to bones suggests that evidence of butchery would be obscured by the activities of scavengers, and the more conservative interpretation may be closer to the truth. It appears reasonable to speculate that they hunted larger animals very infrequently at this period, and most of the diet comprises small animals and plant foods.

Another interpretation that has not been considered in detail yet is that *A. africanus* practiced organized aggressive scavenging like the hyenas. Habitual competitive scavenging would create important selection pressures on a "protohominid" population since individuals who were efficient bipedal runners would be more likely to survive in such a situation. Unfortunately, the fossil record is not likely to throw light on this possibility.

Although the Phase I breccias provide no granulometric evidence for climatic fluctuations during this period, the faunal evidence suggests that *A. africanus* was able to occupy three different habitats during this period, including semidesert, grassveld, and relatively well-watered mountainous country with dense bush cover (Bartholomew and Birdsell 1953; Dart 1964; Boné 1960).

Following *A. africanus* deposits in time are the Phase II breccia at Makapan, and the Middle or Extension Site breccia at Sterkfontein. Whether they are contemporary or accumulated at different times is impossible to determine because their faunas have not been reported separately from Phase I and they cannot be compared. Both caverns were receiving more surface soil and the bone material is sparse compared with the earlier deposits. Presumably both cavern entrances had widened by this time, possibly causing some alterations in the earlier patterns of hominid and animal activities around the original cave mouths. Granulometric analysis of the surface soil found in the breccias suggests that the Makapan habitat was considerably drier than the present, whereas

Sterkfontein was drier during the middle stages of its accumulation only. In the final stages of deposition, Sterkfontein reflects a wetter climate than the present. It is possible that the Makapan pink breccia and the middle stages of the Sterkfontein Middle breccia are coeval.

The Swartkrans pink breccia also contains surface soil that has yielded granulometric data hinting at climatic fluctuations during its accumulation. These fluctuations clearly resemble those of Sterkfontein, and it is possible that the two are in fact coeval.

The Swartkrans fauna is not analyzed fully yet, but has been claimed by all authorities to be later than the three *A. africanus* deposits. This evidence also supports the possibility that Swartkrans and the Sterkfontein Middle breccias are broadly contemporary.

Kromdraai B contains surface-soil materials that reflect a climate distinctly wetter than the present. This may indicate that the deposit overlaps in time with the very end of the Sterkfontein deposition, which shows a trend toward wetter conditions. The only fauna reported from Kromdraai B is a microfaunal sample containing more living species than are found at Swartkrans.

All four deposits are later than the *A. africanus* breccias, and it is probable that they all partly overlap in time. Swartkrans and Sterkfontein Middle brecia may be coeval, with Makapan pink breccia spanning the middle stages of their deposition and Kromdraai B overlapping with the end of Sterkfontein deposition.

They contain stone artifacts, fauna, and remains of *A. robustus (Paranthropus)*. Fragments of another "more advanced" hominid come from Swartkrans and a few isolated teeth from Sterkfontein may represent the same type. *Australopithecus africanus* may also be represented at Sterkfontein and Makapan, but this remains uncertain.

The most abundant hominid in the fossil record of the period is *A. robustus*. There are nearly complete skulls from Swartkrans and Kromdraai representing adults and juveniles as well as numerous fragments and isolated teeth. This hominid is distinct from the earlier specimens both facially and dentally. The face is slightly concave, with a flattened nasal aperture and slightly prognathous mouth. The jaw is heavily built with thick and deep rami and no chin. The supraorbital ridges are flattened and merge back into the sloping frontals. The zygomatic arches are strongly developed. Superficially, the face appears even more apelike than the earlier hominids. Strongly developed sagittal ridges occur in most skulls. The *A. robustus* dentition is typically hominid in overall arrangement, but differs from *A. africanus* in many details: the cheek teeth are very large, with broad, flattened crowns; the canines are extremely small; the incisors are also small and arranged in a straight line across the front of the mouth; the palate is deeper at the back.

Postcranial bones include pelvic fragments, vertebrae, proximal femora, and a thumb bone from Swartkrans. Kromdraai has yielded arm and hand-bone fragments. *Australopithecus robustus* may have stood permanently erect, and adult males may have been slightly taller than *A. africanus*, but not taller than about 5 ft. They probably also weighed more, since some postcranial bones appear to be larger than in *A. africanus*. Detailed comparisons between the pelves and femora of the two hominids yield conflicting results, and it is uncertain whether the *A. robustus* walking mechanism was less efficient (Napier 1964, 1967; Lovejoy and Heiple 1972). Adult brain capacity is about 539 cc.

The *A. robustus* dentition suggests that the diet was dominated by plant foods. Most of the distinctive features of the skull and face are functionally related to the large cheek teeth. The presence of the broad molars and premolars points to a mastication pattern that entailed frequent grinding. Extensively reduced canines and incisors reflect a similar trend. Chipping of the enamel on the cheek teeth has been invoked to support the hypothesis that *A. robustus* ate plant foods only, with subsequent damage from grit in the food. However, damage prior to fossilization is difficult to detect, and grit could have been introduced in a meat diet with the same ease. It is likely that the diet included some meat, but there is no reliable evidence to suggest that organized hunting was a frequent activity. Probably all the *A. robustus* specimens at Swartkrans were introduced as leopard prey, and it remains uncertain whether any of the animals found at this site reflect part of the diet.

Remains of *A. africanus* have not been found in the same deposit with *A. robustus,* and the complete cranium plus palate from the upper Phase I breccia at Makapan may be earlier than the four deposits under discussion. Several loose teeth and the juvenile maxilla fragment from the Sterkfontein Middle breccia have also been classed as *A. africanus*. It is also likely that more complete specimens will be recovered during work in progress on this deposit. At present there is a possibility that some of this material may belong to a "more advanced" hominid, but a final diagnosis must await more complete finds. The possibility that two hominid species occupied the same ecological niche need not imply competition if they were exploiting different kinds of food. However, the evidence for contemporaneity remains insecure.

At Swartkrans the association between *A. robustus* and a more advanced hominid previously labeled *"Telanthropus"* is secure since both come from the same deposit. The new hominid is represented by a nearly complete jaw and the left side of the face, which displays a well developed brow ridge, prominent nasal bones, a reduced mouth region, and a small relatively delicate jaw. The dentition differs from the australopithecines and is closer in arrangement and morphology to living Man. The specimen has been placed in the genus *Homo* but has no specific designation. It has been argued that the stone tools at Swartkrans were made by *Homo sp.* rather than *A. robustus,* and the same argument may apply to the Sterkfontein tools, which include stone artifacts and a bone polisher. Both artifact samples resemble the Developed Oldowan, dated to between 1 and 1.7 million years at Olduvai Gorge, where there is an even earlier phase of stone toolmaking not found in southern Africa. Stone tools from Makapan and Kromdraai are to few to allow comparisons with other samples.

The available fossil record suggests that the hominid population represented in this late group of deposits has become more diverse, and there are clear traces of a stone-artifact technology for the first time in this area. Although toolmaking has been ascribed to *Homo* sp., there is no definite proof that *A. robustus* was not also a toolmaker. It is also unknown whether the two hominids actually competed for territory. Subsequent developments show that the australopithecines became extinct and *Homo* sp. survived with an increasingly elaborate stone-tool technology, suggesting that this genus may have been the more frequent and most successful toolmaker of the two. If they competed for territory, the presence of *Homo* sp. in the area may at least explain the ultimate extinction of the australopithecines.

Unfortunately, the origins of *Homo* sp. are not visible in the fossil record. One possibility is that the *A. africanus* population increased with time, becoming more diversified in behavior, dietary patterns, and skeletal morphology. At one extreme of the varied populations are those that display closer group organization, an omnivorous diet including meat, and efficient bipedal running. Possibly linked with these features is an important increase in brain capacity in relation to the body size. The factors that brought about the isolation of such groups remain uncertain. Selective pressures that might have influenced such a trend would occur in habitats with dense carnivore populations and sparse protection from tree cover. Australopithecine groups would have two alternative life patterns to choose from:

> 1. A vegetarian diet supplemented by small animals. This eliminates the need for competition with large carnivores and scavengers for meat. Group organization is limited to defense against carnivore attack only.
> 2. A diet dominated by meat, in which systematic hunting and competitive scavenging plays an important role.

These activities would select for behavioral and anatomical features like group cooperation, efficient running, increased brainsize, and toolmaking.

It is tentatively suggested that the diversification of the *A. africanus* population could have taken place in areas that experienced a steady increase in carnivore density. One segment of the population adapted to a plant-dominated diet, thus reducing the chances of contact with carnivores. Other groups in the population moved toward increased competition and frequent contact with carnivores, thus bringing about selection for more "human" characters. Eventually, two morphologically distinct hominids would emerge (*A. robustus* and *Homo* sp.), both exploiting the same habitat, but with minimal competition for food. The fact that *A. robustus* was taken more frequently by carnivores is illustrated by the Swartkrans evidence, suggesting that the group eventually succumbed to carnivore predation, thus ending the long australopithecine lineage.

The more successful "hominized" segment of the population survived to form the lineage *Homo,* which is responsible for all subsequent prehistoric remains.

3

The Acheulian
and Related Industries

At present there are only two sites in Africa that provide clear evidence of the technical developments following the Oldowan complex, but neither of these is located in southern Africa. The Oldowan horizons of Beds I–II at Olduvai Gorge, Tanzania are reported to lie below artifact occurrences containing tools known as hand axes and cleavers. These are thought to be a logical development of the flaking processes used to make the protobiface found in the Developed Oldowan of Bed II, Sterkfontein, and Swartkrans (See Fig. 29, page 75). Recent research has shown that horizons containing hand-axes can be found at the same levels as the Developed Oldowan, suggesting that the hand-axe technique was already present before the Oldowan had disappeared from the area.

On the coast of Morocco near Casablanca a complex sequence of horizons linked to ancient raised shorelines has yielded a similar succession to that of Olduvai, but here again it is uncertain whether the hand-axe industries evolved directly out of the underlying Oldowan or from some other unknown origin.

The hand-axe and cleaver are recognized as characteristic tools of several industries found in different parts of Africa. Few of these have been accurately defined yet, and they have been reported under so many different names that the terminology alone becomes a formidable obstacle to the study of this period.

EARLY RESEARCH AND TERMINOLOGY

Names appearing in the literature that refer to this period have been derived from two different sources:

1. French place names: Acheulian, Chellean, Abbevillian, Chelles–Acheul.
2. Local place names: Stellenbosch, Victoria West, Fauresmith, Sangoan, Charaman.

Fortunately many of these have been abandoned and the most recent recommendations on terminology (Bishop and Clark 1967) suggest that only the terms *Acheulian industrial complex* and *Sangoan industrial complex* be used since they alone have been more or less adequately defined.

The term *Acheulian* has been borrowed from a classic archaeological find spot in northwestern France. Two river-gravel quarries outside the village of Saint-Acheul on the Somme River yielded several collections of hand-axes from different levels, together with extinct fauna (Rigollot 1855). Their stratigraphy was studied in detail (Commont 1909), and the village was subsequently quoted as the type site for certain hand-axe collections. An earlier discovery downstream at Abbeville (de Perthe 1849) gave rise to the term "Abbevillian" to describe hand-axes thought to be cruder and earlier than the Acheulian specimens, and the nearby village of Chelles provided the term "Chellean" for similar material. Both terms have lapsed since they are not represented by samples from archaeological contexts and their typological features were not accurately defined. The Acheulian appears to have survived since it is based on a large sample (from possibly primary context) known as the *Atelier Commont* at Saint-Acheul.

Soon after the classic discoveries on the Somme, hand-axes were recognized in South Africa. Sir George Leith is credited with the first discoveries in 1866 (Burkitt 1928), and it is reported that specimens were sent to England for examination in the same year (Goodwin and van Riet Lowe 1929). Early collectors published these implements under an alarming variety of names (*boucher, coup-de-poing,* amygdalith) which reflected their dependence on French terminology. Not until the early twentieth century were there sufficient hand-axe collections available from different parts of the country to permit some comparisons with those of France. Peringuey grouped the South African material under two headings: "Stellenbosch type" and "Orange River type" (Peringuey 1911). His refusal to use the French terminology was supported by Burkitt, Goodwin, and van Riet Lowe in 1928-1929, when they used "Stellenbosch Industries." They replaced the "Orange River type" by the "Victoria West Industry," which was an ill-defined variant reported to contain specialized cores. They also introduced the "Fauresmith Industry" claimed to be later than the Stellenbosch and reported to contain smaller more refined hand-axes. Small hand-axes from surface collections at Hopefield, southwestern Cape Province were also called "Cape Fauresmith."

Later publications proposed a five-stage sequence of development for the Stellenbosch, which was to be followed by two stages of the Fauresmith. These proposals were based on studies of the Vaal River terraces (van Riet Lowe 1937). Ten years later Lowe had abandoned the term Stellenbosch in favor of "The Handaxe Culture" in a paper read at the first Pan-African Congress of Prehistory in 1947 (van Riet Lowe 1952a). Presumably he had realized that the numerous surface scatters from the Stellenbosch district near Cape Town (Seddon 1967) were unreliable samples, and the name was not appropriate. It appears that members of the Congress agreed to adopt the ungainly term "Chelles–Acheul" to describe the same complex. This term was used in Lowe's last analysis of the Vaal sequence, although "Handaxe Culture" also appears (van Riet Lowe 1952b), and "Fauresmith" was retained as a separate and later entity, now divided into three stages. The Victoria West Industry was omitted from this final survey but was quoted as a "technique" rather than a separate industry.

The Chelles–Acheul has lingered on in the literature, with occasional use made of the separate terms Chellean and Acheulian (Leakey 1951). Mason pointed out that the Vaal River evidence was inadequate, and the terminology had become confused (Mason 1961c). However, his suggestion that all the hand-axe industries (and the Developed Oldowan) should be lumped under the term "Acheulian" did not meet with sympathetic response (Clark, Howell, Kleindienst, and Leakey 1962). Reasons for retaining the Chelles–Acheul were based on the report that "Chellean" samples (without cleavers) occurred in the Olduvai beds between the Oldowan and the Acheulian when the first cleavers appeared (L. S. B. Leakey 1951). The cleaver is a bifacially trimmed tool with a butt similar to a hand-axe but with a broad cutting edge instead of a point (Fig. 34). When it was discovered that cleavers occurred at all the levels with hand-axes at Olduvai (M. D. Leaky 1967), the "Chellean" could no longer be justified and the *Chelles*–Acheul became redundant. It is now agreed (Bishop and Clark 1967) that the term "Acheulian industrial complex" should be used in place of Chelles–Acheul, Victoria West, and Fauresmith, all of which should

Fig. 34. Variability in shapes of Acheulian hand-axes, cleavers, knives and picks: (a, b, c, d) lanceolate hand-axes (narrow, shouldered, long, ovate); (e) discoid hand-axes; (f) cordiform hand-axes; (g) triangular hand-axes; (h) double-pointed hand-axes and truncated butts; (i) limande hand-axes; (j) convergent cleavers; (k) divergent cleavers; (l) pointed-butt cleavers; (m) square-butt cleavers; (n) burin-blow bit; (o) side cleaver; (p) knives; (q) picks. (After Kleindienst 1962.)

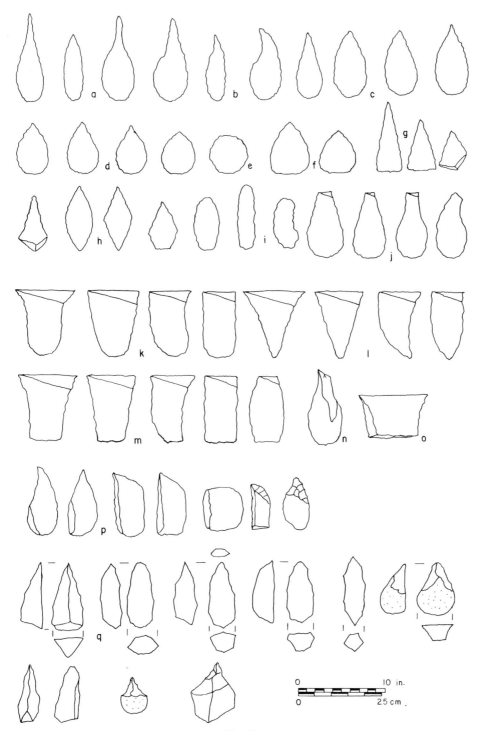

Fig. 34

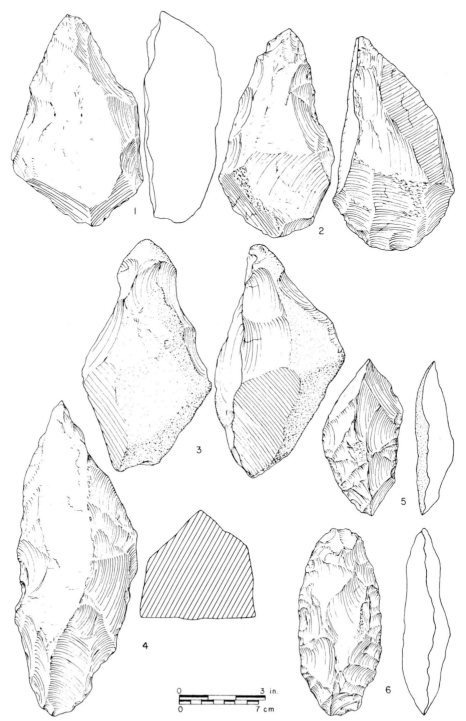

Fig. 35. Tools from Sangoan sites in northeastern Angola: (1, 2, 3, 4) picks from Musolexi; (5, 6) core axes from Catongula. (After Clark 1963.)

be abandoned. The "complex" refers to all the samples in Africa and presumably beyond, and the southern African Acheulian is one "industry" within that complex.

The term *Sangoan* was first applied to artifact collections from surface rubbles in the Sango Bay area on the northwestern shore of Lake Victoria, Uganda, by Wayland in 1920. Similar material was excavated later from a terrace deposit on the Nsongezi River, Uganda, in a stratified horizon overlying Acheulian artifacts (Wayland 1934), and this sequence first demonstrated that the Sangoan was the later industry. Differences between the two remained ill defined, but it was generally recognized that the Sangoan contained a large number of picks and core axes (Fig. 35), which were absent or rare in the Acheulian. The term was soon applied to surface collections from southern Rhodesia (N. Jones 1938), and its position above the Acheulian was confirmed in the Zambesi River valley terrace sequence (Clark 1950a). The lack of detailed definition for the type collection permitted the widespread application of the term and geographical "variants" were proposed on the basis of numerous selected surface collections and very rare excavated samples from geological contexts in river gravels. The proposed variants were: Tugela, Luangwa, Zambesi, and Bembezi, but typological differences among these remained ill defined, and it was soon reported that all four variants could not be distinguished one from another (C. K. Cooke 1962). Although the variants were abandoned, the term "Sangoan" remains in use and has been applied to excavated samples from Angola, Zambia, and Rhodesia, although detailed comparisons with the Sango hills and Nsongezi material are still limited to a few reports (Cole 1967b).

The term *Charaman* has been adopted to describe a large unselected surface sample from the Charama Plateau, Rhodesia (C. K. Cooke 1966a), and it is also represented by sealed samples from caves in the Matopos Hills, Rhodesia. The first excavated sample from Bambata cave was considered to be mixed with hand axes derived from earlier artifact scatters lying outside the cave (N. Jones 1940). The hand axes were therefore removed from the sample and the remainder was called "Proto-Stillbay." Not until a number of similar occurrences had been excavated—particularly Khami (C. K. Cooke 1957b) and Pomongwe cave (C. K. Cooke 1963)—was it realized that hand axes and picks were a persistent feature of the industry. It is now recognized that the Charaman is a late expression of the Sangoan complex in Rhodesia. Although apparently different from the Sangoan in artifact percentages (C. K. Cooke 1966b), its position above a reliable Sangoan sample has not yet been demonstrated. Sangoan material from Rhodesia has recently been called "Gwelan" after an excavated site at Gwelo Kopje, but the name has been extensively criticized since the Gwelo material is no longer available for study (Cooke, Summers, and Robinson 1966).

Both the Sangoan and Charaman occur in the territories north of the Limpopo River, which forms the boundary between Rhodesia and South Africa. To date no reliable sealed samples of either of these have been recovered in South

Africa where the Acheulian is the only acceptable term. The terminology now
used in all these areas can be summarized as follows:

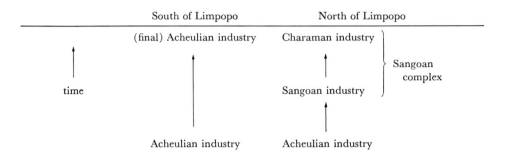

	South of Limpopo	North of Limpopo
	(final) Acheulian industry	Charaman industry
		Sangoan industry
time		
	Acheulian industry	Acheulian industry

All these terms are represented by artifact samples from archeological contexts.
As a general guide to the terms used in earlier literature, the following table is
an attempt to equate abandoned names with those now in use:

Earlier terms (now abandoned)	Terms now in use
Stellenbosch	Acheulian industry
Victoria West	Acheulian industry
Fauresmith	(final) Acheulian industry
Chellean	(early) Acheulian industry
Chelles–Acheul	Acheulian complex
Handaxe Cultures	Acheulian complex
Proto-Stillbay	Charaman industry

It is acknowledged by many workers that the Acheulian industry may display
typological differences in both space and time. Such differences have been inadequately defined, and separate terms to describe geographical variants or chronological phases of the industry have not yet been agreed upon.

THE ACHEULIAN COMPLEX

Acheulian Artifacts

New techniques of flaking stone were introduced during the period of the
Acheulian complex. Compared with the few reliable Oldowan occurrences from
Sterkfontein and Olduvai, it appears that larger blocks of raw material were
used in the Acheulian and larger flakes could be struck from these. Most
Acheulian sites are situated near raw material outcrops, and individual samples
are usually made of one rock type only. Since more Acheulian than Oldowan
samples are available, it appears that a greater variety of rock was employed in
Acheulian times. From the 46 unselected Acheulian samples available from

southern Africa it appears that quartzite and quartz were most commonly used and others include basalt, dolerite, arkose, lydianite, and (1 sample each) silcrete and banded jasper. The last two were carried some distance to the sites. Generally, the sample is composed of whatever rock types are nearest to the site, and those near river gravels with a wide variety of rocks tend to exploit types which will yield relatively large flakes. There is therefore no evidence to suggest a deliberate selection or preference for certain rocks during this period. It appears rather that the nearest workable stone was put to use when needed.

Flaking was carried out by several different methods, each resulting in a core and numerous flakes bearing distinctive features:

1. The block-on-block technique, possibly also used in the Oldowan, in which a large block is held in both hands and struck against the edge of a heavy boulder or "anvil." Flakes removed by this method have large plain platforms, obtuse platform angles, and large cones of percussion, and many are broad and flared. The core may be abandoned while still relatively large. It may be covered with numerous flake scars and sinuous edges produced by alternate flaking. It is thought that spherical cores may be produced by this method.

2. The adjacent-platform technique in which a block is flaked with a hammerstone while held in the hand or rested on the thigh. By using the scar bed of the first blow as the platform for the second blow, a sinuous edge is created on the core.

3. The single-platform technique, as in 2, but the same platform is struck repeatedly to produce endstruck flakes with roughly parallel margins. Rare convergent flakes also may be produced by this method.

4. The discoid technique in which an acute platform angle is prepared around the entire perimeter of a block by repeated flaking. The prepared platform is then struck repeatedly at different points around the perimeter in order to remove flakes from the surface of the core.

5. The Levallois technique in which a block is bifacially trimmed to a definite shape. One part of the perimeter is then trimmed to form a platform at right angles to the length–breadth plane of the specimen. The platform then is struck in such a way that a single flake is removed from the core surface and this flake has an outline which is determined by that of the core (circular, oval, triangular, etc.). The butt of the flake shows clear faceting derived from the prepared platform of the core, and the term "proto-Levallois" has been applied to certain large cores without this faceting. The proto-Levallois core may be struck on one side in such a way that a large flake similar in shape to a hand-axe or cleaver may be removed.

Apart from these "formal" cores, every sample also contains numerous blocks with only one or two flake scars, and there are usually broken, utilized, and incomplete specimens.

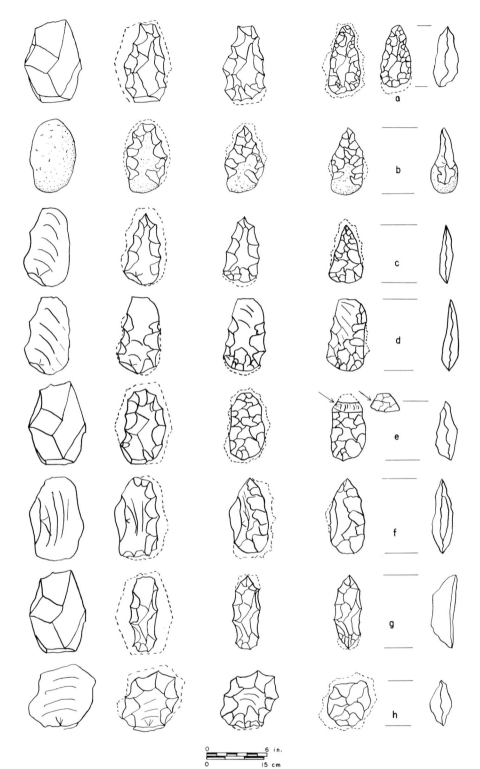

Fig. 36

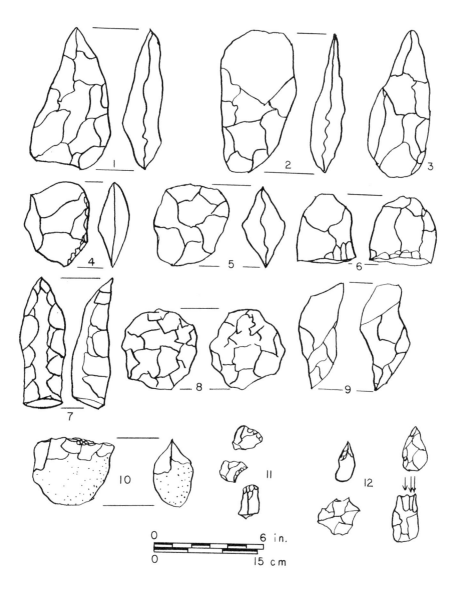

Fig. 37

Fig. 36. Diagrams of hypothetical reduction sequences for Acheulian bifacial tools. In each row the blank appears on the left and the finished tool on the right. (a) thick lanceolate hand-axe made on block; (b) thick lanceolate on cobble; (c) thin lanceolate on endstruck flake blank; (d) cleaver on endstruck flake; (e) tranchet-blow cleaver on block; (f) knife on sidestruck flake; (g) pick on block; (h) discoid on sidestruck flake.

Fig. 37. Diagram of generalized tool types used in the shorter Acheulian typology of Kleindienst (1961, 1962); (1) hand-axe; (2) cleaver; (3) knife; (4) flake scraper; (5) discoid; (6) core scraper; (7) pick; (8) spheroid; (9) other large tool (10) chopper; (11) small scrapers; (12) other small tools.

111

Most tools were formed on flakes of which many were used directly without secondary trimming to modify their shape. Among the more elaborately trimmed tools the types known as the hand-axe and cleaver are the most distinctive. Hand-axes were formed on blocks, cobbles, or large flakes, and the cleavers were usually made on large sidestruck flakes so that part of the sharp flake margin could be used as the cleaver blade. On cleavers made on thick blocks it was necessary to form a cutting edge by means of a transverse blow near the tip of the finished specimen. Those made on cobbles or blocks tend to be thicker than those made on large flakes, as illustrated in the diagrams of Fig. 36. Their shapes vary widely, and numerous attempts have been made to subdivide them into shape classes. Hand-axes and cleavers with one untrimmed lateral margin have been called "knives," and very thick hand-axes with trihedral sections and steep sides have been called "picks." Some of these may be pointed at both ends. Flakes were trimmed to form rough scraper edges and some specimens were deliberately trimmed to form subcircular working edges sometimes called "discoids" (Kleindienst 1961, 1962). Rare points and crude burins (gouging tools) are also reported. Partially trimmed blocks and cobbles that show signs of battering on the flaked edges are usually called "choppers," and battered multiplatform cores have been called "polyhedrals" or "spheroids." The diagram in Fig. 37 illustrates the full range of stone artifacts in the Acheulian. Stone hammers were probably used for most flaking activities, but it has been argued that bone or wooden hammers were used to remove small shallow flakes from certain delicately trimmed specimens. This has been called the "cylinder-hammer" technique, but its significance is doubtful since it has proved impossible to accurately determine the differences between hard- and soft-hammer flake scars. No obvious bone or wood hammers have been recovered with Acheulian samples although other wooden tools have been reported.

The tool types that appear in the Acheulian but are absent in the Oldowan are hand-axes, cleavers, knives, picks, and the larger flake scrapers. The available evidence suggests that certain of the types and features described above were not present in the earlier stages of the Acheulian period, but appeared at different phases of the stylistic evolution of the complex. One such evolutionary scheme was proposed in detail for the Vaal River terraces (Söhnge, Visser, and van Riet Lowe 1937), and the series of typological innovations claimed for this terrace sequence has persisted unchanged in the literature until very recently (Bordes 1968). So many important claims have arisen out of the numerous field reports on these terraces that some discussions of the evidence is necessary.

The Vaal River Sequence

The terraces of the lower Vaal River in the area between Windsorton and Riverview Estates were examined by several workers after the pioneer survey of 1936–1937. Breuil (1943, 1945) pointed out that much of the gravel was derived from the tillites of the ancient Dwyka series, and that pseudotools would there-fore be present in the deposits since pebbles were flaked by glacial action mil-lions of years before man appeared in the valley. H. B. S. Cooke (1946, 1949a) contributed an analysis of the fauna derived from diamond diggings in the grav-els, and Malan (1947) contributed notes on the assumed typological evolution in the area.

The long sequence of Acheulian development proposed for this area is sum-marized in Table 14. The periods represented by wind-blown sand deposition or

Table 14

Original Model of Acheulian Development in the Vaal River Area [a]

Geological event	Industry	Context
Redistributed red sands	Fauresmith III	Surface collections from sands
Youngest gravels (present bed of tributary dongas)	Fauresmith II	Surface collection from donga floors
Downcutting of river and deposi-tion of younger gravels III (present bed)	Fauresmith I	Samples collected from surface of calcified silt
Calcification of silts	Sterile (?)	
Deposition of silts	Sterile	
Current bedded sands	Chelles–Acheul V	Tools collected from surface and spoil
Younger gravels IIB (overlying IIA)	Chelles–Acheul IV	Abraided and fresh tools picked from gravel faces, spoil, and gully floors
Younger gravels IIA (20-ft bench)	Chelles–Acheul III	Abraided and fresh tools picked from gravel faces, spoil, and gully floors
Younger gravels I (40-ft bench)	Chelles–Acheul II	Abraided specimens picked from gravel exposures and diggings spoil
Redistributed red sands over the older gravels	Sterile	
Older gravels derived from basal older gravels to form hill wash (200–50-ft benches)	Chelles–Acheul I and derived Oldowan mixed	Selected specimens from surface and gravels
Red sands calcified	Sterile	
Basal older gravels deposited	Oldowan?	Specimens picked from calcrete matrix. Selected

[a] From van Riet Lowe (1952b).

redistribution were supposed to represent dry periods, whereas phases of downcutting were to represent wet periods or "pluvials." This neat set of interpretations has been entirely demolished (Partridge and Brink 1967). More accurate survey techniques have revealed that only four sets of primary terrace gravels can be isolated at 200, 100, 70, and 40–0 ft above river level. All the "older gravels" are derived hill wash and are not therefore valid as a dating horizon, and the subdivision of the younger gravels cannot be justified by actual examples in the field. It is now apparent that terrace formation, calcification, and wind-blown deposits could have been caused by numerous processes and the authors suggest several such causes: the headward advance of nick points during the erosion cycle normal to any river; the splitting of the cycle across hard-rock barriers in the river valley, warping of the surface during the Pliocene, and the development of nick points due to rapid lowering and stream capture by the Harts River tributary.

The artifacts claimed to be present in the various stages of "Chelles–Acheul" evolution are all surface collections of "typical" specimens taken from the diamond diggers' spoil heaps, thought to have come from certain gravel layers, although some were picked directly from gravel exposures in the diggings. The assessments of these selected samples are entirely subjective and no reliance can be placed on them. To quote Partridge and Brink (1967: 37): "These interpretations are no longer tenable in the light of geomorphological research, and the inferred sequence of events climatic, geological and cultural, based upon them, must now be discarded once and for all."

Similar difficulties accompany the Acheulian sequence claimed for the Zambezi River near Victoria Falls (Clark 1950a). It therefore appears that the two key studies of the Acheulian have not withstood critical inspection by current standards and we are obliged to cast about for suitable excavated sites to replace them. Thus far it has proved impossible to locate a buried series of Acheulian horizons in primary context which cover the entire period of Acheulian evolution. However, a surprising number of unselected Acheulian samples is now available for study although they vary in size and reliability.

Unselected Acheulian Samples

An unselected sample is one that has been recovered in such a way that every specimen showing signs of human workmanship has been collected from the excavation or the surface scatter. This will include a very large percentage of untrimmed flakes without traces of edge damage and any sample without this "waste" component has almost certainly been selected and is numerically distorted by the collector's choice of tools or "typical" specimens. Selected samples of the Acheulian are almost always dominated by hand-axes and cleavers with virtually no waste, and such samples are fairly easily recognized.

The unselected samples that have been mentioned in print are listed in Table 15. The first nine sites listed are possibly primary context floors or "palimpsests,"

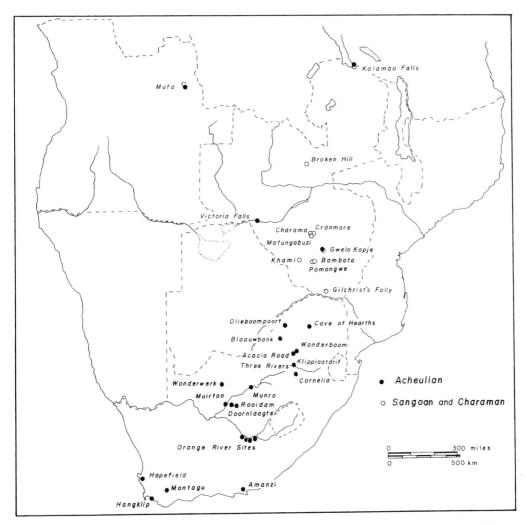

Fig. 38. Distribution map of Acheulian and Sangoan sites in southern Africa from which numerically undistorted samples have been extracted. No attempt is made here to differentiate between samples from archaeological, geological, or surface contexts. For this information the reader may refer to Table 15 (page 116).

which are thick accumulations of artifacts in a concentrated area. The remainder are secondary context or surface sites.

The localities of the 21 sites are shown in Fig. 38. Among those which may be in primary context the artifact samples from Wonderwerk and Munro are too small for the purpose of statistical analysis and one sample from Cave of Hearths may also be inadequate, although they all contain hand-axes and undoubtedly belong to the Acheulian. A brief glance at the references given in

TABLE 15

Unselected Acheulian Samples from Southern Africa

Site	Reference	Context	Associated materials	No. of samples
Kalambo Falls	Clark (1964, 1969)	Open: floors in river silt	Pollen, wood, seed, wooden tools, fruit	10
Cave of Hearths	Mason (1962a)	Cave: deposits, palimpsests, and breccia	Carbon, fauna, and hominid fragment	3
Montagu Cave	Goodwin (1929); Keller (1969b)	Cave: floors, palimpsest	Unburned guano	5
Doornlaagte	Mason (1966, 1967b)	Open: thick palimpsest	Nil	1
Hopefield	Singer and Wymer (1968)	Open: thin palimpsest in sands	Fauna	1
Olieboompoort	Mason (1962a)	Cave: palimpsest in basal rubble	Nil	1
Muirton	Humphreys (1969a)	Open: floor on calcified silt of Vaal River	Nil	1
Munro site	Mason (1969a, d)	Open, thin scatter in calcrete	Bone heaps	1
Wonderwerk	Malan, Cooke, and Wells (1941); Malan and Wells (1943)	Cave: disturbed palimpsest in basal sands	Fauna fragments	1

116

Site	Reference	Context	Organic remains	
Victoria Falls	Clark (1950a)	Site MA-38 collected from gravel exposure	Nil	1
Mufo	Clark (1968)	Collected from gravel exposure	Nil	1
Klipplaatdrif	Mason (1962a)	Collected from gravel exposure and excavated	Nil	2
Three Rivers	Mason (1962a)	Excavated from gravels	Nil	1
Cornelia	van Hoepen (1930) Oakley (1954a)	Collected from disturbed silts and gravels	Fauna (?)	1
Wonderboom	Mason (1957b, 1962a)	Excavated from hill rubble	Nil	3
Acacia Road	Beaumont (1969)	Excavated from hill rubble	Nil	1
Gwelo Kopje	C. K. Cooke (1968)	Excavated from hill rubble	Nil	1
Amanzi	Inskeep (1965b); Deacon (1966a, 1970)	Disturbed spring mound deposits	Plant remains, wood fragments	3
Rooidam	Fock (1968)	Vertically spread through sands from deep pan deposits	Ostrich egg shell (?)	2
Hangklip	Mabbutt (1951); Sampson (1962)	Exposed palimpsest in deposits on 18-m raised shoreline	Nil	1
Blaauwbank	Mason (1962a)	Surface of outwashed gravel	Nil	1
Orange River scheme	Sampson (1969b)	Surface of rubbles	Nil	3

Table 15 reveals that most of the unselected samples now available for study have been excavated quite recently and no systematic survey has been completed. Precise comparisons between sites may be carried out if a standardized typology is used for all of them, but at present there are numerous typologies in use.

Methods of Analysis

The standarized analysis applied to the East African Acheulian (Kleindienst 1961) employs the tool types illustrated in Fig. 37, which have been briefly described above. The typology has been applied to Kalambo Falls, but its use on other sites from South Africa has proved difficult. Modified versions have been used at Montagu, Hangklip, Muirton, and the Orange River scheme. The more detailed account of this typology (Kleindienst 1962) has not been generally accepted since it is apparent that large numbers of subclasses proposed in the long list of types tend to overlap with each other, and the measured boundary between many of them is quite arbitrary. The shorter typology presents fewer hazards and can be made to work effectively although it requires an additional class of "utilized pieces" that have too little edge damage to justify the use of the term "scraper."

An alternative method applied in the Transvaal (Mason 1959, 1962a, 1967b) employs the following types: hand-axes, cleavers, picks, irregular endstruck flakes, irregular sidestruck flakes, quadrilaterals, backed flakes, endscrapers, double sidescrapers, side- and endscrapers, cuboids, irregulars, choppers, anvils, discoids, spheroids, polyhedrons. It is immediately apparent that this typology, based as it is on geometric forms and conventional terms, cannot be directly compared with that of Kleindienst. Although it has been applied by Mason to samples from Cave of Hearths, Klipplaatdrif, Three Rivers, Wonderboom, and Blaauwbank and by Beaumont to Acacia Road, it has not been adopted by other workers in adjacent regions who appear to prefer a modified version of the Kleindienst typology. The main advantage of the method used in the Transvaal is that it can be applied by different workers with reasonably consistent results, but it has been objected that it does not supply enough detail and tends to make most Acheulian samples look alike (Kleindienst 1967). Mason has also measured individual tool types and has presented means and maximum—minimum ranges for lengths of certain types. Although the features chosen for measurement are few, these also can be applied by other workers with reasonably accurate results.

Complex sets of measurements have been taken for hand-axes and cleavers from Acheulian sites in England (Roe 1964, 1968) and presented graphically as scatter diagrams covering every possible shape (Fig. 39). This method overcomes the difficulty of choosing arbitrary boundaries between tool types since statistical testing can be used to determine the real variety in the shapes of these tools. The method also takes into account the fact that the hand-axe shape appears to grade into that of the cleaver (Parkington 1967). Thus far this method has been

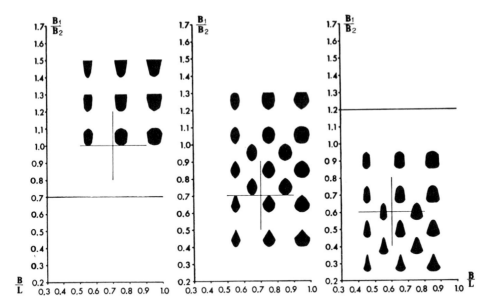

Fig. 39. Display technique proposed by Roe (1964, 1968) based on several measurements of Acheulian bifacial tools. This method partly overcomes the problem of setting up arbitrary boundaries between shapes which grade into one another. B = Breadth; B_1 = Breadth of tip at ⅕ Length; B_2 = Breadth of butt at ⅕ Length; L = Length.

applied to the surface collections from the Orange River scheme but has not yet been used to full advantage in southern Africa. It is likely that any future analyses of Acheulian samples will be concentrated on the procedures proposed by Roe and the various merits and disadvantages of the methods now in use will become less important.

In the present state of Acheulian studies it is clear that only very limited conclusions can be drawn from the analyses available. The two most important aspects of the complex are (1) the typological and stylistic differences between different areas in southern Africa and (2) the changes that took place with the passage of time.

Geographical Distribution

Apart from the few sites already listed, numerous Acheulian find spots have been recorded in southern Africa. Their distribution is shown in the map in Fig. 40, demonstrating clearly that the complex has a very wide distribution, that extends through Africa (Howell and Clark 1964; Clark 1967a) and the rest of southern Europe, southwestern Asia, and India. Unfortunately very little typological information can be gained from the vast number of surface finds in southern Africa and we are obliged to use the few unselected surface samples to discover whether regional differences in artifact design can be detected.

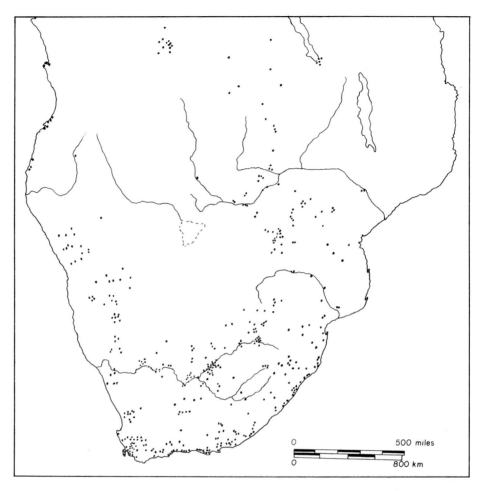

Fig. 40. Distribution map of all recorded Acheulian sites in southern Africa up to about 1965. This type of distribution only reflects the variable intensity of field research efforts in different regions and has no other meaning. Most of the localities displayed here are derived, selectively sampled surface scatters. The exceptions are mapped in Fig. 38 (page 115).

Even the limited information derived from the mass of selected material provides some interesting distribution patterns, such as the apparently restricted territory in which the Levallois and proto-Levallois techniques are found. This rather specialized method occurs in the areas of the Karroo, the western Orange Free State, the Transvaal, and the northern Cape Province. It is apparently absent from the sites of the southern Cape coast and from the areas north of the Limpopo River valley. Its western limits are not clearly defined but specimens have been found as far west as Nakop near Upington (Brain and Mason 1955). Some of the samples found within this south central plateau region also contain signs of the deliberate production of elongated flake blades from prepared single platform cores and other special features such as transverse-blow cleavers and a high proportion of relatively small tools. The latter feature may be related to the now outdated concept of the "Fauresmith" industry.

It is possible (but by no means proven) that the Acheulian in southern Africa is composed of slightly different technical traditions covering the southern Cape coastal belt, the interior plateau region of South Africa, and the savannah region north of the Limpopo Valley. Nothing is yet known of the typology of the western and eastern regions of the subcontinent and the tentative suggestion of a tripart regional subdivision can only be confirmed by a detailed survey of the material now available.

Chronological Changes

Again, lack of detailed analysis of the multilayered sites deprives us of much useful information about typological evolution during this period. A trend common to four sites—Cave of Hearths, Wonderboom, Montagu and Rooidam—is a decrease in overall artifact size with time. One other feature which has been observed at Montagu and Rooidam is an increase in the proportion of broader ovate hand-axes in the upper (and therefore later) layers at the expense of narrow lanceolate hand-axes. Unfortunately these observations cannot yet be placed on a sound metrical basis, and we must again await a systematic survey of all the available material by an analyst using relatively sophisticated techniques such as those now in use for hand-axe and cleaver shape analysis.

It should be emphasized that the terms "Early," "Middle," and "Late" Acheulian that appear so frequently in the literature cannot be justified by the field evidence. The following chronology has been imposed on the available sites in published reports:

Early Acheulian:	Klipplaatdrif, Three Rivers, Acacia Road
Middle Acheulian:	Doornlaagte, Victoria Falls
Later Acheulian:	Kalambo Falls, Cave of Hearths, Montagu, Hopefield, Olieboompoort, Cornelia, Wonderboom, Amanzi, Hangklip, Orange River scheme sites
Final Acheulian or "Fauresmith":	Wonderwerk, Muirton, Rooidam, Blaauwbank

Unfortunately not one of these sites contains a definite sequence with one phase overlying another. This chronological scheme for the whole industry cannot be demonstrated at even one site and is based entirely on rather ill-defined differences in typology. It is assumed that the earlier samples contain few elaborately trimmed tools, a small range of tool types, and a high proportion of miscellaneous utilized flakes and choppers—in fact, an assemblage of tools only slightly more elaborate than the Developed Oldowan. This assumption may eventually prove to be correct but at present we have no primary context Early Acheulian samples clearly related to the excavated EF-HR and TK-II samples from Olduvai Gorge Bed II (M. D. Leakey 1967) or the RHS and MHS samples from Peninj, also in eastern Africa (Isaac 1967a). The three South African sites claimed to be Early Acheulian are all excavated from gravels and hill rubbles, and none of them is represented by large numbers of specimens. For the present it may be wiser to admit that our knowledge of the origins of the Acheulian in this area is very limited indeed.

Dating the Acheulian

Three different dating techniques can be applied to the Acheulian in this area: absolute dating by the radiocarbon technique, relative dating of individual sites by comparing the associated fauna, and indirect dating of coastal sites by relating them to ancient raised shore-line levels.

The numerous attempts to apply the radiocarbon method to wood and char- coal samples associated with Acheulian horizons have met with only limited suc- cess thus far. Carbon samples older than about 50,000 B.P. contain such small quantities of the carbon-14 isotope upon which the age measurement depends, that reliable estimates become virtually impossible. It is likely that the Acheulian tradition disappeared from most parts of southern Africa before 50,000 B.P., and the radiocarbon readings obtained thus far may only indicate that the sites fall beyond the effective range of the method.

By far the largest number of dates has been obtained from the Kalambo Falls floors where artifact concentrations are associated with logs of wood preserved by waterlogging of the silts that cover them. Similar conditions have preserved logs at Amanzi, where readings have been obtained for samples below, at the same level, and above the artifact concentration. The logs provide large enough sam- ples to allow isotope enrichment, a procedure designed to increase the carbon-14 content, thus making it possible to obtain more accurate calculations of very small amounts of residual carbon-14 in the sample. It has proved possible to ex- tend the range of the radiocarbon method back to about 70,000 B.P. by this pro- cedure, but the readings obtained must still be treated as provisional since the enrichment technique is still at the experimental stage.

The date from the Hopefield floor was obtained from bone collagen contain- ing residual carbon-14 in fossil bone fragments found with the artifacts. The technique of collagen dating is also still in an experimental stage and the rela- tively recent date cannot be treated as more than a general indication of the minimum possible age for the site.

The chart shown in Fig. 41 gives the range of available carbon-14 dates in the form of means and standard deviations. We may conclude from this that the Acheulian industry is at the extreme limit and *mainly beyond the limit* of the radiocarbon dating technique, and most of the readings can only be accepted as provisional or experimental attempts to obtain a true age.

The *relative* dating of sites by means of associated fauna depends on the prin- ciple that a site containing a high proportion of extinct species is older than the one containing a high proportion of living species among the animals appar- ently killed and eaten by the Acheulian hunters. The fact that the Acheulian

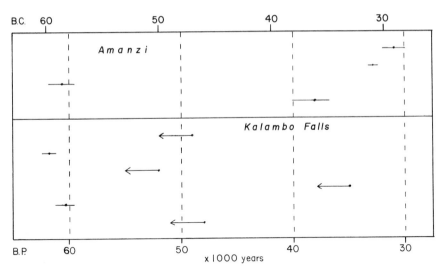

Fig. 41. Radiocarbon readings from Acheulian sites. The means and standard deviations are plotted on a chronometric scale, and the arrows indicate readings published as "greater than" the plotted date. Probably all these readings indicate that Acheulian sites fall at or beyond the upper limits of the radiocarbon dating techniques.

population adapted to a wide variety of environments gives rise to theoretical difficulties since it is probable that the available fauna differed from one region to another. For this reason the fauna of two sites some thousands of miles apart need not be identical even if they are contemporary.

Associated fauna has been recovered from six sites, but one of these (Wonderwerk) has yielded undiagnostic fragments only. The remaining five occurrences include Hopefield, Cave of Hearths, Cornelia, Munro, and the Vaal 70-ft and current (40–1-ft) gravels.

At Hopefield only a very small sample was recovered from the excavated floor and this has not yet been described. It is argued that the vast bulk of the surface material from here belongs to a single fairly long period, namely the Acheulian (Singer and Wymer 1968). Although the total faunal assemblage may be contaminated by later material it is likely that all the extinct species should be associated with the Acheulian. Description of the fauna thus far have been restricted to separate groups: carnivores (Ewer and Singer 1956), rhinoceros (Hooijer and Singer 1960), hippopotamus (Hooijer and Singer 1961), primates (Singer 1962), pigs (Singer and Keen 1955; Keen and Singer 1956), horses (Singer and Inskeep 1961; Singer and Boné 1966), and giraffes (Singer and Boné 1960). A checklist of the species present (Hendey 1969) provides a convenient summary of the collection.

Cave of Hearths Beds I–III yielded a fauna sample in direct association with artifacts all recovered by controlled excavation. This sample is rather small and does not contain as many species as the "mixed" collections taken from the spoil and collapsed deposit found at the site prior to archaeological excavation. It is almost certain that the reliably associated sample does not represent the full range of species originally present in Beds I–III. Only one checklist (H. B. S. Cooke 1962) of their combined contents is available. Cooke considers that the bulk of the material from the spoil-heap collections should be associated with beds I–III so that two separate calculations of the percentage of extinct species are possible on the excavated and the spoil material.

The Cornelia artifacts and fauna are in a gravel body covered by deep silts and overlying a shale bedrock. This site has never been adequately excavated but extensive collections were made from the exposed gravel surface. Because this material occurs in a derived context in the gravels the true association between artifacts and fauna remains open to dispute. The stratigraphy of the site has been briefly reported (Oakley 1954a) and the artifacts (Meiring 1956), and fauna (van Hoepen 1930) have been inadequately described. Fortunately a recent checklist of the fauna (H. B. S. Cooke 1964; Ewer and Cooke 1964) gives a provisional summary of the species present, although this may not be complete.

The Munro site on the Vaal River has provided an enigmatic "bone heap" excavated from the same level as stray Acheulian tools in deep silt. The association between fauna and artifacts is therefore rather loose, and the species present in the bone sample are not yet published.

The very large bone collections from the so-called "younger gravels" of the Vaal River were gathered from diamond-digging spoil and were not recovered *in situ*. It must be assumed that this fauna belongs to the Acheulian period since abundant unrolled artifacts of this industry have been recovered from the same gravels. However, both the circumstances of their recovery and their geological context in the gravels makes it impossible to determine whether this collection has been mixed with much earlier fauna from ancient gravels now reworked into the 70-ft and current gravel deposits (Cooke 1949a, 1964; Wells 1964).

It is probable that the fauna and artifacts are truly associated at all five sites but it is only at the Cave of Hearths that the association is definitely beyond dispute. Outdated faunal lists and terminological difficulties also hamper our knowledge of the Acheulian fauna. Given all these limitations, the results below cannot be considered as solid evidence of the relative ages of the four sites:

Minimum number	Hopefield	Cave of Hearths (I–III)	Cave of Hearths (mixed)	Cornelia	Vaal gravels
Species present:	58	19	48	26	39
Extinct species:	28	9	10	18	20
Extinct species (%):	48.3	47.4	20.8	69.2	51.3

A brief glance at the line of percentages above shows that the fauna from most Acheulian sites contains fewer extinct species than occurred in the australopithecine breccias discussed in the previous chapter. As there are no reliable sites in which the Acheulian has been found overlying an Oldowan occurrence in southern Africa, the fauna provides the only reliable indication that the Acheulian is in fact the later of the two. However, the difference in percentages of extinct species between Acheulian sites could have arisen due to so many other factors that they cannot possibly be used to ascertain which is the older or younger of the four. It is probable that the lists for Cornelia, Vaal, and Cave of Hearths are not complete and the Cave of Hearths (mixed) sample is clearly contaminated by later material from the upper levels of the deposit which contain abundant modern species. The available faunal evidence cannot therefore be used for relative dating although it is potentially valuable for large reliably associated samples discovered in the future.

The third dating approach based on worldwide fluctuations in sea levels during the Pleistocene is potentially useful for coastal sites but has not been fully exploited. The advance and retreat of major glaciations in the northern hemisphere (and possibly the Antarctic) have alternately withdrawn and released huge bodies of water from the oceans, thus causing sea levels to fall and rise. Periods of glacial retreat and high sea level have left traces of ancient shorelines including wave-cut benches and cliffs, beach deposits, and wave-cut caves. On the southern African coast, at least two major benches are recognized. The so-called 60-ft and 20-ft emergences are possibly associated with the 18-m and 8-m shoreline of the European Atlantic and Mediterranean coasts. The corresponding rise in the continental land masses assures that the shorelines of earlier interglacial events stand at a greater elevation than later ones. Thus, the 60-ft (18-m) bench is older than the 20-ft (8-m) level. Several claims for raised beach levels up to 300 ft above sea level have been advanced, but not all these have been widely accepted. A peneplain at about 300 ft has been recognized along considerable stretches of the coast (King 1946), but this is generally agreed to be of Tertiary age and is probably older than the Stone Age period. Several claims have been made for stone artifacts found in beach deposits from the Natal coast, but these have not been adequately documented and it is still impossible to examine their associations.

Cape Hangklip is the only site with an adequately reported geology (Mabbut 1951). The artifact occurrence is situated on and within a black sand deposit that directly overlies the 60-ft bench, and traces of a 20-ft cobble storm beach have been reported below the level of the site. The deposit therefore postdates the 18-m level and predates the 8-m level. These events might be equated with an early and later phase in the glacial retreat of the northern hemisphere usually known as the Riss–Würm Interglacial period. Absolute dates have been obtained from mollusk shells in the beaches at several sites in the Mediterranean. The thorium–uranium (^{230}Th–^{234}U) dating technique has been applied to these, and its range extends far beyond that of radiocarbon (Stearns and Thurber 1965). Readings for the 18-m beach are about 140,000 B.P. and for the 8-m beach around 90,000 B.P. It is possible therefore that the true age of Hangklip falls between these two dates, but this cannot be confirmed until absolute dating is applied to local marine deposits.

The potassium–argon (K–Ar) method, which has been applied to the volcanic tuffs in the Olduvai deposits, has given readings of over 1 million B.P. for the Lower Acheulian. No sites associated with contemporary volcanic deposits have been located in southern Africa, and Olduvai remains the only datable site for the earliest appearance of the Acheulian. It is reported that absolute dating methods are being successfully applied to calcretes (Mason 1967c), but results are not yet available.

Climatic Evidence during the Acheulian Period

The climatic framework proposed for the Vaal River sequence was extended to other sites in southern Africa but could not be confirmed by the field evidence. It is now realized that systematic investigations of soils and vegetation remains are needed to provide adequate indications of climatic change.

The porosity test on dolomitic sand grains described in Chapter 2 was applied to the deposits of Cave of Hearths (Brain 1967e). The sand grains of the lowest Acheulian level (Bed I) contained far more angular grains than a modern sample, and the layers above this suggest a steady decrease in grain angularity with time. The rubble breccia above Bed III, the last Acheulian level, contained a sand of the same angularity as local modern dolomitic soil. A tentative interpretation of this evidence would be that Bed I witnessed a climate with a much higher rainfall than the present and that the rainfall decreased steadily to conditions similar to those of today after the deposition of Bed III. This interpretation can be accepted as provisional since only one Acheulian site has been tested by the method. The underlying principles of the interpretation of grain angularity require further investigation before the Cave of Hearths results can be confirmed.

The waterlogged condition of some of the Kalambo Falls floors has preserved fossil pollen grains in the peaty clays associated with artifacts. Two of the riverbank excavations known as Sites A and B have yielded the best floor fragments and the associated pollens for the lowest floors (6–8 at Site B) suggest a vegetation similar to that found in the valley today: "Brachystegia (dry deciduous) woodland on the basin slopes with reed beds and grass in the valley bottom, with relict patches of moist lowland forest" (Clark 1964: 94). A later floor (5 at Site B) yielded a pollen spectrum that has been interpreted by Clark as "wetter and probably rather cooler." At Site A there is a set of three floor fragments reported to be later than Floor 5 at Site B, on typological and stratigraphic grounds (Clark 1969). The pollens from these levels have been interpreted as a climax stage of the cool–wet trend (Clark and van Zinderen Bakker 1964).

The proposed sequence of floors at this site depends on the assumption that Floor 5 at Site B correlates with Floor 6 at Site A (the lowest above water level). The latter contains a small artifact sample (58 specimens) that is not ty-pologically similar to Floor 5 at Site B. This means that the sequence of floors in the two cuttings may be correlated on geological grounds only and is there-fore still open to some doubt. The small quantities of pollen recovered from some of the analyzed samples (van Zinderen Bakker 1969) also cast some doubt on the climatic interpretations placed on them.

It therefore appears that the results from both Cave of Hearths and Kalambo Falls should be treated with caution as they may be subject to revision when more evidence becomes available. For the present it is interesting to note that the proposed climatic trends for the end of the Acheulian period do not corre-late at the two tested sites. If the interpretations are accepted, it would appear that the climate became wetter in northern Zambia and drier in northern Trans-vaal. Either the two sites do not cover the same period or patterns of past climatic changes in this area are far more complex than we have previ-ously supposed.

Diet and Activities

All the evidence suggests that the Acheulian economy was based on the hunting of available game near permanent water supplies such as river banks, lake shores, or swamp. Most of the artifacts ascribed to this period have been as-sociated with deposits indicating that the original site was positioned near water. Only rarely have sites been found in localities which have other benefits to offer such as natural shelter or raw materials. Some sites such as Wonderboom have been located in a *nek* or gap in a long range of hills. It is tempting to assume that such localities were used as natural funnels where migrating game would tend to concentrate and therefore be more easily trapped.

Since the stone artifacts are definitely associated with animal bones at some sites, we are forced to conclude that most sites are in fact relics of past butcher-ing activities. It has been assumed that the group of hunters and their depen-dents camped around the carcass of some large beast that had been killed, and tools were made on the spot from the nearest available raw materials. However, there is no evidence available from southern Africa to suggest that they moved from one carcass to another. Actually, a wide variety of species are to be found at a single site. Rather enigmatic "bone heaps" have been recovered apparently in association with hand-axes at Munro, and exposed heaps at Hopefield may also be associated with this period but no artifacts were found with them. An-other sealed bone heap from Aloes was reported to have no artifact associations (Gess 1969; Wells 1970b). Bone fragments have been dated to greater than 37,000 B.P. (GX-1280), and Aloes may possibly belong to this period. Unfortu-nately only the Hopefield bone heaps have been reported in adequate detail, but these were surface finds open to all the usual criticisms, including the possibility that they are artificial clusters caused by sand-dune deflation. The contents of all these heaps indicate that several species including carnivores are present in each (Inskeep and Hendey 1966; Singer and Heltne 1966).

In order to gain some insight into the range of animals apparently killed and eaten by the Acheulian hunters, it is useful to examine the list of mammal species found at the four sites where artifacts and bones *may* be associated. The complete list in Table 17 is summarized in Table 16.

There is clearly no evidence to suggest specialized hunting of a few selected animals. It appears that any available meat supply was exploited, and the Acheulian hunting ability apparently extended to the largest and most dangerous animals among the African fauna. The bones of very large beasts (mammoth elephant, rhino, hippo, and giraffe) are absent from the Cave of Hearths perhaps because the site is some distance from likely kill sites near the stream at the bottom of the Makapan Valley. The unusual number of extinct mammoth species from the Vaal River gravels may need to be revised as some of these have been identified on molars only. It is likely that the revised list will reduce their numbers considerably. However, the evidence suggests that large game animals provided much of the Acheulian meat supply.

Whereas the bones of lesser game could be obtained by scavenging from carnivore kills, the presence of the very large animals (presumed to be beyond the hunting capability of carnivores) must reflect organized hunting and probably trapping by man. There is no evidence for the use of pit traps in Acheulian times, but it has been argued (Clark 1959a) that these must have been used to kill the larger animals. It is equally possible that these beasts could be slowed down or trapped by simply driving them into soft muddy deposits. If the faster antelope species were hunted rather than scavenged from carnivore kills, it must

TABLE 16

Mammalian Species Found at Four Acheulian Sites

	No. of mammal species present			
Group	Vaal River	Cornelia	Cave of Hearths	Hopefield
Carnivores	1	—	2	9
Large game (elephant, rhino, and hippo)	7	1	—	4
Horses (zebra, quagga, etc.)	5	4	2	3
Pigs (warthog, bush pig, etc.)	8	5	1	3
Giraffe	1	2	—	2
Buffalo	2	1	1	1
Other large bovids (hartebeest, wildebeest, kudu, sable, etc.)	11	8	6	5
Small antelope (Reduncini, Antilopini, etc.)	4	5	4	4
Other small mammals (primates, hares, porcupine, hyrax, etc.)	—	—	2	7

TABLE 17

Fossil Mammals from Four Acheulian Localities

Order and family	Genus and species	Common name or description	Vaal gravels	Cornelia	Cave of Hearths	Hope-field
Primates	*Papio ursinus*	Chacma baboon	—	—	cf.	—
	Simopithecus	Extinct baboon	—	—	—	×
Carnivora						
Canidae	*Canis mesomelas*	Black-backed jackal	—	—	×	×
	Lycaon picta magnus	Extinct hunting dog	—	—	—	×
Mustelidae	*Mellivora capensis*	Honey badger	—	—	×	×
Viveridae	*Herpeste ichneumon*	Mongoose	—	—	—	×
Hyaenidae	*Hyaena brunnea*	Brown hyena	—	—	—	×
	Crocuta crocuta spelea	Extinct cave hyena	—	—	×	×
	Crocuta crocuta	Spotted hyena	×	—	—	—
Felidae	*Felis serval*	Serval cat	—	—	—	×
	Panthera leo aff. *spelaea*	Extinct cave lion	—	—	—	×
	Meganteron cf. *gracile*	Extinct saber-tooth cat	—	—	—	×
Proboscidea						
Elephantidae	*Gomphotherium* sp.	Extinct mammoth	×	—	—	—
	Archidiskodon subplanifrons	Extinct mammoth	×	—	—	—
	Archidiskodon broomi	Extinct mammoth	×	—	×	—
	Archidiskodon transvaalensis	Extinct mammoth	×	—	—	—
	Loxodonta atlantica	Extinct mammoth	×	—	—	—
	"Loxodonta" zulu	Extinct mammoth	—	—	—	×
Hyracoidea	*Procavia capensis*	Cape dassie or Cape hyrax	—	—	×	—
Perissodactyla						
Rhinocerotidae	*Diceros bicornis*	Black rhinoceros	×	—	—	—
	Ceratotherium simum	White rhinoceros	—	×	×	×
Equidae	*Stylohipparion steytleri*	Extinct horse	?	—	—	×
	Equus quagga	Quagga	×	×	×	—
	Equus burchelli	Burchell's zebra	×	×	—	—
	Equus plicatus	Extinct horse	×	—	×	×
	Equus helmei	Extinct horse	×	—	×	?
	"Eurygnathohippus cornelianus"	Extinct horse	—	×	—	—

(continued)

129

TABLE 17 (continued)

Order and family	Genus and species	Common name or description	Vaal gravels	Cornelia	Cave of Hearths	Hope-field
Artiodactyla						
Suidae	*Mesochoerus lategani*	Extinct bush pig	—	—	—	×
	Mesochoerus paiceae	Extinct pig	×	—	—	×
	"Tapinochoerus" meadowsi	Extinct pig	×	—	—	×
	Tapinochoerus modestus	Extinct warthog	—	×	—	—
	"Kolpochoerus sinuosus"	Extinct warthog?	—	×	—	—
	Orthostonyx sp.	Extinct warthog?	—	×	—	—
	Notochoerus capensis	Extinct warthog	×	—	—	—
	Stylochoerus compactus	Extinct giant bush pig	×	×	—	—
	Stylochoerus altidens	Extinct giant bush pig	×	—	—	—
	Phacochoerus aethiopicus	Warthog	×	cf.	×	×
	Phacochoerus africanus	Warthog	×	—	—	—
Hippopotamidae	*Hippopotamus amphibius*	Hippo	—	×	—	×
	Hippopotamus gorgops	Extinct hippo with protruding orbits	×	×	—	—
Giraffidae	*Libytherium olduvaense*	Extinct short-necked antlered giraffe	×	×	—	×
	Giraffa gracilis	Extinct slender giraffe	—	—	—	×
	Giraffa camelopardalis	Giraffe	—	×	—	—
Bovidae						
Tragelaphini	*Tragelaphus* cf. *strepsiceros*	Extinct kudu	—	—	—	×
	Taurotragus oryx	Eland	×	×	cf.	×
	Strepsiceros strepsiceros	Kudu	?	cf.	cf.	—
Bovini	*"Homioceras" baini*	Extinct giant buffalo	×	×	?	×
	Syncerus caffer	Cape buffalo	×	—	—	—
Reduncini	*Redunca arundinum*	Reedbuck	—	—	cf.	×
	Sylvicapra grimmia	Duiker	×	—	—	—
Hippotragini	*Kobus ellipsiprymnus*	Waterbuck	—	—	cf.	—
	Kobus venterae	Waterbuck	—	cf.	—	—
	Hippotragus spp.	Extinct sable	×	—	—	×
	Hippotragus niger	Sable	×	—	—	—

	Taxon	Common name	1	2	3	4	5
Alcelaphini	*Damaliscus* spp.	Extinct antelope	×	—	cf.	—	—
	Damaliscus cf. *albifrons*	Blesbuck	—	—	?	?	?
	Damaliscus cf. *lunatus*	Tssessebe	—	×	—	×	×
	Damaliscus cf. *pygargus*	Bontebok	—	—	cf.	?	×
	Alcelaphus caama	Hartebeest	—	×	?	cf.	cf.
	Alcelaphus robustus	Extinct hartebeest	—	×	×	?	×
	Connochaetes laticornutus	Extinct wildebeest	—	—	—	×	×
	Connochaetes gnu	Black wildebeest	—	—	—	×	—
	Connochaetes taurinus	Blue wildebeest	×	—	—	—	—
	Lunatocerus cf. *mirum*	Extinct wildebeest?	×	—	—	—	—
Neotragini	*Raphicerus campestris*	Steenbok	×	—	—	—	cf.
Antilopini	*Antidorcas* sp.	Extinct springbok	—	—	—	cf.	×
	Antidorcas marsupialis	Springbok	×	cf.	cf.	×	×
	Aepyceros melampus	Impala	—	—	—	—	—
	Gazella wellsi	Extinct gazelle	×	cf.	×	×	×
	Gazella bondi	Extinct gazelle	—	—	—	—	—
	"*Gazella*" *helmoedi*	Extinct gazelle?	—	—	cf.	×	×
	Gazella sp.	Extinct gazelle	×	—	×	×	—
Lagomorpha	*Lepus capensis*	Cape hare	×	—	—	—	—
Rodentia	*Bathyergus suillus*	Dune mole rat	×	—	—	—	—
	Georychus cf. *capensis*	Cape mole rat	×	—	—	—	—
Hystricoidae	*Hystrix africae-australis*	Porcupine	×	—	—	—	—
Muridae	*Otomys* cf. *saundersiae*	Saunder's otomys	×	—	—	—	—
	Parotomys cf. *brantsi*	Brant's Karroo rat	×	—	—	—	—

be assumed that stalking and the use of the throwing spear had become developed skills by this stage. It is also possible that the lighter game animals were deliberately driven into swampy deposits and stoned. The presence of "charred wooden spear points" at Kalambo Falls remains enigmatic since it is observed that natural weathering of wood by wind-blown sand and even fluviatile sands can produce similar objects. Nevertheless, the fact that such objects were found with Acheulian artifacts strongly favors the possibility that they were man-made. The same argument applies to the "throwing club" and "digging sticks" from Kalambo Falls (Clark 1954b). (See Fig. 42.)

The presence of several carnivore species at Hopefield cannot be explained in terms of environmental factors and it is by no means certain that all the extinct species listed are definitely to be associated with the Acheulian. Carnivores were recovered from bone heaps, and it has been suggested (Inskeep and Hendey 1966) that these were not deliberately hunted but were chance kills caused by artificially poisoning small waterholes.

Small mammals such as hare, hyrax, porcupine, rodents, and shrews form a significant part of the Hopefield fauna, and several birds and reptiles are also known from here. As none of these is reliably associated with the artifacts, we cannot be certain that they formed part of the Acheulian diet. Their small bones are not likely to survive in the gravels of the Vaal or at Cornelia, and only the hyrax was found at Cave of Hearths. Since this may have been introduced by scavengers or owls, there is no reliable evidence to suggest the hunting of small mammals.

Some hint that vegetable foods were collected during this period comes from Kalambo Falls Floor VI, where several local seeds were recovered as well as remains of two edible fruits: an immature fruit of the palm *Borassus aethiopium*, and fruit of *?Chrysophyllum bovinianum*, a montane species not found in the area today, but present at higher and colder altitudes in the adjacent Mafinga Mountains.

Semicircular arrangements of large rocks on the Kalambo Falls floors have been interpreted as possible bases for brush windbreaks, and the presence of leaves and reed remains in these deposits may support this idea. Reeds are also reported to occur in the bottom of depressions or "sleeping hollows" in one floor. Tree bark has been preserved in the deposit, but the suggestion that it was shaped to form carrying trays has not yet been adequately demonstrated (Clark 1962). Large pieces of timber have been recovered from Kalambo Falls and Amanzi, but these show no definite signs of workmanship and their random positions on the floors do not suggest that they were used for constructing wooden shelters.

It has been repeatedly claimed that the Acheulian hunters were familiar with the use of fire, and the evidence from Cave of Hearths and Montagu Cave has been quoted in support of this. It has now been demonstrated that the black layers in the Acheulian deposits at Montagu contain no charcoal, and indeed free

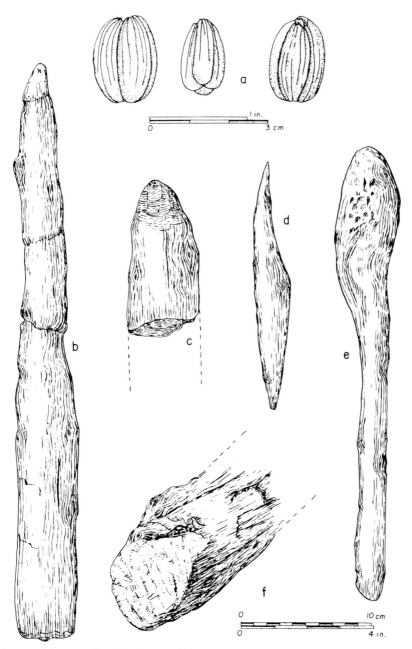

Fig. 42. (a) Three seeds of *Chrysophyllum bovinianum* from Site B at Kalambo Falls; (b, c, d) various wooden objects thought to be deliberately pointed by charring in fire; (e) possible throwing club shaped by charring; (f) end of branch fragment, showing signs of chopping damage (b–e from Kalambo Falls; f from Amanzi).

133

carbon is either absent or so scarce that it is useless for dating purposes. The layers have been tentatively interpreted as "swallow guano" derived from the abundant bird life which inhabits the crevices of the cave roof (Keller 1969b).

The so-called "basal hearth" at the bottom of the Cave of Hearths also contains no free carbon, but over 20% phosphate (P_2O_5), and this has been interpreted as calcined bat guano (Oakley 1954c). The initial guano filling of the cave was accidentally ignited by one of several fireplaces found in Bed I, which is the earliest Acheulian level. Another very large single hearth containing masses of bone fragments was found in Bed III. There is therefore no reason to doubt the evidence for deliberate and controlled use of fire at this site, and the traces from Kalambo Falls are probably acceptable although the problem of natural charring of wood remains to be examined. The presence of "consolidated ash found in association with a burnt clay area" (Clark 1962) at Kalambo Falls has been claimed as a hearth, and this appears to be the most reliable evidence for the local use of fire. The remaining mass of charred wood from Kalambo Falls and the blackened logs from Amanzi Springs *may* indicate the use of fire, but natural weathering also may have played some part. At present it appears reasonable to suppose that Acheulian hunters used fire for warmth and possibly for cooking meat as the charred bones of Cave of Hearths Bed III indicate. The use of fire for deliberate charring and shaping of wooden tools and weapons remains problematic, and no reliable evidence exists for the use of fire during hunting drives.

Considerable doubt surrounds the supposed uses of the various Acheulian stone artifacts although it may be assumed that hand axes and cleavers were employed mainly for butchering activities. The Hopefield excavation yielded 47 hand-axes and 3 cleavers associated with a number of large animal bones. Only 29 cores and 129 flakes were found on this "floor," far too few to suggest the manufacture of the tools on the spot. The most plausible explanation would be that almost all the hand-axes and cleavers were made close to silcrete outcrops some miles from the site, and they were then brought to the scene of butchery. Similar concentrations of hand-axes and cleavers have been reported from Kalambo Falls. It has been frequently assumed that the "heavy-duty" tools (picks and choppers) were used for rough woodworking and possibly for digging pits, and that the small scrapers and other small tools reflect light woodworking activities. It should be stressed that no reliable evidence exists to support these interpretations, and the concept of "activity variants" used to explain the variable tool content of different sites (Kleindienst 1961) remains doubtful since so little is known about chronological changes in Acheulian typology.

The Acheulian Human Type

Only one hominid fragment has been recovered in definite association with Acheulian artifacts in this region. The adolescent mandible from Cave of Hearths Bed III is a badly damaged fragment with the stumps of three incisors,

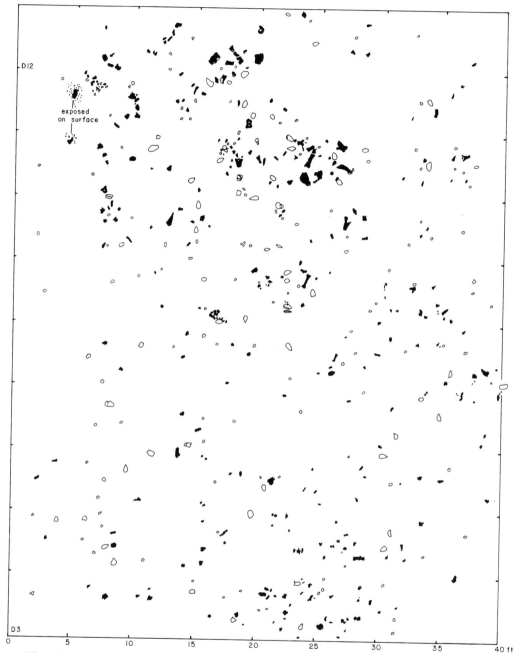

Fig. 43. Distribution of bones (filled) and artifacts (open) on the excavated Acheulian horizon at Hopefield near the locality of the Saldanha skull fragments, which were found on the surface a few hundred yards away. This scatter is typical of many Acheulian "floors" from southern and eastern Africa; it remains impossible to discern the degree of horizontal and vertical disturbance of the material after it was abandoned by the hunters responsible for it. (After Singer and Wymer 1968.)

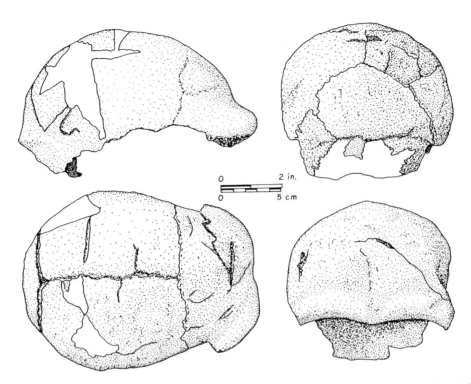

Fig. 44. Right lateral, occipital, top, and frontal views of the Saldanha (Hopefield) skull reconstructed. A mandible ramus fragment was recovered from the same area as the skull fragments. This specimen, like the Broken Hill skull it closely resembles, is generally regarded as a large-brained individual of a late *H. erectus* population.

the right canine and two molars. The second molar is erupted but unworn and the individual's age at death has been estimated at about 12 years (Dart 1948f). The jaw had been broken in two places prior to fossilization. It has been suggested that the height and thickness of the jaw, the absence of any marked "chin," and the enlarged pulp cavities of the teeth may reflect affinities with the Neanderthal human form, but no systematic comparisons have been attempted and it is doubtful whether much useful information could be derived from so small a juvenile specimen.

One other possible Acheulian hominid comes from Hopefield. It is frequently stated that this specimen is associated with the "Cape Fauresmith," an entirely meaningless term that has never been defined. The cranium (26 fragments) and a fragment of ramus belonging to an adult was found lying on the sand surface of this site, and its claimed associations with fauna or artifacts are therefore without any reliable support. On the same surface in the immediate area of the hominid remains were found the bones of extinct animals and silcrete artifacts of little diagnostic value. The artifacts from this site as a whole can be divided into Acheulian and "Middle Stone Age" with rare but obvious later additions. The fauna associated with the "Middle Stone Age" has not been reliably isolated but it is postulated that two groups exist within the collection: an older fauna with a relatively high fluorine and uranium content, and a later group with smaller traces of both elements (Oakley 1957b). It is now accepted that the greater part of the collection belongs to the older group and it is reasonable to assume that this fauna is coeval with the older of the two industries, that is, the Acheulian. As the fluorine and uranium content of the skull is similar to that of the older group of fauna, there is some reason to believe that this hominid should be related to the Acheulian. However, the argument for association is most devious, and we cannot escape the fact that the specimen itself is a surface find subject to all the usual doubts (Fig. 43).

The restored specimen consists of the calvarium without any facial parts (Fig. 44). The most notable features are the pronounced supraorbital ridges, the low sloping frontal region, and the marked ophryonic groove behind the ridges. The parietals are curved, and the occipital region is well rounded although the overall height of the vault appears to be low (Singer 1954, 1957). The specimen has been tentatively assigned to the Neanderthal human type on the basis of its close affinity with the Broken Hill specimen.

THE SANGOAN COMPLEX

Until recently the Sangoan was not represented by a large primary context sample, and for this reason no precise definition of its artifact content was possible. Any sample with a few crude hand-axes and cleavers together with abundant choppers, picks, and core axes made of coarse-grained materials was labeled Sangoan. Thanks to this loose definition a very large number of localities have been recorded from southeastern, central, and western Africa. In southern Africa, where numerous surface collections have been made, certain regional variants have been proposed (Clark 1959a). It has proved impossible to establish accurate typological differences between the claimed Zambezi, Luangwa, Bembezi, and Tugela variants of the Sangoan, and it is now realized that such terminology cannot serve any useful purpose.

To date the only useful sealed samples have been recovered from Kalambo Falls and of these only one (horizon IV in Trench B$_2$) has been published in any detail (Clark 1965). Compared with the five Kalambo Falls Acheulian samples for which an analysis is also available, the Sangoan has an almost identical range of tool types. The only type which does not appear in the Acheulian is the core axe. This is present as a very small proportion (2.2%) of the Sangoan tool assemblage, and it is described as "rough crude handaxe with thick unworked butt and weighing between 2 and 6 lbs" (Clark 1965). Of more importance are the differences in the numerical proportions of the various types common to both the Sangoan and the Acheulian. The Sangoan sample has fewer hand–axes, cleavers, and knives, about the same proportion of "heavy-duty" tools, but the entire industry is dominated by *small scrapers,* a feature never before recognized as important for distinguishing the Sangoan from the Acheulian. It must be stressed that the distinctive features (core axe, few hand–axes–cleavers–knives, abundant small scrapers) hold good for Kalambo Falls but need not stand as general criteria for separating the two complexes.

The chief hindrance to serious study of the Sangoan is the absence of unselected samples. Three collections from Sango Bay "type" area in Uganda have been shown to lack the small-scraper elements found at Kalambo Falls (Cole 1967b), but these were not recovered by excavation and are therefore open to criticism. Excavations at Nsongezi in the same area have revealed a sample dominated by small scrapers and other small tools from the upper rubble. The material is in a geological context and some of it is heavily rolled, but it overlies the M–N horizon with mixed Acheulian and Sangoan elements. The small excavated samples from the upper rubble at Nsongezi may suggest some affinity with the Kalambo Falls B_2 sample, but more reliable material is urgently needed. In southern Africa the unselected samples in Table 18 have been quoted in print.

Of these, the Gwelo Kopje and Bambata samples are no longer available and the Khami and Pomongwe samples are too small for analytical purposes. Far

TABLE 18

Unselected Samples from Sangoan Sites

Site	Reference	Context	No. of samples
Kalambo Falls	Clark (1969)	Excavated from archaeological horizons in ocherous sands at Sites A, B, C, and D on river bank	9
Khami	C. K. Cooke (1957b)	Very small sample excavated base of decomposed granite deposit presumed derived from adjacent granite outcrop slopes	1
Pomongwe	C. K. Cooke (1963)	Small sample excavated from bottom of granitic cave deposit	1
Bambata	Armstrong (1931)	Small sample from bottom of cave deposit. Possibly selected	1
Gwelo Kopje	Gardner and Stapleton (1934), C. K. Cooke (1968)	Excavated from open rubble site overlying possible Acheulian in lower rubble	1
Mafungabusi	C. K. Cooke (1966b)	Partly surface, partly excavated open site in presumed derived context	1
Gilchrist's Folly	C. K. Cooke (1960)	Unselected surface collection	1
Mufo	Clark (1963)	Unselected collections from gravels and sand deposits	1

fewer Sangoan samples exist than in the Acheulian although there are numerous reports of surface discoveries scattered over southern central Africa. No large excavated samples are available from the Zambezi–Luangwa valleys nor from northern Natal. No sites with associated fauna have been discovered, and it is not yet known whether the Kalambo Falls floors reveal any traces of specialized activity.

The Charaman Phase of the Sangoan

Three excavated Charaman samples from the Matopos Hills area of southern Rhodesia are claimed to overly the Sangoan. These are from Bambata, Pomongwe, and Khami where unfortunately the basal "Sangoan" samples are too small to be diagnostic. Cooke has attempted to establish that the Charaman is a later phase of the Sangoan complex in this area on the basis of these three excavations, but it remains unproved that the Charaman levels differ in any way from the traces of "Sangoan" at the base of each of the deposits. Two unselected surface samples and one excavated Charaman site have been compared with the Sangoan collection from Mafungabusi and the differences given in Table 19 were noted (C. K. Cooke, 1966b).

The percentage values suggested that the Charaman contains fewer picks, hand-axes, and other tools (hammers, anvils, choppers, fabricators, etc.) and more points and scrapers. Until these differences have also been established between primary context samples from the same site, we cannot be certain that the Charaman is a chronologically distinct unit. For the present we may only tentatively accept it as a later phase of the Sangoan on the basis of Cooke's three excavations.

Numerous Charaman surface discoveries have been reported from Rhodesia and Zambia, but the only excavated sites besides the three already mentioned

TABLE 19

Comparison of Unselected Surface Samples from Charaman Sites and Mafungabusi [a]

Tool type	Sangoan Mafungabusi	Charaman		
		Charama	Cranmore	Khami
Picks	23.8	15.3	16.1	12.2
Hand-axes	12.3	1.0	1.0	1.0
Points	6.3	17.1	21.0	22.2
Scrapers	32.6	47.2	42.0	46.6
Utilized blades	6.7	8.3	9.9	10.0
Other tools	18.3	11.1	10.0	8.0
Total:	100.0	100.0	100.0	100.0

[a] Values in percentages.

are Redcliff (Brain and Cooke 1967), Twin Rivers (Clark 1971), Broken Hill (Clark, Oakley, Wells, and McClelland 1947) and Katima Mulilo (L. Phillipson 1968). Associated fauna is available from Pomongwe, Redcliff, Twin Rivers, and Broken Hill. (See Table 20.)

Origins and Dating

It has been established beyond all reasonable doubt that the Sangoan complex is later than the Acheulian at Kalambo Falls, Mufo, and probably at Gwelo Kopje, where the stratigraphic positions of the two have been revealed by controlled excavation. The same sequence may be exposed in the walls of some erosion features in the Zambezi River valley (Clark 1950a), but no numerical evidence is available. The same relationship has been established in eastern Africa for several excavations at Nsongezi, Uganda. Several authors have been tempted to assume that the Sangoan is a typological derivative of the Acheulian since they share so many types. It has been suggested that the increase in heavy picks, choppers, and core axes at the expense of refined hand-axes and cleavers reflects an adaptation to a more heavily wooded environment, and the distribution of the Sangoan in central Africa has been evoked to support this hypothesis. It has also been argued that climatic and vegetational changes induced the shift in tool typology at Kalambo Falls (Clark 1964).

Unfortunately the available field evidence provides no clear indication that this took place. Cole's extensive field research in the Orichinga Valley deposits around Nsongezi have revealed no buried sequence in which the Sangoan can be shown to "evolve" directly out of the underlying Acheulian in Uganda. A most important claim for an Acheulian–Sangoan Transitional phase has been put forward by Clark for Kalambo Falls, and this deserves our close attention. The stratigraphy of the two relevant excavations in the riverbank deposits may be summarized as follows:

Site B	Site A
Sangoan Floor B4 – – – – – – –	Sangoan
deposits	"Transitional" Floor A4
eroded	"Transitional" Floor A5
away	"Transitional" Floor A5B
Acheulian Floor B5 – – – – – –	Acheulian Floor 6A
Acheulian Floor 6B	below
Acheulian Floor 7	river
Acheulian Floor 8	level

This implies that the Kalambo Falls provides a continuous sequence passing from Acheulian to Sangoan via three "transitional" levels. Unfortunately the

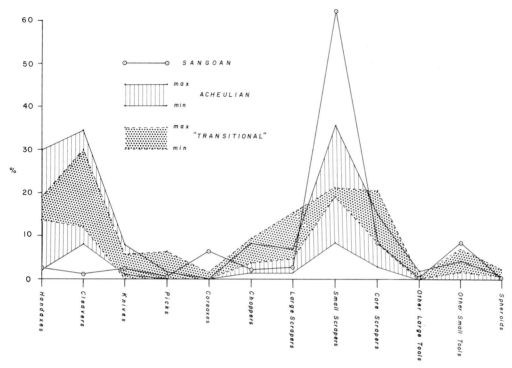

Fig. 45. Percentage frequency distributions for Acheulian, Sangoan, and "Transitional" assemblages from Kalambo Falls. The minimum–maximum range of percentage readings for "Transitional" samples falls within that for Acheulian samples and may not differ substantially from it. The Sangoan sample, in contrast, falls outside the range of the other two groups and is distinguished by a low percentage of cleavers and very high percentage of small scrapers.

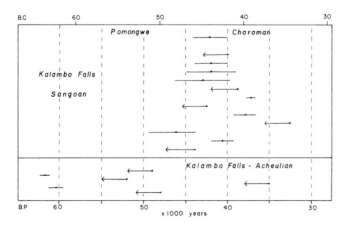

Fig. 46. Radiocarbon readings for Acheulian and Sangoan occurrences at Kalambo Falls, compared with the Charaman reading from Pomongwe. Neither the radiocarbon data nor the available field evidence provide adequate support for the claim that the Charaman is later than the Sangoan phase.

published details and analyses of these three samples suggest that they differ in no way from the underlying Acheulian. The graph in Fig. 45 shows the maximum and minimum percentage of each tool type present in the five Acheulian floors, and the space between the two may be called the *range of variability* of the tool type. When a similar graph is constructed for the three "transitional" samples, it is at once apparent that they fall within the range of variability of the Acheulian and there is therefore no published evidence to justify calling them "transitional." We are therefore forced to concede that the transition has not yet been adequately demonstrated in the field and the true origins of the Sangoan remain unknown.

It has been argued recently that the so-called Lower Acheulian as found in primary contexts at Olduvai and Peninj in eastern Africa could be the typological ancestor of the Sangoan (O'Brien 1969), but no excavations exist at present that might demonstrate such a direct derivation. The available radiocarbon dates for Sangoan levels at Pomongwe, Mufo, and Kalambo Falls suggest that the complex may overlap with the (questionable) Acheulian dates from southern regions but they are almost all later than the Acheulian dates from Kalambo Falls. Unfortunately no dates have been obtained for the claimed "transitional" floors, and it is impossible to determine whether they are in fact intermediate in time between the Acheulian of Floor 6A and the overlying Sangoan. The dates for the Charaman phase at Pomongwe give no indication that this might be a later phase of the Sangoan (Fig. 46).

The Broken Hill Hominid

Broken Hill mine in Central Province, Zambia, comprises a number of opencast workings, one of which caused the complete removal of two dolomite hills, rich in lead and zinc ore. In the base of one hill was a steep tunnel-shaped cave filled with mineralized bone and stone artifacts. Blasting operations loosened a complete human skull from this deposit, and the verbal reports of its discovery suggest that it came from the deepest part of the cave about 60 ft below modern ground level. No controlled excavations of the tunnel fill took place, but a detailed plan and section of this site was recorded before the entire hill was blasted away (Clark *et al.* 1947). The uncontrolled digging and collecting of the cave fill revealed numerous mineralized human bones together with abundant fauna, bone tools, and stone artifacts. The circumstances surrounding the discovery of the complete skull gave rise to doubts about the true association with the material found *in situ,* and further doubts were raised by the observation that the skull and the other bones differed in mineral content. Oakley's detailed study of this problem revealed that such differences could have arisen from variable mineral content in different parts of the deposit, and chemical and radioactive testing revealed that the nitrogen, fluorine, and uranium content of the complete skull was very similar to that of the human bone fragments, bone tools, and animal bones found *in situ* (Oakley 1957b, 1958). On the basis of these findings the association is generally accepted as valid.

The large stone artifact sample from this site was rapidly dispersed in several collections and the complete corpus of material has never been published. It is reported that no hand axes, cleavers, picks, or core axes are present in any collections (Clark *et al.* 1947; Clark 1959b), and the industry was diagnosed as "Middle Stone Age." An exposure in the side of the same open-cast working revealed buried artifacts diffused through superficial deposits about 170 yd from the original cave, and excavations as well as collections of material from the exposed floor produced several of the tool types not found in the cave fill. The claimed stratigraphic sequence from this excavation ("Hope Fountain"–Acheulian–Sangoan–"Proto-Stillbay" is not justified since all the recovered samples are too small for accurate identification (Clark 1959b). Unfortunately no fauna survived in this open site and no connection could be established with the cave material, which was named "Proto-Stillbay" (now Charaman). Some doubt still surrounds the true identity of the associated artifacts because so few have been analyzed. At present it seems most likely that they should be ascribed to the Charaman or Sangoan since no other typological affinities are apparent.

The human remains belong to two individuals. Apart from the complete skull there is a parietal, maxilla, humerus, sacrum, two ilia, a femur, the proximal end of a second femur, two tibiae, and a third recently discovered femur fragment (Clark *et al.* 1968a). The prominent features of the complete skull are the sloping frontal region, pronounced brow ridges, and relatively large capacity (1280 cc) (Fig. 47). There is general agreement that it is closely related to the Hopefield specimen but some debate about the exact affinities of both with the Neanderthal human type from Europe. Recent opinion favors their classification as a subspeices of *Homo sapiens*, possibly differing from *Homo sapiens neanderthalensis* of Europe.

If the associations of both the Broken Hill and Hopefield specimens are accepted, this may hint at a relatively uniform physical type in both the north and south of southern Africa at a time when some divergence in stone artifact design had already taken place.

Broken Hill has also produced published details on the contemporary fauna and diet of the Sangoan complex. An earlier analysis (L. S. B. Leakey 1959) has been revised (Cooke 1964), and 28 mammals have been listed of which 7 (25%) are extinct (Table 20). These include a carnivore *Leptailurus hintoni*, an elephant *Loxodonta africana*, a form of gelada baboon *Simopithecus*, a saber-tooth cat *Machairodus*, a short-necked giraffe *Libytherium olduvaiensis*, a giant buffalo

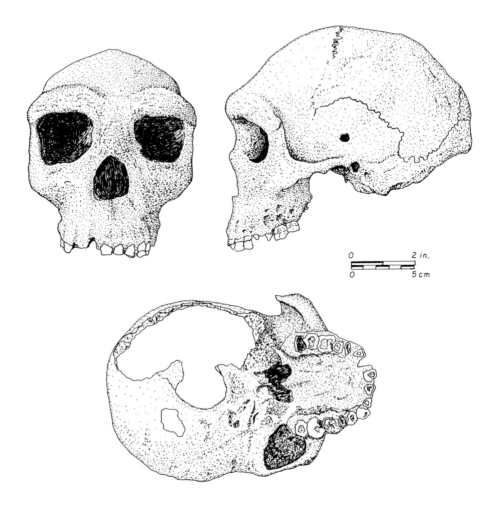

Fig. 47. Frontal, left lateral, and basal view of the Broken Hill skull. The dentition is severely damaged by advanced caries, and the left temporal shows traces of an abscess that has perforated the bone.

Homiocerous baini, and a wildebeest *Connochaetes laticornutus.* The presence of a higher percentage of living species in this fauna supports the interpretation that the site is indeed later than the Acheulian. Like the Acheulian examples there is no suggestion of specialized hunting activities. A grouping similar to that used for the Acheulian sites gives the following numbers: carnivores 7, large game 3, horses 1, pigs 1, giraffe 2, buffalo 1, other large bovids 7, small antelope 1, other small mammals 5. There is of course no proof that all these were hunted by man and the wide range of carnivores and small mammals (rodents and the like) may be a special feature of the cave environment.

TABLE 20

Mammalian and Other Fauna Associated with the Charaman Industry [a]

Genus and species	Description	Broken Hill	Pomongwe	Twin Rivers
Insectivora				
Crocidura cf. *bicolor*	Tiny musk shrew	?	—	—
Primates				
Simopithecus sp.	Extinct baboon	?	—	—
Lagomorpha				
Lepus sp.	Hare	--	3	×
Rodentia				
Pedetes sp.	Spring hare	—	1	—
Saccostomus campestris	Pouched mouse	?	—	—
Otomys irroratus	Swamp rat	?	—	—
Hystrix africae-australis	Porcupine	cf.	1	×
Thryonomys swinderianus	Cane rat	—	1	—
Carnivora				
Canis adustus	Side-striped jackal	cf.	—	—
Herpestes ichneumon	Gray mongoose	×	—	—
Hyaena brunnea	Brown hyena	cf.	—	—
Leptailurus hintoni	Extinct serval cat	×	—	—
Panthera leo	Lion	×	—	—
Panthera pardus	Leopard	×	1	—
Machairodus	Extinct saber-tooth cat	?	—	—
Proboscidea				
Loxodonta africana	Mammoth	×	—	—
Hyracoidea				
Heterohyrax	Extinct giant hyrax	—	3	—
Procavia capensis	Hyrax	—	12	—
Perissodactyla				
Equus burchelli	Burchell's zebra	×	1	××
Equus capensis	Extinct horse	—	1	—
Ceratotherium simum	White rhino	?	—	—
Diceros bicornis	Black rhino	×	—	×
Artiodactyla				
Phacochoerus aethiopicus	Cape warthog	×	1	×
Giraffa camelopardalis	Giraffe	cf.	—	—
Libytherium olduvaiensis	Extinct antlered giraffid	cf.	—	—
Strepsiceros strepsiceros	Kudu	cf.	—	—
Tragelaphus angasi	Nyala	?	—	—
Taurotragus oryx	Eland	×	—	—
"*Homoioceras*" *baini*	Extinct giant buffalo	×	—	—

(continued)

145

TABLE 20 (*continued*)

Genus and species	Description	Broken Hill	Pomongwe	Twin Rivers
Artiodactyla (*continued*)				
Kobus ellipsiprymnus	Waterbuck	—	1	×
Hippotragus niger	Sable	—	1	—
Oryx gazella	Gemsbok	cf.	—	—
Damaliscus albifrons	Blesbok	×	—	—
Damaliscus lunatus	Tsessebe	cf.	1	×
Connochaetes taurinus	Wildebeest	cf.	—	× ×
Sylvicapra grimmia	Duiker	—	3	—
Raphicerus campestris	Steenbok	—	4	—
Litocranius walleri	Gerenuk	cf.	—	—
Syncerus caffer	Cape buffalo	—	—	×
Onotragus leche	Lechwe	—	—	×
Alcelaphus caama	Hartebeest	—	—	×
Redunca arundinum	Reedbuck	—	—	×
Oreotragus oreotragus	Klipspringer	—	—	×
Nonmammalian				
	Rock pigeon	—	1	—
	Ostrich eggshell fragments	—	57	—
	Varanus lizard	—	2	—
	Python	—	2	—
	Tortoise	—	4	—
	Land snail fragments	—	4	—

a Numerals, minimum number of individuals (at Pomongwe).

The fauna associated with the Charaman from Pomongwe cave in the Matopos Hills in Rhodesia displays some remarkable differences. Not only are there only two extinct species, but there is also only one carnivore and only 14 mammals in all. It is now abundantly clear that the Broken Hill deposits contain a fauna which is almost certainly older than that found with the Charaman from Rhodesia. There is therefore some reason to suspect that the Broken Hill cranium belongs to the maker of the Sangoan or perhaps even the later Acheulian Industry. The identity of the small Broken Hill artifact sample can no longer be considered Charaman.

Climatic Evidence during the Sangoan Period

Analysis of pollen samples from the Sangoan levels at Kalambo Falls suggests a decrease in the wooded environment which had developed during the period of the so-called "Transitional" floors. Unfortunately we are left in some doubt about which sample should be precisely associated with the Sangoan levels. However, the published interpretations (Clark 1964, 1966, 1969) suggest that the

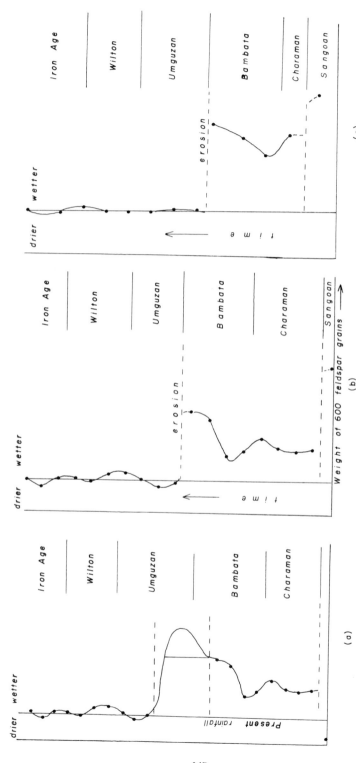

Fig. 48. Fluctuations in runoff from the granite slopes surrounding the Khami Waterworks site, as reflected in the weight of feldspar grains (after Bond 1957). The two sample columns taken from the Khami section revealed an erosional disconformity (b and c). Information on fluctuations during the missing period were inserted by Brain (1969d), based on evidence from the Redcliff site (see Fig. 80, page 218). The suggestion that the Sangoan period witnessed a "wetter" period here conflicts with evidence from Redcliff and Kalambo Falls. A diagram (a) summarizes the revised evidence (after Brain, 1969d).

147

appropriate samples reflect a vegetation similar to that of the present day with possibly even warmer and drier conditions at times.

An experiment carried out on the deposits from the Khami Waterworks in Rhodesia (Bond 1957) has also yielded tentative climatic interpretations. The deposits have accumulated as the result of surface decomposition of the surrounding granite slopes. The detritus has been transported by runoff and deposited in a natural basin now surrounded by bare granite exposures. This deposit is composed of clays and resistant elements such as quartz and feldspars. Since some quartz was undoubtedly introduced by man to the deposit during the manufacture of tools, this material is obviously not suitable as an indicator of runoff strength. Feldspar, on the other hand, is useless for flaking and is probably a reliable indicator of water transport without any human agency.

By weighing samples of feldspar grains taken from different depths in the deposit, it proved possible to plot a graph of fluctuating runoff rates. It is assumed that the carrying capacity of the runoff is directly related to rainfall: an increase in rainfall would increase the runoff, enabling it to carry heavier feldspar grains. Thus, increased sample weight equals increased rainfall.

The results of this ingenious experiment on two separate sample columns are shown in Fig. 48. The plotted curve would suggest that the climate of (supposed) Sangoan levels was considerably wetter than that of today and increased to the extent that the deposit surface was actually eroded. A decreased runoff allowed deposition to begin again during the Charaman period, but the climate remained wetter than the present.

The theoretical difficulties surrounding this interpretation have not been discussed, and it is unfortunate that no similar experiments have been carried out in the numerous granitic cave deposits of this area. Comparative results are urgently needed to test the assumptions basic to this experiment.

At present it is only possible to point out that the interpretations at Khami contradict those from Kalambo Falls, and a great deal of special pleading would be necessary to explain this contradiction. Until more experimental results become available, it will not be possible to do more than guess at the differences between the Acheulian and Sangoan climates.

The pollen spectrum from Mufo (van Zinderen Bakker and Clark 1962) suggest a cooler climate than the present, but produces no reliable indicators of rainfall. The spectrum is dated to about 38,000 B.P., and the associated industry has been called "Late Sangoan–Lower Lupemban."

THE PROBLEM OF ENVIRONMENTAL RESPONSE

It has been forcibly argued in several papers (Clark 1959a, 1962, 1964, 1965; Lee 1963; and others) that the changes in stone artifact design from the Acheulian to the Sangoan came about in response to changes in the environment of the woodland–savannah region of southern central Africa. The argument may be summarized as follows.

Increased rainfall at the end of the Acheulian period in southern central Africa gave rise to changes in the vegetation pattern. The open grassland–savannah that dominates much of the area became closed in with denser tree growth to form a closed woodland–savannah. Woodworking, which already formed part of the activities of the Acheulian population in this area, increased in importance during the so-called Acheulian–Sangoan "transitional" stage, when changes took place in the relative numbers of stone tools present on living floors. The "cutting tools" assumed to be closely related to butchering activities (hand-axes, cleavers, and knives) decrease to be replaced by numerous small flake scrapers assumed to be connected with woodworking. Sangoan samples other than Kalambo Falls appear to be dominated by picks, core axes, and choppers, and these also may be associated with woodworking activities or possibly with the digging of pits.

Unfortunately the available data do not provide very adequate support for this hypothesis. The "transitional" samples have not been shown to differ from the preceding Acheulian in any details although the pollen evidence apparently suggests a denser woodland environment at this period. By the time the Sangoan industry has appeared the pollen evidence for both Kalambo Falls and Mufo suggests dry open grassland–savannah. It may also be argued that abundant wood is available in all environments occupied by hunters in this period, including the semiarid regions to the south where no Sangoan development occurred. The relative abundance of trees need have no influence on the amount of woodworking. In the absence of wooden tools from Sangoan sites, we are forced to rely on the details of edge wear on tools. Since microscopic investigation of this phenomenon has not been possible on either Acheulian or Sangoan specimens, the interpretation placed on tool wear must remain speculative for the present. It is uncertain that the presence of abundant scrapers in an industry reflects woodworking activities.

By the same argument, the decline of the hand-axe, cleaver, and knife should reflect a decline in butchering activities, yet the evidence from Broken Hill suggests that large game animals were killed and eaten exactly as in the Acheulian period. Which tools replaced the hand-axe and cleaver in Sangoan times is far from certain.

A serious difficulty arises out of the lack of definition of the differences between the two complexes and nothing is known yet about the changes in raw material usage during this period. It is probable that more tools were made on blocks and cobbles in Sangoan times rather than on large flakes that form the basis of the "typical" flat Acheulian hand-axes and cleavers. It is quite possible that very many of the small surface discoveries labeled "Sangoan" could equally be regarded as Acheulian made of intractible raw materials. Several such samples exist in the southern regions where they have been called "Late Acheulian" (for example, Cornelia and Amanzi).

Although the causes of the typological changes continue to elude us, it is impossible to ignore the large body of evidence demonstrating that a distinct typological change took place north of the Limpopo River and there is little evidence

TABLE 21

Mason's Subdivision of the Pietersburg Industry [a]

Sites	Cave of Hearths	Mwulu's Cave	Oliboompoort Shelter	Rufus	Kalkbank	Aasvoelkop	Rooirand	Border Cave	Bushman Rock Shelter	Koedoesrand
Epi-Pietersburg	—	—	—	—	—	—	X	X	—	—
Upper Pietersburg	Bed 6–9	—	—	—	X	—	—	X	?	—
Middle Pietersburg	Bed 5	Bed 1–3	Bed 2	X	—	X	—	X	—	—
Lower Pietersburg	Bed 4	—	—	X	—	—	—	—	X	X

[a] From Mason (1957a).

proposed a three-phase chronological subdivision of the industry based on the stratified sequence for the Cave of Hearths, and other excavated samples have been classified within this framework, according to their typological similarity with either the Lower, Middle, or Upper Pietersburg sample from the Cave of Hearths. A summary of this classification is given in Table 21.

The samples from Border Cave (Cooke, Malan, and Wells 1945) have not been analyzed with the standard typology (Eggers 1970); data for Rufus have not been published; and Bushman Rock Shelter (Louw 1969) has been only partially analyzed. Without more adequate documentation these three sites can be included in Mason's framework only on a tentative basis. The standard typological list developed by Mason (1957a, 1962a, 1967b, 1968) for the industry (as

TABLE 22

Typology of Pietersburg Artifact Samples

Tools	Cores	Waste
Sidescraper	Opposed platform	Blade
Frontal scraper	Single platform (narrow)	Blade fragment
Burin	Single platform (broad)	Flake and fragment
Curve-backed knife	Prismatic blade core	
Utilized blade	Discoid core	
Utilized blade fragment	Levallois core	
Utilized flake	Adjacent platform	
	Miscellaneous and broken	

applied to Cave of Hearths, Mwulu, Olieboompoort, Aasvoelkop, and Koedoes-rand) is a model for systematic analysis. However, it obscures several important artifact attributes and has been altered repeatedly to accommodate a larger range of type subdivisions. Its greatest advantage is that it avoids any reference to functional terminology, but depends instead on overall artifact shape. Several terms are borrowed from plane and solid geometry to describe tool forms. This approach produces interesting new combinations of features, but makes it difficult to compare published figures with those from other sites that have been analyzed by a functional typology.

This chapter contains several new departures from the framework summarized in Table 21: some samples have been excluded on the grounds that they belong to a later complex (see Chapter 5), and the term *Pietersburg complex* is used here to embrace not only the Pietersburg industry of the Transvaal, but also numerous sites from elsewhere in South Africa that contain closely related artifact samples. This new grouping has been achieved by applying a standardized typology that differs in several details from that used by Mason (Sampson and Mason 1968).

THE STANDARD TYPOLOGY OF THE PIETERSBURG COMPLEX

The following list of "types" are arbitrary subdivisions of complex feature clusters, some of which undoubtedly grade into one another. The most important factor in the choice of types was that they should be easily recognized by as many other Paleolithic researchers as possible. Almost all the terms below have been used before by other workers.

Each analyzed sample is divided into cores and flakes. The flakes are then divided into two groups: tools (with secondary retouch and/or utilization) and waste (without visible traces of marginal damage). Further subdivision of these categories is given in Table 22.

Detailed descriptions of these types have already been published (Sampson 1968) and will not be repeated here. Schematic diagrams of each type are shown in Figs. 49 and 50. For some numerically larger samples, certain abundant types were measured: the length and breadth of each specimen was extracted and the breadth-to-length ratio calculated.

THE DISTRIBUTION OF INDUSTRIES

The complex is restricted to South Africa only and has not been found north of the Limpopo basin. Numerous surface occurrences have been reported from Botswana (Wayland 1954) and South-West Africa (Fock 1959; MacCalman 1962, 1963), but no excavated samples have been reported from this western portion of the country. Eighteen excavated sites can be grouped within the complex, and

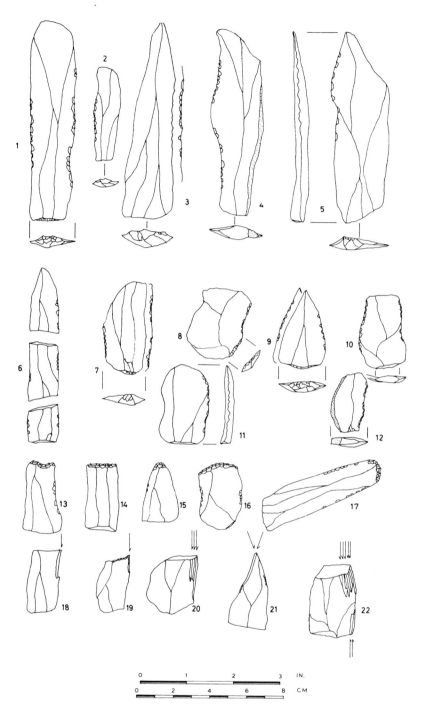

Fig. 49. Tool types used in the analysis of the Pietersburg complex: (1–5) whole trimmed–utilized blades; (6) trimmed–utilized blade fragments; (7–12) trimmed–utilized flakes; (13–17) frontal scrapers; (18–22) burins.

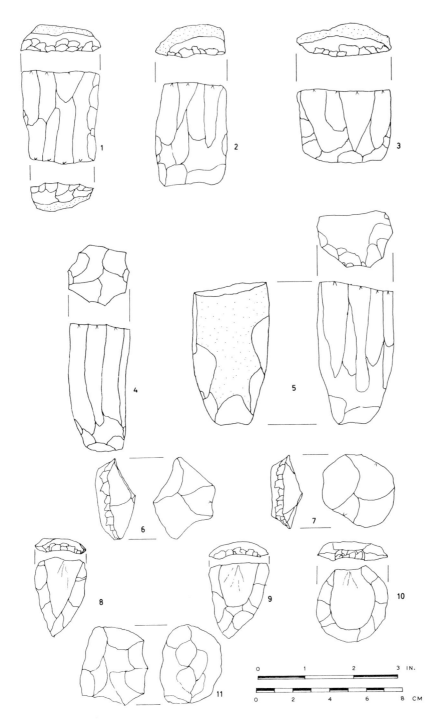

Fig. 50. Core types used in the analysis of the Pietersburg complex: (1) opposed platform; (2) narrow single platform; (3) broad single platform; (4) cylindrical; (5) prismatic; (6) discoid (irregular); (7) discoid; (8–10) Levallois; (11) adjacent platform.

155

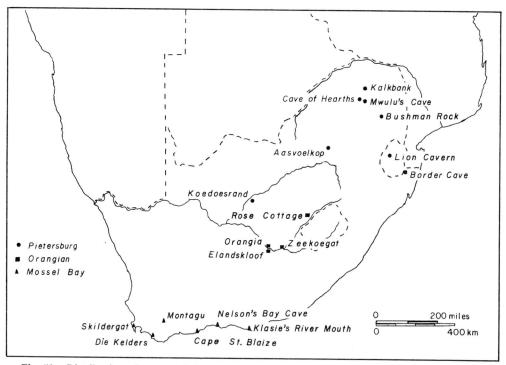

Fig. 51. Distribution of excavated sites ascribed to the three proposed industries of the Pietersburg complex. Although Koedoesrand has been published as Pietersburg (Mason 1962a), it should probably be grouped with the Orangian.

TABLE 23

Classification of Sites in the Pietersburg Complex

Pietersburg industry	Orangian industry	Mossel Bay industry
Cave of Hearths	Orangia I	Cape St. Blaize
Aasvoelkop	Elandskloof 13	Klasie's River Mouth
Rufus?	Zeekoegat 27a	Nelson's Bay Cave
Kalkbank	(surface sites)	Die Kelders
Border Cave	Rose Cottage Cave?	Skildergat
Koedoesrand		Montagu Cave?
Bushman Rock		
Castle Quarry?		
Lion Cavern?		
Mwulu's Cave		

156

numerous surface sites are also known (Fig. 51). The recorded localities fall into three major geographical divisions: the Transvaal highveld, the Orange River valley, and the southern Cape coast. The apparent geographical clustering of these sites is entirely artificial, being a reflection of varied research efforts in these areas. Undoubtedly, many thousands of sites remain to be discovered and analyzed from the intervening areas. Although the distribution data remain fragmentary, it may be assumed that the three groups represent the remains of hunter–gatherer activity in three distinct environments. Although all the sites may be loosely linked in terms of shared stone-flaking technology, they nevertheless represent human adaptations to quite different habitats. Indeed, as might be expected, sites within a single geographical group share a few typological characters which are not found in sites of the other groups. It is *tentatively* proposed that each of these groups be viewed as an "industry" within the Pietersburg complex and that the excavated sites be classified as given in Table 23.

The term "Pietersburg" is retained for the Transvaal group, whereas "Orangian" is adopted from the primary-context habitation at Orangia I on the middle Orange River and is used to describe samples in this region. "Mossel Bay" is a term applied to the material from Cape St. Blaize Cave near the town of that name on the southern Cape coast. The stratigraphy and typology of each group is discussed in the following sections.

THE PIETERSBURG INDUSTRY

The records of ten excavated sites provide data of extremely variable quality which, nevertheless, suggest that they can be tentatively grouped within an industry. Apparently, numerous surface occurrences are known, but none has been analyzed or published (Mason, personal communication), and there are a few dubious samples such as Waterval excavated from derived contexts (Partridge 1964) that may possibly belong within the industry.

Undoubtedly, the site most crucial for our understanding of this industry is the Cave of Hearths in the Makapan valley. First reported by van Riet Lowe (1938, 1943, 1948) it was subsequently excavated during several seasons' work, but the final site report has not yet been published. The stratigraphic sequence of deposits worked out by Mason is not known in detail, but it is apparent that the Pietersburg material overlies the Late Acheulian horizon of Bed 3 (Mason 1962a). It is evidently separated from Bed 3 by a dense scree horizon (Brain 1967e). At present, this is the only site providing adequate stratified evidence for the change from the Acheulian to Pietersburg complex. Since the sterile scree creates a void between the two horizons, nothing is known of their relationship. No typological comparison between Bed 3 and Bed 4 has been published, but a few interesting similarities are reported: the Bed 3 Acheulian contains an unusually high frequency of blades, and one "core" from the Pietersburg of Bed 4 is probably a hand-axe. Although the factors responsible for the disappearance of the Acheulian and its replacement by the Pietersburg must still be investigated, it is suspected that the latter has its technological roots in the local Late Acheulian.

The Cave of Hearths also provides the most complete evidence for the internal evolution of the Pietersburg industry: Beds 4 and 5 are reported to contain two phases, referred to by Mason as the Lower and Middle Pietersburg. Each of the two beds is some 5–6 ft deep and almost certainly represents an accumulation over a very long period. The subdivision of this 10–12 ft of deposits into the two beds is evidently based on a change in artifact content rather than a change in the nature of the sediments. Thus, we lack published evidence to suggest that the two "beds" are distinct geological strata. Each bed was excavated in 1-ft spits and the cultural debris from each of these has been labelled according to depth. Extreme care was exercised to remove spits in accordance with the dip and strike of the deposits, and material near a massively faulted area within both beds was rejected for analytical purposes (Mason, personal communication). Unfortunately, the artifactual content of each spit was not analyzed sepa-

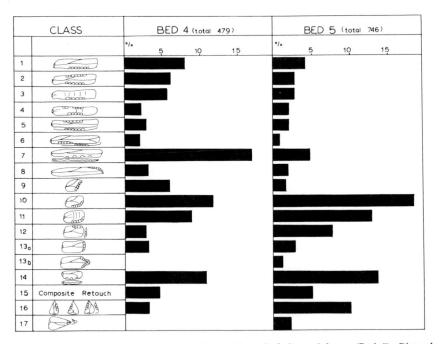

Fig. 52. Typological comparisons between the earlier (Bed 4) and later (Bed 5) Pietersburg samples from Cave of Hearths: (1–7) subtypes of utilized blades and blade fragments classified according to position of edge damage; (8) curve-backed blades and fragments; (9) denticulates; (11–12) utilized flakes; (13a) frontal scrapers; (13b) nosed frontal scrapers; (14) flakes with sinuous retouch; (15) flakes with composite retouch; (16) convergent flakes with utilization; (17) convergent flakes with trimmed–utilized tips.

rately, but several were combined to represent each bed. The percentage changes in tool-and-core types shown in Fig. 52 thus suggest two typologically distinct units. Slower and more subtle changes in typology through time are thus obscured, and it is impossible to tell whether there is a true cultural "break" between Beds 4 and 5. A recent spit-by-spit analysis (Eggers 1970) suggests that several trends present in Bed 4 are simply accelerated in Bed 5, and there is no abrupt typological change between the top spit of Bed 4 and the bottom of Bed 5. The 4–5 unit might therefore be viewed as the best available example of the gradual changes taking place within the Pietersburg stone technology over a very long period: no sharp division between an earlier and later phase can be supported, although there are obvious differences between these two periods if arbitrarily divided.

In its earlier phase, the Pietersburg industry contains a relatively high percentage of utilized flakes, most of which come from discoid or adjacent-platform cores, and very few triangular or convergent forms produced from single-platform cores with broad striking platforms. Together these make up about half the utilized pieces. The remainder of the tool list comprises blades and flake blades, some of which are extremely large, and many of which are broken into fragments. A few struck pieces are roughly fabricated into frontal scrapers or backed knives, but most specimens appear to be merely utilized. At the Cave of Hearths almost all this material is made of quartzite, with rare specimens in quartz, chert, or felsite (Fig. 53). Another excavated sample of the earlier phase is from Koedoesrand: a single-level open site in lydianite rubble (Mason 1962). This assemblage is made exclusively of lydianite, and resembles more closely the earlier phase of the Orangian industry. The site lies 120 miles north of Orangia and 430 miles southeast of the Cave of Hearths. A third Lower Pietersburg sample is reported from recent excavations at Bushman Rock Shelter. Eloff (1969) states that material coming from below the 5-ft level in this deep cave deposit closely resembles the Cave of Hearths Bed 4 sample, but no further details are available.

In the later phase of its development (for example Bed 5) the Pietersburg has undergone several typological changes: large blade production has decreased, giving place to high percentages of flakes (especially convergent forms), and broader, smaller flake blades. The overall decrease in the size of specimens is partially linked to the increased use of chert in the Bed 5 levels since this material cannot produce the large flakes and blades yielded from the most homogenous quartzite. The range of tool types made from these blades remain essentially the same, but the larger number of convergent flakes were used to make a variety of convergent frontal scrapers, some of which have secondary trimming restricted to the extreme tip of the specimen (Fig. 54).

The remaining sites ascribed to this industry appear to contain samples resembling the later phase only. At present, detailed numerical comparisons are possible only for Mwulu's Cave. This high-altitude cave contains nearly 5 ft of

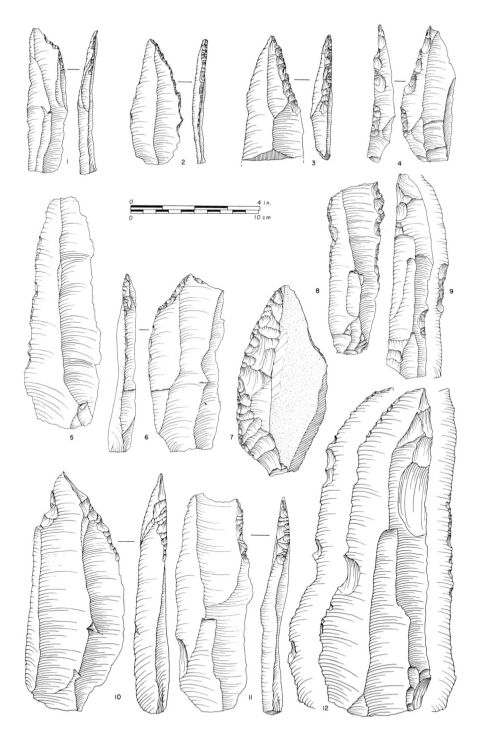

Fig. 53. Specimens from Cave of Hearths Bed 4 (Earlier Pietersburg): (1–4, 6, 10, 11) quartzite blades with blunting retouch on a localized portion of the margin near the tip; (5, 8, 9, 12) blades with coarse retouch and utilization scars on parts of the margin; (7) a unique sidescraper.

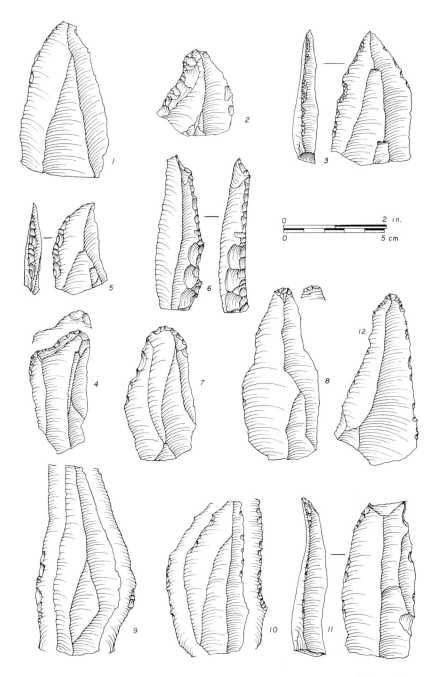

Fig. 54. Specimens from Cave of Hearths Bed 5: (1, 3, 9, 10) convergent flakes with marginal utilization; (2, 4) nosed scrapers; (5, 6) curved-backed knives with blunting retouch on one margin; (8, 12) convergent flakes with trimmed-utilized tips; (11) utilized blade fragment.

deposit in which Tobias (1949) recognized three strata of ash and sand separated by two sterile red sand layers. Stone artifact samples were recovered from each of the ash and sand layers, the lowest of which contains a large sample of the later phase of Pietersburg development. The material was recovered from three excavated spits within the lowest strata, which are evidently more than 3 ft thick in places. The three superimposed samples show remarkably consistent tool percentages and closely resemble those for the Cave of Hearths Bed 5. Quartzite is again the dominant raw material, and the length distribution of whole blades is very similar. Unfortunately, the Mwulu's Cave sample is too small for numerical comparisons.

Among the other listed northern Transvaal sites, Rufus is included by Mason (1962a), but the sample analysis has not appeared in print and detailed comparisons with other samples remain impossible. However, Aasvoelkop Shelter has been shown by Mason to resemble closely the Cave of Hearths Bed 5 materials. Details of the excavation and associations for Aasvoelkop and Rufus are not available.

The inclusion of Border Cave within the Pietersburg complex cannot be justified yet by published numerical data. Cooke *et al.* (1945) isolated a stratified series of three cultural layers within the deep deposits of this cave situated on the border of Swaziland and northern Natal. The lowest horizon ("at bedrock") was reported to contain flakes and blades with very rare secondary retouch and abundant convergent forms. Some of the blades were relatively long (8–9 inches), and the Levallois technique is mentioned. This sample the authors called the "basal industry," which Eggers (1970) has confirmed as closely related to the Cave of Hearths Bed 5, although felsite and not quartzite dominates the raw materials.

Two other Swaziland caves—Lion Cavern and the remarkable Castle Quarry —are reported by Beaumont to contain samples clearly resembling Bed 5, but again no numerical information has been released. Evidently, several other large samples have been excavated and numerous systematic surface collections were made in Swaziland (Boshier and Beaumont 1970), but details of this work are still awaited.

Although no consistent typological analysis of all the samples has been applied, the grouping into a single industry may be justified since Cave of Hearths Bed 5 has been used by each author as the standard sample for comparative purposes. Although future analysis will undoubtedly reveal minor differences between sites, it is already apparent that they display an impressive homogeneity in typological composition.

THE ORANGIAN INDUSTRY

The primary context floor at Orangia on the northern side of the Orange River is taken here as the name for the group of samples in the valley between Bethulie and Petrusville (Fig. 55). A total of 4 excavated samples and 18 surface collections have been recovered from this area which is to be inundated by

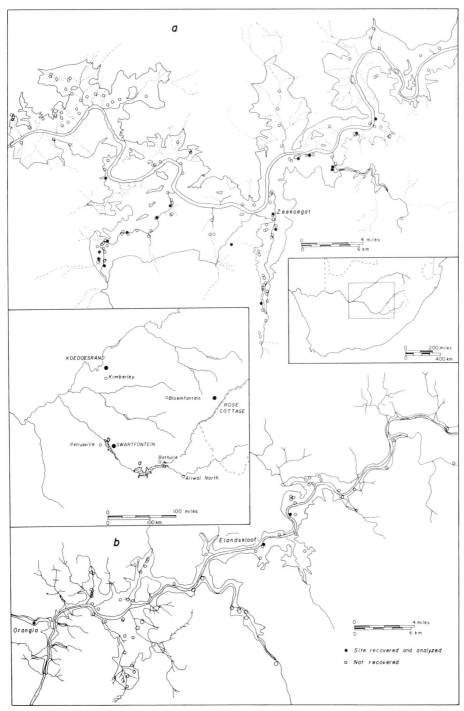

Fig. 55. Distribution maps of Orangian sites in the floodbasins of two dams in the Orange River scheme area. (After Sampson 1968.)

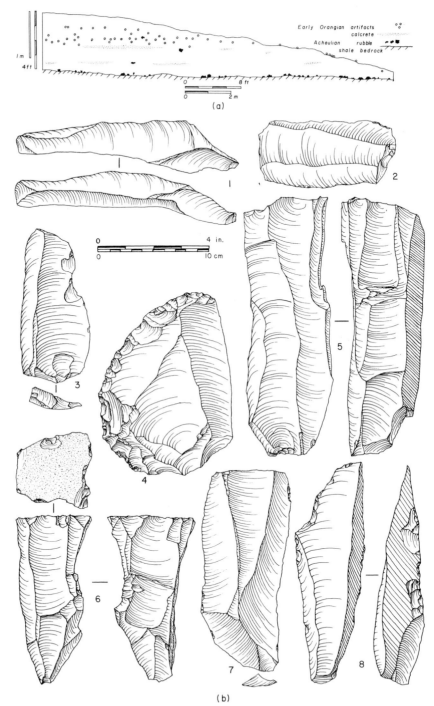

Fig. 56. (a) Section through Elandskloof, showing the position of earlier Orangian specimens overlying an Acheulian horizon and separated from it by sterile sands. (b) Earlier Orangian artifacts from Elandskloof: (1, 2, 3) blade fragments; (4) sidescraper; (5, 6) prismatic blade cores; (7, 8) utilized blade fragments.

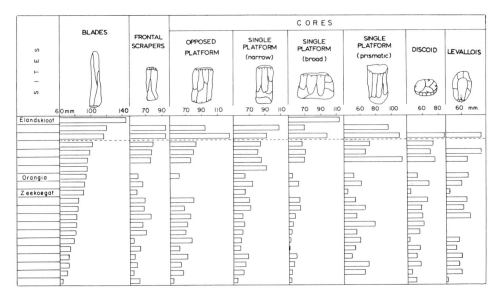

Fig. 57. Mean lengths of blades, frontal scrapers, and various core types from Orangian sites in the Orange River scheme. The dotted line is an arbitrary subdivision into earlier and later phases based on artifact size and minor differences in typology. The subdivision into two phases cannot be adequately supported by stratified field evidence.

two dams. A further 260 surface scatters were recorded but could not be collected for analysis. The identity of these abandoned sites was ascertained by searching for tool-and-core types in the scatter and comparing the range of types for each scatter with that from excavated sites. Their inclusion within the Orangian group is therefore based on the presence or absence of types and not on numerical analysis (Sampson 1968).

The distribution of this industry beyond the limits of the intensively searched area remain unknown since no undistorted samples have been taken from adjacent territory. The selected surface collections from Cradock and Swartfontein may be readily associated with an early phase of the Orangian on the presence–absence of types in the collections, and the Koedoesrand sample may belong in this group rather than the Pietersburg industry for same reasons.

The presently known distribution of the Orangian suggests that it represents the technical debris of hunter–gatherer groups adjusted to a semiarid environment. It differs in several respects from the samples of northern Transvaal and Swaziland. Deep caves are extremely rare in the Karroo, and single-level occupation near streams are the commonest form of archaeological occurrence. These are frequently disturbed or scattered by erosion of the stream banks and multi-layer sites are absent, so that the chronological development of the industry is poorly recorded. The only sites located away from streams—some are miles from

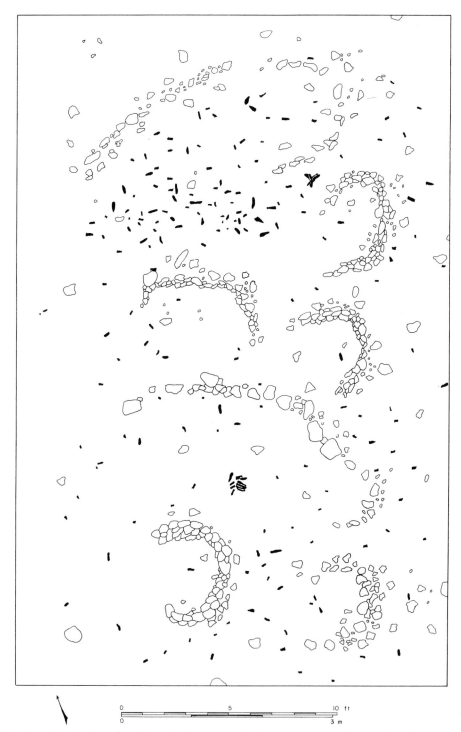

Fig. 58. Distribution of utilized blades and blade fragments in relation to dolerite boulder structures on the primary-context floor at Orangia.

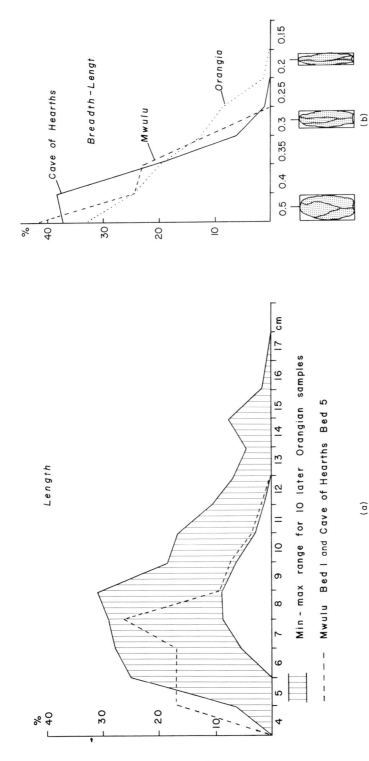

Fig. 59. Metrical comparisons between whole blades from the Pietersburg (Mwulu's Cave and Cave of Hearths) and later Orangian samples. The length distribuitions (a) and breadth-length ratios (b) of blades from the two Pietersburg sites are almost identical and are shown as a single curve.

167

any water source—are the dense surface scatters adjacent to raw material out-crops. Indurated shale (lydianite) was "quarried" by these groups from at least 20 outcrops in the surveyed area, and this rock type was used exclusively for ar-tifacts at all sites. The presence of this hard isotropic rock in virtually unlimited quantities has influenced various features of the Orangian industry; single sites tend to contain enormous quantities of flaked material, much of which shows no sign of utilization or retouch. Presumably, a freshly struck blade or flake would be selected from a heap of flaked pieces, used, then abandoned. If the edge be-came dulled before its task was completed, another fresh specimen was selected from the heap. As lydianite occurs in very large blocks at the outcrop, there are almost no restrictions on the maximum possible size of struck pieces. Thus, the size of specimens at any open site will be determined by cultural tradition *or* distance from the nearest lydianite outcrop.

Elandskloof 13 provides the only evidence for a multiple-phase development of the industry and also demonstrates that the early Orangian overlies a Late Acheulian phase (Fig. 56). Like the Pietersburg industry, nothing is known of the cultural connections between the Orangian and the preceding Acheulian. The Elandskloof excavations reveal a gap in the prehistoric record between these two horizons, which are separated by at least 2 ft of sterile silts. What cul-tural changes took place during this interval remain unknown. On typological grounds it appears that the local late Acheulian contains a high percentage of flake blades and the full range of core types found at early Orangian sites. Like the Pietersburg, it is possible that the Orangian has its technical roots in the local Acheulian. The division of the two Orangian samples from Elandskloof into an early and late phase can be supported on stratigraphic grounds, but both individual samples are too small to provide reliable percentage data for di-rect comparisons. However, measurements of the two samples show that the late phase obviously contains more smaller pieces—a trend similar to that in the Pie-tersburg industry.

Any attempt to arrange these unstratified samples from this area into early and later phases cannot be easily justified on typological grounds. The three samples published as Stage I in the proposed sequence (Sampson 1968) contain no burins or trimmed points, whereas the other sites attributed to Stage II con-tain rare specimens of both types. The Stage I samples contain numerous very large specimens of all types which are not present in Stage II sites, but no clear division into two "stages" based on artifact size alone can be demonstrated by the metric data (Fig 57). Since Elandskloof provides some stratigraphic evidence for a decrease in overall artifact size with time, it is probable that a single, grad-ually changing industry is present, and no clear-cut chronological subdivision is possible. It is likely that different sites were occupied at various stages during the slow development, but the variation of sites based on artifact size should not be taken as a true chronological sequence. Undoubtedly, artifact size was par-tially determined by the distance between the site and the nearest lydianite out-crop, and other factors such as specialized tasks may have occasionally dictated the frequencies of large or small trends on the site.

Of the four excavated sites, only Orangia has yielded a primary-context floor (Fig. 58). About half of the original encampment remained intact in compact silts flanking a small stream flowing into the Orange River. The site is located near the entrance to a narrow ravine, with obvious strategic advantages for the ambush of game animals. The sealed remnant of the floor revealed the presence of seven structures composed of large blocks and cobbles partly enclosing dense artifact scatters, some of which were core heaps and bundles of utilized blades. These scatters lay on the leeward side of the boulders, suggesting that they were arranged to anchor thorn-bush windbreaks for daytime use when winds gust down the ravine from the north. The other five structures were smaller semicircular walls of cobbles lining the east walls of hollows evidently excavated by hand from the original land surface. As these hollows contained almost no artifacts, they may represent sleeping hollows designed for protection against easterly cold air currents known to result from a predawn temperature inversion in the ravine. The extant hollows could accommodate about six adults. Since numerous dolerite cobbles occurred among the disturbed artifacts in the destroyed half of the site, it is assumed that other structures were wrecked by erosion. A conservative estimate for the group size would be about twelve individuals.

It thus appears that the Orangian differs from the Pietersburg industry in raw material usage and the exclusive use of open-site occupation. Both differences merely reflect adjustments to local environmental (particularly geological) conditions. However, several typological differences are also apparent: the very rare occurrence of trimmed points with rounded or thinned butts is a distinct feature of the Orangian industry; true burins are also present; most Orangian sites yield more blades, blade fragments, and blade cores; most whole-blade samples from Orangian sites show that longer, narrower blades were produced in greater quantities (Fig. 59); lower percentages of flakes were produced, and the triangular, convergent flakes (so common in the later phases of the Pietersburg) are extremely rare in the Orangian; the Levallois technique was used at almost all Orangian sites, but is not recorded in the Pietersburg industry. An interesting feature common to both industries is the high frequency of blade fragments from the butt end of the blade. This may suggest that blades were deliberately snapped, and many of the thinner-tipped sections were removed from the site for use elsewhere.

The typological analysis thus reveals that the two groups belong to the same broad technological tradition, and both industries appear to have undergone some reduction in artifact size through time. The underlying causes of this process remain to be investigated. Although a common technology suggests that both groups belong to the same complex, there are several detailed differences that preclude the grouping of all the sites within a single industry.

Finally, the inclusion of Rose Cottage Cave in the Orangian should be considered as a provisional classification only. The fact that it is a cave site situated in a well-watered montane habitat suggests that a close association with the Orangian is unlikely. Furthermore, no numerical analysis of the excavated material has appeared and direct comparisons are impossible. Malan (1952) published a brief description of the deposit resting on a rubble, presumed to be close to bed-rock. The following features of the sample are mentioned: very advanced Leval-lois flakes and blades dominate the assemblage; these are mostly 5–8 inches long; points and sidescrapers are very scarce; secondary retouch is irregular and re-stricted to the margins; trimming on the bulbar surface is rare and bulbar reduction is absent; raw materials include lydianite, sandstone, and chalcedony. Although this limited description fits the Orangian closely, its association with the group must await systematic analysis of the excavated collections. The basal sample is separated from the next overlying assemblage by 18 inches of silts. The short description of this later horizon also fits that of the Orangian, but a shift in raw-material usage is recorded; more chert, chalcedony, and agate was used, and artifacts were smaller.

THE MOSSEL BAY INDUSTRY

The Cape St. Blaize Cave at Mossel Bay first was excavated in 1888 by George Leith (1898) and takes historical precedent as a name site for the group. This se-lected and poorly documented material was distributed among various museums and a small part of Leith's collection was published as the *Mosselbaaisekultuur* by van Hoepen (1932). Later, four undistorted samples were excavated by Goodwin and Malan (1935) from the remaining deposits, thus providing ade-quate material for comparison with other sites.

Regrettably this third group is the most difficult to compare, since detailed analysis of excavated samples are either absent or have not been published yet. Work is still in progress at Nelson's Bay Cave and Die Kelders. All five sites grouped in this industry are large caves located in the seacliffs of the southern Cape coast close to the shore (Fig. 60). Only Skildergat is located about 1 mile from the modern strand. During the period of the Mossel Bay occupation of this area, the active shore line stood at a much lower level so that each site over-looked a broad coastal plain, now inundated by the sea since the post glacial re-treat. The Mossel Bay industry may be expected to reflect local hunter–gatherer adaptations to a wetter, cooler, winter-rainfall habitat with additional food sources at the sea margin. The most abundant raw material in the area is a quartzitic sandstone, which was used almost exclusively. Outcrops extend for miles, so that isolated "quarries" do not occur, as on the lydianite formations on the Orange River. Evidently quartzite cobbles from storm beaches were some-times preferred as raw materials since the weathered cortex (found on most surface outcrops) has been battered away, leaving a fresh, unweathered lump suit-able for transport. The quality of this sandstone varies from place to place; occasionally it is friable and less isotropic so that the production of very long, slender blades becomes impossible. Thus, numerical proportions for this industry may vary from site to site according to the quality of the local sandstone.

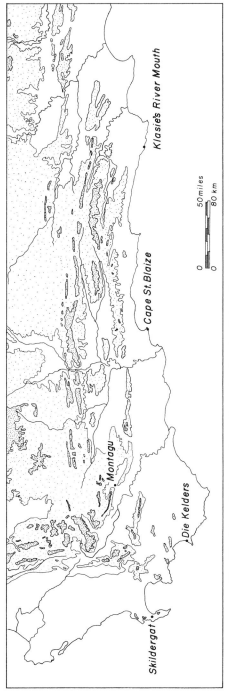

Fig. 60. Map of the southern Cape showing localities of excavated sites yielding samples of the Mossel Bay industry.

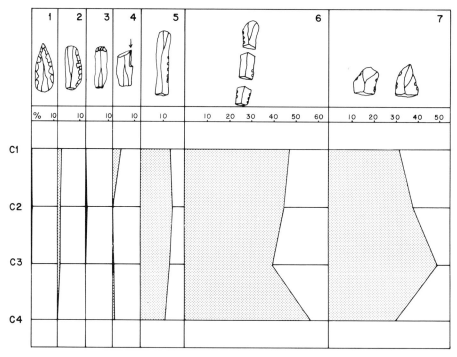

Fig. 61. Vertical distribution of tool types in Cape St. Blaize Cave, Mossel Bay: (1) trimmed points; (2) sidescrapers; (3) endscrapers; (4) burins; (5) trimmed or utilized blades; (6) trimmed or utilized blade fragments; (7) trimmed or utilized flakes. (After Avery and Schweitzer 1969.)

The four samples from Cape St. Blaize Cave are dominated by quartzite with very scarce specimens of quartz, silcrete, chalcedony, and lydianite (Fig. 61). As the raw material usage, tool-type percentages, and range of cores is very similar for each sample, there is no indication that they belong to different phases of the industry. Layer C2 (second from the top) contains a Levallois core and a unifacial trimmed point not found in the other levels, but there are too few to justify a subdivision of the deposit.* Indeed, Keller (1969a) has treated the entire collection as a single sample. Unfortunately this obscures an important trend demonstrated by Goodwin and Malan (1935): the struck pieces from the lowest level (C4) include more large pieces than C1 at the top of the sequence. Clearly, the same trend already recognized in the Pietersburg and Orangian industries was also operating within this industry. However, no examples of the very large blades (200 mm found in the early phases of the other industries) occur at Cape St. Blaize. Indeed, no specimens comparable with the enormous

---

*I am indebted to Messrs. F. Schweitzer and G. Avery of the South African Museum, Cape Town, for their analysis of the Cape St. Blaize Cave samples.

blade from the Cave of Hearths Bed 4 or Elandskloof are found in any of the Mossel Bay caves. The local quartzitic sandstone is, however, capable of producing comparable blades; a small unpublished surface sample from Flesh Bay has yielded several specimens over 200 mm long made of this material.* It is therefore possible that Cape St. Blaize represents a relatively late stage in the industry's development. Comparisons with data from the other industries (see Figs. 52 and 57, pages 158 and 165) suggest that the Mossel Bay differs from the Orangian and Pietersburg industries in a few important typological details: snapped blade fragments take up almost half of the total tool kit; utilized flakes form a much lower percentage; and triangular, convergent flakes are relatively scarce.

An undoubtedly more complete record of the industry's development is represented by the massive accumulation at Klasie's River Mouth caves where a total of 50 ft of deposit has been excavated by J. Wymer (personal communication). Although the analysis of this sequence was completed in 1969, the site monograph has not been published and no numerical data are therefore available. At least 30 ft of mixed sand-with-shells deposit yielded an industry of quartzitic sandstone that resembles in many details that from Cape St. Blaize. This long sequence probably begins in the Klasie's River Mouth cave system soon after the retreat of the sea level from its 20-ft maximum, represented by a distinctive beach shingle on the floor of the cave. The overlying deposits were excavated in 1-ft spits and the contents of each spit subjected to an individual analysis. Wymer recognizes two stages in this long development, based on two definite sequences in different caves. For the excavated layers from the earlier stage the whole blade sample from the bottom to the top layer shows a decrease in size (Fig. 62), and the trend toward small specimens continues in the second stage of the industry's development. Analysis of the very large core samples for these layers has also revealed that blade cores are extremely abundant, whereas the discoid technique is rarely used and the Levallois technique is absent.

The lowermost excavated horizon for Skildergat has been included in this sample on the basis of Jolly's description (1948), and brief inspection of the undescribed sample excavated from the same horizon in 1963 by B. Anthony. A brittle, friable sandstone has been used, and, obviously, fewer blades were produced from this material, there being a higher frequency of flakes struck from adjacent platform and discoid cores. Few specimens show rough irregular trimming of the margins, and utilized pieces are relatively rare. Materials from Nelson's Bay Cave (Inskeep 1965a) and Die Kelders (Schweitzer 1970) are still being analyzed and cannot be compared at present.

The presence of this industry at Montagu Cave, overlying the Acheulian horizons, has not been suggested previously. Keller (1966) proposes that the material from the upper 7 ft of deposit be regarded as Howiesonspoort. However, the lower levels (immediately above the Acheulian) contain all the elements found

*Located in the archaeological collections of the South African Museum, Cape Town.

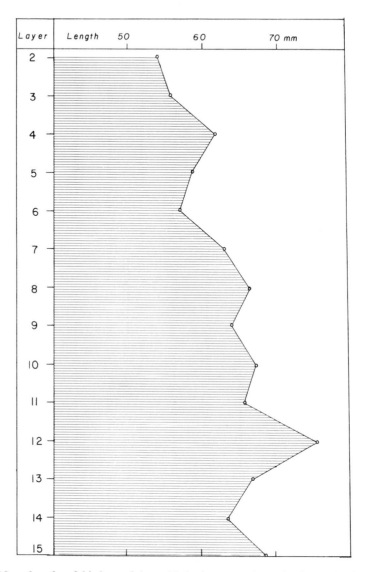

Fig. 62. Mean lengths of blades and large blade fragments from the lowest levels of Klasie's River Mouth. A trend toward smaller blades is apparent here and in the Pietersburg and Orangian sites to the north (J. Wymer, personal communication).

at Cape St. Blaize and few of the characteristic features of the Howiesonspoort industry (see Chapter 6). The large and very thick trimmed segments found in the Montagu layers cannot be regarded as "backed crescents," nor can the curve-backed knives. Although detailed comparisons remain to be worked out, it is apparent that true Howiesonspoort materials may occur only in the *upper 4 ft* of the Montagu deposits. Below this the typological features of the material (overlying the Acheulian) suggest a much closer relationship with the Mossel Bay industry.

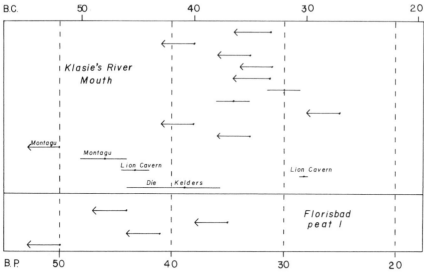

Fig. 63. Radiocarbon readings from sites of the Pietersburg complex compared with those of Florisbad peat I. It is unlikely that any of these readings reflect the true age of their associated artifact samples, which are all older than the upper dating limits of the radiocarbon technique.

It is apparent, therefore, that the Mossel Bay industry is extremely poorly documented at present, and its homogeneity cannot be wholly accepted until more detailed analysis is published. Preliminary analyses of at least three other sites have revealed considerable variation in flaking techniques (R. G. Klein, personal communication), but this is probably related to variability in the quality of raw materials and their cultural significance cannot be assessed for want of more data.

CHRONOLOGY OF THE PIETERSBURG COMPLEX

That the complex is younger in age than the Acheulian has been adequately demonstrated by the stratigraphy of the Cave of Hearths, Elandskloof, and (tentatively) Montagu Cave in each of the three industrial regions. Its stratigraphic position below the Bambata complex is demonstrated at several sites and will be discussed in detail in the following chapter.

Its absolute chronology is documented by a rapidly increasing body of carbon-14 dates. Those available at present are plotted in Fig. 63 together with locality data and standard deviations. Several of these results require comments:

1. *Cave of Hearths:*

    Bed 4   C-926   16,810 ± 960 B.P. (14,861 B.C.)
               C-927   11,700 ± 610 B.P. (9750 B.C.)

Both samples were derived from organic matter extracted from a dark ashy sub-stance in the middle levels of Bed 4. Their readings were obtained during the early stages of development of the carbon-14 dating laboratory technique by Libby (1954). As no charcoal was present in the sample and knowledge of sample contamination was fairly limited at that time, these readings have been rejected by Mason (1962a). It is unfortunate that no further attempts have been made to date Bed 4. Evidence from Bushman Rock Shelter suggests that the Lower Pietersburg is older than 50,000 B.P. and may be at the extreme limit of the carbon-14 dating capacity (Mason, 1969c):

Bed 5   C-924   11,600 ± 700 B.P. (9650 B.C.)

This date was processed at the same time as the others and the sample was a similar unidentified ash substance without trace of visible charcoal. A sample from several feet higher in the sequence yielded an older date. This is rejected for the same reason quoted above.

2. Klasie's River Mouth:

Stage 1. As yet undocumented readings from the lowest layers of this sequence are: >31,200 overlaid by >38,000 B.P. In still later levels of this stage the sequence of readings is: >33,000; >31,000; >31,200 B.P. Details of the sample materials are not available. The repeated dating inversions and "greater than" values detract from their usefulness. All that can be said at present is that Stage 1 is definitely older than 38,000 B.P. Indeed it is likely that this phase is *considerably* older: a similar reading has been obtained for Stage 2 (see below) and this lowest layer of the sequence is resting directly on the beach shingle ascribed to the "20-ft emergence." Absolute dating of this widespread raised beach level (Mabbutt 1957) cannot be ascertained yet: *Mytilus* shell from a 6-m beach at Hout Bay was dated to 47,100 (+2800, −2100) B.P. (GrN-5804). Shell from a 4-m beach level at Melkbosstrand yielded 43,200 (+2000, −1500) B.P. (GrN-5803), and shell from the 3-m level at Nahoon was dated to 29,090 (+410, −390) B.P. (SR-83), (Deacon 1966b). It is likely that these date retreat stages from the 20-ft maximum, which might predate any of the above sites. *If* the 20-ft emergence on the South African coast was formed in response to the same glacial fluctuation that caused the formation of the 8-m beach level in the Mediterranean, western European, and northern African Atlantic coasts, its maximum may be dated to as much as 90,000 B.P. Stearns and Thurber (1965) have obtained dates of this order by the $^{230}U–^{234}U$ method from shells of an 8-m beach at several localities in the Mediterranean.

Stage 2. This is a series of sand and shell layers that overlie Stage 1 uncon-formably. Readings from lower to higher levels are: 30,000 (+1600, −1400) B.P.; 30,450 (+1600, −1400) B.P.; >25,000 B.P. At levels considered to be still later in the depositional sequence, dates of >38,000 and >33,000 B.P. were obtained. Again, the dates conflict with the stratigraphy, thus weakening their value. There is a strong possibility that the entire sequence predates 38,000 B.P.

3. *Montagu Cave:*

178 cm depth	GrN-5134	>50,000 B.P.
	GrN-4728	45,900 ± 2,100 B.P. (43,950 B.C.)

As suggested, the lower layers of this material, reported as "Howiesonspoort" have more features in common with the Mossel Bay industry. Unfortunately it is not yet known whether the two dates quoted are from the lower levels of the Post-Acheulian deposits. A third date, presumably from the upper levels, appears to conform with the known age of the Howiesonspoort assemblage.

4. *Lion Cavern:*

335–410 cm at cave mouth	GrN-5313	43,200 ± 1200 B.P. (41,250 B.C.)
224–290 cm on bedrock in cave	GrN-5020	28,130 ± 260 B.P. (26,180 B.C.)

Another sample reported by Dart and Beaumont (1970) as coming from "further away from the Hill face" (Y-1827) yielded a date of 22,280 ± 400 B.P. and another much younger date (Y-1713), which is rejected by the excavators. No detailed section or information on this site is available yet.

5. *Die Kelders:*

lower layer	GX-1717	31,800 (+5000, −2900) B.P. (29,850 B.C.)
upper layer	GX-1716	11,200 ± 700 B.P. (9250 B.C.)

Schweitzer (1970) states that the two layers are separated by a sterile sand. The readings were obtained from bone samples. The possibility that the sample from the upper layer belongs to a later complex is discussed in Chapter 6.

In summary, it is apparent that the carbon-14 information for the complex is still fragmentary and in many cases surrounded by confusion. At present there is partial evidence to support a date of >50,000 B.P. for Bushman's Rock and (possibly) at Montagu and Rose Cottage caves. A date of 60,000 B.P. or older for the Lower Pietersburg would not appear unreasonable at present. Most of the later dates are suspect and the correct terminal date for the complex cannot be determined since our information is still incomplete.

ASSOCIATED HOMINID REMAINS

Of all the listed sites, only Klasie's River Mouth has yielded fragmentary human skeletal remains. Cranial fragments and teeth were found *in situ* in the Stage 2 levels only. As the analysis of this material has not been released yet, it has not been possible to confirm their superficial resemblance to the more complete cranium from Florisbad.

Florisbad is a deep accumulation of coarse sandy strata intercalcated with black brown organic clays and peats situated above a complex of hot mineral spring vents. Dreyer (1938) conducted extensive but poorly documented diggings in the spring mound near two spring "eyes" that produced abundant fossil fauna, artifacts, and a human cranium with part of the face and maxilla (Dreyer 1936, 1947). His rather confused account of the stratigraphic context of this specimen prompted better-controlled excavation in an adjacent deposit not so severely disrupted by the periodic eruptions from the spring vents (Meiring 1956). The detailed sequence of undisturbed deposits is shown in Fig. 64.

The human fragments were found buried on the edge of a fossil spring "eye," of white sand which had penetrated peat I but had ceased to flow before the deposition of peat II. The cranium was found at the same depth as, but not actually *in situ* in this deposit. The spring "eye" and its contents are therefore older than peat II and broadly contemporary with or slightly younger than peat I, which has furnished a series of conflicting dates: GrN-4208 >48,900; C-850 >41,000; L-271 >35,000; Y-103 >44,000. It is probably reasonable to assume that the specimen is older than 50,000 b.p., and therefore broadly contemporary with the Pietersburg complex. Besides the skull, the white spring sands contained a rich fauna, several dolerite flakes described by Meiring (1956), and numerous dolerite pieces erroneously described as artifacts. Several polyhedral and adjacent-platform flake cores and a few spheroids were also recovered. This very small sample (less than 20 pieces) made of coarse intractible dolerite displays absolutely no resemblance to other samples of the Pietersburg complex. Several wood fragments were also found, including one piece claimed by Clark (1955b) to resemble the systematically ground and roughened handle of a throwing stick, similar to those of throwing clubs made by the Australian aborigines. Until a large stone artifact sample is recovered from the peat I level, the true cultural affinities of the skull cannot be adequately discussed. Van Riet Lowe was given material from the site which included a 250-mm long trimmed point of lydianite, but no recorded depth for the specimen has survived. Its sheer size suggests more affinity with an early phase of the Pietersburg complex, but without further records of its true position in the site, it remains no more than a frustrating hint.

The skull fragments described by Dreyer and Ariëns Kappers (1935) include some 15 fragments, reconstructed to form part of an adult calvarium; most of the right frontal and parts of both temporals conjoin with the upper part of the occipital. Sufficient face fragments exist to allow reconstruction of the right orbit, nasal aperture and maxilla with a partly erupted M^3 (?) and the root sockets of M^2. Isolated teeth were also recovered, but never fully described. The reconstruction suggests a well-rounded cranial profile with a relatively low vault and slightly curved frontal region. Brow ridges are present but not well developed, and the orbits are subrectangular in outline. The fragmentary maxilla suggests that the individual was not prognathous but possessed a relatively flat small face. However, this appearance may be largely the result of reconstruction guesswork since the maxillae conjoin with the other facial fragments at only one

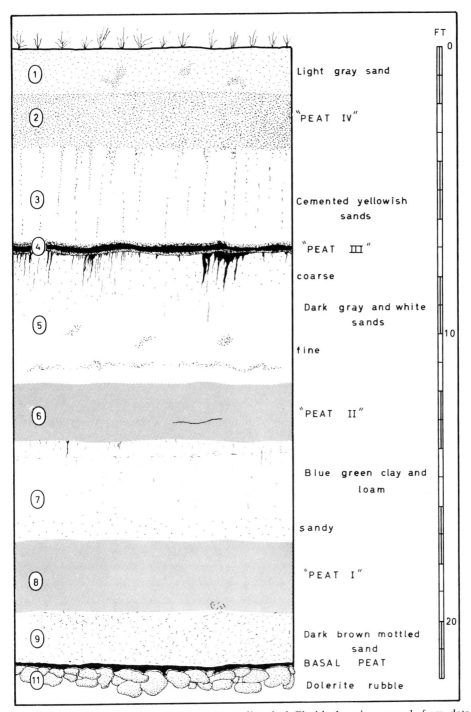

Text labels within figure:

1 — Light gray sand

2 — "PEAT IV"

3 — Cemented yellowish sands

4 — "PEAT III"

coarse

Dark gray and white sands

5

fine

6 — "PEAT II"

Blue green clay and loam

7

sandy

8 — "PEAT I"

9 — Dark brown mottled sand

BASAL PEAT

11 — Dolerite rubble

FT
0
10
20

Fig. 64. Reconstructed section through the undisturbed Florisbad spring mound, from data in van Zinderen Bakker (1957) and Meiring (1956). The Florisbad skull and associated dolerite flakes came from a dead spring eye which had penetrated peat I, but was partly capped by Layer 7. The Florisbad sample of the Bambata complex (see Chapter 5) came from a few inches below peat II.

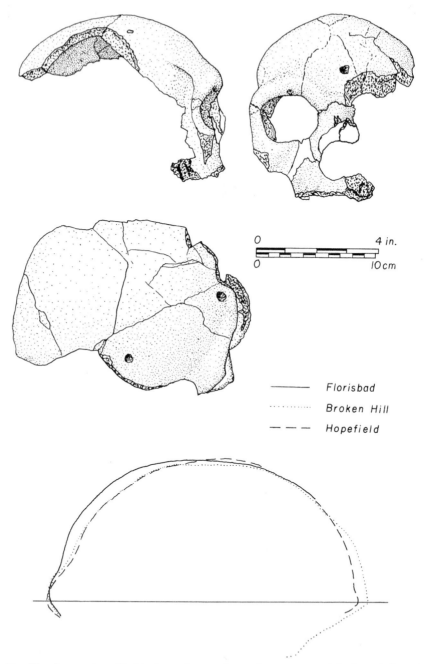

Fig. 65. The fragmentary Florisbad cranium, redrawn from a cast: right lateral frontal and top views. The sagittal section (below) demonstrates that this specimen has greater frontal curvature and less pronounced supraorbital ridges than the essentially similar Saldanha and Broken Hill skulls.

isolated point. The skull bones are relatively thick, and two circular punctate marks occur on the right and left frontals. These are both about 7 mm in diameter and are spaced about 9 cm apart. Although similar in appearance to the punctate marks appearing on the skull of hominid (Sk-54), from Swartkrans (Chapter 2, page 68), both the size and spacing of the Florisbad marks are too large to suggest that they represent large carnivore canine marks. The largest lion in Brain's (1970) measured sample has an upper canine spacing of only 81 mm. The nature of the punctate depressions also suggests that the direction of force that caused the depression on the skull surface came from almost opposite directions. Neither depression seems to have penetrated to the interior of the thick bone, and the cause of these marks requires further investigation.

The status of the Florisbad hominid has been debated extensively. Dreyer (1936, 1947) insisted that it represented an ancestral form of the modern South African Bushmen, a view partially supported by Kappers' analysis of the frontal area of the endocranial cast. This latter case is unfortunately weakened by an ambiguous orientation of the cast (Dreyer and Ariëns Kappers 1935). Drennan (1935, 1937) was the first to propose that it represented a local form of Neanderthal, although possibly ancestral to modern Man. Singer (1958) suggested that it has more in common with the Broken Hill–Hopefield physical type, and that all three should be regarded as neanderthaloid forms (Fig. 65). Only Galloway (1937) has suggested that the Florisbad specimen may represent an *intermediate* form between the Broken Hill–Hopefield type and true *Homo sapiens sapiens,* represented by later fossils from South Africa (see Chapters 5 and 6). The most obvious features supporting his argument may be seen in the cranial profiles shown in Fig. 65: the frontal region is more convex and the brow ridges are less massive than those of the other two fossils. These, together with the apparent foreshortening of the face, would suggest that the Florisbad specimen differs from the other two. All the features suggest a closer affinity with modern Man.

The gross features of the Florisbad skull have been summarized by Galloway as: "a Neanderthal skull with a modern face," and it is clearly not a "typical" Neanderthal form. Unfortunately, the specimen has been almost completely ignored during the last 30 years by students of fossil Man, presumably because its "intermediate" morphology does not lend itself to any straightforward taxonomic classification. Certainly, doubts about its reconstruction, associations and circumstances of discovery will persist, but there can be little doubt that the specimen represents a part of the southern African population which, before 50,000 B.P. was already displaying certain cranial trends that later became distinctive features of the modern human population.

ASSOCIATED FAUNA

Fossil mammalian faunas were recovered in direct association with artifact samples from several sites: Cave of Hearths, Bushman Rock, Klasie's River Mouth, Nelson's Bay Cave, Die Kelders, and Florisbad.

Regrettably, only unreliable species lists are available for Cave of Hearths and Florisbad (H. B. S. Cooke 1964). The Cave of Hearths list (Table 22) includes material from both earlier and later beds so that it fails to provide a true picture of the animals associated with the Pietersburg levels. The Florisbad list (Dreyer and Lyle 1931) is also a mixture of species found in the spring eye, peat I and below peat II. Its usefulness is further reduced since the list of artiodactyls is incomplete.

Of the 31 species listed from Florisbad, only 18 (58%) represent animals still living today. Among the extinct forms are two horses *Equus plicatus* and *E. helmei*; a pig *Stylochoerus compactus* (Ewer 1957a), giant buffalo, *Bubalus bainii*; a waterbuck *Kobus venterae*; an unknown species of roan; a giant wildebeest *Alcelaphus helmei*; two hartebeest *Connochaetes laticornutus* and *C. antiguus* (Hoffman 1953), *Lunatoceras misum*, the gazelle *Gazella bondi*; a hare *Pedetes hagenstadi*; marsh mongoose *Atilax paludinosus*, making a total of 13 extinct species.

It is interesting to note that the pig, giant buffalo, wildebeest, and one hartebeest is also found at the Acheulian site of Cornelia 200 miles northeast of Florisbad. Although the species list is incomplete and no numerical information has been released, it is apparent that Florisbad contains a larger number of extinct species than the Cave of Hearths list (with only 9). It is therefore possible that the Florisbad skull belongs to a very early phase of the Pietersburg or possibly even predates its first appearance.

The only other site with a published list of associated fauna is the open site of Driefontein near Cradock in the northern Cape Province. A small selected sample of artifacts was recovered from 25-ft depth in a coarse gray-green sand lying on shale bedrock. As the tools and mammalian fossils were recovered in 1941 during a well excavation, the circumstances of the find leave much to be desired (Wells 1970a). Although the artifacts resemble in all details those found with the Orangian industry some 100 miles to the north, this diagnosis can only be confirmed by further excavations at this potentially very important site.

The only other fossil fauna locality of interest is the Aloes site near Port Elizabeth on the southern Cape coast. This is a bone deposit capped by a 2-ft thick calcrete, which has been partially removed by Gess (1969). Although no stone artifacts were recovered from the exposed area of bone materials, there is no apparent explanation for the accumulation except that it represents part of a human occupation area. Three quartzite artifacts quoted as being of "Mosselbay type" were recovered from above the calcrete so that no direct association can be demonstrated. Shells of *Achatina zebra* taken from among the bones were used to obtain a date (GX-1280) of 37,000 B.P. with 95% certainty. As usual, with readings of this kind it is impossible to estimate the real age of the site. Again, such site would repay further excavation. The list of species so far recovered has been compiled by Wells (1970b) and is included for comparison in Table 24.

TABLE 24

Fauna from Pietersburg and Possibly Related Sites

Genus and species	Description	Florisbad: Peat I–II. Possibly final Acheulian lithic	Cave of Hearths: Beds 4–9, mixed with later material	Driefontein: Total sample too small and selected	Aloes: No artifacts in association
Primates					
Papio ursinus	Chacma baboon	—	X	—	—
Lagomorpha					
Pronolagus randensis	Red hare	—	X	—	—
Lepus saxatalis	Hare	—	X	—	—
Rodentia					
Xerus sp.		X	—	—	—
Pedetes hagenstadi	Spring hare	X	—	—	—
Tatera sp.	Gerbil	cf.	—	—	—
Otomys irroratus	Swamp rat	X	—	—	—
Myotomys cf. *turneri*		X	—	—	—
Myotomys cf. *unisulcatus*		X	—	—	—
Hystrix africae-australis	Porcupine	—	X	—	—
Carnivora					
Canis mesomelas	Black-backed jackal	—	X	—	—
Myonax cauui	Slender mongoose	X	—	—	—
Atilax paludinosus	Marsh mongoose	cf.	—	—	—
Crocuta crocuta	Spotted hyena	—	X	—	X
Hyaena brunnea	Brown hyena	X	—	—	—
Caracal caracal	Caracal	—	X	—	—
Hyracoidea					
Procavia capensis	Hyrax	—	X	—	—
Perissodactyla					
Equus burchelli	Burchell's zebra	X	—	—	—
Equus quagga	Extinct small horse	—	—	X	X
Equus plicatus	Extinct horse	?	?	X	X
Equus helmei	Extinct horse	X	X	?	X
Diceros bicornis	Black rhino	X	—	—	—
Artiodactyla					
Phacochoerus africanus	Southern warthog	cf.	—	—	—
Phacochoerus aethiopicus	Cape warthog	X	X	X	X
Hippopotomus amphibius	Hippo	X	—	—	—
Giraffa camelopardalis	Giraffe	X	—	—	—
Sivatherium cf.	Extinct giraffe	?	—	—	—
Strepsiceros strepsiceros	Kudu	—	X	—	—

(continued)

TABLE 24 *(continued)*

Genus and species	Description	Florisbad: Peat I–II. Possibly final Acheulian lithic	Cave of Hearths: Beds 4–9, mixed with later material	Driefontein: Total sample too small and selected	Aloes: No artifacts in association
Artiodactyla *(continued)*					
Tragelaphus angasi	Nyala	cf.	—	—	—
Taurotragus oryx	Eland	×	×	×	—
Syncerus caffer	Cape buffalo	—	×	—	—
"Homioceras" baini	Extinct giant buffalo	×	×	×	—
Cephalophus sp.	Blue duiker	cf.	—	—	—
Sylvicapra grimmia	Duiker	×	—	—	—
Kobus sp.	Extinct lechwe	×	—	?	—
Onotragus leche	Lechwe	—	×	—	—
Redunca arundinum	Reedbuck	×	×	×	—
Pelea capreolus	Vaal rhebok	—	×	?	—
Damaliscus albifrons	Blesbok	×	—	—	—
Damaliscus pygargus	Bontebok	?	—	—	—
Damaliscus lunatus	Tsessebe	—	×	—	—
Damaliscus niro	Extinct blesbok	?	?	×	—
Alcelaphus helmei	Extinct giant harte-beest	×	—	×	—
Connochaetes taurinus	Wildebeest	?	×	×	?
Connochaetes antiquus	Extinct wildebeest	×	—	?	—
Oreotragus oreotragus	Klipspringer	—	×	—	—
Oryx gazella	Gemsbok	—	—	×	—
Aepyceros melampus	Impala	—	cf.	—	—
Antidorcas marsupialis	Springbok	?	×	—	×
Gazella bondi	Extinct gazelle	×	×	×	—
Raphicerus campestris	Steenbok	—	—	×	—

Given the unreliability of each of the four samples listed in Table 24, it is impossible to gain any accurate insights into the diet of the hunters responsible for the Pietersburg complex. Publication of more detailed information is urgently needed in this field.

CLIMATIC EVIDENCE FROM PIETERSBURG DEPOSITS

The grain-angularity test carried out by Brain on the Cave of Hearths sediments shows that the sterile rubble underlying Bed 4 contains sand grains with a distribution of angularity similar to that of local surface soils found in the area today. The Bed 4 sediment sample associated with the Lower Pietersburg contains a larger percentage of very angular grains, possibly reflecting the effect of

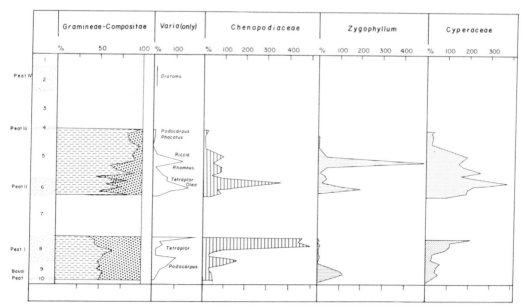

Fig. 66. Pollen diagram of the Florisbad sequence shown in Fig. 64 (page 179). (After van Zinderen Bakker 1957.)

an annual rainfall higher than that of today. The Beds 5–6 sample suggests a definite decrease in angularity during the later phase of Pietersburg occupation in the cave. As already discussed, these results cannot be accepted as conclusive proof of wetter conditions during the early Pietersburg occupation of the area since no data are available from neighboring sites which might support this interpretation.

One possible exception may be the brief granulometric study of the later Pietersburg stratum of Mwulu's Cave (ash and sands III) by King (Tobias 1954). A sample of sand grains examined under a microscope contained a high proportion of rounded grains with dulled surfaces typical of wind-blown sands. This was taken to indicate relatively dry conditions during the lowermost occupation. Evidently, increased aridity is thought to be reflected in the overlying sterile red sand, which contains even more eolian grains. This interpretation coincides with that of Brain's for the coeval Beds 5–6 sample at the Cave of Hearths. It is unfortunate that the Mwulu results were not set up on a quantitative scale since the subjective analysis presented does not permit closer comparison with Bed 5. Although the climatic interpretations of the two deposits coincide, they cannot be accepted as definite facts since both methods have shortcomings which need further investigation.

Finally, the pollen analysis of Florisbad peat I by van Zinderen Bakker (1957) suggests conditions drier than today surrounding the spring itself. The semiarid Karroo scrub (Compositae) occur in about the same proportions as the grass pollens (Gramineae). The modern pollen rain at Bloemfontein only 30 miles to the south contains 90% grass pollens and only 4% scrub. At the top of peat I there is a marked increase in halophytes—plants found consistently around the edge of salt pans. This trend is taken to reflect increased flooding of the area as the result of increased spring activity (Fig. 66). Since peat I is probably older than the Pietersburg complex, this evidence may reflect local climatic conditions before its appearance and at the very beginning of its development.

CONCLUSIONS

The stratigraphic evidence now available from three different regions in South Africa demonstrates that the industry following the late Acheulian is not the so-called "Fauresmith," but a complex without any of the characteristics of Acheulian samples such as hand axes, cleavers, and picks. The discoid, Levallois, and blade-core techniques are used in varying proportions in each of the three regions, and the elaborate secondary trimming of flakes to form repeated tool shapes is virtually absent. Instead, flakes and large blades were used directly without preliminary retouch. The only "formal tools" are rare sidescrapers, frontal scrapers, and burins. The remarkable early phase of the Pietersburg complex is recognized by the presence of extremely large blades, some of which exceed 200 mm in length. Most of the flake tools and cores of this phase are also relatively larger than their equivalents from later levels. The date for its earliest appearance in South Africa may be set at >50,000 B.P., but the limitations of the carbon-14 dating information precludes our estimating how much older than this date it may be.

It is now apparent that a remarkably ancient "blade-and-burin" technology emerged in the high central plateau region of South Africa to the south of the Limpopo basin. Its suggested origins in the local late Acheulian of this area cannot be justified by the excavated sites which have sterile layers separating the two, but the typological trend toward blade production in the late Acheulian at least hints at some connection. The presence of an early phase in the southern Cape coastal belt has not been demonstrated yet, and the possibility that the focus for its emergency lies within the high central plateau (Karroo, Orange Free State, and Transvaal) should be investigated further.

The position of the Florisbad skull within the center of this proposed focus area is of crucial importance. Dated to >50,000 B.P. and probably broadly contemporary with the Broken Hill specimen to the north and the Hopefield cranium to the south, it displays several remarkable features that set it apart from the other two. These features have prompted some authorities to suggest that it is morphologically closer to the modern human type than either its southern or northern counterparts. Thus a tentative overview of prehistoric change during the Post-Acheulian phase (sixtieth millenium?) in southern Africa may be postulated:

1. In the northern woodland–savannah zone of Rhodesia and Zambia the Sangoan–Charaman tradition persisted with obvious Acheulian characters and a flaking technology based upon the Levallois, discoid, and adjacent-platform techniques with only very limited blade production. Still further north in the closed woodland–forest zone of Angola, southern Congo, and possibly the extreme north of Zambia, the Sangoan evidently develops towards a "Lower Lupemban" (see Chapter 5). The human physical type associated with this region is represented by the Broken Hill skull displaying extremely robust features.

2. South of the Limpopo basin on the highveld–grassland–scrub desert regions of the Transvaal, Orange Free State, and Karroo, the Pietersburg complex makes its appearance, as does the Florisbad cranium, displaying more "sapient" morphological characters.

3. On the southern Cape coast, there remains the probability that the Acheulian tradition persisted during this period at sites such as Hangklip, Amanzi, and Hopefield, without the development or frequent use of the discoid or Levallois techniques (Chapter 3). As in the northern woodland zone, the physical type is represented by the extremely robust Hopefield cranium, which closely resembles the Broken Hill specimen.

It is obviously futile to use only these fossils, none of which was found in satisfactory primary contexts, to reconstruct a clear picture of human physical variation during this period. However, the present archaeological evidence points to the independent emergence of a remarkably early blade-and-burin assemblage in central South Africa, and there are therefore grounds for suspecting that the population responsible for this complex may have included some individuals (such as Florisbad) with several "modern" physical traits not found in the populations to the north and south.

This would imply that there was a localized emergence of *Homo sapiens sapiens* or Modern Man in South Africa, which is quite independent of the other postulated foci for his emergence elsewhere in the Old World. McBurney (1967) points out that the Pre-Aurignacian of northern Africa and the Near East is a "blade-and-burin" industry, suggesting a prototype of the Upper Paleolithic consistently associated with the fossil remains of Modern Man. As the Pre-Aurignacian predates the Mousterian and occurs in deposits associated with the end of the Last (Eem) Interglacial, a date of 65,000–60,000 B.P. for the industry is not unreasonable.

The Pietersburg complex represents an independent appearance or a similar technology at the opposite end of the African continent during the same period.

5

The Bambata Complex

Bambata Cave is located in the Matopos Hills in Rhodesia. First excavated in 1929 by Armstrong (1931), it was chosen as the type site for the "Bambata industry," a short-lived term used to describe the artifacts recovered from the lower levels of the cave earth. Armstrong's excavated sample included a series of fine, pressure-flaked points not found in the upper layer of the cave, but his sample includes few tools and no waste and is of limited value today. Later excavations by N. Jones (1940) in this and other caves nearby suggested a chronological development within the industry in which tool manufacture became more refined with time. Again, this subjective interpretation was based on selected specimens from his excavations, and the claim cannot be tested by analysis. In his description of these new finds, Jones elected to abandon the term "Bambata" in favor of "Stillbay," a name coined by Goodwin (1928) to describe a mixed and distorted surface collection from the Cape coast. To distinguish his own material from that of the Cape collections, Jones created the "Rhodesian Stillbay" with an earlier phase called "Proto-Stillbay," now referred to as the Charaman (see Chapter 3). Unfortunately, no adequate description of a "Stillbay" sample from a reliable context on the Cape coast was forthcoming, so that direct comparisons between "Rhodesian Stillbay" and "Stillbay" materials proved impossible. Indeed, the likelihood that samples from two areas some 1600 miles apart would be so alike that they may be ascribed to the same industry now seems remote. With these facts in mind, Cooke, Summers, and Robinson (1966) agreed to abandon the "Rhodesian Stillbay" and return to the "Bambata industry" of Armstrong. This term is presently used to describe samples with a distinctive typology from over 100 sites in Rhodesia, but it has not been applied elsewhere in southern Africa. It is unfortunate that no reliable samples from Bambata itself are available for analytical comparisons with other materials referred to this group. The name is retained because it has historical precedent over any other excavated site, and still contains deposits which should yield an undistorted sample of the industry, if excavated under modern controls. Meanwhile, Cooke has cited a sealed sample from the neighboring Pomongwe Cave as an adequate type sample for this group.

This chapter represents a departure from previous attempts to classify both this and other industries in southern Africa. The Bambata industry of Cooke, Summers, and Robinson is recognized here as just one discrete industry within the Bambata complex that includes other typologically related industries from South Africa. The justification for this new grouping is based on a standardized analysis of several samples from different localities.

TYPOLOGY OF THE BAMBATA COMPLEX

Samples belonging to this complex contain all the various tool types and cores listed for the Pietersburg complex, and there are obviously some technical similarities between the two. However, the Bambata complex contains several important features never found in Pietersburg sites and there are numerous other differences in the percentages of types, size of specimens, and raw material usage. Furthermore, samples of the Bambata complex invariably overlie Pietersburg levels in sites where the two are found together in the same deposits. The artifact types that distinguish Bambata samples from those of the Pietersburg are as follows:

1. *Trimmed points:* flakes or blades with margins trimmed convergently to produce a point. These vary in shape and form according to the initial shape of the blank and the degree of trimming applied to the edge. The following subtypes have been isolated: unifacial points; bifacial points; points with one margin dorsally trimmed and the opposite margin trimmed on the bulbar surface; unifacial points with light bulbar retouch. All these forms differ from the rare trimmed points found in the Orangian industry of the Pietersburg complex since the latter are convergent flakes or blades with reduced or rounded butts and no marginal trimming.

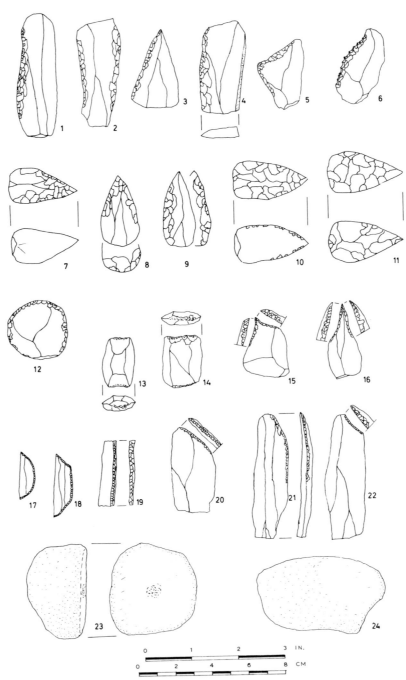

Fig. 67. Tool types of the Bambata complex: (1) sidescraper; (2) double sidescraper; (3) convergent sidescraper; (a) *á dos naturel* sidescraper; (5) angle sidescraper; (6) denticulate sidescraper; (7) unifacial point; (8) unifacial point with reduced butt; (9) point with alternate lateral retouch; (10) unifacial point with bulbar utilization; (11) bifacial point; (12) circular scraper; (13–14) *outils écaillés* (15–16) borers; (20–22) curve-backed knives; (23–24) grind-stones. Types that occur only in the Umguzan–Howiesonspoort levels are: (17) backed crescents; (18) backed trapeziums; (19) backed blades. (See Chapter 6.)

2. *Sidescrapers:* flakes, blades, and blade fragments with one or both margins elaborately retouched, usually on the dorsal surface. Subtypes are: single sidescrapers; double sidescrapers; *à dos naturel* sidescrapers; sidescrapers on convergent flakes; angle sidescrapers; denticulate sidescrapers. The worked edges of all these specimens may vary from convex, through straight, to concave in plan form, but further typological subdivision on this criterion serves little purpose. Although a few sidescrapers occur in most Pietersburg samples, they are far more numerous and show a wider variation in shape and size in the Bambata complex.

3. *Circular scrapers:* flakes with continuous retouch around the entire margin. This may extend over the butt of the specimen, thus imparting a subcircular plan form to the scraper.

4. *Borers:* flakes or blade fragments with steep concave retouch on two opposed margins or two adjacent margins to produce a thick, double-shouldered point.

5. *Outils écaillés:* flakes or blade fragments with one margin or two opposed margins) curved by a large, deep flake scar on one surface of the specimen. This curved edge may be battered or covered with small utilization scars.

6. *Grindstones:* chunks or half-pebbles with one or more facets ground smooth and showing clear parallel striations under an oblique light. The half-pebbles have the flat broken surface ground smooth. The center of the ground face may have a small pit pecked into it. It is seldom possible to distinguish between upper grindstones and broken fragments of the larger lower grindstones.

Schematic diagrams of all the above types are illustrated in Fig. 67.

THE GEOGRAPHIC DISTRIBUTION OF INDUSTRIES

Artifact samples containing the types listed above have been recovered from more than 100 sites in Rhodesia, where the highest density of finds is presently recorded. Relatively few are recorded from Zambia to the north and Botswana to the west. In South Africa the present distribution appears to be sporadic, with some concentration of finds in the Transvaal and southwestern Cape Province. Numerous surface sites are known from South-West Africa (Fock 1959), but no excavated examples are on record yet from the entire western half of the subcontinent. Only excavated or undistorted surface samples are included in the present classification. Their localities are shown on the map in Fig. 68. A tentative grouping of these sites given in Table 25 is based on geographical and typological differences that suggest possible industries within the complex.

The Bambatan industry is found in savannah parkland on the high plateau region between the Zambezi and Limpopo valleys, and surface scatters have been

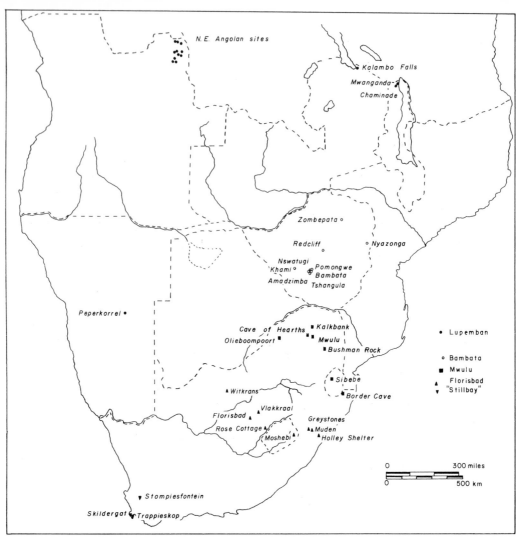

Fig. 68. Distribution of sites yielding excavated or numerically undistorted surface samples of the Bambata complex.

TABLE 25

Industries of the Bambata Complex

Bambatan industry	Mwulu industry	Florisbad industry	Stillbay industry
Zombepata	Mwulu's Cave	Florisbad	Skildergat
Bambata	Cave of Hearths	Rose Cottage	Trappieskop?
Pomongwe	Olieboompoort	Muden	Stompiesfontein?
Amadzimba	Kalkbank	Greystones	
Nswatugi	Bushman Rock	Vlakkraal	
Khami	Border Cave?		
Tshangula	Witkrans		
Nyazongo	Sibebe Shelter?		
Redcliff			
Pfupi			
Mtemwa Rocks			

found in northwestern Botswana (C. K. Cooke 1967). Its distribution probably extends into the Zambezi River valley (Clark 1950a) and even further north where its presence has been reported at the unpublished cave of Twin Rivers. Further north than this, its distribution is extremely uncertain with vague surface traces of possibly related materials from Luano Springs (Sampson 1965) and elsewhere in the Copperbelt area (Gabel 1967).

To the south of this area the "Mwulu" industry takes its name from Mwulu's Cave (Tobias 1949), which yielded the first undistorted sample from sealed context. The presently known distribution includes mountainous and high-plateau grasslands with varied tree cover. Still further south the "Florisbad" industry is a tentative grouping from samples made of lydianite coming from the central plateau and the Drakensburg Mountain region. Finally, the "Stillbay" industry includes one briefly reported sample and unpublished sites from the southwestern Cape Province. The validity of these groups is discussed in the following sections.

THE BAMBATAN INDUSTRY

Of the seven Rhodesian localities listed above, only Khami is an open site while the others are caves. Virtually all the other unpublished localities in Fig. 69 are open sites. At Pomongwe, Bambata, and Khami the Bambata levels directly overlie the Charaman without any apparent sterile layers or disconformity in the deposits, and it is reasonable to assume that it is stratigraphically later than the Charaman, at least in the Matopos area.

Only Pomongwe, Tshangula, and Khami (C. K. Cooke 1957b, 1963) provide samples suitable for analysis. Like the Bambata cave sample, the materials from Nswatugi (N. Jones 1933, 1949) and Nyazongo (Martin 1938) were heavily selected and are of little use. The Amadzimba material recovered by Cooke and Robinson (1954) is unfortunately too small to produce reliable percentage figures and must also be rejected from the analysis. The very large excavated sample from Redcliff (Brain and Cooke 1967) has not been published and cannot be compared.

At the deep cave of Pomongwe the Bambata sequence is located in Layers 13–19 of Cooke's first and second excavations and in Layers 5 and 6 of his third excavation (Fig. 70). Layer-by-layer analysis of these deposits reveal no significant changes in tool typology, as suggested by the percentage graphs of Fig. 71. It may be assumed that the cave was occupied by hunters with a relatively stable lithic technology during this period. Poor-quality vein quartz forms the dominant raw material, but small percentages of numerous other rock types derived from the local granitic and basement rock are also present.

At Tshangula cave some 6.5 miles from Pomongwe the Bambatan sample was recovered from three superimposed layers labeled 4–6, with Level 6 resting directly on bedrock. Analysis again reveals that no typological changes are apparent at this site either, and the material from all three layers may be treated as a single cultural unit.

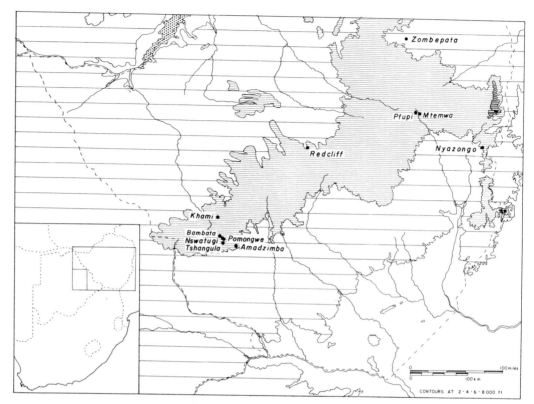

Fig. 69

The Khami Waterworks site is about 50 miles to the west of the Matopos group, but is situated among similar granite outcrops. Bambata samples were recovered from Layer 7 of the feldspathic clay deposits in three arbitrary spits labeled Levels I (lowest), 2, and 3. Again, the graphs show a remarkable level-to-level consistency in tool percentages. Raw materials used at this site include a wide range of rock types found in the Matopos area. The low quality of the local materials at Khami may have influenced both the quality of workmanship and the size distribution of artifacts in these levels.

Metrical analysis of the trimmed points and sidescrapers of compounded levels at each site show that Khami has a higher proportion of shorter, broader specimens. A similar analysis of the original collections of trimmed points from Bambata Cave reveals an unusually high proportion of larger points. In each case this variability in point and scraper dimensions appears to be directly linked to the variable quality of the local raw materials available at each site (Fig. 72).

Thus far, virtually all the information about this industry is restricted to the Matabeleland region of Rhodesia, with nothing more than sporadic surface finds

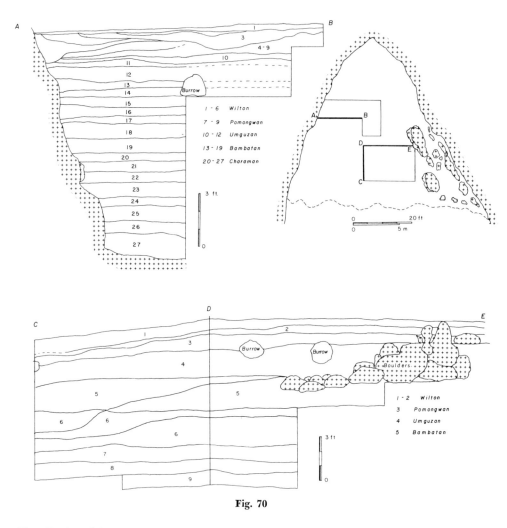

Fig. 70

Fig. 69. Localities of sites that have yielded excavated samples of the Bambata industry, Rhodesia.

Fig. 70. Section through the deposits at Pomongwe Cave, Matopos Hills, Rhodesia showing the stratified sequence of industries.

Fig. 71. Typological comparisons between samples from three industries in the Bambata complex: Mwulu industry (Cave of Hearths, Mwulu's Cave, Olieboompoort), Florisbad industry (Florisbad), Bambata industry (Pomongwe, Tshangula, Khami): (1) trimmed points; (2) sidescrapers; (3) frontal scrapers; (4) circular scrapers; (5) burins; (6) borers; (7) *outils écaillés;* (8) curve-backed knives; (9) utilized blade fragments; (11) utilized flakes; (12) grindstones (figure on page 196).

Fig. 72. Mean and range of length and breadth-to-length ratio: (a) sidescraper; (b) trimmed points. Samples are from Bambata, Mwulu, and Florisbad (figure on page 197).

195

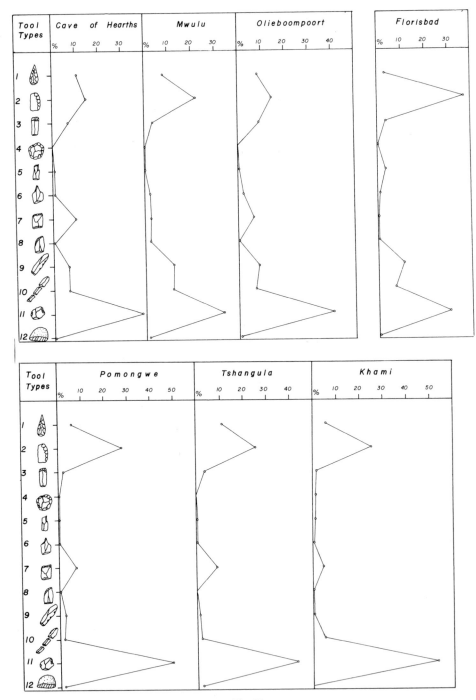

Fig. 71

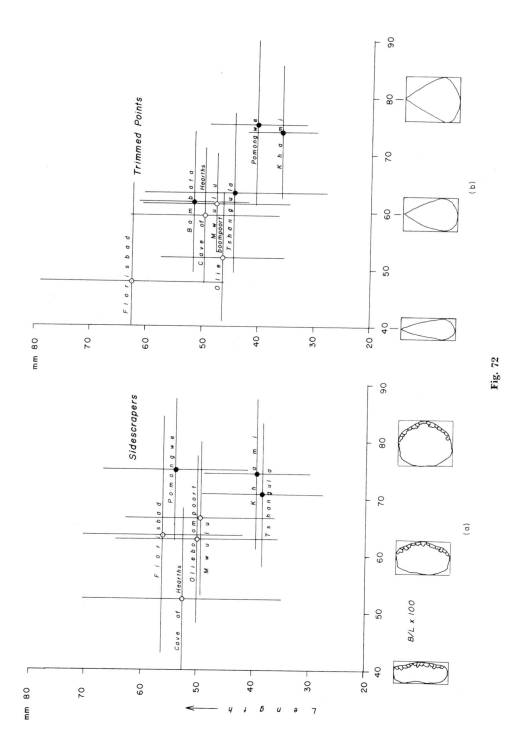

Fig. 72

from further north in Mashonaland. Excavations conducted in the Zombepata
Cave have yielded sealed Bambata materials that should eventually cast more
light on the industry's development in this area (C. K. Cooke, personal communication).

THE MWULU INDUSTRY

Five caves and one open site (Kalkbank) are included. Various terms have
been used to describe the samples listed under this heading, thus obscuring their
similar typologies. The terms previously used to describe the pertinent layers in
each site are listed in Table 26.

The reason for separating the contents of these strata from the Pietersburg industry [as defined by Mason (1957a), and others] is simply that they have a
greater number of features in common with the Bambata industry of Rhodesia
than they have with the Pietersburg industry of the Transvaal (as defined in
Chapter 4). All the samples listed above, with the exceptions of Olieboompoort
and Kalkbank, actually overlie Pietersburg levels and are thus stratigraphically
later than the Pietersburg. Kalkbank is a single-level site, and the Olieboompoort Bed 2 sample overlies an unpublished Late Acheulian rubble presumably
at the base of the deposits.

The "Mwulu" levels in the deep Cave of Hearths deposits occur between 13
and 6 ft in depth from the deposit surface. Arbitrary 1-ft deep spits were removed, and the artifact content of each was labeled and recorded separately,
thus permitting a spit-by-spit analysis. Figure 73 shows the tool-type count for
each spit. The lowest and earliest spit in the sequence (13–12 ft depth) is almost
sterile, and the sample counts for other levels are too small too provide percentage values. There is evidently no trace of typological change within this industry, although the 7-ft deep accumulation must reflect a very prolonged
occupation of the cave. Like the Bambata industry to the north, this probably
reflects a remarkably stable technological tradition. Differences between the Pietersburg levels of Bed 5 and the "Mwulu" levels of Beds 6–8 have been analyzed
elsewhere (Sampson and Mason 1968) and will be briefly summarized here:
trimmed points, burins, borer, *outils écaillés,* and grindstones appear for the first
time in Beds 6–8; there is a large increase in sidescrapers and a proportionate
decrease in utilized flakes in Beds 6–8; more crystalline rocks are used in Beds
6–8; Levallois cores appear and core dimensions are generally smaller in Beds 6–8.

At Mwulu's Cave, the same differences are apparent between the Pietersburg
sample for Bed I and the overlying "Mwulu" sample of Beds II and III. However, there is no change in raw material usage between Beds I and II, in which
quartzite remains the dominant rock type. This persistent use of quartzite in the
earliest "Mwulu" level (Bed II) may have influenced the overall dimensions of
the artifacts which have a breadth-to-length ratio very close to that of the underlying Pietersburg samples of Bed I. Bed II could conveniently reflect an "inter-

TABLE 26

Previous Terminology for Mwulu Industry Sites

Site	Strata	Reference	Previous term
Cave of Hearths	Beds 6–8	Mason (1957a)	Upper Pietersburg
Mwulu's Cave	Beds II–III	Mason (1957a)	Middle Pietersburg
Olieboompoort	Bed 2	Mason (1957a)	Middle Pietersburg
Kalkbank	Brown sand	Mason (1958)	Middle–Later Pietersburg
Bushman Rock Shelter	Layers 28–43	Louw (1969)	Middle Stone Age
Bushman Rock Shelter	Layers 27–43	Mason (1969c)	"Developed" Middle Stone Age
Border Cave	Middle Cave Earth	Cooke *et al.* (1945)	"Normal" Pietersburg
Witkrans	Layer C	Peabody (1954)	Middle Stone Age

mediate" level between the Pietersburg and "Mwlulu" industries, but this interpretation cannot be verified without further excavations (Figs. 74 and 75).

Bed 2 at Olieboompoort Shelter contains an artifact sample that partly resembles that of Mwulu Bed II: a relatively high percentage of quartzite was used, and the length distribution of cores, trimmed points, and blades show that larger tools could be made at this site than at the Cave of Hearths, where more crystalline rock was in use.

The Kalkbank artifacts were recovered from the top of a brown-sand ridge apparently surrounded by white clay. Both deposits are capped by a massive calcrete with an intercalated peat layer (Fig. 76). This unusual geological setting

Bed No.	depth, ft	1	2	3	4	5	6	7	8	9	10	11	12
8	8–9	6	6	2				6		3	1	11	
7	9–10	1	2								2	6	
7	10–11	4	7	2		1		5	1	2	3	15	1
6	11–12	4	4	6		1	2	3		6	3	14	
6	12–13	2										2	

Fig. 73. Vertical distribution of Mwulu industry tools through Beds 6–8 in Cave of Hearths. Key to numerals given in caption of Fig. 71 (page 195).

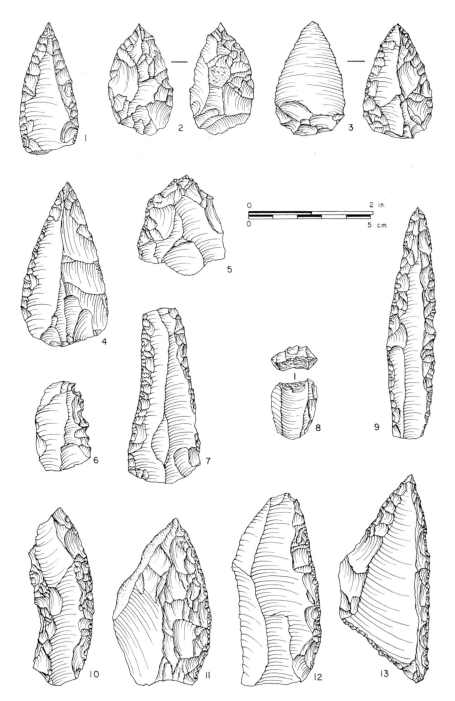

Fig. 74. Tools of the Mwulu industry, Cave of hearths, Beds 6–9: (1) unifacial point; (2) bi-facial point; (3) unifacial point with reduced butt; (4) unifacial point (5, 6) denticulate sidescrapers; (7) double sidescraper; (8) *outil écaillé;* (9) unifacial point; (10–12) side-scrapers; (13) angle sidescraper.

200

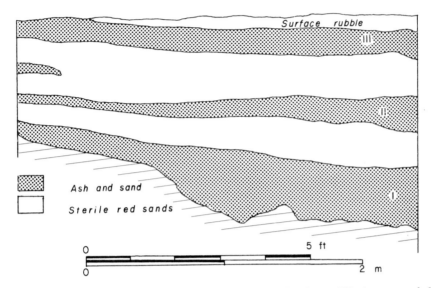

Fig. 75. Section through Mwulu's Cave. The Mwulu sample (Layer III) is separated from the underlying Later Pietersburg sample in Layer II containing elements of both industries. (After Tobias 1949.)

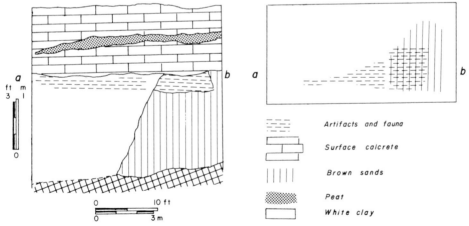

Fig. 76. (Left) Section and (right) plan of Kalkbank. (After Mason 1958.)

has been tentatively interpreted as a hunting camp situated on a sandbar in a vlei or swampy area (Mason 1958). Unfortunately, the artifact sample is too small to be used for analysis, but sidescrapers and grindstones are present together with a few cores, waste flakes, and two perfectly round spheroids produced by a pecking technique. Although further material has been recovered from the site by Mason (1967a), no details are available.

The very deep Bushman Rock Shelter sequence has been analyzed by Louw, who applied Mason's geometric-based typology which cannot be directly compared here. Lydianite is reported to be the dominant rock type, with some quartz and quartzite, but no numerical data have been released. Again, no evidence for typological change through time has been detected in the 3–5-ft deep accumulation of deposits. The presence of three "partly made beads" in these layers cannot be confirmed since Louw simply tabulates these without further description.

The Border Cave sample has been very briefly described by the excavators. Apparently, a gradual typological change is noted between the underlying Pietersburg ("basal industry") and the overlying "Mwulu" sample (normal Pietersburg of the excavators), but this trend has not been verified by the more recent analysis of Eggers (1970). There is an increase in the use of Levallois technique; bifacial and unifacial points (some with butt reduction) are common.

At Witkrans cave near Taung in the northern Cape Province, a single cemented horizon with abundant mammalian fauna has provided a small lydianite artifact sample which has never been fully published. Although too small to provide adequate percentages, the extant collection, now at the University of California, Berkeley, contains the characteristic range of tool and core types. It is included here because of its valuable associations (Peabody 1954).

Although the "Mwulu" group of samples shares a similar range of types with the Bambata industry of Rhodesia, several measureable differences exist between the analyzed samples from these two areas.

1. Trimmed-point samples from the "Mwulu" group include fewer bifacial specimens, more large specimens, and more narrow specimens than are found in the Bambata samples.

2. The sidescrapers from the "Mwulu" samples include more double sidescrapers, more long specimens, and more narrow scrapers than the Bambata samples.

3. More quartzite or lydianite and less crystalline rock (for example quartz) is used at the "Mwulu" sites. Both rock types are isotropic, may be flaked with ease, and are relatively common in the Transvaal, occurring in large blocks. The abundance of these materials in the neighborhood of "Mwulu" sites made it possible to strike longer blades from large cores, thus producing blanks for the larger, narrower points and sidescrapers. Differences in the size and shape of tools thus appear to be clearly limited to the scarcity or abundance of isotropic rocks near the site.

THE "FLORISBAD" INDUSTRY

Of the four excavated samples tentatively listed under this heading, only Florisbad can be compared directly with the Bambata and "Mwulu" industries to the north. The stratigraphic sequence of spring-derived sands and organic clay ("peat") layers is shown in Fig. 64 (page 179).

An unpublished artifact sample from 2–3 inches below the peat II was exca-vated from a possible primary context in the blue-green clay. Although the arti-fact sample was stored separately, the fauna from this level has been mixed with material from a lower stratum in the sequence and cannot be retrieved, since the specimens were not labeled according to depth in the deposits (A. C. Hoffman, personal communication). The excavated sample is very similar to the larger, unlabeled sample recovered by van Hoepen from a sandy "spring eye" in the vi-cinity of Hoffman's excavations, but the latter sample contains more sidescrapers made on broad flakes. In both samples lydianite is used exclusively, and the two samples may be regarded as belonging to the same industry. Although not re-covered by controlled excavations, the small lydianite sample from the Vlakkraal waterhole spoil heap (Wells, Cooke, and Malan 1942) contains the same range of tool and core types found at Florisbad. It is included here as it appears to have important faunal associations, although it should be stressed that both arti-facts and fauna were not observed together *in situ*.

The presence of a similar industry at Rose Cottage Cave above the basal in-dustry cannot be verified without a more detailed analysis of the site than is presently available. Malan (1952) states that the "Upper South African Mago-sian" occurs in a 1-ft thick layer below a thick, near-sterile sand deposit. In con-trast with the underlying industries (tentatively attributed to the Pietersburg complex, Chapter 4) this sample contains more chert, chalcedony, and agate with less sandstone and lydianite. There is an increase in the use of the Leval-lois technique, unifacial points abound, and several specimens have reduced butts. Malan points out that there is a greater variety of tools in the preceding levels but gives no details.

In northern Natal, one excavated, and several complete surface collections have been analyzed by Farnden (1968) and Farnden and Gibbs (1962, 1963) using a typology closely related to, but not exactly like, that used in this chap-ter. Their analysis reveals a tool-type distribution obviously related to that of the Florisbad sample, but detailed numerical comparisons are not possible. Lydi-anite is the dominant raw material used at the sites, which may eventually prove to be a part of a distinctive group within the Bambata complex, including as yet unpublished sites from Swaziland such as Sibebe Shelter, Lesotho (Carter 1969), and possibly Holly Shelter in northern Natal (Cramb 1952). As no adequate data are available from these sites, any further subdivision of the complex would be premature.

The Florisbad sample differs from those of the "Mwulu" industry in relatively few details: the blades produced from lydianite cores are larger and narrower, so that the tool types include an unusually high percentage of long, narrow speci-mens (Fig. 77). Trimmed points are relatively scarce, and most specimens have lateral trimming with reduced butts. Sidescrapers are more abundant, as are bur-ins, whereas *outils écaillés* are relatively scarce. Among the cores are more Leval-lois and prismatic blade cores and notably few discoids.

Although several surface samples of related materials have been found in the Orange Free State, it is interesting to note that no trace of this industry has

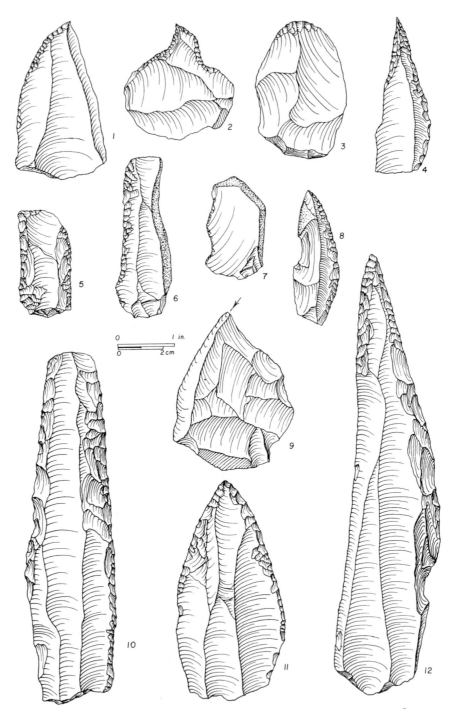

Fig. 77. Tools from below peat II, at Florisbad: (1) curve-backed knife; (2, 4), borers; (3) frontal scraper; (5) double sidescraper; (6) *á dos naturel* sidescraper; (7) utilized flake; (8) sidescraper; (9) burin; (10) double sidescraper; (11, 12) unifacial points.

been located in the Orange River scheme area to the south, nor has it been reported from elsewhere in the semiarid Karroo region of South Africa.

THE "STILLBAY" INDUSTRY

It is only with extreme reluctance that this term is retained here to describe the very poorly documented group of sites listed in Table 25 (page 192). Jolly (1948) only briefly described a "Stillbay" level at Skildergat overlying the basal industry, which was further excavated by Anthony and is tentatively grouped with the Mossel Bay industry in Chapter 4. In his "Stillbay levels" Jolly mentions

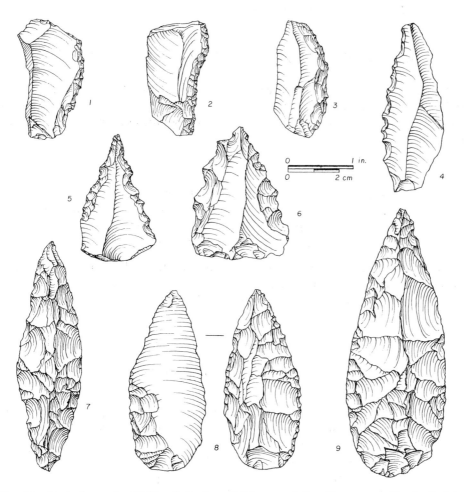

Fig. 78. Tools from the "Stillbay" level at Skildergat: (1–3) sidescrapers; (4) denticulate sidescraper; (5) unifacial point; (7, 9) bifacial points; (8) unifacial point with reduced butt.

the presence of unifacial and bifacial trimmed points only, and no other details were ever released, nor would he permit other workers access to his materials. As this is the only known sealed, numerically undistorted sample of the "Still-bay," its analysis is of extreme importance. Since his death, Jolly's collections have been moved to the South African Museum where, hopefully, they will be analyzed and published. Several mixed and distorted surface collections have been reported from the adjacent Noordhoek and Cape Flats areas (Malan 1938), and a heavily selected sample of bifacial and unifacial points was excavated from a shelter at Trappieskop nearby Skildergat (Fig. 78). Other small excavated samples may occur at Stompiesfontein and other sites in the southwestern Cape mountain belt, but far more research is required to verify not only the status, but the very existence of the so-called "Stillbay."

CHRONOLOGY OF THE BAMBATA COMPLEX

Numerous carbon-14 readings are available from charcoal or other organic materials reported to be associated with artifact samples ascribed to the Bambata complex. Since the dates obtained vary in quality and usefulness, they are discussed individually:

Redcliff:

15-ft level	GrN-5679	41,800 ± 3000 B.P.	(39,850 B.C.)
in Profile B	GrN-5858	40,780 ± 1800 B.P.	(38,920 B.C.)
14-ft level	I-3727	35,500 ± 2700 B.P.	(33,550 B.C.)
16-ft level	I-3728	>39,000 B.P.	

The first two readings came from Layer W reported to be near the top of the "Rhodesian Stillbay" (that is, Bambata) succession. As these dates obtained are consistent, there is no reason to doubt their validity.

Pomongwe:

Layer 13 of first excavation	Sr-39	35,530 ± 780 B.P.	(33,580 B.C.)

Layer 13 is the highest and therefore the latest of the series of Bambata layers at this site. However, the reported depth of the charcoal sample is 7.5 ft below the deposit surface, which is considerably deeper than Layer 13 in the published sections at Pomongwe (see Fig. 70, page 195). Presumably, the sample dates the *later* stages of the Bambata occupation, and correlates well with a similar date from the Redcliff (I-3727). The 6.5-ft sample (no level number given): SR-10 21,700 ± 400 B.P. (19,750 B.C.). Although reported to date the end of the

Bambata occupation of this site, the published depth of the sample does not equate with the depth of the final Bambata layers in the published section.

Witkrans:

Travertine: Lower breccia   UCLA-706   33,150 ± 2500 B.P. (31,200 B.C.)

The depth of the charcoal sample within this deposit has not been reported.

Cave of Hearths:

Bed 6   C-924   15,100 ± 730 B.P. (13,150 B.C.)

Since Bed 6 marks the earliest appearance of the Bambata complex at this site, the reading obtained is surprisingly late. The reading was taken during the early stages of radiocarbon dating development. It shows the same shortcomings as those from Beds 4 and 5, and should be rejected as too young.

Olieboompoort Shelter:

Bed 2   BM-39   >25,000 B.P.
Bed 2   BM-?   >33,000 B.P.

Both readings come from organic nodules recovered at 36–54 in. in depth, about midway through the sequence of Bed 2 deposits. These dates are in accord with those from other Bambata complex sites, but are not particularly useful with their "greater than" values.

Bushman Rock Shelter:

Layer 41   GrN-4855   >45,500 B.C. (?)
Layer 38   GrN-5116   >51,000 B.G. (?)

Vogel (1969) stresses that both samples contained so little carbon-14 that only minimum ages can be given. The apparent dating inversion is therefore of no significance, although the unconventional "B.C." quotes remain unexplained since most values are usually given as Before Present. These are certainly the earliest recorded dates for the complex.

Florisbad:

"Peat II"   L-271C   28,450 ± 2200 B.P. (26,500 B.C.)

As the artifact sample was recovered from the blue-green clays *below* peat II, this carbon sample is not directly associated with the cultural horizon, which is older than the above date.

Rose Cottage:

> 12 ft, 4 in.–12 ft, 6 in.
> and
> 11 ft, 4 in.–12 ft, 10 in.   (SR-116)   >50,000 B.P.

The sample was collected by Beaumont (1963), who reexcavated these deposits but published no further data. If the samples are, in fact, from Malan's "Upper South African Magosian" and not from one of the lower deposits, this reading is in keeping with that from Layer 38 at Bushman Rock.

Sibebe Shelter:

> "Middle Stone Age
> stratum"   GrN-5314   22,850 ± 160 B.P.   (20,900 B.C.)

This site was excavated by Beaumont, but no details have been released. Vogel (1970) reports that the site is 8 km northeast of Mbabane in Swaziland. The charcoal was taken from the upper levels of the 120-cm thick "Middle Stone Age stratum," which contains "well-flaked bifacial points (spears and arrowheads)" and reports a transitional phase between Middle Stone Age and "Second Intermediate." The date presumably belongs to the late stages of occupation in the shelter, and this very inadequate description of the artifact sample does not allow more than a tentative ascription to the Bambata complex.

Kalkbank:

> Laboratory No. ?   >16,000 B.P.

Mason (1967a) has reported this result without details of sample depth or locality. The material used was evidently bone and not charcoal and the result should be treated with caution as little is known of contamination factors. The reading is considerably younger than the others, which is remarkable, considering the number of extinct animal species present at this site.

The array of dates now available suggests that the complex appeared at least 50,000 years ago in South Africa and persisted as a relatively stable technological tradition for a remarkably long period, probably until about 20,000 years ago in some regions. The persistence of this tradition is born out by the relatively deep accumulation of Bambata deposits at several sites.

Although the Bambata industry overlies the Charaman in at least four deposits from Rhodesia, the earliest carbon-14 dates from the related "Mwulu" and "Florisbad" industries overlap with those quoted for the Charaman. It is also extremely interesting to note that these dates overlap with several dates from the

Pietersburg complex, particularly those from sites tentatively grouped as the Mossel Bay industry from the southern Cape coast.

HUMAN REMAINS

At Skildergat an adult burial was uncovered by Mr. V. Peers, who first excavated here, but the burial was never described in detail or photographed *in situ*. The only published accounts of the associations of this skeleton are Peers' sketch sections (Keith 1931), which place the skeleton firmly in the lower "Stillbay" levels. It is reported that the burial was associated with a "laurel-leaf point." Owing to the lack of detailed sections from this site, it has not proved possible to determine whether the skeleton was buried into the "Stillbay" level from the overlying "Howiesonspoort" or the "coarse Stillbay" which follows this. Peers thought that it belonged with the "Stillbay" levels in which it was found.

The postcranial bones of this evidently complete skeleton have never been described, although the overall stature is quoted by Keith (1941) as being 5 ft, 2 inches. Only a cursory analysis of the skull and mandible is available from Keith (1931), and no further work on this specimen has been published. The cranium and face include a combination of features indicating that this is a fossil representative of Modern Man; the estimated cranial capacity is 1600 cc; the frontal bones display a very marked curvature; there are virtually no traces of a supraorbital ridge; there is no sign of an occipital ridge; the cranial profile displays a low vault with a well-rounded curvature and a notably elongated occipital region, giving a total cranial length of 200 mm (Fig. 79). When viewed from the front, there is a notable swelling of the skull low down in the temporal region. The facial bones display relatively small nasal apertures, a prognathous mouth region, and prominent cheekbones. The mandible has a prominent chin, delicate body, and relatively short ascending rami. The dentition is not adequately reported although it is apparently complete. Obviously, a great deal of work remains to be done on this extremely important specimen. Superficial comparisons have suggested that it represents an individual larger in stature, skull size, and cranial capacity than the maximum for the modern Bushman physical type. Attempts to group the Skildergat skull with the so-called "Boskop race" are represented by various inadequately documented specimens from unknown contexts. Without adequate dating associations they cannot be taken seriously at present. Such specimens include the Boskop skull (Haughton *et al.* 1917–1918) the Cape Flats skull (Drennan 1929b), and the Springbok Flats skeleton (Broom 1929).

More reliably associated human fragments occur at Witkrans Cave in the cemented Layer C together with abundant mammalian fossil remains. The unpublished human material comprises two adult molars recently developed from a lump of cemented matrix. Since they have not been reported in detail yet, it is

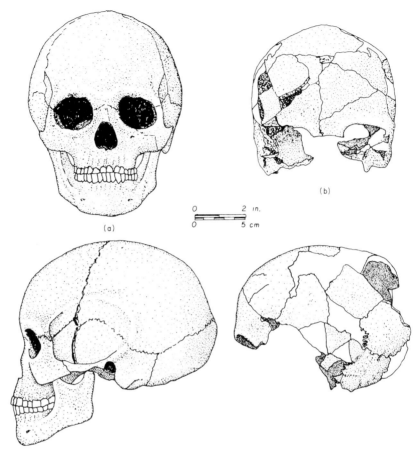

Fig. 79. (a) Fish Hoek skull from Skildergat, frontal and left lateral views. (b) Fragmentary skull from Border Cave, same views.

only possible to point out that they bear a sufficient resemblance to the (also un-published) teeth considered to belong with the Florisbad cranium.

At Border Cave a broken mandible and cranial fragments of an adult were re-covered from the spoil heap of guano diggings, and the correct associations be-tween skull, artifacts, and fauna therefore were lost. Later archaeological excavations yielded a fragmentary infant skeleton *in situ* in the deposits, and the exact level and associated industry is briefly mentioned. Material filling the crev-ices of the adult cranial fragments were considered to be identical with a soft dark earth exposed in the face of the guano diggings in the "normal Pieters-burg" level, but chemical testing and comparisons of the sediments from the skull fragments and the deposit were not carried out. The excavators speculated that the skeleton had been buried into the "normal Pietersburg" from the overlying "Epi-Pietersburg" but this cannot be proved. The exact cultural associations of the adult specimen are therefore unknown, and the associations of the infant skeleton are still unconfirmed.

Neither find has been adequately described. The Border Cave cranium (Wells 1950a) is extremely fragmentary, consisting of the frontal and fragments of the left parietal, temporal, and occipital. The age at death is estimated from suture closure to be about 30 years. Since the skull is so incomplete, and also partially distorted, the metric estimates are of limited use, and the cranial capacity estimate of 1450 cc is not accompanied by a standard deviation. The nonmetric morphology of the skull is of more interest: the frontal region reveals a prominent, nearly vertical forehead, with very weakly developed browridges; the nuchal surface is well rounded and there is no occipital torus; the mastoid process is relatively small. The mandible is small and delicate without any marked trace of alveolar prognathism. The ascending ramus is incomplete, and all the teeth are missing. Numerous postcranial fragments were also recovered from the spoil heap including femoral shafts and a tibia showing a clear "squatting facet" at the distal end.

The excavated position of the infant burial is reported by Cooke *et al.* (1945) to be within the "normal Pietersburg" levels in a very shallow grave. It was definitely not intrusive from the overlying industry which is sealed off by an ash layer at its base from the lower levels. Had the burial been intrusive, this ash layer would have been disrupted by the grave shaft. This comprises the earliest adequate record of a systematic burial in South African prehistory. A remarkable piece of *Conus* shell occurred in the grave fill, but the position of the skeleton is not recorded, nor have drawings or photographs of the find been published. No attempt has been made to determine the age or sex, or measure these remains.

ASSOCIATED FAUNA AND THE BAMBATA DIET

Among the 27 sites listed in Table 25 almost half this number are known to have yielded mammalian faunal fragments in direct association with the artifacts. These are: Bambata, Pomongwe, Tshangula, Redcliff, Cave of Hearths, Kalkbank, Bushman Rock, Border Cave, Witkrans, and Florisbad. In spite of this wealth of material, very little adequate information on the range of associated animals is available. Faunal analyses have been released for Kalkbank (Dart and Kitching 1958) and Bushman Rock (Brain 1969c), but analysis of the Pomongwe fauna is not yet published (C. K. Brain, personal communication). Lists of the specimens present at Cave of Hearths, Border Cave, and Florisbad have been reported but they lack numerical data and are of little use since they reflect the mixed contents of several superimposed layers. The precise associations of the Bambata levels at these sites are therefore obscured. No numerical data are available from Vlakkraal and Witkrans, but the available lists do at least reflect true Bambata associations since Vlakkraal (H. B. S. Cooke 1964) has yielded only one industry and Witkrans has a separate list for the Bambata levels (Peabody 1954; Clark 1971).

In Table 27 species lists for five unmixed faunal samples are compared with each other and with Border Cave, which includes somewhat earlier and later material, as does the Cave of Hearths. All these samples display a remarkable similarity in the range of species present. Artiodactyls dominate each sample and site-to-site differences within this group probably reflect local environmental conditions around each site. The Pomongwe sample contains a notably high proportion of *small mammals* (hyrax, duiker, steenbok) possibly suggesting a less attractive habitat than that reflected at other sites like Vlakkraal and Kalkbank, which were adjacent to a water source and therefore attracted more game. Unfortunately, the Bushman Rock and Witkrans samples are too small to provide a valid comparison. Evidently, most of the tabulated names represent species of living game animals, but a few extinct animals are represented at all the sites. Since the Witkrans artiodactyls have not been analyzed in adequate detail, the number of extinct species cannot be calculated.

Compared with the fauna from Acheulian (and Sangoan) sites, the Bambata samples contain a smaller range of species and a far smaller variety of extinct animals. By this period in the prehistory of southern Africa, some impressive changes in the mammalian fauna have taken place, including the extinction of numerous "giant" forms and an apparent reduction in the range of morphological (and dental) variation in general. Gone are the numerous elephants and giant

TABLE 27

Unmixed Faunal Samples from Five Bambata Sites

	Pomongwe	Bushman Rock	Kalkbank	Witkrans	Vlakkraal	Border Cave (mixed)	Cave of Hearths (mixed)
Primates	—	—	—	1	—	1	1
Lagomorpha	1	—	—	—	—	1	2
Rodentia	2	—	1	3	—	2+	1
Carnivora	1	—	3	4	3	—	3
Hyracoidea	2	—	—	1	—	1	1
Perissodactyla	2	2	4	1	3	2	3
Artiodactyla	13	3	12	7	15	10	15
Total no. of species:	21	5	20	17	21	17+	26
No. of species listed:	21	4	19	17	21	16	31
No. of extinct species:	2	1	4	?	8	2	5

pigs as well as several large artiodactyls. The reasons for these changes must remain a matter for speculation until we gain a better understanding of climatic and vegetational fluctuations during this period. More information on the population genetics, behavior, and ecology of living game animals should also provide valuable insight into this problem. It is tempting to assume that Stone Age hunting activities may have at least partially influenced the large-scale changes in the game population.

The available fossil evidence from Acheulian sites hints at a marked selective bias in hunting activities toward the larger animals, and it may be argued that the Acheulian lithic assemblage is simply a reflection of hominid adaptation to the problem of butchering relatively massive carcasses. The popular view of the Acheulians as "unspecialized" hunters (for example, Clark 1959a, 1970) might be reconsidered in the light of the actual associated faunas. The disappearance of so many large species by the time the Bambata complex appeared may be partly the result of such selectivity over a long period. Although we have no adequate faunal lists for the preceding Pietersburg complex, the "mixed" information from the Cave of Hearths and Border Cave suggests that the large game animals were not brought to these sites during Pietersburg times either. The total absence of elephant and the extreme scarcity of rhino and hippo from Pietersburg and Bambata sites may even suggest a shift in hunting goals in the Post-Acheulian period. Indeed, the range of animals taken at this time would suggest

TABLE 28

Nonmammalian Species at Bambata Sites [a]

Genus and species	Description	Pomongwe	Bushman Rock	Witkrans	Vlakkraal	Cave of Hearths (mixed)
Aves						
Gruidae indet	Crane	—	—	—	—	×
	Rock pigeon	2	—	—	—	—
Struthio sp.	Ostrich (eggshell fragments)	11	10	×	×	×
Reptilia						
Cordylus sp.		—	—	—	—	×
Varanus sp.	Monitor lizard	3	—	×	—	×
Python sebae	Python	×	1	—	—	—
Squamata lacertilia	Rock lizard	1	—	—	—	—
Testudio sp.	Tortoise	5	8	—	—	×
Chelonia	Turtle	—	—	×	—	—
Invertebrata						
Achatina sp.	Land snail	—	13	—	—	×
Inio caffer	Mussel	1	—	—	—	—

[a] Numerals, minimum number of individuals (except shell fragments); ×, present.

TABLE 29

Mammalian Fauna from Bambata Horizons [a]

Genus and species	Description	Pomongwe	Bushman Rock	Kalkbank	Witkrans	Vlakkraal	Border Cave
Primates							
Papio ursinus	Chacma baboon	—	—	—	X	—	X
Lagomorpha							
Lepus sp.	Hare	2	—	—	—	—	X
Rodentia							
Pedetes sp.	Spring hare	1	—	—	4	—	—
species indetermined	Various rodents	1	—	—	X	—	—
Hystrix sp.	Porcupine	1	—	?	1	—	—
Carnivora							
Canis mesomelas	Black-backed jackal	—	—	—	X	—	—
Vulpes chama	Cape fox	—	—	—	—	X	—
Lycaon picta	Hunting dog	1	—	—	—	X	—
Mellivora capensis	Cape honey badger	—	—	—	—	—	—
Crocuta crocuta	Spotted hyena	—	—	2	X	X	—
Panthera pardus	Leopard	—	—	2	—	—	—
Panthera leo	Lion	—	—	1	X	—	—
Felis sp.	Small feline	—	—	—	?	—	—
Hyracoidea							
Procavia capensis	Hyrax	10	—	—	X	—	X
Heterohyrax *	Extinct giant hyrax	1	—	—	—	—	—
Perissodactyla							
Equus burchelli	Burchell's zebra	3	2	6	2	X	X
Equus capensis *	Extinct horse	2	1	4	—	—	—
Equus plicatus *	Extinct horse	—	—	—	—	cf.	X
Equus helmei *	Extinct horse	—	—	X	—	X	—
Diceros bicornis	Black rhino	—	—	2	—	—	—

214

Artiodactyla

Potamochoerus sp.	Bush pig	1	—	—	—	—	—
Phacochoerus aethiopicus	Cape warthog	4	1	8	1	X	X
Phacocheorus africanus	Southern warthog	—	—	—	—	cf.	—
Stylochoerus compactus *	Extinct pig	—	—	—	—	cf.	—
Hippopotamus amphibius	Hippopotamus	—	—	1	—	X	—
Giraffa camelopardus	Giraffe	—	—	—	—	—	—
Strepsiceros strepsiceros	Kudu	1	—	1	—	—	X
Taurotragus oryx	Eland	1	1	1	—	X	X
Syncerus caffer	Cape buffalo	—	—	1	—	—	—
"Homioceras" baini *	Extinct giant buffalo	—	—	1	—	X	X
Kobus ellipsiprymnus	Waterbuck	3	—	2	—	—	X
Sylvicapra grimmia	Duiker	6	—	—	—	cf.	X
Kobus venterae *	Extinct waterbuck	—	—	—	—	X	—
Redunca arundinum	Reedbuck	4	—	—	15	X	X
Hippotragus equinus	Roan	1	—	—	—	—	—
Hippotragus niger	Sable antelope	2	—	—	—	—	X
Damaliscus lunatus	Tsessebe	5	—	cf.	—	—	—
Damaliscus albifrons	Blesbok	—	—	1	5+	X	X
Damaliscus sp. nov.*	Extinct tsessebe	—	—	—	—	X	—
Alcelaphus lichtenstein	Hartebeest	—	1	3	4	—	—
Alcelaphus helmei *	Extinct giant hartebeest	—	—	X	—	cf.	—
Connochaetes taurinus	Wildebeest	1	—	5	10	cf.	—
Oreotragus oreotragus	Klipspringer	4	—	—	—	—	X
Raphicerus campestris	Steenbok	9	—	1	15+	—	—
Aepyceros melampus	Impala	—	—	1	—	—	—
Antidorcas marsupialis	Springbok	—	—	—	—	X	X
Gazella bondi *	Extinct gazelle	—	—	—	4+	X	—

[a] Numeral, minimum number of individuals; X, species present; *, extinct species.

a more random selection of any available foodstuffs and a more systematic exploitation of different microhabitats surrounding this sites.

The evidence to support such an interpretation is of special interest. It is now apparent that several nonmammalian species occur at Bambata sites and it may be assumed that they formed an intrinsic part of the diet (Table 28).

Such additions to the Bambata diet suggest, if anything, a less specialized approach to exploitation of the habitat than is evident from Acheulian sites. Unfortunately, most of our information on Bambata food refuse is restricted to cave sites or centralized "base camps" near water, such as Vlakkraal or Kalkbank. It may be argued that larger animals such as elephant, rhino, or hippo could have been killed and butchered at some distance from the caves, and only the flesh would have been brought back after the massive bones of these animals had been stripped and abandoned. Such activity would no doubt distort the archaeological evidence of dietary range at the site itself.

It might be expected that such butchery sites would contain relatively high percentages of large bones and fewer stone tools of a less formal design than those recovered from cave sites. Although the fossil record includes several bone accumulations apparently not associated with stone tools, these all contain a relatively wide range of species similar to those found at cave sites (Table 29). It may be postulated that these represent "base camps" near which suitable rocks were not available and no stone flaking took place. Dart and Kitching (1958) have proposed that bone would have served as a substitute raw material in such cases, and their analysis of the Kalkbank fauna has been submitted as evidence for such activity. Although one-third of the bone assemblage has been gnawed by porcupine, they point out that there is a marked disproportion in the survival rate of different body parts from various specimens. Following the dicta of the "osteodontokeratic" hypothesis, it is concluded that systematic selection and breakage by the hunters can explain these discrepancies (see Chapter 2). The survival rate for the different parts of the bovid skeleton at this site closely resembles that from Makapansgat and the gnawed goat-bone sample analyzed by Brain. Unfortunately, figures for distal–proximal survival of the Kalkbank bones have not been published, so that detailed comparisons are not possible. Without denying the use of bone at this site by the human occupants, there can be little doubt that gnawing of the camp refuse by carnivores and other scavengers has greatly distorted our view of any human activities involving bone tools.

EVIDENCE FOR CLIMATIC CHANGE

The relatively deep deposits containing the Bambata samples at several sites lend themselves to granulometric and other analyses of possible signs of climatic change during this period. Quantitative investigations of the deposits from Redcliff (Brain 1969d), Khami (Bond 1957), Cave of Hearths (Brain 1957e) and Florisbad (van Zinderen Bakker 1957) have each been based upon entirely independent analytical principles, and it is remarkable that these experiments have yielded such similar interpretations. The Redcliff deposits were tested for percentage of jasper grains, weight percentage of coarser particles, and weight percentage of calcium carbonate. These were chosen respectively as likely to indicate: intensity of hillslope erosion occurring in the cave catchment area, carrying capacity of water flowing through the cave entrance, and carbonate precipitation within the deposits. As explained in previous chapters, the Khami analysis is based on the weights of feldspar grains transported by water flowing from the surrounding granite amphitheatre. The Cave of Hearths analysis recorded variations in grain angularity, and at Florisbad the fluctuations in fossil pollens were investigated.

At Redcliff, the Bambata levels between 13 and 25 ft were sampled, at 1-ft intervals, and the fluctuations in coarse grains, jasper, and $CaCO_2$ are shown in Fig. 80. In the early stages of the Bambata occupation their percentage values (when compared with the values for the modern local soil) suggest that the hillside runoff and erosion was relatively greater than at present, reflecting a thin vegetation cover and weak anchorage of the soil. Later in this occupation series, there is a marked trend toward slower erosion rates, possibly reflecting conditions similar to, or wetter than, the present.

The Khami evidence has been taken to reflect conditions which are comparatively wetter than today. However, there is again a notably "drier" phase reflected in the deposits of the earlier levels of the Bambata accumulations. Remarkably, a similar pattern emerges from the somewhat confused samples from the Cave of Hearths. Here the samples from Beds 5 and 6 have been mixed to yield a sand-grain porosity range that suggests a climatic sequence wetter than that of today. In the mixed sample from Beds 7–9 there is an increase in the range of grain porosity which is taken to suggest an increase in annual precipitation. It must be stressed, however, that this bald summary of the results and their interpretation tends to obscure the justifiably cautious manner in which each analysis has been treated by Brain and Bond. Both authors present their analysis as experimental or pioneer attempts to extract climatic data and their interpretations are offered in the most tentative terms, without any claim to a final or conclusive judgment. At each site there exist a number of factors other than the climatic fluctuations shown in Fig. 80. Among these are changes in slope gradient adjacent to the site and changes in the gradient of the surface of occupational deposits. Since these (and other depositional processes) cannot be assessed or quantitatively analyzed, several serious doubts about the "climatic" interpretations may be raised. Considering the number of unknowns in this problem, it is all the more remarkable, therefore, to note that the results from each of the three sites has yielded a similar interpretation of climatic change during the Bambata period.

With this trend in mind, it is of great interest to note the qualitative observations by C. K. Cooke (1963) of the Bambata levels at Pomongwe and Tshangula. At both sites the lower portions of the Bambata deposits contain a large amount of clastic scree derived from the granite roof and walls of each cave. Passing upward through the deposits the density of the scree blocks was seen to

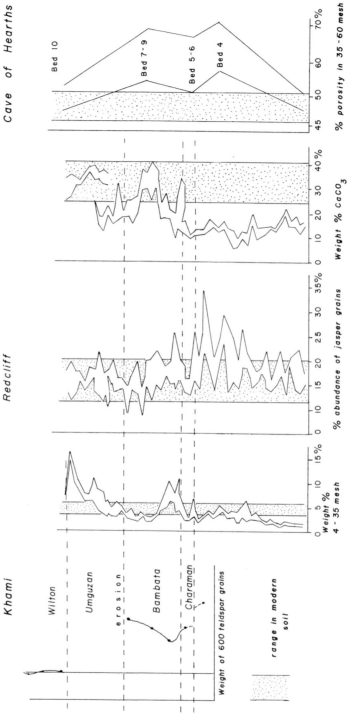

Fig. 80. Tentative correlation of granulometric studies of sediments (after Brain 1969d); and Cave of Hearths (Brain 1967e). from three archaeological sites: Khami (after Bond 1957); Redcliff

increase progressively. The possibility that spalling of the granite roof surface is largely influenced by changes in temperature and humidity cannot be lightly dismissed. Since the same trend was observed at both sites, it is unlikely that the increase in roof spalling through time is simply the result of some local geological quirk in cave structure. Although not on a quantitative basis, these two observations tend, nevertheless, to support the interpretation of climatic change presented by Brain and Bond.

Again, the microscopic analysis of rounded sand grains from Mwulu Beds II and III by King (Tobias 1954), although purely qualitative, tends to confirm the trend suggested by the other sites. Bed II, which is taken here on typological grounds to represent a very early stage of development of the "Mwulu" industry, contains numerous rounded grains which increase considerably in the overlying sterile red sand and become relatively scarce in Bed III. If the author's interpretation is correct, namely that the increase in rounded grains reflects an increase in eolian activity due to low vegetation coverage and relatively dry conditions outside the cave, the same assumed "dry-to-wet" trend emerges.

Finally, the pollen analysis of peat II at Florisbad reveals that the lowest sample in this layer (a few inches above the "Florisbad" sample) contains over 80% grass pollens and less than 20% Karroo scrub pollens, suggesting a higher mean annual rainfall than the area presently enjoys. Thereafter, the grass–scrub pollen ratios fluctuate, the grasses dominating all the higher peat II samples. There is also a rapid increase in halophyte pollens, which are taken to reflect an increase in the amount of standing water and also an increase in spring activity. This renewal in spring activity evidently reaches a peak near the top of peat II and during the deposition of the overlying clays. Although postdating the "Florisbad" artifact sample, probably by a fairly short period, this evidence suggests a similar trend towards wetter conditions, since the spring's activity is known to be controlled by local water-table fluctuations.

Similar evidence of spring eruption following the Bambata occupation at Rose Cottage may also be mentioned here. A 7-ft deep sterile sand has accumulated above this level, also strongly hinting at a rise in the local water table surrounding the cave.

To summarize, there are at least four quantitative analyses and several other qualitative reports that have been invoked as evidence of climatic change. At present it is clear that each case study on its own cannot be accepted as conclusive proof of such a change, but it is nevertheless remarkable that several different methodological approaches have produced a similar, albeit tentative, interpretation: (1) in the early stages of the Bambata tradition (from about 45,000 to 50,000 B.P.) annual rainfall was somewhat higher than at present in various areas, (2) mean annual rainfall increased with time during the Bambata period. Both conclusions can only be confirmed by further quantitative analysis of deposits from other Bambata sites.

STATUS AND RELATIONS WITH THE PIETERSBURG COMPLEX

Both the basic technology, range of tool designs, and the chronology of this complex suggests a close parallel with the loosely grouped industries from northern Africa, the Levant, and Europe, known as the Mousterian. It is now apparent that the general assumption found in most introductory textbooks on paleolithic prehistory—the "Stillbay" is the South African equivalent of the Upper Paleolithic period in Europe and the Levant—is substantially incorrect. Certainly, the available carbon-14 dates suggest that the Bambata technical tradition may have persisted in some areas after about 38,000 B.P., thus becoming broadly contemporary with the early part of the European Upper Paleolithic tradition. However, the major portion of its existence now appears to fall between 50,000 and 30,000 B.P., suggesting that it is the South African equivalent of the Mousterian complex to the north of the Sahara.

Apart from the still inadequate numerical analyses used to define the Bambata complex, there remains the extremely important problem of its relationship to the Pietersburg tradition described in the previous chapter. Samples ascribed to the Bambata group are stratigraphically later than the Pietersburg at no less than six caves, yet there is considerable overlap in the carbon-14 dates. If there is a true chronological overlap between the two, such a persistent stratigraphic relationship should not be expected. Sites with Pietersburg layers overlying Bambata material should also be expected. However, this is not the case, and the evidence presents a serious contradiction between the stratigraphic and carbon-dating record.

Given the present inadequacies of the analysis and records pertinent to this problem, at least three different explanations for dating contradictions may be presented. First, it may be argued that the actual age of the Pietersburg complex is near the extreme limits of the dating range of the carbon-14 technique, and the existing Pietersburg dates are mostly faulty or inadequate. Certainly, among numerous dates quoted from Pietersburg deposits, more than half the readings are merely "greater than" values while others appear to be definitely contaminated for various reasons. If the true age of the Pietersburg complex proved to be >50,000 B.P., the apparent chronological overlap with the Bambata would disappear and there would be no conflict with the stratigraphic evidence. However, there are several dates within the 45,000–30,000 B.P. range that cannot be faulted, and still others may be even younger. There is, therefore some reason to suppose that the two complexes do indeed overlap in radiocarbon age.

The second approach would be to deny the existence of two discrete complexes and treat all the recorded samples as one vast, variable complex: the so-called "Middle Stone Age" of previous literature with local or regional stratigraphic sequences. Any site with both Pietersburg and Bambata samples *in situ* is reported to contain consecutive phases of one local industry: thus, the Bambata becomes the "Middle Pietersburg" or "Upper Pietersburg" as presented by

Mason. Implicit in this model is the assumption that a particular phase of the local industry will display site-to-site variability or even layer-to-layer variability within one site. The variables will include: raw material, flaking technology, formal tool typology—in short, all those features that distinguish Pietersburg from Bambata artifact samples. To justify such variability the concept of "activity variants" is repeatedly invoked, yet the rare associated faunas give no hint of site-to-site differences in hunting or butchering activities. This approach thus obscures the very marked typological differences between Pietersburg and Bambata samples, and ignores the relatively abundant stratigraphic evidence which demonstrates that the Bambata is a later complex.

The third approach involves a compromise. Given that the early stages of the Pietersburg date to about 60,000 B.P. and given that the Bambata makes its appearance at about 50,000 B.P. in the eastern Transvaal and eastern Orange Free State, it is apparent that the Pietersburg complex persisted for a considerable period in other parts of South Africa after the advent of the Bambata tradition. Evidently, the areas where the Pietersburg technology continued in use during the "Bambata period" include the southern Cape coast, and the Karroo region, where no occurrence of a Bambata site has ever been reported after many years of research. Only this explanation will accommodate both the stratigraphic and carbon-14 dating evidence. The ultimate appearance of the "Stillbay" sample at Skildergat in the southwestern Cape Province may be understood when more systematic fieldwork has been completed in the western portion of South Africa. For the present, it can be tentatively postulated that the Bambata complex may have originated from some local development within the "Mwulu" area and dispersed to other parts of the country, excluding the semiarid interior and the southern Cape coastal region. The previously held view that the Bambata industry had purely local origins in the preceding Charaman ("Proto-Stillbay") no longer appears tenable in the light of recent work on the chronology and typological differences between the two industries.

Hopefully, this interpretation will be tested in the not too distant future by more thorough and complete numerical analyses of all the available Pietersburg and Bambata samples. Meanwhile, the present meager survey of the data is presented as the first step toward clarifying the confused status of the "Middle Stone Age."

RELATIONSHIP WITH THE LUPEMBAN INDUSTRY

Although the distribution of Lupemban sites lies mainly to the north of the area covered by the present work, there are nevertheless a few samples reported as "Lupemban" from southern Angola, South-West Africa, northern Zambia, Malawi, and the Transvaal. The chronological and technical relationship between this industry and the Bambata complex therefore deserves some attention.

TABLE 30

Typology of Lupemban Artiban Artifact Samples

| | Sangoan–Lower Lupemban | | | |
	Musolexi–Caimbo LMU and I levels (%)	Camafufo LMU and I levels (%)	Catongula LMU and I levels (%)	Mussolegi Luaco 6 28–12-m levels (%)
Tool types				
Hand-axes	—	1.5	2.1	17.6
Hand-axe–choppers	12.6	5.8	13.3	—
Picks	28.6	25.0	9.1	41.1
Core choppers	—	13.2	23.0	11.8
Core scrapers				
single	3.8	2.9	6.3	—
double	0.8	4.4	2.1	—
circular	5.5	8.8	11.2	—
end and side	3.4	—	2.1	—
Core axes, various	2.1	5.8	15.4	23.5
Lanceolate points, various	0.8	1.5	4.2	5.9
Polyhedral stones	5.9	20.6	2.1	—
Tranchets	—	—	—	—
Flake scrapers				
various	—	—	—	—
Burins	—	—	—	—
Battered lumps	29.5	8.3	8.4	—
Hammerstones	6.7	1.5	0.7	—
Grindstones	—	—	—	—
Anvils	—	—	—	—
Tool sample totals:	**237**	**68**	**143**	**17**
Core types [a]				
Single platform	—	1	1	—
Double platform	2	—	—	—
Multiplatform	—	—	—	—
Conical	—	—	—	—
Biconical and protobiconical	6	1	3	—
Discoid	13	3	20	1
Other	—	—	—	—
Core sample totals:	**21**	**5**	**24**	**1**

[a] Values in the core type and waste sections are numerical (as are all totals); other values in percent, as given in the column heads.

	Upper Lupemban							South-West Africa		Malawi sites	
Luxilo 1	Chachimba	Mbalabala	Chingufo	Matafari	Furi 1	Cauma	Mussolegi-Luaco 6 12–6-m levels	Peperkorrel	Chaminade 1A, 12 and 3	Mwanganda
(%)	(%)	(%)	(%)	(%)	(%)	(%)	(%)	(%)	(%)	(%)
—	—	3.3	—	3.2	3.1	7.3	—	—	—	—
—	—	—	—	10.8	12.5	2.4	—	—	—	—
24.1	—	—	—	8.8	9.4	7.3	—	15.3	3.1	—
—	—	—	—	2.5	—	4.9	10.0	—	6.5	—
—	—	—	—	—	—	—	—	2.8	3.7	1.4
—	—	—	—	—	—	—	—	2.8	3.7	1.4
—	—	—	—	—	—	—	—	4.2	3.7	1.4
—	—	—	—	—	—	—	—	2.8	3.1	1.4
60.5	87.0	82.8	95.0	35.5	43.8	34.0	30.0	39.5	1.2	5.4
14.9	11.9	8.8	3.5	4.9	12.5	17.0	40.0	1.4	5.6	—
—	1.5	—	—	3.2	—	2.4	—	—	—	—
—	—	0.7	1.4	0.6	—	7.3	—	—	—	—
—	—	4.7	—	24.6	15.6	17.0	20.0	31.0	64.5	80.0
—	—	—	—	—	—	—	—	—	4.9	4.1
—	—	—	—	1.3	—	—	—	—	—	2.7
—	—	—	—	1.9	3.1	—	—	—	—	—
—	—	—	—	1.3	—	—	—	—	—	2.7
—	—	—	—	1.9	—	—	—	—	—	—
450	67	149	286	158	32	41	10	72	162	74
—	—	—	—	1	1	—	7	—	—	3
—	—	—	—	1	2	—	—	—	—	—
—	—	—	—	4	2	3	—	15	—	1
—	—	—	—	1	1	—	—	10	—	1
—	—	—	—	3	8	1	7	—	—	2
—	—	27	—	21	5	39	6	—	—	13
3	4	12	3	—	—	—	6	1	—	—
3	4	39	3	31	19	43	26	26	—	20

(continued)

TABLE 30 (*continued*)

	Sangoan–Lower Lupemban			
	Musolexi–Caimbo LMU and I levels	Camafufo LMU and I levels	Catongula LMU and I levels	Mussolegi Luaco 6 28–12-m levels
	(%)	(%)	(%)	(%)
Waste [a]				
Flakes–plain platform	61	46	26	9
Prepared platform	12	3	—	5
Fragments	4	66	1	—
Redirecting blades	2	—	1	—
Waste sample totals:	**79**	**115**	**28**	**14**
Raw materials				
Quartz	54.9	51.1	33.0	58
Quartzite	30.5	41.0	41.5	16
Gres polymorphe	13.1	5.1	20.5	16
Chalcedony	1.5	2.8	5.1	—
Chert	—	—	—	—
Sample totals:	**259**	**117**	**176**	**51**

[a] Values in the core type and waste sections are numerical (as are all totals); other values in percent, as given in the column heads.

The industry takes its name from a diamond-mining exposure on the Lupemba stream near Tshikapa in southern Kasai (Breuil 1944). Although sealed in alluvial silts, the artifacts sample from this type site was not recovered by controlled excavations, and only a small selected tool collection was obtained. However, a few larger undistorted samples were referred to this group, particularly the materials excavated by Colette (1931) from the upper levels of Kalina Point, Kinshasa. The term was soon adopted to describe selected samples from Kenya and the numerous collections from both surface and sealed contexts in northeastern Angola (L. S. B. Leakey 1949). Subsequently reports of Lupemban finds in this area by Janmart (1947, 1948, 1953) and Breuil and Janmart (1950) are blighted by the absence of any numerical data by which the reader might gain some indication of the range, percentage composition, and variety of tool types within the industry. A similar absence of quantitative data greatly reduces

| | Upper Lupemban | | | | | | South-West Africa | | Malawi sites | |
Luxilo 1 (%)	Chachimba (%)	Mbalabala (%)	Chingufo (%)	Matafari (%)	Furi 1 (%)	Cauma (%)	Mussolegi-Luaco 6 12–6-m levels (%)	Peperkorrel (%)	Chaminade 1A, 12 and 3 (%)	Mwanganda (%)
—	—	—	—	61	21	20	33	—	50	—
8	100+	25	65	32	10	2	22	—	38	—
3	—	—	—	9	—	2	9	28	12	—
—	1	—	1	1	—	14	—	—	—	—
11	101+	25	66	103	31	38	64	35	100	241
—	—	—	—	—	—	—	31	—	50	46
—	—	—	—	—	—	—	6.5	100	49	53
—	—	—	—	—	—	—	62.5	—	—	—
—	—	—	—	—	—	—	—	—	—	1
—	—	—	—	—	—	—	—	—	1	—
—	—	—	—	—	—	—	107	312	—	314

the value of Mortelmans' (1962) claim for a four phase development of the industry in the western Congo basin. Only J. D. Clark (1963, 1966, 1968) has produced percentage analyses of large collected samples from the Lunda region of northeastern Angola. Of the more than 80 claimed Lupemban occurrences from the Companhia de Diamantes concession area, no indisputable evidence of a primary-context floor has survived. However, several of the earlier reports hint at small buried scatters in the "redistributed sands" or on old land surfaces evidently overlying river gravels. Clark has applied a standardized typology to a total of three "Lower Lupemban–Sangoan" samples and another nine samples, which are reported on stratigraphic grounds to be later in the sequence, and are labelled "Upper Lupemban."

The details of this standardized typology and the type percentages for each site are listed in Table 30. Brief inspection of this at once demonstrates that all

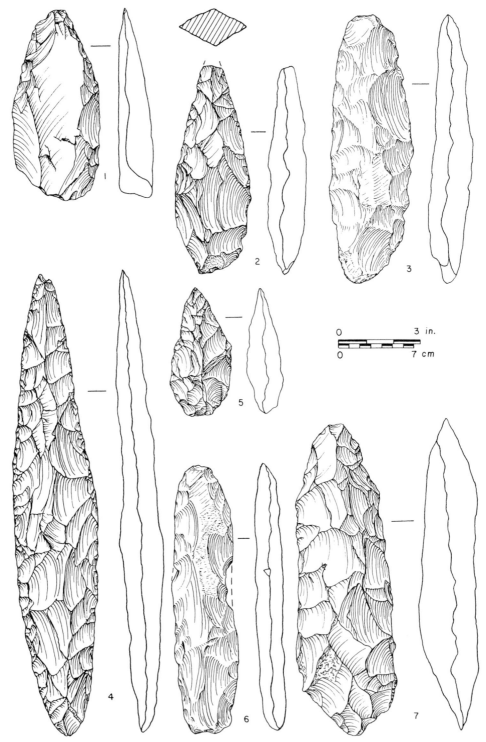

Fig. 81. Unifacial and bifacial points ascribed to the Lower Lupemban, northeastern Angola: (1, 3, 5, 6) Catongula; (4) Musolexi; (7) Muazanza. (After Clark 1963).

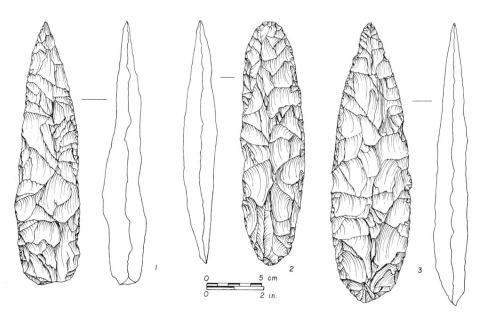

Fig. 82. Bifacial points ascribed to the Upper Lupemban, northeastern Angola: (1) Tijolaria; (2) Cammissele; (3) Toca. (After Clark 1968.)

the samples are from disturbed, geological contexts in which the individual artifacts are vertically distributed through several feet of sands and gravels. Apart from their broad typological homogeneity, they are of limited value. No associated fauna or human remains have been recovered although a wood-and-peat deposit in the lower part of the 3–4-m gravels (thought to contain the "Lower Lupemban–Sangoan" at adjacent sites) has yielded dates of 34,000 B.P. (UCLA-16a) and 38,000 ± 2500 B.P. (UCLA-168) . A pollen spectrum from the same deposit is reported to contain a high proportion (38%) of grasses, which is taken by van Zinderen Bakker (1963) to reflect a relatively lower annual rainfall than the present. Similar conditions have been reported from the broadly contemporary pollen spectrum at Kalambo Falls (see Chapter 3) in the "Sangoan" levels.

From the "flats gravels" at Mufo, another peat-and-wood sample has yielded a date of 14,503 ± 560 B.P. (C-581) and a pollen spectrum of a cool ravine forest cover (van Zinderen Bakker 1963) , indicating both moister and cooler conditions than the present. Although these data are reported to be directly associated with an "Upper Lupemban" tool sample, this is not described or analyzed and the validity of the diagnosis cannot, therefore, be tested. Until primary-context floors are excavated in direct association with charcoal, there must remain some doubt about the precise chronology of the Lupemban. Nevertheless, Clark's pioneer attempts to standardize the typology and stratigraphy of the Lupemban in this area have proved to be an invaluable contribution to an understanding of the previously confused terminology and descriptions for this area (Figs. 81 and 82).

Furthermore, his work has allowed MacCalman and Viereck (1967) to compare their surface collections from Peperkorrel, South-West Africa, with those of the "type" area more than 1000 miles to the north. The Peperkorrel collection comes from a quartzite hillslope rubble and is interpreted by the authors as a "factory" site. Although the part containing the most tools is a numerically distorted sample, it nevertheless shows the same range to types found in the Angolan samples and the metric distribution of selected tool types is used to support the authors' opinion that this is an extreme southerly "outlier" of the Lupemban. Since the recorded distribution of the Lupemban has been previously restricted to the tropical forest zones of Africa, the claim for its presence at a position enjoying only 10–15 inches of mean rainfall is remarkable. Once again, the absence of reliable sealed samples prevents any conclusive interpretation of the meaning of the apparent discrepancy in Lupemban distribution.

The presence of the Lupemban at Kalambo Falls has been reported by Clark (1969) from sealed contexts in several rubble layers, although details have not been released on the typological similarities with the "type" collections. Evidently the samples have been "typologically separated" from the rubbles overlying the Sangoan deposits in all four sites, which comprise a total of eight trenches. At all four sets of trenches rubble I is present and can be locally split into two stratigraphic subunits called rubbles Ia and Ib, respectively. In areas where the two rubbles cannot be divided, it is known as rubble I composite. In a few localities the rubble can be split into three levels of which the lowest is labelled rubble Ic. Scattered charcoals from rubble Ic in trench AI have yielded a series of readings (L-3991): 30,500 ± 2000 B.P.; 27,500 ± 2300 B.P. (humic acid extract). Clark has suggested that this date may be too old, and that the charcoals were derived from underlying levels. Since his judgment is based on unpublished typological grounds, it cannot be evaluated precisely. The rubble complex apparently contains a mixture of Lupemban (various stages) and "Magosian" at Sites A and B, so that they are of minimal value. At Sites C and D no "Magosian" is reported, so that the Lupemban samples are uncontaminated. However, all this material occurs in a geological context and cannot be regarded as an absolutely reliable example of the local Lupemban.

In trench A4 a "Lower Lupemban" sample is provisionally named from a clay-with-rubble below the rubble I complex. Scattered charcoal from this deposit yielded a date (GrN-4648) of 31,660 ± 600 B.P. Although two pollen samples are reported as associated with the "Lupemban" in the same trench, in fact they both derive from clays *underlying* the rubble complex by 1.5 ft, and presumably predate the Lupemban horizon. Both spectra are dominated by grasses (50 and 66%) and are taken to reflect conditions similar to the present, or slightly wetter. Any further assessment of the Lupemban material from this site must await future publications of the lithic materials. The same details are needed from the two Congo sites: Lemba dated to 30,000 B.P. (Lv-99) and Basoko River dated to 30,000 B.P. (Lv-97), both reported by Dossin (1962).

Perhaps the first true primary-context "floors" tentatively ascribed to the Lupemban are the Mwanganda elephant-butchering site (Clark and Haynes 1970) and the series of three horizontal artifact concentrations from Chaminade IA (Clark, Haynes, and Mawby 1967). At Mwanganda, the small tool assemblage (see Fig. 83 and Table 30) is scattered among the bones of a single elephant and clearly represents the detritus of a specialized activity. It is hardly surprising, therefore, that several tool types listed for the Angolan "type" Lupemban are missing from this assemblage. A similar case may exist for the Chaminade "concentrations" which are evidently dominated by flakes without any trace of edge damage. Unfortunately, no trace of faunal remains has survived with this material, and they have been interpreted as "workshop" localities with relatively few worked tools remaining.

Undoubtedly, as more primary-context information emerges for the Lupemban, it will become increasingly apparent that site-to-site variations in tool percentages are to be expected as more is learned of different activities during this period. For the present, however, the Lupemban can only be viewed as a typological phenomenon represented in the "type" areas by the least reliable samples. These are nearly all derived from mixed or distorted collections, taken partly from *in situ* and partly from the surface or spoil heaps. They are invariably derived from geological contexts in which individual specimens are scattered through great depths of deposits. None of the published data demonstrates a close association between artifacts and charcoal or pollen samples, and the assumed chronology and environmental data for the industry can be viewed as only very tenuous.

In spite of all these shortcomings, there remains the relatively consistent tool-type distribution of the Lupemban, which clearly differs considerably from that of the Bambata complex to the south, where the presence of hand axes, picks, core axes, gouges, core scrapers, and bifacial "Lupemban" points is unknown. This considerable divergence in typology between the two regions would seem sufficient grounds to classify the Lupemban as a separate industrial complex with its own industries, phases, and activity variants, as yet to be worked out in detail in the future.

With the major differences in mind, it is difficult to equate the two "Later Sangoan" or "Lupemban" samples claimed by Mason (1962a) from Linksfield and Primrose Ridge in the southern Transvaal. These are two surface collections from hillslope situations near Johannesburg. Mason has been at pains to demonstrate that they differ from both Cave of Hearths Bed 5 and other Pietersburg samples, but it remains impossible to compare these samples with samples from the "Mwulu" industry which it appears to resemble at least in the range of tool types. There are evidently a wide range of trimmed-point types and a higher percentage of *à dos naturel* sidescrapers in these two samples, but the usual plea for more detailed comparisons must be stated again in this case. At present it seems that the Linksfield and Primrose Ridge sites are more likely to represent some variations within the Bambata complex rather than another "southern outlier" of the Lupemban.

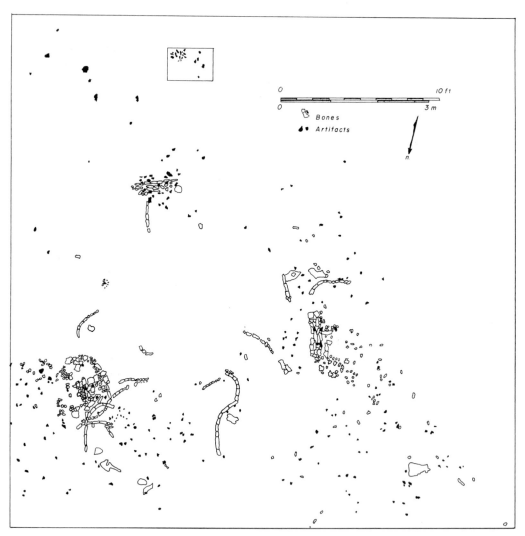

Fig. 83. Plan of the elephant-butchery site at Mwanganda, ascribed to the Lupemban industry. (After Clark and Haynes 1970.)

6

Howiesonspoort
and Related Sites

The Howiesonspoort Shelter about 30 miles inland from the southern Cape coast near Grahamstown was excavated in the early 1920s by J. Hewitt, who recovered an apparently homogenous artifact sample from some 18 inches of deposit. Stapleton and Hewitt (1927–1928) reported that the same variety of tools was to be found at all depths between the deposit surface and bedrock, and they suggested that the shelter had been occupied by a single group of people over an unknown period. Following the normal procedure for that time, they omitted any numerical breakdown of the excavated sample but published instead a series of "typical" artifacts representing the Howiesonspoort. Although it is no longer certain whether Hewitt kept all the lithic material from the site or selected in favor of "typical" specimens, his extant collection would repay further analysis. A remaining fragment of the deposit has been excavated recently by H. Deacon and J. Deacon (personal communication) using more rigorous controls, and this work has confirmed Hewitt's original suggestion that a single homogenous sample is present. The site, therefore, represents the earliest discovery of a presumably complete artifact sample of an industry not previously described and, as

such, it is an appropriate choice for a name site to describe that industry
(Fig. 84).

Recognizing this fact, Goodwin (1929) proposed that the name be adopted to
describe a "variant" in which he included several surface sites from the southwestern Cape coast. Since all these are selected collections from unrelated and
probably mixed contexts, they contributed nothing toward clarifying this new
discovery. Of far greater importance is the still unpublished stratum reported by
Jolly (1948) to contain "Howiesonspoort" material at Skildergat cave, an occurrence first observed by Peers who originally excavated there. Subsequently, the
name has been applied to excavated materials from five other caves in the southwestern Cape region, but no systematic comparison of all this material has been
undertaken yet.

To date, the term has not been applied outside this region, although it has
been recognized as broadly contemporary with the so-called "Modderpoort variant" of the eastern Orange Free State and the so-called "Rhodesian Magosian"
by Malan (1946, 1949a, 1952, 1957). Unfortunately, this correlation could be
supported by only qualitative judgments on typology and presumed stratigraphic
sequences at that time, and both these terms have been abandoned for want of
reliable support.

This chapter, while avoiding the application of the term "Howiesonspoort"
outside the southwestern Cape region, attempts to show the marked similarity
between samples from this area and those from sites distributed over the northern interior. As usual, the inevitable absence of any standardized typology makes
it impossible to give any insight into the quantitative relationships between
"similar" samples from different sites. Sufficient information has been obtained,
however, to compile a table of presence or absence, using the same typology applied in Chapter 5 to define the Bambata complex (see Table 32). Only samples
excavated from sealed contexts are included among the 15 sites listed in the
analysis, and their positions are given in the map in Fig. 85. Scores of surface
collections from South-West Africa and elsewhere have been excluded from the
typological list for want of adequate collecting controls and analytical reporting.
Such collections include those reported by Malan (1949b) and Fock (1959) as
"Magosian" or "Second Intermediate", and also the collections from the Zambezi
valley (Clark 1950a) and Botswana (C. K. Cooke 1967).

It is already apparent that an alarming variety of names is in current use to
describe materials similar in typological composition. Several other names have
been applied to various samples in the past, although some consensus on terminology does appear to be emerging for this period. The distribution map shows
two geographical site clusters named "Howiesonspoort" in the southern Cape
and "Umguzan" in Matebeleland, with two sites between these areas as yet not
ascribed to either group. A summary of previous published terminologies for the
17 excavated samples is given in Table 31.

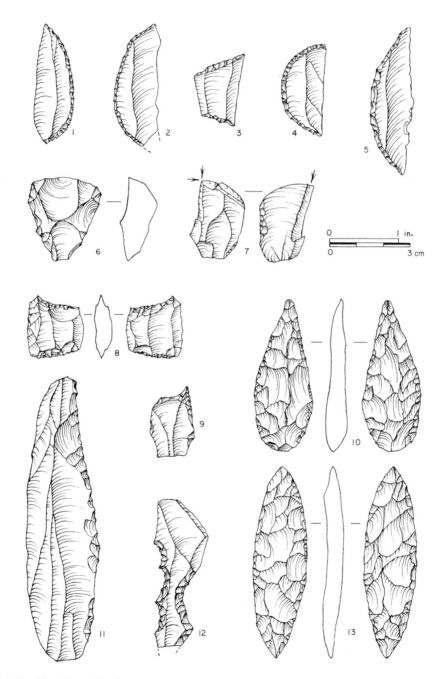

Fig. 84. Tools from Howiesonspoort sites: (1, 2, 4, 5) backed crescents; (3) backed trapezium; (6) utilized Levallois core; (7) burin; (8) *outil écaillé;* (9) borer; (10, 13) bifacial point; (11) sidescraper; (12) double sidescraper. Speciments 2, 3, and 5 are from Howiesonspoort; all others are from Tunnel Cave.

233

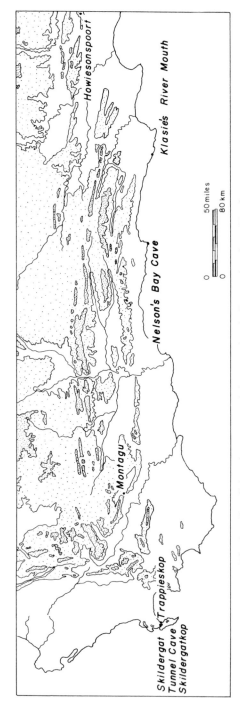

Fig. 85. Localities of caves containing samples similar to that from Howiesonspoort.

TABLE 31

Terminology for 17 Howiesonspoort and Umguzan Sites

Site	Depth or layer	Reference	Sample published as:
1. Mumbwa	Lower cave earth 2.5–7 ft	Clark (1942)	Rhodesian Stillbay industry
2. Pomongwe	7–13 and 4	C. K. Cooke (1963)	Rhodesian Magosian
3. Khami	Layer 6, Levels 1–5	C. K. Cooke (1950, 1953, 1955, 1957b)	Second Intermediate—Magosian industry
		Jones and Summers (1946)	Magosian
4. Bambata	1 ft 9 in.–5 ft	N. Jones (1940, 1949)	Upper Bambata
5. Amadzimba	Decomposed granite 18–30 in.	C. K. Cooke and Robinson (1954)	Rhodesian Stillbay industry
6. Nswatugi	Ocherous granite sand 1–4 ft	N. Jones (1933)	Upper Bambata zone
7. Sitanda Dam	A–2, 3, and 4	C. K. Cooke and Garlake (1968)	Tshangula (Magosian)
8. Zombepata		C. K. Cooke (1971)	Tshangula (Magosian)
9. Cave of Hearths	8–5 ft	Mason (1962a)	Upper Pietersburg
10. Border Cave	Below rubble	C. K. Cooke et al. (1945)	Epi-Pietersburg
11. Howiesonspoort	0–18 in.	Goodwin and van Riet Lowe (1929)	Howiesonspoort variant
12. Klasie's River Mouth	Layers 21–10	Singer and Wymer (in press)	Howiesonspoort
13. Skildergat	—	Jolly (1948)	Cape Peninsula Magosian
14. Skildergatkop	0.7–1.2 m	Malan (1955b)	
15. Tunnel Cave	0–68 in.	Malan (1955b)	
16. Trappieskop	0.95–1.0 m	Goodwin (1953)	
17. Montagu Cave	Layer 2, upper layers	Keller (1969b)	Howiesonspoort

THE UMGUZAN GROUP OF SITES

Those listed as 11–17 in Table 31 have been ascribed to the Howiesonspoort, and 2–8 to the *Umguzan*. The latter term was proposed by Cooke, Summers, and Robinson (1966) to describe the Matabeleland group, but this choice has been criticized since the name is taken from an implementiferous gravel site on the Umguza River near Sawmills (N. Jones 1924). The sample from this locality is neither complete, nor in primary context, and cannot be used as a reference for numerical comparisons. Instead, the very large excavated sample from Pomongwe has been used for definitive description of the industry. C. K. Cooke (1968) was later persuaded to employ the name "Tshangula" in its place, but this choice is equally unfortunate, since the presence of this industry in the Tshangula cave deposit remains in doubt and, if present, is too small to provide a percentage analysis (Fig. 86).

The name "Umguzan" is retained here because the Sawmills discovery has historical precedence over all other sites, including the so-called type site of the "Magosian"—a term which has been used until recently to describe the group.

The rejection of the Magosi rock cistern in Uganda as a type site for this material is justified on various grounds. First described by Wayland and Burkitt (1932) and reanalyzed by Clark (1957a), it was again excavated and found to contain more than one industry. The original Magosian sample is therefore a mixture of industries and as such, is entirely invalid as a typological reference (Cole 1967a). In retrospect, the widespread use of the term "Magosian" in southern Africa now appears somewhat surprising considering the vast distance separating the two regions. The lack of any absolute chronology and the complete absence of quantitative controls were criticisms presented by Hole (1959) in an important paper which deserved closer attention at the time.

A few additional samples from reliable sealed contexts have been compared with one or more of the above sites, but too little typological information is available for inclusion in Table 31 are as follows:

Site	Reference	Sample published as:
Kalambo Falls	Clark (1969)	Magosian
Redcliff	Brain and Cooke (1967)	Rhodesian Magosian
Sibebe Shelter	Vogel (1970)	Transitional MSA– Second Intermediate
Tshangula	C. K. Cooke (1963)	Magosian

TYPOLOGY

The same type list used in describing the Bambata complex can be applied here, (see Table 32), but two important additions occur in the list: backed blades and backed crescents. The backed blades are small blades usually not

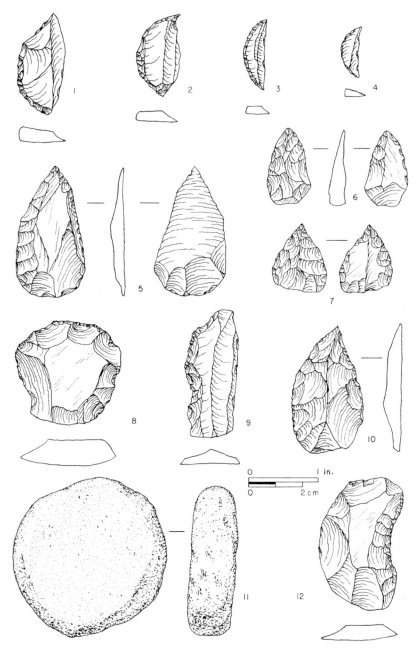

Fig. 86. Umguzan tools from Pomongwe: (1–4) backed crescents; (5) unifacial point with reduced butt; (6, 7) bifacial points; (8) circular scraper; (9) sidescraper; (10) unifacial point; (11) grindstone; (12) sidescraper.

TABLE 32

Tool Types Present in Howiesonspoort and Related Sites

	Nsalu	Leopard's Hill	Mumbwa	Nata River	Pomongwe	Khami	Bambata	Amadzimba	Cave of Hearths	Border Cave	Howiesonspoort	Klasie's River Mouth	Skildergat	Skildergatkop	Tunnel Cave	Trappieskop
Tools																
Trimmed points	X	X	X	X	X	X	X	X	X	X	X	?	X	X	X	X
Sidescrapers	X	X	X	X	X	X	X	X	X	—	X	X	X	—	X	X
Frontal scrapers	X	X	X	X	X	X	X	X	X	X	X	X	—	X	—	X
Circular scrapers	X	X	—	—	X	X	—	—	—	—	—	?	—	—	—	—
Burins	—	—	X	—	X	X	X	X	X	—	X	X	X	—	X	X
Borers	—	—	—	—	X	X	—	X	X	—	—	—	—	X	—	—
Outils écaillés	X	X	X	—	X	X	X	—	X	—	X	X	X	X	X	—
Curve-backed knives	X	X	X	—	X	X	—	X	X	X	X	X	—	—	—	X
Backed crescents	?	X	X	X	X	X	X	X	X	X	X	X	X	X	X	X
Backed blades	X	X	X	X	X	X	X	X	X	X	X	X	X	X	X	X
Utilized blades	X	X	X	—	X	X	X	X	X	X	X	X	X	X	X	X
Utilized flakes	X	X	X	—	X	X	—	X	X	—	X	X	—	X	X	X
Grindstones	X	X	X	—	X	X	—	?	X	—	X	—	—	—	—	—
Other types	X	X	—	—	X	X	—	X	X	—	—	X	—	X	X	—
Cores																
Blade cores	X	X	X	X	X	X	X	X	X	X	X	X	X	X	X	—
Discoid cores	X	X	X	X	X	X	—	X	X	—	X	X	—	X	X	X
Levallois cores	?	X	X	X	X	X	X	X	X	—	X	X	X	?	—	X

larger than 1 inch, with one lateral margin blunted by the backing technique. Both size and shape vary considerably. The backed crescents have one margin backed in a convex plan form, so that the backing intersects the opposite margin at both tips. These are rarely larger than 1 inch long, and their shape varies.

UMGUZAN AND BAMBATAN TYPOLOGICAL DIFFERENCES

As the Umguzan is reported from levels directly overlying the Bambatan in at least four sites from Rhodesia, it may be assumed to reflect technological changes following the Bambatan in that area. For this reason, detailed changes between the two are of considerable interest. Cooke (1968) has presented a standardized analysis of three Umguzan levels and two from the Bambatan, all of which contain very large samples and therefore provide reasonable percentage proportions for each type (Table 33). This table suggests several differences between the two

TABLE 33

Tool Types [a, b]

Types	Bambatan		Umguzan		
	Pomongwe (%)	Khami (%)	Pomongwe (%)	Khami (%)	Sitanda (%)
Microlithic					
Anvils	—	—	0.1	—	0.3
Microliths	—	—	10.9	29.5	16.1
Burins	—	—	—	0.7	0.1
Borers	—	—	0.4	1.1	0.7
Points	—	—	0.8	1.5	0.1
Battered crystals	—	—	8.3	—	0.1
Macrolithic					
Points	14.8	19.5	14.8	18.8	11.8
Plain anvils	3.4	10.2	4.1	0.4	1.5
Bipolar anvils	—	1.7	0.7	1.5	0.1
Pebble tools	1.5	2.4	0.5	0.7	0.3
Burins	5.1	2.4	—	3.6	0.4
Borers	0.5	0.9	2.3	1.5	0.4
Adzes	—	1.9	—	—	—
Backed blades	8.2	3.8	2.4	10.6	11.5
Backed flakes	—	—	—	1.1	0.1
Crescents	5.6	2.6	0.8	1.5	0.5
Saws	6.7	3.1	0.8	1.1	0.3
Kasouga flakes	1.5	1.2	4.2	—	0.1
Gouges	—	—	4.9	—	0.5
Rubbers/grindstones	—	0.5	—	1.8	—
Scrapers					
Side-	19.0	15.0	15.0	6.6	25.5
End-	12.3	6.1	8.9	4.4	13.3
Notched	6.7	10.2	6.1	4.4	8.7
Compound	8.2	14.2	8.5	4.4	5.9
Circular	6.2	3.3	5.4	4.4	3.0
Tool totals:	**195**	**421**	**745**	**271**	**749**
Core types					
Thin radial	19.3	30.3	40.3	49.0	51.8
Thick radial	78.0	63.9	35.4	20.8	23.5
Polyhedral	—	2.2	—	4.4	7.3
Triangular	1.3	3.2	0.4	2.6	2.6
Blade	1.9	0.4	17.4	12.8	8.1
Microcores	—	—	6.7	10.1	6.9
Core totals:	**758**	**760**	**826**	**455**	**423**

[a] After C. K. Cooke (1968).
[b] Totals, numbers; all other values are percentages.

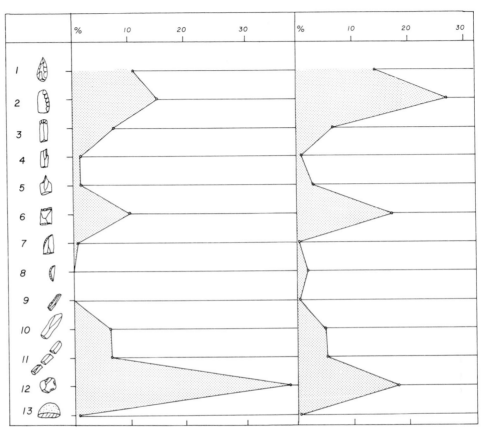

Fig. 87. Cave of Hearths: tool type percentage frequencies for Beds 6–8 (left) and Bed 9 (right).

industries, but these cannot be accepted as definitive, particularly since the Pomongwe and Khami values differ remarkably from those first published in the original site reports. Rubbers and/or grindstones are in fact present in the Bambatan sample from Pomongwe, not Khami, and of more importance, the so-called "crescents" and "backed blades" from both Bambatan samples refer to partially backed knives or à dos naturel specimens, and do not conform in any way to the definitions of these two types given above. True backed crescents and blades do not appear until the Umguzan levels, although a few specimens may be found in the topmost spits of the Bambata, probably the result of admixture. Ultimately, only two major typological changes can be detected with the disappearance of the Bambatan and the advent of the Umguzan:

1. The appearance of true backed blades and backed crescents. Although the backing technique was known and used in the Bambatan for *localized* blunting of part of a flake or blade margin (the curve-backed knife), it is not until the Umguzan that totally backed margins appear.

2. There is a marked decrease in the overall dimensions of all artifacts when the Umguzan appears. In Cooke's typology, this change is reflected in the presence of "microlithic" versions of several Bambatan types. Evidently, smaller flakes were required as blanks for the manufacture of various flake tools, and for this reason most Umguzan cores were flaked down to a smaller size before rejection. Curiously, this change does not appear to be related to any very marked changes in raw material usage. At Khami there is a slight increase in the amount of agate and chalcedony with the first appearance of the Umguzan, but vein quartz and opal breccia remain the dominant raw materials used at this site.

Although numerical comparisons between the two industries are virtually absent, it is nonetheless of great interest to survey the comments and observations of excavators at some of the other caves listed above. Only Cave of Hearths provides quantitative information on typological changes between the two horizons. As the samples from the 13–8-ft levels are ascribed to the Bambata complex, it is likely that the overlying 8–5-ft levels will be closely related to the Umguzan. As the graphs in Fig. 87 show, true backed elements appear for the first time above the 8-ft level, and there is a notable increase in the frequency of small cores above the same level. This decrease in dimensions is apparent among both the tools and the waste flakes, but has not been placed on a metrical basis.

At the two other caves where similar samples overlie levels related to the Bambata complex—namely, Border Cave and Skildergat—exactly the same changes have been observed. At Border Cave, the excavators note that in the "Epi-Pietersburg" (overlying the Bambatan):

> Several highly developed and specialized tools occur, the most numerous of these being backed blades made on fragments of Levallois blades . . . In most cases the secondary "backing" was executed by using the main cleavage face of the flake as striking platform . . . . The backing, in the majority of specimens, is confined to the extremities of the arcs . . . [Cooke, Malan, and Wells 1945: 8].

This sample differs from the Umguzan samples already discussed in a few important details: small triangular pressure-flaked points are present, there is "an abundance of long narrow and slender ribbonlike blades with prepared striking platforms," (Cooke, Malan, and Wells 1945: 9), and burins are reported to be absent. Although the detailed analysis of Eggers (1970) is not yet available, it is already apparent that this sample cannot be directly related to the Umguzan group: although it shares the same range of tool types, there are, nevertheless, important differences in the proportions of tools and frequencies of flaking techniques being used.

At Skildergat, Jolly notes that the "Magosian" (Howiesonspoort) differs from the underlying "Stillbay" (Bambata) in that it contains large backed blades and crescents, and the trimmed points and cores are notably smaller. At two other caves in the Cape coastal region, Montagu and Klasie's River Mouth, the Howiesonspoort overlies samples referred in Chapter 4 to the Pietersburg complex.

Montagu does not show any marked disconformity between the bottom of the Howiesonspoort and the top of the preceding industry, nor is there any sterile deposition between them that might suggest a temporary pause in occupation at the cave. At Klasie's River Mouth, on the other hand, the Howiesonspoort layers are readily distinguished from the preceding Mossel Bay deposits: a thick series of black hearths are banked up against a massive rock fall which caps the underlying sands-with-shell that contains the Mossel Bay. There is also a sharp increase in the use of chalcedony at the bottom of this Howiesonspoort hearth sequence—a trend that increases through the series of hearths and diminishes toward the top.

Exact differences between the Umguzan and Howiesonspoort remain to be worked out. Although they evidently share the same range of tools and core techniques, it is already clear that more crystalline rock was used among the Rhodesian groups, particularly vein quartz and chalcedony. The Howiesonspoort group, although using far more chalcedony and silcrete than is found in the earlier Mossel Bay samples, nevertheless utilized large quantities of quartzite, especially at localities where crystalline rock was scarce. Another marked feature of the Howiesonspoort is the persistent occurrence of very long blades, some of which have been backed. It is probable that the production of such specimens in Rhodesia is impossible due to the intractable nature of most of the crystalline raw materials.

CHRONOLOGICAL PROBLEMS

Although little evidence of such a debate has yet appeared in print, it is widely believed that the carbon-14 dating of the samples variously named "Second Intermediate" or "Magosian" is problematical. Most of the confusion has been caused by the total absence of any adequate definition of what is meant, but these terms and various samples with dates greater than 40,000 B.P. have been ascribed to one or other name without adequate supporting data. In particular, Keller (in press) has ascribed the lower occupation horizons of Layer 2 at Montagu to the "Second Intermediate" when in fact they are more closely related to the Mossel Bay industry and may belong to the Pietersburg complex. His suggestion that there are no significant differences between the top and the bottom of the layer (containing seven occupation horizons) cannot be accepted. The so-called "backer crescents" from Horizons 6 and 7 at the bottom of the layer are in fact thick, wedgelike fragments that are known from other Mossel Bay samples. They are neither crescent nor were they made by the backing technique.

A similar error in definition has entered the literature in the form of the "Upper South African Magosian" from Rose Cottage Cave. Malan (1952) makes no mention of the backing technique from this level at all, and his short description conforms far more closely with the type list from the Bambata complex. Mason (1969c) is correct in pointing out the affinity between this sample and the equally ancient Bushman Rock occurrence: their similarity is probably typo-logical as well as chronological.

In fact, the Umguzan–Howiesonspoort chronology shows (with one doubtful exception) a uniformity which is consistent with its stratigraphic position fol-lowing the Bambata complex. Following the procedure in previous chapters, each reading is listed separately.

Pomongwe:

3 ft 9 in. depth   SR-11   15,800 ± 200 B.P. (13,850 B.C.)

This sample comes from the top of the Umguzan sequence at Pomongwe and therefore dates the end of the occupation rather than the beginning, which by interpolation with the preceding Bambatan readings should date to about 20,000 B.P.

Howiesonspoort:

I-1844   18,740 ± 320 B.P. (16,190 B.C.)

Klasie's River Mouth:

Layer 19   >18,400 B.P.
Layer 17   28,100 ± 1500 B.P. (26,150 B.C.)

The obvious inversion between these two selected dates is only one problem in an otherwise bewildering array of readings from several different hearths in this complex. The others (from bottom to top) are >34,000, >32,000, >35,000, >37,000, >38,000, >35,000, and >38,130 B.P. from Layer 8 at the top of the sequence. The persistent inversions and "greater than" readings reflect the same inconsistencies seen in the entire series of deposits at this site. As the most meticulous care was taken to obtain only large charcoals for these readings, contamination either prior to or during deposition must be invoked to explain the erratic sequence. The selection of the two dates from Layers 19 and 17 cannot be justified on any grounds other than the fact that they fall into an overall chronological sequence for the Klasie's River Mouth deposits viewed as a whole.

Montagu Cave:

Layer 2; horizon 1?, near top   23,200 ± 180 B.P. (21,250 B.C.)
Layer 2; between horizons 5 and 6   19,100 ± 110 B.P. (17,150 B.C.)

The reliability of these dates is also open to question in view of their inversion.

Holley Shelter:

24–30 inches   BM-30   18,200 ± 500 B.P. (16,250 B.C.)

Like Sibebe Shelter (Vogel 1970) it remains uncertain whether this sample belongs with the group or not since too little information is available on its typology. Certainly the above date would suggest that it is at least contemporary. Another reading (BM-34) of 4400 ± 150 B.P. from the 18–24-inch levels must be discounted as contaminated—probably by later charcoal from the overlying layers.

Newhof-Koewas:

$$19,800 \pm 450 \text{ B.P. } (17,850 \text{ B.C.})$$

The sample reported by Viereck (1967) is a calcrete associated with a "developed Middle Stone Age." Since its tool-type composition is not reported, its inclusion in this group cannot be accepted.

ASSOCIATED FAUNA AND DIET

Although more than half the listed artifact samples were recovered in direct association with mammalian fauna, the usual absence of published information on bone remains must be once again noted. As previously mentioned, species lists have been released for combined layers from only a few of the deeper caves so that faunal evidence for a single cultural horizon is obscured. From Mumbwa, a very small and fragmentary collection has been reported: zebra, hyena, reedbuck, hartebeest, and warthog are present. The importance of more detailed faunal analysis is again demonstrated by Brain's analysis of the Pomongwe collections. Numerical comparisons between the associated fauna of the Bambata and overlying Umguzan levels here revealed important clues for and understanding of the technological changes which distinguish the two horizons. With the advent of the Umguzan, several larger game animals disappear from the deposits: *Equus capensis* an extinct horse, waterbuck, leopard, roan antelope, kudu, reedbuck, and a few smaller animals such as honey badger, cane rat, and porcupine. Individual counts for both layers may be compared in Table 34.

Obviously, the evidence from only one site cannot be accepted as conclusive for a shift in the pattern of the local diet. Fortunately, this same trend has been confirmed in the still unpublished faunal analysis for Klasie's River Mouth. Evidently, the larger game animals found in the lower Mossel Bay sequence have mostly disappeared by the advent of the Howiesonspoort hearth complex, which contains mainly bones of smaller antelope in the springbok–duiker size range.

The fact that a similar shift in faunal content has occurred in two regions separated by over 1000 miles can hardly be dismissed as coincidental. Improved analysis of the faunas from some of the deeper sites such as Cave of Hearths and Border Cave would help to further confirm this trend, as would full publication of other sites like Redcliff and Klasie's River Mouth.

Two possible interpretations may be suggested: (1) a shift in the distributions of species in the game population as a whole; (2) selection by the Umguzan

TABLE 34

Faunas of the Bambatan and Umguzan Levels, Pomongwe [a]

Genus and species	Description	Bambatan	Umguzan
MAMMALIAN			
Lagomorpha			
Lepus sp.	Hare	2	3
Rodentia			
Pedetes sp.	Springhare	1	1
Hystrix sp.	Porcupine	1	—
Carnivora			
Mellivora capensis	Cape honey badger	1	—
Hyracoidea			
Procavia capensis	Hyrax	10	10
Heterohyrax	Extinct giant hyrax	1	6
Perissodactyla			
Equus burchelli	Burchell's zebra	3	3
Equus capensis	Extinct horse	2	—
Artiodactyla			
Potomochoerus sp.	Bush pig	1	1
Phacochoerus aethiopicus	Cape warthog	4	5
Strepsiceros strepsiceros	Kudu	1	—
Taurotragus oryx	Eland	1	—
Sylvicapra grimmia	Duiker	6	3
Kobus ellipsiprymnus	Waterbuck	3	—
Redunca arundinum	Reedbuck	4	—
Hippotragus equinus	Roan	1	—
Hippotragus niger	Sable	2	4
Damaliscus lunatus	Tsessebe	5	2
Connochaetes taurinus	Wildebeest	1	4
Oreotragus oreotragus	Klipspringer	4	3
Raphicerus campestris	Steenbok	9	5
NONMAMMALIAN			
Rock pigeon		2	1
Vulture		—	1
Francolin		—	1
Tortoise		5	9
Monitor lizard		3	2
Python		1	3
Rock lizard		1	1
Ostrich eggshell fragments		11	69
Mussel shell fragments		1	1

[a] Numerals represent minimum numbers of individuals.

hunters of smaller species from a stable game population. As there is no reliable evidence to support the concept of deliberate choice of animals in either this or any preceding industry, it seems more likely that the Umguzan (and the broadly contemporary Howiesonspoort to the south) partly reflects hunting adaptations to a changing game population. Such a proposition assumes that the hunters took random samples from the local game population at all times. A decrease in the number of large species in the population would, therefore, be reflected in the hunter's sample. Differences between the tool kits of the Bambatan and Umguzan may be at least partly explained in the light of such adaptations from large to small animal hunting.

ASSOCIATED DEPOSITS AND CLIMATIC IMPLICATIONS

As previously discussed (Chapters 3, 5) the only quantitative analyses of deposits are from Khami and Redcliff. Brain's data from Redcliff shows a dramatic increase in the proportions of large sand grains in the Umguzan levels—a trend that peaks near the top of these deposits. The percentage abundance of jasper grains fluctuates within the range for modern local soils while the percentage of $CaCO_3$ decreases sharply in at least one locality. This evidence is taken tentatively to reflect an increase in the carrying capacity of water flowing into the cavern at the time that these deposits were accumulating and this in turn may reflect an increase in mean annual rainfall (see Fig. 80, Chapter 5, page 218). As already pointed out, this interpretation, if taken on its own, cannot withstand critical examination, since numerous other local processes have not been accounted for in the analysis. However, the results and their interpretation coincide remarkably with those of Bond's work at Khami where the trend toward increased number of large feldspar grains (reflecting increased rainfall runoff velocity) at the top of the Bambata levels is abruptly halted by a disconformity in the deposits. It was assumed that runoff velocity increased sufficiently by this stage to actually start eroding the deposits which had accumulated during the Umguzan occupation of the site. A similar truncation of the Umguzan levels at Tshangula Cave has been reported by C. K. Cooke (1963), who points out that only a very small sample of artifacts has survived as a result of surface erosion, presumably caused by spring eruptions at the back of the cave.

In Pomongwe nearby, the Umguzan deposits are banked up against a massive scree fall derived from a partial collapse of the granite roof of the cave. Although local structural weaknesses in the roof could be responsible for such a collapse, the possible influences of climatic change, particularly an overall increase in rainfall and/or more frequent and intense frosting of the cave-roof surface during winter nights, must be considered. In Chapter 5 it was noted that a steady increase in roof spalls in the underlying Bambatan deposits had been observed, so that the roof collapse may be viewed as a culmination in a trend rather than a random or sporadic accident of the cave's history. Obviously, if viewed in isolation, any climatic interpretation of such a rock fall must be considered as merely speculative, but similar falls have been reported in direct association with the Umguzan levels at Bambata, Zombepata, and Madiliyangwa. The likelihood that all four caves suffered partial collapse during this period as a result of random weathering processes seems remote in the extreme. Examination of deposits from still farther afield provides remarkable confirmation of some overall influence affecting cave formation at this time: the "Epi-Pietersburg" from Border Cave is capped by a massive roof collapse, and the Howiesonspoort hearths at Klasie's River Mouth are banked up against a similar boulder fall.

Two other sites provide indirect evidence of depositional changes during this period: Rose Cottage Cave contains a deep, near-sterile sand overlying the Bambatan horizon. This hiatus in the cave's occupation is explained by the apparent eruption of a spring from a fissure at the back of the deposits which made the cave uninhabitable, while ejecting the deep accumulations of sands. A charcoal sample from 176-cm depth in this accumulation has provided a reading (GrN-5300) of 25,640 ± 220 B.P., suggesting that the spring was active during the period under discussion. The second site to provide indirect evidence is Florisbad, where the pollen diagram for peat III dated to 19,530 ± 650 B.P. (L-271D) suggests a decrease in halophytes around the spring itself. This is taken by van Zinderen Bakker to reflect a decrease in spring activity by this date, but it may simply reflect a decrease in the area of *standing* (saline) water. Of greater importance is the culmination at this date of a trend toward increased grass pollens at the expense of Karroo scrub pollen. By the peat III level, the spectrum contains almost 100% Gramineae, suggesting a mean annual rainfall even higher than that at present.

It is now apparent that granulometric and chemical changes, widespread rockfalls, deposit truncation, spring eruptions, and pollen changes all reveal fairly marked shifts in depositional events during this period. It is difficult to explain such changes in terms other than climatic ones, since no other environmental process can be invoked to explain such widespread alterations. Certainly, an increase in mean annual rainfall would suffice to cause the features already listed. Unfortunately, there is no adequate evidence to suggest an overall decrease in mean annual temperature as well for this period. Any attempt to correlate this "event" with the (apparently contemporary) Main Würm maximum of the northern European glacial sequence would be rash in our present state of uncertainty.

The possible influence of such climatic change on the game population of southern Africa at this time should form a fascinating topic for future research. For the present, the paucity of adequate analyses allows little more than loose speculation in this field.

POST-HOWIESONSPOORT OCCURRENCES IN THE SOUTH
AND POSSIBLE CONNECTIONS

At Klasie's River Mouth on the southern Cape coast the black hearth layers of the Howiesonspoort levels are immediately overlain by a sand and shell deposit several feet thick and containing an artifact sample made of quartzite, and closely resembling the preceding Mossel Bay industry. No numerical information on the assemblage is available yet, but it is apparent that it consists entirely of blades, blade fragments, and flakes. The discoid and Levallois techniques are apparently absent, and the cave sample contains only single-platform and prismatic-blade cores. A few convergent blades have been lightly trimmed to form points and rare backed pieces occur in the lower levels, probably derived from the underlying Howiesonspoort levels. But for the absence of discoid and Levallois cores, the sample would conform to the basic typology of the Pietersburg complex. Its occurrence after the Howiesonspoort in this area is therefore of extreme interest, as it suggests the *reappearance* of a relatively early lithic technology at a much later date. It has been provisionally labeled "Middle Stone Age 3" by the excavators (J. Wymer, personal communication) and has two inverted carbon dates that are of limited value. The lower of the two samples yielded 11,685 ± 450 B.P., but its reliability remains uncertain.

On the same coast it is worth noting that Peers originally reported the occurrence of a "coarse Stillbay" overlying the Howiesonspoort levels at Skildergat. Keith (1931) reports that it contains tools of poorer workmanship than the much earlier Stillbay levels but fails to give any details. Jolly (1948), while attempting to refute Peer's original stratigraphic interpretation of the sequence, was obliged to report that he had uncovered at least 1 ft of midden deposits between the top of the Howiesonspoort levels and the bottom of the much later Wilton industry. As the presence of such a deposit embarrassed his claims for close evolutionary relationships between the Howiesonspoort and Wilton, he omitted to report on the artifactual content of the intervening layers—presumably containing Peer's "coarse Stillbay." Although this is the only other example that might parallel the stratigraphic evidence from Klasie's River Mouth, it is worth noting the blade-dominated assemblages from Die Kelders were dated at 11,200 ± 700 B.P. and possibly related material from Nelson's Bay Cave dated at 18,060 ± 550 B.P. (UW-175). Indeed, both caves may suggest a (perhaps unbroken) continuation of the Mossel Bay technology all through the Bambata and Howiesonspoort periods. The apparently coeval occupation of this area by peoples practicing markedly different technologies remains to be explained.

At least two other sets of evidence invite comparisons with this phenomenon. First, there is the artifact sample in the Rose Cottage sequence that immediately overlies the sterile spring-ejected sands which are dated to the Howiesonspoort period. This so-called "Pre-Wilton" sample is composed entirely of small utilized blades struck from agate, jasper, and chalcedony blade cores, all of which are relatively small since these rock types can be obtained only in small lumps. Its relatively simple technology, limited typology, and stratigraphic position argue for some connection with the blade-dominated samples from the Cape coast.

The second group that invites comparison is the so-called "Middle Stone Age phase 3" group from the Orange River scheme (Sampson 1968) among which is Zeekeogat 27. This primary-context floor is located in a stratum overlying calcified alluvial silts, which have yielded Orangian material a few hundred yards distant from the floor. The artifacts from this, and four other complete surface samples, reveal a simple typology comprising utilized blade, blade fragments, and flakes struck from prismatic and cylindrical blade cores. Formal shaped tools are absent, as are the discoid and Levallois technique. Lydianite was the dominant raw material and most specimens are larger than those found in the "Pre-Wilton" sample of Rose Cottage. However, several jasper and agate microblade cores and numerous very small slender blades struck from these have also been found at Zeekoegat 27, suggesting closer affinities with the Pre-Wilton than are apparent at first. Numerical analyses of the five samples are given in Table 35.

TABLE 35

Analysis of Possible Post-Howiesonspoort Samples [a]

	Schalkwyks-kraal 24A	Zeekoegat 12	Zeekoegat 27	Zeekoegat 15	Groenfontein 3
Tool types					
Trimmed points	—	—	—	1.8	0.3
Sidescrapers	—	—	0.9	0.2	—
Frontal scrapers	—	1.2	0.8	3.6	0.5
Burins	—	—	0.3	—	—
Utilized blades	18.9	16.5	21.4	22.4	20.0
Utilized blade fragments	28.2	36.5	47.2	25.0	17.1
Utilized flakes	52.8	46.0	29.3	46.5	62.0
Tools (totals):	53	85	965	112	375
Core types					
Opposed platform	—	—	—	(1)	—
Single platform					
(narrow)	(3)	(3)	6.1	(3)	17.0
(broad)	—	—	—	(2)	33.9
Adjacent platform	—	(2)	11.0	(4)	31.2
Prismatic blade	(4)	(7)	73.0	(6)	18.3
Cylindrical blade	(1)	—	9.8	(1)	—
Cores (totals):	8	12	82	17	71

[a] Totals and numerals in parentheses, numbers; all other values, percentages.

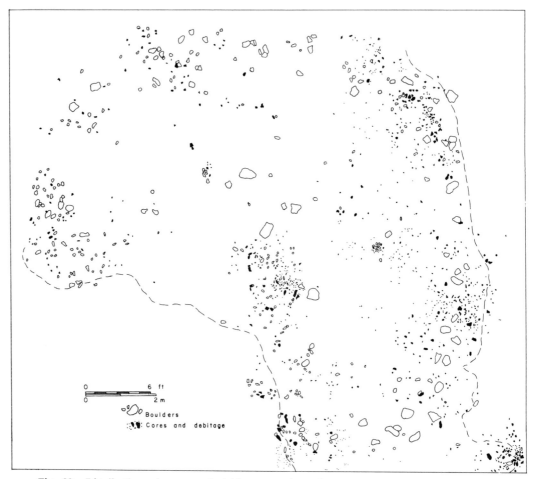

Fig. 88. Distribution of cores and debitage on the primary-context floor at Zeekoegat 27, possibly of post-Howiesonspoort date.

The horizontal distributions of material on the Zeekoegat 27 floor (see Fig. 88) suggest a temporary encampment probably within a 30-ft diameter circular enclosure of thornbushes weighted down with dolorite boulders. Only the circle of boulders has survived together with four main flaking foci containing dense scatters of waste flakes, heaps of cores, hammerstones, and apparent "handfuls" of blades. Like the Orangia I floor of an earlier date, this find suggests a localized cultural adaptation to a harsh environment without adequate caves or rock shelters.

It is of interest to note that no trace of any Howiesonspoort-like assemblage could be located in this area. Furthermore, there appears to be a total absence

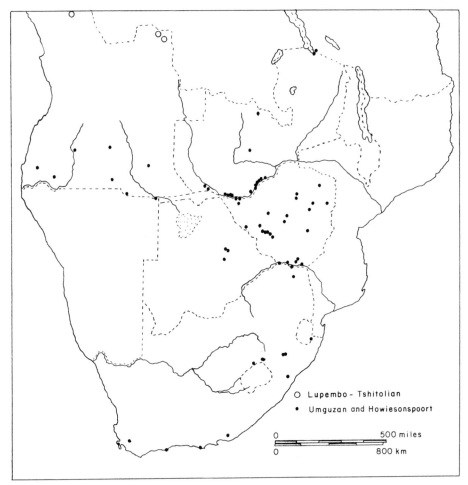

Fig. 89. Distribution of claimed "Second Intermediate" localities: Howiesonspoort and related occurrences. Most localities are represented by small surface scatters. (After Clark 1964.)

of any trace of such material from the entire semiarid plateau known as the Karroo. Even if the localities of dubious and otherwise unusable "Second Intermediate" find spots were plotted on the map, as in Fig. 89, there remains a notable blank in this region. Perhaps the Pietersburg complex persisted in this area during the period when better-watered adjacent regions were occupied by hunters producing the Bambata and later the Howiesonspoort–Umguzan lithic tradition. The alternate emergence of an entirely blade-dominated industry in the Orange River valley may be closely connected with the reappearance of a similar typology on the Cape coast and to the east in the foothills of the Lesotho Mountain ranges.

CONTEMPORARY SITES IN NORTHERN ZAMBIA

Although surface collections of Umguzan come from several localities in the Zambezi valley, evidently eroding from the "Kalahari Sands II" at Jafuta Farm (Clark 1950a) no primary-context discoveries have been reported. Further north it is probably found in the basal deposits of Mumbwa, Nsalu, and Leopard's Hill Cave. Associated carbon-14 dates at Leopard's Hill are: 23,600 ± 360 B.P. (UCLA-1429A), 22,600 ± 510 B.P. (UCLA-1429B), and 21,550 ± 950 B.P. (GX-0957). Although descriptions of the Nsalu and Leopard's Hill samples are available (Miller 1969a), the sample from Twin Rivers dated to 22,800 ± 1000 B.P. (UCLA-229) cannot be ascribed to this group with any confidence. Until all these samples are subjected to the same analysis, it will remain impossible to compare them with the derived "Magosian" from Kalambo Falls. Here the overlying date is only 9500 ± 210 B.P. (L-395D), but this cannot be taken as the true age of the sample.

Although sharing a similar array of types with the Umguzan to the south, this term has not previously been used in Zambia. Its adoption in this region cannot be justified without further analysis of both Rhodesian and Zambian materials.

RELATED SITES IN ANGOLA

An excavated site from southern Angola has yielded a sample with typological characters closely resembling those of the Umguzan to the south: Menongue (França, 1960) is a disturbed sample in geological context, recovered from 70 cm of fluviatile sands resting on shale bedrock which forms a midstream island on the Cuèbe River. Two large surface collections have been reported by de Almeida and França (1965) from Cuangar and Derico near the southern border, but neither has been described. The limited descriptive information from Menongue suggests a close typological resemblance to the Zambezi valley collections.

In the north a group of samples has been described by J. D. Clark (1963) under the term *Lupembo–Tshitolian,* suggesting an intermediate development following the still poorly reported Lupemban complex of the Lunda region. Several Lupembo–Tshitolian samples were reported to have come from the surface of the 3–4-m terrace, the surface of the "flats gravels," and the surface of marginal laterites associated with these deposits, but none has been excavated from sealed contexts (although all were capped by redistributed sands). No numerical analyses were possible as the samples were both selected, too small, or gathered *in situ* and from spoil heaps. This is unfortunate. Such samples would have probly not derived or greatly disturbed since the time that the ridge was occupied, in stratigraphic deposits directly overlying the gravels with Lupemban material.

TABLE 36

Tool Typology of Lupembo–Tshitolian Samples

	Mbalambala	Matafari	Congui-Mongi
Tool types			
Hand-axe–choppers	11	—	8
Picks	23	—	2
Core scrapers	24	1	2
Flake scrapers			
side-	27	3	2
double	—	1	2
hollow	41	1	2
Short endscrapers	29	—	—
Core axes, various	164	8	6
Points			
bifacial lanceolate	—	1	—
bifacial pointed	—	3	—
bifacial double-pointed	—	1	—
unifacial pointed	2	1	—
tanged	1	2	—
incomplete	3	—	—
Tranchets	5	1	4
Backed blades and crescents	1	—	—
Backed flakes	4	—	—
Utilized flakes, various	20	—	—
Hammer stones	6	—	3
Grindstones	1	—	—
Tool sample totals:	**362**	**23**	**31**
Core types			
Single platform	44	3	4
Double platform	9	—	2
Multiplatform	66	—	2
Biconical	94	—	11
Discoid	107	8	27
Prepared subtriangular	14	—	2
Core sample totals:	**334**	**11**	**48**
Waste types			
Endstruck flakes			
long	29	6	13
short	117	—	13
Subtriangular flakes	—	1	—
Irregular flakes	964	10	87
Redirecting flakes	7	—	—
Waste sample totals:	**1117**	**17**	**113**

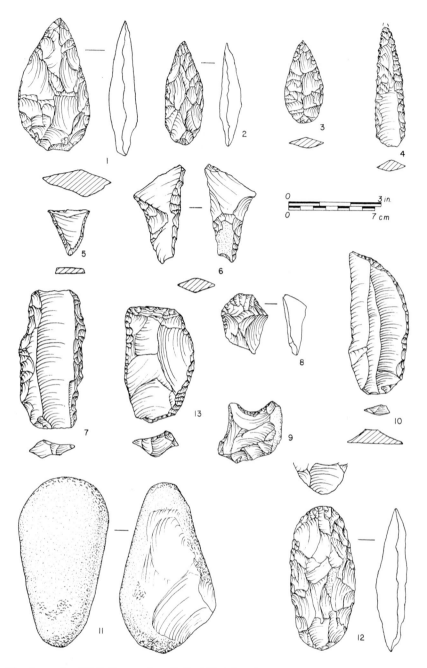

Fig. 90. Lupembo–Tshitolian tools: (1–4) bifacial points; (5, 6) *petits tranchets*; (7, 13) double sidescrapers; (8) frontal scraper; (9) notched scraper; (10) backed crescent; (11) hammerstone; (12) core axe with tranchet bit. All specimens are from Mbalambala Ridge.

That they are younger, and occurred later than the Lupemban is beyond dispute, but their association with a wood sample dated to 11,189 ± 490 B.P. (C-580) from the gravel surface at Mufo cannot be accepted, since the wood was not in direct association with an artifact collection. Considering the lack of information about the artifacts and the context of the dated wood, this cannot be taken as evidence for the absolute age of the Lupembo–Tshitolian.

It is regrettable that the very large unselected surface collection from Mbalambala could not be compared with one of these sealed assemblages in order to verify that it resembles them in typological detail. As it is, this surface collection represents the only large recorded sample that has not suffered distortion by selective collecting practices. The Mbalambala assemblage was sampled from a very dense surface scatter on a ridge north of Dundo township. Although probably not derived or greatly disturbed since the time that the ridge was occupied, this site affords absolutely no opportunity for assessing the stratigraphic relationship between the collected sample and the Lupemban finds from elsewhere. There is no way of proving that it is younger than the Lupemban except on typological grounds—an approach no longer encouraged in prehistoric studies.

Only two sealed samples can be compared with the "type" assemblage: the first is from the redistributed sands III at Matifari. This is immediately suspect since it has been separated from an Upper Lupemban in the same deposits on the basis of patination differences. The second site is Congui-Mongi where gravels were evidently "mixed" through a laterite crust covering them. Unfortunately, there are so few tools at this site that percentage comparisons cannot confirm that Mbalambala resembles this sample in all details. Typological lists are presented for all three sites in Table 36.

The major features by which the Mbalambala collection may be distinguished from other Lupemban samples (see page 253) are as follows: *gres polymorphe* is the only rock material used; trimmed points are more abundant and varied in shape; rare backed flakes and blades are present; utilized flakes occur; there is a greater frequency of smaller narrower flakes; there are more smaller tools, particularly scrapers, hand-axe–choppers, and core axes (see Fig. 90).

At present there are no adequate grounds for demonstrating that these distinctive features are not the consequence of a Lupemban technology applied exclusively to *gres polymorphe*. Both the size distribution of specimens and the apparent "refinement" of certain types could be the result of using a superior raw material and need not indicate that it is later in age than the Lupemban. Until further stratified data are recovered, the status of the Lupembo–Tshitolian concept must remain in some doubt. Similar ascriptions for surface samples from elsewhere in Angola (Clark 1966), as well as the small artifact sample from Chambuage found *in situ* a few inches above a possible wooden implement (Clark 1968), should also be treated with caution.

CONCLUSIONS

Although so many excavated sites have yielded undisturbed samples that may be compared with original Howiesonspoort material, the inevitable absence of a standardized typology and numerical analyses robs us of the opportunity to formulate an adequate interpretation of this phase in prehistory. It is only possible to point out that two main geographical groups emerge from the preceding synthesis: the Howiesonspoort of the southern Cape coast, and the Umguzan which may include not only the Rhodesian sites, but also Cave of Hearths, some Zambian caves, and Menongue. In the intervening zone, related surface collections are known from South-West Africa and Botswana, but not in the semiarid Karroo. Similar material has been recorded from Border Cave, but it is concluded that no adequate evidence has been presented to demonstrate the presence of related material from Rose Cottage Cave. Finally, the Angolan evidence for the Lupembo–Tshitolian remains rather limited, although further field investigations will no doubt demonstrate its validity and its close typological links with the preceding Lupemban complex of the Congo basin.

At both Umguzan and Howiesonspoort sites as well as a few other localities dated to this period, there is evidence for shifts in depositional processes such as roof collapses, surface erosion, granulometric changes, and pollen-rain trends. It is tentatively concluded that this unusually widespread occurrence must be at least partly the result of fairly far-reaching climatic changes, presumably including increases in mean annual rainfall and, perhaps, a decrease in mean annual temperature with more extensive winter frosts. Although indications of such an event have been found at several sites, it must be noted, however, that such evidence has not been reported from numerous others containing either Howiesonspoort or Umguzan materials. To what extent these negative reports are the result of inadequate observation and recording can only be assessed by further research into this problem.

Another interesting area for future research is the apparent change in the composition of mammalian fauna found with Howiesonspoort and Umguzan artifacts. The evidence from two sites analyzed thus far suggests a decrease in the number of larger game animals in these layers, possibly indicating changes in wildlife population as a whole. Whether such changes could have been brought about by selective hunting over many thousands of years prior to the appearance of the Howiesonspoort–Umguzan groups is by no means clear at present. Already there is some hint of an inherent contradiction in the evidence that suggests an overall increase in rainfall for this period, but a decrease in larger game at the same time. Obviously, this interesting problem will repay further investigation.

Actually, such changes in the palaeoenvironment are of more than passing importance. *If* larger animals had indeed become relatively scarce at this time, patterns of game exploitation by local hunting groups, of necessity, must have changed in some respects. Emphasis on the hunting of smaller and swifter-running antelope might require new tactics and new weapons, particularly lighter projectiles. Both the reduction in tool size and the advent of true backed blades and microliths (presumably used as spear or arrow barbs) at about 25,000 B.P. may suggest such a technical adaptation. It remains uncertain whether or not the bow and arrow was known during the Bambata period, but its use by Umguzan hunters may be inferred both from the presence of very small backed microliths, presumably too small to barb a spear, and also the presence of the first true cylindrical-sectioned ground and polished bone points from both Pomongwe, Klasie's River Mouth, and Leopard's Hill.

That vegetable foods played an important part in the diet can be assumed, although evidence for this is indirect. As in the preceding Bambatan period, grindstones were used, presumably for a variety of processes, some of which included food processing. One important innovation connected with vegetable food gathering, which may also be ascribed to this period is the bored stone. C. K. Cooke (1955) reported the presence of a small bored stone from the Umguzan levels at Khami, another comes from Leopard's Hill Cave and a third from Nsalu. No other sites have yielded examples of this new type. Its use in southern Africa is widespread and almost universal hereafter, and it is still in use among Kalahari Bushmen as a digging-stick weight.

Finally, there remains the awkward problem of the status and classification of this group of sites. Stratigraphic, chronometric, and typological evidence lend overwhelming support to the idea that the Umguzan represents a local development out of the preceding Bambatan industry, perhaps as a response to important changes in the local environment and food sources. Although recognized in earlier literature as a discrete "culture" with a distinctive typology which separates it from the Bambatan, it now appears unreasonable to classify it as an industry. There are far more similarities than differences between the Bambatan and Umguzan and the appearance of backed blades and crescents in the latter of the two should not be taken as a *major* technological change. For this reason it is proposed that the original classification of N. Jones (1940) should now be preferred: that the Umguzan be viewed as a later phase of the Bambatan industry which should be referred to as the *Umguzan phase*.

However, any attempt to force the Howiesonspoort group into a similar category would be entirely premature. Although reported to overlie the "Stillbay" at Skildergat and to resemble it in several details, its position has not yet been adequately demonstrated nor has the "Stillbay" been defined. Indeed, the apparently early carbon-14 dates as well as the scarcity of trimmed points and the marked emphasis on blade-production in the Howiesonspoort group may argue for the existence of a discrete industry in this region. Unfortunately, the resolution of this problem hinges almost entirely on the reanalysis of the Skildergat materials, a task which has yet to be undertaken. Possible connections with the "Stillbay" are further obscured by confused evidence for human skeletal associations at the site. Until carbon-14 dating of parts of the Skildergat skeleton is carried out, its true cultural associations must remain a source for speculation.

7

The Oakhurst Complex

Neither the terminology nor the concepts outlined in this chapter have appeared in earlier literature on the southern African Stone Age. The Oakhurst complex is a new and tentative proposal designed to accommodate a large body of recently excavated material which could not be adequately placed in earlier systems of classification. Certain older finds are reexamined and shown to resemble closely the recent discoveries.

Oakhurst is a cave about 4 miles inland from the southern Cape coast, some 13 miles east of the town of George. Its excavation by Goodwin (1938) is an important landmark in the development of local prehistoric studies, since he maintained a high standard of excavation and recording previously unknown in southern Africa. Over 10 ft of cave fill was excavated in a series of 20 superimposed levels, most of which varied in thickness between 3 and 9 inches and conformed to the dip and strike of the deposit. All artifacts and mammalian fauna from each level were recovered and recorded separately. Burials and their associations were treated as discrete units, and the stratigraphic links between burial pits and the levels from which they were dug out have been analyzed in careful detail. Goodwin's campaign set a new standard for subsequent excavations in local cave deposits, and it is entirely fitting that Oakhurst be chosen as type name for the new complex (Sampson 1971b).

However, the reasons for this choice extend beyond mere historical sentiment. Goodwin isolated a lithic sample found only in the lowermost levels of the cutting (60–126 inches), directly underlying the obviously microlithic Wilton series which dominates the upper levels (see Chapter 8). This basal sample, therefore, represents the earliest discovery of the industry that precedes the Wilton complex in southern Africa. The excellent layer-by-layer analysis presented by Schrire (1962) reveals a relatively simple typology with abundant large convex scrapers of various forms together with a few endscrapers, *outils écaillés*, pebble choppers, and numerous utilized flakes. In his original report, Goodwin erroneously referred this sample to the "Smithfield B," a very late industry from the interior that belongs to the historic period and has nothing in common with the basal Oakhurst sample (see Chapter 9). Unfortunately, this erroneous ascription (and Goodwin's failure to recognize that he had discovered a hitherto unknown industry) has led to considerable confusion in classification and terminology. Considering the extreme simplicity of the sample's typology as well as the coarse quality of its raw materials, Goodwin's failure to perceive its significance is quite understandable.

It is now apparent that this quartz-and-quartzite assemblage actually resembles the "Smithfield A" from the interior in numerous details (see page 268). Because the "A" group of surface samples is made of lydianite, the resemblance is not apparent upon superficial examination, and presumably Goodwin had no opportunity to handle large samples of "Smithfield A" prior to his Oakhurst report. This similarity was realized by Louw (1960), who referred a Pre-Wilton sample from Matjes River Cave to the "Smithfield A," but his opinion has been ignored entirely by subsequent authors on account of the inferior excavations and reporting of this site. Only recently has it proved possible to demonstrate that the "Smithfield A" of the interior also precedes the Wilton (Sampson 1967b) so that the connection now can be demonstrated.

THE STANDARD TYPOLOGY

A total of 29 tool types has been used in a systematic classification of artifact samples thought to belong to this complex. Detailed descriptions of each type have appeared elsewhere (Sampson 1970), and the type list is summarized in Table 37. Diagrammatic representations of each type are shown in Fig. 91.

The basic flaking technology places great emphasis on the production of large broad flakes from adjacent-platform and large single-platform cores, many of which appear to have been used subsequently as hammers, since their margins display extensive battering. Blade production is minimal, and the few specimens

TABLE 37

Oakhurst Complex Tool and Core Types

Tool types		Core types
Endscrapers	Sidescrapers (types 1–5)	Single platform (broad)
Side- and endscrapers	Sidescraper fragments (convex, straight, and angle)	Single platform (narrow)
Small endscrapers	Steep scrapers	Adjacent platform
Core hammers	Frontal scrapers (1)	Multiplatform
Flake scrapers	Frontal scrapers (2)	Discoid
Backed adzes	Battered fragments	Subcircular plain platform
Pebble adzes	Fabricators (side and end)	Subcircular prepared platform
Trimmed–utilized blades	Picks–reamers	
Trimmed–utilized flakes	Grindstones	
Outils écaillés	Bored stones	
Straight-backed points		

found in most samples are broad, irregular, and are probably accidental byproducts of the flaking process. In each sample there is a high frequency of flakes with large unfaceted platforms. Also, the original rock cortex may form part of the dorsal surface of the flake. Either whole flakes or fragments of large flakes were marginally trimmed to form the various scrapers found in the type list, and numerous flakes were evidently used directly without prior marginal trimmings.

DISTRIBUTION AND CLASSIFICATION OF THE OAKHURST COMPLEX

So many excavated samples are now known to share the typological characters listed above, that some attempt must be made to isolate regional groups within the complex. At present, three such groups may be recognized, and these are tentatively labeled in Table 38.

The locality of each of these sites is shown in Fig. 92. The *Oakhurst industry* is proposed for the presently known samples from the southern Cape coastal region only. These, and possibly other unpublished assemblages, are made of quartz, quartzite, sandstone, and very rare fragments of silcrete or chalcedony. A few samples are associated with bone work, shell beads, and pierced shells.

Fig. 91. Tool types of the Oakhurst complex: (1) endscraper; (2) side- and endscraper; (3) small endscraper; (4) core hammer; (5) sidescraper; (6) backed adze; (7) pebble adze; (8) utilized blades; (9) utilized flakes; (10) *outlis écaillés;* (11) small convex scraper; (12) straight-backed point (11 and 12 very rare); (13) circular scrapers; (14) sidescrapers (1); (15) sidescrapers (2); (16) sidescrapers (3); (17, 18) sidescrapers (4); (19–21) sidescraper fragments; (22) steep scrapers; (23) frontal scrapers (1): (24) frontal scrapers (2); (25) battered pieces; (26, 27) "fabricators"; (28) picks–reamers; (29) grindstone.

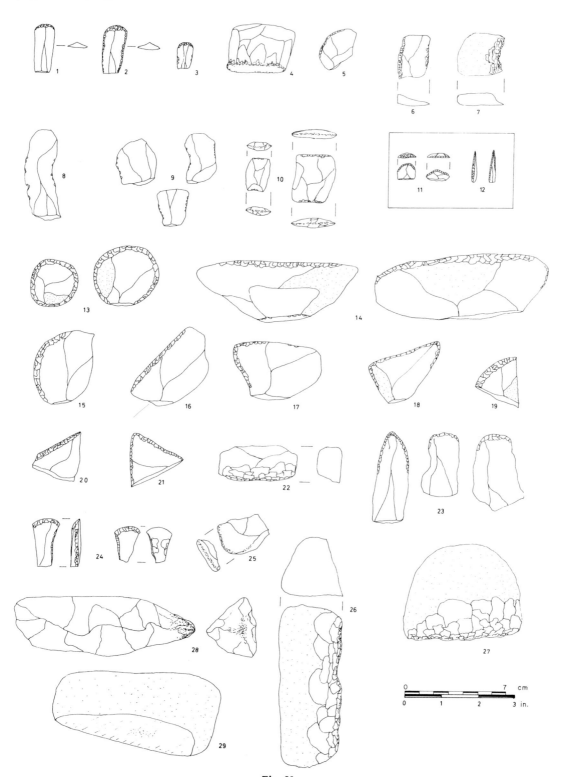

Fig. 91

TABLE 38

Tentative Terminology for Industries in the Oakhurst Complex

Oakhurst industry	Lockshoek industry	Pomongwan industry
Oakhurst (60–100 in.)	Nqamakwe Cave (Layer C)	Pomongwe (Layers 7–10; Layer 3)
Matjes River (Layer D)	Umgazana (strata 1–14)	Tshangula (Layer 2)
Glentyre (42–72 in.)	Karridene	Makunkubi Farm
Melkhoutboom (4.0–6.5 ft)	Zeekoegat 13 (lower level)	Surface sites
Uniondale (?)	Wonderwerk (13–20 in.)	
Welcome Woods (?)	Glenferness (12–48 in.)	
Nelson's Bay Cave (2.3–3.0 m)	Hennops River (31–40 in.)	
	Uitkomst (Bed 1)	
	Rufus (Bed 2) (?)	
	Magazine (Bed 1) (?)	
	Bushman Rock (Layers 3–28)	

Fig. 92. Distribution of excavated sites that have yielded samples ascribed to the Oakhurst complex.

The *Lockshoek industry* includes numerous samples made almost exclusively of lydianite and distributed over southeastern, central, and northern South Africa. More than 100 surface sites belonging to this group have also been recorded and further regional subdivisions may prove necessary when more is known of its westerly distribution.

The *Pomongwan* has been found in Matabeleland and northeastern Botswana, although its presence is suspected over a wider area to the north, possibly extending into Zambia. In this region a wide variety of Basement rock types was used, including agate, jasper, chalcedony, opal breccia, quartz, and quartzite.

The composition and associations of each of these proposed industries is examined below.

THE OAKHURST INDUSTRY

The five samples in this group have been variously named by different authors, thus leading to unnecessary confusion (Table 39). Four samples evidently reflect the earliest occupation at each site. Their stratigraphic position above the Howiesonspoort horizon has been demonstrated only at Nelson's Bay Cave. Of still more importance is their chronological relationship to the Post-Howiesonspoort blade complex discussed on pages 248–251. Once again, the inadequately published excavations from Skildergat may hold the clue to this problem: undisturbed material from the 1-ft deep midden *between* the Howiesonspoort and the Wilton levels may represent either the blade complex or the Oakhurst industry, or possibly both of these. It is of interest to note that bedrock was never reached at either Oakhurst, Glentyre, or Matjes River, and the possibility that still earlier industries are represented at all three sites has never been investigated. Goodwin (1938) mentions the presence of "Middle Stone Age" specimens in the deposit below 112 inches at Oakhurst, but these have not been found in the collections. His field notes also mention similar finds from Glentyre.

Since all five samples underlie extensive Wilton samples, there can be little doubt that the Oakhurst industry immediately precedes the Wilton in this area. Associated radiocarbon dates are in good agreement with this.

As so much confused terminology has surrounded these four samples in the past, each will be inspected in detail before they are compared. The Oakhurst material was recovered in seven superimposed units, details of which appear in Table 40.

The only nonlithic artifacts recovered are a cylindrical-sectioned bone point and three "shell crescents" of doubtful human manufacture. The dominant raw material is vein quartz, with limited use made of quartzite cobbles from an adjacent stream bed. Obviously, the individual spit samples are too small, and they cannot be combined to provide adequate percentage data. There may be

TABLE 39

Previous Terminology for Oakhurst Industry Samples

Site	Depth	Reference	Previous name
Oakhurst	60–100 inches	Goodwin (1938)	Smithfield B
		Fagan (1960)	Late Wilton
		Schrire (1962)	Smithfield B
Glentyre	42–72 inches	Fagan (1960)	Late Wilton
Matjes River	4–16 ft	Louw (1960)	MR variant of Smithfield A
Melkhoutboom	—	H. J. Deacon (1969a)	Basal industry or Pre-Wilton
Nelson's Bay Cave	2.3–3.0 m	R. Klein (1971, personal communication)	"Pre-Wilton"

TABLE 40

Tool Types from Oakhurst Industry Levels in Oakhurst Shelter [a]

Level (inches)	Tool sample total	Small convex scraper	Large convex scrapers	Duckbill scrapers	End-scrapers	*Outils écaillés*	Pebble choppers	Saws
60–64	186	10	149	—	—	22	2	2
64–68	37	2	30	2	—	1	2	—
68–73	21	—	13	3	—	2	3	—
73–77	5	1	4	—	—	—	—	—
Sterile								
82–88	10	—	6	—	3	1	—	—
88–100	13	1	8	—	1	3	—	—
100–112	1	—	1	—	—	—	—	—
Totals:	**273**	**14**	**211**	**5**	**4**	**29**	**7**	**2**

[a] After Schrire (1962).

a chronological division into an earlier and later unit separated by the sterile sand.

Glentyre is a shallow shelter formed in a granite cliff only a few miles from Oakhurst. Although Goodwin excavated here, he never published his finds. However, his detailed field notes have survived. The analysis presented by Fagan provides no spit-by-spit analysis of the lower sample, which Goodwin recognized to be very similar to that from Oakhurst. Fagan has provided the following typology for the composite sample from between 42 and 72 inches depth; flake scrapers 69%; pebble scrapers 17.2%; miscellaneous retouched flakes 7.8%; utilized pieces 6.2%. Only 65 tools were recovered, together with 138 cores and 272 waste flakes. Obviously, this sample lacks the typology which would allow comparisons with Oakhurst.

Undoubtedly, the most important sample comes from Matjes River, where abundant bone work and other organic remains were recovered in association

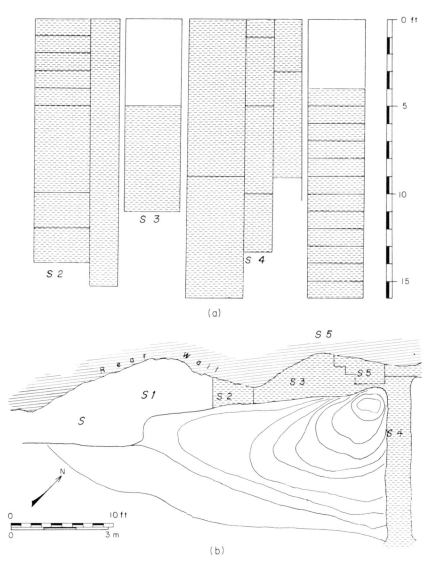

Fig. 93. (a) Correlation of excavated spits in Layer D in Matjes River Shelter. (b) Plan of the shelter showing localities of the various excavations.

with the lithic assemblage. The published account of the contents of "Layer D" (about 12 ft of deposit) fails to provide any spit-by-spit analysis, nor does it point out the extremely variable quality of different excavations carried out in this "layer" (Inskeep 1961). Of the six different areas excavated in various campaigns (S and S 1–5 in Fig. 93) only Site 5 provides samples of any possible use. One-foot deep spits were removed from the center rear of the deposits, where the strata are horizontal and conform with the excavated spit orientation (Hoffman 1958). As shown in Fig. 93, the excavated units recovered from adjacent sites are

TABLE 41

Spit-by-Spit Analysis of Site 5

Site 5 (ft depth):	4–5	5–6	6–7	7–8	8–9	9–10	10–11	11–12	12–13	13–14	14–15	15–16
Tools (totals):	(45)	(43)	(104)	(111)	(41)	(35)	(23)	(4)	(13)	(6)	(8)	(2)
Endscrapers	2	2	20	19	10	4	—	—	—	—	—	—
Side- and endscrapers	3	—	5	1	—	—	—	—	—	—	—	—
Core hammers	—	1	5	3	2	—	—	—	—	—	—	—
Backed adzes	1	—	—	1	1	—	—	—	—	—	—	—
Trimmed–utilized blades	3	6	9	13	4	2	4	—	—	—	1	—
Trimmed–utilized flakes	4	5	16	19	7	14	6	2	8	—	3	1
Outils écaillés	8	8	1	2	1	3	1	—	1	1	—	—
Small convex scrapers	2	—	2	—	—	—	—	—	—	—	—	—
Circular scrapers	—	—	1	1	—	1	—	—	—	—	—	—
Sidescrapers												
(1)	2	—	1	2	1	—	2	—	—	—	—	—
(2)	2	—	2	5	1	3	1	—	—	—	—	—
(3–4)	—	—	2	3	—	2	—	—	—	—	—	—
Sidescraper fragments												
convex	1	—	1	4	3	1	3	1	—	—	—	—
straight	—	—	1	2	—	—	—	—	—	—	—	—
angle	—	—	1	1	1	—	—	—	—	—	—	—
Steep scrapers	1	2	2	1	3	—	—	—	—	3	1	—
Frontal scrapers (1)	5	10	20	29	—	—	—	—	1	1	—	—
Frontal scrapers (2)	—	—	2	1	—	—	—	—	—	—	—	—
Battered fragments	1	1	4	—	1	—	—	1	—	—	—	—
Fabricators (1)	4	1	5	2	—	—	—	—	1	—	1	—
Fabricators (2)	1	—	1	1	1	4	3	1	1	1	1	—
Picks	—	—	—	—	1	—	—	—	—	—	—	—
Grindstones	1	—	—	—	—	—	—	—	—	—	—	—
Ocher palette	—	1	1	1	4	—	—	—	1	—	—	—
Muller–hammers	3	6	1	—	1	3	3	—	1	1	1	1
Cobble "choppers"	1	—	1	—	—	—	—	—	—	—	—	—

266

Materials

No. of specimens in chalcedony or quartz	9	12	7	8	3	3	—	—	—	—	—	—
Cores (totals):	(5)	(5)	(9)	(4)	(2)	(2)	(1)	(—)	(4)	(—)	(2)	(—)
Single plain-platform	2	—	2	—	—	1	—	—	2	—	2	—
Single prepared-platform	—	—	2	1	—	—	—	—	—	—	—	—
Discoid	—	—	1	2	—	—	—	—	2	—	—	—
Adjacent-platform	3	5	4	1	2	1	1	—	—	—	—	—
Waste (totals):	(39)	(22)	(74)	(66)	(19)	(77)	(24)	(10)	(48)	(12)	(32)	(14)
Blades and blade fragments	5	10	26	14	3	4	1	—	—	—	2	1
Flakes	31	9	44	45	16	58	14	5	32	10	25	10
Broad flared flakes	3	3	4	7	—	15	9	5	16	2	5	4
Bone artifacts												
Ground-edge axe–adzes	1	1	—	1	—	—	—	—	—	—	—	—
Awls and awl fragments	9	3	4	4	3	6	—	—	—	—	—	—
Cylindrical Bone point fragments	6	1	3	5	—	—	—	—	—	—	—	—
Polished bone tubes	1	1	1	1	1	2	—	—	—	—	—	—
(?) Leister prong	—	1	—	—	—	—	—	—	—	—	—	—
Rib mattock	—	1	—	—	—	—	—	—	—	—	1	—
Spatulas (ground)	—	—	—	—	—	1	1	—	—	1	—	—
Ornaments												
Pendants	1	—	2	—	—	—	—	—	—	—	—	—
Pierced shells	3	1	8	—	1	—	1	—	—	—	—	—
Incised ostrich egg	—	—	—	—	1	—	—	—	—	—	—	—
Polished bone ring	—	—	—	—	1	—	—	—	—	—	—	—

so deep that they become meaningless. An analysis of each spit in Site 5 is given in Table 41 in which the standard typology is introduced.

Table 41 suggests that Layer D contains two superimposed cultural units, and not one, as stated by Louw. The main differences between these units are as follows.

Lower Unit (10–16 ft): a sparsely distributed sample of artifacts made entirely of quartzite. The basic technology includes the production of plain-platform flakes with a high proportion of flared specimens with large butts, struck from single plain-platform cores. The very rare blades in this sample have irregular outlines, large plain butts, and are probably the chance products of flaking. The tools are dominated by miscellaneous utilized flakes, and there are a few true sidescrapers in the upper spits. Bone work includes only two ground rib

TABLE 42

Tool Typology for Four Oakhurst Industry Samples

	Oakhurst, 60–100 in. (%)	Glentyre, 42–72 in. (counts)	Matjes River D	
			4–10 ft (%)	10–16 ft (counts)
Endscrapers	2.9	2	17.9	—
Side- and endscrapers	1.8	2	2.3	—
Core hammers	0.4	2	2.8	—
Backed adzes	1.1	1	0.5	—
Pebble adzes	0.4	2	0.2	—
Trimmed–utilized blades	4.4	4	8.0	5
Trimmed–utilized flakes	22.5	14	16.9	—
Outils écaillés	10.7	5	6.6	4
Small convex scrapers	4.4	2	0.5	—
Circular scrapers	1.8	1	0.8	—
Sidescrapers (1)	—	—	3.4	2
Sidescrapers (2)	12.5	—	3.4	1
Sidescrapers (3 and 4)	4.8	—	1.8	—
Sidescraper fragments				
convex	10.0	9	2.5	4
straight	4.1	—	0.8	—
angle	0.7	—	0.8	—
Steep scrapers	4.8	2	2.6	5
Frontal scrapers (1)	7.7	5	16.1	1
Frontal scrapers (2)	1.8	1	0.8	—
Battered fragments	—	2	1.3	1
Fabricators (1)	1.1	1	3.0	3
Fabricators (2)	1.1	4	2.0	1
Picks	—	—	0.2	—
Grindstones	—	1	0.2	—
Palettes	0.4	1	1.8	7
Muller–hammers	—	4	2.8	—
Tools (totals):	**271**	**65**	**369**	**34**

fragments which resemble spatulae, and there are also a few bone fragments with cut marks on the surface. The lower levels of the adjacent (less reliable) digs confirm the absence of bone work and the range of tool types present.

Upper Unit (4–10 ft): a relatively rich sample of artifacts dominated by quartzite but with about 5–10% made of siliceous rocks (chalcedony and vein and crystal quartz). The basic technology includes some emphasis on the production of quartzite blades from single-platform cores. There is no evidence to suggest that these specimens (waste and tools) were brought in from outside the shelter. Rare imported Mossel Bay specimens show surface weathering and are easily distinguished from the specimens included in Table 41. The tools include a high proportion of endscrapers, frontal scrapers, and numerous sidescraper forms. Abundant and varied bone working appears, as well as shell and bone ornaments. There is no evidence to suggest better preservation of bone at this level since shell and small fauna are equally well preserved in both units.

Each sample may belong to the same industrial tradition, but the upper unit perhaps suggests a developed phase. The reappearance of blade production in this same level may reflect the continued persistence of the blade-dominated tradition on the southern Cape coast already mentioned in the Klasie's River Mouth sequence.

Melkhoutboom is a cave in the Zuurberg range to the east of Grahamstown some 35 miles inland from the southern Cape coast. First excavated by Hewitt (1931b), it has been recently reexamined by H. J. Deacon (1969a). Although a restricted area (10 by 3 ft at the surface) has been excavated near the back of this cave, sufficient material has been recovered from below the Wilton levels to present some useful comparisons. An ashy complex about 2.5 ft deep and resting on bedrock has provided nearly 2000 specimens, of which only a very small proportion shows signs of use. No vertical subdivision of the sample has been provided and the published typology provides very limited details: 61 trimmed flakes; 2 miscellaneous retouched pieces; 2-edge-ground stones on ocher fragments, 2 anvils; ?1 *outil écaillé;* 7 cores. The rest are untrimmed flakes, chips, and chunks. Ostrich eggshell beads and marine shell (*Nassa* sp.) beads were also recovered. Continuing excavations at this site will shortly produce further details and a wider array of types. Comparisons with similar Pre-Wilton levels from Uniondale and Welcome Woods should then prove possible. Unfortunately, insufficient published information is available yet from these last two sites. Also, the basal layer of Wilton Shelter may contain a related sample (Deacon 1969). Similarly, a related sample is reported from Nelson's Bay Cave, where work is still in progress.

For the present, only four reliable samples can be compared by using the standardized typology. Of these, the basal unit for Matjes River is too small to provide adequate picture of the whole assemblage. The four are listed in Table 42.

The two largest samples obviously differ considerably in their proportion of sidescrapers and end–frontal scrapers, but the meaning of such differences remains obscure. Since quartzite is the dominant raw material used in Matjes River D, it is probable that larger endstruck flakes could be produced here, thus allowing the manufacture of more endscrapers, but other factors may also have caused such differences.

THE LOCKSHOEK INDUSTRY

The term *Lockshoek* is employed here with some reluctance. The name is derived from a farm on the Riet River in the Orange Free State, where van Riet Lowe (1929) first isolated a large, evidently unmixed surface scatter of his "Smithfield A." Although Lockshoek was chosen as the type site for the industry, the actual farm name has not previously been used in the literature. Reasons for rejecting the term "Smithfield A" are discussed in Chapter 9. Regrettably, the Lockshoek type site has been virtually destroyed by selective gathering of "typical" tools, which were removed to numerous different museums. The largest extant collection is at the National Museum, Bloemfontein. It contains some thousands of tools, but the percentage values for these are quite meaningless since they only reflect the early collectors' bias. The name "Lockshoek" is proposed here not because it represents a reliable type sample but rather because it provides the earliest recorded definition of the industry. Subsequent analysis of numerous complete samples found about 100 miles south of Lockshoek (Sampson 1970) has shown the original description by van Riet Louw (1929) to be accurate in almost every detail.

The tentative grouping of sites within this industry is summarized in the map in Fig. 94. Unfortunately the standard typology has been applied to only a few samples within this vast area. More analytical work is necessary to demonstrate any typological homogeneity. Such homogeneity is only tentatively claimed here on the basis of presence or absence of tool types at each site. Further work on these samples may demonstrate the need for additional subdivision of the group. Inevitably, the terms under which the different samples have been published vary considerably from site to site, and it is necessary to summarize these first (Table 43).

The stratigraphic position of this group is somewhat variable and many samples in the list come from basal strata in their deposits. Layer C at Nqamakwe is preceded by Layer D, a sterile scree and boulder layer, which is in turn underlaid by Layer E, an ash layer with artifacts closely resembling the Howieson-spoort typology. Zeekoegat 13 is a partially sealed sample that overlies a fluviatile silt containing a late blade-dominated sample a few yards away at Zeekoegat 15. The Wonderwerk sample overlies a massive rock fall that may equate with the widespread roof collapse features noted at several other caves to be associated with the Howiesonspoort–Umguzan horizon. Underlying the rock fall at Wonderwerk is a small sample of undiagnostic specimens including a few discoid and Levallois cores and presumably linked with the Bambata complex, although

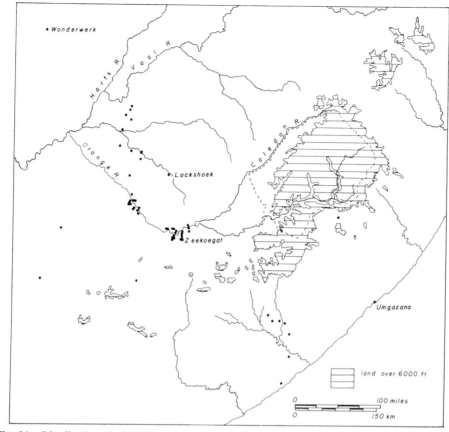

Fig. 94. Distribution of sites ascribed to the Lockshoek industry within the Oakhurst complex. All except Wonderwerk and Umgazana are surface scatters.

TABLE 43

Previous Terminology for Lockshoek Industry Sites

Site	Depth	Reference	Previous name
Nqamakwe Cave 22	Layer C	Laidler (1934)	
Umgazana	Layers 1–14	Chubb, King, and Mogg (1934)	Umgazana variant of the "Smithfield A"
		van Riet Louw (1936)	Smithfield P
Karridene		Cramb (1934)	Smithfield
Zeekoegat 13	Lower level	Sampson (1967b)	Later Stone Age Phase I
Orange River Scheme surface sites		Sampson (1970)	Later Stone Age Phase I
Wonderwerk	Brown earth 13–20 in.	Malan and Wells (1943)	Smithfield A
Glenferness	12–48 in.	Mason (1962a)	Smithfield ?
Hennops River	31–40 in.	Mason (1962a)	Middle Smithfield
Uitkomst	Bed I	Mason (1962a)	Earlier–Middle Smithfield
Rufus	Bed 2	Mason (1962a)	Middle Smithfield ?
Magazine	Bed I	Mason (1962a)	Earlier Smithfield
Kruger Cave		Mason (1969)	Later Stone Age
Bushman Rock	Layers 3–28	Louw (1969)	Later Stone Age

this association cannot be confirmed without further investigation of the deposits. Among the Transvaal sites, the Rufus sample is reported to overlay an unpublished layer with specimens related to the Bambata complex. The same relationship exists at Bushman Rock, where Layer 28 represents the end of the "Mwulu" sequence and the beginning of the Lockshoek series.

Only 16 inches below Layer 28 (dated to about 12,500 B.P.) comes a sample dated to >50,000 B.P., and deposition during this period has either been very slow or, quite possibly, there has been an erosion of the deposit surface, perhaps coinciding with the depositional "event" of about 20,000 B.P. discussed in the preceding chapter. It should be stressed, however, that no evidence for a disconformity in the Bushman Rock deposits have been reported and this problem cannot be adequately discussed until granulometric studies have been carried out. Finally, a small unpublished sample was recovered from Bed 10 at Cave of Hearths. Overlying the Umguzan-related Bed 9, this later material has been called "Smithfield" by Mason (1962a) and can at present be only tentatively grouped with the Lockshoek until more details are released.

The Lockshoek is overlaid by the Wilton sample at Zeekoegat 13, but at Wonderwerk and Bushman Rock, it is followed by an unnamed industry related to the "Smithfield" as defined in Chapter 9. At Umgazana it is followed by layers containing a similar lithic typology, but with the important addition of ceramics. This is discussed in Chapter 10.

Unfortunately, the standard typology has been applied only to Zeekoegat 13 and the series of complete surface collections in the Orange River scheme area. Percentage values for these samples are compared in Sampson (1970). For the listed sites outside this area, only the range of tool types can be recorded for want of more complete published data. The Nqamakwe, Umgazana, and Karridene samples are selected and cores and waste were not kept by the excavators. The Wonderwerk sample is too small to provide percentage data.

Figures for the Orange River scheme samples reveal that they fall into two main groups labeled X and Y–Z (Sampson 1970), the first of which is dominated by utilized flakes, whereas the second includes samples with more sidescrapers and/or endscrapers. Whether this apparent dichotomy reflects functional variations within the industry, or some chronological change in typology as seen in Matjes River D, cannot be resolved at present for want of more adequate stratified sites in this heavily eroded area.

Unlike the Oakhurst industry, the Lockshoek sites have yielded relatively little bone work. One important exception is Umgazana, which has yielded a selected range of bone work including three cylindrical bone points, large bone points with beveled butts, thick, biconical bone points, club-headed awls, *lissoirs*, bone polishers, several ground-edged and pierced fragments, and a fine-stemmed bone point (Fig. 95). This evidently rich coastal cave is also reported to yield abundant grass bedding and vegetation in an excellent state of preservation. This occurs also at Matjes River, Nelson's Bay, and Melkhoutboom. Bone point

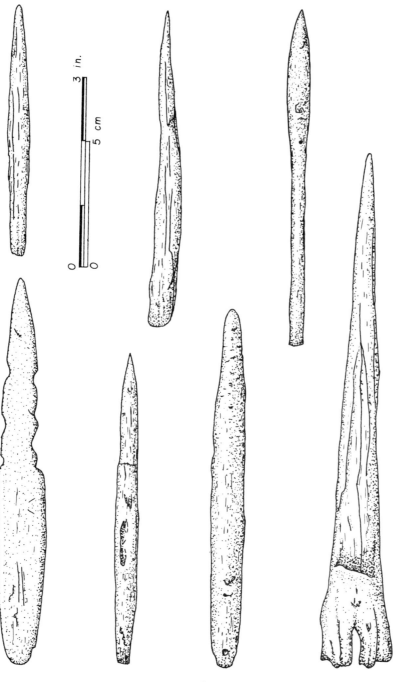

Fig. 95. Bone artifacts from the Lockshoek sample at Umgazana Cave, Pondoland.

273

fragments with incised chevron and crosshatching decoration were found at Wonderwerk, and ostrich eggshell beads were found at Bushman Rock.

The geographical distribution of the Lockshoek industry no doubt extends far beyond the areas from which sealed samples have been obtained. Goodwin and van Riet Lowe (1929) list several surface finds from the Orange Free State, northern and eastern Cape Provinces, and farther westward into the Great Karroo. Mason (1962a) and Malan and van Niekerk (1955) list several surface occurrences from the Transvaal. Although its presence in South West Africa is reported, no adequate examples have been described.

TABLE 44

Cooke's Type List for Pomongwe [a] and Shimabala

| | Pomongwe | | |
	First excavation Layers 7–10	Third excavation Layer 3	Shimabala Zambia
Tools			
Duckbill scrapers	10	4	2
Detaching hammers	15	3	9
Utilized flakes	—	2	18
Burins	1	—	1
Lames écaillés	—	5	21
Circular scrapers	459	116	21
Thumbnail scrapers	—	41	6
Sidescrapers	1	14	33
Notched scrapers	2	5	14
Scrapers various	—	13	3
Fabricators	6	2	5
Mullers	—	3	1
Anvils	17	7	—
Grooved stones	1	—	—
Borers	—	1	3
Chopping tools	1	—	26
Bone work			
Bone points and fragments	3	11	—
Cut bone fragments	—	2	—
Notched bone fragments	—	3	—
Ornaments			
Tortoise carapace pendant	—	1	—

[a] From C. K. Cooke (1963).

THE POMONGWAN INDUSTRY

This industry was introduced to the literature by Cooke *et al.* (1966) when it became apparent that the Umguzan horizons at Pomongwe Cave and elsewhere were immediately followed by an industry containing abundant subcircular scrapers and very few other tool types. At first referred to as the "scraper horizon" by the excavator (Cooke 1963), it was soon realized that the assemblage resembles the "Early Smithfield" of South Africa. However, the local name was preferred. Samples of the industry have been found in layers between the Umguzan and the overlying Wilton at two sites, Pomongwe and Tshangula.

It is suspected that the Pomongwan occurred in a similar sequence at Bambata cave, but this requires confirmation by further excavation at the site (C. K. Cooke, personal communication). Numerous additional surface discoveries have been made over the last few years, but no further publications have appeared. At present, its distribution is restricted to Rhodesia with probable outliers in northeastern Botswana.

Only one typological summary has appeared in which C. K. Cooke (1963) uses a type list not directly comparable with the standard typology (Table 44).

The large numbers of thumbnail scrapers in the third excavation are absent from the list of the first where they may have been included with the circular scrapers. Cooke's illustrations suggest that the circular scrapers cover several of the scraper types listed in the standard typology. At Tshangula, the Pomongwan levels yielded bone points, a pierced mussel shell pendant, and abundant ostrich eggshell beads.

CHRONOLOGY OF THE OAKHURST COMPLEX

At present about 20 associated carbon-14 dates have been obtained from seven of the listed sites. As dates are available from each of the three industries, the chart in Fig. 96 is arranged to show the remarkable consistency of the readings for all three. Details of the dated samples are listed below:

Matjes River:

Layer D	L-336H	11,250 ± 400 B.P. (9300 B.C.)
	L-336G	10,500 ± 400 B.P. (8500 B.C.)
	GrN-5061	9780 ± 60 B.P. (7630 B.C.)
	GrN-5871	10,030 ± 55 B.P. (8080 B.C.)

Unfortunately, the exact positions of each of these dated samples within Layer D were never published. Samples L-336H and L-336G were taken from midway through the deposits and must approximately date the interface between the lower and upper units. GrN-5061 is a shell sample.

Melkhoutboom:

> 5 ft depth   GaK-1538   10,500 B.P. (8550 B.C.)

The sample comes from about midway through the lower deposits containing the "basal industry."

Uitkomst:

> Bed 1–2 interface   BM-?   9844 ± 200 B.P. (7894 B.C.)

Sample comes from the bottom of the overlying Iron Age deposit and is taken by Mason (1962a) to reflect contaminations from the underlying Bed I level.

Bushman Rock:

Layer 28a	142 cm	GrN-4816	12,510 ± 105 B.P.	(10,560 B.C.)
Layer 28b	142 cm	GrN-5873	12,470 ± 145 B.P.	(10,520 B.C.)
Layer 27	137 cm	GrN-4815	12,160 ± 95 B.P.	(10,210 B.C.)
Layer 21	99–100 cm	GrN-4814	12,090 ± 95 B.P.	(10,140 B.C.)
Layer 12	61–69 cm	GrN-4813	9940 ± 80 B.P.	(7990 B.C.)
Layer 9	30 cm	GrN-4854	9510 ± 55 B.P.	(7560 B.C.)
Layer 3	15 cm	GrN-5874	9570 ± 55 B.P.	(7620 B.C.)

Louw (1969) describes Layer 28 as "Middle Stone Age," that is, belonging with the "Mwulu" sample. Of the 34 recorded artifacts from this level, only one "hemilemniscate" (?trimmed point) is reported; otherwise there are no other diagnostic pieces which would exclude it from the Lockshoek sample. As already suggested, this may be a partially mixed interface. Of great interest is a comment by Vogel (1970) reporting that the sample from Layer 28a came "from the top of a *gravel layer*"—perhaps a trace of the depositional hiatus mentioned above.

Pomongwe:

> Layer 3   SR-12   9400 ± 100 B.P. (7450 B.C.)

This reading is from a charcoal sample. The surrounding "white ash" has yielded readings that are younger and probably contaminated by secondary carbonates. The position of this sample in the layer suggests that the date represents a late stage in the Pomongwan occupation of the cave.

Tshangula:

> top of white ash layer   UCLA-692   12,200 ± 250 B.P. (10,250 B.C.)

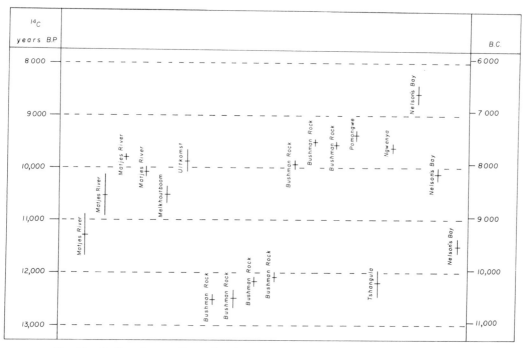

Fig. 96. Radiocarbon readings of various samples ascribed to the Oakhurst complex.

ASSOCIATED FAUNA AND DIET

Among the numerous sites attributed to the Oakhurst complex at least 15 have yielded mammalian fauna in association with the Oakhurst artifacts. It is unfortunate that almost no attempt has been made to isolate species in the Oakhurst layers from those in earlier or later deposits. As a result, the species lists provided for Oakhurst Shelter and Glentyre (Wells 1960) fail to differentiate between material from Oakhurst layers and overlying Wilton layers. Similar mixed reports have appeared for Wonderwerk and Pomongwe. Only at Bushman Rock is it possible to compile a list of species associated purely with the Lockshoek industry (Brain 1969c). These data are given in Table 45 together with the mixed Oakhurst-plus-Wilton species lists from Pomongwe, Oakhurst, Glentyre, and Matjes River (Hoffman 1958), all of which need reanalysis. Indeed, the Matjes River fauna has been so ruthlessly selected and arbitrarily described that it is doubtful whether the present information is of much use.

In spite of the variable quality of the lists, a few interesting points deserve our attention. First, the game surrounding the three coastal sites included hippo,

TABLE 45

Faunas of the Oakhurst Complex

Genus and species	Description	Bush-man Rock	Po-mongwe (mixed)	Oak-hurst (mixed)	Glen-tyre (mixed)	Matjes River (mixed)
MAMMALIAN						
Primates						
Papio ursinus	Chacma baboon	—	—	—	×	—
Lagomorpha						
Lepus sp.	Hare	2	10	—	—	—
Rodentia						
Hystrix africae-australis	Porcupine	—	—	×	—	—
Otymys sp.	Swamp rat	—	—	×	—	—
Carnivora						
Panthera pardus	Leopard	—	—	—	×	—
Genetta sp.	Genet	—	—	×	×	?
Myonax pulverulentus	Gray mongoose	?	—	—	×	?
Lutra sp.	Otter	—	—	—	—	×
Hyracoidea						
Procavia capensis	Cape hyrax	5	26	×	—	×
Heterohyrax	Extinct hyrax	—	9	—	—	—
Perissodactyla						
Equus burchelli	Burchell's zebra	9	—	—	—	—
Equus cf. *quagga*	Quagga	—	—	×	×	—
Artiodactyla						
Potamochoerus sp.	Bush pig	—	—	×	×	×
Phacochoerus aethiopicus	Cape warthog	7	—	—	—	—
Hippopotamus amphibius	Hippopotamus	—	—	—	×	×
Strepsiceros strepsiceros	Kudu	4	—	—	—	—
Taurotragus oryx	Eland	—	—	—	×	—
Tragelaphus sp.	Bushbuck	—	—	—	—	×
Syncerus caffer	Cape buffalo	—	—	×	×	×
Sylvicapra grimmia	Duiker	3	3	—	—	×
Cephalophus caerulus	Blue duiker	—	—	×	—	—
Redunca arundinum	Reedbuck	9	—	—	—	—
Hippotragus niger	Sable	4	—	—	—	—
Hippotragus leucophaeus	Bloubok	—	—	×	×	—
Damaliscus lunatus	Tsessebe	1	—	—	—	—
Alcelaphus caama	Hartebeest	5	—	—	×	—
Connochaetes taurinus	Wildebeest	6	—	—	—	—
Oreotragus oreotragus	Klipspringer	—	1	—	—	×
Raphicerus campestris	Steenbuck	3	3	cf.	cf.	×
Aepyceros melampus	Impala	4	—	—	—	—
Orycteropus afer	Ant bear	—	1	—	—	—

(continued)

278

TABLE 45 *(continued)*

Genus and species	Description	Bush-man Rock	Po-mongwe (mixed)	Oak-hurst (mixed)	Glen-tyre (mixed)	Matjes River (mixed)
NONMAMMALIAN						
Guinea fowl		—	1	—	—	—
Vulture		—	1	—	—	—
Francolin		—	1	—	—	—
Other birds		—	—	✕	✕	✕
Tortoise		24	11	✕	✕	✕
Monitor lizard		4	8	—	—	—·
Python		2	2	—	—	—
Rock lizards		—	—	—	—	—
Ostrich eggshell fragments		57	239	✕	✕	✕
Land snail fragments		22	123	—	—	—
Freshwater mussel fragments		1	—	—	—	—·
Donax mussels		—	—	✕	✕	✕
Oyster		—	—	✕	✕	✕
Solen razorshells		—	—	✕	✕	✕
Limpet		—	—	✕	✕	✕
Other marine mollusks		—	—	✕	✕	✕
Fish		—	—	?	—	✕

bush pig, and Cape buffalo, none of which was recovered from Pomongwe and Bushman Rock. Evidently the composition of the Cape coastal fauna at this period closely resembled that of historic times when distinctive species such as quagga, bloubok, and blue duiker were first recorded. Also of interest is the paucity of mammals found at Pomongwe. Comparisons with Bushman Rock suggest that the later occupants of Pomongwe were consuming mainly small animals such as hare, hyrax, and very small antelope. This list contrasts sharply with that of Bushman Rock, which includes numerous large game animals. Any attempt to interpret this difference would be premature. Differences in game density or climatic sequence may both be responsible, but other factors must be considered: both caves have been partially excavated so that the complete horizontal scatter of bones in each Oakhurst deposit is unknown. Although excavations took place near the back wall of each site, there remains the possibility that the published species lists may be the result of sampling errors caused by limited excavation. Furthermore, if Pomongwe was used not as a base camp, but only as a temporary shelter during hunting trips at this period, it is likely that only small animals would occur in the deposits. Perhaps further excavations could resolve this problem.

Marine mollusks were evidently eaten at the three coastal caves, but all excavators report that the Oakhurst levels contain relatively few specimens when compared with the dense shell midden forming the overlying Wilton layers.

At Bushman Rock abundant charred marula seed cases were found at all levels down to Layer 14 in which an acacia thorn was also recovered. Layer 9 is described as a marula seed "dump," and Layer 12 contained a high concentration of the same seed. Marula nuts were also found at Pomongwe. Although vegetable matter has been reported from all three coastal sites as well as Melkhoutboom, no analysis of edible fruit has appeared yet. No doubt application of the flotation technique in future excavations will reveal further remains.

HUMAN BURIALS AND THE ASSOCIATED PHYSICAL TYPE

Thus far, only the coastal caves have yielded human burials belonging to Oakhurst complex. The remarkable scarcity of inhumations at caves from the interior of southern Africa may suggest that burial took place outside the cave in the Lockshoek or Pomongwan regions, but this can only be demonstrated by the discovery of datable burials from the interior. The numerous coastal burials are of extreme importance but their value has been marred by the variable quality of excavation, recording, and description. Each site is discussed in turn.

The cranial measurements of six skulls from Matjes River D have been published by Louw, who made no attempt to examine the provenance of the material he was presenting. The available field notes dealing with some of the burials, as well as the accession lists, suggest that at least four of the six specimens are truly associated with Layer D, but it is impossible to ascribe individuals to the upper or lower units. The remaining two are not sufficiently documented and there is now no way of ascertaining their associations. All the skeletal material and the documentation require complete reanalysis. There are also fragments of other individuals from this layer, not mentioned in Louw's monograph.

Oakhurst: In the 60–100-inch levels of the deposits Goodwin reported: Grave IV at 88–105 inches; Grave V at 115 inches; Grave XIII at 68 inches; Grave XIV at 68 inches; Grave XV at 115 inches; Grave XVI at 106 inches. Some of these could have been buried into this level from a surface forming at a later date, and the skeletons would, therefore, be associated with a later industry. Goodwin reports that one grave shaft penetrated a black carbon layer, which conveniently sealed the Oakhurst Industry deposits: Grave VII, therefore, was buried through the top of the deposit from an overlying level.

The burials given in Table 46 can be firmly associated with Oakhurst levels and of these, Nos. 5, 13, and 15 have been measured and described by Drennan.

Glentyre: Grave 3 (72-inch depth) and Grave 5 (also 72-inch depth) can both be firmly ascribed to Oakhurst at this site. There were no grave goods, but the skull from Grave 3 was covered by two cobblestones. No measurements are available.

TABLE 46

Burials at Oakhurst

Grave no.	Skeletal content	Other contents
IV	1 juvenile (not analyzed)	Stone artifacts, gravestone.
V	1 juvenile (No. 5)	Ocher on skull and sacrum, gravestone.
XIII	1 juvenile (No. 13)	Ivory palette, double-pierced nacre pendant, tortoise shell, ostrich egg. Ocher on limbs and skull.
XIV	1 adult (not analyzed)	5 gravestones.
XV	1 adult (No. 15), quartz flake embedded in left side of occipital bone	Stone artifacts, pierced limpet and ostrich eggshell beads on pelvis. Ocher on skull and pelvis.
XVI	1 infant (not analyzed)	Gravestone. Whole burial coated in ocher.

Umgazana: Three burials, probably adults, were found in Layer 12 presumably buried into it from Layer 13. All three skeletons disintegrated and were abandoned.

Karridene: The skeleton was found in the sands directly below the surface sample and was probably buried from the original "floor" before it was covered and reexposed by the wind. The human remains have been measured and reported by Galloway and Wells.

The skeletal remains for this complex are all concentrated on the Cape coast, where burial in caves appears to have been relatively common. The contracted bodies were sprinkled or heavily coated with ocher and buried with artifacts and sometimes covered with flat stones. Evidence of food bones in these graves has not yet been clearly demonstrated.

Including the destroyed burials from Umgazana, altogether 17 individuals have been found. Specimens of adult crania from which measurements have been published are few: Matjes River Layer D, Nos. 1–6; Oakhurst, Nos. 5, 13, 15; Karridene. This list gives a total of 10 specimens that can be ascribed to Oakhurst samples with reasonable certainty. Unfortunately, the Matjes River specimens have not been sexed, and only a few measurements for the skulls (and none for the postcranial bones) have been published. For this reason, detailed comparisons between skeletal samples from the three sites are not yet possible, but the following skull indices and dimensions can be compared: maximum cranial length, cranial breadth and length; auricular height and length index; auricular height and breadth index. Graphic examples of each index are given in Fig. 97.

In the scatter diagrams pairs of indices are compared in order to test whether the samples of skulls yield different or similar clusters of measurements. A brief

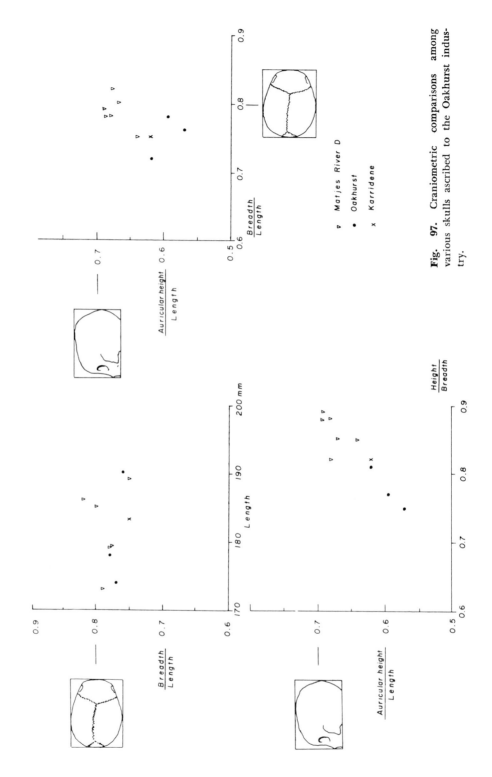

Fig. 97. Craniometric comparisons among various skulls ascribed to the Oakhurst industry.

▽ Matjes River D

● Oakhurst

× Karridene

inspection of the diagrams reveals that the three female crania from Oakhurst are similar to the specimens from Karridene, but these four specimens taken together form a separate cluster from the Matjes River sample in two of the three diagrams. The Matjes River crania have higher vaults than the others, and there are more broader skulls in the same sample. It is possible that other differences in the postcranial skeletons also exist, and more work is urgently needed on these specimens. At present, it is possible to state that the human type of the Oakhurst industry on the Cape coast does not suggest a very uniform skull morphology, but the significance of the differences cannot be discussed since the samples are small and the metrical data are limited.

The only complete cranium representing the Cape coastal population of a period earlier than Oakhurst is the Skildergat specimen, which is probably associated with Howiesonspoort or the overlying "coarse Stillbay" of Peers. Only limited data have been published by Keith, but these are sufficient to show that the Skildergat specimen is longer than any of the Oakhurst specimens. It is low vaulted and not quite outside the range of the Oakhurst scatter. Again, the amount of information is too limited to allow us to draw meaningful conclusions from this comparison, but the diagrams do suggest that the Skildergat specimen need not be a direct ancestor of the Oakhurst type since it falls outside the size range of these specimens.

OAKHURST DEPOSITS AND THEIR SIGNIFICANCE

A curious feature of many of the cave deposits from which Oakhurst samples have been excavated is the presence of massive white layers of carbonates and charcoal. The various excavators have remarked on the presence of "ash." Among the five sites listed under the Oakhurst industry, Matjes River Layer D was also called "the burned layer," referring to the abundance of charcoal and ash levels. Oakhurst has a series of dense charcoal layers intercalated with deep bands of white ash or carbonate. At Glentyre a 9-inch deep black deposit and "ashy soil" is reported to contain "pavement" of cobblestones, possibly representing a hearth area. This band is enclosed in an interlocking mass of white ash layers. A remarkably similar network of overlapping ash deposits is found at Melkhoutboom near the bottom of the excavation and at Nelson's Bay Cave.

Among sites attributed to the Lockshoek industry, the Umgazana Strata 1–14 comprise a complex mass of charcoal lenses and carbonate layers, whereas Layer C at Nqamakwe is described as a 1-ft deep complex of compressed carbon and white ash layers alternating with sand lenses. The Uitkomst sample was recovered from a "fireplace," at Glenferness the artifacts came from a "white ash," and the Hennops River sample from a "hard white ash." In the Bushman Rock sequence (Layers 3–28) there is a continuous accumulation of variegated hearth lines containing black, dark brown, light gray, buff, and white "ash" lenses of which some are partially cemented.

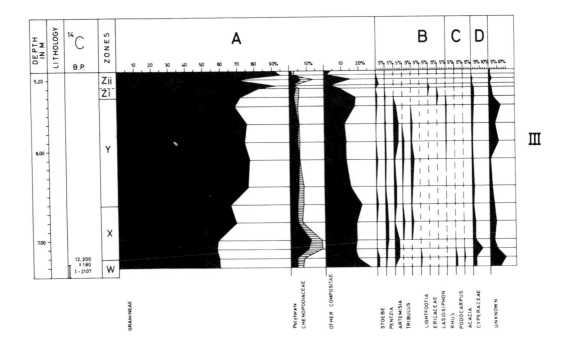

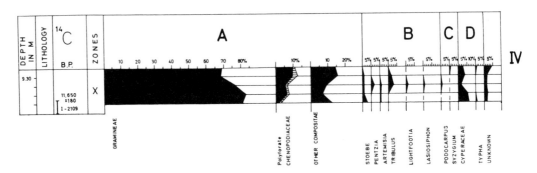

Fig. 98. Pollen diagram of sediments from Aliwal North suggesting vegetal changes in this area during the period of the Oakhurst complex. (After Coetzee 1967.)

Finally, Pomongwe levels at both Pomongwe Cave and Tshangula are both described as "white ash with rare charcoal specks." Of the complete list of cave sites for which any published details are available, only the Wonderwerk report contains no mention of this remarkably consistent feature. It is unfortunate that no adequate charcoal analyses of these deposits have been carried out to determine whether or not they do indeed represent "ash" as so many authors have assumed. Cooke (1963) points out that Pomongwan white ash layers closely resemble wood ash, particularly that of dried woods which burn rapidly, leaving very little charcoal. His suggestion that the layers at Pomongwe and Tshangula represent the debris of a local bush fire appears unlikely in the light of the repeated occurrence of this phenomenon elsewhere. Such dense hearth complexes can only reflect a new aspect of the Oakhurst hunters' activities. If large bonfires were repeatedly built inside the caves during this period, some explanation for this behavior should be sought. There is absolutely no reliable evidence to suggest any overall temperature changes for this period of 12,000–9000 B.P. Indeed, all the relevant cave deposits contain notably fewer roof spalls than occurred in the preceding Howiesonspoort and Umguzan strata. The pollen spectrum from Aliwal North (Coetzee 1967) provides the only possible indication of temperature changes during this period (see Fig. 98). Prior to 12,000 B.P. certain cold-adapted plant species occurred at lower altitudes than previously found in this area, but thereafter the vegetation reflects a variable dry–warm regime, probably reaching an optimum at about 11,500 B.P. It is unlikely, therefore, that a decrease in mean annual temperature during Oakhurst times can be invoked to explain the apparent increase of cave hearths during the period. At present it is only possible to point out that the Oakhurst patterns of cave occupation differ from those of earlier industries.

POSSIBLY RELATED SITES IN ZAMBIA

Between 12,000 and 9000 B.P. the heavily wooded territory of northern Zambia was occupied by groups practicing a fully microlithic stoneworking technology known as "Nachikufu I." This lithic tradition differs considerably from the relatively simple Oakhurst complex, and displays closer stylistic connections with the Wilton complex treated in the following chapter. However, very little is presently known of the prehistory of southern Zambia or the Zambesi valley during this period. It may be expected that traces of the Pomongwan Industry would occur in this region, but no stratified sites have yet been recovered which might reveal the sequence of events following the Umguzan phase. At present only one excavated sample from Zambia appears to be related to the Pomongwan group in Rhodesia. This is Shimabala Quarry only a few miles south of Lusaka. A narrow clay-filled fissure exposed by parting of the limestone quarry face was found to contain mammalian fauna and artifacts (Sampson 1963). The excavated sample (mainly of quartz) is of limited value as it occurred in a derived context, and publication has been delayed since the identity of the sample was not previously recognized. An analysis of the tool assemblage, using Cooke's typology appears in Table 44 together with the figures from Pomongwe Cave. Faunal remains with the Shimabala sample include: leopard, hyena, zebra (abundant), warthog, hippo, kudu, buffalo, duiker, reedbuck, roan, hartebeest, wildebeest, and impala. A few fragments of ostrich egg were recovered, but no small mammals or nonmammalian bone. The composition of this assemblage has more in common with Bushman Rock than Pomongwe.

AVAILABLE EVIDENCE FROM ANGOLA

Clark (1965, 1966) has described a "Second Intermediate Coastal Variant" from Palmeirinhas, south of Luanda. This is an unselected surface collection apparently weathering from a clay–sand that overlies the local 20-m sea-cut platform. No organic associations were recovered, and the industry is undated. Quartz is the dominant raw material. Only 26 tools and 32 utilized pieces were recovered, and the published typology does not allow direct comparisons with Pomongwan or elsewhere. Core scrapers, "fabricators," and large sidescrapers dominate the sample. Although too small to provide adequate percentage data, the sample appears to have more types in common with the Oakhurst complex than with the preceding Umguzan. However, the paucity of material and the unreliable context of the sample do not permit any definite ascription. Similar shortcomings prevent a diagnosis of six other small surface collections in the Luanda area. It must be concluded, therefore, that no adequate evidence has been found yet to suggest the presence of this complex in Angola.

OAKHURST ORIGINS AND RELATED PROBLEMS

It is now apparent that stoneworking techniques in southern Africa underwent complex changes between about 13,000 and 12,000 B.P. By this time the array of types found in the Umguzan–Howiesonspoort have virtually disappeared. Evidently no known prehistoric groups were making trimmed points or backed blades and crescents, nor were the Levallois or blade-core techniques in use. In their place appeared a lithic tradition based on the production of large plain-platform flakes from adjacent-platform cores. Flakes were either used directly or marginally trimmed to form a variety of scraper forms. In those sites with adequate conditions for preservation, ground and polished bone armatures, awls, and jewelry make their first convincing appearance, as do pierced and ground ostrich eggshell beads. Bored stones and reamers appear at many sites for the first time. Although ocher pencils, ocher-stained grindstones, and ocher-covered inhumations have been recovered, there is still no convincing evidence to suggest that rock paintings were executed by the Oakhurst peoples. Elaborate burial was practiced, at least on the Cape coast, where the individual was placed in a flexed position lying on one side in a shallow grave and frequently covered by grindstones. Both artifacts and food bones may occur in the grave fill. While the human skeletal type is unquestionably *H. sapiens sapiens* and displays several morphological characters that superficially resemble the modern Kalahari Bushman, the term "Proto-Bushman" previously applied to the group is of little value since no evolutionary connection can possibly be demonstrated.

Fig. 99. Tools and ornaments from the Oakhurst industry: (1–3) endscrapers; (4) circular scrapers; (5–9) sidescrapers; (10–12) pierced shell pendants; (11) pierced bone pendant; (13–15) cylindrical bone points; (16–20) ivory mattocks; (17) polished bone tube; (18, 19) bone awls. The specimens are from Oakhurst, Glentyre, and Matjes River.

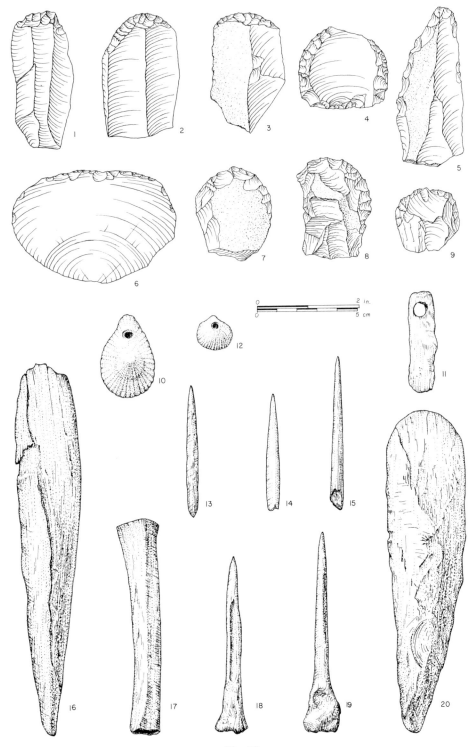

Fig. 99

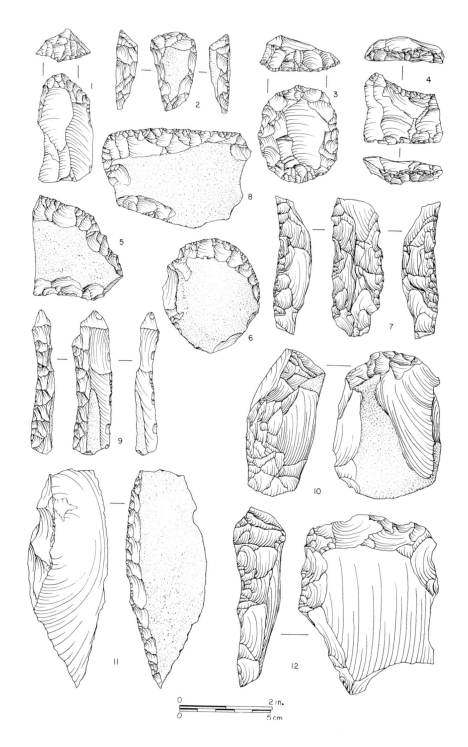

Fig. 100

The factors that brought about the material culture changes summarized above remain obscure at present for want of more detailed information about environmental, dietary, and population changes between the fourteenth and twelfth millenia. Probably different sets of factors were operating in each of the three areas studied thus far, and there is no reason to seek a common cause for the emergence of the Oakhurst, Lockshoek, and Pomongwan industries.

It has been noted previously that the Oakhurst industry may overlap in time with the (as yet unnamed) Post-Howiesonspoort blade industry found at Klasie's River Mouth and possibly elsewhere. Until more carbon-14 dates are made available for each group of samples and their stratigraphic positions have been demonstrated within one deposit, no clear picture of their relationship can emerge. The possibility that the two "industries" represent activity variations of a single local population needs to be considered, but there is very little evidence that might favor this hypothesis rather than one that postulates two separate industries practiced by different peoples. In Matjes River D the upper unit contains clear evidence of blade production and the use of blades as blanks for end-scrapers by people practicing the Oakhurst technology. No trace of blademaking has been recovered from the sparse lower unit sample deposited by the first occupants of the cave. Even if the two groups eventually prove to be of the same local industry, there remains the unresolved problem of how and why they replaced the Howiesonspoort.

One obvious possibility is the arrival in this area of a new hunting group already equipped with the Oakhurst technology. It certainly appears that several large caves in the Cape coastal region were occupied for the first time by Oakhurst groups. Also, there can be little doubt that the skeletal sample from Oakhurst levels shows no very striking resemblance to the earlier human skeleton from the Howiesonspoort or "Stillbay" levels at Skildergat. However, if an invasion hypothesis is to be invoked, some convincing source area for the new population is needed and no such evidence exists in the archaeological record at present.

The origins of the Lockshoek industry are similarly obscured by the lack of suitable field data. Its stratigraphic position above the Howiesonspoort, Umguzan, or other unnamed samples seems reasonably consistent, and no overlap in carbon-14 dates has occurred so far. Thus, the "activity variant" hypothesis need not apply in this area. Unfortunately, the absence of associated skeletal material remains, and the inadequacy of the environmental data prevents any discussion of Lockshoek origins.

Finally, the Pomongwan has been found to be consistently younger than the Umguzan, which it replaced at possibly about 13,000 B.P. The faunal data for Pomongwe Cave suggest a decrease in the amount of large game hunted after this period, but the associated faunas from Bushman Rock and Shimabala sug-

---

Fig. 100. Tools from the Lockshoek industry: (1) frontal scraper (1); (2) frontal scraper (2); (3) circular scraper; (4) *outil écaillé*; (5) sidescraper fragment; (6) circular scraper; (7, 9) backed adzes; (8) sidescraper (4); (10) battered piece; (11) sidescraper (1); (12) steep scraper.

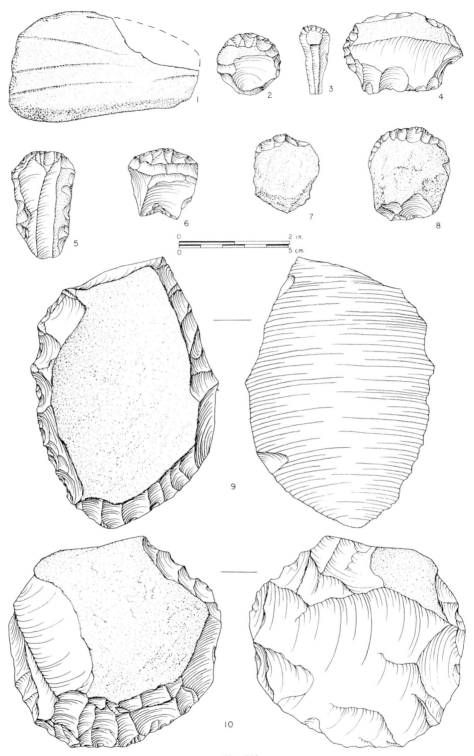

Fig. 101

Fig. 101. Tools from the Pomongwan industry, Pomongwe Cave: (1) grooved stone; (2) circular scraper; (3) endscraper; (4) sidescraper; (5) side- and endscraper; (6–8) sidescrapers; (9) sidescraper (4) ; (10) core hammer.

gest that the dietary shift at Pomongwe may have been a strictly local phenomenon. Supposed adaptations to a depleted game population will not suffice to explain the advent of the Pomongwan technology. Diffusion or invasion hypotheses are equally hampered by the lack of associated skeletal material. Hopefully, the origins of this complex will be pursued by researchers during the next decade. The present chapter can do little more than point out the problem and encourage recognition of a stage in southern African prehistory for which no adequate terminology has previously existed. While not wishing to impose the terms suggested here, it is to be hoped that some, at least, will be generally adopted to replace the confusing array of names now in use to describe essentially similar artifact assemblages (see Figs. 99, 100, and 101) .

8

The Wilton
Complex

The Wilton Rock Shelter from which this complex takes its name is located several miles west of Howiesonspoort about 30 miles inland from the southern Cape coast. Hewitt (1921) described the excavations conducted by Stapleton, Kilroe, and himself over a five-day period during which they recovered four skeletons and removed some 4 ft of deposit before reaching bedrock. Hewitt's opinion that the deposit represented a single stratum containing one homogenous assemblage was supported by Burkitt (1928), who visited the shelter, and the name "Wilton" was formally adopted by Burkitt, Goodwin, and van Riet Lowe during a meeting of the British Association at Pretoria in 1926. Following the standards of description and analysis considered appropriate for the times, Burkitt listed the tools found at Wilton without numerical data. Although they probably kept all the material recovered during the work, it is impossible to divide the extant collection according to depth within the deposit. The proportions of tool types in this original collection are summarized in Fig. 102. Other elements mentioned by Burkitt included: bored stones, palettes, rough pottery, and ostrich eggshell beads. Recent excavations reported by Deacon and Brooker

(1969) indicate that the original collection is a mixture of probably four recognizable stages of development within a single lithic tradition. There is no single homogenous assemblage, but a complex series of stylistic changes covering some 6000 years of local prehistory.

In the absence of a precise description for the type-site material, workers in adjacent areas were soon reporting similarities between Wilton and their own discoveries. Goodwin and van Riet Lowe (1929) restricted the name to surface finds from the Cape coastal region, but Goodwin tentatively suggested that it might be present in almost all parts of South Africa, South West Africa, and Botswana. He also pointed out similarities between Wilton and several excavated sites from the Matopos Hills, Rhodesia some 900 miles to the north. Burkitt (1928) supported this link with Rhodesia and mentioned similar material still farther afield in Kenya and Uganda. Their example was soon followed by local workers. N. Jones (1949) adopted the term in Rhodesia, Clark (1942) used it to describe finds from Mumbwa in Zambia, L. S. B. Leakey (1931) used it in Kenya, O'Brien (1939) in Uganda, and Clark (1954a) in Somalia. None of these reports attempted a detailed numerical comparison between the local "Wilton" sample and that from the type site. Although tool lists and percentage analyses were presented for several sites in South Africa, Rhodesia, Zambia, and Somalia, the inevitable lack of standardized typology makes detailed comparisons impossible. It is quite apparent that a "Wilton" sample from the shores of Lake Victoria in Uganda will not precisely resemble one from the vicinity of Cape Town in South Africa, and no doubt earlier authors fully realized this. However, all the published samples share several typological features that would allow them to be loosely grouped at the "technocomplex" level. Thus, the Wilton industrial complex may be a legitimate term in all the above regions, but several local industries must surely occur within this complex.

The task of isolating and describing the different industries of the Wilton complex in southern Africa has progressed in a very haphazard fashion, hampered, as always, by the absence of agreed analytical procedures. Although standardized typologies have emerged for some geographical regions, these cannot be compared one to another. In this chapter, the various typologies are examined in an attempt to isolate those features that allow us to identify each industry.

DISTRIBUTION AND NOMENCLATURE
OF THE WILTON COMPLEX INDUSTRIES

A tentative grouping of 55 sites yielding samples related to the Wilton complex is presented in Table 47. Given the present inconsistency in definition and analysis of this array of sites, any further geographical subdivision would be rash. No doubt stylistic differences exist between Wilton sites from South-West

TABLE 47

Organization of Sites and Industries in the Wilton Complex

Coastal Wilton	Interior Wilton	Matopan	Pfupian	Zambian Wilton	Nachikufan
Wilton 0–60 in.	Rose Cottage	Pomongwe	Pfupi	Mumbwa	Nachikufu Cave
Oakhurst	Riversmead I–IX	Tshangula	Nyazongo	Gwisho A	Nachikufu Shelter
Glentyre 0–42 in.	Zaayfontein V–XIV	Khami	Mtemwa Rocks	Gwisho B	Nsalu
Matjes River Layer C	Glen Elliott IV–VIII	Gokomere	Surface sites	Lusu	Bimbe
Nelson's Bay Cave	Holmsgrove III–V	Amadzimba		Makwe	Chifubwa
Melkhoutboom 0–40 in.	Blydefontein I–VIII	Nswatugi		Nakapapula	Leopard's Hill
Welcome Woods	Zeekoegat, lower level	Bambata		Kamusongolwa	Mwela Rocks
De Hangen		Madiliyangwa			Chaminade
Uniondale	Lemoenfontein	Calder's Cave		Kotakota	Fingira
Montagu, Layer I		Dombazanga		Siasuntwe	Mbande
Skildergat					
Trappieskop				Kandande	
Klipkop		Hillside		Donke	
Nqamakwe C, III					
Umlaas group					
Tongaat group					
surface sites					

TABLE 48

Stratigraphic Correlation of Coastal Wilton Sites

Phase	Wilton	Melkhoutboom	Glentyre	Oakhurst	Matjes River	Other samples
Ceramic	Layer 1	0–13 in. (Pottery Wilton)	0–6 in. (Pottery Wilton)	0–9 in. (Pottery Wilton)		Surface sites, De Hangen
Developed	Layer 2	?13–24 in. (Pottery Wilton)	6–12 in. (Developed Wilton)	9–18 in. (Developed Wilton)	Layer C, Site 5	Umlaas group ("Smithfield C")
Classic	Layer 3	?24–38 in. (?Prepottery Wilton)	12–21 in. (Normal Wilton)	18–36 in. (Normal Wilton)	Layer C, Site 5	Nqamakwe C, Layers II–III
Early	Basal layer	?	21–42 in. (Smithfield C)	36–60 in. (Smithfield C)	Layer C, Site 5	Montagu Layer 1

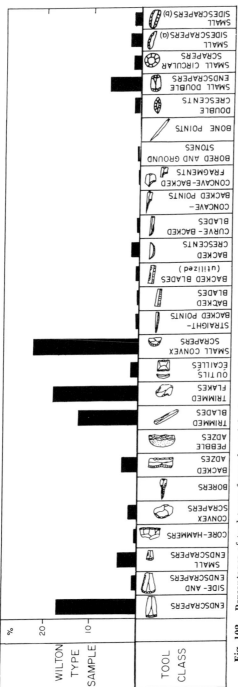

Fig. 102. Percentages of tool types from the original excavations at Wilton Shelter. This sample is a mixture of all phases combined.

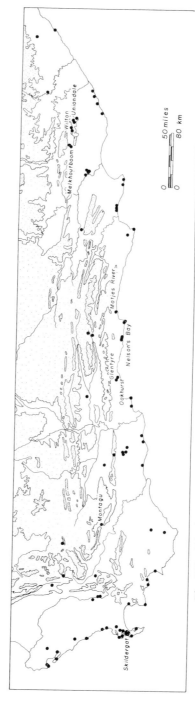

Fig. 103. Distribution of all reported Wilton sites in the southern Cape. The excavated sites are named.

295

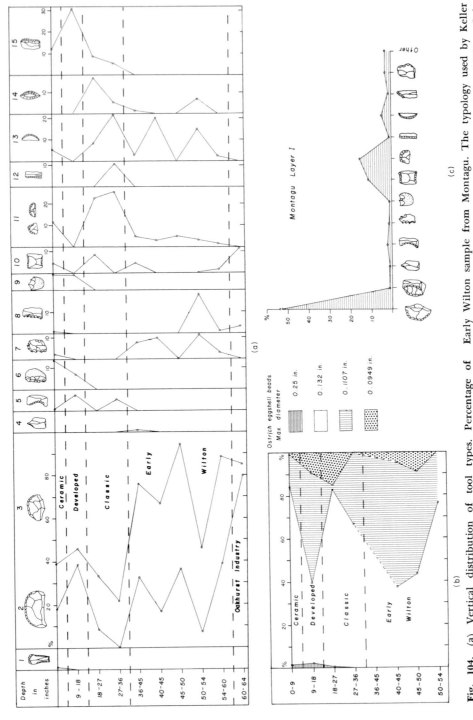

Fig. 104. (a) Vertical distribution of tool types. Percentage of tool types changes through time in the Wilton levels of Oakhurst Shelter. (b) Variations in the diameter of ostrich eggshell beads in the various phases of the Wilton levels. (c) Distribution of tool types in the Early Wilton sample from Montagu. The typology used by Keller (1969b) at Montagu differs from that used by Schrire (1962) at Oakhurst, so that precise comparisons are not yet possible.

Africa and those from the southwestern Cape, but the inevitable lack of numerical comparisons does not allow a separation at present. Each of the above industries is treated individually in the following sections.

THE COASTAL WILTON

Typology

The range of tool types recovered from Wilton Shelter (Fig. 102) must suffice to summarize the typology of the Coastal Wilton. Comparisons between samples have not been attempted, chronological subdivision of coastal Wilton deposits lacks standardization, and terminologies vary from one site to another. It will be observed that a few Oakhurst tool types persist into this complex, but these occur in diminished frequencies only in the early stages of the Wilton development. It is apparent that the Wilton industry and, indeed, the entire complex is essentially of microlithic character. The elements that distinguish Wilton from any other prehistoric assemblage are the abundant microblades and small flakes, which have been either marginally trimmed to form small convex scrapers and sidescrapers, or blunted to form a variety of microlithic backed bladelets, crescents, points, and other forms. These easily recognized traits have led to the recording and collecting of numerous Wilton samples along the South African coast, where wind-eroded sites and shell middens related to this industry are extremely common. The resulting record suggests a high density of finds (Fig. 103), but a variable amount of useful information. Since so many surface scatters have been selectively collected, their exact positions in the stylistic evolution of the Wilton remains unknown. Only a few professional excavations have yielded adequate information about chronological subdivision and correlations have been hampered by the uneven use of different terms. A tentative attempt to order the more reliable Wilton data from excavated or totally collected samples is given in Table 48. Four phases—Early, Classic, Developed, and Ceramic —are tentatively suggested to describe the Wilton development through time. In the following table samples from various sites are described according to depth, but the terms used by their excavators are included in brackets.

Similar subdivisions may prove possible for other sites, particularly Skildergat, Nelson's Bay, Welcome Woods, and Uniondale when these samples have been analyzed. The positions of the other listed sites within this framework remain obscure for want of detailed analyses. It should be stressed here that the basis for such chronological subdivisions of the Coastal Wilton is tentative and subject to some adjustment after systematic analysis. The present outline has not been placed on a numerical basis although the Oakhurst data provide some helpful indications of tool-type fluctuations through time (Fig. 104). However, it is not yet known whether the other sites share similar fluctuations, although subjective inspection of these materials suggest that they may follow the same general evolution.

Chronological Subdivision: Phases

The *Early Wilton* may be generally recognized by the presence of relatively abundant large sidescrapers, steep scrapers and core hammers, many of which are made of quartzite, quartz, or sandstone. These may constitute over half the tool kits and display little or no homogeneity in shape or design. There are no features that distinguish these specimens from similar tools in the preceding Oakhurst industry. Early Wilton samples may also be characterized by a relatively high frequency (perhaps 30% of all tools) of large utilized flakes without formal design. Like the larger scraper elements, these are mostly of quartzite or sandstone and are also a common feature of the preceding Oakhurst technology. The remainder of the Early Wilton tool assemblage includes relatively few (5–10%) small convex scrapers, small sidescrapers, small circular scrapers, *outils écaillés,* and scarce (about 5%) backed microliths including backed crescents, double crescents, backed bladelets, and backed points usually with backing along two parallel or converging margins. Silcrete, chalcedony, crystal quartz, and chert are the preferred raw materials. Grindstones, reamers, bored stones, and cylindrical bone points may occur, as well as bone awls, mattocks, tubes, beads, shell pendants, ostrich eggshell beads, and engraved ostrich eggshell fragments. Two numerical analyses of Early Wilton samples from Oakhurst (Schrire 1962) and Montagu (Keller 1969b) are given in Fig. 104.

The so-called *Classic Wilton* differs from the preceding phase in the numerical proportions of a few tool types and suggests a shift in the use of certain raw materials. The larger heavy scraper elements decrease in frequency or disappear completely, and large utilized flakes are less numerous. They are replaced by an increased proportion of small convex scrapers (about 30–40%), small sidescrapers, small circular scrapers, and backed adzes may also increase slightly. The backed microlithic elements now make up between 15 and 25% of the tools with a wider range of forms represented. Essentially, the major changes in tool design between the Early and Classic phases indicate a decrease in the dimensions of stone scrapers of all types. The majority of Classic Wilton scrapers are too small to be effective while hand-held and must have been hafted on to wood or bone handles. Numerous specimens were recovered from Melkhoutboom and Matjes River with a mastic of unknown materials (presumably vegetable gums) still adhering to their surfaces, indicating the method of attachment to the handle. Complete hafted specimens have been recoverd from somewhat dubious contexts at several sites (Deacon 1966c; Hewitt 1912), although it is by no means certain which of these came from Wilton levels (Fig. 105). It is also assumed that the numerous backed microliths were hafted in slotted wooden arrows and served as barbs projecting from the shaft. Although several backed crescents and backed bladelets have been recovered with adhering mastic, no complete examples of the so-called "composite" arrowhead have been recovered yet. The precise

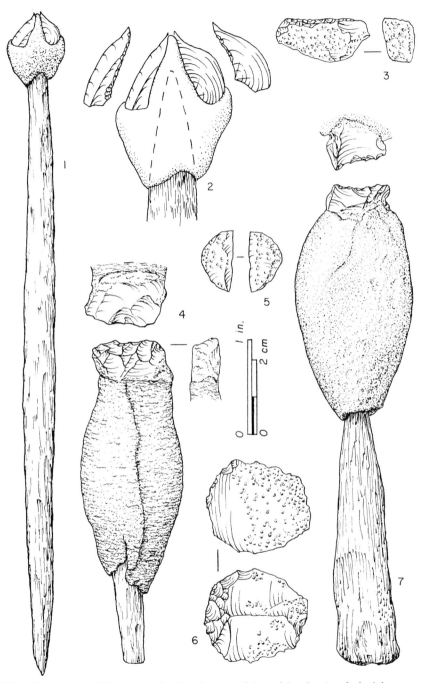

Fig. 105. Hafted microlithic tools: (1, 2) sidestruck flakes of bottle glass hafted in wax on a whittled wooden arrow shaft made by modern Bushmen (after Goodwin (1944); (3) backed adze with traces of mastic adhereing to the backed margin, from Melkhoutboom; (4) backed adze mounted in mastic handle from Plettenberg Bay; (5) backed crescent with mastic adhering to backed margin and faces, from Melkhoutboom; (6) small endscraper with mastic handle, from Plettenberg Bay.

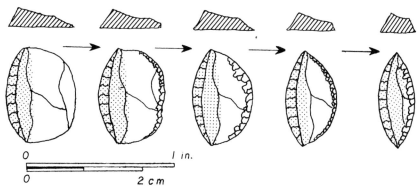

Fig. 106. Diagram of reduction process by which a backed flake mounted in mastic is blunted and refurbished repeatedly until the margin of the working edge retreats to the mastic. The jettisoned specimen then resembles the double crescent, covered with mastic (stippled area).

method of hafting therefore, remains a subject for speculation, although a few relatively recent "composite" arrowheads with glass armatures have been collected from the historic Bushmen (Clark 1959a; Goodwin 1945) see Fig. 105. Other tool types yielding specimens with adhering mastic include small backed adzes and the so-called double crescent, which is now generally thought to represent a heavily utilized backed flake. This was eventually rejected when the utilized edge had been repeatedly resharpened by flaking and had retreated back to the mastic in which the true backed margin was embedded, as shown in Fig. 106. This type may constitute over 5% of the tool kit and is a distinctive feature of the Coastal Wilton sequence. It occurs only rarely in the industries of the interior.

In the *Developed Wilton* there occurs a reversal in the trend that occurred between the Early and Classic phases. The proportion of coarse-grained rocks increases, and there is a subsequent trend towards the manufacture of large sidescrapers from flakes of these materials. Large utilized flakes also proliferate, as do core scrapers, core choppers, and serrated pieces. There is also a noticeable increase in the frequency of endscrapers at a few sites, at the expense of the smaller (hafted) scraper types. Backed microliths remain, and in some assemblages the backed crescent may be entirely absent although backed bladelets and points persist. At a few sites, rare bifacial pressure-flaked points on very small flakes make their first appearance. In summary, the developed Wilton reflects a breakdown in the homogeneity of design shown by samples from the Classic phase: a wider range of types is present, each forming a small percentage of the assemblage, and individual types display a wider range of morphological and size variation than is apparent in the Classic phase.

Although this trend has been recognized in at least five Coastal Wilton sites, it is by no means certain that it represents a universal phenomenon in the Cape coastal region. Presumably in areas where the only suitable materials are small pieces of crystalline or other isotropic rock, the "microlithic" character of the

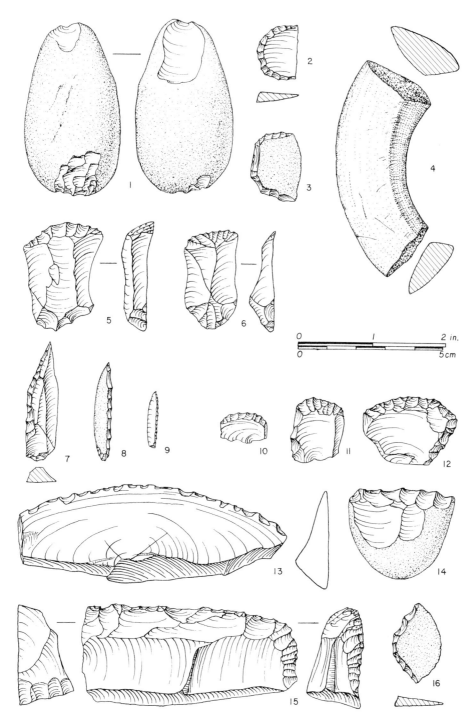

Fig. 107. Tools from the Umlaas group of sites, tentatively ascribed to the Developed phase of the Coastal Wilton: (1) bipolar flaked pebble; (2, 3) deep backed crescents; (5, 6) end-scrapers; (7, 8, 9) backed points; (10–12) small convex scraper; (13) utilized flakes; (14) pebble adze; (15) backed adze; (16) backed flake.

Classic phase may have been retained for a longer period. The interior mountain ranges of the Cape Folded Belt may reflect such a situation.

Inclusion of the 22 surface collections labelled "Umlaas variant of the Smithfield C" by Schoute-Vanneck and Walsh (1961) within this phase cannot be justified on a numerical basis, as the authors give only the range of tool types
found at each site (Fig. 107). The group is tentatively included here on typological grounds only as it displays the features described above.

Finally, the *Ceramic Wilton* refers to the later levels of the Developed Wilton
which yield, in addition to stone artifacts, sherds of pottery. No changes in the
proportions of tool types during this phase have been detected. Sherds have been
described from Oakhurst (Schofield 1938b), Glentyre (Fagan 1960), and Melkhoutboom (Deacon 1969a). The presence of sherds in later Wilton levels is also
reported from Nelson's Bay Cave (Inskeep 1965a) and Skildergat (Jolly 1948).
Parkington and Poggenpoel (1971) also describe sherds associated with a late
Wilton industry from De Hangen in the southwestern Cape Province mountains. Here it is evident that the stone industry has retained a "microlithic"
character similar to that of the Classic phase, presumably a response to the limited size of isotropic raw materials available in the vicinity of the site. Although
sherds have been recovered *in situ* with Wilton samples from other sites, these
are not yet reported. There can be no doubt that pottery was used by the groups
responsible for the final stages of the Wilton development in this region. It has
been recovered repeatedly by controlled excavations, and there is no reason to
suppose that the sherds are intrusive from later occupations of the sites. These
numerous examples of firm associations between pottery and late Wilton assemblages help to support the numerous claimed surface associations between sherds
and Wilton artifacts recovered from shell middens along the southwestern Cape
coast. An extremely valuable survey by Rudner (1968) lists all known Ceramic
Wilton shell middens in this region. Their distribution is mapped in Fig. 103
(page 295).

Although the sherds recovered *in situ* are mostly small specimens (Fig. 108),
it is apparent that they represent a surprising variety of forms and sizes of vessels. This impression is amply reinforced by the surface collections from the shell
middens, specimens of which are shown in Fig. 109. Virtually no physical or
chemical analyses of this material have been carried out. Visual inspection of the
sherds shows that the vessel walls were built up by hand from a variety of clays,
tempered with quartz sands, grits, broken sherds, or crushed marine shell. Firing
temperatures were uneven but always relatively low, and most sherds are fairly
soft or friable. There is no evidence to suggest the use of a wheel or firing kiln.
Most sherds display matte surfaces with a blotchy buff-gray coloring, and the
interior body is black, indicating an uneven firing in an open hearth. The use of
a true slip has not been reported, but black burnished outer surfaces are known.
Grooving of the wet clay surface near the rim was occasionally practiced, but the
resulting decoration of parallel lines is irregular and poorly controlled.

The most characteristic vessel form from this group is a conical-based pot with
rounded shoulders and a vertical or sloping neck. Either a raised boss or, more

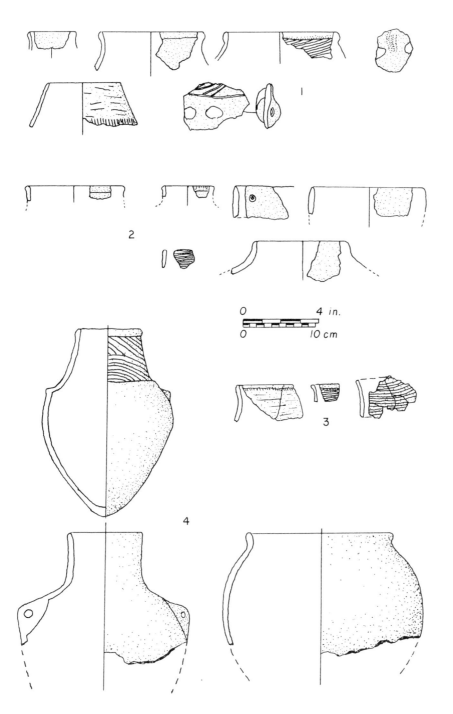

Fig. 108. Potsherds recovered from *in situ* with the Ceramic Wilton samples in the southern Cape coastal region: (1) De Hangen; (2) Melkhoutboom; (3) Glentyre; (4) Oakhurst.

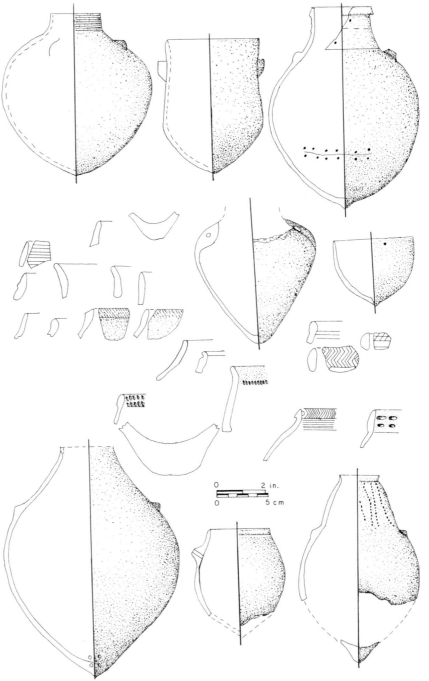

Fig. 109. Whole ceramic vessels reported by J. Rudner (1968) from the surfaces of shell middens containing Wilton artifacts on the southwestern Cape coast.

frequently, a reinforced lug may occur at two or three points around the shoulder. Incised decoration is usually restricted to the neck, common forms being horizontal or diagonal lines, impressed dots, or combinations of these. The pot rim is frequently rolled, everted, or flattened at the tip, and small incisions may occur along the rim itself. Other pot shapes recognized by Rudner are bowls and bag-shaped pots, either with or without pierced and reinforced lugs. Rimsherds with drilled holes are also recorded.

It must be admitted that the process by which later Coastal Wilton groups acquired pottery remains obscure. Independent invention seems the least likely explanation as the ceramic technology appears in this region for the first time with an already homogenous set of stylistic features. These point to a longer history of design and development elsewhere. Nor need this imply that the pottery (or sherds) were obtained from adjacent or migratory Iron Age groups such as the so-called Hottentots, as suggested by several authors. If ceramics were entering Late Coastal Wilton deposits through barter, raiding, or theft from another cultural group, it is likely that metal objects would also occur in Ceramic Wilton levels, but these have not been detected. There is no evidence which might refute the claim that the pottery was actually manufactured by late Wilton peoples, but the necessary technical skills were evidently acquired from adjacent groups with a longer history of potmaking. Exactly who those groups may have been remains an interesting objective for future research.

Besides the lithic and ceramic features of the Coastal Wilton, there persists through all the proposed phases a vigorous boneworking tradition which has not yet been adequately studied. Chipped and ground bone mattocks, adzes, and digging sticks have been reported from Matjes River C and several midden sites. Other ground and polished bone objects from Matjes River C include: (1) a large pierced rib fragment with beveled end, possibly designed for use as a hafted adze, (2) a flat elliptical polished bone plaque drilled at two points near the center (Fig. 110). Both here and at other sites the most abundant bone-work forms are polished bone awls, and "spatulas" with ground and beveled edges. Matjes River Layer C has also yielded several long slender club-headed pins. Ground and polished bone beads also occur at several sites. Bone tubes with polished or incised outer surfaces are fairly common, some with beveled rims. Fifteen open-ended bone shafts from Matjes River C have one or more holes drilled into the side wall of the shaft. Louw (1960) lists these as "flutes" although their true function is unknown. Ostrich eggshell fragments, some with incised lines on the outer surface, occur at almost every Wilton site. Again, no systematic study of this material has taken place, but common incised decorative motifs are chevrons, hatching and "ladder" designs.

At Matjes River and Oakhurst, whole ostrich eggshells were recovered with pierced ends. These presumably served mainly as water containers. Another extremely common element at Wilton sites is the ostrich eggshell bead, which

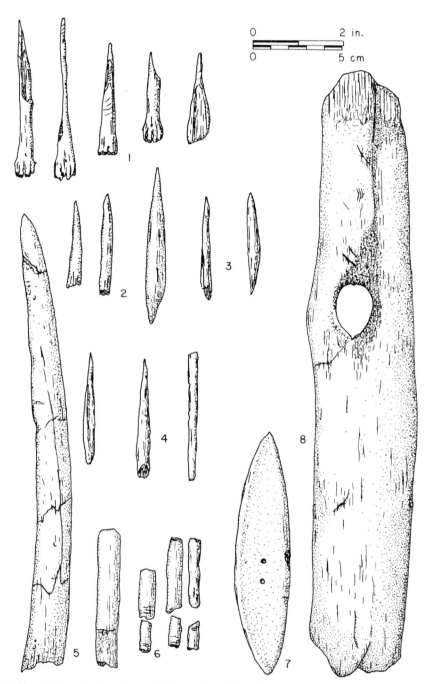

Fig. 110. Bone work from Coastal Wilton sites: (1) awls; (2–4) cylindrical points; (5) ground and polished rib fragment; (6) polished and decorated tubes; (7) polished and double-drilled fragment (?pendant); (8) pierced and ground mattock with beveled blade (top). The specimens are from Matjes River and Oakhurst.

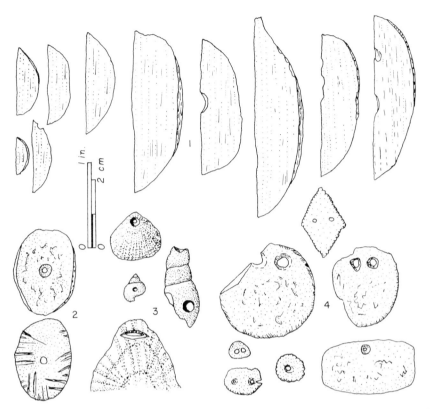

Fig. 111. Ornaments of marine and ostrich eggshell from Coastal Wilton sites: (1) shell crescents, possibly of human manufacture; (2) drilled and engraved mollusk fragments; (3) pierced marine mollusks; (4) drilled, polished, and nicked pendants of mollusk and ostrich eggshell. The specimens are from Oakhurst Shelter.

has been recorded in all stages of manufacture. Schrire (1962) has noted that the beads from the Wilton levels at Oakhurst tend towards larger maximum diameters in the Classic phase. Louw (1960) also notes that Wilton beads are markedly larger than the preceding Oakhurst beads of Matjes River D, but his observations were not placed on a numerical basis. Presumably most beads were simply strung as single rows or twisted ropes and used as ornamental necklaces, but Meiring (1953) reports the discovery of bead arrangements that suggest a complex plaiting to form an "apron" of beads around the pelvic area of a human burial in Matjes River D. Unfortunately no photographic record of this arrangement was recovered, although Goodwin (1938) managed to photograph a similar "apron" fragment *in situ* at Oakhurst. Apart from bone and ostrich egg beads rare specimens of ivory, pierced teeth, tortoise shell, shale, and possibly clay beads have been reported.

The use of marine shells as beads and pendants is well documented for all phases of the Coastal Wilton. Whole shells—either *Patella* limpets or one of the *Burnupena* group—were pierced by a short incision and presumably suspended without further alteration. Many others, including small white mussels *Donax serra* and even smaller periwinkels of the *Oxystele* group, were similarly pierced and strung. Probably the most common form of shell pendant is a white mussel fragment with a beveled and nicked margin and two holes drilled off center, usually through the thicker portion of the shell. A similar design has been applied to larger fragments of the venus' ear, *Haliotis sanguineum,* which forms a large flat pendant with a blue-green irridescent nacre of remarkable beauty. Another recurrent form is the so-called shell crescent (Fig. 111) found only in Wilton deposits containing large quantities of marine molluscan debris. These are usually large crescent-shaped fragments of brown mussel *Perna perna* or black mussel *Choromytilus meridionalis,* with the straight margin formed by the edge of the shell, and the convex margin suggesting deliberate snapping. Whether or not these objects could be formed by natural patterns of mussel breakage is still being debated. If they are true artifacts, no obvious function is apparent at present.

Artifacts in other materials have been reported from Melkhoutboom by Hewitt (1931b) and Deacon (1969a, b). Wooden pegs were found wedged into crevices of the rock shelter wall and others were found in the deposit, a few of which were positioned vertically and in close association with grass, which may have been used as a binding material. Most of the excavated pegs were associated with grass bedding. Twigs and side branches had been removed by ring cutting and snapping at the base, and long curved wooden shavings found among the grass bedding point toward an efficient whittling technique. Several pegs had been finished off by brief charring of the point. Various whittled sticks and points were also recovered, including a fire-drill stick with the characteristic charred impressions. Abundant cut reeds (*Cyperus textilus*) were recovered, as was an unidentified notched reed presumably used as an arrow shaft. Unfortunately, the opposite end is charred so that no details of armature hafting has survived. *Cyperus textilus* was split and teased out to make cord of both two-strand and four-strand twist, and several knotted pieces have been recovered, pointing to the use of grass netting. A netting fragment with a 10-mm mesh and made from two-strand cord has also survived. Abundant stems of the reed *Phragmites communis* Trin. were found in short cut stem lengths. Numerous specimens were split. Such material may be the by-product of arrow-shaft manufacture. Teased out and rolled bark fibers were also used as cord and grass stems occur in knotted bunches suggesting use as a binding material. Grass bedding includes the stems, bases and especially the inflorescences of *Themdea triandra,* *Koeleria cristata,* and *Danthomia* sp. (or *Pentasehistes* sp.). At caves near to the present coastline the use of *Zostera* sea grass as bedding has been noted at Oakhurst, Glentyre, and Matjes River.

Only one fragment of worked leather was found at Melkhoutboom, but better-preserved leather work is reported by Parkington and Poggenpoel (1971) from the Ceramic Wilton deposits of the small montane rock shelter at De Hangen, where a roll of four leather patches stitched together was found screwed up in a wad of grass. One side of the fragment displays careful tailoring in the form of a dart or tuck, suggesting that it may have been part of a garment or possibly an arrow quiver. De Hangen has yielded a similar array of wooden pegs, digging sticks, fire drills, whittled fragments, wood shavings, reed arrow shafts, matting fragments, fiber cords, knitted cords, bound fibers, and bedding grass. A parcel of marine shells wrapped in a larger leaf was also recovered intact.

Chronology

The carbon-14 chronology of the Coastal Wilton may be constructed from the following readings:

Wilton:

Middle levels	I-2565	4860 ± 115 B.P.	(2910 B.C.)
Upper levels	Gak-1540	2270 ± 100 B.P.	(320 B.C.)

These date the Classic and Developed phases, respectively. A reading of 8260 ± 720 B.P. (Gak-1541) for the Early phase may be suspect since the reading is taken from a bone sample derived from human skeletal material "near bedrock" but otherwise poorly documented. The date is probably acceptable but needs to be checked by charcoal dates from the same level.

Nelson Bay:

60-cm level	GrN-5702	2925 ± 35 B.P.	(975 B.C.)
50-cm level	GrN-5715	2540 ± 50 B.P.	(590 B.C.)
40-cm level	GrN-5703	1930 ± 60 B.P.	(A.D. 20)

Vogel (1970) reports that all three dates come from Wilton midden material near the entrance to this deep cave. If the tentatively proposed phase sequence outlined above emerges from the analysis of this material, the dates will probably cover the Classic and Developed phases. The sample dated to A.D. 20 comes from just below the earliest ceramic levels of the midden deposits.

De Hangen:

On bedrock	CAR-I/1	1850 ± 50 B.P.	(A.D. 100)
Hearth in pit	CAR-I/6	485 ± 45 B.P.	(A.D. 1465)
Main ash concentration	CAR-I/3	380 ± 45 B.P.	(A.D. 1570)
Main ash concentration	CAR-I/7	350 ± 50 B.P.	(A.D. 1600)
Hearth in grass layer	CAR-I/4	90 ± 50 B.P.	(A.D. 1860)

Montagu:

Layer I   7100 ± 45   B.P.   (5150 B.C.)

Matjes River:

Bottom of			
Layer C	L-336E	7750 ± 300 B.P.	(5800 B.C.)
Middle of			
Layer C	L-336F	5400 ± 250 B.P.	(3450 B.C.)
	GrN-5888	3555 ± 35 B.P.	(1605 B.C.)

The value of these readings is considerably diminished by the absence of adequate sample records. No measured depths were recorded when the first two charcoal samples were taken (A. C. Hoffman, personal communication), and the last reading comes from a shell sample merely recorded as the "highest level" by Vogel (1970). Without further analysis of the artifacts from Site 5 at this cave, it may be only tentatively assumed that the readings cover the Early and Classic phases.

Although much work needs to be completed in order to confirm the exact correlations between dates and proposed phases, the Coastal Wilton carbon-14 chronology shows a reasonable homogeneity, which confirms its stratigraphic position following the Oakhurst industry.

Diet and Associated Fauna and Flora

Like other aspects of this industry, patterns within the Coastal Wilton diet remain very poorly documented, although detailed analysis of food remains at a few sites is now under way. Although it is known that food sources from the sea and littoral were intensively exploited by the hunter–gatherer groups occupying all the listed coastal caves and shell middens, virtually no numerical data have been presented. As mentioned in the previous chapter, faunal lists are frequently confused with the Oakhurst associations, and dietary changes between the two industries remain almost completely unknown except for a few casual observations by various authors.

Goodwin (1938) notes that the Oakhurst deposits reveal a change in shell content at about the 60-inch level that happens to mark the interface between the Oakhurst Industry and the overlying Early phase of the Wilton. Whereas the midden below 60 inches is dominated by oyster and razor shells with almost no fish remains (2 burned otoliths), the midden above this interface is dominated by "regular piles" of white mussel, which are superceded by black mussels. Fish remains are again present, but scarce. It is the 36 inch level marking the first appearance of the Classic phase, where fish remains begin to increase and become extremely abundant in the Developed and Ceramic phases. Goodwin

(1946) has suggested that the use of tidal semicircular stone fish traps on rocky coastlines may have developed at this time, but these features cannot be accurately dated. Figure 112 maps the recorded distribution of fish traps along the coast. Boulders were piled up across narrow inlets and embayments at low tide so that large fish crossing over the artificial barrier at the subsequent high tide would be trapped for the duration of the following low tide. During this time it is relatively easy to catch larger fish in the shallows, and many traps are still in use today.

It is of great interest to note that the deposits at Glentyre are described by Goodwin in a similar manner—below the 42-inch level (marking the end of the Oakhurst industry accumulation). Razor shells dominate the midden materials, and fish remains are absent. Above this, oyster and razor shells are the dominant forms, and fish are still absent. At the 24-inch level, fish traces appear but remain scarce through the Early phase of the Wilton. At 18–20 inches, the level at which the Classic phase appears, the quantity of fish bones increases rapidly and white and black mussels become the dominant shellfish. In the Ceramic levels, fish remains are even more abundant than mollusks. If similar trends exist at other Wilton sites on the coast, they have not been reported. Nor is there any clear picture of the range of animals hunted near these sites. Although mollusks tend to dominate most midden deposits of this period in both caves and open sites, there is no reason to believe that they formed a dominant role in the diet. However, it is evident at all the deeper sites that game animals occur

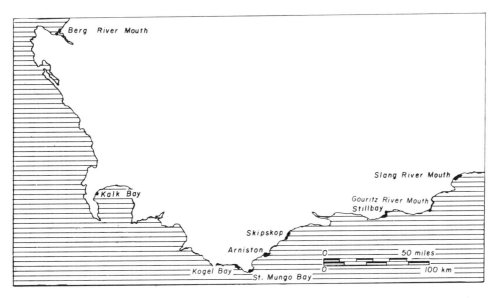

Fig. 112. Distribution of coastal fish traps on the southwestern Cape coast. (After information in Goodwin 1946, and Rudner 1968.)

in greater abundance in the preceding Oakhurst levels. The lack of numerical support for the various authors' observations rather spoils their case, but faunal analyses being presently conducted will probably confirm that game animals are less abundant in Wilton deposits. It has also been observed that there is a more limited range of species present, most of which are small forest-adapted animals. However, much work remains to be done in this field and it is not yet possible to confirm that the advent of the Coastal Wilton technology corresponds exactly with a decrease in hunting activity and an increase in exploitation of shoreline food sources.

The pattern of diet revealed at Coastal Wilton shelters situated inland in the Cape Folded Belt obviously differs from that of the littoral sites. Marine mollusks occur with all the inland samples, but these are restricted in both number and variety, the white mussel *Donax serra* being the most commonly found. At such distances from the coast (usually over 30 miles) it is unlikely that the few shells recovered at each site represent a food source. Deacon (1969a) points out that thick fragments of this shell provides suitable material for the manufacture of shell beads similar to those made from the ubiquitous ostrich eggshell. Whether such occurrences inland reflect coastal–inland movements of single groups or casual trade contacts between two groups—one littoral and one montane—cannot be discussed adequately until evidence of seasonal occupation from both areas has been confirmed. Parkington and Poggenpoel (1971) have demonstrated that the tooth-eruption pattern of hyrax jaws at De Hangen indicate that most hyrax were killed during the summer months, but evidence of winter abandonment of montane sites has not been detected yet. Similarly, evidence for winter occupation of coastal sites is not forthcoming. Even if seasonal coastal–montane transhumance is to be expected on theoretical grounds as several authors have claimed, no entirely convincing evidence of this has been presented.

The only quantitative faunal analysis for a montane site is that of De Hangen (Table 49). Small animals dominate the list with the exception of an eland and an equid. The extremely interesting presence of domestic stock in this assemblage may reflect raids on either European or Hottentot groups in adjacent areas. Hyrax and tortoise dominate the list. Abundant plant remains have also been recovered from the montane sites, many of which are parts of numerous edible species (Fig. 113), Deacon's (1969b) list from Melkhoutboom is given in Table 50.

The edibility of *Jatrophon capensis* and *Hyposus* sp. remains uncertain. *Pappea capensis* is an oil source and *Oxalis* sp. is also medicinal. Although the outer flesh of *Encephalartos* sp. is edible, the kernel is poisonous. Another rather abundant poisonous plant recovered from Melkhoutboom is *Boophone disticha* Herb, represented by inner and outer bulbar leaves.

Keller (1969) also reports the presence of probably poisonous plant remains from Layer I of Montagu. Corm scales of *Morea* sp. or *Homeria* sp. were probably pounded in a small, stone-based pit in the cave's deposit surface. At De Hangen, poisonous plant remains include the toxic seeds of *Toxicodendron capense*

TABLE 49 Fauna from De Hangen

Genus and species	Description	Minimum no. of individuals
Papio ursinus	Chacma baboon	1
Procavia capensis	Hyrax	64
Lepus sp. or *Pronolagus* sp.	Hare	6
Raphicerus sp.	Steenbok–grysbok	6
Oreotragus oreotragus	Klipspringer	3
Sylvicapra grimmia	Duiker	1
Antidorcas marsupialis	Springbok	1
Taurotragus oryx	Eland	1
Bos taurus	Domestic cattle	1
?*Ovis* sp. or *Capra* sp.	Domestic sheep–goat	1
Equus sp.	An equid	1
Herpestes pulverulentus	Mongoose	8
Genetta tigrina	Genet	2
Mellivora capensis	Honey badger	1
?*Canis mesomelas*	Black-backed jackal	1
Hystrix africae-australis	Porcupine	1
?*Tatera* sp.	Gerbil	Several
?*Graphiurus* sp.	Doormouse	Several
Testudo (*Chersine*) *angulata* (+ spp. ?)	Tortoise	313
?	Lizard	Present
?	Snake	Present
?	Frog	Present
?Numididae–Phasianidae	Guinea fowl–francolin	1
?	Freshwater fish	Present
Marine mollusk: *Haliotis, Patella, Turbo, Mytilus, Cypraea, Bullia, Nassa, Donax*		Present

TABLE 50 Plant Remains from Melkhoutboom [a]

Genus and species	Parts surviving	Relative abundance
Bulline sp. (?*B. alooides*)	Rootstock	X
Cyperus usitatus Burch.	Basal leaf sheaths and corms	X
Oxalis sp. (?*O. umbricata*)	Basal leaf sheaths	X X X X
Hyposus sp. (?*H. argentea*)	Contractile roots, rootstock, basal leaf sheaths	X X X X
Morea sp. (?*M. edulus* or *M. polystachya*)	Corm scales	X X X X
Babiana sp.	Corm scales	X
Watsonia sp. (?*W. angusta*)	Corm, corm scales, stems, and leaves	X X X X
Freezia sp. (?*F. corymbosa*)	Corms, corm scales	X X X X
?*Amarantus hybrides*	Single leaf, stem	X
Encephalartos sp.	Kernel and leaves	X
Schotia afra (L.) Shunb.	Pods and seeds	X X X
Harpephyllum caffrum Bernh.	Pip	X X
Pappea capensis (Spring)	Fruit in localized area	X X
Podocarpus falcatus (Thumb.)	Fruit (invariably broken open)	X X X
Cassine sp. (?*C. aethiopicus*)	Fruit	?
Jatrophon capensis Sond.	Fruit coats	X X

[a] From Deacon (1969b).

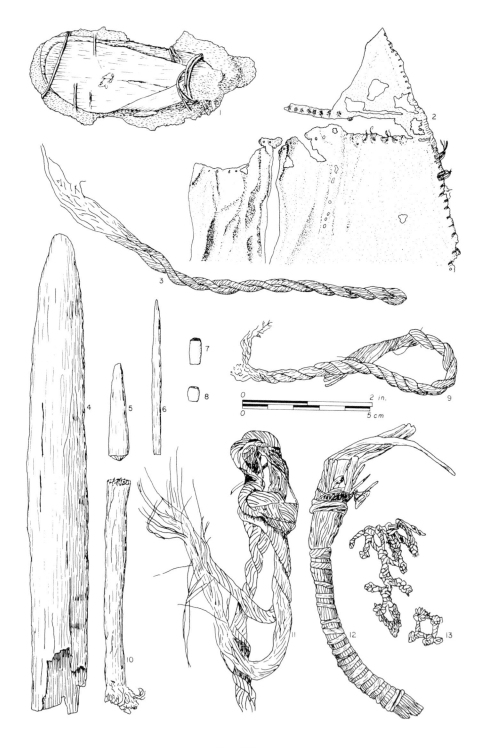

Fig. 113

TABLE 51   **Plant remains from De Hangen**

Genus and species [a,b]	Common name	Parts surviving	Edible parts	De Hangen: relative abundance
Restio setiger	Rushes	Male inflorescences	Seed	✕
Willdenovia striata	Rushes	Seeds and seedcases	Seed	✕
Cannamois sp.	Rushes	Seeds	Seed	✕
Ficinia sp.	Rushes	Inflorescences	Seed	✕
Leucodendron sp.	Bush	Seeds and seedcases	Seed	✕✕✕
Dioscorea elephantipes	Hotnotsbrood	Tuber casing	Tuber flesh	✕✕✕
Euclea tomentosa	Baboon cherries	Seeds and leaves	Fruit	✕✕
Euclea linearis	Bush	Seeds and leaves	Fruit	✕✕✕
Olea africana	Wild olive	Seeds	Fruit	✕✕✕
Rhus sp.	Taaibos	Seeds	Fruit	✕✕✕
Secale cereale	Domestic rye	Stems and ears	Seeds	✕✕✕
Pelargonium spp.	Red bulb	Tuber casings	Tuber flesh	✕✕
Brabeium steliatifolium	Wild almond	Fruit casings	Nuts	✕✕
Carpobratus edulis	Sour fig	Dried stems	Fruit	✕
*Moraea sp.	Hottentot's onion	Corms and sheaths	Corms	✕✕✕
Homeria sp.	Uyntjies	Corms and sheaths	Corms	✕✕✕
*Babiana sp.	Uyntjies	Corms, sheaths, and seeds	Corms	✕✕✕
*Watsonia sp.	Hotnotsbrood	Corms and sheaths	Corms	✕✕✕

[a] From Parkington and Poggenpoel (1971).
[b] Asterisk indicates species present at Melkhoutboom.

(*Hyaenanche globosa*) and abundant seeds of *Ricinus communis,* the castor oil plant, which is not indigenous and must reflect the early European contact in the Southwestern Cape. The edible plant remains from De Hangen include only three forms found at Melkhoutboom, suggesting a very detailed knowledge of local plant life. Table 51 gives Parkington and Poggenpoel's (1971) report.

The presence of domestic rye in this list further demonstrates some form of contact with early European settlers in this region. It is significant that most edible plants in this montane area are scarce during the winter months but abundant in late spring and summer.

Human Remains

Human skeletal material associated with the Coastal Wilton is relatively abundant. J. Rudner (1968) has again provided a valuable survey of burials associated with the Ceramic phase, but most of these have been destroyed by vandals,

Fig. 113. Artifacts of organic materials from Coastal Wilton sites: (1) mussel shell wrapped in leaf and bound with sinew; (2) fragment of stitched hide; (3, 9, 11, 12) grass twine fragments; (4) digging stich tip fragment; (5) wooden point, possibly a fire-drill tip; (6) wooden arrowhead; (7, 8) drilled seed beads; (10) battered wooden wedge; (13) fragments of twine netting. The specimens are from De Hangen and Melkhoutboom.

with a few important exceptions. Evidently, on-site inhumation was frequently practiced at this time. Almost all the available skeletal materials suffer from inadequate documentation of exact provenance and grave association. Only at Oakhurst and Glentyre are the notes that accompany the material adequate enough to indicate the relative positions of individual burials within the Wilton accumulation.

In Oakhurst, two skeletons were buried from the Early phase into the underlying Oakhurst industry deposits, and a number of graves occur within the Early phase itself. Some of these may be intrusive from later phases. In all, a total of 6 graves may tentatively be associated with the Early phase, and these yielded the remains of at least 13 different indivuduals, although many of them are so fragmentary that they are of little value. Only 3 adult skulls were sufficiently intact to provide measurements. The repeated disturbance of later graves, as well as the crushing effect of gravestones, has destroyed or disturbed much of the material. In the overlying Classic Wilton levels, there are the graves containing 5 individuals, but some of these may be intrusive from the Developed or Ceramic horizons. One grave occurs in the Developed levels, again, possibly intrusive from above. Details of the graves and their contents are given in Table 52.

Given the complexity of so many interlocking grave fills no definite associations between phases and burials can be reached. The skeletons, nevertheless, represent the population responsible for the Wilton industry as a whole, regardless of phase.

At Glentyre the published documentation is of less use. Grave 4 at a 35-inch depth is situated in the Early phase, but it is not known whether this was intrusive. A pile of gravestones and disturbance by burrowing animals has virtually destroyed the skeleton.

For Matjes River Layer C, the field notes are so inadequate as to leave serious doubts about the burials' provenance. Meiring (1937) accepted that the "Wilton" skulls which he analyzed were all from Layer C, but he provides no documented proof of their positions.

Although the grave goods with each burial were recovered and labeled, individually, it is unfortunate that Louw (1960) published none of these data. Other sites in which the excavators have reported the discovery of such burials include Wilton, Melkhoutboom, Nelson's Bay, and Skildergat. None of the other finds was either reported or documented.

Craniometric data on the Coastal Wilton population are presently restricted to five skulls from Oakhurst (four male, one female) and eight skulls from Matjes River Layer C (not sexed).

The diagrams in Fig. 114 show that two Wilton skulls from Oakhurst are shorter than the others, also that the Matjes River sample contains mainly larger-headed specimens. In terms of crude shape distribution, the two samples overlap completely, and there is every reason to presume that both samples are drawn from the same population. When the data from both samples combined

TABLE 52

Graves and Contents Associated with Wilton Phases at Oakhurst Shelter

Phase	Grave no.	Depth, etc.	Skeletal contents	Other contents
Early	III	Sealed beneath white ash at 48 inches	1 adult (No. 3)	Nil
	VI	Grave complex intruded into the top of Phase I at 60–67 inches	2 adults (Nos. 6, 6a) 6 other (fragmentary)	Abundant grave Goods (see Goodwin)
	VIII	58 inches	1 adult and other fragments	Nacre pendant, tortoise shell
	X	60 inches	1 adult (crushed)	Several gravestones, ostrich egg, bored stone, ostrich eggshell beads
Early?	XI	Buried into Phase I at 69 inches	1 adult (not analyzed)	Slate palette
	XII	61 inches	1 youth	4 pierced shells, 3 nacre pendants and beads, all at the neck
Classic VII or later?		50-inch depth, soft infilling cut into underlying shell midden	1 child (No. 7) (not analyzed)	4 gravestones (1 grindstone), shell and stone crescents, 3 ostrich eggs (bored), ocher on skull, *Donax* shells along spine, girdle of ostrich eggshell beads
	IX	43-inch depth, soft infilling cut into shell midden	3 children (Nos. 9, 9A, and 9B)	Quartz crystals on left orbit, 1 specimen with ocher on cranium; 1 specimen on sea-grass bed, 2 shell pendants at neck
Developed?	XVII	57-inch depth buried into midden	(not analyzed)	Water-tortoise carapace on left arm
	I	24 inches	1 adult male (No. 1)	Nil

317

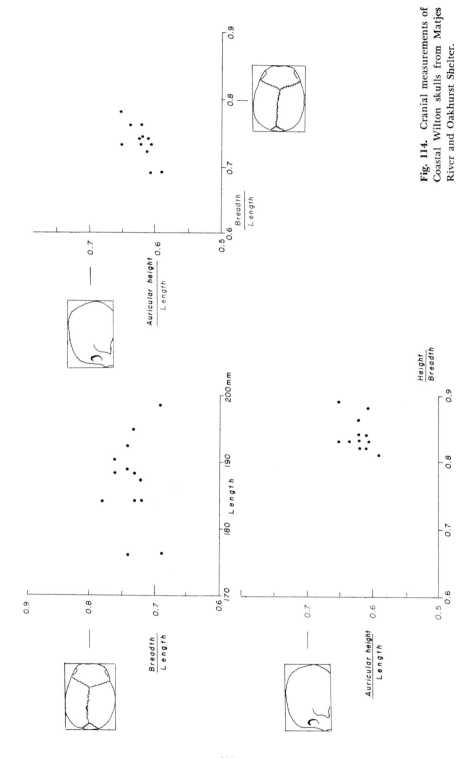

Fig. 114. Cranial measurements of Coastal Wilton skulls from Matjes River and Oakhurst Shelter.

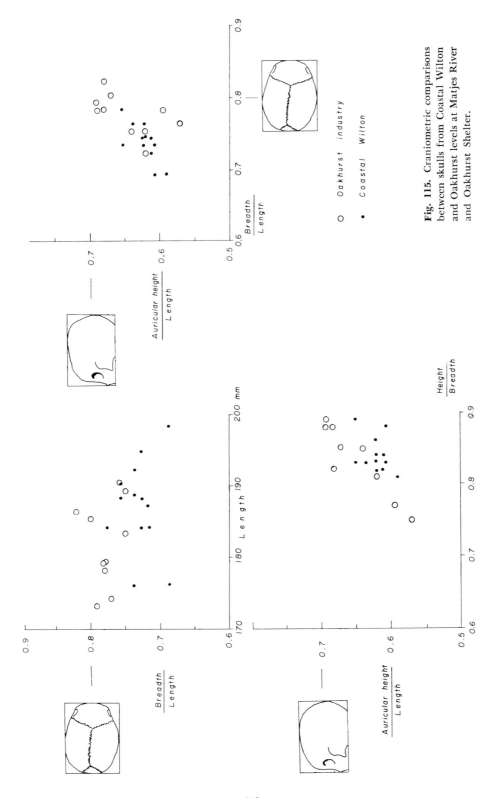

Fig. 115. Craniometric comparisons between skulls from Coastal Wilton and Oakhurst levels at Matjes River and Oakhurst Shelter.

○ *Oakhurst industry*

● *Coastal Wilton*

319

are compared with the same set of data for the preceding Oakhurst population, as shown in Fig. 115, a number of interesting points emerge:

1. Most Wilton skulls are narrower than Oakhurst skulls and display a wider range of variation in length.
2. The crude shape indices suggest an overlap between the Wilton sample and the Oakhurst sample *from Oakhurst Shelter only.*

The skulls associated with the Oakhurst industry of Matjes River Layer D clearly differ from those of the combined Wilton sample in that more specimens have higher and broader cranial vaults. It is most disappointing that further metrical comparisons are not possible at present for want of sufficient standardized information, particularly on the postcranial material. If the few indices plotted here show such marked changes at Matjes River, it is likely that other differences will emerge with further analysis of the abundant material. The possibility that the advent of the Coastal Wilton and the waning of the Oakhurst industry is linked partly to human population movement at this time should be seriously considered. Further osteometric work on these samples should prove rewarding.

Any attempt to explain the emergence, development or survival of the Coastal Wilton at this stage will have to be revised in the near future in the light of the research campaign currently being carried out in this area by several archaeologists and related specialists. The factors underlying the emergence of a microlithic stone technology early in the sixth millenium B.C. are obviously complex and at present only dimly perceived. Both environmental and population changes must be considered.

The Environment

It has been noted already in the preceding chapter that most of the larger game animals hunted by the makers of the Oakhurst industry could only have existed on the broad coastal plain which then separated the large shelters from the contemporary shoreline. Since a worldwide rise in sea level took place between the ninth and eighth millenia B.C. as a result of the postglacial retreat in the northern (and possibly southern) hemisphere, it is reasonable to assume that the local coastal plains were submerged at this time. By 8000–7000 B.C. the shelters were located close to the sea; the surrounding terrain would have been hilly with densely forested ravines, and the game herds previously supported by the coastal plain would have disappeared from the scene. Any hunters exploiting the terrain around these large shelters would be obliged to adapt radically new strategies of exploitation, or move from the area. It is of great importance to note that these changes took place more than a millenium *before* the appearance of the Early Wilton microlithic technology. The gradual adoption of microlithic tools after about 5500 B.C. is evidently not a reflection of adjustments to this new environmental pattern. Any such adjustments in exploitation patterns took place during the later stages of the Oakhurst industry. What the Early Wilton phase *may* partly reflect is an increased efficiency in exploitation through time, but dietary details for this and the immediately preceding final Oakhurst levels are sadly inadequate so that no details of shifts in food remains are yet known for this crucial period.

Another aspect of the trend toward a microlithic technology is the concomitant shift in the use of rock types in this region—yet another field of investigation for which we lack adequate numerical data. Descriptive accounts at most sites where both Oakhurst and Wilton samples have been recovered reveal that the microlithic elements are made almost invariably of siliceous rocks such as silcrete or chalcedony whereas larger tools are of coarse-grained rocks. Because silcretes and the like are less abundant and occur in small nodules or pebbles, evidently greater effort was expended in finding such materials. Also, there is no reason to suppose that the flooding of the coastal plain made it any easier to find these rocks, most of which are probably derived from the tertiary sediments now forming the offshore seabed. If the new Wilton technology reflects an aspect of increased efficiency in the hunting-and-gathering system of this area, this is not readily apparent from the rock-type evidence, which suggests an increased effort to obtain suitable raw materials for microliths.

If no environmental changes during the sixth millenium B.C. have been detected in these field data, the possibility of human population movements during this period remains to be considered. The extremely limited craniometric evidence from Matjes River hints at physical differences between the Wilton and preceding Oakhurst skeletal samples, each of which display notable homogeneity. No such homogeneity exists in the Oakhurst and Wilton skeletal material from Oakhurst Shelter, nor do they display the craniometric differences observed in the Matjes River samples. Although it remains possible that this conflicting evidence may reflect differences in measuring techniques or simply variable skill in the reconstruction of damaged or distorted skulls, there remains the possibility that the data from the two caves represent a real difference. Without an exhaustive biometric survey of the material no firm conclusion may be drawn. At present the evidence from Oakhurst suggests a static population undergoing technical change, whereas the Matjes River data suggests a change in physical type at the time that the Wilton technology begins to replace the Oakhurst. Reconstruction of events around such limited data is a hazardous procedure, but further work may reveal that the Oakhurst population acquired the microlithic technology though localized borrowings from incoming groups already equipped with this cultural tradition.

The subsequent development of the Coastal Wilton after the Early phase poses other intriguing problems. Between about 3000 and 2000 B.C. the lithic technology becomes almost entirely microlithic in character, but the reasons underlying this trend are not really understood. Fagan (1960) suggests that this reflects an increasing technical adaptation to intensive fishing practices as suggested by the faunal evidence from Oakhurst and Glentyre. The presence of a similar trend at montane shelter sites up to 40 miles from the coast does little to support this hypothesis. Evidence of contemporary population shifts or changes in exploitation patterns has not been gathered and no alternative explanations can be offered at present. Equally mysterious is the reappearance of larger flakes, pebble choppers, and sidescrapers in the Developed Wilton on the coast. The possible interplay of two contemporary lithic traditions (microlithic and macro-lithic) will be discussed more fully in Chapter 10.

THE INTERIOR WILTON

This provisional term if applied to Wilton-related occurrences found in various parts of the South African interior (including Lesotho and Swaziland), Botswana, and the interior of South-West Africa. So sparse is the field evidence for this vast area that no regional classification or terminology can be presented. Several different environments, varying from arid desert through semiarid, thorn-veld, bushveld, and savannah to riverine woodland or alpine pasture are represented. Obviously, different sets of hunter–gatherer strategies for exploiting the food sources to these regions may be predicted. It is therefore logical to expect the area to yield a number of different industries. Figure 116 maps all the published reports of Wilton-related stone tool samples, with the excavated sites designated by name. This record has accumulated gradually over the last fifty years in so haphazard a manner that virtually nothing useful can be gleaned from it other than the overall distribution of finds. Many of the major sources from which the map is compiled merely state that "Wilton" artifacts occur at a certain number of places, without enumerating the tool kit or any other related facts. Some excavation reports are equally vague.

Only in the area of the Orange River scheme are there sufficient data to reveal the detailed development of a Wilton-related industry. It replaces the Lockshoek industry in the middle reaches of the Orange River valley and undergoes a series of typological changes through time. Rock-shelter sites yielding evidence of its development are mapped in Fig. 117. The analyses of these excavations (Sampson 1967a, b, c, 1969a, 1970; Sampson and Sampson 1967) demonstrate a complex development that can be conveniently subdivided into four phases similar to the system tentatively applied to the Coastal Wilton. The excavated samples representing the four phases are enumerated in Table 53. Of the seven sites listed above, Zeekoegat 13 is the only open site. This is also the only locality where the Early Wilton phase has been found in its stratigraphic position over-lying a sample of the Lockshoek industry.

Typology

The complete range of tool types recognized in this industry is illustrated in Fig. 118. Percentage values for each tool type in every phase of all the sites have been calculated. A summary of these data is given in the composite graphs in

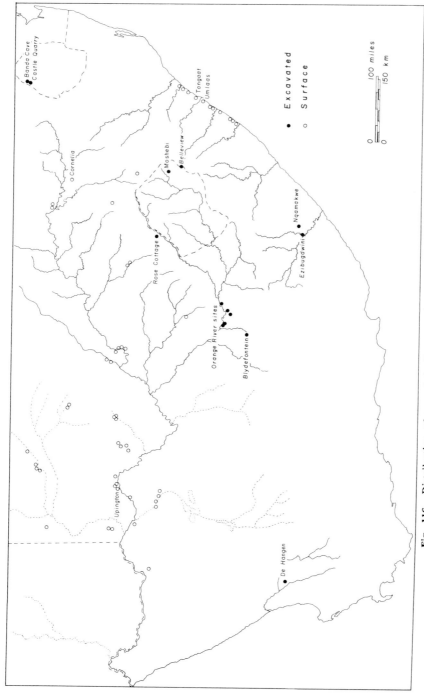

Fig. 116. Distribution of reported sites tentatively ascribed to the Interior Wilton.

Excavated ●
Surface ○

Banda Cave
Castle Quarry
Cornelia
Moshebi
Belleview
Tongaat
Umlaas
Nqamakwe
Ezibugdwini
Rose Cottage
Orange River sites
Blydefontein
Upington
De Hangen

100 miles
150 km

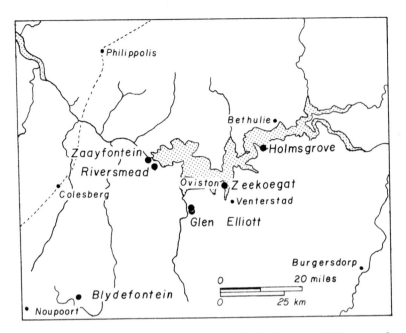

Fig. 117. Localities of excavated rock shelters containing Interior Wilton samples in the Orange River scheme area.

Fig. 119, in which the maximum–minimum percentage range for each tool type in all four phases is given.

The *Early phase* contains large scrapers, core hammers, fabricators, and utilized flake elements, all made of lydianite and all typical of the Lockshoek industry. However, the Early phase also contains low percentages of small convex scrapers, *outils écaillés* and various backed microliths made from small bladelets struck from agate, chalcedony, or jasper pebbles. Pebbles of these materials can be obtained only from the gravels of the Orange River, where they are abundant but of variable quality. They are also very small, seldom exceeding 5 mm in diameter. Analysis of these Early phase samples has shown that the proportion of microlithic tools and crystalline rock to lydianite Lockshoek-type scrapers is partly determined by the distance of the site from the river bank and its gravel source.

In the *Classic phase* the Lockshoek elements dwindle and eventually disappear. The lithic assemblage is now fully microlithic, using between 90 and 40% crystalline pebbles, the proportion again determined by distance from the river gravels. At Blydefontein, some 45 miles from the gravel source, some quartz was used, but lydianite dominated the Classic phase sample. Some tools, especially the small convex scrapers, are bigger since they are made on larger flakes. A very similar trend has already been described for the Coastal Wilton phase.

TABLE 53

Stratigrahic Correlation of Interior Wilton Sites [a]

Phase	Previous terms (Sampson 1970, etc.)	Zeekoegat 13	Zaay-fontein	Rivers-mead	Blyde-fontein	Glen Elliott Shelter	Glen Elliott Crevice	Holms-grove
Ceramic	Later Stone Age Phase 5	—	V–VI	I–II	I–II	IV–VI	II	III–VI
Developed	Later Stone Age Phase 4	—	—	III–IV	III–IV	VII	—	—
	Phase 3–4 transitional	—	—	V	V	—	—	V
Classic	Later Stone Age Phase 3	—	VII–IX	VI–IX	VI–VII	VIII	—	—
Early	Later Stone Age Phase 2	Upper level	X–XIV	—	—	—	—	—

[a] Roman numerals represent excavated spits or levels.

325

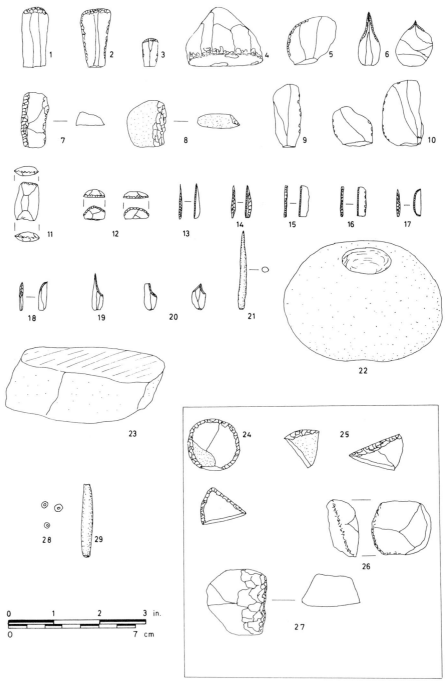

Fig. 118. Tool types of the Interior Wilton of the Orange River valley. Numbers 24–27 occur in the earlier phase only.

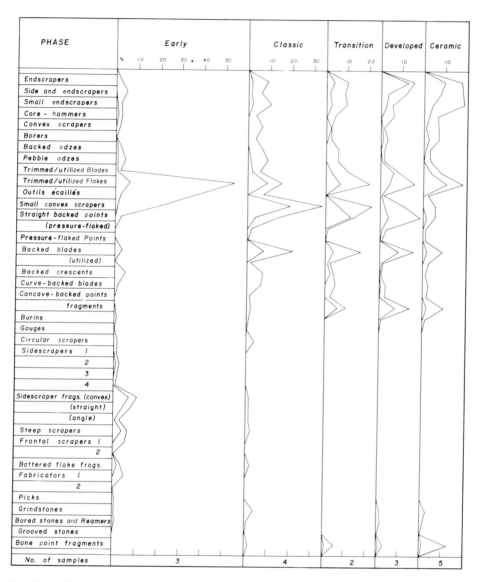

Fig. 119. Minimum–maximum range of percentages for each tool type of the various phases of the Interior Wilton of the Orange River valley.

However, unlike the Coastal Wilton, the *Developed phase* in the middle Orange River valley displays an entirely new development. The use of lydianite takes preference over crystalline raw materials once more, but the latter are not totally abandoned. As lydianite occurs in large blocks, both the cores and flakes are generally larger than those in the preceding phase. One result of this trend is that small convex scrapers become gradually larger and begin to take on the appearance of small endscrapers. These become steadily bigger and more elongated with time. Also, the blades used as blanks from which backed microliths are manufactured become longer so that the blade butt is frequently snapped off and discarded during the backing process. Thus, concave-backed fragments (and some true microburins) increase in number. Among the various backed forms, points and bladelets increase at the expense of single crescentic forms, but no other changes are noted. It thus emerges that Developed phases of the Coastal Wilton and the interior, particularly the middle Orange River, differ considerably in typological content, showing a distinct stylistic divergence.

In the *Ceramic phase* small pressure flaked leaf point arrowheads become a rare but consistent feature of the tool kit, and small potsherds occur for the first time. Almost all these are too small to permit reliable reconstruction of the pottery form, but they make a perfect match with two isolated bowls found near the Riet River less than 100 miles to the north (Fig. 120). These are wide bowls with curved undecorated sides and straight rims. The walls are extremely thin and evenly fired to form a gray-buff matte surface both inside and out. Firing temperature was high and well controlled. The clay body of the bowl is tempered with fine river sand and very little grass. There can be little doubt that this relatively sophisticated ware does *not* represent the earliest potmaking efforts of the local Wilton hunter–gatherers. The only possible explanation for its presence here is that either whole pots or sherds were acquired from groups in adjacent territory who had already developed potmaking skills. Whether such contemporary neighbors were Stone Age or Iron Age peoples remains to be determined, but the latter seems more likely, especially in view of the small iron arrowhead stem and copper fragment found in the Ceramic phase at Zaayfontein Shelter.

Nonlithic artifacts include only rare fragments of cylindrical bone arrow points, bone awls, beads of ostrich eggshell or bone, and pierced shell pendants made of freshwater mollusk. The extreme paucity of bone work is one of the significant differences between this industry and the Coastal Wilton. Other Coastal Wilton features that are missing are double crescents, small double endscrapers, small circular scrapers, small sidescrapers, and shell crescents.

Unfortunately, the detection of similar stylistic developments elsewhere in the interior, is largely frustrated by the near-total absence of comparable published data. Beaumont (1963) recognized three phases within the Wilton deposits at Rose Cottage Cave, of which the third and latest phase contains pottery and may equate with the Ceramic phase on the middle Orange River. The identity of the preceding two phases at Rose Cottage remains obscure for want of any typological information. Only the ratio of "scrapers" to "quadrilaterals" is reported (Schoonraad and Beaumont 1968) and is obviously of little use. Similar reports of a Wilton-associated group of sites from Swaziland hint at stylistic developments, but nothing else is known of these other than a series of carbon-14 dates (Vogel 1970) from Banda Cave and Castle Quarry.

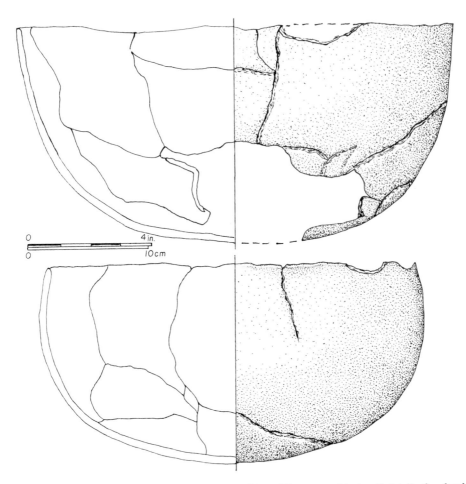

Fig. 120. Two ceramic bowls found on the Riet River. These resemble in all details the sherds recovered with the Ceramic phase of the Interior Wilton of the Orange River valley.

Further evidence of stylistic change in the Wilton from Moshebi's Shelter, Lesotho is reported by Carter (1969). Spits 4–6 of the excavation are without pottery, but above Spit 4 the first sherds appear, as do several pressure-flaked tanged arrowheads. Probably a Classic–Developed–Ceramic sequence exists here also, with a localized development of the tanged arrowhead form. The known distribution of this distinctive type has been summarized by Humphreys (1969b) from records of stray finds in Lesotho, the Orange Free State, and the northeastern Cape Province.

Nearer to the coast, but still within the general distribution of the Interior Wilton, Laidler (1933, 1936) has reported two early excavations at Ezibugdwini cave and Nqamakwe Shelter C in the Transkei. His description of the content of each excavated layer suggests that a Classic–Developed sequence resembling that of the Orange River scheme group of sites was uncovered here. Further excavations will be needed to confirm this correlation.

To the west, only the Upington surface site (I. Rudner 1953) can be ascribed to the Ceramic phase with any certainty, as can several other collections from the northern Cape Province and South-West Africa (Rudner and Rudner 1959; Rudner and Grattan-Bellew 1964). However, this area still entirely lacks adequate excavated data. Similar inadequacies accompany the Botswana data (F. Malan 1950). In the Brandberg area of South-West Africa recent excavations by Sandelowsky have yielded Wilton-related material, and MacCalman (1965) reports the presence of a Late Wilton associated site with copper beads.

At the present time Wilton occurrences from the Orange Free State and Transvaal are surprisingly few, although surface collections such as Riverton and Cornelia demonstrate its presence in the Vaal valley. Only at North Brabant shelter in the Waterberg district of the northeastern Transvaal has a complete sample been excavated. Schoonraad and Beaumont (1968) suggest that the potsherds and glass beads with this sample are properly associated and there is every reason to believe that the shelter contains a local expression of the Ceramic phase. Metal fragments and porcelain beads in the same deposit hint strongly at a relatively late Iron Age contact situation in this area.

From the observations listed above it is now apparent that much work remains to be done on the Interior Wilton. Intensive excavation campaigns in restricted areas of Lesotho, Botswana, South-West Africa, and Swaziland are in progress at present and will no doubt help to clarify the various regional patterns which must exist within this vast complex.

Diet and Associated Fauna

Understandably, few insights into dietary patterns or seasonal strategies are available yet from this material. An uneven and incomplete analysis of associated fauna from the Orange River scheme shelters reveals that numerous small mammals are represented, including springbok, steenbok, porcupine, and hyrax. Curiously, almost no large mammals are present, but the bulk of the bone remains include an astonishing range of small animals including ten different rodents, frogs, fish, crab, turtle, freshwater mollusks, tortoise, leguaan, snakes, lizards, gecko, and birds. Ostrich eggshell is also consistently present. It is almost certain that this material is only a partial reflection of the Interior Wilton diet in the valley, but it is quite apparent that maximum use was made of all local food sources, however small in size. In contrast, the North Brabant fauna includes buffalo, impala, duiker, zebra, leopard, warthog, and Cape hunting dog, as well as some smaller animals (hyrax, porcupine, lizards, tortoise, and birds).

Chronology

The chronology of Interior Wilton sites overlaps entirely with that of the Coastal Wilton, but fails to survive into the historic period. Several radiocarbon dates are available.

Riversmead:

Level IX (Early)	GX-0724	2530 ± 105 B.P. (580 B.C.)
Level V (Developed)	GX-0665	2285 ± 115 B.P. (335 B.C.)
Level XX (Ceramic)	GX-0723	2645 ± 95 B.P. (695 B.C.)

The Level II reading is too old to represent the Ceramic phase and may be rejected as contaminated with older carbon.

Zaayfontein:

Level X (Early–Classic)	SR-160	3270 ± 115 B.P. (1320 B.C.)
Level X (Early–Classic)		(1985 B.C.)
Level VII (Ceramic ?)	GX-0666	730 ± 75 B.P. (A.D. 1220)
Level VI (Ceramic ?)		(A.D. 1520)

Rose Cottage:

36–46 cm	GrN-5299	6850 ± 45 B.P. (4900 B.C.)
20–25 cm	GrN-5298	1100 ± 30 B.P. (A.D. 850)
(Ceramic)		

Blydefontein:

Level VIII (Classic)	SR-152	3650 ± 120 B.P. (1690 B.C.)
Level VI (Classic)	SR-142	3090 ± 100 B.P. (1140 B.C.)
Level III (Developed)	SR-132	1980 ± 120 B.P. (30 B.C.)

Banda Cave:

Lower level	Y-1714	5890 ± 80 B.P. (3940 B.C.)

Castle Quarry:

170 cm	Y-1829	3970 ± 120 B.P. (2020 B.C.)
	GrN-5022	2860 ± 35 B.P. (910 B.C.)

Further dates from Lesotho (P. Carter, personal communication) include 230 B.C. from Moshebi's Shelter; a neighboring shelter named Bellview has yielded readings of 1330 B.C. and A.D. 360.

Few positive conclusions may be drawn from this rather fragmentary record. It is at least clear now that the South African interior was inhabited by numerous hunter–gatherer groups whose lithic technology underwent stylistic changes that are partly parallel to those of the Coastal Wilton period. Faunal evidence, such as it is from this period, suggests a comparable efficiency in the exploitation of all available food resources. Whereas marine or littoral foods were used at the coast, stream and riverine fauna were evidently collected in the interior. Regular movements by hunter–gatherer bands may be inferred for the semiarid regions, but concrete evidence for such patterns has not been detected yet. Exactly what physical relationships, if any, existed between the Coastal and Interior Wilton populations remains a subject for speculation only. Evidently inhumation within the domestic litter of a settlement was not commonly practiced by Interior Wilton groups, and for this reason nothing is known of the physical appearance of these people. Presumably burial took place in isolated graves without clear surface indications, and these have remained undetected up to the present.

THE MATOPAN INDUSTRY

Cooke *et al.* (1966) proposed that this term be adopted to describe all stone artifact assemblages from the southern and southwestern region of Rhodesia, which had previously been called "Southern Rhodesian Wilton." Nearly 200 localities have been discovered, but only 10 are excavated sites, the remainder comprising surface scatters that have not been systematically sampled. There are, in addition, a few excavated sites which have not been reported.

Typology

Although a systematic analysis of all the reliable collections from this area was begun a few years ago, this work is not complete and no details have been released. The only published numerical analyses are those from Khami (C. K. Cooke 1957b), Amadzimba (Radcliffe-Robinson and Cooke 1950; Cooke and Robinson, 1954), Hillside (Simons 1968), Calders Cave (Cooke *et al.* 1966), and Dombazanga (Robinson 1964), and different type lists have been employed in each report so that direct numerical comparisons between sites are quite impossible. However, sufficient published data exist to allow certain general observations about the distinctive characters of the Matopan (Figs. 121, 122, 123). First, a Preceramic and Ceramic phase can be recognized at several sites, but virtually no important tool changes have been observed during the industry's development. This means that the overall appearance of the Preceramic and Ceramic phases are virtually the same: essentially microlithic assemblages. No equivalent of the "Developed" phase has been detected in this area. C. K. Cooke (1957b) has argued for a three-phase development of the Matopan at Khami, based on his excavation and analysis of the upper granitic deposits of this stratified open site. Three superimposed assemblages were recognized:

Khami Waterworks	Original terminology	New designation	Tool totals
Layer 3	Upper Southern Rhodesian Wilton	Matopan (Ceramic)	86
Layer 4	Middle Southern Rhodesian Wilton	Matopan (Preceramic)	79
Layer 5	Lower Southern Rhodesian Wilton	Matopan ?	31

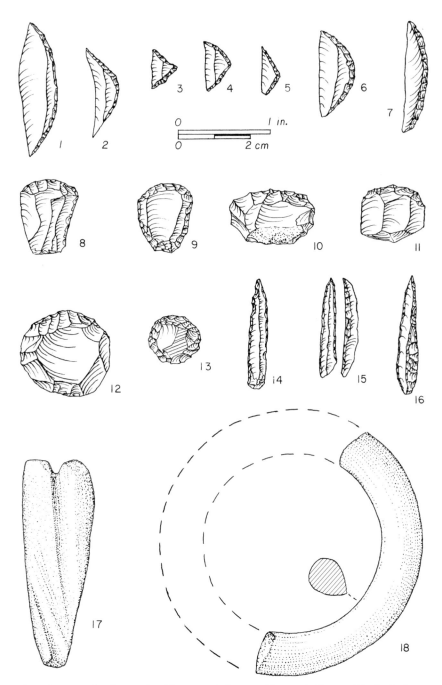

Fig. 121. Stone tools from the Matopan industry, Nswatugi Cave: (1) backed crescent; (2) eared backed crescent; (3–5) backed triangular gometrics; (6, 7) backed crescent; (8, 9) small endscrapers; (10, 11) small convex scrapers; (12, 13) circular scrapers; (14–16) straight-backed points; (17) grooved stone; (18) ground stone ring fragment.

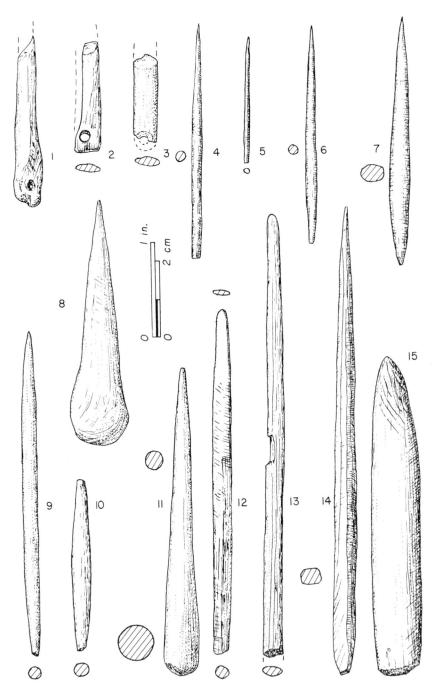

Fig. 122. Bone work from the Matopan industry: (1–3, 8–14) Amadzimba caves; (4–7) Pomongwe; (15) Nswatugi.

334

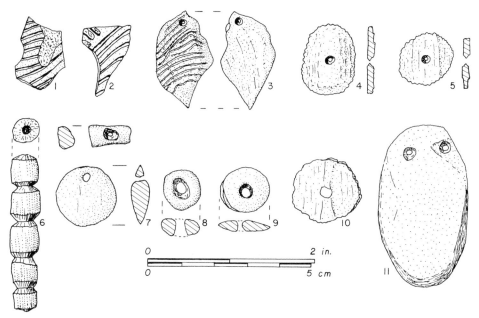

Fig. 123. Ornaments from the Matopan industry: (1–3) engraved fruit-husk fragments; (4–5, 10) drilled tortoise carapace; (6–9) drilled bone and ivory; (11) ground and double-drilled shale pendant. Specimens (1–5) are from Pomongwe and (6–11) are from Amadzimba.

Unfortunately, the tool samples are too small to allow any typological distinctions to be made between each assemblage, and there is certainly no clear evidence for separating Layer 5 from Layer 4. Similarly, at Hillside Shelter there are no apparent typological differences between Preceramic and Ceramic phases although the contents of no less than six separate levels have been analyzed with admirable attention to detail. Tool types for Hillside Shelter are given in Table 54.

Far more distinctive is the pottery from the Ceramic phase of the Matopan, which displays very close affinities with early Iron Age wares found in the same region. There can be little doubt that the presence of such sherds in the upper levels of several Matopan deposits represents the first contact with incoming Iron Age groups who were later to absorb the aboriginal Stone Age hunters into their own (radically different) culture. Iron Age occupation middens actually overlie Ceramic-phase Matopan deposits at several sites. demonstrating a complete change in the archaeological record. The associated pottery has been variously named Bambata ware, Gokomere ware or (now preferred) Leopard's Kopje ware. Sherds show a characteristic stamp decoration, serrated rims, or crosshatched and parallel grooves in the wet clay.

TABLE 54

Hillside Shelter Tool Types

Tool types	0–2 in.	2–4 in.	4–8 in.	8–12 in.	12–16 in.	16 in.–bedrock
			Depth			
Endscrapers	—	1	5	7	3	—
Fabricators	—	—	1	5	1	—
Sidescrapers	—	1	3	2	1	3
Adze blades	—	—	—	2	—	—
Utilized blades	—	—	—	4	—	—
Blade scrapers	—	—	—	3	—	—
Thumbnail scrapers	—	—	9	25	21	3
Backed crescents	1	1	17	14	17	2
Double-backed crescents	—	—	2	4	3	—
Backed blades	—	—	—	1	—	—

Chronology

The paucity of associated fauna and the total absence of human skeletal remains with the Matopan is still a severe handicap, but a few carbon-14 dates have been processed:

Pomongwe:

    Layer 2 (burned marula nut)   SR-14   7610 ± 110 B.P. (5660 B.C.)

Amadzimba:

    1–12-inch depth   BM-57   4200 ± 150 B.P. (2250 B.C.)

Calder's Cave:

    Layer 3 (Ceramic phase)   UCLA-929   1970 ± 80 B.P. (20 B.C.)

Dombazanga:

    8–10 inches (Ceramic phase)   SR-15   1220 ± 100 B.P. (750 B.C.)

Although few in number these dates adequately demonstrate that the Matopan is the close contemporary of the Wilton and makes its earliest appearance at Pomongwe during the same millenium that South Africa witnessed the emergence of a microlithic technology. But the failure of the Matopan to "develop" in a like manner must be at least partly linked with the relatively early advent of Iron Age groups in Rhodesia at about A.D. 100 or possibly as much as a century earlier.

Although isolated groups of Matopan hunter–gatherers persisted in the area until much later, their hold on this territory was rapidly undermined and they were either absorbed, eliminated, or displaced by the technically more efficient Iron Age population. It seems unlikely that this industry survived into the historic period, and this view is confirmed by the available carbon-14 dates.

THE PFUPIAN INDUSTRY

To the north and east of the Matopan area occurs a sparse scatter of Wilton-related finds that Cooke *et al.* (1966) have designated the Pfupian industry, after the excavated sample from Pfupi Rock Shelter near the Rusawi River in Mashonaland, Rhodesia. Remarkably little is known of this industry, and the only published samples include Pfupi and Mtemwa Rocks (K. R. Robinson 1952), Nyazongo Mountain Shelter (Martin 1938), Ziwa Mountain East and West Shelter, Nyangombe River, and Cituma Rocks (K. R. Robinson 1958). The case for delineating a separate industry from this sparse information remains extremely weak. Nevertheless, Cooke and his co-workers propose that all localities previously called "Southern Rhodesian Wilton" occurring north of 18° south and east of 30° east on their published survey map (Summers and Cooke 1959) should be renamed Pfupian. It therefore appears that the distinction between Matopan and Pfupian has been drawn largely on georgraphical distribution rather than on sound typological differences between samples from the two regions. The authors do suggest, however, that several tool types in Pfupian artifact samples are distinctive of this area: ground stone axes (K. R. Robinson 1938), bored stones, double backed crescents, geometric microliths, and small bifacial points (Fig. 124). As most of these types have been reported from the Matopan area as well, albeit as rare elements, the claimed differences may not be as clear-cut as at first supposed. Until a standardized numerical analysis is released, it will remain difficult to assess the exact typological differences between these two areas. Numerical analysis of Pfupian samples is somewhat varied in design, but are briefly summarized in Table 55.

Not only are some samples rather small, but the types claimed to be distinctive elements of the Pfupian are not all consistently present at every site. It also appears that there are not yet sufficient field data to suggest the presence of Preceramic and Ceramic phases similar to those of the Matopan. In spite of the lack of a carbon-14 chronology for the area, the stratigraphic position of each of the above samples shows that the Pfupian immediately underlies, and therefore precedes, the Iron Age occupation of every site. There can be little doubt that they are broadly contemporary with the Matopan to the south and west and must represent the occupation debris of related hunter–gatherer groups. Until more sites are discovered and excavated in Mashonaland, nothing definite will be known of the Pfupian–Iron Age contact, of the interaction between the two cultures, nor of the fate of the Pfupian groups. The earliest traces of Iron Age settlement in the Inyanga district of eastern Rhodesia dates to about A.D. 300 when intrusive groups manufacturing pottery known collectively as Ziwa ware first appear in the archaeological record. Presumably Pfupian groups persisted in the

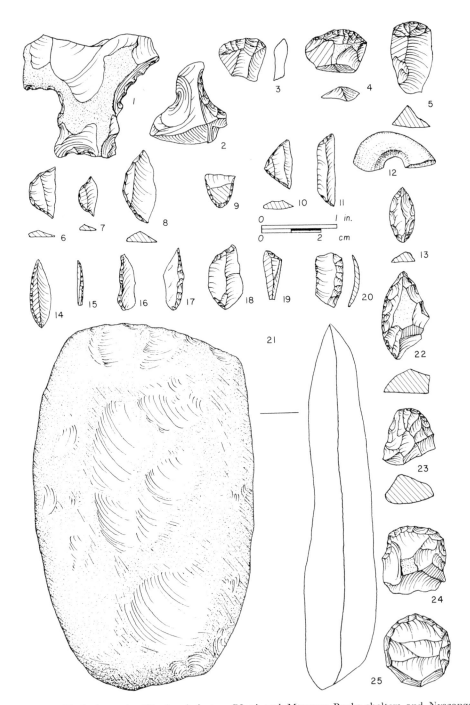

Fig. 124. Tools from the Pfupian industry, Pfupi and Mtemwa Rocks shelters and Nyazongo Mountain Cave: (1, 2) strangulated scrapers; (3, 4) small convex scrapers; (5) endscraper; (6–8) backed crescents; (9) deep backed crescent; (10) back triangle; (11) double oblique truncated bladelet; (12) bored stone fragment; (13) backed adze; (14) curve-backed point; (16–20) backed microlithic; (21) grooved stone axes; (22–24) small convex scrapers; (25) circular scrapers.

TABLE 55

Tool Types for Various Pfupian Sites

	Pfupi (12–18 in.)	Mtemwa Rocks (12–24 in.)	Ziwa East (12–24 in.)	Ziwa West (12–18 in.)	Nyan- gombe (0–6 in.)	Cituma Rocks (12–46 in.)	Nya- zongo
Scrapers	41	178	19	1	×	23	—
Borers	7	2	—	—	—	2	—
Outils écaillés	2	—	—	—	—	—	—
Backed points	11	15	1	—	—	1	—
Backed blades	6	28	14	5	×	30	—
Backed crescents	30	18	18	3	×	8	×
Double crescents	1	—	—	—	—	2	—
Backed triangle	2	2	—	—	—	—	—
Trapeziums	10	2	2	1	—	1	—
Petits tranchets	2	—	—	—	—	1	—
Small foliate points	—	—	—	—	1	—	—
Bored stones	—	—	—	1	—	—	—
Ground stone axes	—	3	—	1	—	—	×
Burins	4	10	—	—	—	1	—
Bone points	—	—	4	2	—	2	—
Totals:	116	258	58	14	—	71	—

mountainous areas for centuries after this time, but evidence of their durability has not been detected yet from excavated data. The present lack of faunal associations and human skeletal remains contributes further to the enigmatic status of the Pfupian which may be accepted only with reservations as a discrete cultural entity.

THE ZAMBIAN WILTON

Although numerous excavated samples and surface scatters of Wilton-like material have been reported from north of the Zambezi Valley, detailed comparisons between sites have not been published. At present the distribution of sites ascribed to the Zambian Wilton is restricted mainly to the westerly part of Zambia, but there is evidently a partial overlap with the contemporary Nachikufan cultural area which is broadly delineated as northern and eastern Zambia. Without closer analysis it will remain difficult to review the possible relationships between the two industries. Certainly, the available literature on sites located in central Zambia, between the Nachikufan and Zambian Wilton regions, shows no convincing evidence of two distinctive typological entities. Future work will no doubt blur the ascribed differences between the two areas.

Undoubtedly, most Zambian Wilton sites are located either in the Zambezi valley itself or within the broad drainage basins of the Zambezi headwaters and its large tributary, the Kafue River (Fig. 125). The sites themselves of course represent the refuse and flaking debris of hunter–gatherer groups who exploited several different niches including open grassy floodplain, riverine gallery forest, and the parkland savannah with its typical mosaic structures of woods and intervening open grassland. To both the north and east the tree cover becomes much denser, forming an almost continuous woodland. It is therefore obvious that the Zambian Wilton is not restricted to a single type of environment, but occurs in both open grassland and dense woodland.

The most important excavated sites are Mumbwa Cave (Clark 1942), Gwisho Spring Mound (Gabel 1963a, 1965), and Nakapapula Cave (D. W. Phillipson 1969). Other excavated sites with important associated carbon-14 dates are Kamusongolwa Kopje (D. W. Phillipson 1965), the Lusu and Siasuntwe middens

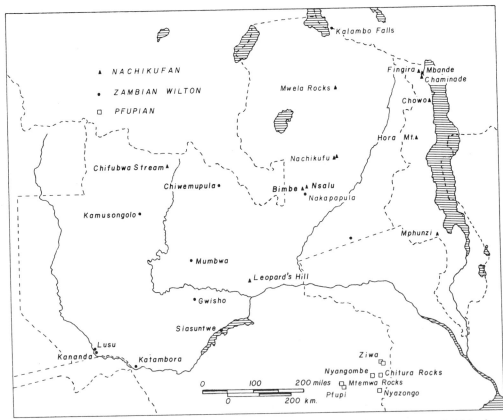

Fig. 125. Distribution of excavated sites in northeastern Rhodesia, Zambia, and Malawi ascribed to the Wilton complex.

(D. W. Phillipson 1964), and Makwe Shelter (Lofgren and Phillipson 1966; D. W. Phillipson 1970), although numerical analyses of this material have not been published. Several useful surface scatters have been reported from the upper Zambezi by Bond and Clark (1954), and Clark (1950a) reports at least 20 localities from the red silts of the Zambezi banks upstream from the Victoria Falls. Among these Katombora Road has been analyzed by Inskeep (1959).

Typology

As several different type lists have been employed by different authors to describe their material, percentage comparisons between assemblages are somewhat difficult. However, the shorter list of tool types presented by D. W. Phillipson (1969) provides an extremely useful basis for describing the overall characters of the Zambian Wilton lithic assemblages (see Table 56). Although the values for Mumbwa and Katombora are approximations derived from alternative published typologies, they nevertheless suffice to show that considerable site-to-site variations exists between assemblages called by the same name. It should also be stressed that these values represent gross characters derived from samples taken at all depths in the various excavated deposits. Another typology employed by Gabel (1965) to compare Gwisho with Mumbwa is given in Fig. 126.

Clear evidence of stylistic changes through time in the Zambian Wilton is virtually absent, although multilevel data are available for Nakapapula and Gwisho. Percentage changes for each type through time are given in Fig. 127. Whereas the lithic tradition at Nakapapula shows remarkable stability over a long period, the Gwisho evidence suggests a gradual increase in the frequency of backed crescents at the expense of large scrapers. Grindstones are also more frequent near the bottom of the mound deposits, but it is unlikely that these represent a chronologically significant feature of the industry's development (Fig. 127).

Unfortunately, no comparable data for the 2-ft deep accumulation of Wilton deposits at Mumbwa are available. Certainly it seems possible that Nakapapula and Gwisho represent the long-term accumulations of two independent hunter–gatherer groups each with its own minor stylistic characters.

Of the two sites, only Nakapapula has a Preceramic and Ceramic phase, while Gwisho Mound A was evidently abandoned long before the advent of the Iron Age. The uppermost three levels of the Nakapapula shelter deposits contained abundant potsherds associated with the lithic materials. Unlike other Ceramic phase sites, two stratified groups of sherds can be recognized here. The earlier group comprises large and small rounded vessels with concave or shouldered necks and inverted rims. Decoration is restricted to the neck where false-relief chevron stamping and straw impressions have been applied. Parallel grooves are common, some forming triangular or pendant loop patterns, filled with straw impressions. Chevron patterns also occur on the beveled rims (Fig. 128). This

TABLE 56

Tool Types for Various Zambian Wilton Sites [a]

	Nakapapula	Gwisho Mound A	Mumbwa	Katombora
Crescents	29.3	58.0	8.8	63.8
Backed blades	7.2	1.7	36.5	7.3
Points	2.5	0.6	0.9	0.8
Convex scrapers	13.9	14.8	16.1	22.6
Concave scrapers	9.7	0.3	1.4	4.1
Burins	1.8	0.2	11.4	—
Outils écaillés	11.8	10.2	—	—
Lames écaillés	1.8	4.7	5.4	—
Kasouga flakes	2.5	—	0.7	—
Adzes	2.2	1.1	—	—
Utilized crystals	4.3	—	—	—
Bored stones	1.8	—	0.5	—
Polished axes	0.4	0.3	0.5	—
Grindstones	4.0	5.0	×	—
Others	5.7	3.1	19.9	1.6
Sample totals:	**279**	**882**	**254**	**124**

[a] Numerical values are percentages.

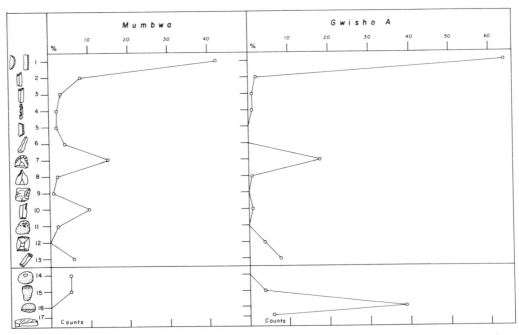

Fig. 126. Typological comparisons between the Zambian Wilton samples from Mumbwa and Gwisho A: (1) backed crescents and backed blades; (2) oblique truncated blades; (3) concave-end blades; (4) notched blades; (5) trapeziums; (6) blades; (7) convex scrapers; (8) truncated flakes; (9) kasouga flakes; (10) burins; (11) hammerstones; (12) *outils écaillés;* (13) end-scrapers; (14) bored stones; (15) ground stone axes; (16) upper grindstones; (17) lower grindstones. (After Gabel 1965.)

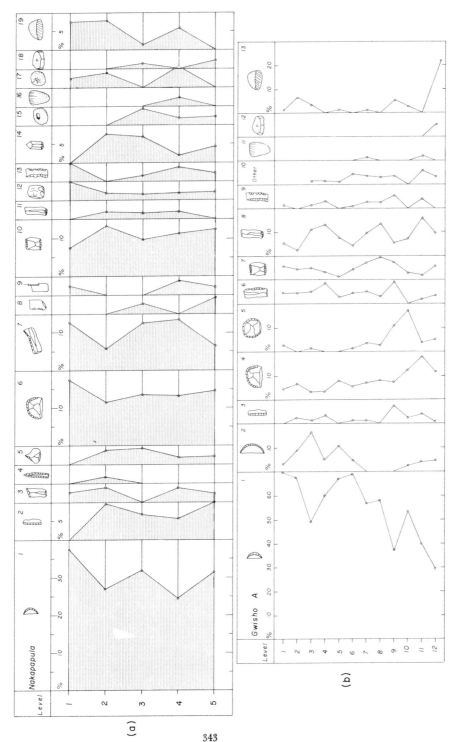

Fig. 127. The vertical distribution of tool types in the Zambian Wilton at Nakapapula and Gwisho A, following two different typologies presented by Phillipson (1969) for Nakapapula and Gabel (1965) for Gwisho A. (a) Nakapapula: (1) backed crescent; (2) backed bladelet; (3) truncated bladelet; (4) backed point; (5) borer; (6) hollow scraper; (7) sidescraper; (8) trimmed blade; (9) burin; (10) *outil écaillé*; (11) *lame écaillé*; (12) Kasouga flake; (13) backed adze; (14) chisel; (15) bored stone; (16) ground stone axe; (17) ground palette (18) grindstone; (19) muller. (b) Gwisho A: (1) small backed crescent; (2) large backed crescent; (3) backed bladelet; (4) convex scraper; (5) circular scraper; (6) backed blade; (7) *outil écaillé*; (8) *lame écaillé*; (9) backed adze; (10) other; (11) ground stone axe; (12) grindstone; (13) muller.

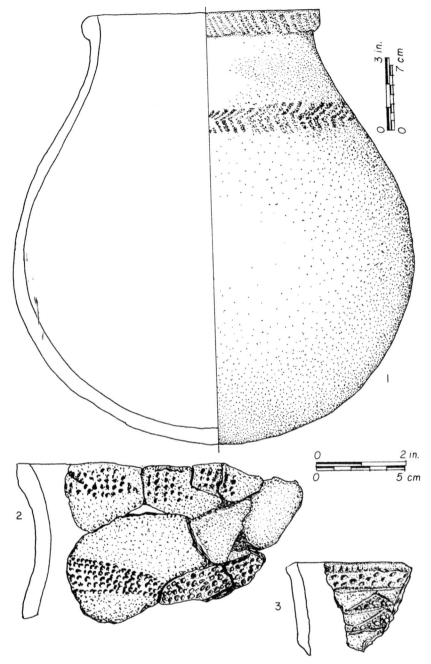

Fig. 128. Early Iron Age (2 and 3) and Recent Iron Age (1) ceramics at Nakapapula, suggesting prolonged contact between Zambian Wilton hunters and adjacent Iron Age groups.

ware is completely characteristic of the earliest Zambian Iron Age, which has been recorded from Kalambo Falls as early as A.D. 345 and appears in southern Zambia in several well-established village mounds by the middle of the first millenium A.D. It is probably reasonable to assume that limited contacts and barter between the Wilton and Early Iron Age groups is reflected in the upper levels of Nakapapula. In the top few inches of deposit there is a marked change in potsherd types. Here the vessels show the same characters as those made by Lala women today. Large rounded pots with concave necks and everted rims are the commonest form, and only one bowl is reported. The characteristic decoration is combstamping, which forms a band on the rim. A second band of segmental black designs may occur on the neck or shoulder. D. W. Phillipson (1969) suggest that this material is of recent Iron Age origin since the shelter is known to have been used as a Lala refuge during the Ngoni raids of the nineteenth century. The sherds were probably trampled into the top of the Wilton deposits and are not therefore in true association.

Associated Artifacts

Nonlithic artifacts are relatively scarce in the Zambian Wilton. Clark (1950a) notes the presence of ostrich eggshell beads without mentioning specific sites, but little else was known of this aspect of the material culture prior to the excavation of Gwisho.

Although abundant beads of the freshwater mollusk *Unio* come from Gwisho, ostrich eggshell was not used, evidently because ostrich was entirely absent from the Kafue Flats at this time. Gabel (1965) points out that none of the backed microliths from the stone tool assemblage are suitable for bead drilling and suggests that wood or bone drills were used here rather than backed points. Evidence of other shell or bone ornaments has not been reported from here or any other Zambian Wilton site, and these are perhaps unknown in this region. Bone tools are also remarkably scarce: five hippo phalanges used as rubbers, and a small crude bone awl from Gwisho represent all that is presently known of Zambian Wilton bone work.

On the other hand the evidence for wood working at Gwisho exceeds all other Wilton sites in both quantity and degree of preservation. Fagan and van Noten (1966) point out that the permanently saturated conditions of the spring mound deposits are ideal for the preservation of hard woods. Even twigs and leaves have survived. The woods used at Gwisho include the following. Rhodesian teak, *Baikiaea,* was for digging sticks, points, arrowheads, and possibly a bow stave. *Dalbergia* was also used for a digging stick and *Brachystegia boehmii* Taub. was frequently used for arrowheads. Other rarely used woods include *Brachystegia* cf. *speciformis* Benth. and *Celtis* sp. In each case the wood appears

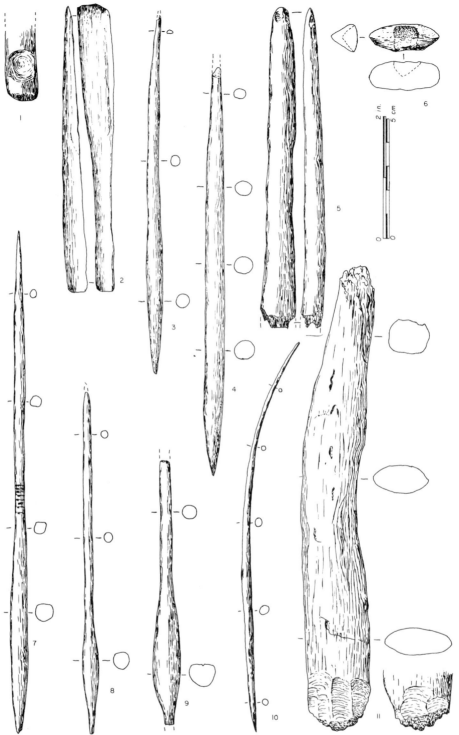

Fig. 129. Wooden tools from Gwisho A: (1, 6) fire-drill sockets; (2) spatula; (3, 4, 7–10) arrowpoints; (11) ?digging stick fragment.

to have been chosen for hardness or flexibility according to the tool type required. Figure 129 shows the range of wooden tools found at Gwisho. Included
are arrowheads, link shafts, miscellaneous points, digging sticks, spatulas, fire-
drill bases, and numerous whittled and ring-cut fragments. A few fragments
have been interpreted as bow staves, although no complete bows are present. A
more complete bow is reported from the neighboring Gwisho Mound B, where
over 50 wooden tools have been recovered, including possible wooden eating
utensils (Gabel 1965). Details of this second excavation are not yet available.

Chronology

The carbon-14 chronology of the Zambian Wilton again shows substantial
overlap with dates to the south.

Gwisho A:

8-ft depth	M-1324	4650 ± 150 B.P. (2700 B.C.)
8-ft depth	M-1323	4450 ± 150 B.P. (2500 B.C.)
8-ft depth	UCLA-173	4230 ± 100 B.P. (2350 B.C.)
5-ft depth	UCLA-174	4700 ± 100 B.P. (2750 B.C.)

Gwisho B:

1.7–1.8-m depth	GrN-4307	4785 ± 70 B.P. (2835 B.C.)
0.6–0.62-m depth	GrN-4306	3680 ± 70 B.P. (1730 B.C.)
0.45–0.47-m depth	GrN-4305	3660 ± 70 B.P. (1710 B.C.)

Siasuntwe:

Sample eroding from midden	UCLA-727	2010 ± 80 B.P. (60 B.C.)

Lusu:

No sample data	C-830	2025 ± 230 B.P. (75 B.C.)
	C-839	2136 ± 150 B.P. (186 B.C.)

Kamusongolwa:

Upper levels of Wilton	SR-95	4000 ± 105 B.P. (2050 B.C.)

Nakapapula:

Level 5 (12–15 inches)	GX-737	3280 ± 90 B.P. (1330 B.C.)
Level 3 (6–9 inches)	GX-535	1180 ± 100 B.P. (770 B.C.)
Level 3 (3–6 inches)	GX-767	910 ± 85 B.P. (A.D. 1040)

Makwe:

Horizon 2	SR-204	5010 ± 90 B.P.	(3060 B.C.)
Horizon 2	GX-1555	4815 ± 120 B.P.	(2865 B.C.)
Horizon 3i	SR-205	4580 ± 95 B.P.	(2630 B.C.)
Horizon 3i	GX-1554	4485 ± 110 B.P.	(2535 B.C.)
Horizon 3ii	GX-1553	4645 ± 110 B.P.	(2695 B.C.)
Horizon 4i	GX-1552	5430 ± 140 B.P.	(3480 B.C.)
Horizon 4ii			
(Ceramic phase)	GX-1551	1730 ± 110 B.P.	(A.D. 220)

Kandanda (Phillipson 1970) :

5-ft level	SR-203	3,690 ± 85 B.P.	(1740 B.C.)
	SR-202	3,360 ± 95 B.P.	(1410 B.C.)
	SR-201	3,450 ± 80 B.P.	(1500 B.C.)
	SR-199	1,835 ± 50 B.P.	(A.D. 115)
	SR-198	2,130 ± 55 B.P.	(180 B.C.)
Ceramic phase	GX-1579	490 ± 90 B.P.	(A.D. 1460)
Ceramic phase	GX-200	465 ± 85 B.P.	(A.D. 1485)

Although no readings predating 4000 B.C. have been obtained, it is reasonable
to predict that the lowermost levels of Nakapapula are of this order, whereas the
earliest levels of the Zambian Wilton at Makwe may be considerably older. Unfortunately, the relationship between the earliest Wilton and the preceding industry remains vague. At Kandanda, Donke, and Mumbwa it overlies lithic samples obviously related to the Bambata or Umguzan while at Makwe the
preceding industry may be related to the Oakhurst complex. Until more carbon-
14 dates become available for the period between 20,000 and 5000 B.C. in southern Zambia, the emergence of the Wilton in this area will remain enigmatic. On
the other hand, the contact period between Wilton hunter–gatherers and the
Early Zambian Iron Age groups is reasonably well documented. Potsherds appear at Nakapapula during the third century A.D. and somewhat later in the
Zambezi River valley sites. Potsherds are also reported from Lusu dated to the
second century B.C., a remarkably early date for this association. Since it contradicts the dating of the Iron Age–Wilton contact elsewhere, this reading may be
regarded with some reservations at present, although it may not be totally unacceptable in the light of the Calders Cave date of 20 B.C. for this event.

Diet and Associated Fauna

Details of the dietary range and exploitation patterns employed by Zambian
Wilton groups are somewhat hindered by poor bone preservation at most sites
and the lack of numerical analysis for the few where preservation conditions are
adequate. The fauna present at two sites are listed in Table 57.

TABLE 57

Fauna Associated with Two Zambian Wilton Sites

Genus and species	Description	Gwisho A	Mumbwa
Cercopithecus sp.	Monkey	Scarce	—
Hystrix africae-australis	Porcupine	Scarce	×
Mellivora capensis	Honey badger	Doubtful	—
Loxodonta africana	Elephant	Scarce	—
Equus burchelli	Zebra	Abundant	×
Diceros bicornis	Black rhino	Moderately abundant	—
Potamochoerus sp.	Bush pig	Scarce	—
Phacochoerus africanus	Warthog	Abundant	×
Hippopotamus amphibius	Hippo	Scarce	—
Strepsiceros strepsiceros	Kudu	Moderately abundant	×
Tragelaphus scriptus	Bushbuck	Scarce	—
Taurotragus oryx	Eland	Doubtful	×
Syncerus caffer	Cape buffalo	Abundant	—
Redunca arundinum	Reedbuck	Abundant	×
Hippotragus equinus	Roan	Scarce	×
Alcelaphus lichtensteini	Hartebeest	Doubtful	—
Connochaetes taurinus	Wildebeest	Abundant	×
Oreotragus oreotragus	Klipspringer	Doubtful	—
Raphicerus sp.	Grysbok–steenbok	Scarce	—
Aepyceros melampus	Impala	Abundant	—
Ourebia ourebia	Oribi	Doubtful	—
Cephalophus sp.	Blue duiker	—	×

The lists reflect a remarkable emphasis on the game animals which were evidently abundant on the Kafue Flats during this period. Curiously, the most common modern species are not represented in the lists: various carnivores, baboons, and lechwe. There is also a quite remarkable absence of small animals including fish, reptiles, amphibians, and birds, although fish and lechwe are apparently present in Mound B. The only other riverine food source at Mound A appears to be the freshwater gastropod *Lanistes* and the bivalve *Cafferia* as well as the *Unio* already mentioned. Fragments of the land snail *Achatina* are also present. From this evidence it appears that Gwisho was essentially a hunting base from which the Wilton group preyed on herd animals on the surrounding grassy floodplain of the Kafue Flats. The same pattern emerges for the Mumbwa Caves, which contains a similar range of bones. It is interesting to note that this pattern is not reported from the south where the mixed Pomongwan–Wilton faunal assemblage from Pomongwe Cave contains virtually no large animals. The Gwisho–Mumbwa dietary range also contrasts sharply with that of the Orange River sites, where a great variety of small animals were exploited. In many ways the economic pattern reflected by Gwisho and Mumbwa resembles more closely the big-game hunting activities of earlier industries. What remains to be discovered is whether these two sites were periodically, perhaps seasonally, abandoned when game herds moved elsewhere. It is entirely possible that both sites reflect only a limited facet of a complex set of exploitation strategies based on seasonal movements from one favorable niche to another.

Certainly, hunting was not the only activity carried out from Gwisho where nuts, husks, and kernel fragments of the vegetable-ivory palm *Hyphaene ventricosa* were recovered in great numbers. Equally numerous were whole and broken marula nuts, *Sclerocarya caffra,* and the large flat seeds of the musaule tree, *Guibourtia coleosperma*. Several other unidentified seeds and reeds were also recovered, including fragmentary patches of reeds arranged in crosswise layers over each other. Undoubtedly more important evidence can be extracted from this material. The only other mention of vegetable foods in the Zambian Wilton is a pit filled with mungongo nuts reported by L. Phillipson (1970) from the late levels of Kandanda. Two charred post holes from this same site yield the only hint of simple structures or windbreaks used by these people. Although similar structures may be present in the Gwisho deposits, they have not been reported as such. Leaves, twigs, brush, and branches are present, but no artificial patterns within this material were recognized during excavations.

Human Remains

Not only is Gwisho unique in its preservation of organic materials, but it has also yielded 14 human burials as well as other fragments. A further 19 burials are reported from Mound B, but no description of these is available yet (Gabel 1962, 1963a, b). The layout of the Gwisho Mound A burials is shown in Fig. 130. The orientation and position of individual skeletons is consistently horizontal, but no other regular patterns can be detected. Both extended or semiflexed on the side, dorsally extended or semiflexed, and vertically extended positions are present. Apart from ocher smears on a few individuals, no other grave associations were recovered, and capstones were absent. Two skeletons were headless and others had bones missing, suggesting partial disturbance by burrowing animals and possible human interference. Skeletons 1–3 may have been buried together in the same shallow pit. The consistently haphazard burial procedures used at Gwisho may be contrasted with the more regular flexed burials with abundant grave goods and capstones found at Coastal Wilton sites.

Comparisons between the best-preserved Gwisho skeletons and those from Oakhurst (all levels) are of interest, but poor preservation has reduced the number of comparable measurements (see Fig. 131). Calculations of stature for the two samples reveal the following: Gwisho males (7) 159.2–169.5 cm, Oakhurst males (8) 161.8–165.8 cm; Gwisho females (3) 138.8–152.4 cm; Oakhurst females (4) 153.6–159.7 cm.

Whereas the two male samples overlap, the Oakhurst female sample contains consistently taller individuals. The small sample size, however, prevents any general conclusions being drawn from these figures, and comparisons with the very

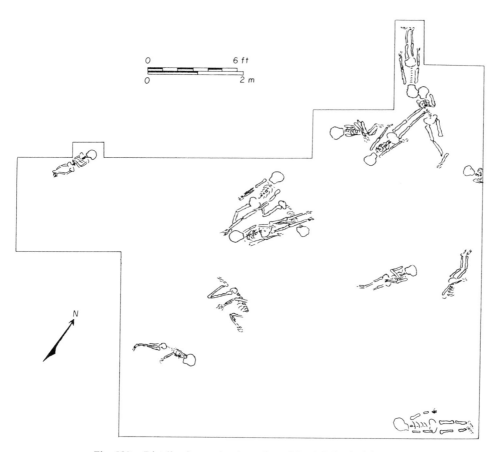

Fig. 130. Distribution and orientation of burials in Gwisho A.

large Wilton population from Matjes River Layer C is not possible for want of any adequate postcranial survey of this material. Craniometric comparisons between 5 reasonably complete adult skulls from Gwisho and the 13 skulls from Wilton levels at Oakhurst and Matjes River Layer C do however, suggest a consistent overlap between the two samples.

Wells (1950b) mentions the discovery of at least 16 individual burials recovered in pioneer excavations at Mumbwa by Dart and del Grande (1931), but most of these were no more than soil shadows with a few fragmentary teeth. Two or three badly damaged skulls were recovered from the upper Wilton levels, but no measurements are available. Although the Zambian Wilton population is relatively well represented, more published data are needed before a reliable evaluation can be made of its affinities with contemporary peoples on the southern Cape coast. The limited measurements presently available hint strongly at a close affinity, but confirmation is required.

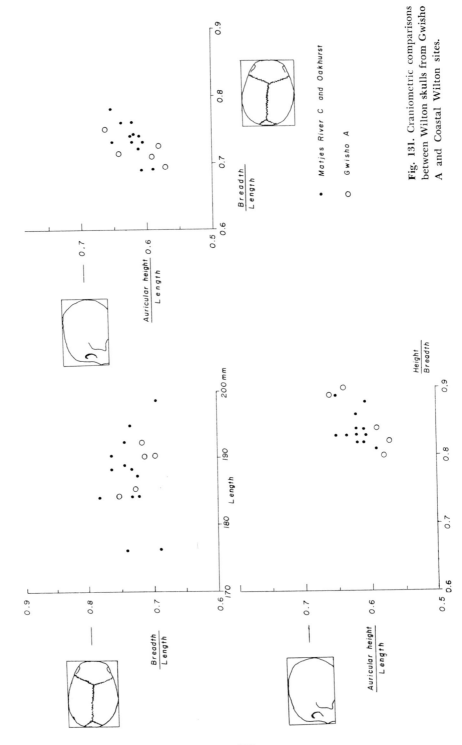

Fig. 131. Craniometric comparisons between Wilton skulls from Gwisho A and Coastal Wilton sites.

• *Matjes River C and Oakhurst*

○ *Gwisho A*

There remains, in addition, the problem of cultural affinities between the Zambian Wilton and the Pfupian to the south. It is already apparent that the typological composition of each industry is far from consistent between sites. If their typological characters are so variable, it is surely reasonable to expect a considerable overlap between the two industries. Indeed, the present published figures from both areas do little to encourage one in the belief that they *are* indeed two distinct industries. Both contain scrapers and backed crescents in abundance, similar rare backed microlithic shapes (triangles, trapeziums, points, and so forth) crop up sporadically in each region, as do ground axes and bored stones. Admittedly bone work and jewelry are extremely rare in the Zambian Wilton, but these elements can hardly be said to be a common feature of the Pfupian either. Like so many others, this problem can only be resolved by more systematic and detailed analysis of all the available materials.

THE NACHIKUFAN INDUSTRY

The name for this group of northern Zambian sites is taken from the Nachikufu Cave about 30 miles south of Mpika in Northern Province. Clark (1950c) introduced the term in describing the carefully excavated artifact samples not only from the type site but also from Nsalu and Bimbe in the same region. In this initial report it was proposed that the industry be divided into three phases based on the stratigraphic sequence recognized at each site. Although type lists for each phase were presented, no numerical data were employed in the description. The same name and chronological scheme was applied to subsequently excavated sites from Mwela Rocks, Chifubwa Stream (Clark 1958), Leopard's Hill, and a shelter immediately adjacent to Nachikufu Cave.

Typology

The systematic survey of all this material by Miller (1967, 1969a) has made this the best-documented of all the Wilton-related industries of southern Africa and serves as a model for future research on this complex. Miller's typology comprising a list of 27 tool types has been used to classify the contents of 7 major sites, which have been correlated on the basis of stratigraphy, typological similarities, and carbon-14 dating (see Table 58).

Each proposed phase of the industry's development is therefore represented by more than one sample and it becomes possible to investigate the range of typological variability of each of the phases as demonstrated graphically in Fig. 132.

Phase I samples are consistently dominated by ill-made backed bladelets and other backed microliths including crescents, geometrics, and backed flakes. Convex chunk scrapers are abundant in some, but not all sites. Phase IIA is characterized by an increase in the proportion of all scrapers and an increase in backed flakes over other microliths. In Phase IIB samples the microliths are reported to

	Leopard's Hill	Nachikufu Cave	Nachikufu Shelter	Nsalu	Mwela Rocks	Bimbe	Chifubwa Stream
Phase IIIB	—	—	×	—	—	×	—
Phase IIIA	×	×	×	×	×	×	—
Phase IIB	×	—	—	—	—	×	—
Phase IIA	×	×	×	—	×	—	—
Phase I	×	×	×	×	×	—	×

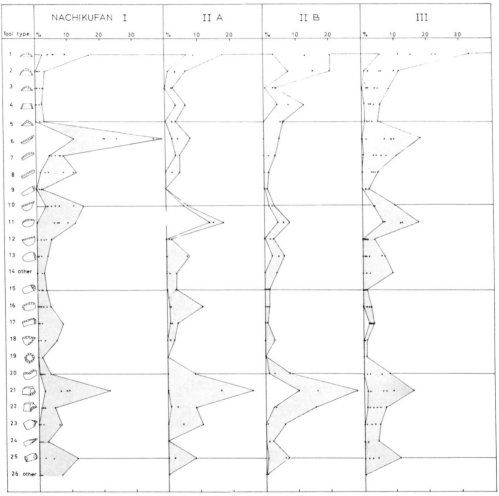

Fig. 132. Range of percentages of each tool type in the four phases of the Nachikufan industry: (1) crescents; (2) deep crescents; (3) eared crescents; (4) trapeziums; (5) triangles; (6) backed points; (7) convex backed bladelets; (8) backed blades; (9) truncated blades; (10–13) truncated flakes; (14) other truncated pieces; (15) endscrapers; (16) sidescrapers; (17) side–endscrapers; (18) convergent sidescrapers; (19) circular scrapers; (20) concave scrapers; (21) convex chunk scrapes; (22) concave chunk scrapers; (23) nosed scrapers; *(*24) drills; (25) *outils écaillés;* (26) other.

be dominated by deep and eared crescents, but scrapers display variable proportions from site to site. Phase II samples display remarkably little consistency in percentage values from one site to another and most of them have potsherds or iron in true association with the artifacts.

Chronology

Visual inspection of the graphs in Fig. 132 leave no doubt that there is considerable overlap between samples from different phases and all but the earliest phase display remarkably little stylistic homogeneity from one site to another. The arrangement of phases as outlined in the table above is therefore open to alternative interpretations. However, the carbon-14 chronology of the industry goes some way to support a sequential development for the industry as a whole.

Mwela Rocks:

4.5–7.0 ft	Phase I	Y-808		
		charcoal	10,820 ± 340 B.P.	(8870 B.C.)
		alkali	11,700 ± 280 B.P.	(9750 B.C.)
3.0–3.5 ft	Phase IIA	Y-625	8640 ± 240 B.P.	(6690 B.C.)
2.5–3.0 ft	Phase IIB	Y-805		
		charcoal	7320 ± 200 B.P.	(5370 B.C.)
		alkali	7200 ± 700 B.P.	(5250 B.C.)

Chifubwa Stream:

post-Phase I	C-663	6310 ± 250 B.P.	(4325 B.C.)

Nachikufu Shelter:

5–7 ft	Phase IIIA	Y-799	1060 ± 100 B.P.	(890 B.C.)
2–3 ft	Phase IIB and Iron Age	Y-796	200 ± 100 B.P.	(A.D. 1750)

Nachikufu Cave:

3.0–3.5 ft	post-Phase I	Y-620B	9720 ± 550 B.P.	(7770 B.C.)
2.5–3.0 ft	Phase IIB	Y-791	5630 ± 550 B.P.	(3980 B.C.)
1.5–2.0 ft	Phase IIB	Y-619	4830 ± 320 B.P.	(2850 B.C.)
		Y-619A	5000 ± 200 B.P.	(3050 B.C.)
0.5–1.0 ft	Phase III and Iron Age	Y-618	300 ± 200 B.P.	(A.D. 1650)

Kalambo Falls:

Site C, 3.5–4.0-ft level	Phase ?	GrN-4224	3920 ± 40 B.P.	(1970 B.C.)
Site C, 3.5–4.0-ft level	Phase ?	GrN-4225	3850 ± 40 B.P.	(1900 B.C)
Site C, below Iron				
Age level	Phase ?	GrN-4223	2730 ± 40 B.P.	(780 B.C.)
Site A, 1-ft level	Phase ?	GrN-4226	2470 ± 40 B.P.	(520 B.C.)

Leopard's Hill:

Levels 37–39	Phase I	UCLA-1291	16,400 ± 265 B.P.	(14,450 B.C.)
Level 27	Phase I	GX-0957	21,550 ± 950 B.P.	(19,600 B.C.)
Level 14	Phase IIA	UCLA-1290	9700 ± 85 B.P.	(7750 B.C.)

Of extraordinary interest are the very early dates associated with Phase I. Unfortunately the tool samples from the lowest levels of Leopards Hill are extremely small and the full complement of Phase I tool types are not recorded here, although backed bladelets, backed flakes, and chunk scrapers are undoubtedly present, and a bored stone fragment comes from Level 27. Unfortunately, the dating inversions between Levels and 37–39 detract somewhat from the reliability of these readings. Nevertheless, the Phase I tool kit appears to have disappeared by about 7000 B.C. at three sites at least, and the reading (Sr-45) of 13,300 ± 250 B.P. or 11,350 B.C. from near the bottom of Kamusongolwa Kopje may also refer to a Nachikufu Phase I sample, but this has not yet been described (D. W. Phillipson 1965).

Phase IIA dates cluster between 7750 and 5250 B.C., whereas Phase IIB readings fall between 3980 and 2850 B.C., thus fully supporting the stratigraphic separation for the two. Phase III dates are considerably younger and reveal an unexpected gap in the carbon-14 record lasting three millenia. It is now apparent that the carbon-14 chronology in no way conflicts with the composite stratigraphic record first proposed by Clark and supported by Miller.

However, the relatively poor agreement between percentage values for different sites within any single phase has been pointed out already. Typological homogeneity for each phase is lacking, and samples can be regrouped according to degrees of similarity. Sampson and Southard (1972) have compared the percentage values of each sample with those of the other 17 samples and generated an "index of agreement" for every pair of samples that measures the amount of similarity between the two (W. S. Robinson 1951). Following the procedure laid out by Craytor and Johnson (1968) and Johnson (1968), the index for every pair was placed in a Q matrix and sorted to produce a one-dimensional seriation of the 18 samples based on clusters of most-similar samples. The results of this experiment are shown in the dendrogram of Fig. 133. Although most Phase I samples cluster as a homogenous group, the typological distinction between Phase II and III and their subdivisions is not apparent. Instead, there emerge from the analysis six clusters of like samples each dominated by a few characteristic tool types. The clusters and their dominant tool types are summarized in

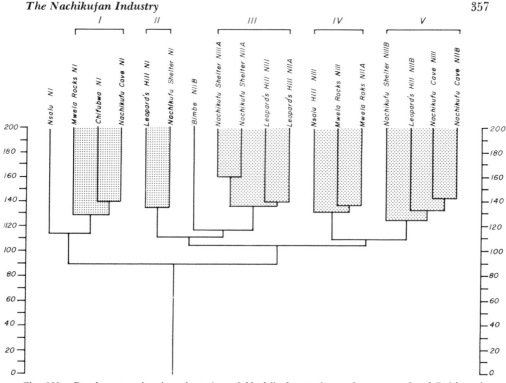

Fig. 133. Dendrogram showing clustering of Nachikufan tool samples on a scale of Robinson's (1951) index values. The Roman numerals indicate clusters of similar samples.

Fig. 134. This diagram simply demonstrates that there are three rather different kinds of Phase I samples, each dominated by a characteristic array of tool types that probably reflects specialized tasks rather than regional styles. Although Phase IIA and IIB samples cluster separately, there are obviously different kinds of samples from each of these phases—again probably task-specific. Of interest is the fact that Phase III fails to emerge as a separate typological entity but is spread across three different clusters which it shares with both Phase IIA and IIB samples.

It is now clear that the Nachikufan industry did not simply evolve through a series of typological phases at the same rate in all parts of north Zambia. In any given phase different shelters appear to have been occupied by groups concentrating on a limited number of activities for which only a few stone tool types were needed. Some shelters were repeatedly used over long periods for the same set of tasks so that Phase II and III do not merge clearly as different typological units. Whereas Phase I can be readily distinguished from Phases II–III, most of the fine subdivisions between Phases II and III themselves may be the result of activity variations from site to site rather than purely chronological changes in design.

Unfortunately, the real nature of their tasks cannot be investigated without a more detailed survey of the associated fauna at each site. Whereas it is tempting to assume that samples dominated by small backed microliths are in some way

Nachikufan Phases of Clark and Miller	N I	N I	N IIA	N III	N IIA	N III	N IIB	N III

Sites:	Nachikufu Cave Nsalu Hill	Nachikufu Shelter Leopard's Hill	Nachikufu Shelter ⟶ X Leopard's Hill ⟶ X	Mwela R. ⟶ X Nsalu	Nachikufu Cave ⟶ X Leopard's Hill Nachikufu Shelter

CLUSTER	I	II	III	IV	V

Fig. 134. The dominant tool types in each cluster of similar Nachikufan samples. Rank order 1 indicates types with the highest percentage frequencies.

linked with hunting activities, this cannot be demonstrated without some knowledge of the associated faunal remains. Likewise, the samples dominated by convex chunk scrapers may be linked to equipment-maintenance activities, but
again this assumption must be examined with prior knowledge of the amount
and variety of faunal remains with this sample.

Fauna

Clark (1959a) reports that abundant fauna occur in Nachikufu Shelter, but
no other information has been released. Present are: hartebeest, wildebeest, sassaby, duiker (2 species), reedbuck, roan antelope, eland, buffalo, cane rat, mole
rat, spring hare, tortoise, lizard, carnivore (indet), black rhinoceros, Burchell's
zebra, and warthog (2 species). Most of the larger animals also occur at the
Zambian Wilton sites of Gwisho and Mumbwa (sassaby excepted), but rodents,
tortoise and lizard remains have not been reported elsewhere in Zambia. The
only vegetable remains reported from Nachikufu sites are carbonized seeds of
Uapaca kirkiana.

Human Remains

Associated human skeletal remains are equally scarce. Leopard's Hill has
yielded extremely damaged fragments (Clark 1950b) and a better preserved skeleton was recovered from Chipongwe (Clark 1955a) with a small artifact sample
that may belong with the Nachikufan group but cannot be identified with any
certainty.

Affinities

In spite of the rather unbalanced quality of the Nachikufan data, several important points emerge. Of the greatest interest is the presence of an undoubted
microlithic industry in northern Zambia prior to 7000 B.C. and possibly extended
as far back in time as about 16,000 B.C., although such extreme antiquity for the
Nachikufan Phase I is still subject to confirmation by further dating. The origins of this early phase cannot be ascertained, but the preceding industry at
Nsalu and Leopard's Hill has been reported as "Magosian" (that is, related to
the Umguzan of Rhodesia). A "Magosian" containing small foliate points and
backed crescents occurs in a derived context at Kalambo Falls below Nachiku-
fan-related material, but this also has yet to be described in detail and is dated
to only 9550 ± 120 B.P. or 7600 B.C. (L-395D). If this date is correct and the artifact sample is not mixed (both are possible), the local "Magosian" would be a
contemporary of Phase I only a 130 miles to the south. The implications of this
cannot be discussed until the Kalambo Falls data were verified. *If* the northern
Zambian equivalent of the Umguzan does indeed contain an array of backed microliths, this region will be the only one in southern Africa where some form of

typological continuum between the Umguzan and the Wilton samples can be detected. Exactly why backed bladelets and points should have been preferred in this closed woodland environment at so early a date must remain a subject for speculation until more is learned of Nachikufu I exploitation strategies.

Phases II–III of the Nachikufan industry displays a much closer resemblance to the Zambian Wilton with its abundant backed crescents and scrapers, although Nachikufu Phase IIA dates may be still older than the earliest Wilton samples. Certainly, Phase IIB and III samples display a striking resemblance to the Preceramic and Ceramic phases of the Zambian Wilton, and more detailed comparisons between these are urgently needed. Indeed the presence of a long "Wilton" development at Nakapapula, which is less than 20 miles from Bimbe and Nsalu, simply underlines the typological and terminological confusion that has emerged from the lack of standardized analytical procedures. At present it appears extremely likely that supposed differences between the Zambian Wilton and Nachikufu Phases II–III will prove to be far less clear-cut than previously stated.

Phase III may be best regarded as a continuation of the complex range of Phase II assemblages after the time of the first Iron Age contact. Miller (1969b) has pointed out that Nachikufan hunter–gatherers were replaced by Iron Age groups at Kalambo Falls by A.D. 345 and at Leopard's Hill Cave by A.D. 535. However, complete submergence of the Nachikufan groups after the Iron Age arrival is not to be inferred from these two entirely localized events. It is abundantly clear that Nachikufan hunters continued to occupy this territory alongside Iron Age settlements for a considerable period and evidence for partial interaction and exchange between the two is relatively widespread. Characteristic Early Iron Age potsherds appear in Nachikufan levels at several sites, whereas at Nsalu Hill other typical Iron Age elements occur, including glass beads, coiled copper wire, and an iron arrowhead stem. Iron arrows also occur in the top levels of Mwela Rocks. Of still greater interest is the evidence for the actual smelting of iron by late Nachikufan groups. Filmer and Mills (1968) report the presence of a small lithic assemblage with Early Iron Age pottery and slag dating to A.D. 890 ± 95 (GX-1010) and A.D. 815 ± 130 (GX-1009). This level is overlain by Iron Age midden. At Nachikufu Shelter the Phase II sample has slag in its upper levels, and remains of a smelting furnace were recovered 1 m below the deposit surface. Coiled copper wire occurs nearer to the surface. Sherds and slag also occur in the adjacent Nachikufu Cave near the surface, but they are questionably associated with the lithic assemblage.

Finally, there is some reason to assume that a few small groups of these people persisted in isolated pockets on the Muchinga escarpment into the nineteenth century. Evidently the Lala tribe records the presence of a small people in this area prior to their arrival (Vansina 1966), and Clark (1950b) has pointed out that the Batwa of the swamps of Lake Bangweulu, the Lukanga swamps, and the Kafue Flats are probably remnants of this Stone Age population.

CONTEMPORARY SITES IN MALAWI

Several recently excavated samples from Malawi are reported to show typological affinities with the Nachikufan of Zambia, but no detailed analyses are available yet. The relevant sites are Fingira (Robinson and Sandelowsky 1968a, b), Mphunzi Shelter (Miller 1971), Hora Mountain Cave (Clark 1956), Chowo (Miller 1969b), Mabande Court, and Chaminade Ch-3 (Clark 1967b). Both a Preceramic and a Ceramic stage have been recognized, but the typological composition of lithic samples evidently varies considerably from one site to another. Chaminade Ch-3 is a Preceramic open site located on the edge of the Rift. It contains backed crescents, blades, backed flakes, small scrapers, and larger elements such as choppers, core scrapers, and grindstones. In contrast to this, the broadly contemporary occupants of Fingira Shelter at the southwestern end of the Nyika Plateau were making cruder microliths including deep crescents, trapezium geometrics, small steep scrapers, and grindstones. No doubt, geographically separated groups each producing various task-specific assemblages will be revealed by the projected survey and analysis of all this material.

The carbon-14 chronology for the area is still restricted to Preceramic sites only:

Chaminade Ch-3:

UCLA-1240   3450 ± 80 B.P. (1500 B.C.)

Fingira Hill:

UCLA-1250   3260 ± 80 B.P. (1310 B.C.)
UCLA-1259   3430 ± 80 B.P. (1480 B.C.)

Mbande Court:

A-785   4080 ± 100 B.P. (2130 B.C.)
A-783   2220 ± 120 B.P. (270 B.C.)

Chowo:

SR-127   2125 ± 120 B.P. (175 B.C.)

The readings serve to demonstrate that these assemblages are contemporary with the Nachikufan Phase II, but there is no evidence available yet to suggest that they are the same. The presence of diminutive convex scrapers in large numbers in Malawi sites may suggest a general stylistic character for the region as a whole, but this can only be confirmed when the analysis presently under way is completed.

The Ceramic phase sites of Hora Mountain and Mphunzi Shelter both contain potsherds distributed through 1–2 ft of deposits and directly associated with lithic materials. Slag is also reported from Hora Mountain. Chowo has a Ceramic phase horizon overlying the dated Preceramic sample quoted above, and it in turn is covered by purely Iron Age deposits. The sherds from the Preceramic horizon are similar to those from the Early Iron Age settlement of Phopo Hill -dated to A.D. 295± 95 (SR-128). Evidently, the Stone Age–Iron Age contact in Malawi was quite as early as that in northern Zambia, and the Stone Age populations survived alongside the Iron Age settlements in a similar manner.

Associated fauna is available from Fingira Hill, and two burials are reported from the same deposits. Both individuals, as well as the skelelton from Hora Mountain (Wells 1957), are of short stature and are typical of the terminal Stone Age physical type, but metrical comparisons with more southerly skeletal populations must await publication of metrical data. Any further comment on the Malawi evidence at this stage of research would be premature.

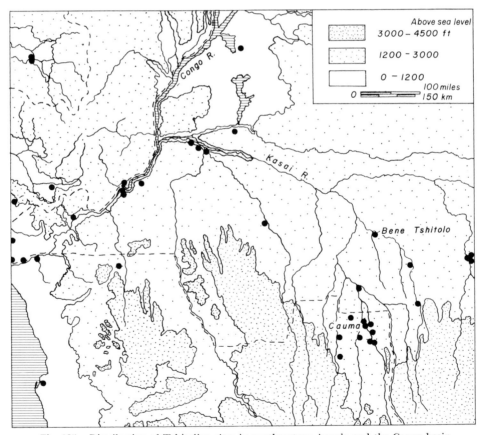

Fig. 135. Distribution of Tshitolian sites in northeastern Angola and the Congo basin.

THE STATUS OF THE
TSHITOLIAN INDUSTRY IN ANGOLA

Although this industry is really a cultural expression of the lower Congo basin, its presence in northeastern Angola nonetheless brings it within the geographical limits of the present study. Clark (1965, 1966) lists ten occurrences from northeastern Angola and three others from elsewhere in northern Angola (Fig. 135). Although two phases—a Lower and Upper Tshitolian—are postulated on the basis of collections taken from the sides of erosion gullies, no single site has yet provided sealed samples of each phase directly superimposed. Actually, only one site in this group has been excavated by Clark (1963), who suggests that the sample should be ascribed to the Lower Tshitolian on typological grounds. This important occurrence is at Cauma on the right bank of the Chiumbe River, where an apparently primary-context Tshitolian flaking scatter

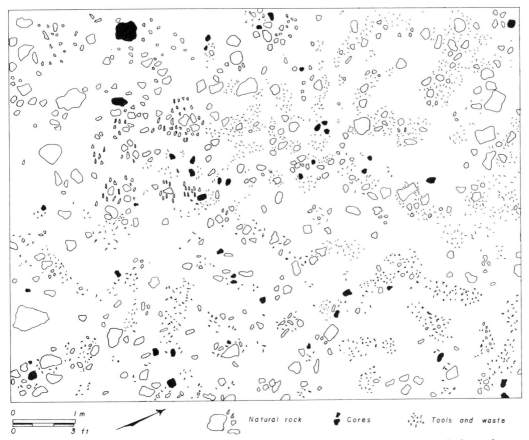

0 ═══ 1 m
0 ═══ 3 ft

Natural rock   Cores   Tools and waste

Fig. 136. Artifact scatter at Cauma, the only site reported to yield a sealed undisturbed sample of Tshitolian artifacts. (After Clark 1963.)

TABLE 59

Cauma Tool Types *a*

	Count	Percent
Hand-axes and hand-axe–choppers	9	2.3
Core choppers	3	0.8
Core axes		
bifacial long	11	2.8
bifacial short	20	5.1
unifacial long	9	2.3
unifacial short	10	2.5
fragments	13	3.3
Diminutive bifaces	3	0.8
Utilized flakes	13	3.3
Scrapers		
core	1	0.3
side-single	9	2.3
side-double	9	2.3
end-	18	4.6
hollow	23	5.8
Backed blades and flakes	5	1.3
Microliths	3	0.8
Petits tranchets		
single-edge retouch	91	23.2
double-edge retouch	124	31.5
Hammer or pestle stones	11	2.8
Anvil	1	0.3
Grindstones	4	1.0
Miscellaneous	2	0.5
Total:	**392**	99.9

a From Clark (1963).

was exposed below 1.5 m of redistributed sands. Below the artifact "floor" was another 1 m of sands, which capped the 10-m gravels and bench of the river. The flaking floor was excavated and plotted over a 6 by 8-m area (Fig. 136), and is thus only a sample of what was undoubtedly a much larger scatter. The exposed section revealed dense clusters of flakes, all of which are unrolled, but many show signs of fire cracking, presumably produced by the heating action of a bush fire that occurred shortly after the material was laid down. In places, the underlying gravels protrude upwards into the level of the "floor" and contain rolled, thickly patinated specimens that are tentatively attributed to an earlier occurrence. These are excluded from the analysis.

The Cauma excavation thus provides the only sealed, numerically undistorted sample of the northeastern Angolan Tshitolian industry. Clark's analysis reveals the composition given in Table 59. A total of 395 cores and 11,884 waste flakes and fragments was also recovered, but no charcoal or organic associations. Table 59 makes it abundantly clear that the Tshitolian differs in almost every respect from any known industry in the Wilton complex and should be regarded as belonging to a completely different cultural province. The other related collections from this area confirm this conclusion. Iondi and Lussaca contain additional types such as foliate and tanged points, with apparently larger numbers of backed blades, crescents, and large trapezium forms. Clark has suggested that Cauma may lack these elements because it represents a specialized workshop site, but the limited area of the floor exposed by excavation may be the real explanation for their absence from the sample. The existence of an Upper Tshitolian cannot be verified by any valid material from the area.

Although carbon-14 dates have been obtained from wood samples in the lower stream gravels (UCLA-171) 4700 ± 100 B.P., and from above the upper flats terrace (UCLA-167) 6840 ± 130 B.P., these should not be regarded as dependable dates for the Tshitolian since both samples were in fact taken from sterile deposits. Obviously systematic fieldwork on the Tshitolian has only just begun.

CONCLUSIONS AND OVERVIEW

Origins

It is now possible to state with some confidence that the technical origins of the Wilton complex are no longer to be sought in a vague entity previously called the "Second Intermediate." The term was used to imply a transitional stage in the prehistory of southern Africa during which Bambata-related industries acquired the techniques for making backed blades and backed crescents. These types, so it was thought, were increasingly preferred until eventually stone industries almost everywhere were dominated by them. Thus, the Wilton emerged by gradual evolution out of industries like the Howiesonspoort, Umguzan, and other entities now abandoned for want of adequate field data. The processes that caused this supposed evolution could not be investigated, but it was widely assumed that it took place at a fairly constant rate in all areas. This tacit agreement about a steady rate of lithic "evolution" is amusingly illustrated by remarks in several papers summarizing the so-called Later Stone Age. For some years now, new carbon-14 dates associated with Wilton or Oakhurst samples have been sourly greeted as "too old," although no evidence of contamination or admixture could be produced.

This chapter concludes that very few, if any, early dates for the Wilton complex are contaminated. What is needed is a revised interpretation of Wilton origins to accommodate the new evidence.

Undoubtedly, the Howiesonspoort groups who hunted on the Cape coastal plains 20,000 years ago were completely adept at making blunt-backed tools and produced a wide repertoire of shapes including crescents, straight-backed blades, curve-backed knives, trapeze forms, and obliquely backed pieces. Almost all of these are larger than any of the equivalent shapes found in a Coastal Wilton assemblage. However, the field data now at our disposal entirely support the hypothesis that all knowledge of these techniques had completely disappeared by about 16,000 B.C. and cannot be detected in this area again until their reintroduction (in diminutive forms) at about 6000 B.C. At this time the Oakhurst tool types are seen to dwindle via the early phase of the Wilton as microlithic types began to increase. The origins of the Coastal Wilton are not to be found in the Howiesonspoort sites.

Nor are the origins of the Matopan industry in Rhodesia to be found in the Umguzan since the Pomongwan, the local expression of the Oakhurst complex, can be shown to have intervened in this territory between about 13,000 and 6000 B.C. during which time no knowledge of backing techniques can be detected. Elsewhere, in the South African interior the Lockshoek industry precedes the Wilton during the same period, although the exact date of the first Wilton appearance has not yet been obtained. The so-called "Pre-Wilton" at Rose Cottage is a misnomer and contains no backed elements which might suggest a forerunner of the Interior Wilton.

In southern Zambia it is probable that a Pomongwan-like technology was practised immediately prior to the first appearance of the Zambian Wilton at perhaps 6000 B.C. although Makwe is the only shelter where this has been demonstrated.

However, in the denser subtropical woodland of northern Zambia the lithic technology between 14,000 and 7000 B.C. is fully microlithic and almost completely unlike the Oakhurst complex, which is its southern contemporary. The Nachikufan Phase I provides the only evidence for the persistence of a true microlithic technology during this period. By 7000 B.C. this had given rise to the Phase II situation, where convex chunk scrapers dominate the microlithic forms which are now best represented by backed crescents. This new combination of elements so commonly found in Phase IIA samples is broadly similar to that found in the Zambian Wilton, Pfupian, and the Early phase of the various Wilton industries to the south. Since the earliest dated appearance of the new microlithic technology in the Matopos, northeastern Cape, and southern Cape coast does not exceed 6000 B.C., some explanation of this time lag is required.

It now appears that the available field data may support the following hypothesis: the microlithic technology (which is simply one stage in the composite hafting of stone armatures in arrow shafts) was favored by hunter–gatherers living in the northern Zambian woodland savannah during the period when all the (presently studied) territory to the south was being utilized by groups without any knowledge of these techniques. In archaeological terms this means that the Nachikufan Phase I and the Oakhurst complex are broad contemporaries. After about 7000 B.C. there is evidence for interaction between these two areas, and it is not unreasonable to assume that the appearance of abundant scrapers in the Nachikufan Phase IIA is at least partly the result of contact with Oakhurst technology. In return, the microliths, particularly backed crescents, were adopted by groups in southern Zambia and Rhodesia, and the new techniques are found alongside the Oakhurst tool kit on the southern Cape coast by 6000 B.C. Thus, the Early phase of the Wilton may represent a period of dispersal southwards of microlithic elements into the waning Oakhurst complex.

In the Classic phase of the various Wilton industries microliths (often made of locally scarce crystalline rocks) become more numerous at the expense of larger Oakhurst-related scraper types. Again, the typological shift occurs earlier in northern Zambia than in the south. The Nachikufan Phase IIB emerges between 4000 and 3000 B.C., the Zambian Wilton between 3000 and 2000 B.C., the Matopan at about 2000 B.C., the Interior Wilton at about 2000 B.C., and the Coastal Wilton between 3000 and 2000 B.C. Of course, the processes which caused these technical changes in each region may not have been identical, but again a southward diffusion of ideas may have been partly responsible.

Another problem intimately related to the origins of the Wilton is the actual physical movements of peoples during this period. Unfortunately, no biometric studies of the relevant skeletal populations have been aimed specifically at this problem, so that remarkably few skeletons can be directly compared. However, basic craniometric comparisons have shown that the Cape Coastal Wilton and Zambian Wilton skeletons display a similar range of head shapes, but both differ markedly from the Oakhurst populations at Matjes River. Before any final conclusions can be drawn about the existence of Oakhurst and Wilton "races," more material must be recovered and analyzed. If a southward migration of a mainly dolichocephalic racial stock brought the Wilton into South Africa, adequate supporting evidence for such an event is still lacking.

Iron Age Contacts

Evidently, most areas of southern Africa were occupied by Wilton-related groups by about 1000 B.C. with the interesting exception of the Transvaal and possibly pockets of the northwestern Cape, Botswana, and perhaps the southern Cape coast. After about 300 B.C. the Coastal and Interior Wilton of South Africa begin localized changes in design that cause them to look less and less alike. The Developed phase in each area is partly related to shifts in raw material usage, but the real underlying cause of these changes remains to be investigated. In Rhodesia and Zambia, no such developments have been found during this period. Finally, evidence of the southward movement of the earliest Iron Age groups is reflected in the Ceramic phase of the whole Wilton complex. Potsherds, and sometimes other bartered goods such as metal objects and glass beads, appear in the Nachikufan III and Zambian Wilton between A.D. 700 and 800. Still earlier contacts may have been established to the south where country less hostile to Iron Age stockherders was rapidly colonized. Thus, potsherds appear in Wilton deposits at A.D. 200 at Makwe and 20 B.C. at Calders Cave.

Although Iron Age groups were present in Swaziland as early as A.D. 400, contact with the Wilton may not have occurred until later when the Iron Age population had increased in the South African interior. Thus, sherds do not appear at Rose Cottage until A.D. 850. On the southern Cape coast, however, a characteristic local ware appears for the first time during the first century A.D. This occurrence is almost certainly linked to the early penetration of South West Africa by potmaking peoples for which no adequate archaeological evidence exists. Metal occurs in a Wilton context at Numas Shelter at A.D. 80, and an Iron Age occupation in Eros Shelter, Klein Windhoek, is dated (GrN-5297) to 1745 ± 35 B.P. or A.D. 105.

The survival of groups practicing a Wilton technology into the historical period still remains in some doubt. In Zambia and Rhodesia all traces of this tradition were obliterated by the spread of Iron Age material culture, which extended even to the pockets of hunter–gatherer *Batwa,* who resisted absorptions into adjacent Iron Age communities. Only De Hangen Shelter in the southwestern Cape mountains presents an undoubted Ceramic Wilton industry dated to A.D. 1600, perhaps just overlapping with the first Dutch settlement at Kaap de Goede Hoop in 1652. Whether the troublesome *Bosjesmannen* who raided this settlement from the mountains still practiced Wilton flaking methods is impossible to determine from the extant documents dealing with these encounters.

ROCK ART AND THE WILTON COMPLEX

In the previous chapter it was noted that no example of the very abundant rock art in southern Africa can be reliably associated with samples from the Oakhurst complex. At that time red ocher was ground with stone mullers, and human burials were occasionally coated with this material.

With the appearance of the Wilton, several reliable associations between artifact samples and rock paintings and engravings become evident. To establish rock art associations requires special conditions and sometimes ingenious methods of investigation. Most obvious is the recovery of painted or engraved slabs or cave wall surfaces actually covered by Wilton samples. Alternately, a fallen roof slab with paintings on its undersurface may cap a Wilton deposit, indicating that the paintings were executed during Wilton times—or earlier if another industry underlies the Wilton. The most frequent association, although less reliable, is the occurrence of rock art on the walls and roof of a cave or shelter that contains a Wilton industry and no other.

Of the sites discussed in this chapter, the following have yielded one of these associations:

Wall buried by deposits: Chifubwa Stream, Nakapapula, De Hangen
Painted slab in deposits: Matjes River
Painted wall with only Wilton in the deposits: Nachikufu, Nsalu, Riversmead, Blydefontein, Wilton

Numerous other sites contain rock paintings, but these deposits also contain other industries besides those of the Wilton complex—either earlier or later ones. Doubtless, many of these paintings were in fact executed by Wilton groups but methods have still to be developed by which the archaeologist can determine exactly which paintings are to be ascribed to each horizon. Since some ambiguity exists about all the other painted sites, they cannot be included in the present list.

Rock art studies in southern Africa have only recently acquired adequate descriptive and analytical procedures pioneered by Maggs (1967) and admirably adapted to rock-engraving sites by Fock (1970). But the new techniques have not yet been widely applied, although excellent systematic surveys are in progress (for example, Vinnicombe 1967). So vast is the descriptive literature on this subject that it must of necessity fall outside the scope of the present work. Several major works including Summers (1959), Willcox (1956, 1963), C. K. Cooke (1969), Lee and Woodhouse (1971), and Rudner and Rudner (1970) may be consulted for various discussions of this material and full bibliographies. Although of enormous potential use to the prehistorian, the bulk of this vast corpus of material cannot be adequately dated, and very few recorded rock-art sites have been excavated, so that their cultural associations are largely unknown.

Of the few Wilton complex sites given above remarkably little has been published on the rock art. At Nakapapula and the Nachikufan sites a distinctive set of abstract motifs occurs. These include dots, lines, and gridlike patterns, together with rare monochrome animal and human outlines. One important painting at Nachikufu depicts a man carrying a bow and arrow. Red, purple, and black are the dominant colors, but the exact identification of pigments is unknown. An abstract engraving occurs at Chifubwa Stream.

Although most of the paintings in the Matopos area are almost certainly of Wilton age, no firm associations have been established yet. These are succinctly discussed by C. K. Cooke (1957a, 1959), who points out that not only are a wide variety of animals depicted on the granite walls of the caves, but human figures provide abundant information on details of dress, utensils, bags, weapons, decorations, hunting methods, social or ritual behavior, and possibly totemic beliefs. Undoubtedly the paintings of Rhodesia are richer and more varied in content, style, approach, and choice of colors than any sites in Zambia.

Still further south on the Orange River, sites contain both naturalistic and abstract paintings. At Riversmead, a group of white monochrome antelope are overpainted by a red finger-painted "grid," which may hint at some stylistic change during the Wilton occupation. Grids are also present at Blydefontein and many other local (undated) shelters among which are a few which overlie naturalistic polychrome figures of animals. D. W. Phillipson (personal communication) has demonstrated that grids in northern Zambia are persistently linked with the Iron Age contact, and it is not unreasonable to assume that they are linked with the Ceramic phase in the Orange River as well, although what the significance of these forms may be is beyond our grasp.

Finally, the coastal sites are not all described in detail. Animals, human figures, and human handprints abound at both Wilton and De Hangen, but numerical analyses have not been released. The Matjes River specimen is a painted gravestone with blurred human figures only (Meiring 1953).

Whether or not Wilton groups were responsible for the mass of engraved sites in the South African interior remains to be proved. Although these sites are frequently quoted as being of non-Wilton origin, the extent of Wilton penetration into most of this area is still entirely unknown. Such statements must therefore be regarded as premature.

9

The Smithfield Complex of the South African Interior

The earliest Iron Age groups to appear in the archaeological record of southern Africa apparently had little effect on the material culture of adjacent hunter–gatherers. No doubt during the first 800 years or so of the Christian era such Iron Age communities were relatively small and sparsely scattered. Under such conditions, it may be reasonable to conclude that their pastoral and agricultural activities made scarcely any impact on the ecological balance of their habitat. Presumably, they passed unnoticed by the majority of the thinly scattered hunter–gatherer population, whose food sources were in no way jeopardized and whose daily round remained undisturbed by the appearance of fugitives from Iron Age conflicts. Only the presence of potsherds and rare metal items with the Ceramic Wilton betrays any knowledge of their presence. Obviously, some indigenous groups maintained direct bartering relationships with the Iron Age population, whereas more distant groups acquired pottery (and perhaps potmaking techniques) through contacts with neighboring Late Wilton areas.

Of course, this view of social relations in the first millenium A.D. is a gross overgeneralization that obscures many regional changes. These are, at present, only dimly perceived in the archaeological record. Probably the most important single factor during this period was a steady growth of the Iron Age population. Such growth can only be inferred since the evidence for numbers, size, and density of Iron Age settlements in Zambia, Rhodesia, and South Africa is still being gathered. (Iron Age archaeology in Mozambique, Angola, and South-West Africa is still virtually nonexistent.) A slow but steady population increase within the farming communities is suggested by the expansion and increased complexity of the great stone-wall complexes of Rhodesia and the Transvaal, of which Zimbabwe and Mapungubwe are the best known. Also, in southern Zambia the characteristic village-mound accumulations become steadily larger and more numerous. In all these regions changes in ceramic styles and metalworking techniques hint at population movements. By the end of the first millenium A.D. it is likely that the Iron Age populations of Zambia, Rhodesia, and the Transvaal were larger and occupied more favorable habitats than the Stone Age hunter–gatherers. Whereas numerous bands of the latter survived in so-called "marginal" habitats (with resources not suited to pastoralism and farming), their material culture became increasingly influenced by Iron Age elements.

During the first half of the second millenium A.D. the remnant Stone Age groups continued to be absorbed by the expanding Iron Age economy, except in those areas which were hostile to farming. Typical of such areas were high mountain ranges, swampland, and closed forest belts with excessively heavy tsetse-fly infestations. After about A.D. 1500, the archaeological record of these northerly territories is entirely dominated by the Iron Age, and many of the caves and rock shelters previously occupied by Nachikufan or Ceramic Wilton hunter–gatherers are either abandoned or filled with Iron Age debris. These include potsherds, metal objects, iron slag fragments, glass beads (traded from the eastern African coast), and abundant faunal remains including relatively scarce bones of domestic livestock. Whereas this stratigraphic pattern holds good for the cave deposits of Malawi, Zambia, and Rhodesia, it does not apply to the Stone Age record of the South African interior during the same period. Here, Stone Age groups survived longer and their lithic technology displays clear Post-Wilton developments peculiar to different regions.

TERMINOLOGY AND EARLY RESEARCH

The term "Smithfield" has a long and confused history in South African archaeology. It is used in this chapter to describe *only* that group of industries that postdate the Wilton complex of the South African interior. It has, however, been used in a far wider sense by earlier workers using very inadequate field data. Its continued use, therefore, requires some brief justification.

Smithfield is a small town in the southern Orange Free State. In the late nineteenth century a heavily selected surface collection of lydianite artifacts was made by a Dr. Kannemeyer (1890) from the banks of the town "drain," actually a small stream flowing through the town. His collection, now housed in the South African Museum, contains several Orangian specimens, numerous typical Oakhurst scrapers and abundant endscrapers, side- and endscrapers, and scarcer types without any trace of the patination found on the Orangian and Oakhurst groups. The collection is obviously mixed, and the continued use of the term "Smithfield" may rightly be challenged on these grounds alone. It is, however, so entrenched in the literature that its removal may do more harm than good. It is retained here for historical reasons and not because Smithfield provides an adequate "type" sample.

Subsequent use of the term has been critically examined by Inskeep (1967) and Sampson (1969a) and will be only briefly recounted here: C. van Riet Lowe made numerous selected surface collections from the Riet River survey in the 1920s, during which he isolated two industries he thought to be evolutionary phases of the Smithfield industry. Later he published (Goodwin and van Riet Lowe 1929) detailed descriptions of the range of tool types found in three "variations" of the Smithfield industry. These were:

Smithfield A: type site, Lockshoek Farm, Orange Free State
Smithfield B: type site, Avalon Farm, Orange Free State
Smithfield C: type site, Ventershoek Shelter, Orange Free State

"Smithfield A" and "B" both occurred in the Orange Free State and northern Cape, whereas "Smithfield C" was restricted to the foothills of Lesotho and the eastern Orange Free State. Other regional categories were proposed: "Smithfield N" by Goodwin (1930) and van Riet Lowe (1936) for northern Natal; "Smithfield P" by van Riet Lowe (1936); and "Coastal Smithfield" by van Riet Lowe (1946) and Schofield (1936a) for the southeastern coastline. Not one of these terms was represented by a sealed unselected artifact sample recovered under controlled conditions. It is inevitable that the term came to be used in all parts of South Africa by amateur and professional archaeologists alike. It is hardly surprising that the chronological ordering of Smithfield "variations" have become the subject of several conflicting reports, as have the stratigraphic relations between Smithfield and Wilton industries (see Table 60).

Such conflicting results are the consequence of inadequate definitions and subjective comparisons between assemblages. The differences of opinion reflected in this table can be readily resolved by numerical analysis of unselected samples. Recent work suggests that van Riet Lowe's "Smithfield A" is a local regional

TABLE 60

Proposed Sequences of Smithfield Samples

Sites	Orange Free State surface collections (Goodwin and van Riet Lowe 1929)	Matjes River (Louw 1960)	Oakhurst and Glentyre (Goodwin 1938)	Transvaal sites (Mason 1962a)
Later	Smithfield C	Smithfield B	Wilton	Later Smithfield
	Smithfield B	Wilton	Smithfield C	Middle Smithfield
Earlier	Smithfield A	Smithfield A	Smithfield B	Earlier Smithfield

expression of the Oakhurst complex—a term proposed for the first time in Chapter 7, where "Smithfield A" is referred to the Lockshoek industry within the Oakhurst complex. Available carbon-14 dates suggest that this industry disappeared after about 7000 B.C. It therefore has no obvious connections with the Smithfield B or C, which do not appear in the Smithfield region until about A.D. 1600.

In this chapter, only the labels B–C, and N will be retained.

REGIONAL SUBDIVISIONS OF THE COMPLEX

The groups given in Table 61 are tentatively proposed as regional subdivisions of the Smithfield complex. The sites are mapped in Fig. 137. Inevitably, most usable samples have been taken from the eastern half of the country, although many more "Smithfield" occurrences have been reported without adequate descriptions. No industrial terminology has been proposed because too few comparative analyses have been undertaken between regions.

"SMITHFIELD B" SITES OF THE ORANGE RIVER VALLEY AND ADJACENT AREAS

In the area of the Verwoerd Dam some 60 miles southwest of Smithfield, a series of 4 excavated samples and 12 large surface occurrences have been analyzed. Numerous other surface sites have been plotted, but could not be salvaged and are now flooded by the Verwoerd and Vanderkloof Dams. Their distribution is mapped in Fig. 138. All samples were published (Sampson 1967b, 1970) under the provisional term: "Later Stone Age Phase 6." The stratigraphic position of this industry above the Wilton is beyond dispute in this area as it overlies the Ceramic phase at Zaayfontein, Glen Elliott Shelter, Glen Elliott Crevice, and Holmsgrove.

TABLE 61

Regional Subdivisions of the Smithfield Complex

Brandberg, South-West Africa	Northern Cape	Transvaal	Eastern Cape– Orange Free State	Lesotho–Natal highlands	Smithfield N
Brandberg shelters	Wonderwerk	Magabeng	Zaayfontein	Moshebis	Holley Shelter
Surface sites	Witkrans	Olieboompoort	Glen Elliott	Cathkin Peak	Warmbad
	Little Witkrans	Pietkloof	Holmsgrove	Giant's Castle	Nqutu
	Surface sites	Groenvlei	Ventershoek	Belleview?	Pigeon Rocks
		Munro	Orange Free State	Brotherton	Muden
		Matluassi (Dobazanga)	surface sites		New Amalfi
		North Brabant	Tafelberg Hall		Karkloof
		Bushman Rock	Nquamakwe		
			Ezibugdwini		
			Oudefontein		

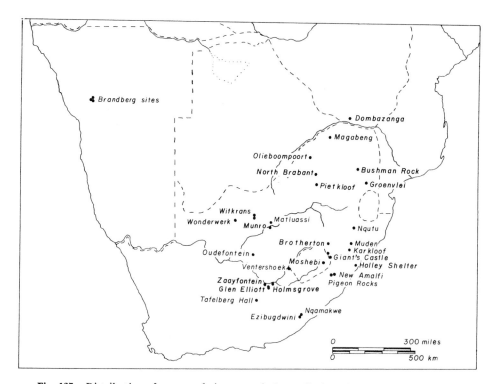

Fig. 137. Distribution of excavated sites tentatively ascribed to the Smithfield complex.

Its typological characters are given in Tables 62 and 63; the characteristic stone tools are illustrated in Fig. 139. The four excavated samples were associated with fragmentary cylindrical bone points, numerous bone flakes, ostrich eggshell beads, glass, and metal beads. Rare tobacco pipe bowls of soapstone, clay, and sandstone were also encountered, as well as a clay cattle figurine. Metal fragments were also present.

All sites contained abundant sherds derived from a standardized bowl form with a flat bottom and vertical walls. Sherds are relatively thick, very poorly and unevenly fired, and tempered with scarce grit or broken sherds and abundant grass stems. The exterior walls are frequently decorated by parallel, but poorly controlled, lines of stamp impressions. This friable ware is easily distinguished from the local Wilton Ceramic phase bowls, the sherds of which are generally much thinner (Fig. 140) and better fired.

These Smithfield samples also differ from the Ceramic Wilton in lithic typology: the small backed microlithic elements are very rare or completely absent. In those sites where organic preservation is sufficient (especially the Glen Elliott sites), there is a very marked increase in cylindrical bone point fragments in the Smithfield layers. Presumably the small stone barbs were replaced by the more simple bone arrow armatures at this time.

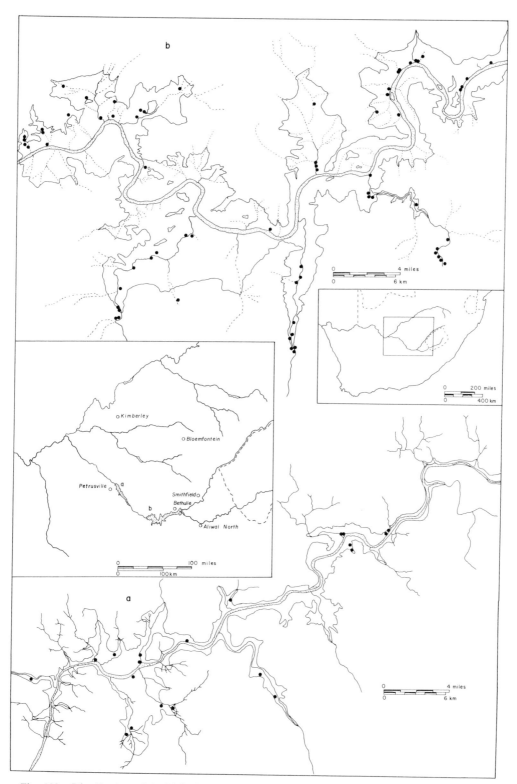

Fig. 138. Distribution of Smithfield B sites in the two dam floodbasins of the Orange River scheme.

TABLE 62

Analysis of Smithfield B Samples from the Orange River

Tool types	Vaalbank 9	Zeekoegat 1	Evergreen 12	Evergreen 15A	Evergreen 22	Vlakdrif 1	Vlakdrif 2	Vlakdrif 3	Schalkwykskraal 1	Schalkwykskraal 14	Schalkwykskraal 24C	Inhoek 8	Rolfontein 22
Endscrapers	23.0	14.0	15.2	6.5	16.8	22.8	25.5	13.2	24.8	8.5	9.3	19.8	5.6
Side- and endscrapers	26.3	23.1	18.3	7.6	17.6	23.5	23.1	19.9	28.5	19.6	18.8	19.5	10.1
Small endscrapers	13.7	5.4	6.0	0.55	5.6	9.1	8.2	4.0	4.75	2.8	5.6	6.4	1.2
Core hammers	3.1	3.4	3.4	4.9	1.7	10.6	6.4	0.7	9.5	2.0	1.9	1.4	3.5
Convex scrapers	3.4	4.0	5.7	4.9	16.8	9.1	3.6	11.6	6.7	10.6	4.8	6.7	10.7
Borers	2.4	0.7	1.2	1.1	3.4	1.5	—	0.4	—	2.5	1.9	3.5	1.2
Backed adzes	0.4	2.7	1.8	1.1	1.7	—	4.1	3.3	—	1.8	1.6	2.7	2.1
Pebble adzes	2.5	2.0	0.2	2.3	—	0.8	—	0.7	2.9	1.8	—	0.6	1.1
Miscellaneous trimmed blades	2.1	6.4	3.1	12.0	1.7	3.0	4.5	2.2	2.9	7.0	5.0	2.6	7.1
Miscellaneous trimmed flakes	13.3	34.2	35.6	54.8	27.0	10.6	19.1	40.0	13.1	37.1	49.0	24.6	46.5
Outils écaillés	0.7	1.0	0.75	1.1	1.7	2.3	—	1.5	1.9	0.8	0.5	2.5	1.8
Small convex scrapers	2.6	1.0	4.1	—	3.4	4.5	2.7	2.6	—	3.3	0.8	6.2	6.0
Straight-backed points	—	0.7	0.45	—	—	—	—	0.4	0.9	1.0	—	0.52	0.3
Backed crescents	—	0.3	1.2	—	—	—	—	—	—	—	—	0.21	0.9

Curve-backed blades	0.6	0.7	0.27	—	—	—	—	—	—	—	—	0.12	—
Concave-backed points and fragments	0.3	—	0.07	—	—	—	—	—	—	—	—	0.21	0.3
Grindstones	2.1	—	—	—	—	—	—	—	—	0.8	0.3	0.3	0.3
Upper grinders (oblique edge)	0.5	—	—	—	—	—	0.45	—	0.9	—	—	0.08	—
Pallette fragments	0.1	—	—	—	—	—	—	—	—	0.25	—	0.25	0.3
Grooved stones	0.1	—	—	—	—	—	—	—	0.9	—	—	—	—
Bored stones	0.2	—	—	—	—	—	0.45	—	—	—	—	0.12	—
Reamers	2.2	0.7	1.4	1.1	3.4	0.9	—	0.4	1.9	0.8	0.3	1.3	1.5
Miscellaneous hammerstones	0.6	—	—	1.1	—	—	—	—	—	0.5	—	0.3	—
Burins and gouges	—	—	—	—	2.3	0.8	—	—	—	—	—	—	—
Sample totals:	**1687**	**299**	**1327**	**183**	**119**	**132**	**220**	**278**	**107**	**399**	**376**	**2425**	**336**
Core types													
Microblade cores	9.3	7.0	4.5	—	—	—	1.6	(1)	—	8.5	(1)	9.0	6.3
Other microcores	5.1	5.6	7.1	(2)	(2)	—	1.6	(3)	—	22.0	—	21.5	25.4
Blade cores	4.2	18.4	7.7	—	—	—	9.7	(4)	—	3.4	—	4.7	6.3
Single plain-platform	20.0	19.8	16.8	(4)	(18)	—	45.3	(2)	(3)	15.2	(5)	7.7	11.1
Single prepared-platform	15.5	1.5	11.0	(1)	(1)	—	8.0	(1)	—	8.5	(3)	5.2	6.3
Adjacent-platform	15.5	14.1	18.6	(5)	(6)	—	24.1	(2)	(3)	16.9	(8)	9.4	12.7
Miscellaneous cores	30.3	33.7	34.1	(6)	(1)	—	9.7	(5)	(1)	25.5	(5)	42.5	31.8
Totals:	**334**	**71**	**155**	**(18)**	**(28)**		**62**	**(19)**	**(7)**	**59**	**(22)**	**233**	**63**

[a] Those values in parentheses represent counts, not percentages.

TABLE 63

Agate and Jasper Tools and Cores from Various Smithfield B Sites from the Orange River

Sites	Agate and jasper tools (%)	Agate and jasper cores (%)	Total agate and jasper (%)
Vaalbank 9	8.4	15.3	9.5
Zeekoegat 1	7.7	31.0	12.2
Evergreen 12	6.8	23.0	8.5
Evergreen 22	6.7	—	5.8
Vlakdrif 1	5.3	1.7	6.3
Vlakdrif 2	2.3	1.6	2.1
Vlakdrif 3	6.6	15.8	7.2
Schalkwykskraal 1	0.9	—	0.9
Schalkwykskraal 14	9.8	33.6	12.9
Schalkwykskraal 24C	0.6	—	0.5
Inhoek 8	11.0	54.1	14.6
Rollfontein 22	11.9	58.7	19.3

The two available carbon-14 dates for the earliest levels of the Smithfield B in the area are as follows:

Glen Elliott Shelter:

Level III	SR-121	90 ± 90 b.p. (a.d. 1860)
	GX-1295	235 ± 30 b.p. (a.d. 1715)

They suggest that the industry appeared in this part of the Orange River valley during the seventeenth century A.D. and it therefore belongs to the protohistoric period. As no evidence exists for an Iron Age incursion into the valley, there can be little doubt that the so-called *Bosjesmannen* or Bushmen (first encountered by white explorers and migrant farmers) were the makers of the Smithfield B artifacts. A drawing of these people by Charles Bell in 1834 (Fig. 141) reveals several pieces of equipment made of materials that have not survived in the archaeological record. These include leather headgear, sandals, skirts, a reed mat used as a windbreak, quivers, arrows, bows, hunting spears (with heads of unknown materials), large (metal?) earrings, and a pipe.

Although the Smithfield hunter–gatherer population was severely reduced by European punitive expeditions, the majority probably was absorbed by the white farmsteads that proliferated in the valley during the early nineteenth century. Prior to their absorption (and their disappearance from the rock shelters) a short period of contact between the two groups is reflected in the uppermost layers of the shelter deposits, which contain tools of bottle glass, wire, and metal within the Smithfield B assemblage.

Only very few rock paintings can be ascribed to Smithfield B with any certainty. Glen Elliott Shelter contains finger-painted grids in red ocher and

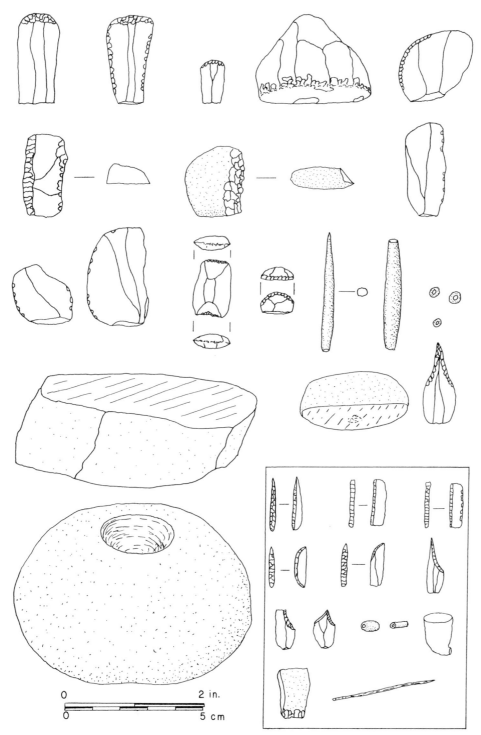

Fig. 139. Tool types of the Smithfield B in the Orange River valley. The items in the lower left group are very rare and occur in only a few samples (backed microliths, glass beads, bottle-glass scrapers, soapstone pipe bowls, wire arrowpoints).

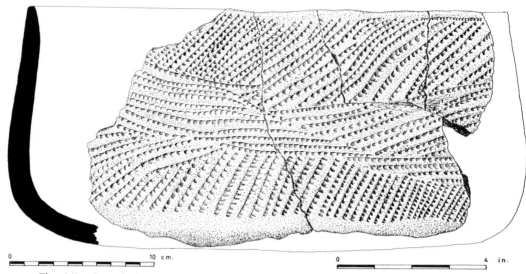

Fig. 140. Ceramic bowl type associated with Smithfield B sites at the eastern end of the Orange River scheme area and the Smithfield C of Ventershoek Shelter.

Fig. 141. Redrawn from a sketch by Charles Bell in 1834. Makers of the Smithfield B in a rock shelter to the south of the Orange River scheme area. Several items of material culture are recorded here that do not survive in the archaeological record: reed screen, quivers, bows, spears, arrows, sandals, caps, cloaks, and earrings.

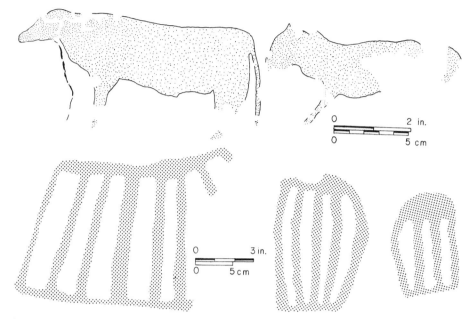

Fig. 142. Rock paintings in red ocher, firmly associated with the Smithfield B at Glen Elliott Shelter.

amorphous animals, one of which has a lead tied around the neck and may represent a domestic cow. Numerous other shelters in the area contain "grid" paintings, and rare representations of domestic animals, possibly also dating to this period (Fig. 142).

Historical accounts make it clear that European-owned domestic livestock formed part of the "Bushmen" diet, but no bones of such animals have been recovered from Smithfield B deposits. The dietary range reflected in the associated fauna shows little difference from that of the preceding Ceramic Wilton, comprising small mammals, reptiles, birds, amphibians, fish, crabs, mollusks, and ostrich eggs. It is obvious from historical accounts that large game animals including hippo were eaten at this time, but again, no archaeological evidence for this or the vegetable component of the diet has survived.

Some 80 miles south of this area, Tafelberg Hall shelter excavated by Hewitt (1931a) would have provided a more reliable "type" sample than the surface scatter chosen by van Riet Lowe. Hewitt's material includes the characteristic pottery, bone work, beads, and metal fragments. Several paintings including grids, circles, dots, animals, and humans occur on the walls and on a fallen slab in the deposit. The associated fauna included the same variety listed above plus some larger species such as warthog, zebra, and hartebeest. Plant materials included a small monocotolydon root and corm sheaths of a small iridaceous plant.

Still farther south, Laidler (1933, 1934) describes excavated samples from the Transkei region that clearly relate to the Smithfield B. Horizon I at Nqamakwe Shelter C overlies the Developed Wilton; the stone artifacts include abundant endscraper forms, core hammers, and no backed microliths; glass beads, stamp-impressed potsherds, and bone points were also recovered. At Nqamakwe Cave B the same association of materials overlies a thick basal tufa. Here the Smithfield assemblage also contains wooden pegs, a fire drill, and pierced mollusk orna-ments. The associated fauna is similar to that of the Orange River shelters. One important feature of Nqamakwe Cave B is that the potsherds were found only in the top layers of horizon I. This would suggest the presence of a Preceramic Smithfield horizon, not found in the Orange River area. A similar situation ex-ists at Ezibugdwini Cave: horizons 1–2 containing a typical Smithfield B lithic assemblage with bone work and pottery caps the sequence; horizon 3 is a 3-inch thick sterile hearth; horizon 4 contains endscraper forms and no trace of pottery or backed microliths; Horizon 5 contains a Developed Wilton assemblage. Thus, the Smithfield B is preceded by a Preceramic Smithfield phase in horizon 4. Farnden's (1966) small excavations at New Amalfi in Natal may represent a similar Preceramic phase. Unfortunately, very little numerical evidence has been presented, and the published Transkei typologies cannot be compared directly with those of the Orange River sites. Further excavations will be needed in this area before the presence of a "Preceramic Smithfield" can be fully confirmed.

To the north of the Orange River, only Humphreys and Maggs' (1970) work at Oudefontein is sufficiently detailed to allow comparisons here. A surface scat-ter of artifacts was collected from among a group of burial cairns. Artifact analy-sis shows close affinities with the Smithfield B of the Orange River sites. Pot-sherds, bone work, and glass beads were also associated. The site provides the only plausible association between human skeletal remains and the Smithfield. Two adult skeletons were found in flexed positions in shallow graves covered with large stones. On the skull of Burial I were found a flat copper pendant, an os-trich eggshell bead headband, and fragments of hair matted with specularite.

Another probable Smithfield B burial is one from Eagle's Nest on the Modder River, where van Riet Lowe (1926) reported a crouched adult burial excavated through a very dense surface site (Fig. 143). A complete (undescribed) pot rested near the feet, and an ostrich eggshell bead necklace was draped around the neck. Unfortunately, no metrical studies have been carried out on any of the skeletal material, and we may only assume that they represent the so-called "Bushman" population of the South African interior.

Actually, the distribution of reported Smithfield B surface sites is far more ex-tensive than that shown in Fig. 137 (page 376), but no analytical data have been presented with the original reports. Figure 144 maps the generalized infor-mation on surface sites from Fock (1965) and Goodwin and van Riet Lowe (1929), combined with unpublished distributions from the Transkei and eastern Cape. The westerly extension of similar sites remains unknown.

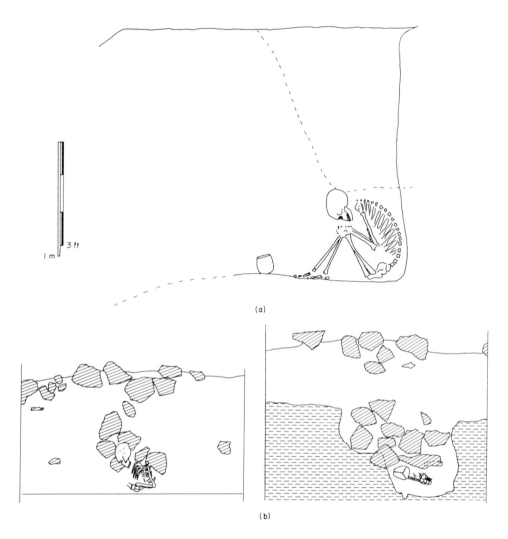

Fig. 143. Sections of burial pits through surface scatters of Smithfield B material: (a) Eagle's Nest, Riet River; (b) Oudefontein.

Plotted on this same map are the sites originally referred to as "Smithfield C" by van Riet Lowe (Goodwin and van Riet Lowe 1929). Examinations and analysis of the type site, Ventershoek (Sampson 1970) has confirmed van Riet Lowe's opinion. This "variation" simply reflects an adaptation of the Smithfield B technology to a new set of raw materials including small igneous pebbles and poor-quality lydianite found in the Caledon River valley. Any use of the term "Smithfield C" outside the area is invalid. The Ventershoek assemblage contains more smaller tools, but otherwise resembles the Smithfield B of the Orange

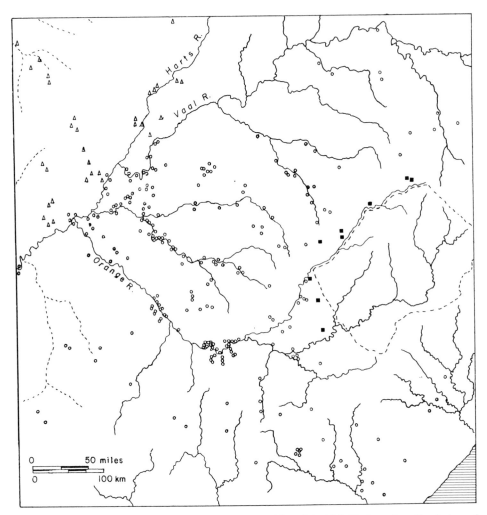

Fig. 144. Distribution of all available recorded localities of Smithfield sites after Goodwin and van Riet Lowe (1929), Sampson (1970), Fock (1965), and unpublished records. Smithfield C sites (squares) are restricted to the Caledon Valley. The industry in the Harts Valley has not been adequately described.

River in all details (Fig. 145). Since the eastern Orange Free State and Lesotho foothills presented suitable environments for migrant pastoralists, the Smithfield population in this area was in direct conflict with intrusive Iron Age cattle keepers, who are depicted on the walls of Ventershoek and many other unpublished shelters (Fig. 146). Frequently, direct conflicts between the two groups are depicted, battles and cattle raids forming a recurrent theme.

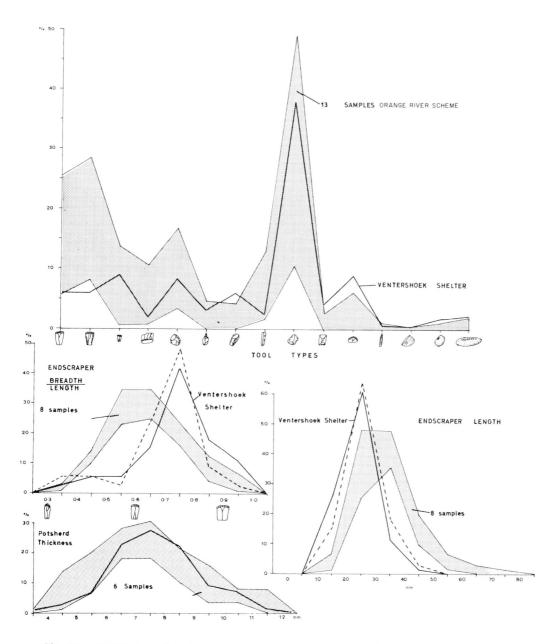

Fig. 145. Distribution of tool types, endscraper measurements, and potsherd thickness of the Smithfield C at Ventershoek Shelter compared with the minimum–maximum range for Smithfield B sites in the Orange River scheme area. Tool types (left to right): endscraper, side- and endscraper, small endscraper, core hammer, convex scraper, borer, backed adze, utilized blade, utilized flake, *outil écaillé*, small convex scraper, double-backed point, slate palette fragment, hammerstone, grindstone.

387

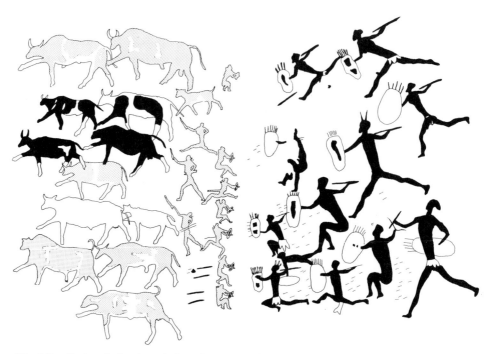

Fig. 146. Rock painting in a shelter about 60 yards east of the Ventershoek Shelter. Diminutive red figures (probably the makers of the Smithfield C) are driving off with sticks a herd of black, white, and red cattle evidently stolen from the black figures on the right, who are carrying typical Nguni shields and short spears. These individuals are advancing into a rain of arrows that have made contact with at least one of their members, who is lying down. A rear guard of small red men are firing into the oncoming Nguni warriors. This is an eloquent document of the conflict situation between terminal Smithfield groups and expanding Iron Age cattle keepers.

Another adaptation of the Smithfield B technology to cherty and crystalline raw materials occurred in the northwestern group of sites mapped in Fig. 146. The excavated samples from Wonderwerk (Malan and Wells 1943), Witkrans, and Little Witkrans (Peabody 1954). In all these (unanalyzed) samples the end-scrapers are notably smaller than those from Smithfield B sites in the Orange Free State and Karroo, where lydianite is the dominant raw material.

SMITHFIELD SITES IN THE TRANSVAAL

Mason (1962a) presented a distribution of "Later Smithfield" samples in the Transvaal that closely resemble the Smithfield B to the south. Only a few of these have been published in any detail: Olieboompoort Bed 3 and Magabeng

TABLE 64

Artifacts from Various Transvaal Smithfield Sites

	Olieboom-poort (Bed 3)	Magabeng (Bed 1)	Munro (AC 200)	North Brabant (stratum)	Bushman Rock (Layers 1–2)	Pietkloof	Groenvlei	Dombazanga (0–4 in.)
Endscrapers	X	X	X	X	X	X	—	X
Side- and endscrapers	X	X	X	X	—	X	—	X
Small endscrapers	X	X	X	X	X	X	—	X
Core hammers	X	X	X	X	X	X	—	X
Convex scrapers	?	?	X	X	X	X	—	X
Borers	?	?	?	—	—	—	—	—
Backed adzes	?	?	X	X	—	?	—	—
Trimmed flakes and blades	X	X	X	X	X	X	—	X
Small convex scrapers	X	?	X	X	X	X	—	X
Outils écaillés	X	X	X	X	X	X	—	X
Grindstones	X	—	X	X	X	X	—	—
Grooved stones	X	—	X	X	—	X	—	—
Bored stones	—	—	X	—	X	X	—	—
Bone awls	X	X	—	X	—	X	—	X
Cylindrical bone points	X	X	—	X	X	X	—	—
Ostrich eggshell beads	X	—	—	X	—	X	—	X
Pendants	X	—	—	X	X	X	—	—
Glass beads	—	—	—	X	—	X	X	X
Stamp-impressed pottery	—	—	—	X	X	X	X	X
Plain pottery	—	—	X	X	X	—	—	X
Metal fragments	—	—	—	X	—	—	—	—
Raw material in decreasing frequency	Agate Quartz Chalcecony	Quartz	Chalcedony Jasper Agate Quartz	Chert Quartz	(No data)	?	?	?Quartz ?Lydianite

389

(Mason 1962a), and Munro (Mason 1969a, b). Other described samples come from North Brabant Shelter (Schoonraad and Beaumont 1968), Bushman Rock Shelter (Louw 1969), Pietkloof (Mason 1951), Groenvlei (Malan and van Niekerk 1955), and Dombazanga (K. R. Robinson 1964), which is just north of the Limpopo and actually located in Rhodesia.

As usual, the absence of a standardized typology defeats all attempts to compare these assemblages with each other or with those further south. Only the range of tool types can be given without numerical data (Table 64). Both at Dombazanga and Bushman Rock samples have not previously been ascribed to the Smithfield complex. In each case the excavators reported these levels as "mixed" Iron Age and underlying Stone Age material.

Whereas the typological range of these sites clearly overlaps with that of the Orange River sites, there are some important features peculiar to the Transvaal group. First, the dominant rock types used are all siliceous, intractable forms yielding smaller flakes. Most stone artifacts in these Transvaal assemblages, therefore, tend to be smaller than their equivalent types from the Smithfield of the Orange Free State and Orange River, where lydianite is used almost exclusively. Second, there exists at Magabeng, Olieboompoort, and Matluassi a distinct Preceramic form of the Smithfield. The carbon-14 dates for some of these sites are of great interest:

Olieboompoort:

  BM-42   820 ± 150 B.P. (A.D. 1080)

Magabeng:

  BM-31   1020 ± 150 B.P. (A.D. 930)

Both dates suggest that the Smithfield technology was already present in the Transvaal at the time when Developed or Ceramic Wilton groups existed in Rhodesia to the north, and in the Orange River valley to the south. This may partly explain the absence of any convincing Wilton assemblage from the Transvaal. At Dombazanga the "Smithfield" from the top 4 inches of the cave deposit overlies a Ceramic Wilton dated to A.D. 750 ± 100 (SR-15). However, the immediate technical ancestry of the Preceramic Smithfield in the Transvaal remains unknown since it lies on bedrock at Magabeng and Matluassi, and follows a pronounced unconformity at Olieboompoort. Some authors, particularly Mason (1962a), have assumed that it evolved directly from the Oakhurst complex (called "Earlier Smithfield"), but not a single site is known from the Transvaal that contains adequate dated assemblages representing the period between about 6000 B.C. and A.D. 1000 Smithfield-related samples overlie Oakhurst horizons at Bushman Rock and Wonderwerk, but these sites cannot support an Oakhurst origin for the Smithfield because the intermediate period is not represented clearly at either site. Although it is unreasonable to assume that the Transvaal region was not occupied during this period, it is necessary to admit that the direct ancestry of the Transvaal Smithfield remains unknown.

SMITHFIELD SITES OF NATAL AND THE ADJACENT HIGHLANDS

Unfortunately, no adequate survey of claimed Smithfield N sites has been compiled, and the distribution of surface collections remains unknown. Figure 147 shows the location of published samples, including surface collections mentioned by Malan (1955a)), Davies (1947, 1949, 1951, 1952), Goodwin (1930),

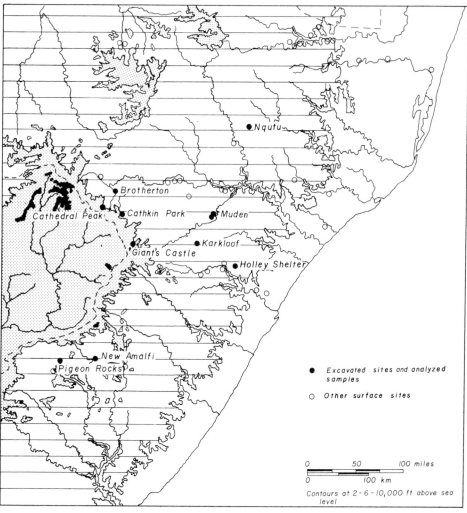

Fig. 147. Distribution of excavated sites reported to have yielded samples of the Smithfield N industry in Natal.

TABLE 65

Tool Types of Three Natal Smithfield Sites [a]

Tool types	Muden 2, open site (%)	Muden 1, rock shelter (%)	Karkloof, open site (%)
Endscrapers	17.1	12.2	26.0
Transverse endscrapers	1.6	1.9	—
Duckbill endscrapers	1.2	4.1	—
Micro endscrapers	0.2	0.5	—
Thumbnail endscrapers	3.2	3.6	—
Core scrapers–trimming stones	3.2	2.2	1.3
Sidescrapers	21.6	17.1	21.5
Double sidescrapers	0.6	1.2	—
Circular–horseshoe scrapers	1.8	1.7	—
Multiple scrapers	1.0	—	—
Borers	0.8	1.9	—
Miscellaneous trimmed flakes and blades	—	0.5	2.0
Outils écaillés	0.2	0.7	—
Strangulated scrapers	15.1	25.0	13.7
Hollow scrapers	27.6	21.1	35.2
Side–hollow scrapers	0.4	2.2	—
End–hollow scrapers	0.4	0.2	—
Micro–hollow scrapers	3.3	3.1	—
Ground stone ring	—	0.2	—
Choppers	0.4	0.5	—
Sample totals:	**502**	**416**	**153**

[a] Data from Farnden (1965, 1969).

van Riet Lowe (1936), and other isolated reports (Stein 1933; Wells, 1933; King and Chubb 1932a; Lebzelter and Bayer 1928; P. G. Brien 1932b; K. Brien 1935). Obviously, none of these reports contained any adequate analysis of the Smithfield N, and it is only recently that the numerical characters of three surface samples have become available, thanks to the efforts of Farnden (1965, 1969); they are given in Table 65.

Although not analyzed by a system comparable with that of the Orange River sites, it is nevertheless apparent that all three samples contain a high proportion of hollow scraper forms not found in Smithfield B assemblages. It is unfortunate that neither ceramics nor organic remains were recovered with these samples, nor is there any way to fit them into a local stratigraphic sequence. Cramb's (1952) sample from the upper levels of Holley Shelter also includes bone work, potsherds, glass beads, and a wooden point, but there is unfortunately no numerical analysis. The Warmbad excavations are reported by van Riet Lowe (1947) to have yielded grindstones, mullers, grooved and bored stones, and a stone arm

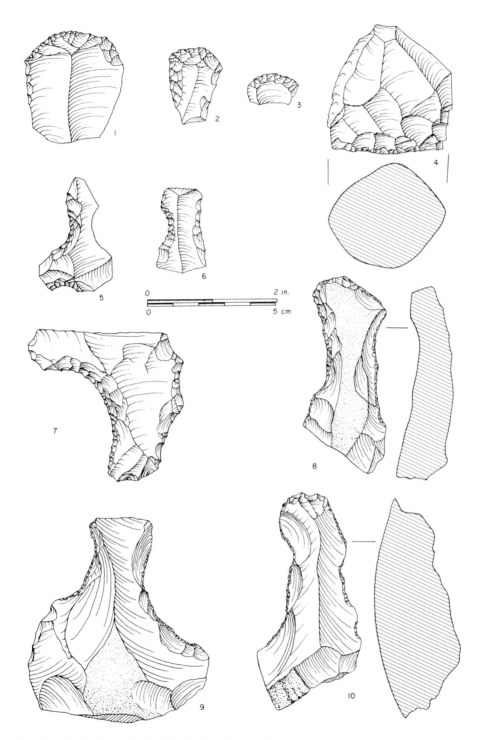

Fig. 148. Tools from the Smithfield N industry. The large hollow and strangulated scrapers (5–10) are features that do not occur in the B and C regions. Sites in the highland and Drakenberg foothills contain only diminutive examples of this type.

TABLE 66

Artifact Analysis of Giant's Castle Rock Shelter

	Level (cm)					
	0–30	30–45	45–60	60–75	75–90	Totals
Flaked stone tools						
Notched scraper						
single	4	14	7	—	1	26
double	—	9	6	—	—	15
triple	—	—	—	1	—	1
Notched scraper and endscraper	—	1	—	—	—	1
Notched scraper and sidescraper	—	—	4	—	—	4
Notched scraper, end- and sidescraper	—	—	1	—	—	1
Point	—	1	1	—	—	2
Thumbnail scraper	3	14	11	3	3	34
Endscraper (other than thumbnail)	4	35	18	10	3	70
Sidescraper	1	—	1	—	2	4
Double sidescraper	—	—	1	—	—	1
Rectangular flake, worked all round	—	—	—	—	1	1
Crystal split as chisel	—	—	1	—	—	1
Long microlithic backed blade	—	—	—	1	—	1
Broad scraper (concave–convex?)	—	—	1	—	—	1
Totals:	**12**	**74**	**52**	**15**	**10**	**163**
Other artifacts						
Microlithic core	—	2	3	—	1	6
Bone point (piece)	—	2	4	2	—	8
Bone link shaft (piece)	—	1	—	—	—	1
Pottery (sherd)	14	10	—	—	—	24
Paint grindstone						
upper	1	—	—	—	—	1
lower	—	1	—	—	—	1
Grindstone	1	—	—	—	—	1
Grindstone, piece	4	2	—	—	—	6
Whetstone (?)	2	—	—	—	—	2
Sandstone fragment, serrated edges	1	—	—	—	—	1
Wooden button	1	—	—	—	—	1
Metal cylinder	1	—	—	—	—	1
Boot eyelet	—	—	1	—	—	1
Wooden bead (?)	—	—	—	—	1	1
Yellow ocher, piece	1	—	—	—	—	1
Orange ocher, piece	—	—	—	1	—	1
Middle Stone Age flake reused in Late Stone Age	—	—	—	—	1	1

ring, palettes, and a ground and polished stone axe with the industry. Bone work included awls, arrowpoints, and a large cylindrical ivory point (Fig. 148).

In the highland region of Natal, only the Giant's Castle shelter (Willcox 1957) has been analyzed in sufficient detail to allow any diagnosis. Table 66 suggests the presence of both a Ceramic and Preceramic phase, but unfortunately, no carbon-14 dates are available for the site. The dominant rock type in use here was chalcedony, with some lydianite and quartzite. The industry, although containing several hollow and strangulated scraper forms found in the Smithfield N sites, clearly has far more in common with the Smithfield B–C complex to the north. The Cathkin Peak collections (Stein 1933) presumably occupy a similar "marginal" position between the Smithfield "B–C" and "N" regions, as does Beaumont's (1967) undescribed sample from Brotherton Shelter. Evidently, potsherds were present as well as an intrusive Iron Age burial. At Moshebi's Shelter (Carter 1969) the top three spits are dated to A.D. 1690 and contain tanged pressure-flaked points, glass beads, ceramics and bone work, small endscrapers, and rare backed blades. King and Chubb (1932b) report a similar typology from a Drakensberg rock shelter.

Of great importance is the presence of a preceramic level of the Smithfield N at this site, inviting further investigations. Davies (1951) mentions the presence of possible preceramic levels at Nqutu Cave as well as a polished stone axe, but none of this material has been described. Malan's (1955a) excavations at Pigeon Rocks also lack any description. Obviously, much additional field research is needed in this area.

If the presence of a preceramic Smithfield N is confirmed by later excavations, like those presently being conducted by Carter (1969, 1970), the technical origins of this industry will require further investigation. Like the Transvaal, little is known of the cultural tradition prevalent in the Natal interior during the period about 6000 B.C. to A.D. 1000. Davies (1951) has suggested that Nqutu demonstrates an Oakhurst ("Smithfield A") origin for the Smithfield N, since a comparable sample is reported from below the preceramic "N" levels but without adequate publication this can hardly be claimed as conclusive evidence.

SOUTH-WEST AFRICA

J. Rudner (1957) reported that several rock shelters in the Brandberg area contained Wilton industries overlaid by a scatter of crude scrapers and pottery that was concentrated on or near the surface. He named this superficial Post-Wilton horizon the Brandberg Culture, which has been reported from no less than 25 sites in the Brandberg range by Viereck (1968). Unfortunately, no information has been released on exactly how many of these samples are from excavated contexts overlying the Wilton, nor have adequate numerical analyses been presented. Apart from abundant utilized flakes of lydianite, the industry evidently consists of endscrapers, side- and endscrapers, sidescrapers, hollow

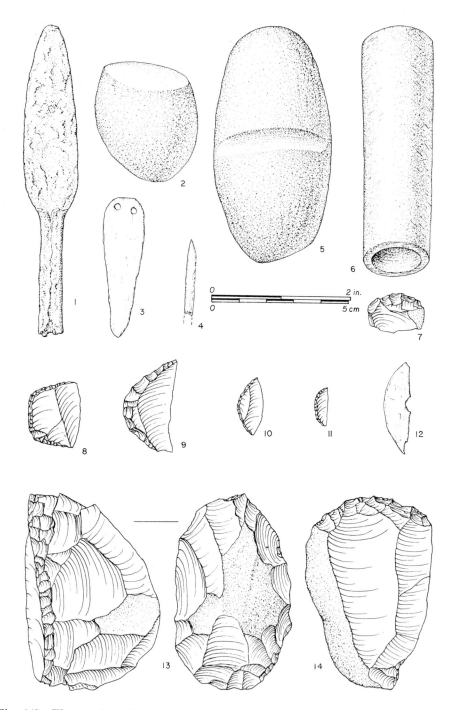

Fig. 149. The so-called "Brandberg" industry evidently contains numerous backed microlithic pieces (8–11), which strongly suggest that it cannot be distinguished on typological grounds from the preceding Wilton in this area. Associations include metal objects (1) and ground stone pipes (6).

scrapers, steep scrapers, core hammers, mullers, grindstones, bored and grooved stones, ground stone pallettes, stone pipes, bone work, shell beads and pendants, glass beads, and rare metal fragments. The sherds represent rough bag-shaped pots, some with lugs, spouts, and pointed bases (Fig. 149).

Unfortunately, Viereck's (1967) insistence that these samples represent a regional variant of the "Damaraland Culture" has done little to clarify their status. Within this group he includes (unanalyzed) surface collections from the Erongo Mountains (made of porphyry, basalt, and quartzite) and from southeastern Damaraland (made of quartzite, quartz, and chalcedony). Since none of this material has been analyzed, it remains impossible to evaluate his claims for such widespread stylistic similarity in this region. The relationship of the so-called "Damaraland" samples to the Wilton has not been demonstrated outside the Brandberg. Since backed microliths occur in many of the claimed sites, further evidence is needed to show why they should not be ascribed to the (earlier?) Wilton complex.

A more acceptable claim is that the "Brandberg" groups of samples were made by the Bergdama, as no doubt were several of the others reported from adjacent regions. J. Rudner (1957) points out that these enigmatic negroid hunter–gatherers were reported to be living in the Brandberg (Guerig 1891) and Erongo Mountains (Galton 1853) in the nineteenth century, having been driven out or absorbed by Herero and Hottentot migrants who entered Damaraland earlier in the century (Vedder 1938). The recurrent association of "Brandberg" artifacts with stone hut circles in the Brandberg and Neuhof—Kowas areas may further support this assumption. Viereck (1963) and Jipsen (1961–1965) report finding remains of grass and wood windbreaks within the stone circles, suggesting that some sites at least belong to the historical period, as indicated by

Phillips Cave surface:
$$\text{R-23} \quad 280 \pm 80 \text{ B.P. (A.D. 1670)}.$$

The sample was taken from a surface hearth and dates the final occupation of the cave. However, the underlying sample (12 tools) reported by Martin and Mason (1954) is dated as follows:

Phillips Cave:
$$\text{tufa 2 ft} \quad \text{C-9-11} \quad 3368 \pm 200 \text{ B.P. (1148 B.C.)}$$

and has far more in common with the "Brandberg" typology than it does with the coeval Wilton complex. A similar parallel exists for

Windhoek Zoo Park Gardens:
$$\text{elephant tusk} \quad \text{SR-34} \quad 5200 \pm 140 \text{ B.P. (3250 B.C.)}$$

Details of this elephant-kill site are not available, but MacCalman (1965) reports that only quartz scrapers and choppers are present, without backed elements. The possibility that the "Brandberg" group has a local technical ancestry quite independent of the Wilton complex should be investigated further. The striking resemblance between the lithic technology of the Brandberg–Damaraland groups of sites and that of the Oakhurst complex also begs numerous questions.

FAUNA ASSOCIATED WITH SMITHFIELD SAMPLES

The published data are summarized in Table 67. Several other sites have produced (unpublished) fauna and of those given in Table 67 only Wonderwerk and North Brabant represent complete analyses. This means that additional species are almost certainly represented in the other collections. It is unfortunate that the richest sample—Wonderwerk—is largely out of context and almost certainly contains earlier material mixed in with it, hence the much wider range of artiodactyls represented.

In spite of all the usual shortcomings of the published evidence, Table 67 at least reveals that the Smithfield dietary range follows the same pattern as that of the Wilton and Oakhurst complexes: intensive exploitation of all local food resources *including* a wider range of small animals from different niches. Large game animals are not abundant at the listed sites, but warthog, springbok, zebra, and buffalo occur at several localities.

A TENTATIVE INTERPRETATION

Considering the very high density of Smithfield sites, and their relatively rich artifactual content, it is somewhat surprising that this recent period of South African prehistory remains so poorly understood. The recovery of more sealed samples with associated fauna, plant remains, carbon-14 dates and rock art should obviously receive priority, but the many thousands of rich surface sites along rivers and watercourses should not be ignored.

At present it is only possible to point out that the Smithfield B–C and N sites *with ceramic associations* represent the debris of some of the activities of hunter–gatherers loosely termed "Bushmen" whom the first European explorers and farmers encountered. Thus, the Smithfield industry belongs partly to the prehistoric period and partly to history. The task of evaluating the archaeological data in the light of the historical record has yet to be undertaken when more published sites are available. So abundant is the archaeological record for the period that it should prove possible to isolate territorial groups by studies of the

TABLE 67

Fauna Associated with Various Smithfield Sites

Genus and species	Description	Glen Elliott Shelter	Glen Elliott Crevice	Ventershoek	Moshebi's Shelter	Tafelberg Hall	Witkrans	Powerhouse Cave	Wonderwerk	North Brabant
MAMMALS										
Insectivora										
Crocidura sp.	Shrews	×	×	×	—	×	—	×	—	—
Primates										
Papio ursinus	Chacma baboon	—	—	—	×	—	×	—	×	—
Lagomorpha										
Lepus capensis	Cape hare	×	?	×	—	—	—	×	—	—
Rodentia										
Pedetes sp.	Spring hare	×	?	×	—	—	—	—	—	—
Otomys sp.	Swamp rat	×	—	×	—	×	—	—	—	—
Other rodents		×	×	×	×	×	×	—	—	—
Hystrix africae-australis	Porcupine	×	?	×	—	—	—	×	×	×
Carnivora										
Canis sp.	Dog	—	—	—	×	—	—	—	—	—
Lycaon picta	Hunting dog	—	—	—	—	—	—	—	—	—
Mellivora capensis	Honey badger	?	—	—	—	—	—	—	×	—
Herpestes ichneumon	Mongoose	×	—	—	—	—	—	—	—	—
Hyaena brunnea	Hyena	—	—	—	—	—	—	—	cf.	—
Panthera pardus	Leopard	—	—	—	—	—	—	—	—	×
Hyracoidea										
Procavia capensis	Hyrax	×	×	×	×	—	×	—	—	—
Perissodactyla										
Equus quagga	Quagga	—	—	—	—	—	×	×	×	—
Equus burchelli	Zebra	?	—	?	—	×	—	—	×	×
Ceratotherium simum	White rhino	—	—	—	—	—	—	—	×	—
Diceros bicornis	Black rhino	—	—	—	—	—	—	—	×	—

(continued)

TABLE 67 (*continued*)

Genus and species	Description	Glen Elliott Shelter	Glen Elliott Crevice	Ventershoek	Moshebi's Shelter	Tafelberg Hall	Witkrans	Powerhouse Cave	Wonderwerk	North Brabant
Artiodactyla										
Phacochoerus aethiopicus	Cape warthog	?	?	—	—	×	×	×	×	×
Phacochoerus africanus	Southern warthog	—	—	—	—	—	—	—	×	—
Tragelaphus angasi	Nyala	—	—	—	—	—	—	—	×	—
Taurotragus oryx	Eland	—	—	—	—	—	—	—	×	—
Syncerus caffer	Cape buffalo	?	—	—	—	—	—	×	×	×
Cephalophus sp.	Blue duiker	?	—	?	—	?	—	—	—	×
Sylvicapra grimmia	Duiker	—	—	—	—	—	—	—	cf.	—
Kobus ellipsiprymnus	Waterbuck	—	—	—	—	—	—	—	×	—
Pelea capreolus	Vaal rhebok	—	—	—	×	—	—	—	—	—
Hippotragus equinus	Roan	—	—	—	—	—	—	—	cf.	—
Oryx gazella	Gemsbok	—	—	—	—	—	—	—	×	—
Damaliscus cf. *pygargus*	Bontebok	—	—	—	—	—	—	—	×	—
Alcelaphus caama	Hartebeest	—	—	—	—	×	—	—	×	—
Connochaetes taurinus	Wildebeest	?	—	?	—	—	—	—	cf.	—
Antidorcas marsupialis	Springbok	×	?	×	—	×	—	?	×	—
Aepyceros melampus	Impala	—	—	—	—	—	—	—	—	×
NONMAMMALIAN										
Tortoise		×	×	×	—	×	—	—	×	×
Turtle		?	—	—	—	—	—	×	×	×
Lizards		×	×	×	—	—	×	—	—	—
Monitor		—	—	—	×	—	×	×	—	—
Snake		×	×	×	—	—	—	—	—	—
Small birds		×	×	×	×	—	—	—	—	×
Large birds		—	—	—	×	—	—	—	—	×
Ostrich egg		×	×	×	×	×	×	×	×	—
Frogs		×	×	×	—	—	—	—	—	—
Toads		×	×	×	—	—	—	—	—	—
Fish		×	×	×	×	—	×	×	—	—
Crab		×	×	×	—	—	×	×	—	—
Riverine mollusks		×	×	×	—	×	×	×	—	—

distribution of ceramic and artifact styles. Detailed patterns of food exploitation should also be revealed by the data.

Considering the large number of sites already plotted, the almost total absence of reliably associated human skeletal remains appears quite incongruous. Burials are available from Oudefontein, Modderpoort and probably from some earlier "Smithfield N" excavations, but no "Smithfield population" can be adequately defined in taxonomic terms. For this reason, the relationship between the Smithfield "Bushmen" of historical sources and the preceding Wilton-related population remains a subject fit only for speculation. Unfortunately, the artifactual associations of the large "Bushmen" skeletal samples housed in museums and medical schools are completely unknown.

Another important question remains to be discussed: Are the cultural origins of the Smithfield to be found in the preceding Wilton? In the Orange River valley it has been demonstrated that some local Ceramic Wilton elements persist into the Smithfield period; certain rock art styles (especially grid motifs), abundant endscraper forms, and the almost exclusive use of lydianite. However, the material changes which take place when the Smithfield first appears are more obvious: backed microliths disappear, bone arrow armature production increases, a distinctive pottery style appears (almost certainly of domestic manufacture, not traded in from elsewhere), and glass trade beads and metal work appear. In this area, at least, the available evidence does not point to a straightforward stylistic evolution, but a marked influx of new ideas (and possible people) into the area.

It is suggested that these changes should be viewed as a peripheral consequence of the Iron Age domination of the northern territories after about A.D. 1000. The Transvaal, although widely infiltrated by Iron Age settlers by this date, nevertheless contained several hunter–gatherer groups who were not yet in contact with Iron Age technology and were not using pottery (Magabeng, Olieboompoort, Matluassi). Nor were they using backed microlithic arrow armatures like the Developed or Ceramic Wilton groups to the north and south of the Transvaal. As Iron Age domination in the Transvaal expanded, contact between the two cultures became inevitable, and several later Stone Age sites reveal the same lithic technology now associated with characteristic stamp-impressed pottery and traded materials such as glass beads and metal work. The Smithfield B–C complex to the south may, therefore, reflect the diffusion of ideas (and perhaps even population movements) from the Transvaal, where surviving Stone Age groups came under increasing pressure from an expanding Iron Age population. By the seventeenth century A.D. the techniques of potmaking would certainly have been acquired, as well as glass trade beads and metal fragments.

It may be argued that the Preceramic levels of either the Smithfield N or "Damaraland" group of sites could serve equally well as possible focal points for the origin of the complex, but neither of these groups appears to resemble the Smithfield B–C industry in typological details or pottery styles. It is more likely, therefore, that these other Preceramic Smithfield foci may have given rise to the local protohistoric industries of northern Natal and the Brandberg. The complex pattern of cultural influences already revealed by the scanty evidence at our disposal can be most conveniently summarized in diagrammatic form (see Fig. 167, Chapter 10, page 437). It is apparent that in the extreme south, the inland hunter–gatherers were little influenced by these changes and we find the Ceramic Wilton persisting into the historic period at De Hangen. On the South African coastline an equally complex pattern of changes was taking place during this period.

10

The "Strandloper" Sites of the South African Coast

The first European settlers who colonized the southwestern Cape during the second half of the seventeenth century A.D. encountered several different groups of indigenous hunter–gatherers. Contacts with the "Bushmen" groups of the mountainous interior were infrequent and often hostile, but it was the coastal inhabitants who first attracted the settlers' attention. In 1653 the *Journal of Van Riebeeck* (Thom 1952) mentions that:

> . . . Table Valley was annually visited by three tribes of people, similar in dress and customs. One is called the Strandloopers, or . . . Watermen, because they live on mussels which they find on the rocks and some roots from the earth. As far as we have observed they are not above 40 or 50 in number and . . . have no cattle. The second kind are those from Saldanha . . . who arrive here every year with countless cattle and sheep. The third kind were called by him (i.e. Harry the interpreter) Fishermen, who after the departure of the Saldanhamen arrive here with cattle only and no sheep, and who subsist by fishing, without boats, from the rocks with little fishing lines. On this they are very keen. . . . They live beyond the mountains east of the Cape. . . .

403

Although the journal of the colony's first Governor is littered with accounts of meetings, trading, and negotiations with a few members of this coastal society, his writings fail to reveal any clear picture of their everyday activities (Goodwin 1952).

A particularly troublesome omission is the absence of any reference to their migratory habits during the course of the year. It has proved impossible to determine from historical sources whether they moved seasonally along the coastline (as the later name "Strandlooper" or "Strandloper" implies) or between coast and interior in their quest for food supplies. The *Journal* has hinted at the existence of two distinct indigenous groups, one adapted to the mountainous interior ("Bushmen") and the other to a coastal habitat (*Strandlooper*). Written records leave no clue to their racial affinities, economic or social relations, or territorial boundaries. The possibility that the Strandlopers and the "Bushmen" may have been one and the same people encountered at different times of the year (and exploiting two different habitats) is never once mentioned. Such details will have to be recovered from the archaeological record if the problem is to be resolved. It is obvious that we should define "Strandloper" in archaeological terms before the question can be approached.

Like so many other areas of Stone Age research, fieldwork connected with protohistoric and historic coastal settlement has progressed in a haphazard fashion based mainly on accidental discovery and selective digging. Only a few excavations reflect any awareness that the "Strandloper" concept is based on an ill-defined name that poses more problems than it answers. This situation has been greatly aggravated by the widespread looting of coastal shell mounds and midden-filled caves by amateur skull hunters and a few quasi-professional individuals whose irresponsible digging methods have done untold damage to many of the richest sites. Nevertheless, many thousands remain intact, and a systematic excavation program is urgently needed.

TERMINOLOGY

Indeed, so few of the excavations in coastal midden sites provide adequate published data that it is not yet possible to recognize either regional or chronological subdivisions. Several different terms have been employed to describe stone artifact samples from those deposits that have *not* yielded obvious Wilton assemblages. Common to most of these non-Wilton samples are large flake scrapers, various heavy-duty elements (like choppers, anvils, and grindstones), bone work, and pottery. The lithic elements in such assemblages include so few elaborately flaked, formal tool types that few authors have risked comparisons with inland industries, particularly the Smithfield. The only safe conclusion to be drawn is that they contain no microlithic elements. Inevitably, several different terms have been introduced to describe such samples (see Table 68).

Although the (apparently redundant) term "Later (late) Stone Age" is currently popular for describing non-Wilton midden assemblages, the word "Strand-

TABLE 68

Terminology for Various Strandloper Sites

Sites	Reference	Term introduced
Tsitsikamma Caves	FitzSimons (1926)	Strandloper
Umgazana Cave, various	Chubb *et al.* (1934)	Smithfield A (Umgazana var.)
	Laidler (1935)	Shellmound cultures
Six surface collections, Northern Natal	Schofield (1936a)	Coastal Smithfield
Windhoek Cave	Grobbelaar and Goodwin (1952)	Final Stone Age
Logie's Rock Cave	Rudner and Rudner (1954)	Sandy Bay
Matjes River Shelter	Louw (1960)	Smithfield B (Matjes River variant)
Scott's Cave	Deacon and Deacon (1963)	Late Stone Age
Andrieskraal Shelter	J. Deacon (1965)	Later Stone Age

looper" has persisted, for example, van Noten (1965) and H. J. Deacon (1969c). It has also been used to describe Wilton occurrences, for example, Hewitt's (1921) reference to the Wilton type site and Rudner's (1968) use of the term to include any shell-mound site with pottery. However, in this chapter it will be used as a provisional term to describe any non-Wilton assemblage from a coastal shell midden that postdates the Oakhurst complex. If there is a "Strandloper complex" with regional industries, insufficient data exist to support such a concept.

Since the South and South-West African coastline passes through so many different environments, it cannot be viewed as a single habitat. However, a similar *range* of marine, littoral, and terrestrial food sources would be available at almost all points along this coast. It might be reasonable, therefore, to expect later hunter–gatherers to use broadly similar exploitation tactics anywhere along the shoreline, with perhaps minor regional differences. Hopefully, these differences may be partly reflected in the cultural remains of two or more adjacent groups. If such evidence exists, we are not yet able to extract it from the patchy archaeological record, with any confidence. All that is possible at present is to assess the results of research on the four major zones: the Atlantic coast, the southwestern Cape, the southern Cape coast, the Natal coast. Whereas these form convenient geographical subdivisions, they should not be taken as cultural units containing discrete "industries."

THE ATLANTIC COAST

This is the desertic shoreline extending southwards from Walvis Bay to the northern edge of the winter-rainfall zone at about St. Helena Bay (Fig. 150). Archaeological exploration has not yet extended north of Walvis Bay. J. Rudner

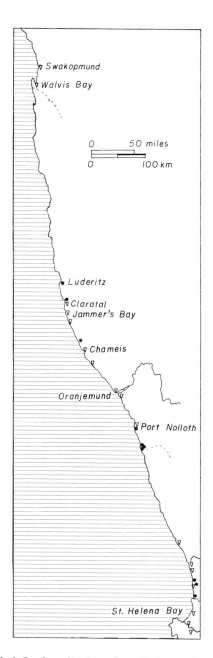

Fig. 150. Distribution of "Strandloper" midden sites and Ceramic Wilton middens on the Atlantic Cape coast. See Fig. 152 (page 409) for the key. (After Rudner 1968.)

(1968) briefly described surface finds on shell middens from eight sites, all yielding pottery forms similar to those from Ceramic Wilton middens on the same coast (Fig. 151) with conical bases, reinforced lugs, spouts, and varied decorative motifs on the neck. No survey of lithic materials from those sites has been published, but there are brief descriptions of small selected samples from Claratal,

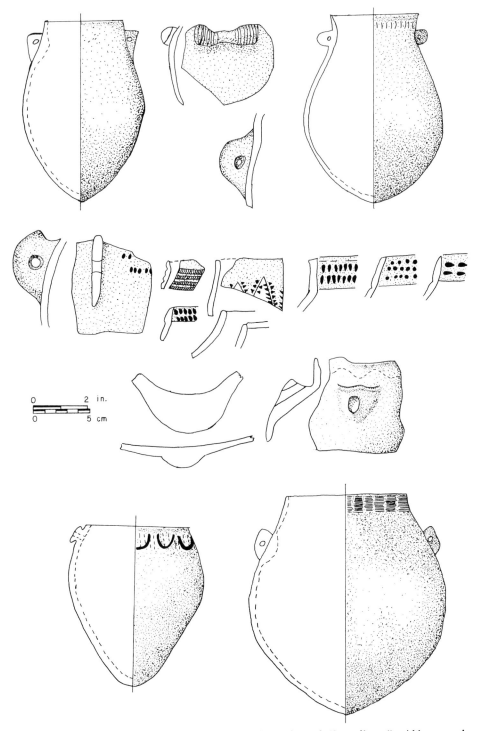

Fig. 151. Whole pots and sherds collected from the surface of "Strandloper" middens on the Atlantic Cape coast.

Jammer's Bay, and Chameis (Rudner and Grattan-Bellew 1964). Human skeletal remains were removed from the Walvis Bay middens, but never published.

Several early travelers record sighting Strandlopers on this stretch of coast. Bartholomew Dias landed at Luderitz Bay and Oranjemund in 1487 and met Strandlopers at both places. Bode may have landed at Jammer's Bay when he encountered Hottentot-speaking Strandlopers in 1677 (Vedder 1938). Although it may be suspected that those people were responsible for the middens at these sites, no connection has been proved. Similar doubt surrounds the connections between the middens of Walvis Bay and the Topnaar Strandlopers recorded by Alexander (1838) and several later travelers (Colson 1905).

Evidently Strandlopers survived on this coast until a much later date than elsewhere in South Africa. Martin (1872) records their presence on the Namaqualand coast in 1858, Schultze-Jena (1907) records "Hottentots" living at the coast near Port Nolloth between 1903 and 1905 and also at Luderitz in 1903. As late as 1938 H. Martin recorded shell middens with the standing remains of five whalebone huts north of Swakopmund (J. Rudner 1968), and Dart (1955c) reported three surviving Strandlopers from Sessfontein in the Kaokoveld.

Although midden sites are known to be abundant on this coast, systematic archaeological investigations are lacking. Recent (unpublished) excavations from South-West Africa should help to explain the true relationship between Wilton and non-Wilton midden sites. These may reflect seasonal or other activity variations of a single culture; they could represent the remains of two contemporary but culturally distinct groups; or they may represent two industries of different ages. All three alternatives may apply to different sections of this vast coastline. Only excavation can determine which alternative pattern should apply in any given point along the shore (Sydow 1967).

Since the sparse historical record suggests various (and conflicting) accounts of the physical and cultural affinities of the west coast Strandlopers, the recovery of adequate skeletal samples is also essential. The frequently quoted view that they were "Hottentots" who, disposed of their livestock, were moving to the coast and mingling with local "Bushmen" groups has no very sound basis. Neither term can be adequately defined and both have been used in this region to describe races, cultural groups or economic systems. Wilson and Thompson (1969) suggest that both terms should be avoided.

THE SOUTHWESTERN CAPE

The shoreline from St. Helena Bay to Cape Agulhas has been summarized by J. Rudner (1968). As shell mounds have been the object of discussions for at least a century, for example, Martin (1872), over 100 sites are now known and several have been excavated. Surface material has been collected from almost all of them, and at least 70 sites have yielded potsherds. Of these, about 30 have

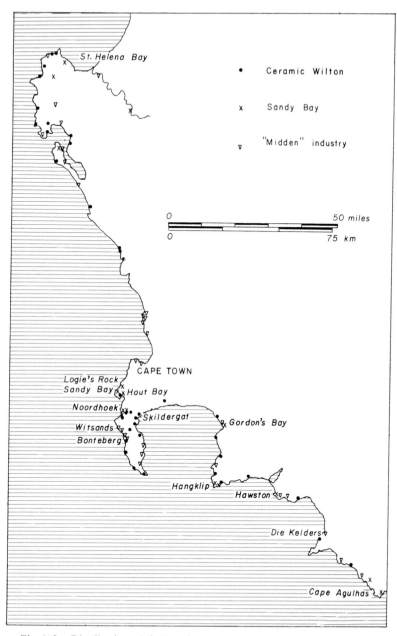

Fig. 152. Distribution of shell middens on the southwestern Cape coast.

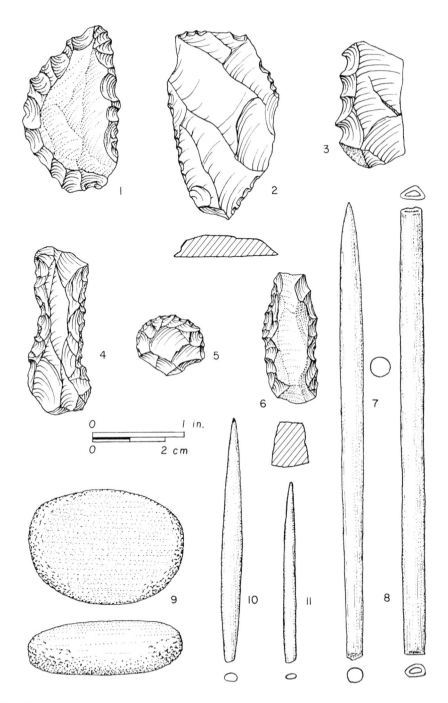

Fig. 153. Artifacts from the Sandy Bay industry at Logie's Rock Shelter: (1) denticulate sidescrapers; (2) utilized flake; (3) denticulate piece; (4, 6) backed adzes; (5) small convex scraper; (7, 10, 11) bone points, (8) bone tube; (9) muller.

TABLE 69

Artifact Analysis of 10 Sandy Bay Sites [a]

Tool types	Sandy Bay, Site 1 (no.)	(%)	Sandy Bay, Site 2 (no.)	Hout Bay (no.)	(%)	Noord-hoek (no.)	Gordon's Bay (no.)	(%)	Hang-klip West (no.)	Hang-klip East (no.)	Haws-ton (no.)	Arnes-ton (no.)	Het Kruis (no.)
Endscrapers	12	4.0	6	4	4.1	2	4	2.8	2	—	—	—	5
Small endscrapers	7	3.3	—	—	—	1	3	2.1	2	2	14	7	—
Sidescrapers	21	7.0	6	8	8.3	12	29	20.0	16	4	20	6	27
Small sidescrapers	23	7.5	10	6	6.2	2	12	8.4	6	9	5	4	13
Backed adzes (slugs)	240	78.9	41	77	80.1	19	85	59.5	36	18	12	5	9
Bored stones	—	—	2	1	1.2	—	2	1.4	1	1	1	—	—
Grooved stones	1	0.3	—	—	—	—	8	5.6	—	—	—	—	—
Sample totals:	**304**	100%	**65**	**96**	100%	**36**	**143**	100%	**63**	**34**	**52**	**22**	**54**

[a] From Rudner and Rudner (1954).

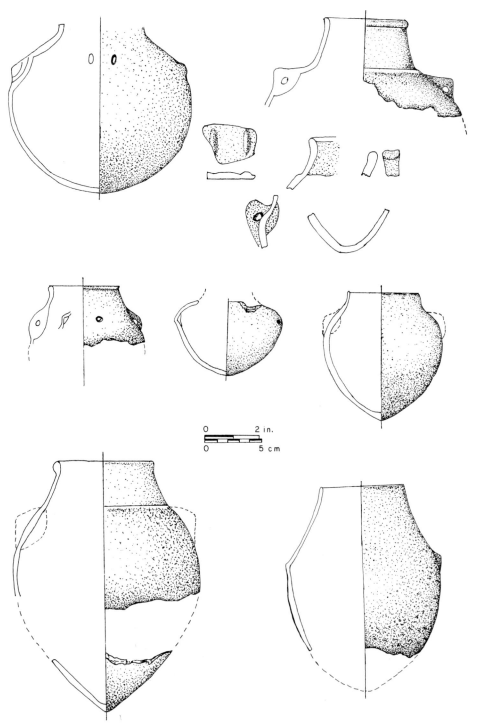

Fig. 154. Whole pots and sherd collected from middens containing artifacts of the Sandy Bay industry.

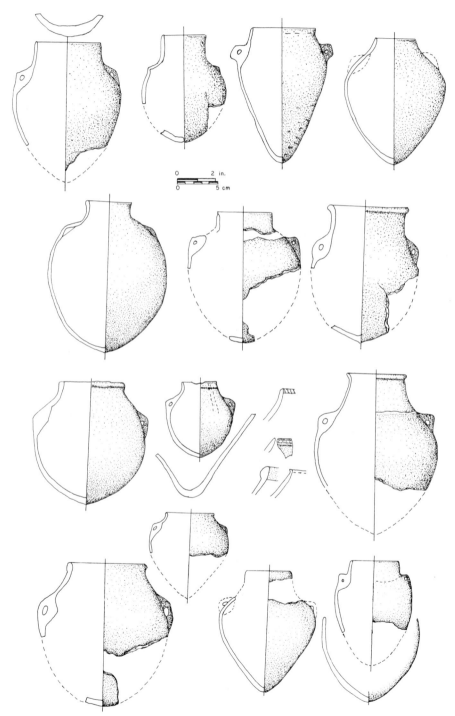

Fig. 155. Whole pots and sherds collected from shell mounds containing the "midden" industry on the southwestern Cape coast. (After Rudner 1968.)

Wilton artifacts tentatively associated with them. The remaining middens all provided small collections of quartz or quartzite choppers, hammers, flakes, grindstones, and rare bone work and ornaments, but the only detailed descriptions concern the ceramic finds (Fig. 152).

Rudner and Rudner (1956) have summarized surface collections from the Cape peninsula, which they grouped under the name "Sandy Bay industry," taking as the type site a large surface scatter of artifacts and potsherds from a totally eroded midden near the shore at Sandy Bay. Unfortunately, the excavations of an adjacent intact midden by Johnson (1951) were not analyzed so that this *in situ* material cannot be used for reference. Only the small excavated assemblage from Logie's Rock Shelter (Rudner and Rudner 1956) can be cited as a possible sealed example of the industry. At present there are no faunal or human skeletal associations, nor are the described samples dated, so that the relationship of this group of sites to the local ceramic Wilton cannot be examined. Far more work will be needed to determine whether the Sandy Bay group represents a discrete cultural tradition, a later industry, or merely an activity (or regional) variant of the Wilton in this area.

Sandy Bay assemblages contain abundant quartzite flakes struck from beach cobbles. Besides these, there are bored and ground stones and numerous sidescrapers, and endscrapers and worked-out adzes termed "slugs" by Rudner. They are made of quartzite, quartz, or silcrete (Fig. 153). Whereas these forms are certainly present in Wilton samples, they are not recorded as a dominant form. Rudner and Rudner's (1954) analysis of ten Sandy Bay collections suggests that these are usually the most abundant forms of worked pieces (Table 69).

It is not clear whether these are selected samples. Items such as core choppers, grindstones, hammerstones, and miscellaneous trimmed flakes are excluded from the published lists. Potsherds were recovered from all sites. The larger sherds (Fig. 154) tentatively associated with Sandy Bay middens resemble those from local ceramic Wilton sites and numerous other shell mounds yielding samples termed "Late Stone Age" or "Crude midden industry" by Rudner (Fig. 155). No numerical analyses of these latter have appeared, and their organic associations are unknown. Human burials have been recovered from over a dozen middens, but again, no study of this material has been published, apart from the thorough analysis of the Bok Baai skeleton by Singer (1955). Its exact cultural associations are unfortunately not described (Rudner and Rudner 1955).

Apart from van Noten's (1965, 1967) trench in the Gordon's Bay midden, all other excavated sites are caves or shelters. A most valuable contribution by Maggs and Speed (1967) on the Bonteberg Shelter includes a numerical analysis of two superimposed artifact samples (see Table 70).

Although the type list differs from Rudner's, the two have sufficient in common to suggest that the Bonteberg samples do not closely resemble the Sandy Bay group. However, at least one "scraper" form from Layer 2 is actually a backed adze and Rudner (*personal communication*) is of the opinion that this later ceramic layer belongs with the group.

TABLE 70

Artifact Analysis of Two Samples from Bonteberg Shelter [a]

	Layer 1, lower (%)	Layer 2, upper (%)
Tool types [b]		
Scrapers	2.1	5.3
Core scrapers	11.2	1.7
Utilized flakes	25.8	26.6
Utilized crystals	11.7	41.5
Modified quartzite flakes	19.6	2.1
Backed crescents	—	4.2
Outils écaillés	1.7	2.1
Flake choppers	10.0	—
Core choppers	6.7	1.7
Bifacial pieces	2.8	1.7
Hammers and pebbles	4.5	7.4
Pebble tools	1.1	2.1
Grindstones	2.8	5.3
Sample total:	**179**	**94**
Other artifacts		
Potsherds	—	32
Ostrich eggshell beads	1	86
Bone work	—	2
Ocher	30	45
Glass bead	—	5
Animal remains [c]		
Large mammals: baboon, eland, small antelope, seal	2	55
Small mammals: hyrax, mongoose, insectivores, rodents	51	1009
Birds	1	10
Torto	31	677
Fish	30	724

[a] From Maggs and Speed (1967).

[b] Tool type analyses given as percentages.

[c] Numerals indicate identifiable fragments, not individuals.

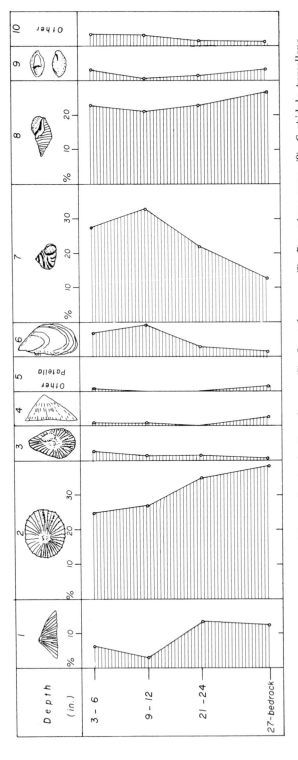

Fig. 156. Vertical distribution of shellfish remains in the Bonteberg Shelter: (1) *Patella granularis;* (2) *P. granatina and occulus;* (3) *P. cochlear;* (4) *P. argenvilli;* (6) *Chloromytilus meridionalis;* (7) *Oxysteles spp.;* (8) *Burnupena spp.;* (9) *Crepidula porcellana.* (After Maggs and Speed 1967.)

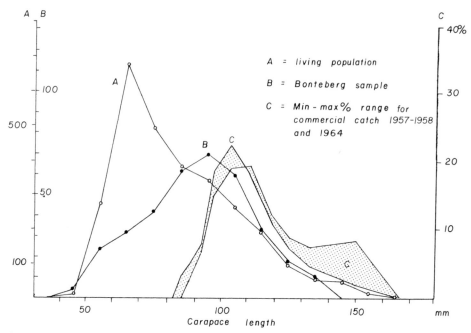

Fig. 157. Analysis of crayfish *Jasus lalandi* carapace length from the Bonteberg sample, which evidently represents an exploited population.

The Bonteberg analysis has also provided limited dietary information (see Table 70). The more detailed analysis of shellfish remains from a restricted area of the excavation is shown in Fig. 156. Two species of limpet were most frequently eaten by the occupants at both the preceramic and ceramic levels, and there is no clear evidence of fluctuations through time in species availability or size. Grindley's (1967) excellent analysis of crayfish mandibles suggests that the sample came from a heavily exploited population. Also the presence of a few very large individuals at all levels may suggest occasional diving, netting or spearing activity in order to obtain such specimens from deep crevices in the coastal rocks (Fig. 157).

It is regrettable that comparable data have not been produced from nearby cave excavations at Witsands (Drennan 1931) or Smitswinkel Bay (Maggs and Speed 1967), both of which have produced pottery and very abundant and varied bone work—a feature almost entirely missing from Bonteberg. A ground stone axe head from Witsands appears to be the only one of its kind from this area (Fig. 158).

The presence of a preceramic industry at Bonteberg is confirmed by similar samples from Gordon's Bay midden (Van Noten 1965, 1967) and Die Kelders

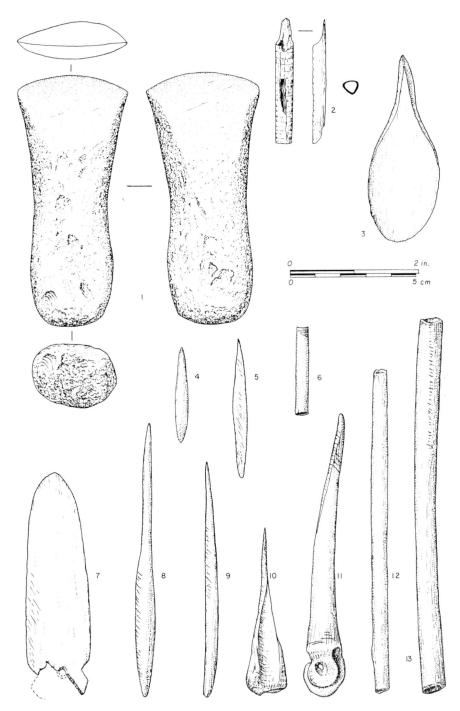

Fig. 158. A polished stone axe (1) and bone work (3–13) from Witsands Cave. Specimen 2 (bone work) is from Gordon's Bay.

Cave (Schweitzer 1970), but no numerical comparisons are possible at present. Only the associated carbon-14 dates suggest that they may be broadly coeval:

Bonteberg:

Layer 1	SR-167	4045 ± 100 B.P.	(2555 B.C.)
Layer 2b (bottom)	SR-166	2050 ± 95 B.P.	(100 B.C.)

Both dates are from shell samples. A reading of 100 B.C. for the first appearance of pottery in the extreme southwestern Cape is somewhat surprising, and the validity of this date may be questioned. However, nothing is known of the age of the earliest pottery-using groups in the western Cape, and the question remains open.

Gordon's Bay:

upper Level 1	GrN-4372	2700 ± 40 B.P.	(750 B.C.)
Level 2	GrN-4373	2980 ± 60 B.P.	(1030 B.C.)
lower Level 3	GrN-4374	3220 ± 55 B.P.	(1270 B.C.)

Die Kelders:

upper	GX-1685	1465 ± 100 B.P.	(A.D. 485)
? lower	GX-1686	2020 ± 95 B.P.	(70 B.C.)
	GX-1687	1960 ± 95 B.P.	(10 B.C.)
	GX-1688	1960 ± 95 B.P.	(10 B.C.)

All readings are from charcoal samples. The uppermost date comes from a ceramic midden, thus throwing doubt on the early date (on shell) from Bonteberg. Besides the abundant quartzite non-Wilton stone artifacts from Die Kelders there is also abundant bone work and ornaments reminiscent of Witsands.

An increasing body of evidence suggests that the southwestern Cape coast was inhabited by groups practicing a simple non-Wilton flaking technology at the time that the Wilton complex dominated vast tracts of southern Africa, including the adjacent southern Cape coast. Although several Wilton samples have been collected from the southwestern Cape region, none has been dated and it is still not clear whether both toolmaking traditions were in use here at exactly the same time. The only *in situ* sample comes from Skildergat, where Jolly (1947) reports that ceramic Wilton with reworked European gunflints overlay a "conventional" midden industry *with pottery* to a depth of 13 inches. In a later report, Jolly (1948) omits any mention of pottery from the midden, nor did the original excavators recover any trace of sherds (Peers and Peers 1926). As Jolly presents no data in support of his published sequence, it is impossible to judge the validity of his interpretation.

Although 11 skeletons were recovered from the Skildergat midden horizon, little is known of them beyond the descriptions of Peers and Peers (1926), who mentions that all were crouched burials lying on their sides, many with ostrich eggshell bead necklaces and one adult female with the fragmentary remains of a leather pouch near the pelvic region. Some metric data have been provided by Keen (1942) and Drennan (1929a). Although fragmentary material has come from most of the other excavated sites, this has not been described in detail.

Obviously, the southwestern Cape will continue to be a problematic area until we have more excavation reports of a standard comparable with that on Bonteberg Shelter. At present there is evidence for a preceramic technology dating from before 2000 B.C. which resembles that of the preceding Oakhurst complex rather than the contemporary Wilton. Yet Wilton sites are common enough and may be contemporary. Also ceramic Wilton and ceramic "Strandloper" middens occur close together, yet nothing definite is known of their relationships. Furthermore, there is the Sandy Bay group of sites, which must be broadly contemporary, although differing in artifact typology from either of the others. The early historical record provides no ready solution to these problems, other than to point out that different groups occupied the coast.

The presence of stock-herding "Hottentots" as revealed by van Riebeeck and others further complicates the picture, and it is distressing to note that no definite "Hottentot" sites can be identified in the archaeological record, so that their origins, technology, and contribution to late coastal culture remains to be investigated. Goodwin (1952) has summarized their dealings with the European settlers and (Goodwin 1956) the evidence for Hottentot metal working, but it is still uncertain whether they used stone tools. An archaeology of the "Hottentots" has not yet developed.

THE SOUTHERN CAPE COAST

Between Cape Agulhas and the Transkei coast some hundreds of shell midden sites have been discovered, but the position of only about 70 (all with ceramics) have been mapped (J. Rudner 1968). An exhaustive survey of this coast is urgently needed as middens are being rapidly destroyed by erosion and the strip development of resort towns (Fig. 159).

Rudner's survey, although limited to ceramic middens and based on surface collections only, is of some importance as it shows that no Ceramic Wilton sites have been found east of Matjes River. In this stretch of coast his typological separation of Ceramic Wilton and Sandy Bay collections appears to break down,

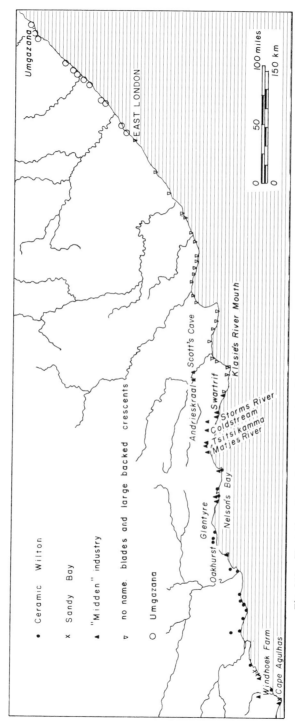

Fig. 159. Tentative clustering of industries along the southern Cape coast. (After Rudner 1968.)

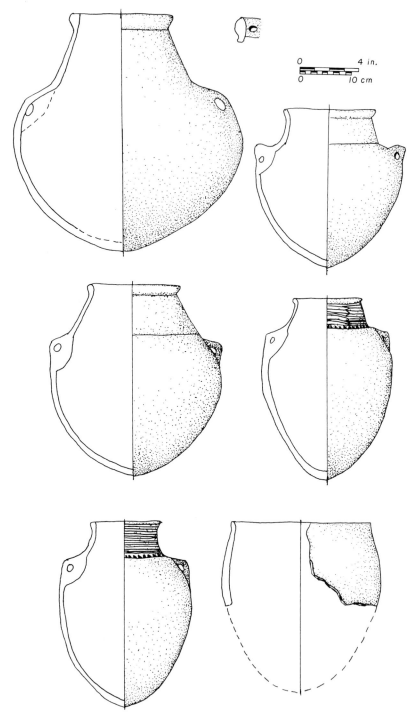

Fig. 160. Whole pots and sherds collected from shell mounds on the southern Cape coast reported to contain artifacts of the "midden" industry. (After Rudner 1968.)

422

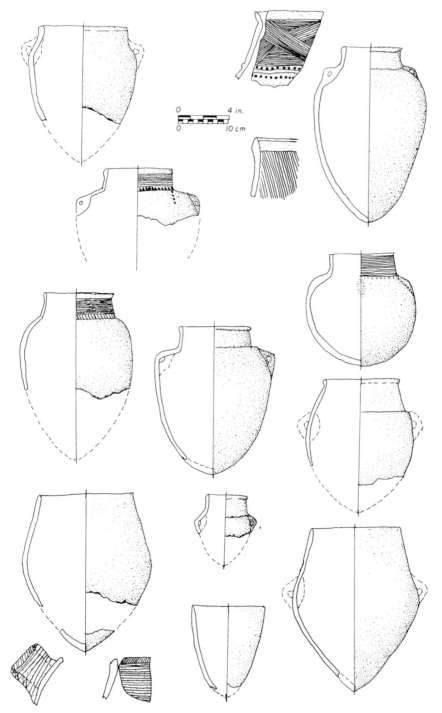

Fig. 161. Whole pots and sherds collected from shell mounds on the southern Cape coast reported to contain an unnamed lithic industry with blades and large backed crescents. (After Rudner 1968.)

423

perhaps weakening his case for a distinct Sandy Bay tradition on the southwestern coast.

To the east of Matjes River his surface collections suggest a distinctive non-Wilton artifact assemblage, including utilized quartzite flakes, convergent flakes, blades, and "giant backed crescents" presumably used as flake adzes (see Fig. 160). No numerical analysis of this evidently local midden industry has appeared, and Rudner's variable terminology (Late Mossel Bay, Magosian, Middle Stone Age, and the like) does little to clarify its typological characters. The apparently associated pottery (Fig. 161) also includes a few distinctive forms not found to the west, particularly the large spouted pots and small shouldered vessels.

From the East London district onward, lydianite (indurated shale) outcrops occur on the coast. Surface collections from middens along this stretch include a range of sidescraper types identical to those found in the Lockshoek industry (Chapter 7), but several collections include ceramics, an association that will be discussed later.

Whereas the surface collections suggest interesting regional differences in typology, the absence of sealed associations and dated assemblages detracts enormously from their value. Several cave and midden deposits have been excavated, but these provide assemblages different from those described by Rudner. Excavated sites include: Windhoek Farm Cave (Grobbelaar and Goodwin 1952); Nelson's Bay Cave (Inskeep 1965a); Matjes River Shelter (Louw 1960); Coldstream Cave (Peringuey 1911); Knysna Heads Cave (Bain 1880); Klasie's River Mouth (Singer and Wymer 1969); Andrieskraal I Shelter (J. Deacon 1965); Scott's Cave (Deacon and Deacon 1963); Storms River Mouth Cave and Swartrif Midden (Deacon 1969c); the Tsitsikamma Caves (FitzSimons 1923a, b, 1925); and Umgazana Cave (Chubb *et al.* 1934). Inevitably, different type lists have been used at each site, so that detailed comparisons between assemblages are difficult, particularly as the earlier excavators kept only small selected samples and very poor records.

With the exception of Umgazana (Levels 14–30) these assemblages contain very few elaborately shaped tools and do not fit most typological analyses. The type list prepared by J. Deacon (1965), as given in Table 71, is employed here to compare excavated samples.

Of these, only Klasie's River Mouth may resemble the surface collections briefly described by Rudner, but no figures have been published for this assemblage. The available evidence suggests both the Preceramic and Ceramic phases are present on the coast, with the two superimposed at Nelson's Bay Cave, Klasie's River Mouth, and (?) some of the Tsitsikamma Caves. Only at Matjes River is the Ceramic phase found overlying a Developed Wilton at the top of Layer C. East of Matjes River the preceramic levels are "nonmicrolithic" in character and have more features in common with the earlier Oakhurst industry.

TABLE 71

Type List from Various Southern Cape Coastal Sites [a]

	Windhoek Farm Cave	Nelson's Bay Cave	Matjes River Shelter, Layer B	Coldstream Cave	Klasie's River Mouth, Cave 5	Andrieskraal I Shelter	Scott's Cave	Swartrif Midden	Storms River Mouth	Tsitsikamma Caves
Endscrapers	—	X	5	X	—	2	—	—	—	—
Core scrapers–hammers	—	X	8	X	X	6	14	—	—	—
Sidescrapers	X	X	1	X	X	7	—	—	—	—
Convex scrapers	X	X	6	X	—	14	—	—	—	—
Notched scrapers	—	X	4	X	X	7	—	—	—	—
Outils écaillés	—	X	1	—	—	23	—	—	—	—
Utilized flakes	X	X	69	X	X	59	212	X	X	—
Pebble scrapers	X	X	10	X	X	34	7	X	X	—
Palettes	—	—	3	X	—	4	1	—	—	—
Grooved stones	X	—	—	—	—	4	—	X	—	—
Bored stones	X	X	3	X	—	7	—	—	X	—
Grindstones	X	X	X	X	X	25	1	X	X	—
Polished stone axes	X	—	—	—	—	—	—	—	—	—
Ground-edged pebbles	—	X	X	X	—	3	—	X	X	—
Pecked hammerstones	X	X	14	X	X	14	—	X	—	—
Battered quartz crystals	—	X	—	X	—	32	—	—	—	—
Sample totals:			124+			241	235			
Ocher pencils	—	X	X	X	—	3	X	—	—	—
Ocher-stained pebbles and slabs	—	X	X	X	Paintings	8	—	—	—	—
Potsherds	X Upper levels	X Upper levels	X	X	Upper levels	—	1671	—	—	Upper levels

[a] From J. Deacon (1965).

425

That they are contemporary with the Wilton at Matjes River Level C and elsewhere cannot be doubted:

Nelson's Bay Cave:

GrN-5702	2925 ± 35 B.P.	(975 B.C.)
GrN-5715	2540 ± 50 B.P.	(590 B.C.)

Klasie's River Mouth, Cave 5:

GX-1378	4110 ± 160 B.P.	(2160 B.C.)
GX-1397	2885 ± 105 B.P.	(335 B.C.)

Klasie's River Mouth, main cave:

GX-0969	2525 ± 85 B.P.	(575 B.C.)
GX-0971	2795 ± 85 B.P.	(845 B.C.)

This group of dates overlaps with those from the preceramic levels at Bonteberg, Gordon's Bay, and Die Kelders, all of which contained a similar range of stone artifacts.

A few Ceramic-phase dates are also available:

Nelson's Bay Cave:

GrN-5703	1930 ± 60 B.P.	(A.D. 20)

Scott's Cave:

bedrock	SR-82	1190 ± 100 B.P.	(A.D. 760)
top 3 inches	Y-1425	360 ± 80 B.P.	(A.D. 1590)

The Nelson's Bay Cave date again hints at a surprisingly early appearance of pottery in the southern Cape, but (like the Bonteberg Layer 2B date), this will need confirmation by further readings.

It has been repeatedly stressed that the lithic assemblages from these sites resemble the Oakhurst industry rather than the local (and contemporary) Coastal Wilton. The usually rich associated bonework and shell ornaments, however, includes the same range of types found in both the contemporary industries (see Table 72).

Implements of other organic materials are reported from only two sites. From Windhoek Farm cave comes a wooden "trap trigger" (Fig. 162) and several items of twisted grass (*Cyperus textilis*) including cordage, two-stranded rope, knotted netting, a complete bracelet, and the knotted edge of a mat. From among the dense grass bedding of the Scott's Cave deposits come 4 wooden pegs, 3 fire sticks, and 16 other objects including whittled points, bow-stave fragments, a blunt-ended bird bolt, and several worked ends. *Cyperus textilis* cordage includes knotted and whipped fragments. Leather thong fragments include knotted pieces. There is also a piece of sewed leather.

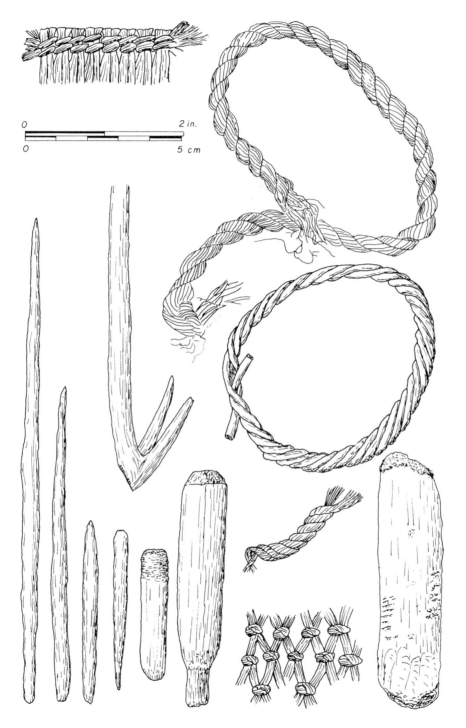

Fig. 162. Wooden tools and grass matting, twine, and netting from Windhoek Farm and Scott's Cave.

TABLE 72

Nonlithic Artifacts from Southern Cape Coastal Sites

	Windhoek Farm Cave	Nelson's Bay Cave	Matjes River Shelter, Layer B	Coldstream Cave	Andrieskraal Shelter I	Scott's Cave
Tools						
Polished bone tubes	X	X	X	X	—	X
Polished bone arrow points	X	X	X	X	X	—
Polished bone shaft fragments	X	X	X	X	X	—
Polished bone awls	X	X	X	X	X	X
Ivory link shaft–points	—	X	X	X	X	—
Ivory shaft fragments	—	—	X	—	X	—
Ivory–bone spatula	—	?	X	X	X	—
Ivory–bone mattock	—	—	X	—	—	—
Bone flakes	—	X	X	—	X	X
Bone fabricators	X	X	X	—	X	X
Ornaments						
Ostrich eggshell beads	X	X	X	X	X	X
Marine shell beads	—	X	X	X	X	X
Bone and ivory beads	—	—	X	—	X	—
Pierced marine shells	—	X	X	X	—	X
Nacre pendants	—	X	X	X	X	—
Ostrich eggshell pendants	X	—	X	—	X	—
Tortoiseshell pendants	—	—	X	—	—	—
Pottery bead	—	—	—	—	—	X

M. J. Wells (1965) identified several plant remains among the Scott's Cave bedding, including roots, bulbs, tuber corms, rhizomes, stems, fruit, seeds, leaves, bark, inflorescences, and thorns. Besides *C. textilis* there are bulbs of *C. usitatus* (uintjies), nearly all of which are crushed, suggesting that they were used as food. *Freesia* corms with young leaves indicate that they were dug up in late winter; *Cliffortia illicifolia*, a stream bank shrub, was probably used as bedding, as were the grasses *Cynodon dactylon* Pers.; *Setaria neglecta* de Wit, *Digitaria* sp.; and *Danthonia* sp., probably picked in summer, as was *Cyperus sphaerospermus* Schrad. An edible plant *Amarantus paniculatus* L. also occurs here as well as *Dioscorea, Watsonia, Aloe, Acacia karroo, Emex australis,* the reedlike palmiet *Priorium serratum*, and leaves of the ironwood *Vepris undulata*. None of this material has been carried any great distance to the cave, and most of the grasses were picked between August and April during summer.

Details of the dietary pattern at any of these sites remain rather vague. Shellfish collecting obviously played an important part in the diet, even at Scott's

TABLE 73

Shellfish Remains from Storm River Sites [a]

	Storms River Site 1		Storms River Site 2		Storms River Site 3		
	No.	%	No.	%	No.	%	Comments
Edible inclusions							
Patella argenvillei	48	6.4	—	—	6	1.0	Limpets (edible but
Patella barbara	68	9.1	9	2.0	20	3.2	indigestible)
Patella cochlear	130	17.4	72	15.9	61	9.7	
Patella longicosta	260	34.8	51	11.3	84	13.4	
Patella oculus	51	6.8	27	6.0	39	6.2	
Patella tabularis	26	3.5	4	0.9	4	0.6	
Perna perna	71	9.5	154	34.0	272	43.2	Mussels (edible)
Turbo sarmarticus	71	9.5	50	11.0	61	9.7	Alikreukel (edible)
Oxystele tigrina	6	0.8	48	10.5	48	7.6	Winkels (edible)
Oxystele sinensis	11	1.5	26	5.7	34	5.4	
Haliotis sanguineum	6	0.8	2	0.4	—	—	Siffie (edible)
Haliotis midae	—	—	10	2.2	—	—	Perlemoen (edible)
Sample totals:	**748**		**453**		**629**		
Other inclusions							
Balanus maxillarus	2		—		—		Barnacles
Tetraclita serrata	—		—		2		
Dinoplax gigas	1		—		—		Chitons
Thias capensis	1		—		—		
Thias squamosa	—		—		1		
Burnupena cincta	13		—		17		(Active predator)
Burnupena lagenaria	5		—		—		Welks
Burnupena sp.	4		—		—		(Scavenger)

[a] From H. J. Deacon (1969c).

Cave, where the occupants collected abundant freshwater mollusks. However, several mammalian species were hunted, including large and small antelope, carnivores, and rodents. Fish and tortoise were commonly taken as well, but more details are needed to assess the importance of hunting against collecting of seafoods.

H. J. Deacon (1969c) has provided an excellent analysis of shellfish and fish remains from Storms River Mouth and Swartrif (see Tables 73 and 74). The presence of two grooved line sinkers in the Swartrif midden has encouraged Deacon to suggest that the represented fish were partly caught on lines, whereas others (less commonly caught today) were killed by localized cold current upwellings. When analyses of this quality become standard practice in coastal excavations, a far clearer picture of Strandloper activity should emerge.

TABLE 74

Fish Remains from Various Southern Cape Coastal Sites [a]

	Fish remains				
	Premaxilla		Dentaries		Minimum number of individuals
Identification	Left	Right	Left	Right	
Storms River Site 1, Mouth cave midden					
Diplodus trifasciatus	1	1	2	—	2
Pomatomus saltator	—	—	1	2	2
Rhabdosargus sarba[b]	—	—	4	1	4
Diplodus sargus[b,c]	6	3	2	—	6
Chrysoblephus laticeps	2	7	2	3	7
Chrysoblephus gibbiceps[b]	—	1	1	—	1
Lithognathus lithognathus	—	—	1	1	1
Lithognathus mormyrus[b]	—	—	1	2	2
Pachymetopon grande[b]	1	—	—	—	1
Sample totals:	**10**	**12**	**14**	**9**	**26**
Storms River Site 2, Swartrif Midden					
Rhabdosargus sarba[b]	—	1	—	—	1
Diplodus sargus[b,c]	20	15	14	10	20
Diplodus trifasciatus	—	1	—	—	1
Chrysoblephus laticeps	2	4	1	—	4
Sample totals:	**22**	**21**	**15**	**10**	**26**

[a] From Deacon (1969c).
[b] Easily caught.
[c] Maybe killed by upswellings of cold water.

The physical characters of the Strandloper population of this zone are still imperfectly known. Craniometric data have been published from very few sites including Matjes River Layer B, Windhoek Farm, and a series of caves in the Tsitsikamma area (Laing 1925; Laing and Gear 1929; Wells 1929; Wells and Gear 1931). Unfortunately, both the excavations and reports on these sites (FitzSimons 1923a, b, 1925, 1926) were such that the associations of the extant material are in doubt and even the whereabouts of the individual caves remain ambiguous (Schauder 1963; Turner 1970).

Only a few basic craniometric features of this excavated sample can be compared for want of more published details. Figure 163a first compares the skull dimensions of Strandloper finds. In Fig. 163b these are treated as a single population and compared with the equivalent metrical ratios of the Coastal Wilton sample and the Oakhurst sample (Fig. 163c). This very inadequate glimpse of the available material can only serve to pose important questions rather than

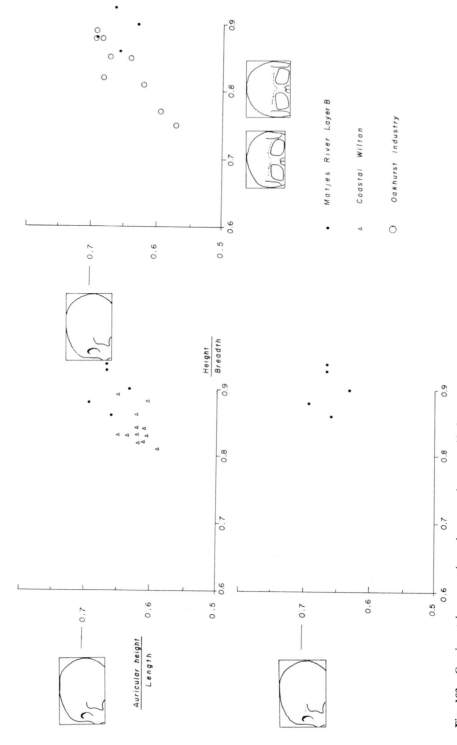

Fig. 163. Craniometric comparisons between three stratified groups of skulls from Matjes River, and Oakhurst: (top left) Coastal Wilton and Matjes River Layer B; (top right) Oakhurst Industry with Matjes River Layer B.

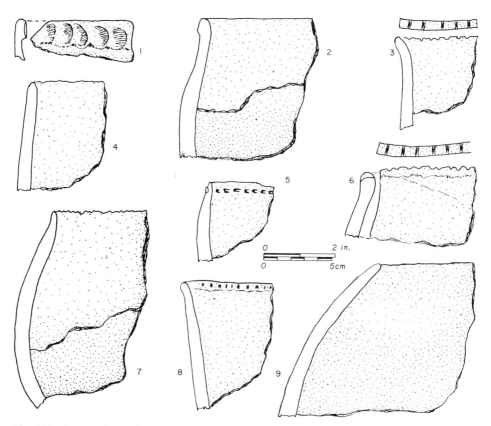

Fig. 164. Pottery from Zigzag and Umgazana caves: (1, 5, 7, 9) sherds from the ceramic levels of Umgazana Cave; (2, 3, 4, 6, 8) sherds from Zigzag Cave near Umgazana.

provide ready answers. It is apparent that the basic cranial morphology of the Strandloper samples has more in common with the Oakhurst sample than with the Wilton group. Since skull shape may be influenced by environmental factors, it is doubtful whether these similarities and differences have any genetic significance. The apparent similarity in skull morphology between Oakhurst and late Strandloper samples can, of course, only be confirmed by examination of much larger samples. The problem is a vital one, since the technical and cultural similarities between the Oakhurst industry and later Strandloper artifact samples are already clear. The significance of these connections is discussed in the concluding section (pages 435–438).

Unfortunately, the skeletal material from Umgazana has not survived. Here the selected Lockshoek sample from the lower deposits (Layers 1–14) is directly overlain with an *identical* lithic sample associated with abundant pottery (Schofield 1938c) sharing distinctive traits not present at sites further west (Fig. 164). Again, Umgazana suggests a continuity for the Oakhurst complex on the southern Cape coast, perhaps into the historical period.

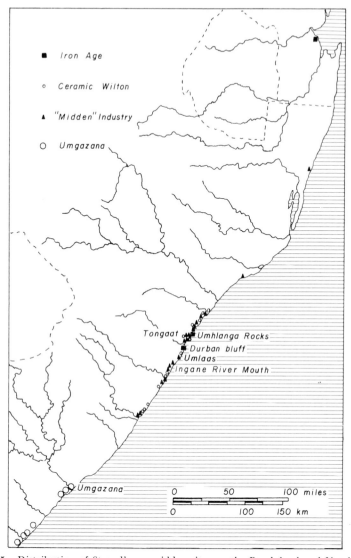

Fig. 165. Distribution of Strandloper midden sites on the Pondoland and Natal coast.

THE NATAL COAST

The distribution of published midden sites is mapped in Fig. 165 and has been compiled from several brief surveys: P.G. Brien (1932a), King and Chubb (1932a), Schofield (1935, 1936a, b, 1938a), Schoute-Vanneck (1958), Schoute-Vanneck and Walsh (1959), and van Riet Lowe (1946).

Of these, only Midden A at Ingane River Mouth, has been excavated and adequately described by Schoute-Vanneck and Walsh (1959). Stone artifacts include

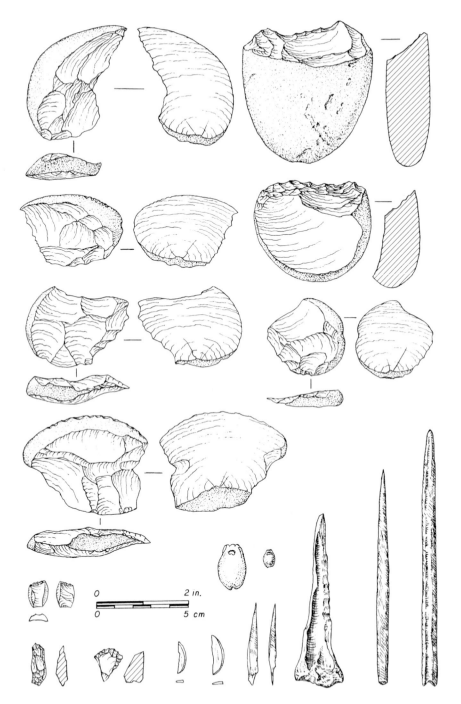

Fig. 166. Ingane River Mouth: a typical set of Strandloper midden artifacts, dominated by flaked cobbles, utilized flakes, and various bone working, ornaments, and rare smaller scrapers and *outils écaillés*.

flaked pebbles of sandstone, lydianite, and silicified tillite; large utilized flakes struck from the pebbles; rare flake scrapers; small quartz scrapers; *outils écaillés;* and utilized bladelets. Bone work includes cylindrical polished points, awls, spatulas, and flaked fragments. There are also pierced shell ornaments, beads and shell crescents, and rare ostrich eggshell beads. A single potsherd is claimed to be "intrusive." Among the fauna are 18 species of shellfish (of which *Mytilus perna* is dominant), abundant small fish remains, large and small antelope, rodents, and insectivores (Fig. 166).

Three adjacent middens provided Iron Age pottery, but no flaked artifacts. Middens with abundant Iron Age pottery, a few grindstones and no other associations have also been reported from Durban Bluff (Schoute-Vanneck 1958) and Umhlanga Rocks (Beater and Maud 1963). Several other middens with only Iron Age ceramics have been noted along the northern Natal coast extending into Mozambique (van Riet Lowe and Wells 1944). Although it is quite possible that Iron Age groups practiced a littoral subsistence economy, no adequate archaeological investigation of the problem has been undertaken. Associated human skeletal sample and a series of carbon-14 dates would greatly assist our understanding of the changes from Stone Age to Iron Age material culture on the Natal coast.

CONCLUSIONS

Because the term "Strandloper" refers to a highly developed set of littoral exploitation strategies, it obviously has too broad a meaning to be applied to a related group of lithic assemblages. Strandloper strategies were employed by the makers of the Oakhurst, Coastal Wilton, and later sites. Certainly there is no single "Strandloper industry" and a terminology for later non-Wilton assemblages is needed.

Whereas too little research has been carried out on the western and eastern coasts, work on southern Cape coast sites has demonstrated that a relatively simple Oakhurst-like flaking technology was practiced on several middens during the Wilton period. Several local researchers have repeatedly insisted in print that such sites must represent a specialized or seasonal activity of the local population (for example, H. J. Deacon 1969c; Inskeep 1967; Maggs and Speed 1967; and others). In their opinion, adjacent middens and inland caves containing Wilton assemblages, therefore, would represent yet another aspect of the same population's activities. The presence of rare marine shell ornaments in coast-range caves is frequently invoked as evidence of such population movements, which, it is implied, would be a logical procedure to avoid exhausting littoral food supplies, particularly shellfish.

Much evidence suggests that this assumption is invalid. The range of faunal material from Wilton and non-Wilton middens is identical: shellfish collecting is invariably supplemented by fishing and hunting of all available game animals. The same range of subsistence activities took place on both kinds of midden. Thus, the differences in artifact content are more likely to reflect two distinct stone-flaking traditions that represent two independent populations. Obviously, they exploited the littoral by using every available food source.

One tacit assumption of the "transhumance" school of interpretation is that littoral food sources would be too quickly exhausted if utilized constantly. Most shell mounds are dominated by one or two molluscan species that thrive close to the site, suggesting that a certain shell bank was repeatedly visited and cropped. Middens were not semipermanent settlements, as their structure invariably shows; thus, bands of shells representing single "crops" are frequently sandwiched between lenses of windblown sand that drifted over the midden at times when the surface was abandoned. If one shellfish source showed signs of exhaustion, it would be just as logical to move *along* the shore to another, rather than turning inland away from a major food supply.

The archaeological evidence suggests that intensive exploitation of coastal resources began with the Oakhurst industry about 10,000–8000 B.C. (any possibly earlier sites are now drowned by the postglacial rise in sea level at this time). The Oakhurst tool kit with its wide range of bone tools and equipment for processing vegetable foods was no doubt developed to cope with all aspects of coastal resources. It has been suggested in previous chapters that it represents a permanent coastal population fully adapted to this way of life. What is now emerging from the archaeological record is that this industry persisted on the extreme southern coast of Africa for several millenia after its contemporaries—the Lockshoek and Pomongwan industries—had disappeared from the interior. Whereas the Wilton technology came to dominate the interior, its influence on the southern Cape coast is not apparent east of Matjes River. Even on the southwestern coast where Wilton middens are common, the Oakhurst tradition may have persisted alongside the Wilton. Later in its Developed and Ceramic phases, the Coastal Wilton contains fewer microliths and a greater proportion of simple flake scrapers, trimmed pebbles, and utilized flakes, perhaps suggesting a new extension of the Oakhurst technology. No Ceramic Wilton middens have been reliably dated to the historic period. It is likely that this technical tradition had disappeared from the Cape coast by the seventeenth century A.D. when the first European contact was established and the historical period begins. Only in the mountainous interior did the Wilton tradition persist, as shown at De Hangen (Fig. 167).

At present it seems most probable that the montane "Bushmen" of van Riebeeck's *Journal* were indeed a distinct ethnic group, belonging to the Wilton technical tradition, while his "Strandlopers" belonged to an even older tradition with its roots in the Oakhurst complex. If the existence of an intrusive "Wilton population" in the southwestern Cape Province is accepted, their sojourn on the coastal strip may have been relatively brief, after which the indigenous population reasserted its hold over this littoral.

If this rough patchwork of cultural and skeletal evidence is combined, there is some reason to suspect that the Strandlopers represented are an extremely ancient and isolated Stone Age group, briefly influenced by Wilton ideas (and the genes of the "Wilton population").

Probably, the ceramics found in Strandloper middens were acquired from so-called "Hottentots," who were highly mobile potmaking, metal-using stock herders, whose temporary encampments cannot yet be recognized in the archaeological record. There is no reason to doubt that some middens, particularly those on the Atlantic coast, were actually made by destitute Hottentot groups, but they betray no distinctive cultural features. On the Natal coast, certain middens were formed by fugitive Iron Age groups who adopted a Strandloper subsistence after losing property and livestock. Here at least, the distinctive pottery and absence of flaked stone supports the interpretation.

The ultimate fate of the historical Strandlopers was less frequently violent than that of the interior "Bushmen" of the Smithfield complex. By the mid-

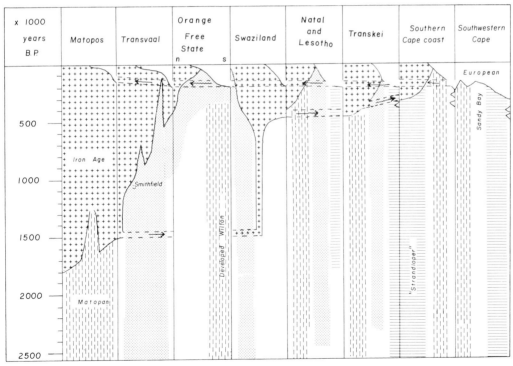

Fig. 167. Tentative diagram displaying the complex set of culture contacts in different regions of southern Africa at the close of the Stone Age and the beginning of the historical period.

eighteenth century the Strandlopers are no longer mentioned in the chronicles of the Cape colony. Epidemics introduced from European ships appear to have reduced their numbers quite rapidly, and most of the survivors were absorbed as farm or domestic labor. Only a few stragglers continued to live on the beaches of the southwestern Cape coast, now employed to dig away their own ancestors' shell middens. With these they fed the lime kilns put up by van Riebeeck's men to provide mortar for the fortress and settlement. In so doing Africa's last Stone Age people may have taken most of their history with them before they were finally obliterated by the European advance.

11

Doubts and
Speculations

Among the new hypotheses appearing in the preceding chapters are several that merit further critical appraisal. A few others could be tentatively expanded. This final chapter therefore attempts to evaluate certain interpretations and to offer some alternatives. As field research expands, some of these will probably become redundant, but no apology is necessary. Obviously the mere synthesis of facts is a sterile exercise unless accompanied by insights into the events under investigation. However blurred or distorted by inadequate data, such interpretations may be of some use even if they act only as foils for further criticism. Much of what follows is little more than guesswork propped up by fragments and hints, but without this no clear direction can emerge for future research. To remain silent, with the excuse that more and better evidence is needed, would defeat the purpose of this work.

THE SIGNIFICANCE OF *Australopithecus africanus*

In Chapter 2, the scattered data from the australopithecine-bearing breccias have been manipulated to suggest that *A. africanus* remains represent the earliest known true hominids in southern Africa. It is important that the reader recognize that such manipulation is only possible because the field evidence is so imprecise. The case for broad correlations between Taung, Sterkfontein lower, and Makapan gray breccias rests entirely on an assessment of the mammalian fauna and granulometry. The fact that all three units contain *A. africanus* only, without traces of stone toolmaking, cannot be used to support such correlations since it is precisely these features which we wish to compare.

Neither the faunal nor the granulometric data offer a watertight case. The mammalian fossil assemblages differ markedly in composition since each reflects a different habitat. Furthermore, the artiodactyl list from Sterkfontein is probably incomplete, and Churcher (1970) has shown that *Equus capensis* (*E. helmei*) is present in the Sterkfontein Type Site, but absent from the other two. The orthodox view that Taung and Sterkfontein Type Site are close in time may require future revision. Unfortunately, we cannot determine whether the giant horse remains come from all levels of the lower breccia. The three assemblages may be viewed as broadly coeval, but we have insufficient evidence to allow a precise age ranking (Sampson 1971a).

The correlation of upper deposits at Sterkfontein and Makapan with Swartkrans and Kromdraai B is also weakly supported, there being no clearly defined assemblage from the Makapan pink or red-brown breccias. Similarities between the granulometric curves of the four deposits may be fortuitous. It remains likely that factors other than climatic fluctuations have caused the observed changes and Butzer (1971) has suggested that changes in slope gradient may be partially responsible for the granulometric curves. This objection, however, does not help us to understand why the curves are so alike in some cases. Although it remains impossible to prove that the four deposits are contemporary, there can be little doubt that they are all later in time than the three assemblages discussed above. Thus, in spite of numerous weaknesses in the evidence, it appears reasonably certain that deposits containing *A. africanus* only without stone working are earlier than those containing *Homo* sp., *A. robustus,* and traces of *A. africanus* with stone tools.

If *A. africanus* is indeed a fully erect biped, the lack of evidence for stone working behavior requires some comment. That no stone tools have been discovered at Taung, Sterkfontein Type, or Makapan gray breccia can, of course, be ascribed to chance. If it is accepted that *A. africanus* is in fact the *earliest* hominid, this absence takes on a a greater significance. There may now be some reason to suspect that the species was truly incapable of stone tool manufacture. Furthermore, its capacity to reshape mammalian skeletal parts for use as tools or weapons remains in doubt. Even the rammed, wedged, and locally abraded specimens from Makapan (which could not be discussed as the product of gnawing by carnivores) may now be questioned. Observations by Zapfe (1939, 1966) on the gnawing behavior of the caged spotted hyena and the valuable work of Kruuk (1966) and Sutcliffe (1970) on eastern African spotted hyenas in the wild show that this animal does indeed cause bone accumulations. Furthermore, rammed and wedged fragments occur in partly digested, regurgitated lumps, evidently brought back to the lair to feed the young. In these same collections occur specimens with localized surface abrasions and holes caused by the erosive action of gastric juices. There now appears to be no damaged element from the Makapan gray breccia found that cannot be explained in terms of natural nonhominid activity.

One further question arises from this case: Is *A. africanus* the only australopithecine at all three sites? Tobias (1967a) has shown that a few *A. africanus* cheek teeth from Sterkfontein and Makapan fall within the range of *A. robustus* measurements, but these are not characteristic of the latter's truly giant molars and premolars. This sample is so small that most authorities prefer to regard it as representing a large (male?) *A. africanus* rather than the robust species. Their inclusion in the *A. africanus* collections suggests a wider morphological variation for this species than is generally recognized.

BIPEDAL STATUS FOR *Australopithecus robustus?*

Evidence has been slowly accumulating, mainly from eastern African sites, to suggest that *A. robustus* may not have been capable of permanent bipedal locomotion. Broom's early reservations about the appearance of the *A. robustus* ischium are once more gaining attention. Several factors may now be considered: the length of the ischium does not clearly suggest a pelvic adaptation to permanent bipedal gait; humerus and radius fragments are extremely long, suggesting an arm length similar to that of modern humans; the epiphyses of finger bones hint at adaptation to part-time knuckle-walking; the cranial capacity has been shown to fall within the range of modern gorillas. These, together with the evidence already brought forward by Robinson, serve to reopen Broom's original case for a separate generic status (*Paranthropus*) for this material. The dietary hypothesis is further supported by Jolly's (1970a, b) work on grass-eating baboons, which suggests that groups with a specialized diet comprising grass blades, seeds, rhizomes, small leaves, bulbs, and ground-dwelling arthropods display most of the dental and cranial features that distinguish the robust from the gracile australopithecines.

It now appears more probable that the robust form represents a distinct population of partly bipedal, partly knuckle-walking primates adapted to grazing in an open, treeless niche.

PREDATION AT THE AVEN MOUTH: AN ALTERNATIVE ROLE

It is widely believed that the great wealth of material in the breccias is the result of chance preservation. It is also possible that the sites themselves may have played a significant role in hominid evolutionary processes.

If the aven or fissure mouth consistently attracted leopards from the surrounding grasslands, as Brain has suggested, it is also likely that an array of scavengers would be attracted to the same locality. Among these we might expect hyenas, other large carnivores, and australopithecines, all intent upon driving the leopard from its kill slung across a tree limb above the fissure. Of these three it seems likely that australopithecines may have been the more successful. *If* competitive scavenging was to become a regular feature of australopithecine behavior, it is likely that this niche would have exerted pressures on the behavior of the scavenging group. Success and survival in such a niche would require more frequent display of group aggression, organized attack, stone throwing, club wielding, and mutual support among members of the group. Individuals less adept at bipedal running and quick judgment or timing stand less chance of survival in this situation. Thus, several hominid characters involving behavior, anatomy, and mental agility will be favored by accelerated selection.

Brain has suggested that several agents contributed bones to the five sites: leopards, hyenas, porcupines, owls, saber-tooth cats, and australopithecines, with leopards contributing the most. However, several large carnivores including lions,.leopards, hyenas, and saber-tooth cats also occur in the accumulations. Although accidental deaths may account for some of these, it is plausible that competitive scavenging would increase the frequency of such deaths among this group. The evidence for australopithecine scavenging activities, if it exists, cannot be discerned from the available record. Read's (1971) claim to have revealed such activity at Makapan is without foundation as no attention is paid to the role of alternative scavengers. The search for such evidence may be the central focus for future research.

This line of speculation would therefore suggest an alternative role for the breccia caves; not only were they possible traps, but they also acted as a crucial niche in which adjacent australopithecine groups would have been subjected to accelerated "hominization" through competitive scavenging. How we should recognize such activity in the fossil record has yet to be determined.

AUSTRALOPITHECINES AS PART
OF THE AFRICAN FAUNA

Students of human origins have concentrated, understandably, upon those anatomical and behavioral features that distinguish man from nonhuman primates. By isolating such sets of characters we may hope eventually to understand the mechanism and process by which nonhuman traits were replaced by human ones. Serious discussion of the actual *process* of "hominization" has only just begun and is purely hypothetical. Research aimed at testing such hypotheses tends to be extremely specialized and usually deals with functional anatomy or primate behavior in the wild. So narrow is the focus of our interest that we tend to forget that the early hominids were an integral part of a much larger and fantastically varied game population. Any changes on other parts of the mass were likely to influence the fate of the hominids contained within it.

Of crucial importance are the relationships between the large predators and their prey, including game herds and primates. A third group affected by this relationship is the scavengers. The numbers, dimensions, hunting tactics, killing patterns, and specialized niches of a single large carnivore species are dependent upon the food sources available to it and upon the competition from other carnivores. Even intraspecific competition can affect the fate of the species. In turn, large carnivores by selective killing have the potential to mold behavioral and anatomical traits in the prey species, including primates. Factors that might cause carnivores to hunt and kill primates more frequently are: a decrease in alternative food sources such as game herds; more frequent harrassment from a growing scavenger population; growth of competing carnivore populations; growth of primate populations. Thus, selective pressures could be brought to bear upon the early hominids via large carnivores responding to the interplay of population dynamics in the African fauna as a whole.

It is interesting to note that the carnivores and nonhuman primates from the breccias suggest several important changes with time. Most obvious are trends toward size increase among the baboons of the later deposits. At the same time there is an incredible proliferation of predatory hyenas, some of which are giant forms. Large lion- and leopardlike forms also appear for the first time, and only one fairly small saber-tooth cat survives into the later stages. It is suggested that such changes may reflect real shifts in the local animal population.

An increase in the total number of carnivores in the region would inevitably lead to further adaptations in specialized niches, presumably giving rise to speciation. Probably the success of the hyenids at this time arose out of adaptations to both hunting and scavenging niches. Inevitably such development would have some impact on the primate population, and the trend toward giganticism in the baboons may be a response to such changes. Increased harrassment by hyenas may conceivably have caused leopards to concentrate on primate kills that are lighter and more readily dragged into trees.

One cannot help but observe that it was during this same period that the hominid population displays its greatest morphological diversity. The mechanisms underlying that diversity should be sought in an understanding of game population dynamics. The foregoing are little more than brief and grossly oversimplified guesses in a field outside the author's competence. However, they serve to point up the fact that we have no long-term studies of large carnivore predation in the wild. Nor do we know anything about the frequency of predation on large primates in various habitats. While it is still possible, such surveys might be usefully carried out with the aid of electronic tracking devices.

A LOCAL EVOLUTION?

As Ewer (1957b) has observed, the faunas of Taung, Makapan, and Sterkfontein Type Site include more extinct species than the fauna of Olduvai Gorge Bed I of eastern Africa. Although direct faunal comparisons between eastern and southern Africa will always remain tenuous, it appears likely that Swartkrans and Kromdraai have more in common with Olduvai Bed I and may be broadly contemporary. If this correlation is accepted, a reasonable date for the beginning of their accumulation would be 2–1.5 million years ago, if the potassium–argon dates from the bottom of Olduvai are accepted. Bed I, like the South African sites, has yielded a diversified hominid sample and abundant stone tools. A similar array of evidence is emerging from Koobi Fora and Ileret East of Lake Rudolf, and there is now some reasonable claim that hominid evolution after 2 million B.P. followed parallel patterns in both eastern and southern Africa.

However, the dated material from the lower Omo beds north of Lake Rudolf must be broadly contemporary with the *A. africanus* sites of South Africa, that is, between about 3.5 and 2 million years. The Omo hominid remains, although mainly dental and fragmentary jaw material, point quite clearly to a diversified population including very massive *A. robustus* types, gracile australopithecines, and even smaller-toothed specimens tentatively ascribed to the genus *Homo*. Such an array contrasts sharply with the South African evidence which suggests a much narrower range of morphological variation during the same period.

Australopithecus africanus may represent a local specialized population out of which the later diversity emerged. Alternately, the concentration of *A. africanus* in the three sites could conceivably reflect some specialized predation habit of a large carnivore that sampled only gracile specimens from the whole population. A third possibility is that diversification (speciation?) of the hominids took place earlier in eastern Africa than in southern Africa, possibly due to the earlier proliferation of carnivores in this region.

THE ORIGINS OF *Homo erectus* AND THE ACHEULIAN

Although skeletal material ascribed to *Homo erectus* is firmly associated with Acheulian artifacts at sites in eastern and northern Africa, no such connection can be established to the south. Possibly the Broken Hill, Hopefield, and Cave of Hearths specimens represent relatively late examples of this population, but these already display characters (including a larger brain capacity) not typical of the northern specimens.

Numerous students of the Acheulian have pointed to its typological uniformity, widespread geographical distribution, and consistent associations with the bones of large game animals. Whereas it has been widely assumed that the complex "evolved" out of the Oldowan, it is seldom asked why or by what processes this might have happened. Similar questions surround the emergence of *H. erectus* and his probable dispersal into new habitats in Europe and eastern Asia.

Evidently the australopithecines of south-central Africa had already diversified 2 million years ago. At one extreme of their range of variability were groups displaying "human" behavior patterns more frequently. This segment of the population, by definition, was best adapted to withstand predation and even to compete with large carnivores by scavenging and infrequent killing of smaller animals and juvenile game. By constant association with and observation of large carnivore tactics, true hunting strategies were far more likely to emerge in this segment than elsewhere in the population.

Protection from predation by organized resistance would no doubt have helped this part of the population to increase faster than the other segments. They may ultimately have collaborated with large carnivores in the extermination of the rest of the population. Thus, the range of variability became narrowed down about 500,000 years ago with the extinction of the small-brained and robust forms. *Homo erectus* could conceivably be the end product of such a process.

Again, this is an overbrief and too simplistic view of a crucial event. Innumerable other factors no doubt contributed to the anatomical changes, one of which may have been a marked increase in the sheer physical strength of the individual. Isaac (1967b) has pointed to the pronounced increase in the size of struck flakes in the Lower Acheulian, in contrast to the (contemporary?) Developed Oldowan technology. It is possible that this change reflects more than just manual dexterity. The production of larger flakes was obviously linked to the need for hand-axes and cleavers, both tools that are assumed to reflect a cultural response to the problems of dismembering large carcasses.

ALTERNATIVE VIEWS
ON THE PIETERSBURG COMPLEX

Although typological similarities between sites included in this complex can be demonstrated, there is still insufficient evidence to prove that they are all contemporary. Indeed, several of the associated carbon-14 dates would suggest that some sites overlap in time with the Bambata complex. If this overlap could be proved, the case for a discrete complex would be considerably weakened. There remains the possibility that some Pietersburg sites are nothing more than specialized work places of hunter–gatherer groups also responsible for Bambata sites elsewhere. If this relationship could be proved, considerable damage might be done to the hypothesis that the Pietersburg represents a distinctive Pre-Bambata tradition.

At present the stratigraphic evidence from Cave of Hearths, Mwulu's Cave, Border Cave, Rose Cottage Cave, and possibly Skildergat argues against contemporaniety for the two complexes. The carbon-14 dates for this period are so inconsistent that they should not be preferred to the stratigraphic evidence. Whereas the Pietersburg tradition may have persisted in the semiarid Karroo region into the Bambata period of the north, such contemporaneity has yet to be proved by absolute dating.

THE BAMBATA COMPLEX
IN WIDER PERSPECTIVE

Several authors have observed that the Bambata (or "Stillbay") of southern Africa should be regarded as contemporary with the sequence of Upper Paleolithic industries from Europe. An uncritical survey of the associated carbon-14 dates might suggest that this was indeed the case. However, an increasing number of dates reveal that some Bambata samples may be as old as 50,000 years or even older, thus casting doubt on many of the later dates. If the Bambata complex proves to be this old, it should be equated rather with the Middle Paleolithic industries of Europe. Indeed one cannot help but be struck by the remarkable typological affinities between many Bambata samples and those from the Mousterian of Europe and northwestern Africa or the Levalloiso–Mousterian of southwestern Asia and northeastern Africa. Of course, this comparison must await formal demonstration by an analyst conversant with the standardized Mousterian typology established by Bordes (1959) and applied almost universally to the Mousterian complex. No doubt several localized differences will emerge, but most of these could be ascribed to the fact that flint is not available in southern Africa where less tractible cryptocrystalline rocks were widely used.

If the Bambata is regarded as a local expression of Mousteroid technology, we might expect it to be associated with hominid remains of Neanderthal type, but this has yet to be demonstrated.

CARBON-14 DATING
AND THE HOWIESONSPOORT PROBLEM

So numerous are the carbon-14 readings from claimed Howiesonspoort levels in excess of 30,000 B.P. that one is prompted to wonder whether there may in fact be another extremely early "Howiesonspoort" tradition on the southern Cape coast besides the one appearing at about 20,000 B.P. At least three alternative arguments may be proposed:

    1. The older readings are the result of sample contamination by ancient or "dead" carbon. There is no shred of evidence that might support this claim, and such contaminations in cave deposits are virtually unknown.

2. The younger readings are all contaminated and should be disregarded; this includes the date from the type site. Such contamination is certainly possible, but still unproved. *If* all the Howiesonspoort samples are older than 30,000 B.P., we should have to reconsider their position within the framework of Stone Age chronology.

3. Most of the dates are correct—what is at fault is the grouping of all samples under a single unit: the Howiesonspoort. In the present absence of a numerical survey, such an error is entirely possible.

If there are in fact two (chronologically separated) industries both erroneously labeled "Howiesonspoort" on the southern Cape coast, we must conclude that the complexities of culture change here are still beyond the prehistorian's grasp.

HOPES AND HESITATIONS: SOUTHERN AFRICA IN PALEOLITHIC PREHISTORY

It has been frequently suggested that the earliest hominids are found in large numbers in eastern and southern African sites simply because the two areas offer unique conditions for the preservation of Lower Pleistocene fossils. Protagonists of this argument usually wish to point out that australopithecines have not been found in Europe and Asia because contemporary deposits have not survived. This of course implies that very early hominids were indeed present in both continents. Such talk is nonsense.

Kurtén (1968) has summarized no less than 20 Lower Pleistocene (Villafranchian) sites containing massive mammalian fossil accumulations from Europe. Several of these are limestone cavern breccias no doubt formed by broadly similar depositional processes to those which shaped the South African sites. Not one has yielded hominid remains or legitimate flaked stone artifacts. The total number of European fossil-bearing sites of Lower Pleistocene date still exceeds that known from sub-Saharan Africa. It is surely more than coincidental that no European australopithecines have been discovered?

Among the scanty claims for the presence of stone artifacts in association with Villafranchian faunas in Europe are: Grotte du Vallonet, l'Escale and Montière in France; Bugiuleşti, Dirjov, and Farkaşele in Romania; and Gerasimovka in southern Russia. With the exception of Vallonet on the Riviera coast, none of these claims survives critical examination. From Asia the only acceptable association comes from el'Ubeidiyeh in Israel. None of the claims from the Soan and Narbada rivers of India occurs with fauna, nor do those from the Irrawaddy in Burma. In Java the Sangiran hominid maxilla and the Modjokerto infant cranium are both from beds claimed to contain Villafranchian fauna, and australopithecine status has been proposed for the infant. Unfortunately the date of the associated Djetis fauna is still disputed. Only Vallonet and el'Ubeidiyeh offer completely convincing evidence of Lower Pleistocene hominid activity outside Africa. It is suggested that both localities represent the peripheral dispersal of the earliest hominid population out of the savannah belts of southern central Africa, which can still be regarded as the legitimate place of origin for mankind.

Although South Africa offers none of the fine stratified, dated primary-context evidence of the eastern African sites, it has nonetheless provided the largest body of hominid fossils so far and offers a unique insight into one of the niches in which the hominizing process could have operated.

The remarkable technical uniformity achieved by the Acheulian hominids has been traced to southwestern Asia, southern and western India; also to south and eastern Europe (where contemporary non-Acheulian groups have also been claimed to exist). Olduvai Gorge in Tanzania still offers the best opportunity for examining the technical origin of the Acheulian and its links with the (contemporary?) Developed Oldowan. If related technical changes did indeed take place elsewhere in the Oldowan world, we have no evidence of them. Apparently genuine early Acheulian sites occur in northwestern Africa, Spain, southern France, and Israel, but there is no proof that these evolved *locally* from the preceding Oldowan. In South Africa, only Swartkrans offers some hint of a transition between the two complexes.

Our present evidence would suggest that Acheulian groups dispersed into northwestern Europe and possibly into southern Asia some time after the first Acheulian appearance in Africa. Even cursory examination of the very incomplete distribution maps for the Acheulian strongly suggest that southern Africa maintained possibly the densest human population in the world during this period. As such, it held the greatest potential for further technical innovation; several sharply contrasting habitats were occupied, prompting local adaptations to cope with special regional problems of survival. Unfortunately the earliest appearance of the Proto-Levallois technique and true blade production cannot be firmly dated, but sufficient evidence exists to suggest that both were practiced by Acheulian groups on the vast central plateau of South Africa. Late in the Acheulian period, these local traditions were diverging so dramatically that no trace of the earlier conformity remained. Similar divergence has been observed elsewhere in Africa, Europe, and southwestern Asia, but only in a very limited area is it possible to detect the emergence of a blade-producing tradition from the final Acheulian. On the Levantine coast of the Mediterranean the sites of Adlun, et Tabun, and the inland site of Jabrud have yielded a pre-Mousterian industry with small hand-axes, choppers, large blades, blade cores, and burins. The Pre-Aurignacian is also found at Haua Fteah on the Libyan coast. No trace of such a development has been recovered from any of the surrounding regions, which were presumably occupied by groups practicing a Levallois technology.

Although still poorly documented, it is already apparent that similar innovations took place, probably during the same period (this has yet to be dated), in the high semiarid Karroo region of South Africa. Whereas it is suspected that the Pre-Aurignacian of southwestern Asia was accompanied by significant genetic changes in the local Acheulian population (forming an ancestral stock for modern Man), no skeletal evidence is forthcoming to demonstrate this point. For this reason the Florisbad skull is all the more significant as it hints at morphological changes which suggest very early shifts in the population of the South African plateaus toward modern features. In neither the technical nor the evolutionary sense can South Africa be regarded as a "backwater" during this period.

During the subsequent emergence of the Mousterian complex of Europe, northern Africa, and southwestern Asia, it seems most likely that the Bambata and Lupemban complexes dominated sub-Saharan Africa. If a Neanderthal population was responsible for these two, we have no field evidence to prove it. Again, there is no evidence to suggest that southern Africa had "fallen behind" other regions in either technical innovations or the development of hunting strategies. Indeed, the existence of sophisticated blade-based industries on the southern Cape coast (the Howeisonspoort) between 50,000 and 40,000 B.P., as well as the persistence of blade industries on the Orange River, strongly suggest a rigorous innovative culture complex not apparent from the Paleolithic record elsewhere at this period.

Certainly the most remarkable "local" development in southern Africa was the disappearance of the Howiesonspoort–Umguzan traditions and their replacement by the nonmicrolithic Oakhurst complex (perhaps as early as 12,000 B.P.) made by peoples already showing some resemblance to the indigenous population of the much later historical period. Apart from the quite dramatic changes in technology, there occurs a marked shift in subsistence strategies away from hunting to a more broad-based hunter–gatherer economy. This change has direct parallels in the postglacial adaptations of the contemporary European population and also the prefarming cultures of southwestern Asia.

It is only at this stage that southern Africa failed to develop strategies similar to the remainder of the Old World. With the abundance of game animals, vegetable, riverine, and littoral food resources, no pressures occurred to develop alternative economic patterns. The scarcity of readily domesticated local species, and the vast distances and physical barriers cut this region off from the farming practices of northern and central Africa, and indigenous farming culture failed to develop. Instead, the diverse peoples of the Wilton complex emerged, in which hunter–gatherer economics were further refined. The behavior of local food sources was closely studied over several millenia and carefully cropped to allow maximum leisure without destroying the source itself. The elegance of such subsistence strategies, still practiced by the Bushmen of the Kalahari today, cannot be matched by any of the disastrous practices of the farming world. The failure of the southern African population to develop farming, permanent settlements, urbanism, metallurgy, and higher technology can, of course, be claimed as evidence of "backwardness" within the nineteenth century concept of "Progress." But the modern descendants of the Smithfield population have conserved aspects of human experience which are increasingly difficult to discover in the back streets of civilization. With their seemingly incredible leisure periods, their prolific creativity, Rabelaisian humor and appetites, their dagga and their dancing, the Bushmen seem enviably content with their lot. They do not of course make convincing Noble Savages, suffering like other humans from the usual repertoire of ailments. If left alone, they may survive yet while the civilized portion of our species discovers new and beastlier ways to destroy itself. We might profit by listening to the laughter from the Stone Age with closer attention.

Bibliography

Abel, W.
  1931   Kritische Untersuchungen über *Australopithecus africanus* Dart. *Morphologiese Jahrbuch* **65**, 4, 539–640.
Alexander, A. J.
  1956   Bone carrying by a porcupine. *South African Journal of Science* **52**, 257–258.
Alexander, J. E.
  1838   *An expedition of discovery into the interior of Africa, through the hitherto undescribed countries of the Geat Namaquas, Boschmans and Hill Damaras performed under the auspices of Her Majesty's Government and the Royal Geographical Society, and conducted by Sir James Edward Alexander*. London: Colburn.
Alimen, H.
  1957   *The Prehistory of Africa*. London: Hutchinson.
Anderson, J. M.
  1968   The cultural implications of the Rhinoceros teeth from the limeworks, Makapansgat. *Palaeontologia Africana* **11**, 85–97.
Armstrong, A. L.
  1931   Rhodesian Archaeological Expedition (1929): Excavation in Bambata Cave and researches on prehistoric sites in Southern Rhodesia. *Journal of the Royal Anthropoligical Society of London* **120**, 4, 715–721.

451

Ashton, E. H.
 1950   The endocranial capacities of the Australopithecinae. *Proceedings of the Zoological Society of London* **120**, 4, 715–731.

Ashton, E. H., and S. Zuckerman
 1951   Some cranial indices of *Plesianthropus* and other primates. *American Journal of Physical Anthropology* n.s. **9**, 3, 283–296.

 1952   Age changes in the position of the occipital condyles in the chimpanzee and gorilla. *American Journal of Physical Anthropology* n.s. **10**, 3, 277–288.

 1956a   The base of the skull in immature hominoids. *American Journal of Physical Anthropology* n.s. **144**, 611–624.

 1956b   Age changes in the position of the Foramen Magnum in hominoids. *Proceedings of the Zoological Society of London* **126**, 315–325.

 1956c   Cranial crests in the Anthropoidea. *Proceedings of the Zoological Society of London* **126**, 581–634.

Avery, G., and F. Schweitzer
 1969   Cape St. Blaize. In C. G. Sampson. "Aspects of the Stone Age sequence in Southern Africa," pp. 201–205. Unpublished Ph.D. thesis, Oxford University.

Bain, T.
 1880   Bone caves at Knysna. *Cape Monthly Magazine* **2**, 255–256.

Barbour, G. B.
 1949   Makapansgat. *The Scientific Monthly* **69**, 3, 141–147.

Bartholomew, A., and J. B. Birdsell
 1953   Ecology and the protohominids. *American Anthropologist* **55**, 4, 481–498.

Beater, B. E., and R. R. Maud
 1963   The occurrence of a coastal midden near Umhlanga Rocks, Natal. *South African Archaeological Bulletin* **18**, 69, 21–23.

Beaumont, P.
 1963   Two interesting artefacts from Rose Cottage Cave. *South African Archaeological Bulletin* **18**, 70, 60–61.

 1967   The Brotherton Shelter. *South African Archaeological Bulletin* **22**, 1, 85, 27–30.

 1969   A very early Stone Age site at Northcliff extension 2, Johannesburg. *South African Journal of Science* **65**, 3, 65–71.

Bishop, W. W., and J. D. Clark (Editors)
 1967   *Background to Evolution in Africa.* Chicago: University of Chicago Press.

Bond, G.
 1957   The geology of the Khami Stone Age sites. *Occasional Papers of the National Museum, Southern Rhodesia* **3**, 21a, 44–55.

Bond, G., and J. D. Clark
 1954   The Quaternary sequence in the Middle Zambezi valley. *South African Archaeological Bulletin* **9**, 36, 115–130.

Boné, E. L.
 1955a   Une clavicule et un nouveau fragment mandibulaire, d'*Australopithecus prometheus*. *Palaeontologia Africana* **3**, 87–101.

 1955b   Un second fragment bipariéto-occipital de l'Australopithèque de Makapansgat (N. Transvaal). *Zeitschrift für Morphologie und Anthropologie* **47**, 2, 217–220.

 1956   Un nouveau pariétal droit d'un jeune Australopithèque (*A. prometheus*) de Makapansgat. *Zeitschrift für Morphologie und Anthropologie* **48**, 1, 71–78.

 1959   Quelques spécialisations dentaires du groupe préhumain des Australopithèques et leurs implications évolutives. *Revue Belge de Science Dentaire* **14**, 4, 581–590.

 1960   La signification écologique de la faune des mammifères fossiles des grottes à Australopithèques. *Mammalia* **24**, 2, 286–300.

Boné, E. L., and R. A. Dart
  1955   A catalog of australopithecine fossils found at the Limeworks, Makapansgat. *American Journal of Physical Anthropology* n.s. **13**, 4, 621–624.

Bordes, F.
  1959   Typologie du Paléolithique ancien et moyen. *Publications de l'Institut de Préhistoire de l'Université de Bordeaux, Mém. 1.*
  1968   *The Old Stone Age.* New York: McGraw-Hill.

Bosazza, V. L., R. J. Adie, and S. Brenner
  1946   Man and the Great Kalahari Desert. *Journal of the Natal University College Scientific Society* **5**, 1–9.

Boshier, A. K.
  1965   Effects of pounding by Africans of north-west Transvaal on hard and soft stones. *South African Archaeological Bulletin* **20**, 79, 131–136.

Boshier, A. K., and P. B. Beaumont
  1970   Nuclear antiquity—2: Beyond the mists of mining. *Nuclear Active.* S. A. Atomic Energy Board. **24**, 1–12.

Brain, C. K.
  1956   Some aspects of the ape-man period in the Transvaal. *South African Museums Association Bulletin* **6**, 171–176.
  1957   New evidence for the correlation of the Transvaal ape-man-bearing cave deposits. *Proceedings of the Third Pan-African Congress on Prehistory, Livingstone, 1955* 143–148.
  1958   The Transvaal ape-man-bearing cave deposits. *Memoirs of the Transvaal Museum* **11**.
  1965   Comments on a visit to Makapansgat limeworks, December 1962. *South African Archaeological Bulletin* **20**, 79, 110–111.
  1967a   The Transvaal Museum's fossil project at Swartkrans. *South African Journal of Science* **63**, 9, 378–389.
  1967b   Hottentot food remains and their bearing on the interpretation of fossil bone assemblages. *Scientific Papers of the Namib Desert Research Station* **32**, 6, 1–11.
  1967c   New light on old bones. *South African Museums Association Bulletin* **9**, 1, 22–27.
  1967d   Bone weathering and the problem of bone pseudo-tools. *South African Journal of Science* **63**, 3, 97–99.
  1967e   Procedures and some results in the study of Quaternary cave fillings. In *Background to Evolution in Africa,* edited by W. W. Bishop and J. D. Clark, pp. 285–301. Chicago: University of Chicago Press.
  1968   Who killed the Swartkrans ape-men? *South African Museums Association Bulletin* **9**, 4, 127–139.
  1969a   The contribution of Namib Desert Hottentots to an understanding of australopithecine bone accumulations. *Scientific Papers of the Namib Desert Research Station* **39**, 4, 13–22.
  1969b   The probable role of leopards as predators of the Swartkrans australopithecines. *South African Archaeological Bulletin* **24**, 3, 4, 95, 96, 170–171.
  1969c   Faunal remains from the Bushman Rock Shelter, Eastern Transvaal. *South African Archaeological Bulletin* **24**, 2, 94, 52–55.
  1969d   New evidence for climatic change during the Middle and Late Stone Age times in Rhodesia. *South African Archaeological Bulletin* **24**, 3, 4, 95, 96, 127–143.
  1970   New finds at the Swartkrans australopithecine site. *Nature (London)*, **225**, 5238, 1112–1119.

Brain, C. K., and C. K. Cooke
  1967   A preliminary account of the Redcliff Stone Age cave site in Rhodesia. *South African Archaeological Bulletin* **21**, 84, 171–182.

Brain, C. K., and R. J. Mason
 1955   A later African Chelles–Acheul site near Nakop, south Kalahari. *South African Ar-chaeological Bulletin* **10**, 37, 22–25.

Brain, C. K., and J. T. Robinson
 1953   A geological note on the australopithecine-bearing deposit at Swartkrans. *Congrés Géologique International, Section V. Alger, 1952* 55–56.

Brain, C. K., C. van Riet Lowe, and R. A. Dart
 1955   Kafuan stone artefacts in the post australopithecine breccia at Makapansgat. *Nature (London),* **175**, 4444, 16–18.

Breuil, H. E. P.
 1943   On the presence of quartzites mechanically broken (sometimes simulating human workmanship) in the Dwyka Tillites and their derivation in the Older Gravels of the Vaal. *South African Journal of Science* **40**, 285–399.

 1944   (1) Le Paléolithique au Congo Belge d'après les recherches du Docteur Cabu.
         (2) Les industries Paléolithiques de la terrasse de 15 metres et d'un chenal secondaire comble, Plaine de Piedmont de Leopoldville, d'après les fouilles et photographie du Docteur Cabu. *Transactions of the Royal Society of South Africa* **30**, 143–174.

 1945   Pseudo-implements from the glacial conglomerates at Nooitgedacht, dist. Kimberly. *South African Journal of Science* **41**, 397–399.

Breuil, H. E. P., and J. Janmart
 1950   Les limons et graviers de l'Angola du nord-est et leur contenu archéologique. *Museu do Dundo, Publicações Culturais No. 5.* Lisbon: Diamang.

Brien, K.
 1935   The Late Stone Age in Natal. *South African Journal of Science* **32**, 500–505.

Brien, P. G.
 1932a   Coastal archaelological sites near Durban. *South African Journal of Science* **29**, 742–750.

 1932b   A description of preliminary excavations in a rock shelter at Isipofu. *South African Journal of Science* **29**, 751–755.

Broom, R.
 1909   On evidence of a large horse recently extinct in South Africa. *Annals of the South African Museum* **7**, 281–282.

 1925   On the newly discovered South African man-ape. *Natural History* **25**, 4, 409–418.

 1929   The Transvaal fossil human skeleton. *Nature (London)* **123**, 3098, 415–416.

 1934   On the fossil remains associated with *Australopithecus africanus. South African Journal of Science* **33**, 471–480.

 1936a   A new fossil anthropoid skull from South Africa. *Nature (London)* **138**, 3490, 486–488.

 1936b   The dentition of *Australopithecus. Nature (London)* **138**, 3495, 719.

 1937a   On some new Pleistocene mammals from limestone caves in the Transvaal. *South African Journal of Science* **33**, 750–768.

 1937b   Notices of a few more fossil mammals from the caves of the Transvaal. *Annals and Magazine of Natural History* **20**, 509–514.

 1937c   The Sterckfontein, ape. *Nature (London)* **139**, 3512, 326.

 1938   The Pleistocene anthropoid apes of South Africa. *Nature (London)* **142**, 3591, 377–379.

 1939a   A restoration of the Kromdraai skull. *Annals of the Transvaal Museum* **19**, 327–329.

 1939b   The dentition of the Transvaa! Pleistocene anthropoids, *Pleisianthropus* and *Paranthropus. Annals of the Transvaal Museum* **19,** 303–314.

 1939c   A preliminary account of the Pleistocene carnivores of the Transvaal caves. *Annals of the Transvaal Museum* **19**, 331–338.

1939d   The fossil rodents of the limestone caves at Taungs. *Annals of the Transvaal Museum* **19**, 315–317.

1940   The South African Pleistocene Cercopithecid apes. *Annals of the Transvaal Museum* **20**, 89–100.

1941a   Mandible of a young *Paranthropus* child. *Nature (London)* **147**, 3733, 607–608.

1941b   On two Pleistocene golden moles. *Annals of the Transvaal Museum* **20**, 215–216.

1942   The hand of the ape-man, *Paranthropus robustus. Nature (London)* **149**, 3784, 513–514.

1945a   A new primitive hyaena from Sterkfontein. *South African Museums Association Bulletin* **3**, 273.

1945b   Age of the South African ape-men. *Nature (London)* **155**, 3935 ,389–390.

1947   The mandible of the Sterkfontein ape man *Plesianthropus. South African Science* **1**, 1, 14–15.

1948a   The giant rodent mole, *Gypsorhynchus. Annals of the Transvaal Museum* **21**, 47–49.

1948b   Some South African Pliocene and Pleistocene mammals. *Annals of the Transvaal Museum* **21**, 1–38.

1949a   Another new type of fossil ape-man. *Nature (London)* **163**, 4132, 57.

1949b   Jaw of the ape-man *Paranthropus crassidens. Nature (London)* **163**, 4154, 903.

1951   *Finding the Missing Link.* London: Watts.

Broom, R., and A. R. Hughes

1949   Notes on the fossil baboons of the Makapan caves. *South African Science* **2**, 9, 194–196.

Broom, R., and J. S. Jensen

1946   A new fossil baboon from the caves at Potgietersrust. *Annals of the Transvaal Museum* **20**, 337–340.

Broom, R., and J. T. Robinson

1948   Size of the brain in the ape-man. *Plesianthropus. Nature (London)* **161**, 4090, 438.

1949a   The lower end of the femur of *Plesianthropus. Annals of the Transvaal Museum* **21**, 181–182.

1949b   A new type of fossil baboon, *Gorgopithecus major. Proceedings of the Zoological Society of London* **119**, 2, 379–386.

1949c   A new type of fossil man. *Nature (London)* **164**, 4164, 322–323.

1949d   A new mandible of the ape-man *Plesianthropus transvaalensis, American Journal of Physical Anthropology* n.s. **7**, 1, 123–127.

1949e   Thumb of the Swartkrans ape-man. *Nature (London)* **164**, 4176, 841–842.

1950a   A new sub-fossil baboon from Kromdraai, Transvaal. *Annals of the Transvaal Museum* **21**, 242–245.

1950b   Further evidence of the structure of the Sterkfontein ape-man *Plesianthropus. Memoirs of the Transvaal Museum* **4**, 11–83.

1950c   Man contemporaneous with the Swartkrans ape-man. *American Journal of Physical Anthropology* n.s. **8**, 2, 151–155.

1950d   Notes on the pelves of the fossil ape-men. *American Journal of Physical Anthropology* n.s. **8**, 4, 489–494.

1950e   Note on the skull of the Swartkrans ape-man *Paranthropus crassidens., American Journal of Physical Anthropology* n.s. **8**, 3, 295–303.

1952   Swartkrans ape-man: *Paranthropus crassidens. Memoirs of the Transvaal Museum* **6**, 1–123.

Broom, R., J. T. Robinson, and G. W. H. Schepers

1950   Sterkfontein ape-man *Plesianthropus. Memoirs of the Transvaal Museum* **4**, 1–117.

Broom, R., and G. W. H. Schepers
　1946　The South African fossil ape-men: the Australopithecinae. *Memoirs of the Transvaal Museum* **2**, 1–272.

Burkitt, M. C.
　1928　*South Africa's past in stone and paint.* London and New York: Cambridge University Press.

Butzer, K. W.
　1971　Another look at the australopithecine cave breccias of the Transvaal. *American Anthropologist* **73**, 5, 1197–1201.

Campbell, B. G.
　1964　Quantitative taxonomy and human evolution. In *Classification and human evolution,* edited by S. L. Washburn, pp. 50–74. London: Methuen.

Campbell, B. G.
　1968　Justification and controversy: motives for research. *South African Journal of Science* **64**, 2, 60–63.

Carter, P. L.
　1969　Moshebe's shelter: excavation and exploitation in Eastern Lesotho. *Lesotho Notes and Records* **8**, 13–23.
　1970　Late Stone Age exploitation patterns in Southern Natal. *South African Archaeological Bulletin* **25**, 2, 98, 55–58.

Cartmill, M.
　1967　The early Pleistocene microfaunas of sub-Saharan Africa and their ecological significance. *Quaternaria* **9**, 169–198.

Chitty, D.
　1934　A laboratory study of pellet formation in the short-eared owl *(Asio flammeus)*. *Proceedings of the Zoological Society of London* **108A**, 96–99.

Chopra, S. R. K.
　1962　The innominate bone of the Australopithecinae and the problem of erect posture. *Bibliographica Primatologica* **1**, 93–102.

Chubb, E. C., G. B. King, and A. O. D. Mogg
　1934　A new variation of Smithfield culture from a cave on the Pondoland coast. *Transactions of the Royal Society of South Africa* **22**, 4, 245–270.

Churcher, C. S.
　1956　The fossil Hyracoidea of the Transvaal and Taungs deposits. *Annals of the Transvaal Museum* **22**, 477–501.
　1970　The fossil Equidae from the Krugersdorp caves. *Annals of the Transvaal Museum* **26**, 6, 145–148.

Clark, J. D.
　1942　Further excavations (1939) at the Mumbwa Caves, Northern Rhodesia. *Transactions of the Royal Society of South Africa* **29**, 3.
　1950a　*The Stone Age cultures of Northern Rhodesia, with particular reference to the cultural and climatic succession in the Upper Zambezi Valley and its tributaries.* Cape Town: South African Archaeological Society.
　1950b　A note on the pre-Bantu inhabitants of Northern Rhodesia and Nyasaland. *South African Journal of Science* **47**, 80–85.
　1950c　The newly discovered Nachikufu Culture of Northern Rhodesia and the possible origin of certain elements of the South African Smithfield Culture. *South African Archaeological Bulletin* **5**, 19, 86–98.
　1954a　*The prehistoric cultures of the Horn of Africa; an analysis of the Stone Age cultural and climatic succession in the Somalilands and eastern parts of Abyssinia.* London and New York: Cambridge University Press.

1954b   An early Upper Pleistocene site at the Kalambo Falls on the Northern Rhodesia/ Tanganyika border. *South African Archaeological Bulletin* **9**, 34, 51–56.

1955a   Human skeletal and cultural material from a deep cave at Chipongwe, Northern Rhodesia. I. The cultural remains. *South African Archaeological Bulletin* **10**, 40, 107–114.

1955b   A note on a wooden implement from the level of Peat I at Florisbad, Orange Free State. *Reseaches of the National Museum, Bloemfontein* **1**, 6, 135–140.

1956   Prehistory in Nyasaland. *The Nyasaland Journal*, **9**, 1, 92–119.

1957a   A re-examination of the industry from the type site of Magosi, Uganda. *Proceedings of the Third Pan-African Congress on Prehistory, Livingstone, 1955* 228–241.

1957b   *Proceedings of the Third Pan-African Congress on Prehistory, Livingstone, 1955,* edited by J. D. Clark. London: Chatto & Windus.

1958   The Chifubwa Stream rock shelter, Solwezi, Northern Rhodesia. *South African Archaeological Bulletin* **13**, 49, 21–24.

1959a   *The prehistory of Southern Africa.* London: Pelican.

1959b   Further excavations at Broken Hill, Northern Rhodesia. *Journal of the Royal Anthropological Institute* **89**, 2, 201–232.

1962   The Kalambo Falls prehistoric site: An interim report. *Actes du IVe Congrès Panafricain de Préhistoire et de l'étude du Quaternaire, Léopoldville, 1959* 195–201.

1963   Prehistoric cultures of northeast Angola and their significance in tropical Africa. *Museu do Dundo, Publicações Culturais No. 62.* Lisbon: Diamang.

1964   The influence of environment in inducing culture change at the Kalambo Falls prehistoric site. *South African Archaeological Bulletin* **20**, 76, 93–101.

1965   The distribution of prehistoric cultures in Angola. *Actas del V Congreso Panafricano de Prehistoria y de estudio del Cuaternario. Tenerife, 1963* **1**, 225–309.

1966   The distribution of prehistoric culture in Angola. *Museu do Dundo, Publicações Culturais No. 73.* Lisbon: Diamang.

1967a   *Atlas of African prehistory.* Chicago: University of Chicago Press.

1967b   Interim report on the archaeology of the Malawi, Rungwe and southern Rukwa regions. In Clark, J. D., C. V. Haynes and J. E. Mawby, "Interim report on palaeoanthropological investigations in the Lake Malawi rift." Unpublished manuscript.

1968   Further palaeo-anthropological studies in Northern Lunda. *Museu do Dundo, Publicações Culturais, No. 78.* Lisbon: Diamang.

1969   *Kalambo Falls prehistoric site,* Vol. I. Cambridge: University Press.

1970   *The prehistory of Africa.* London: Thames & Hudson.

1971   Human behavioral differences in Southern Africa during the Late Pleistocene. *American Anthropologist* **73**, 5, 1211–1236.

Clark, J. D., D. R. Brothwell, R. Powers, and K. P. Oakley

1968a   Rhodesian man: Notes on a new femur fragment. *Man* **3**, 1, 105–111.

Clark, J. D., G. H. Cole, G. L. Isaac, and M. R. Kleindienst

1968b   Precision and definition in African archaeology. *South African Archaeological Bulletin* **21**, 83, 3, 114–121.

Clark, J. D., and C. V. Haynes

1970   An elephant butchery site at Mwanganda's Village, Karonga, Malawi, and its relevance for Palaeolithic archaeology. *World Archaeology* **1**, 3, 390–411.

Clark, J. D., C. V. Haynes, and J. E. Mawby

1967   "Interim report on palaeo-anthropological investigations in the Lake Malawi rift." Unpublished manuscript.

Clarke, R. J., F. C. Howell, and C. K. Brain

1970   New finds at the Swartkrans australopithecine site (cont'd). More evidence of an advanced hominid at Swartkrans. *Nature (London)* **225**, 5239, 1219–1222.

Clark, J. D., F. C. Howell, M. R. Kleindienst, and L. S. B. Leakey
  1962   Letter to the editor. *South African Archaeological Bulletin* **17**, 67, 199.
Clark, J. D., K. P. Oakley, L. H. Wells, and J. A. C. McClelland
  1947   New studies on Rhodesian Man. *Journal of the Royal Anthropological Institute* **77**, 1,
          7–32.
Clark, J. D., and E. M. van Zinderen Bakker
  1964   Prehistoric culture and Pleistocene vegetation at the Kalambo Falls, Northern Rhode-
          sia *Nature (London)* **201**, 4923, 971–975.
Coetzee, J. A.
  1967   Pollen analytical studies in East and Southern Africa. *Palaeoecology of Africa,* Vol.
          III. Cape Town: Balkema.
Cole, G. H.
  1967a   A re-investigation of Magosi and the Magosian. *Quaternaria* **9**, 153–168.
  1967b   The later Acheulian and Sangoan of Southern Africa. In *Background to evolution in
          Africa,* edited by W. W. Bishop and J. D. Clark, pp. 481–528. Chicago: University of
          Chicago Press.
Colette, J. R. F.
  1931   Eassi biométrique sur la station préhistorique de Kalina (Congo Belge). *Compte
          Rendu du XVᵉ Congrès International d'Anthropologie et d'Archaeologie Prèhistoire,
          Paris,* 278–285.
Colson, R.
  1905   The Port Nolloth kitchen-middens. *Man* **5**, 93, 166–168.
Commont, V.
  1909   Saint-Acheul et Montières. *Memoires de la Sociéte Geologique Nord Lille* **6**, 3; *La
          Revue Prèhistorique,* 4ᵉ année, No. 10.
Cooke, C. K.
  1950   The Middle Stone Age site at Khami, Southern Rhodesia: A further examination.
          South African Archaeological Bulletin **5**, 18, 60–68.
  1953   Examination of ash-filled pits in the Magosian deposit at Khami. *Occasional Papers of
          the National Museum, Southern Rhodesia* **2**, 18, 529–531.
  1955   The occurrence of the bored-stone in the Magosian Industry, and some unusual Ma-
          gosian implements from the Khami area of Southern Rhodesia. *South African Ar-
          chaeological Bulletin* **10**, 38, 53–54.
  1957a   The prehistoric artist of Matebeleland: His materials and techniques as a basis for
          dating. *Proceedings of the Third Pan-African Congress on Prehistory, Livingstone,
          1955* 282–294.
  1957b   The Waterworks site at Khami, Southern Rhodesia: Stone Age and Proto-historic. *Oc-
          casional Papers of the National Museum, Southern Rhodesia* **3**, 21a, 1–60.
  1959   Rock art in Matabeleland. In *Prehistoric rock art of the Federation of Rhodesia and
          Nyasaland,* edited by R. F. H. Summers. Salisbury.
  1960   Report on archaeological sites Bubye/Limpopo valleys of Southern Rhodesia. *South
          African Archaeological Bulletin* **15**, 59, 95–109.
  1962   The Sangoan industries of Southern Rhodesia. *South African Archaeological Bulletin*
          17, 68, 212–230.
  1963   Report on Excavations at Pomongwe and Tshangula Caves, Matopo Hills, Southern
          Rhodesia. *South African Archaeological Bulletin* **18**, 71, 73–151.
  1964   Unusual implements from an open eroded site near Inyanga, Southern Rhodesia.
          South African Archaeological Bulletin **19**, 73, 17.
  1966a   Re-appraisal of the industry hitherto named Proto-Stillbay. *Arnoldia* **2**, 22, 1–14.
  1966b   The archaeology of the Mafungabusi area, Gokwe, Rhodesia. *Transactions of the
          Rhodesian Scientific Association* **51**, 51–78.

1967 A preliminary report on the Stone Age of the Nata River, Botswana. *Arnoldia* **2**, 40, 1–10.

1968 The Early Stone Age in Rhodesia. *Arnoldia* **3**, 39, 1–12.

1969 *Rock art of Southern Africa.* Cape Town: Books of Africa.

1971 Excavation in Zombepata Cave, Sipolilo District, Mashonaland, Rhodesia. *South African Archaeological Bulletin* **26**, 3 & 4, 103 & 104, 104–127.

Cooke, C. K., and P. S. Garlake

1968 The Tshangula (Magosian) site at Sitanda Dam, Tshipise Tribal Trust Lands, Beit Bridge, Rhodesia. *Rhodesian Schools Exploration Society (Matebeleland Branch) 18th Expedition: Siyanje* 22–34.

Cooke, C. K., and K. R. Robinson

1954 Excavations at Amadzimba Cave located in the Matopos Hills, Southern Rhodesia. *Occasional Papers of the National Museum, Southern Rhodesia* **2**, 19, 699–728.

Cooke, C. K., R. Summers, and K. R. Robinson

1966 Rhodesian prehistory re-examined: Part I, the Stone Age. *Arnoldia* **2**, 12, 1–7.

Cooke, H. B. S.

1938 The Sterkfontein bone breccia—a geological note. *South African Journal of Science* **35**, 204–208.

1946 The development of the Vaal River and its deposits. *Transactions of the Geological Society of South Africa* **49**, 243–259.

1947 Some fossil Hippotragine antelopes from South Africa. *South African Journal of Science* **43**, 226–231.

1949a Fossil mammals of the Vaal River deposits. *Memoirs of the Geological Survey of the Union of South Africa* **35**, III, 1–117.

1949b The fossil Suina of South Africa. *Transactions of the Royal Society of South Africa* **32**, 1–44.

1950 A critical revision of the Quaternary Perissodactyla of Southern Africa. *Annals of the South African Museum* **31**, 393–476.

1952 Quaternary events in South Africa. *Proceedings of the First Pan-African Congress on Prehistory, Nairobi, 1947* 26–36.

1962 Notes on the faunal material from the Cave of Hearths and Kalkbank. In *Prehistory of the Transvaal*, pp. 447–453. Johannesburg: Witwatersrand University Press.

1964 Pleistocene mammal faunas of Africa, with particular reference to Southern Africa. In *African ecology and human evolution*, edited by F. C. Howell and F. Bourlière, pp. 65–116. London: Methuen.

1967 The Pleistocene sequence in South Africa and problems of correlation. In *Background to evolution in Africa*, edited by W. W. Bishop and J. D. Clark, pp. 175–184. Chicago: University of Chicago Press.

1968 Evolution of mammals on Southern continents. II. The fossil mammal fauna of Africa. *Quarterly Review of Biology* **43**, 3, 234–264.

Cooke, H. B. S., B. D. Malan, and L. H. Wells

1945 Fossil man in the Lebombo Mountains, South Africa: The "Border Cave," Ingwavuma district, Zululand. *Man* **45**, 3, 6–13.

Cooke, H. B. S., and L. H. Wells

1947 Fossil mammals from the Makapan valley, Potgietersrust. III: Giraffidae. *South African Journal of Science* **43**, 232–235.

Cramb, J. G.

1934 Smithfield implements from a Natal coastal site. *Transactions of the Royal Society of South Africa* **22**, 1, 205–223.

1952 A Middle Stone Age industry from a Natal rock shelter. *South African Journal of Science* **48**, 181–186.

Craytor, W. B., and L. Johnson
  1968   Refinements in computerized item seriation. *Bulletin of the Museum of Natural History, University of Oregon No. 10* 1–22.

Dale, M. M.
  1948   New fossil Suidae from Limeworks quarry Makapansgat, Potgietersrust. *South African Science* **11**, 5, 114–117.

Dale, M. M., and D. Tobiansky
  1947   Fossil mammals from the Makapan valley, Potgietersrust. II: Suidae. *South African Journal of Science* **43**, 304.

Dart, R. A.
  1925a   *Australopithecus africanus:* the man-ape of South Africa. *Nature (London)* **115**, 2884, 195–199.

  1925b   A note on Makapansgat: A site of early human occupation. *South African Journal of Science* **22**, 454.

  1926   Taungs and its significance. *Natural History* **26**, 3, 315–327.

  1929   A note on the Taungs skull. *South African Journal of Science* **26**, 648–658.

  1934   Dentition of *Australopithecus prometheus*. *Folia Anatomica Japonica* **12**, 207–221.

  1948a   A (?) promethean *Australopithecus* from Makapansgat valley. *Nature (London)* **162**, 4114, 375–376.

  1948b   The Makapansgat proto-human *Australopithecus prometheus*. *American Journal of Physical Anthropology* n.s. **6**, 3, 259–283.

  1948c   The adolescent mandible of *Australopithecus prometheus*. *American Journal of Physical Anthropology n.s.* **6**, 4, 391–411.

  1948d   An adolescent promethean australopithecine mandible from Makapansgat. *South African Science* **2**, 73–75.

  1948e   An *Australopithecus* from the Central Transvaal. *South African Science* **1**, 11, 200–201.

  1948f   The first human mandible from the Cave of HearthS, Makpansgat. *South African Archaeological Bulletin* **3**, 12, 96–98.

  1949a   The cranio-facial fragment of *Australopithecus prometheus*. *American Journal of Physical Anthropology* n.s. **7**, 2, 187–213.

  1949b   The first pelvic bones of *Australopithecus prometheus:* Preliminary note. *American Journal of Physical Anthropology* n.s. **7**, 2, 255–257.

  1949c   Innominate fragments of *Australopithecus prometheus*. *American Journal of Physical Anthropology* n.s. **7**, 3, 301–333.

  1949d   A second adult palate of *Australopithecus prometheus*. *American Journal of Physical Anthropology* n.s. **7**, 3, 335–338.

  1949e   The bone-bludgeon hunting technique of *Australopithecus*. *South African Science* **2**, 150–152.

  1949f   The predatory implemental technique of *Australopithecus*. *American Journal of Physical Anthropology* n.s. **7**, 1, 1–38.

  1952   Faunal and climatic fluctuations in Makapansgat valley: Their relation to the geological age and promethean status of *Australopithecus*. *Proceedings of the First Pan-African Congress on Prehistory, Nairobi, 1947* 96–106.

  1954a   The adult female lower jaw from Makapansgat. *Nature (London)* **173**, 4398, 286–287.

  1954b   The second, or adult, female mandible of *Australopithecus prometheus*. *American Journal of Physical Anthropology* n.s. **12**, 3, 313–343.

  1954c   The significance of Makapansgat. *Zeitschrift für Morphologie und Anthropologie* **46**, 2, 119–123.

  1955a   *Australopithecus prometheus* and *Telanthropus capensis*. *American Journal of Physical Anthropology* n.s. **13**, 1, 67–96.

1955b   The first australopithecine fragment from the Makapansgat pebble culture stratum. *Nature (London)* **176**, 4473, 170–171.

1955c   Three Strandlopers from the Kaokoveld coast. *South African Journal of Science* **51**, 175–179.

1956a   The myth of the bone-accumulating hyaena. *American Anthropology* **58**, 1, 40–62.

1956b   Cultural status of the South African man-apes. *The Smithsonian Report for 1955* 317–338.

1957a   The Makapansgat australopithecine osteodontokeratic culture. *Proceedings of the Third Pan-African Congress on Prehistory, Livingstone, 1955* 161–171.

1957b   The osteodontokeratic culture of *Australopithecus prometheus. Memoirs of the Transvaal Museum* **10**, 1–105.

1958a   The minimal bone–breccia content of Makapansgat and the australopithecine predatory habit. *American Anthropologist* **60**, 5, 923–931.

1958b   Bone tools and porcupine gnawing. *American Anthropologist* **60**, 4, 715–724.

1958c   A further adolescent australopithecine ilium from Makapansgat. *American Journal of Physical Anthropology* n.s. **16**, 4, 473–479.

1959a   A tolerably complete australopithecine cranium from the Makapansgat pink breccia. *South African Journal of Science* **55**, 325–327.

1959b   The first *Australopithecus* cranium from the pink breccia at Makapansgat. *American Journal of Physical Anthropology n.s.* **17**, 1, 77–82.

1959c   Further light on australopithecine humeral and femoral weapons. *American Journal of Physical Anthropology* n.s. **17**, 2, 87–93.

1959d   Osteodontokeratic ripping tools and pulp scoops for teething and edentulous australopithecines. *Journal of the Dental Association of South Africa* **14**, 5, 164–178.

1960a   The place of antelope cannon-bones (or metapodials) in australopithecine economy. *Zeitschrift für Wissenschaftliche Zoologie* **68**, 1–15.

1960b   The bone tool-manufacturing ability of *Australopithecus prometheus. American Anthropologist* **62**, 1, 134–143.

1960c   The persistence of some tools and utensils found first in the Makapansgat grey breccia. *South African Journal of Science* **56**, 71–74.

1961a   Further information about how *Australopithecus* made bone tools and utensils. *South African Journal of Science* **57**, 127–134.

1961b   An australopithecine scoop made from a right australopithecine upper arm bone. *Nature (London)* **191**, 4786, 372–373.

1962a   The Makapansgat pink breccia australopithecine skull. *American Journal of Physical Anthropology* n.s. **20**, 2, 119–126.

1962b   A cleft adult mandible and the nine other lower jaw fragments from Makapansgat. *American Journal of Physical Anthropology* n.s. **20**, 3, 267–286.

1962c   The most complete *Australopithecus* skull from the pink breccia at Makapansgat. *Actes du IVe Congrès Panafricain de Préhistoire et de l'étude du Quaternaire, Léopoldville, 1959* 237–240.

1962d   Stalactites as a tool material for the australopithecines: A missing cultural link between skeletal and stone tool-making, from the Makapansgat stalactitic cavern. *Illustrated London News* **241**, 6493, 1052–1055.

1962e   Substitution of stone tools for bone tools at Makapansgat. *Nature (London)* **196**, 4852, 314–316.

1963   The carnivorous propensity of baboons. *Symp. Zool. Soc. Lond.* **10**, 49–56.

1964   The ecology of the South African man-apes. In *Ecological studies in Southern Africa,* edited by D. H. S. Davis, pp. 49–66. Den Haag: Dr. W. Junk.

1965a   Recent discoveries during excavation preparations at Makapansgat. *South African Archaeological Bulletin* **20**, 79, 148–158.

1965b   Australopithecine cordage and thongs. In *Homenage a Juan Comas en su 65 Aniversario*, Vol. II, pp. 43–61. Mexico City: Editorial Libros de Mexico.

1965c   Pounding as a process and the producer of other artefacts. *South African Archaeological Bulletin* **20**, 79, 141–147.

1967   A Chisenga kudu cranial chalice. *South African Journal of Science* **63**, 198–200.

Dart, R. A., and N. del Grande

1931   The ancient iron-smelting cavern at Mumbwa. *Transactions of the Royal Society of South Africa* **29**, 4, 81–89.

Dart, R. A., and J. W. Kitching

1958   Bone tools at the Kalkbank Middle Stone Age site and the Makapansgat australopithecene locality, Central Transvaal. Part 2. The osteodontokeratic contribution. *South African Archaeological Bulletin* **13**, 51, 94–116.

Davies, O.

1947   Recent exploration of Stone Age sites in Natal. *Transactions of the Royal Society of South Africa* **31**, 325.

1949   Notes from Natal. *South African Archaeological Bulletin* **4**, 15, 87–94.

1951   Archaeology of Natal. *Natal Region Survey Volume I* 1–29. Cape Town: Oxford University Press.

1952   *Natal archaeological studies*. Pietermartizburg.

Davis, D. H. S.

1959   The barn owl's contribution to ecology and palaeoecology. *Ostrich, Suppl. No. 3, Proc. 1st Pan-Afr. Ornith. Congr.* 144–153.

1962   Distribution of the Southern African Muridae, with notes on some of their antecedents. *Annals of the Cape Provincial Museums (Natural History)* **2**, 56–76.

Deacon, H. J.

1966a   The Early Stone Age occupation at Amanzi springs, Uitenhage district, Cape Province. M.A. thesis submitted to Archaeology Dept., University of Cape Town.

1966b   The dating of the Nahoon footprints. *South African Journal of Science* **62**, 111–113.

1966c   Note on the X-ray of two mounted implements from South Africa. *Man n.s.* **1**, 1, 87–90.

1967   Two radiocarbon dates for Scott's Cave, Gamtoos valley. *South African Archaeological Bulletin* **22**, 2, 86, 51–52.

1969a   Melkhoutboom Cave, Alexandria District, Cape Province: a report on the 1967 investigation. *Annals of the Cape Provincial Museums (Natural History)* **6**, 13, 141–169.

1969b   Plant remains from Melkhoutboom Cave, South Africa. *Actes du VIe Congrès Panafricain de Préhistoire et de l'étude du Quaternaire. Dakar, 1967,* in press.

1969c   Two shell midden occurrences in the Tsitsikama National Park, Cape Province: a contribution to the study of the ecology of the Strandloopers. *Koedoe* (publication of the National Parks Board, S. Africa), in press.

1970   The Acheulian occupation at Amanzi Springs Uitenhage district, Cape Province. *Annals of the Cape Provincial Museums (Natural History)* **8**, 2, 89–189.

Deacon, H. J., and M. Brooker (Editors)

1969   South Africa. *Council for Old World Archaeology, Surveys and Bibliographies Area 13* No. IV, 1–15.

Deacon, H. J., and J. Deacon

1963   Scott's Cave: a Late Stone Age site in the Gamtoos valley. *Annals of the Cape Provincial Museums (Natural History)* **3**, 96–121.

Deacon, J.

1965   Part I: Cultural material from the Gamtoos valley shelters (Andrieskraal I). *South African Archaeological Bulletin* **20**, 80, 193–200.

de Almeida, A., and J. C. França
- 1965   Le Magosien du sud de l'Angola. *Acts del V Congreso Panafricano de Prehistoria y de estudio del Cuaternario. Tenerife, 1963* 1, 117–126.

de Graaf, G.
- 1958   A new chrysochlorid from Makapansgat. *Palaeontologia Africana* 5, 21–27.
- 1961   A preliminary investigation of the mammalian microfauna in Pleistocene deposits of caves in the Transvaal system. *Palaeontologia Africana* 7, 59–118.

de Perthe, M. B.
- 1849   *Antiquités celtiques et antédiluviennes.* Vol. I. Paris: private printing.

de Villiers, H.
- 1965   Part II: Skeletal remains from the Gamtoos valley. *South African Archaeological Bulletin* 20, 80, 201–205.

Dossin, J. M., *et al.*
- 1962   Louvain natural radiocarbon measurements. *Radiocarbon* 4, 97–98.

Drennan, M. R.
- 1929a   Preliminary note on the Skildergat No. 4 skeleton. In "Preliminary report on the archaeology of the Fish Hoek-Noord Hoek valleys," edited by A. J. H. Goodwin. Unpublished manuscript.
- 1929b   An Australoid skull from the Cape Flats. *Journal of the Royal Anthropological Institute* 59, 417.
- 1931   A ground stone axe from a Cape rock shelter. *Transactions of the Royal Society of South Africa* 19, 45–48.
- 1935   The Florisbad skull. *South African Journal of Science* 32, 601–602.
- 1937   The Florisbad skull and brain cast. *Transactions of the Royal Society of South Africa* 24, 1, 103–114.

Dreyer, T. F.
- 1936   The endocranial cast of the Florisbad skull—a correction. *Soölogiese Navorsong van die Nasionale Museum, Bloemfontein* 1, 3, 21–23.
- 1938   The archaeology of the Florisbad deposits. *Argeologiese Navorsings van die Nasionale Museum, Bloemfontein* 1, 8, 65–77.
- 1947   Further observations on the Florisbad skull. *Soölogiese Navorsing van die Nasionale Museum, Bloemfontein* 1, 5, 183–190.

Dreyer, T. F., and C. U. Ariëns Kappers
- 1935   A human skull from Florisbad, Orange Free State. *Koninklijke Akademie van Wetenschappen, Amsterdam* 38, 1, 119–128.

Dreyer, T. F., and A. Lyle
- 1931   *New fossil mammals and man from South Africa.* Bloemfontein: National Museum.

Eggers, V.
- 1970   "Border Cave." Unpublished Ph.D. thesis. University of California, Berkeley.

Eloff, J. F.
- 1969   Bushman Rock Shelter, Eastern Transvaal: Excavations 1967–8. *South African Archaeological Bulletin* 24, 2, 94, 60.

Ewer, R. F.
- 1954a   Some adaptive features in the dentition of hyaenas. *Annals and Magazine of Natural History* 7, 188–194.
- 1954b   The fossil carnivores of the Transvaal caves. The Hyaenidae of Kromdraai. *Proceedings of the Zoological Society of London* 124, 565–585.
- 1955a   The fossil carnivores of the Transvaal caves. The Lycyaenas of Sterkfontein and Swartkrans, together with some general considerations of the Transvaal fossil Hyaenids. *Proceedings of the Zoological Society of London* 124, 839–857.

1955b The fossil carnivores of the Transvaal caves. The Hyaenidae, other than *Lycyaena,* of Swartkrans and Sterkfontein. *Proceedings of the Zoological Society of London 124,* 815–837.

1955c The fossil carnivores of the Transvaal caves: Machairodontinae. *Proceedings of the Zoological Society of London 125,* 587–615.

1956a The dating of the Australopithecinae: Faunal evidence. *South African Archaeological Bulletin* 11, 42, 41–45.

1956b The fossil suids of the Transvaal caves. *Proceedings of the Zoological Society of London 127,* 527–544.

1956c The fossil carnivores of the Transvaal caves: Canidae. *Proceedings of the Zoological Society of London 126,* 97–119.

1956d The fossil carnivores of the Transvaal caves: Felidae. *Proceedings of the Zoological Society of London 126,* 83–95.

1956e The fossil carnivores of the Transvaal caves: Two new viverrids, together with some general considerations. *Proceedings of the Zoological Society of London 126,* 259–274.

1957a The fossil pigs of Florisbad. *Researches of the National Museum, Bloemfontein* 1, 10, 239–257.

1957b Faunal evidence on the dating of the Australopithecinae. *Proceedings of the Third Pan-African Congress on Prehistory, Livingstone, 1955* 135–142.

1957c Some fossil carnivores from the Makapansgat valley. *Palaeontologia Africana* 4, 57–67.

1958a The fossil Suidae of Makapansgat. *Proceedings of the Zoological Society of London* 130, 329–372.

1958b Faunal lists for the sites of Sterkfontein, Swartkrans, Kromdraai A and Makapan limeworks. Appendix A In The Transvaal ape-man-bearing cave deposits, edited by C. K. Brain, *Memoirs of the Transvaal Museum* 11, 127–130.

Ewer, R. F., and H. B. S. Cooke
  1964 The Pleistocene mammals of Southern Africa. In *Ecological studies in Southern Africa,* edited by D. H. S. Davis, pp. 35–48. The Hague: Dr. W. Junk.

Ewer, R. F., and R. Singer
  1956 Fossil carnivora from Hopefield. *Annals of the South African Museum* 42, 335–347.

Fagan, B. M.
  1960 The Glentyre Shelter and Oakhurst re-examined. *South African Archaeological Bulletin* 15, 59, 80–94.

Fagan, B. M., and F. L. van Noten
  1966 Wooden implements from Late Stone Age sites at Gwisho hot-springs, Lochinvar, Zambia. *Proceedings of the Prehistoric Society of Great Britain* 32, 246–261.

Farnden, T. H. G.
  1965 Notes on two Late Stone Age sites at Muden, Natal. *South African Archaeological Bulletin* 20, 1, 77, 19–23.

  1966 Excavation of a Late Stone Age shelter at New Amalfi, East Griqualand. *South African Archaeological Bulletin* 21, 3, 83, 122–124.

  1968 Notes on Middle Stone Age sites in the Muden/Keats drift areas of Natal. *South African Archaeological Bulletin* 21, 3, 83, 122–124.

  1969 A Late Stone Age site in the Karkloof, Natal. *South African Archaeological Bulletin* 23, 4, 92, 147–149.

Farnden, T. H. G., and W. D. Gibbs
  1962 A Middle Stone Age site near Pietermaritzburg, Natal. *South African Archaeological Bulletin* 27, 65, 30–31.

  1963 Notes on Middle Stone Age sites on the Bushmans River at Escourt. *South African Archaeological Bulletin* 28, 69, 24–26.

Filmer, N. T., and E. A. C. Mills
 1968   Chondwe—an Iron Age Site south-east of Ndola. *Archaeologia Zambiana* **10**, 4.
FitzSimons, F. W.
 1923a   The cliff dwellers of Tsitsikamma. *South African Journal of Science* **20**, 541.
 1923b   Bushmen of the Zuurberg. *South African Journal of Science* **20**, 501.
 1925   Palaeolithic man in South Africa. *Nature (London)* **116**, 3021, 615.
 1926   Cliff dwellers of Tsitsikamma: results of recent excavations. *South African Journal of Science* **23**, 813.
Fock, G. J.
 1959   Survey of archaeological research in South West Africa. *South African Archaeological Bulletin* **14**, 53, 9–18.
 1965   Die Verbreitung vorgeschichtlicher Kulturen in der Nordlichen Kapprovinz, Sudafrika. *Sonderdruck aus Fundberichte aus Schwaben, Neue Folge* **17**, 11–20.
 1968   Rooidam, a sealed site of the First Intermediate. *South African Journal of Science* **64**, 153–159.
 1970   The rock-art site at Eindgoed. *South African Archaeological Bulletin* **25**, 2, 98, 71–72.
França, J. C.
 1960   Primeira nota sobre a jazida Magosiense de Vila Serpa Pinto (Angola). In *Estudios sobre Pré-história do Untramar Português*, edited by J. C. França and A. de Almeida, No. 16, pp. 13–106. Lisbon.
Freedman, L.
 1957   The fossil Cercopithecoidea of South Africa. *Annals of the Transvaal Museum* **23**, 121–262.
 1961a   New cercopithecoid fossils, including a new species from Taung, Cape Province, South Africa. *Annals of the South African Museum* **46**, 1–14.
 1961b   Some new fossil cercopithecoid specimens from Makapansgat, South Africa. *Palaeontologia Africana* **7**, 7–45.
 1965   Fossil and subfossil primates from the limestone deposits at Taung, Bolt's Farm and Witkrans, South Africa. *Palaeontologia Africana* **9**, 19–48.
Gabel, C.
 1962   Human crania from the Later Stone Age of the Central Kafue Basin, Northern Rhodesia. *South African Journal of Science* **58**, 307–314.
 1963a   Lochinvar Mound: a Later Stone Age camp-site in the Kafue Basin. *South African Archaeological Bulletin* **18**, 70, 40–48.
 1963b   Further human remains from the Central African Later Stone Age. *Man* **63**, 44, 38–43.
 1965   *Stone Age hunters of the Kafue: the Gwisho A Site*. Boston: University Press.
 1967   Archaeology in the Western Copperbelt. *South African Archaeological Bulletin* **22**, 1, 85, 3–14.
Galloway, A.
 1937   The nature and status of the Florisbad skull as revealed by its non-metrical features. *American Journal of Physical Anthropology* **23**, 1, 1–16.
Galton, F.
 1853   *Narrative of an explorer in tropical South Africa*. London.
Gardner, T. and P. Stapleton
 1934   Gwelo Kopje—S. Rhodesia. Description of a section through the implementiferous talus. *Transactions of the Rhodesian Scientific Association*. **33**, 1, 4–14.
Gear, J. H. S.
 1926   A preliminary account of the baboon remains from Taungs. *South African Journal of Science* **23**, 731–747.

George, M.
  1950   A Chalicothere from the Limeworks quarry of the Makapan valley, Potgietersrust district. *South African Journal of Science* **46**, 241–242.

Gess, W. H. R.
  1969   Excavation of a Pleistocene bone deposit at Aloes near Port Elizabeth. *South African Archaeological Bulletin* **24**, 1, 93, 31–32.

Goodwin, A. J. H.
  1928   An introduction to the Middle Stone Age in South Africa. *South African Journal of Science* **25**, 410–418.

  1929   The Montagu Cave: A full report of the investigation of the Montagu rock-shelter. *Annals of the South African Museum* **24**, 1, 1–16.

  1930   A new variation of the Smithfield culture from Natal. *Transactions of the Royal Society of South Africa* **19**, 1, 7–14.

  1935   Klip Kop Cave, Hermanus. *Annals of the South African Museum* **24**, 211–219.

  1938   Archaeology of the Oakhurst Shelter, George. *Transactions of the Royal Society of South Africa* **25**, 3, 229–324.

  1945   Some historical Bushman arrows. *South African Journal of Science* **41**, 429–443.

  1946   Prehistoric fishing methods in South Africa. *Antiquity* **79**, 134–139.

  1952   Jan van Riebeeck and the Hottentots, 1652–1662. *South African Archaeological Bulletin* **7**, 25, 1–53.

  1953   Two caves at Kalk Bay, Cape Peninsula. *South African Archaeological Bulletin* **8**, 31, 59–77.

  1956   Metal working among the early Hottentots. *South African Archaeological Bulletin* **11**, 42, 46–51.

Goodwin, A. J. H., and B. D. Malan
  1935   Archaeology of the Cape St. Blaize Cave, and raised beach, Mossel Bay. *Annals of the South African Museum* **24**, 111–140.

Goodwin, A. J. H., and C. van Riet Lowe
  1929   The Stone Age cultures of South Africa. *Annals of the South African Museum* **27**, 1–289.

Greenwood, M.
  1955   Fossil Hystricoidea from the Makapan valley, Transvaal. *Paloeontologia Africana* **3**, 77–85.

Gregory, W. K., and M. Hellman
  1939   The dentition of the extinct South African man-ape *Australopithecus (Plesianthropus) transvaalensis* Broom; a comparative and phylogenetic study. *Annals of the Transvaal Museum* **19**, 339–373.

Grindley, J. R.
  1967   The Cape rock lobster *Jasus lalandii* from the Bonteberg excavation. *South African Archaeological Bulletin* **22**, 3, 87, 94–102.

Grobbelaar, C. S., and A. J. H. Goodwin
  1952   Report on the skeletons and implements in association with them from a cave near Bredasdorp, Cape Province. *South African Archaeological Bulletin* **7**, 27, 95–107.

Guerig, G.
  1891   *Deutsch Südwest-Afrika, Reissenkizzen.* Hamburg.

Haughton, S. H.
  1917–   Preliminary note on the ancient human skull-remains from the Transvaal. *Transac-*
  1918   *tions of the Royal Society of South Africa* **6**, 1–8.

  1925   A note on the occurrence of a species of baboon in limestone deposits near Taungs. *Transactions of the Royal Society of South Africa* **12**, lxviii.

1947   Note on the australopithecine-bearing rocks of the Union of South Africa. *Transactions of the Geological Society of South Africa* **1**, 55–62.

1964   The australopithecine fossils of Africa and their geological setting. *Raymond Dart Lectures. Lecture 1.* Johannesburg: Witwatersrand University Press.

Hendey, Q. B.
1969   Quaternary vertebrate fossil sites in the Southwestern Cape Province. *South African Archaeological Bulletin* **24**, 3 & 4, 95 & 96, 96–105.

Hendey, Q. B., and R. Singer
1965   Part III: The faunal assemblages from the Gamtoos Valley Shelter. *South African Archaeological Bulletin* **20**, 80, 206–213.

Hewitt, J.
1912   Note on two remarkable implements presumably of Strandlooper origins. *Albany Museum Records* **2**, 4, 282–283.

1921   On several implements and ornaments from Strandlooper sites in the Eastern Province. *South African Journal of Science* **18**, 454–467.

1931a   Discoveries in a Bushman cave at Tafelberg Hall. *Transactions of the Royal Society of South Africa* **19**, 2, 185–196.

1931b   Artefacts from Melkhoutboom. *South African Journal of Science* **28**, 540–548.

Hoffman, A. C.
1953   The fossil Alcelaphines of South Africa—genera *Peloroceras, Lunatocerus* and *Alcelaphus. Researches of the National Museum, Bloemfontein* **1**, 3, 41–56.

1958   New excavations at Matjes River Rock Shelter. *South African Museums Association Bulletin* **6**, 342–348.

Hole, F.
1959   A critical analysis of the Magosian. *South African Archaeological Bulletin* **14**, 56, 126–134.

Holloway, R. L.
1970   Australopithecine endocast (Taung specimen, 1924): A new volume determination. *Science* **168**, 966–968.

Hooijer, D. A.
1959   Fossil rhinoceros from the Limeworks Cave, Makapansgat. *Palaeontologia Africana* **6**, 1–13.

Hooijer, D. A., and R. Singer
1960   The fossil rhinoceroses from Hopefield. *Zoologiese Mededelingen van het Rijksmuseum Natural History* **37**, 8, 113–129.

1961   The fossil hippopotamus from Hopefield, South Africa. *Zoologiese Mededelingen van het Rijksmuseum Natural History* **37**, 10, 157–165.

Hopwood, A. T., and J. P. Hollyfield
1954   An annotated bibliography of the fossil mammals of Africa (1742–1950). *Fossil Mammals of Africa* **8**, 194.

Howell, F. C.
1955   The age of the australopithecines of southern Africa. *American Journal of Physical Anthropology* n.s. **13**, 4, 635–662.

Howell, F. C., and J. D. Clark
1964   Acheulian hunter-gatherers of Sub-Saharan Africa. In *African ecology and human evolution,* edited by F. C. Howell and F. Bourlière, pp. 458–533. London: Methuen.

Hrdlička, A.
1925   The Taungs ape. *American Journal of Physical Anthropology* **8**, 379–392.

Hughes, A. R.
1954a   Habits of hyaenas. *South African Journal of Science* **51**, 156–158.

1954b   Hyaenas versus australopithecines as agents of bone accumulation. *American Journal of Physical Anthropology* n.s. **12**, 4, 467–486.

1958   Some ancient and recent observations on hyaenas. *Koedoe* **1**, 105–114.

Humphreys, A. J. B.

1969a   Later Acheulean or Fauresmith? A contribution. *Annals of the Cape Provincial Museums (Natural History)* **6**, 10, 87–101.

1969b   Four bifacial tanged and barbed arrowheads from Vosburg. *South African Archaeological Bulletin* **24**, 2, 94, 72–74.

Humphreys, A. J. B., and T. M. O'C. Maggs

1970   Further graves and cultural material from the banks of the Riet River. *South African Archaeological Bulletin* **25**, 3 & 4, 99 & 100, 116–126.

Inskeep, R. R.

1959   A Late Stone Age camping-site in the upper Zambezi valley. *South African Archaeological Bulletin* **14**, 55, 91–96.

1961   Review of the prehistory of the Matjes River Rock Shelter. II. The archaeology. *South African Archaeological Bulletin* **16**, 61, 30–31.

1965a   University of Cape Town excavations at Plettenburg Bay. *Scientific South Africa* **2**, 12, 575–582.

1965b   Earlier Stone Age occupation at Amanzi: A preliminary investigation. *South African Journal of Science* **61**, 229–242.

1967   The Late Stone Age in Southern Africa. In *Background to evolution in Africa*, edited by W. W. Bishop and J. D. Clark, pp. 557–582. Chicago: University of Chicago Press.

Inskeep, R. R., and Q. B. Hendey

1966   An interesting association of bones from the Elandsfontein fossil site. *Actas del V Congreso Panafricano de Prehistoria y de estudio del Cuaternario. Tenerife, 1963* **2**, 109–124.

Isaac, G. L.

1967a   The stratigraphy of the Peninj Group—early Middle Pleistocene formations west of Lake Natron, Tanzania. In *Background to evolution in Africa*, edited by W. W. Bishop and J. D. Clark, pp. 229–257. Chicago: University of Chicago Press.

1967b   Discussion in Leakey, M.D.: Preliminary survey from Beds I and II, Olduvai Gorge, Tanzania. In *Background to evolution in Africa*, edited by W. W. Bishop and J. D. Clark, pp. 446. Chicago: University of Chicago Press.

Janmart, J.

1947   Stations préhistoriques de l'Angola du Nord-Est. Anlayse géologique, climatologique et préhistorique d'un sondage fait en bordure de la rivière Luembe (Angola du Nord-Est). *Museu do Dundo, Publicações Culturais No. 1.* Lisbon: Diamang.

1948   "La station préhistorique de Candala (District de la Lunda, Angola du Nord-Est)" e estudos sobre préhistoria da Lunda. *Museu do Dundo, Publicações Culturais No. 2.* Lisbon: Diamang.

1953   The Kalahari Sands of the Lunda (N. E. Angola), their earlier redistributions and the Sangoan Culture. *Museu do Dundo, Publicações Culturais No. 20.* Lisbon: Diamang.

Jipsen, H.

1961–   *Prehistoric living sites in the inner Brandberg.* Parts I, II, III. Windhoek.
1965

Johnson, J. P.

1907a   *The Pre-historic period in South Africa.* London: Longmans, Green & Co.

1970b   *The Stone Age implements of South Africa.* London: Geological Magazine.

Johnson, L.

1968   Item seriation as an aid for elementary scale and cluster analysis. *Bulletin of the Museum of Natural History, University of Oregon. No. 15* 1–46.

Johnson, T.

1951   The excavation at Sandy Bay. *South African Archaeological Bulletin* **6**, 22, 58.

Jolly, C. J.

1970a   The seed-eaters: A new model of hominid differentiation based on a baboon analogy. *Man* n.s. **5**, 1, 5–26.

1970b   The large African monkeys as an adaptive array. In *Old World monkeys: Evolution systematics and behavior,* edited by J. R. Napier and P. H. Napier, pp. 139–174. New York: Academic Press.

Jolly, K.

1947   Preliminary note on new excavation at Skildergat, Fish Hoek. *South African Archaeological Bulletin* **2**, 5, 11–12.

1948   The development of the Cape Middle Stone Age in the Skildergat cave, Fish Hoek. *South African Archaeological Bulletin* **3**, 12, 106–107.

Jones, N.

1924   On the Palaeolithic deposits of Sawmills, Rhodesia. *Journal of the Royal Anthropological Institute* **54**, 276–286.

1933   Excavations at Nswatugi and Madiliyangwa, and notes on new sites located and examined in the Matopo Hills, Southern Rhodesia. *Occassional Papers of the Rhodesian Museum* **1**, 2, 1–44.

1938   The Bembesi industry. *Occasional Papers of the National Museum, Southern Rhodesia* **1**, 7, 7–31.

1940   Bambata Cave: A reorientation. *Occasional Papers of the National Museum, Southern Rhodesia* **1**, 12, 11–28.

1949   *The prehistory of Southern Rhodesia: An account of the progress of the research from 1900 to 1946.* Cambridge: University Press.

Jones, N., and R. F. H. Summers

1946   The Magosian culture of Khami, near Bulawayo, Southern Rhodesia. *Journal of the Royal Anthropological Institute* **76**, 1, 59–68.

Jones, T. R.

1936   A new fossil primate from Sterkfontein, Krugersdorp, Transvaal. *South African Journal of Science* **33**, 709–728.

Kannemeyer, D. R.

1899   Stone implements of the Bushmen. *Cape Illustrated Magazine* **1**, 120–130.

Keen, E. N. and R. Singer

1956   Further fossil Suidae from Hopefield. *Annals of the South African Museum* **42**, 350–360.

Keen, J. A.

1942   Report on a skeleton from Fish Hoek Cave. *South African Journal of Science* **38**, 301–304.

Keith, A.

1931   *New discoveries relating to the antiquity of man.* London: Williams and Norgate.

1941   Description of "The Fish Hoek Man." In *Guide to the Peer's Cave: Tunnel Cave and rock shelters at Skildergat, Fish Hoek,* edited by H. S. Jager, p. 12. Cape Town: Fish Hoek Municipality.

Keller, C. M.

1966   "Archaeology of the Montagu Cave." Unpublished Ph.D. thesis. University of California, Berkeley.

1969a   Mossel Bay: A redescription. *South African Archaeological Bulletin* **23**, 4, 92, 131–140.

1969b   Report on excavations at Montagu Cave, C. P., South Africa. *Actes du VIe Congrès Panafricain de Préhistoire et de l'étude du Quaternaire. Dakar 1967*, in press.

Kern, H. M., and W. L. Straus
1949   The femur of *Plesianthropus transvaalensis. American Journal of Physical Anthropology* n.s. **7**, 1, 53–77.

King, G. B., and E. C. Chubb
1932a   Remarks on some stone implements and Strandlooper middens of Natal and Zululand *South African Journal of Science* **29**, 765–769.
1932b   Stone implements from a rock-shelter in the Drakensberg. *South African Journal of Science* **29**, 768–769.

King, L. C.
1946   *South African scenery.* Edinburgh: University Press.
1951   The geology of Makapan and other caves. *Transactions of the Royal Society of South Africa* **33**, 121–150.

Kitching, J. W.
1951   A new species of Hippopotamus from Potgietersrust. *South African Journal of Science* **47**, 209–211.
1952   A new type of fossil baboon *Brachygnathopithecus peppercorni. South African Journal of Science* **49**, 15–17.
1953   A new species of fossil baboon from Potgietersrust. *South African Journal of Science* **50**, 66.
1963   A fossil *Orycteropus* from the Limeworks quarry, Makapansgat, Potietersrust. *Palaeontologia Africana* **8**, 119–121.
1965   A new giant Hyracoid from the Limeworks quarry, Makapansgat, Potgietersrust. *Palaeontologia Africana* **9**, 91–96.

Kitching, J. W., L. H. Wells, and E. Westphal
1948   Fossil Cercopithecoid primates from Limeworks quarry, Makapansgat, Potgietersrust. *South African Science* **1**, 9, 171–172.

Kleindienst, M. R.
1961   Variability within the Late Acheulian assemblage in Eastern Africa. *South African Archaeological Bulletin* **16**, 62, 35–52.
1962   Components of the East African Acheulian assemblage: analytical approach. *Actes du IVe Congrès Panafricain de Préhistoire et de l'étude du Quaternaire, Léopoldville, 1959* 81–111.
1967   Discussion in R. J. Mason: Questions of terminology in regard to the study of Earlier Stone Age cultures in South Africa. In *Background to evolution in Africa*, edited by W. W. Bishop and J. D. Clark, pp. 768. Chicago: University of Chicago Press.

Kruuk, H.
1966   A new view of the hyaena. *New Scientist* **30**, 849–851.

Kurtén, B.
1960   The age of the Australopithecinae. *Stockholm Contributions in Geology* **6**, 2, 9–22.
1962   The relative ages of the australopithecines of Transvaal and the pithecanthropines of Java. In *Evolution and Hominisation*, edited by G. Kurth, pp. 74–80. Stuttgart: Gustav Fischer Verlag.
1968   *Pleistocene mammals of Europe.* London. Weidenfeld & Nicolson.

Laidler, P. W.
1933   Dating evidence concerning the Middle Stone Age and a Capsio-Wilton culture in the south-east Cape. *South African Journal of Science* **30**, 530–542.
1934   The archaeological and geological sequence in the Transkei and Ciskei. *South African Journal of Science* **31**, 535–546.
1935   Shell mound cultures. *South African Journal of Science* **32**, 500–571.

1936   A Late Stone Age cave deposit in the Transkei. *South African Journal of Science* **33**, 888–892.

Laing, G. D.
1925   A further report on the Tsitsikamma material. *South African Journal of Science* **22**, 455.

Laing, G. D., and J. H. Gear
1929   A final report on the Strandlooper skulls found at Tsitsikamma. *South African Journal of Science* **26**, 575.

Lavocat, R.
1957a   La faune de rongeurs des grottes à Australopithèques. *Palaeontologia Africana* **4**, 69–75.
1957b   Sur l'âge des faunes de Rongeurs des grottes a Australopithèques. *Proceedings of the Third Pan-African Congress on Prehistory, Livingstone 1955* 133–134.
1967   Les microfaunes du quaternaire ancien d'Afrique orientale et australe. In *Background to evolution in Africa,* edited by W. W. Bishop and J. D. Clark, pp. 67–72. Chicago: University of Chicago Press.

Leakey, L. S. B.
1931   *Stone Age Cultures of Kenya Colony.* Cambridge: University Press.
1936   *Stone Age Africa: an outline of prehistory in Africa.* London.
1949   Tentative study of the Pleistocene climatic changes and Stone-Age culture sequence in northeastern Angola. *Museu do Dundo, Publicações Culturais No. 4.* Lisbon: Diamang.
1951   *Olduvai Gorge; a report on the evolution of the Hand-axe Culture in Beds I–IV.* London and New York: Cambridge University Press.
1959   A preliminary re-assessment of the fossil fauna from Broken Hill, N. Rhodesia. Appendix in J. D. Clark, Further excavations at Broken Hill, North Rhodesia. *Journal of the Royal Anthropological Institute* **89**, 2, 225–230.
1960   Recent discoveries at Olduvai Gorge. *Nature (London)* **188**, 4755, 1050–1052.
1968   The earliest toolmakers. In *Prelude to East African history,* edited by M. Posnansky, p. 30. London: Oxford University Press.

Leakey, L. S. B., P. V. Tobias, and J. R. Napier
1964   A new species of the Genus *Homo* from Olduvai Gorge. *Nature (London)* **202**, 4927, 7–9.

Leakey, M. D.
1967   Preliminary survey of the cultural material from Beds I and II, Olduvai Gorge, Tanzania. In *Background to evolution in Africa,* edited by W. W. Bishop and J. D. Clark, pp. 417–446. Chicago: University of Chicago Press.
1970   New finds at the Swartkrans australopithecine site (cont'd). Stone artefacts from Swartkrans. *Nature (London)* **225**, 5239, 1222–1225.

Lebzelter, V., and F. A. H. Bayer
1928   Stone Age cultures on the Zululand highveld and in Northern Natal. (Preliminary report). *Annals of the Transvaal Museum* **12**, 280–284.

Lee, D. N., and H. C. Woodhouse
1970   *Art on the rocks of Southern Africa.* Cape Town: Purnell.

Lee, R. B.
1963   The population ecology of man in the Early Upper Pleistocene of Southern Africa. *Proceedings of the Prehistoric Society of Great Britain* **29**, 235–257.

Le Gros Clark, W. E.
1947   Observations on the anatomy of the fossil Australopithecinae. *Journal of Anatomy, (London)* **81**, 300–333.
1952   A note on certain cranial indices of the Sterkfontein skull No. 5. *American Journal of Physical Anthropology* n.s. **10**, 1, 119–121.
1955   *The fossil evidence for human evolution.* Chicago: University of Chicago Press.

Leith, G.
  1898   On the caves, shell-mounds and stone implements of South Africa. *Journal of the Royal Anthropological Institute* **28**, 258–274.
Libby, W. F.
  1954   Chicago radiocarbon dates V. *Science* **120**, 733–742.
Lofgren, L., and Phillipson, D. W.
  1966   Makwe. *Archaeologia Zambiana* **7**, 4–5.
Louw, A. W.
  1969   Bushman Rock Shelter, Ohrigstad, Eastern Transvaal: A preliminary investigation. *South African Archaeological Bulletin* **24**, 2, 94, 39–51.
Louw, J. T.
  1960   Prehistory of the Matjes River Rock Shelter. *National Museum, Blosmfontein. Memoirs No. 1.*
Lovejoy, C. O., and K. G. Heiple
  1972   Proximal femoral anatomy of *Australopithecus. Nature (London)* **235**, 5334, 175–176.
Mabutt, J. A.
  1951   Cape Hangklip—a study in coastal geomorphology. *Transactions of the Royal Society of South Africa* **34**, 1, 17–24.
  1957   Some Quaternary events in the winter rainfall area of the Cape Province. *Proceedings of the Third Pan-African Congress on Prehistory, Livingstone 1955* 6–13.
Maberly, A. C. T.
  1951   *Animals of the Kruger National Park.* Bloemfontein.
McBurney, C. B. M.
  1967   *The Haua Fteah (Cyrenaica) and the Stone Age of the South-East Mediterranean.* London and New York: Cambridge University Press.
MacCalman, H. R.
  1962   Gungans, an Early Middle Stone Age site in the Windhoek district. *Cimbebasia* **3**.
  1963   The Neuhoff-Kowas Middle Stone Age, Windhoek district. *Cimbebasia* **7**.
  1965   Carbon 14 dates from South West Africa. *South African Archaeological Bulletin* **20**, 80, 215.
MacCalman, H. R., and A. Viereck
  1967   Peperkorrel, a factory site of Lupemban affinities from central South West Africa. *South African Archaeological Bulletin* **22**, 2, 86, 41–50.
Maggs, T. M. O'C.
  1967   A quantitative analysis of the rock art from a sample area in the western Cape. *South African Journal of Science* **63**, 100–104.
Maggs, T. M. O'C., and E. Speed
  1967   Bontberg Shelter. *South African Archaeological Bulletin* **22**, 3, 87, 80–93.
Maguire, B.
  1965   Foreign pebble pounding artefacts in the breccias and the overlying vegetation soil at Makapansgat limeworks. *South African Archaeological Bulletin* **20**, 79, 117–130.
  1968   The lithic industry in the Makapansgat limeworks breccias and overlying surface soil. *Palaeontologia Africana* **11**, 99–126.
Malan, B. D.
  1938   The Middle Stone Age of the Cape Peninsula: The Hardy collection. *Bureau of Archaeology, Survey Series No. 3* 1–26. Pretoria.
  1946   The distribution and chronology of the Modderpoort culture. *South African Journal of Science* **42**, 254–260.
  1947   Flake tools and artefacts in the Stellenbosch–Fauresmith transition in the Vaal River valley. *South African Journal of Science* **43**, 350–362.
  1949a   Magosian and Howieson's Poort. *South African Archaeological Bulletin* **4**, 13, 34–36.

1949b Two new South African Magosian occurrences in Natal and South West Africa. *South African Journal of Science* **46**, 88–91.

1952 The final phase of the Middle Stone Age in South Africa. *Proceedings of the First Pan-African Congress on Prehistory, Nairobi 1947* 188–194.

1955a A preliminary account of the archaeology of East Griqualand. *Bureau of Archaeology, Survey Series No. 8* 1–26, Pretoria.

1955b The archaeology of Tunnel Cave and Skildergat Kop, Fish Hoek. *South African Archaeological Bulletin* **10**, 37, 3–9.

1957 The term "Middle Stone Age." *Proceedings of the Third Pan-African Congress on Prehistory, Livingstone 1955* 223–227.

Malan, B. D., H. B. S. Cooke and L. H. Wells

1941 A preliminary account of the Wonderwerk Cave, Kuruman dist. *South African Journal of Science* **37**, 300–312.

Malan, B. D., and J. C. van Niekerk

1955 Die Later-Steentyd in Transvaal. *South African Journal of Science* **51**, 231–235.

Malan, B. D., and L. H. Wells

1943 A further report on the Wonderwerk Cave, Kuruman. *South African Journal of Science* **40,** 258–270.

Malan, F.

1950 A Wilton site at Kai Kai, Bechuanaland Protectorate. *South African Archaeological Bulletin* **5,** 20, 140–142.

Martin, C.

1938 A rock shelter on Nyazongo Mountain, Penhalonga district, Southern Rhodesia. *Occasional Papers of the Queen Victoria Museum Library, No. 1* 1–18.

Martin, H., and R. J. Mason

1954 The test trench in the Phillips Cave, Ameib, Erongo Mountains, South West Africa. *South African Archaeological Bulletin* **9**, 36, 148–151.

Martin, P. D.

1872 Stone implements and shell caves. *Cape Monthly Magazine* **5**, 53–55.

Mason, R. J.

1951 The excavations of four caves near Johannesburg. *South African Archaeological Bulletin* **6**, 23, 71–79.

1957a The Transvaal Middle Stone Age and statistical analysis. *South African Archaeological Bulletin* **12**, 48, 119–143.

1957b Preliminary note on an Earlier Stone Age site at Wonderboom south: Pretoria. *South African Journal of Science* **53**, 431–434.

1958 Bone tools at the Kalkbank Middle Stone Age site and the Makapansgat australopithecine locality. Central Transvaal: Part I. The Kalkbank site. *South African Archaeological Bulletin* **13**, 51, 85–93.

1959 Some South African Stone Age cultures. *Nature (London)* **183**, 4658, 377–379.

1961a The earliest tool-makers in South Africa. *South African Journal of Science* **57**, 13–16.

1961b *Australopithecus* and the beginning of the Stone Age in South Africa. *South African Archaeological Bulletin* **16**, 61, 8–14.

1961c The Acheulian culture in South Africa. *South African Archaeological Bulletin* **16**, 63, 107–110.

1962a *Prehistory of the Transvaal: a record of human activity.* Johannesburg: Witwatersrand University Press.

1962b Australopithecines and artefacts at Sterkfontein. Part II. The Sterkfontein stone artefacts and their maker. *South African Archaeological Bulletin* **17**, 66, 109–126.

1965 Makapansgat limeworks fractured stone objects and natural fracture in Africa. *South African Archaeological Bulletin* **20**, 1, 77, 3–16.

1966 The excavation of Doornlaagte Earlier Stone Age camp, Kimberley district. *Actas del V Congreso Panafricano de Prehistoria y de estudio del Cuaternario. Tenerife 1963* **2**, 187–188.

1967a Prehistory as a science of change; new research in the South African interior. *Occasional Papers of the Archaeological Research Unit, Johannesburg* **1**, 1–19.

1967b Analytical procedures in the Earlier and Middle Stone Age cultures in Southern Africa. In *Background to evolution in Africa,* edited by W. W. Bishop and J. D. Clark, pp. 737–764. Chicago: University of Chicago Press.

1967c The archaeology of the earliest superficial deposits in the Lower Vaal Basin near Holpan, Windsorton district. *South African Geographical Journal* **49**, 39–56.

1968 Cultures, technology and analytical procedures in African prehistory. *Pan-Afr. Congr. Prehist. Commission on Nomenclature Bull.* **1**, 22–23.

1969a The Oppermansdrif Dam archaeological project—Vaal basin. *South African Archaeological Bulletin* **24**, 3 & 4, 95 & 96, 182–192.

1969b Experimental attribute analysis of Later Stone Age artefact assemblages from Munro's site AC 200–250, Oppermansdrif and Olieboompoort Bed 3, Western Transvaal. *Occasional Papers of the Archaeological Research Unit, Johannesburg* **5**, 1–18.

1969c Tentative interpretations of new radiocarbon dates for stone artefact assemblages from Rose Cottage Cave, O. F. S. and Bushman Rock Shelter, Tvl. *South African Archaeological Bulletin* **24**, 2, 94, 57–59.

1969d The Oppermansdrif Dam archaeological project—Vaal Basin. *Occasional Papers of the Archaeological Research Unit No. 3 Johannesburg* 1–14.

Mayr, E.

1942 *Systematics and the origins of species from the viewpoint of a zoologist.* New York: McGraw-Hill.

1949 Speciation and selection. *Yearbook of Physical Anthropology* **5**, 180–185.

1951 Taxonomic categories in fossil hominids. *Cold Springs Harbor Symposium on Quantitative Biology* **15**, 109–117.

1964 The taxonomic evolution of fossil hominids. In *Classification and human evolution,* edited by S. L. Washburn, pp. 332–346. London: Methuen.

Meester, J.

1955 Fossil shrews of South Africa. *Annals of the Transvaal Museum* **22**, 271–278.

Meiring, A. J. D.

1937 The "Wilton" skulls of the Matjes River Shelter. *Soölogiese Navorsing van die Nasionale Museum* **1**, 6, 51–94.

1953 The Matjes River Shelter: Evidence in regard to the introduction of rock painting into South Africa. *Navorsinge van die Nasionale Museum, Bloemfontein* **1**, 3, 77–84.

1956 The macrolithic culture of Florisbad. *Researches of the National Museum, Bloemfontein* **1**, 9, 205–237.

Mendrez, C.

1966 On *Equus (Hippotigris)* cf. *burchelli* (Gray) from Sterkfontein Extension; Transvaal, South Africa. *Annals of the Transvaal Museum* **25**, 91–97.

Miller, S. F.

1967 The archaeological sequence of the Zambian Later Stone Age. *Actes du VIᵉ Congrès Panafricain de Préhistorie et de l'étude du Quaternaire. Dakar 1967.* In press.

1969a "The Nachikufu industries of the Later Stone Age in Zambia." Unpublished Ph.D. thesis, University of California, Berkeley.

1969b Contacts between the Later Stone Age and the Early Iron Age in Southern Central Africa. *Azania* **4**, 81–90.

1971 Mphunzi Shelter, a Later Stone Age site in Malawi. In press.

Mollet, O. D. v. d. S.

1947   Fossil mammals from the Makapan valley: 1, primates. *South African Journal of Science* **43**, 295–303.

Mortelmans, G.

1962   Le Quaternaire du Congo occidental et sa chronologie. *Actes du IVᵉ Congrès Panafricain de Préhistorie et de l'étude du Quaternaire, Léopoldville, 1959* 97–132.

Napier, J. R.

1959   Fossil metacarpals from Swartkrans. *Fossil Mammals Afr.* **17**, 1–18.

1964   The evolution of bipedal walking in the hominids. *Archives de Biologie (Liège)* **75**, 673–708.

1967   The antiquity of human walking. *Scientific American* **216**, 56.

Oakley, K. P.

1954a   Study tour of early hominid sites in Southern Africa, 1953. *South African Archaeological Bulletin* **9**, 35, 75–87.

1954b   The dating of the Australopithecinae of Africa. *American Journal of Physical Anthropology* n.s. **12**, 1, 9–27.

1954c   Evidence of fire in South African cave deposits. *Nature (London)* **174**, 4423, 261–262.

1956   The earliest fire-makers. *Antiquity* **30**, 118, 102–107.

1957a   Dating the australopithecines. *Proceedings of the Third Pan-African Congress on Prehistory, Livingstone 1955* 155–157.

1957b   The dating of the Broken Hill, Florisbad and Saldanha skulls. *Proceedings of the Third Pan-African Congress on Prehistory, Livingstone 1955* 76–79.

1958   The dating of Broken Hill (Rhodesian Man). In *Hundert Jahre Neanderthaler, Neanderthal Centenary, 1856–1956*, edited by G. H. R. von Koenigswald, pp. 265–266. Utrecht: Kemink en Zoon.

O'Brien, T. P.

1939   *The prehistory of the Uganda Protectorate.* London and New York: Cambridge University Press.

1969   Sangoan origins, a suggested "Earlier" Acheulian derivation. *South African Archaeological Bulletin* **23**, 4, 92, 143–144.

Oppenheimer, A.

1964   Tool use and crowded teeth in Australopithecinae. *Current Anthropology* **5**, 5, 419–421.

Oxnard, C. E.

1968   A note on the fragmentary Sterkfontein scapula. *American Journal of Physical Anthropology* n.s. **28**, 2, 213–217.

1969   Evolution of the human shoulder: Some possible pathways. *American Journal of Physical Anthropology* n.s. **30**, 3, 319–331.

Parkington, J. E.

1967   Some comments on the comparison and classification of archaeological specimens. *South African Archaeological Bulletin* **22**, 3, 87, 73–79.

Parkington, J. E., and C. Poggenpoel

1971   Excavations at De Hangen, 1968. *South African Archaeological Bulletin* **26**, 1 & 2, 101 & 102, 1–36.

Partridge, T. C.

1964   A Middle Stone Age and Iron Age site at Waterval, north west of Johannesburg. *South African Archaeological Bulletin* **19**, 4, 76, 102–110.

1965   A statistical analysis of the Limeworks lithic assemblage. *South African Archaeological Bulletin* **20**, 79, 112–116.

Partridge, T. C., and A. B. A. Brink

1967   Gravels and terraces of the Lower Vaal River Basin. *South African Geographical Journal* **49**, 21–38.

Peabody, F. E.

1954   Travertines and cave deposits of the Kaap escarpment of South Africa, and the type locality of *Australopithecus africanus* Dart. *Bulletin of the Geological Society of America* **65**, 671–705.

Peers, V., and B. Peers

1926   Peers A/101 1926—Skildergat. Unpublished manuscript.

Peringuey, L.

1911   The Stone Ages of South Africa. *Annals of the South African Museum* **8**, 1–218.

Phillipson, D. W.

1964   Zambian radiocarbon dates. *Archaeologia Zambiana* **1**, 4–6.

1965   Zambian radiocarbon dates, May–August, 1965. *Archaeologia Zambiana* **4**, 2.

1969   The prehistoric sequence at Nakapapula rockshelter, Zambia. *Proceedings of the Prehistoric Society of Great Britain* **35**, 172–202.

1970   Makwe. *Archaeologia Zambiana* **12**, 5–6.

Phillipson, L.

1968   Middle Stone Age material from sites near Katima Mulilo on the Upper Zambezi. *South African Archaeological Bulletin* **23**, 3, 91, 90–101.

1970   Excavations at Kandanda and Donke. *Archaeologia Zambiana* **12**, 3–5.

Pocock, T. N.

1969   Appendix I. In The new Witwatersrand University excavations at Sterkfontein, edited by P. V. Tobias and A. R. Hughes. *South African Archaeological Bulletin* **24**, 3 & 4, 95 & 96, 168–169.

Radcliffe-Robinson, K., and C. K. Cooke

1950   Some unusual elements in the Wilton industry in the Matopos area of Southern Rhodesia. *South African Archaeological Bulletin* **5**, 19, 108–114.

Read, C. E.

1971   The ecological study of faunal remains in archaeology. Unpublished Ph.D. thesis, University of California, Los Angeles.

Rigollot, Dr.

1855   *Mémoire sur des instruments en silex trouvés à Saint-Acheul, près d'Amiens*. Amiens.

Robinson, J. T.

1949   Some observations on the systematic position of the Australopithecinae. *South African Journal of Science* **46**, 83–87.

1952a   The australopithecines and their evolutionary significance. *Proceedings of the Linnean Society, London* **3**, 196–200.

1952b   The australopithecine-bearing deposits of the Sterkfontein area. *Annals of the Transvaal Museum* **22**, 1–19.

1953a   *Telanthropus* and its phylogenetic significance. *American Journal of Physical Anthropology* n.s. **11**, 4, 445–501.

1953b   The nature of *Telanthropus*. *Nature (London)* **171**, 4340, 33.

1954a   The genera and species of the Australopithecinae. *American Journal of Physical Anthropology* n.s. **12**, 2, 181–200.

1954b   The australopithecine occiput. *Nature (London)* **174**, 4423, 262–263.

1954c   Nuchal crests in australopithecines. *Nature (London)* **174**, 4443, 1197–1198.

1956   The dentition of the Australopithecinae, *Memoris of the Transvaal Museum* **9**, 1–179.

1958a   Cranial cresting patterns and their significance in the Hominoidea. *American Journal of Physical Anthropology* n.s. **16**, 4, 397–428.

1958b   The Sterkfontein tool-maker. *Leech* **8**, 3, 4, 5, 94–100.

1959   A bone implement from Sterkfontein. *Nature (London)* **184**, 4686, 583–585.

1961   The australopithecines and their bearing on the origin of man and of stone tool-making. *South African Journal of Science* **57**, 3–13.

1962a   Australopithecines and the origin of man. *The Smithsonian Report for 1961* 479–500.

1962b   Australopithecines and artefacts at Sterkfontein. Part I. Sterkfontein stratigraphy and the significance of the extension site. *South African Archaeological Bulletin* **17**, 66, 87–108.

1962c   The origins and adaptive radiation of the australopithecines in *Evolution und Hominisation,* edited by G. Kurth, pp. 120–140. Stuttgart.

1965   *Homo "habilis"* and the autralopithecines. *Nature (London)* **205**, 4967, 121–124.

1967   Variation and the taxonomy of the early hominids. *Evolutionary Biology* **1**, 69–100.

1970   New finds at the Swartkrans australopithecine site (cont'd). The new early hominid vertebrae from Swartkrans. *Nature (London)* **225**, 5239, 1217–1219.

in press   *Early hominid posture and locomotion.* Chicago: University of Chicago Press.

Robinson, J. T., and R. J. Mason

1957   The occurrence of stone artefacts with *Australopithecus* at Sterkfontein. *Nature (London)* **180**, 4585, 521–524.

Robinson, K. R.

1938   A note on a ground stone axe. *Proceedings of the Rhodesian Scientific Association* **36**, 163–164.

1952   Excavations in two rock shelters near the Rusawi River, Central Mashonaland. *South African Archaeological Bulletin* **7**, 27, 108–129.

1958   Some Stone Age sites in Inyanga district. In *Inyanga; prehistoric settlements in Southern Rhodesia,* edited by R. Summers, pp. 270–309. London and New York: Cambridge University Press.

1964   Dombazanga rock shelter, Mtetengwe River, Beitbridge, Southern Rhodesia; excavation results. *Arnoldia* **1**, 7, 1–14.

Robinson, K. R., and B. H. Sandelowsky

1968a   Fingira: preliminary report. *Dept. Antiq. Publ* **3**, Zomba, Malawi.

1968b   Further work in the Iron Age of Northern Malawi. *Azania* **3**, 107–145.

Robinson, W. S.

1951   A method for chronologically ordering archaeological deposits. *American Antiquity* **16**, 4, 293–301.

Roe, D. A.

1964   The British Lower and Middle Palaeolithic: Some problems, methods of study and preliminary results. *Proceedings of the Prehistoric Society of Great Britain* **30**, 245–267.

1968   British Lower and Middle Palaeolithic handaxe groups. *Proceedings of the Prehistoric Society of Great Britain* **34**, 1–82.

Rudner, I.

1953   Decorated ostrich egg-shell and stone implements from the Upington area. *South African Archaeological Bulletin* **8**, 31, 82–84.

Rudner, I., and J. Rudner

1954   A local Later Stone Age development. *South African Archaeological Bulletin* **9**, 35, 103–107.

1955   II. Archaeology of a coastal dune area at Bok Baai. *South African Archaeological Bulletin* **10**, 39, 86–91.

1956   Excavation of the Logie's Rock cave, Llundudno. *South African Archaeological Bulletin* **9**, 43, 77–80.

1959   Wilton sand-dune sites in Northwestern Cape and South West Africa. *South African Archaeological Bulletin* **14**, 56, 142–145.

Rudner, J.

1957   The Brandberg and its archaelogical remains. *Journ. der S.W.A. Wiss. Gesellschaft, Windhoek* **12**, 7–44, 81–84.

1968   Strandloper pottery from South and South West Africa. *Annals of the South African Museum* **49**, 2, 441–663.

Rudner, J., and P. Grattan-Bellew

1964   Archaeological sites along the southern coast of South West Africa. *South African Journal of Science* **60**, 67–79.

Rudner, J., and I. Rudner

1970   *The hunter and his art: A survey of rock art in Southern Africa.* Cape Town: C. Struik.

Sampson, C. G.

1962   The Cape Hangklip main site. *Journal of the University of Cape Town Science Society* **5**, 15–24.

1963   Paper read at V Congr. Panafr, Prehist. Tenerife, 1963.

1965   A preliminary report on the Luano spring deposits, Northern Rhodesia. *South African Archaeological Bulletin* **20**, 1, 77, 29–33.

1967a   Excavations at Zaayfontein Shelter, Norvalspont, Northern Cape. *Researches of the National Museum, Bloemfontein* **2**, 4, 41–119.

1967b   Zeekoegat 13: A Later Stone Age open-site near Venterstad, Cape. *Researches of the National Museum, Bloemfontein* **2**, 5–6, 211–237.

1967c   Excavations at Glen Elliot Shelter, Colesberg district, Northern Cape. *Researches of the National Museum, Bloemfontein* **2**, 5–6, 125–209.

1968   The Middle Stone Age industries of the Orange River Scheme area. *National Museum, Bloemfontein. Memoirs* **4**, 1–111.

1969a   Aspects of the Stone Age sequence in Southern Africa in the light of recent research in the Orange River Scheme area. Unpublished D.Phil. thesis, Oxford University.

1969b   The Acheulian Industry in the Orange River Scheme area. *Researches of the National Museum Bloemfontein,* in press.

1970   The Smithfield Industrial Complex: further field notes. *National Museum, Bloemfontein. Memoirs* **5**, 1–172.

1971a   Sequential dating of the South African australopithecine-bearing breccias. Paper read at Section F of the 70th Annual Meeting of the American Anthropological Association, New York.

1971b   The Oakhurst Complex: proposals for a pre-Wilton complex in Southern Africa. Paper read at the First Congress of African Archaeologists, Urbana.

Sampson, C. G., and R. J. Mason

1968   Two analyses of the Middle Stone Age industries from the Cave of Hearths and Olieboompoort Shelter, Northern Transvaal. *Occasional Papers of the Archaeological Research Unit, Johannesburg* **2**, 1–14.

Sampson, C. G., and M. E. Sampson

1967   Riversmead Shelter: excavation and analysis. *National Museum, Bloemfontein. Memoirs* **3**, 1–111.

Sampson, C. G., and M. D. Southard

1972   Variability and change in the Nachikufan industry of Zambia. *South African Archaeological Bulletin* in press.

Schauder, D. E.

1963   The anthropological work of F. W. FitzSimons in the Eastern Cape. *South African Archaeological Bulletin* **18**, 70, 52–59.

Schofield, J. F.

  1935   Natal coastal pottery from the Durban district: A preliminary survey. *South African Journal of Science* 32, 509–527.

  1936a A hitherto undescribed pebble culture of the Later Stone Age from the Natal coast. *Annals of the Durban Museum* 3, 5, 81–95.

  1936b Natal coastal pottery from the Durban district: a preliminary survey. Part II. *South African Journal of Science* 33, 993–1009.

  1938a Pottey from Natal. *South African Journal of Science* 35, 382–395.

  1938b Part V. The pottery. In Archaeology of the Oakhurst Shelter, George, edited by A. J. H. Goodwin. *Transactions of the Royal Society of South Africa* 25, 3, 295–301.

  1938c A description of the pottery from the Umgazana and Zig-zag caves on the Pondoland coast. *Transactions of the Royal Society of South Africa* 25, 327–332.

Schoonraad, M., and P. Beaumont

  1968   The North Brabant shelter, North Western Transvaal. *South African Journal of Science* 64, 319–331.

Schoute-Vanneck, C. A.

  1958   The shell middens on the Durban Bluff. *South African Archaeological Bulletin* 13, 50, 43–54.

Schoute-Vanneck, C. A., and R. C. Walsh

  1959   The shell middens at the Ingane River mouth, Natal south west. *South African Archaeological Bulletin* 14, 54, 43–55.

  1961   The Umlaas variant of the Smithfield C culture. *South African Archaeological Bulletin* 16, 64, 137–143.

Schrire, C.

  1962   Oakhurst: a re-examination and vindication. *South African Archaeological Bulletin* 17, 67, 181–195.

Schultze-Jena, L. S.

  1907   *Aus Nomaland und Kalahari*. Jena: Fischer.

Schweitzer, F. R.

  1970   A preliminary report of excavations of a new cave at die Kelders. *South African Archaeological Bulletin* 3 & 4, 99 & 100, 136–138.

Seddon, D.

  1967   Some Early Stone Age surface sites around Stellenbosch, S. W. Cape. *South African Archaeological Bulletin* 22, 2, 86, 57–59.

Senyürek, M. S.

  1941   The dentition of *Plesianthropus* and *Paranthropus*. *Annals of the Transvaal Museum* 20, 293–302.

Shaw, J. C. M.

  1937   Evidence concerning a large fossil *Hyrax*. *Journal of Dental Research* 16, 1, 37.

  1938   The teeth of the South African fossil pig *(Notochoerus capensis* syn. *meadowsi)* and their geological significance. *Transactions of the Royal Society of South Africa* 26, 25–37.

  1939a Growth changes and variations in Warthog third molars and their palaeontological significance. *Transactions of the Royal Society of South Africa* 27, 51–94.

  1939b Further remains of a Sterkfontein ape. *Nature (London)* 143, 3612, 117.

  1940   Concerning some remains of a new Sterkfontein primate. *Annals of the Transvaal Museum* 20, 145–156.

Simonetta, A.

  1957   Catalogo e sinominia annotata delgi ominoidi fossil ed attuali (1758–1955). *Atti di Societe Toscana, Scienze Naturale* 64, 53–112.

Simons, H. A. B.
   1968   A Late Stone Age occupation site in the Hillside area of Bulawayo. *South African Ar-chaeological Bulletin* **23**, 2, 90, 45–49.

Singer, R.
   1954   The Saldanha skull from Hopefield, South Africa. *American Journal of Physical An-thropology* n.s. **12**, 3, 345–362.

   1955   III. A report on the Bok Baai skeletal remains. *South African Archaeological Bulletin* **10**, 39, 91–93.

   1957   Investigations at the Hopefield site. *Proceedings of the Third Pan-African Congress on Prehistory, Livingstone, 1955* 175–182.

   1958   The Rhodesian, Florisbad and Saldanha skulls. In *Hundert Jahre Neanderthaler, Neanderthal Centenary, 1856–1956,* edited by G. H. R. von Koenigswald, pp. 52–62. Utrecht: Kemink en Zoon.

   1962   *Simopithecus* from Hopefield, South Africa. *Bibliographica Primatologica* **1**, 43–70.

Singer, R., and E. L. Boné
   1960   Modern giraffes and fossil giraffids of Africa. *Annals of the South African Museum* **45**, 375–548.

   1966   Hipparion in Africa. *Quaternaria* **8**, 187–191.

Singer, R., and P. G. Heltne
   1966   Further notes on a bone assemblage from Hopefield, South Africa. *Actas del C Con-greso Panafricano de Prehistoria y de estudio del Cuaternario. Tenerife, 1963* **2**, 261–264.

Singer, R. and R. R. Inskeep
   1961   A complete fossil equid skull from Hopefield, C. P. *South African Archaeological Bul-letin* **17**, 65, 23.

Singer, R., and E. N. Keen
   1955   Fossil suiformes from Hopefield. South Africa. *Annals of the South African Museum* **42**, 160–179.

Singer, R., and J. Wymer
   1968   Archaeological investigations at the Saldanha skull site in South Africa. *South African Archaeological Bulletin* **23**, 3, 91, 63–74.

   1969   Radiocarbon date for two painted stones from a coastal cave in South Africa. *Nature (London)* **224**, 5218, 508–510.

   in   Middle Stone Age occupational settlements on the Tzitzikama coast, eastern Cape
   press Province, South Africa.

Söhnge, P. G., D. J. L. Visser, and C. van Riet Lowe
   1937   The geology and archaeology of the Vaal River Basin. *Memoirs of the Geological Survey of the Union of South Africa* **35**, 1–184.

Sollas, W. J.
   1926   On a sagittal section of the skull of *Australopithecus africanus. Quarterly Journal of the Geological Society of London* **82**, 1–11.

Stapleton, P., and J. Hewitt
   1927– Stone implements from a rock shelter at Howieson's Poort near Grahamstown. *South
   1928   African Journal of Science* **24**, 574–587; **25**, 399–409.

Stearns, C. S., and D. L. Thurber
   1965   Th^{230}–U^{234} dates of Late Pleistocene marine fossile from the Mediterranean and Moroccan littorals. *Quaternaria* **7**, 29–42.

Stein, H. B.
   1933   Stone implements from the Cathkin Peak area. *Bantu Studies* **7**, 159–181.

Straus, W. L.

1948 The humerus of *Paranthropus robustus*. *American Journal of Physical Anthropology* n.s. **6**, 3, 285–311.

1950 On the zoological status of *Telanthropus capensis*. *American Journal of Physical Anthropology* n.s. **8**, 4, 495–498.

Summers, R. F. H. (Editor)

1959 *Prehistoric rock art of the Federation of Rhodesia and Nyasaland*. Salisbury: National Publications Trust.

Summers, R., and C. K. Cooke

1959 Archaeological survey of Rhodesia. *Annual Report of the Historical Monuments Commission (Bulawayo)* Supplement 1, Map 5.

Sutcliffe, A. J.

1970 Spotted Hyaena: Cruncher, gnawer, digester and collector of bones. *Nature (London)* **227**, 5263, 1110–1113.

Sydow, W.

1967 The pre-European pottery of South West Africa. *Cimbebasia Memoir* **1**.

Thom, H. B. (Editor)

1952 *Journal of Jan van Riebeeck*. Cape Town: Van Riebeeck Society.

Tobias, P. V.

1949 The excavation of Mwulu's Cave, Potgietersrust district. *South African Archaeological Bulletin* **4**, 13, 2–13.

1954 Climatic fluctuations in the Middle Stone Age of South Africa as revealed in Mwulu's Cave. *Transactions of the Royal Society of South Africa* **34**, 2, 325–334.

1964 The Olduvai Bed I Hominine with special reference to its cranial capacity. *Nature (London)* **202**, 4927, 3–4.

1965 *Australopithecus, Homo habilis*, tool-using and tool-making. *South African Archaeological Bulletin* **20**, 80, 167–192.

1967a The cranium and maxillary dentition of *Australopithecus (Zinjanthropus) boisei*. In *Olduvai Gorge*, edited by L. S. B. Leakey. Vol. II. Cambridge: University Press.

1967b Cultural hominization among the earliest African Pleistocene hominids. *Proceedings of the Prehistoric Society of Great Britain* **33**, 367–376.

1968 Cranial capacity in anthropoid apes. *Australopithecus* and *Homo habilis*, with comments on skewed samples. *South African Journal of Science* **64**, 81–91.

1969 Man's past and future. *Raymond Dart Lectures, Lecture 5*. Johannesburg: Witwatersrand University Press.

Tobias, P. V., and A. R. Hughes

1969 The new Witwatersrand University excavation at Sterkfontein. Progress report, some problems and first results *South African Archaeological Bulletin* **24**, 3 & 4, 95 & 96, 158–169.

Tobias, P. V., and J. T. Robinson.

1966 The distinctiveness of *Homo habilis*. *Nature (London)* **209**, 5027, 953–960.

Tobias, P. V., and G. H. R. von Koenigswald

1964 A comparison between the Olduvai hominines and those of Java and some implications for hominid phylogeny. *Nature (London)* **204**, 4958, 515–518.

Toerien, M. J.

1952 The fossil hyaenas of the Makapansgat valley. *South African Journal of Science* **48**, 293–300.

1955 A sabre-tooth cat from the Makapansgat valley. *Palaeontologia Africana* **3**, 43–46.

Turner, M.

1970 A search for the Tsitsikamma Shelters. *South African Archaeological Bulletin* **25**, 2, 98, 67–70.

Tuttle, R. H.
 1967 Knuckle walking and the evolution of hominoid hands. *American Journal of Physical Anthropology* n.s. **26**, 171–206.

van Hoepen, E. L. N.
 1930 Fossiele perde van Cornelia, O. V. S. *Palaeont. Navorsinge Nas. Mus. Bloemfontein* **2**, 13–24.

 1932 Die Mosselbaaise Kultuur. *Argeologiese Navorsings van die Nasionale Museum, Bloemfontein* **1**, 4.

van Noten, F.
 1965 Strandloopers van de Kaap de Goede Hoop. *Afrika-Terveuren* **3**, 4, 58–60.

 1967 Excavations at Gordon's Bay. *Inventaria Archaeologica Africana* **SA1–5**.

van Riet Lowe, C.
 1926 The Modder River man and his possible relation to the Smithfield industry. *South African Journal of Science* **23**, 887–891.

 1936 The Smithfield "N" culture. *Transactions of the Royal Society of South Africa* **23**, 4, 367–372.

 1937 The archaeology of the Vaal River Basin. *Memoirs of the Geologica! Survey of the Union of South Africa* **35**, 61–184.

 1938 The Makapan caves; an archaeological note. *South African Journal of Science* **35**, 371–381.

 1943 Further notes on the Makapan caves. *South African Journal of Science* **40**, 289–295.

 1946 The Coastal Smithfield and bipolar technique. *South African Journal of Science* **42**, 240–246.

 1947 A ground axe from Natal. *Transactions of the Royal Society of South Africa* **31**, 4, 325–331.

 1948 Cave breccias in the Makapan Valley. *Robert Broom Commemorative Volume*, pp. 127–131. Cape Town: Royal Society of South Africa.

 1952a The development of the Hand-axe culture in South Africa. *Proceedings of the First Pan-African Congress on Prehistory, Nairobi, 1947* 167–177.

 1952b The Vaal River chronology. An up-to-date summary. *South African Archaeological Bulletin* **7**, 28, 135–149.

van Riet Lowe, C., and L. H. Wells
 1944 *A contribution to the prehistory of Moçambique and report on material from kitchen-middens near the mouth of the Limpopo River.* Lourenço Marques: Comissão dos Monumentos e Reliquias Históricas de Moçambique.

Vansina, J.
 1966 *Kingdoms of the Savanna.* Madison.

van Zinderen Bakker, E. M.
 1957 A pollen analytical investigation of the Florisbad deposits (South Africa). *Proceedings of the Third Pan-Arican Congress on Prehistory, Livingstone, 1955* 56–67.

 1963 Analysis of pollen samples from north-east Angola. In *Prehistoric cultures of N. E. Angola and their significance in Tropical Africa*, edited by J. D. Clark, pp. 213–217. Lisbon: Diamang.

 1969 Appendix I. Summary of analysed pollen samples: Kalambo Falls. In *Kalambo Falls*, edited by J. D. Clark, Vol. I, pp. 232–235. London and New York: Cambridge University Press.

van Zinderen Bakker, E. M., and J. D. Clark
 1962 Pleistocene climates and cultures in north-eastern Angola. *Nature (London)* **196**, 4855, 639–642.

Vedder, H.

1938   South West Africa in early times. London: Oxford University Press.

Viereck, A.

1963   Junge Erongo-Kultur und Bergdamavolk. *Mitteilungen der S. W. Wiss. Gesellschaft, Windhoek* **4 & 5.**

1967   The Damaraland culture. A "Later Stone Age" horizon in South West Africa. *Journ. der S.W.A. Wiss. Gesellschaft, Windhoek* **21,** 13–31.

1968   *Die Spuren der alten Brandbergbewohner.* Windhoek: S.W.A. Wissenschaftlichen Gesellschaft.

Vinnicombe, P.

1967   Rock-painting analysis. *South African Archaeological Bulletin* **22,** 4, 88, 129–141.

Vogel, J. C.

1969   Radiocarbon dating of Bushman Rock Shelter, Ohrigstad district. *South African Archaeological Bulletin* **24,** 2, 94, 56.

1970   Groningen radiocarbon dates IX. *Radiocarbon* **12,** 2, 444–471.

von Hemmer, J. H.

1965   Zur nomenklatur und verbreitung des genus *Dinofelis* Zdansky, 1924 *(Theraclurus* Piveteau, 1948). *Palaeontologia Africana* **9,** 75–89.

von Koenigswald, G. H. R.

1948   Remarks on the lower canine of *Plesianthropus transvaalensis Broom. Robert Broom Commem. Vol.* Special Publ. Roy. Soc. S. Afr., 159–164.

1961   *Australopithecus* und das Problem der Geröllkulturen. *Dt. Gerells. Anthrop. Tübingen* 139–152.

Washburn, S. L.

1957   Australopithecines: the hunters or the hunted? *American Anthropologist* **59,** 4, 612–614.

Washburn, S. L., and B. Patterson

1951   Evolutionary importance of the South African "man-apes." *Nature (London)* **167,** 4251, 650–651.

Wayland, E. J.

1934   Rifts, rivers, rains and early man in Uganda. *Journal of the Royal Anthropological Institute* **44,** 333–352.

1954   Outlines of prehistory and Stone Age climatology in the Bechuanaland Protectorate. *Acad. Roy. des Sciences Coloniales, Brussels* **25,** 4, 3–47.

Wayland, E. J., and M. C. Burkitt

1932   The Magosian culture of Uganda. *Journal of the Royal Anthropological Institute* **62,** 369–390.

Webb, G. L.

1965   Notes on some Chalicothere remains from Makapansgat. *Palaeontologia Africana* **9,** 49–73.

Wells, L. H.

1929   Fossil Bushmen from the Zuurberg. *South African Journal of Science* **26,** 806.

1933   A find of stone implements from Estcourt, Natal: with remarks on some specimens from the Weenen district. *Bantu Studies* **7,** 221–225.

1950a   The Border Cave skull, Ingwavuma district, Zululand. *American Journal of Physical Anthropology* n.s. **8,** 2, 241–243.

1950b   Appendix C. Fossil man in Northern Rhodesia. In *The Stone Age cultures of Northern Rhodesia,* edited by J. D. Clark, pp. 143–150. Cape Town: South African Archaeological Society.

1951   A large fossil klipspringer from Potgietersrust. *South African Journal of Science* **47,** 167.

1957   Late Stone Age human types in Central Africa. *Proceedings of the Third Pan-African Congress on Prehistory, Livingstone, 1955* 183–185.

1960   Mammalian remains from Late Stone Age sites in the George-Knysna area. *South African Journal of Science* **56**, 306.

1964   The Vaal River "Younger Gravels" faunal assemblage. *South African Journal of Science* **60**, 88–91.

1970a   A Late Pleistocene faunal assemblage from Driefontein, Cradock district, C. P. *South African Journal of Science* **66**, 59–61.

1970b   The fauna of the Aloes Bone deposit: a preliminary note. *South African Archaeological Bulletin* **25**, 1, 97, 22–23.

Wells, L. H., and H. B. S. Cooke

1957   Fossil Bovidae from the Limeworks quarry, Makapansgat, Potgietersrust. *Palaeontologia Africana* **4**, 1–55.

Wells, L. H., H. B. S. Cooke, and B. D. Malan

1942   The associated fauna and culture of the Vlakkraal thermal springs, O. F. S. *Transactions of the Royal Society of South Africa* **29**, 3, 203–233.

Wells, L. H. and H. S. Gear

1931   Cave dwellers of the Outeniqua Mountains. *South African Journal of Science* **28**, 444,

Wells, M. J.

1965   An analysis of plant remains from Scott's cave in the Gamtoos Valley. *South African Archaeological Bulletin* **20**, 2, 78, 79–94.

Willcox, A. R.

1956   *The rock paintings of the Drakensberg*. London: Max Parrish.

1957   A cave at Giant's Castle game reserve. *South African Archaeological Bulletin* **12**, 47, 87–97.

1963   *The rock art of Southern Africa*. Johannesburg: Nelson.

Wilson, M., and L. Thompson (Editors)

1969   *The Oxford history of South Africa. I. South Africa to 1870*. London: Oxford University Press.

Wolberg, D. L.

1970   The hypothesized osteodontokeratic culture of the Australopithecinae: a look at the evidence and the opinions. *Current Anthropology* **11**, 1, 23–37.

Wolpoff, M. H.

1968   "Telanthropus" and the single species hypothesis. *American Anthropologist* **70**, 3, 477–493.

1971   Is the new composite cranium from Swartkrans a small robust Autralopithecine? *Nature (London)* **230**, 5293, 398–401.

Young, R. B.

1925   The calcareeous tufa deposits of the Campbell Rand from Boetsap to Taungs native reserve. *Transactions of the Geological Society of South Africa* **28**, 55–67.

Zapfe, H.

1939   *Palaeobiologica* **7**, 111.

1966   *Denkschr. Ost. Akad. Wiss.* **112**, 109.

Zuckerman, S.

1928   Age-changes in the Chimpanzee with special reference to growth of brain, eruption of teeth and estimation of age, with a note on the Taungs ape. *Proceedings of the Zoological Society of London (1928)* 1–42.

1950a   South African fossil anthropoids. *Nature (London)* **165**, 4199, 652.

1950b   South African fossil hominoids. *Nature (London)* **166**, 4212, 158–159.

1950c   Taxonomy and human evolution. *Biological Review* **25**, 935.

1951a   Comments on the dentition of the fossil australopithecinae. *Man* **51**, 38, 20.

1951b   The dentition of the Australopithecinae. *Man* **51**, 61, 32.

1954   Correlation of change in the evolution of the higher Primates. In *Evolution as a process,* edited by J. Huxley, A. C. Hardy and E. B. Ford. pp. 300–352. London: Chatto & Windus.

Zuckerman, S., E. H. Ashton, C. E. Oxnard, and T. F. Spence

1967   The functional significance of certain features of the inominate bone in living and fossil Primates. *Journal of Anatomy (London)* **101**, 3, 608.

Index

Numbers in italics refer to the pages on which the complete references are cited.

A

Aasvoelkop, 152, 153, 156, 162
Abbeville, 103
Abbevillian, 103
Abel, W., 43, *451*
Acacia karroo, 428
Acacia Road, 117, 118, 121
Achatina sp., 146, 213, 279, 349
Achatina zebra, 182
Acheulian, 9, 102–136, 137, 138, 139, 140,
    142, 143, 146, 148, 149, 157, 158, 168,
    173, 174, 175, 177, 182, 186, 187, 212,
    213, 216, 444, 448, 449
  analytical procedures for, 118–119
  and associated fauna, 127–132
  and associated hominids, 134–135
  dating of, 122–126, 141
  distribution of, 119–21
  Early, 108, 121, 122
  Final, 9, 108, 121, 183

Acheulian (*contd.*)
  history of research, 102–104, 107–108
  Late, 9, 121, 149, 157, 158, 168, 186
  Lower, 74, 126, 142, 445
  Middle, 121
  origins of, 444–445
  and raw materials, 109
  technology of, 108, 112
  terminology of, 102–104, 107–108, *see also*
      Terminology
  typical, 9
  typologies of, 118–119
Acheulian complex, *see* Acheulian
Acheulian industrial complex, *see* Acheulian
Activity variants, 134
Adie, R. J., 22, *453*
Adjacent platform cores, 152, 159, 173, 178,
    249, 259, 260, 267, 286, 379
Adlun, 448
À dos naturel sidescrapers, 191, 230
Adze blades, 336